本报告整理
由中国社会科学院哲学社会科学创新工程
（2016-2018KGYJ055）资助

本报告出版
得到国家重点文物保护专项补助经费的资助

洛阳盆地中东部先秦时期遗址

1997—2007年区域系统调查报告

3

中国社会科学院考古研究所
中澳美伊洛河流域联合考古队　编著

科学出版社
北京

内 容 简 介

1997—2007年，中国社会科学院考古研究所与澳大利亚、美国等国家的大学和研究机构合作，对中国古代文明产生和发展的腹心地区——洛阳盆地中东部近1120平方千米的区域，开展了区域系统调查。期间共发现遗址（或地点）456处，采集到大量先秦时期的遗物。调查结果表明：这些遗址涵盖了先秦时期的各个阶段，显示了该区域约从公元前6000年左右至公元前200年左右近6000年的社会发展图景，展示了早期中国文明核心区从零星分布的聚落到王朝统治中心的社会发展轨迹。

本书适合于考古学、历史学的相关研究者及大专院校相关专业师生参考、阅读。

图书在版编目(CIP)数据

洛阳盆地中东部先秦时期遗址：1997—2007年区域系统调查报告：全4册 / 中国社会科学院考古研究所，中澳美伊洛河流域联合考古队编著. —北京：科学出版社，2019.9

ISBN 978-7-03-062470-3

Ⅰ.①洛… Ⅱ.①中… ②中… Ⅲ.①文化遗址–调查报告–洛阳–先秦时代 Ⅳ.①K878.05

中国版本图书馆CIP数据核字（2019）第212272号

责任编辑：张亚娜 / 责任校对：邹慧卿
责任印制：肖 兴 / 封面设计：美光制版

科学出版社 出版
北京东黄城根北街16号
邮政编码：100717
http://www.sciencep.com

中国科学院印刷厂 印刷
科学出版社发行　各地新华书店经销

*

2019年9月第 一 版　　开本：889×1194　1/16
2019年9月第一次印刷　　印张：136 3/4　插页：8
字数：3900 000

定价：1800.00元（全4册）

（如有印装质量问题，我社负责调换）

Pre-Qin Period Sites in the East and Central Luoyang Basin:

The Systematic Regional Archaeological Survey Report (1997-2007)

Institute of Archaeology, Chinese Academy of Social Sciences
Sino-Australian-American Collaborative Archaeological Team of the Yiluo River Valley

Science Press
Beijing

研 究 编

第四章　伊洛地区复杂社会的兴衰：聚落形态的时空变化[①]

伊洛地区是黄河流域中华文明的核心区域，经历了早期国家形成和中国古代王朝诞生的过程。数十年的考古工作发现和发掘了若干重要的青铜时代及历史时期的大型遗址，尤其是二里头遗址的发掘引起了数十年来对夏商文明起源的研究和争论。但是，长期以来我们对整个地区中小型遗址分布及史前社会发展情况了解不足，因此迫切需要对区域性的社会进化过程进行细化分析，特别是从新石器时代早期到青铜时代晚期。伊洛地区调查项目旨在解决这一问题。该项目由中澳美伊洛河流域联合考古队和中国社会科学院考古研究所河南二里头工作队进行，从1997年到2007年进行了系统的全覆盖调查。调查范围覆盖了伊洛地区1120平方千米的面积，记录了从旧石器时代到青铜时代的456个地点，提供了伊洛地区的聚落分布景观和不断变化的社会政治格局。本章分析新石器时代和青铜时代（公元前6000—前200年；从裴李岗文化到东周）451个遗址的聚落模式，提供至今最完整的、近6000年时间跨度内古代聚落分布的时空关系。两个考古队曾经各自发表调查的初步结果[1]，本章的目的是将这些资料进行整体的综合分析。

第一节　气候与环境背景

伊洛河流域是一个肥沃的冲积平原，北临黄河，三面环山，计有崤山、熊耳山、伏牛山和嵩山等天然屏障。伊河和洛河从西南向东北流过盆地，在注入黄河之前合二为一，形成伊洛河。一方面，肥沃的冲积平原保证了农业的高产，可满足密集的人口需要。另一方面，伊洛盆地属于相对封闭的地理环境，有利于军事防御[2]。但是该地区绝非与外界隔绝，因为丰富的水系把盆地与周围地区有效地连接起来。洛阳之所以成为九朝古都，与其地理位置的优势密切相关。

[①] 本章由刘莉、陈星灿、华翰维（Henry T. Wright）、许宏、李永强、陈国梁、赵海涛、金河范（Habeom Kim）、李炅娥（Gyoung-Ah Lee）执笔。本章节为报告整理过程中撰写，英文版已经发表。部分数据与资料编中的统计数据不完全一致，系未根据最终统计结果进行修改。另为尊重已发表之原文，体例和注释也未与前文统一，特此说明。

中国北方的黄土地区经历了一个温暖湿润的中全新世气候最适宜期（约8000～5000 cal. BP），为新石器文化的发展创造了有利条件，但是这一时期也经历了持续不断的气候波动。从全新世晚期开始（约4200 cal. BP），出现了不稳定的干冷气候[3]。对洛阳盆地沉积物钻孔的孢粉学和岩性学分析表明，全新世时期，这一地区的植被从阔叶落叶林（9230～8850 cal. BP）转变到草原-草甸植被（8850～7550 cal. BP），然后到草原稀疏树木（7550～6920 cal. BP）[4]。伊洛地区的地质考古调查揭示了中全新世期间与人类土地利用相关的一系列景观变化。中全新世早期显示稳定的自然景观，土壤发育，地下水位高；早期新石器裴李岗人群对自然环境的影响十分有限。随后，中全新世晚期（7300～4100 cal. BP）迅速转向山坡侵蚀和山谷冲积增加，表明人类加剧了对自然环境及土地的利用和管理。这种变化与仰韶中、晚期开始强化的粟作农业生产及水稻田的首次出现时间相吻合。大约4000 cal. BP之后，一些集水区的河谷下切导致冲积平原变窄，谷地内的湿地沉积物消失。这一变化与全新世晚期华北地区由于夏季季风减弱而出现的较为干燥的气候相对应。然而，这种看似不利的气候条件却是该地区第一个国家级社会组织（二里头文化）出现的环境背景[5]。很明显，气候环境和人类活动之间的相互作用是理解社会发展的关键因素之一，这个问题将在下面进一步讨论。

第二节　研究方法

聚落形态考古学旨在了解决定一个地区遗址分布的因素[6]。基于系统化区域调查的聚落形态考古学促进了对世界许多地区古代社会进程的了解。这种研究方法在中国也被成功地应用在一些研究项目中，如山东东南部[7]、内蒙古赤峰地区[8]及河南安阳洹河地区[9]的区域性调查。伊洛地区调查项目也是其中之一，该项目系统地记录了各个时期遗址的分布情况，在调查期间还收集了主要来自灰坑的浮选样本，用于植物考古分析[10]和^{14}C测年。

衡量区域性的社会复杂化程度，需要采用量化方法。我们用遗址数量、最大遗址面积和聚落等级三个变量来分析伊洛地区从裴李岗文化到周代的社会发展进程。其中遗址数量可反映人口密度，而最大中心遗址面积和聚落等级反映了人口密度及社会结构的复杂程度。一般认为当一个区域内可观察到二至三级聚落等级时，其社会组织结构大致处于简单酋邦和复杂酋邦时代，而一个具有四级或更多聚落等级的区域系统，很可能标志着国家的形成[11]。

在调查中确定遗址范围和记录遗址面积至关重要。根据伊洛地区的地理环境，如长期农耕和水土流失造成的地貌改变，我们一般以100米距离内至少有3至5片同时期的陶片作为界定一个遗址的最低标准。除此之外，我们也重视其他的背景因素，比如遗址形成过程和微景观因素的考察。在大多数情况下，我们都以遗迹现象如灰坑、墓葬、陶窑和房基等的存在作为判断遗址的确切依据。调查时使用全球定位仪（GPS）确定遗址准确位置。遗址的边界则在整个地区调查完毕和遗物的年代确定以后在地图上加以确认。不同文化、不同时期的遗址面积互异，判断遗址范围主要依地面陶片的分布情况。调查所发现的陶片作为我们判断年代的主要标尺；为确定重要遗址的时空分布，有时也使用洛阳铲取得必要的地下资料[12]。

伊洛地区的遗址可分为两类。

（1）单一型：一个遗址中仅发现一种考古学文化遗存，这种遗址的面积比较容易测定。

（2）复合型：一个遗址中发现多种文化遗存。调查中发现的绝大多数遗址都是复合型，这种情况对估计遗址中各个考古文化时期的分布面积造成困难。

由于遗址的保存状态和考古遗存在地面暴露的情况不同，对遗址范围的测定有三种情况：

（1）一个遗址中各个文化时期的分布范围能够确定。

（2）整个复合型遗址只记录了一个总分布面积。

（3）一个遗址中有些文化时期的分布范围能够确定，但有些时期不能确定。

为了方便计算并侧重分析较大遗址的等级分布，当我们分析遗址面积数据时，所有等于和小于9万平方米的遗址都被视为单一型遗址，因为它们在聚落等级分析中都被归类为最低层次的小村庄（裴李岗期除外）。较大的遗址可能代表区域中心，因此，我们将大于9万平方米的遗址分为两类进行分析：单一型遗址组和复合型遗址组。在复合型遗址组中，有一些较大的遗址的文化遗存具有长期的延续性，并有相对明确的各文化分布面积，我们将这类遗址归为单一型遗址进行分析。这种区分有助于我们观察直方图中遗址群聚合的趋势。两种遗址类别的分布在直方图中分别显示，但我们对聚落等级的分析基于单一型遗址的分布。这一分析方法是为了尽可能不遗漏那些很可能是中心聚落的大遗址，同时也避免将不能确定准确范围的复合型遗址误定为中心聚落。因此，我们在地图上标出的大中型中心聚落是比较保守的估计。另外，有些大型遗址的范围可分为遗物分布集中的核心区和最大范围分布区，如二里头（分别为300万和540万平方米）和金钟寺（分别为34万和83万平方米）。为了计算的一致性，我们只使用核心区的范围。有些多元文化遗址中的早期文化层有重要遗迹，但由于受到晚期人类活动的破坏，无法估计遗址面积。在这种情况下，我们根据出土遗迹和遗物来讨论遗址的性质。

为了建立伊洛地区准确的考古学年代序列，我们将55个新石器时代和青铜时代的浮选样本进行加速器质谱（AMS）测年，并使用OxCal v.3.2软件校正AMS日期[13]。然后使用求和概率分布方法（Summed Probability Distributions，以下简称SPD）来聚合^{14}C年代，以显示按时间顺序排列的绝对年代的连续性和不连续性模式。使用'rcarbon' R 软件制作SPD图像[14]。

第三节　聚落分布和^{14}C年代

本节基于伊洛地区调查数据库中新石器至青铜时代451个遗址的信息进行聚落形态分析，涵盖的考古学文化为裴李岗晚期、仰韶、龙山、二里头、二里岗、殷墟、西周和东周，时间跨度近6000年。以下我们将分析每个文化时期的遗址分布状态和相关的^{14}C测年时代。

一、裴李岗文化时期

根据发现的陶片遗存，共有16个遗址被确定为裴李岗文化晚期，其中8个与仰韶早期共存，意味着人类居住的延续性。这些遗址都很小（0.2万～9万平方米），位于不同的地形环境中，从山坡、黄土塬地，到河谷的洪泛平原。在我们调查之前，河南考古工作者在巩义市西南部的瓦窑嘴发现了一个较大的裴李岗晚期遗址（17万平方米）[15]。该遗址位于我们的调查区域之外。由于发掘后的居民区建设，遗址现已不复存在。因此，我们无法验证其面积。如果发表的信息正确，瓦窑嘴则是伊洛地区已知最大的裴李岗遗址。另外，位于盆地西部的西石桥东（076）（9万平方米）也比其他遗址（0.2万～2.5万平方米）大得多。这两个遗址可能在东北部和西部的二级聚落等级的分布区域中具有中心聚落的地位（图4.1a、图4.2）。

裴李岗时期的经济表现为广谱生计形态，以狩猎、采集野生植物和粟作农业为特征。铁生沟遗址（图4.1a-2）出土的炭化植物及磨盘、磨棒上的残留物分析表明人们的食物包括驯化和野生谷物、橡子、豆类和块茎植物[16]。

裴李岗文化（不包括贾湖类型）的年代大约为 6200～5000 cal. BC。这些测年结果均来自伊洛地区以外一些遗址的木炭样本[17]。在我们的调查中，从两个裴李岗遗址获得了测年结果。府店东（Y124）样本（5557～5380 cal. BC，来自木炭；图4.1a-3）的年代相当于裴李岗文化晚期，而府店东南（Y118）样本的年代（4228～3982 cal. BC，来自炭化粟；图4.1a-4）则接近仰韶文化早期（图4.3，表4.1）。这两个地点相距约500米，两遗址的陶器类型相似。如果府店东（Y124）的木炭样本来自老炭，其^{14}C年代可能比遗址的实际年龄稍早。府店东南（Y118）样本的测年晚于裴李岗文化年代，可能表明裴李岗风格的陶器在伊洛地区某些遗址一直被生产和使用到仰韶早期。由于测年样本太少，目前无法做进一步解释。未来需要获得更多的裴李岗遗址的测年。

二、仰韶文化时期

我们共记录了228个仰韶文化遗址。大多数遗址可以进一步分为仰韶早期、中期和晚期，但54个遗址只能归属于仰韶文化。仰韶早期遗址稀少（N=20），但在仰韶中期（N=77）和晚期（N=146）阶段，遗址数量显著增加。6个仰韶早期的单一型遗址面积均小于6万平方米，表明人口密度非常低，与裴李岗晚期相似。我们分析了142个面积比较确定的仰韶中、晚期遗址的聚落等级分布情况，包括95个单一型仰韶和47个复合型遗址。

这些单一型遗址在直方图（图4.2）中分布为两组：

（1）10个相对较大的遗址为区域中心聚落（19万～34万平方米，包括武屯东南、苗湾C、赵城、景阳岗、保庄西北、寺沟、东王河北、纲常、金钟寺、灰嘴东）；

（2）85个小型遗址为小村庄（≤13万平方米）。

第四章 伊洛地区复杂社会的兴衰：聚落形态的时空变化

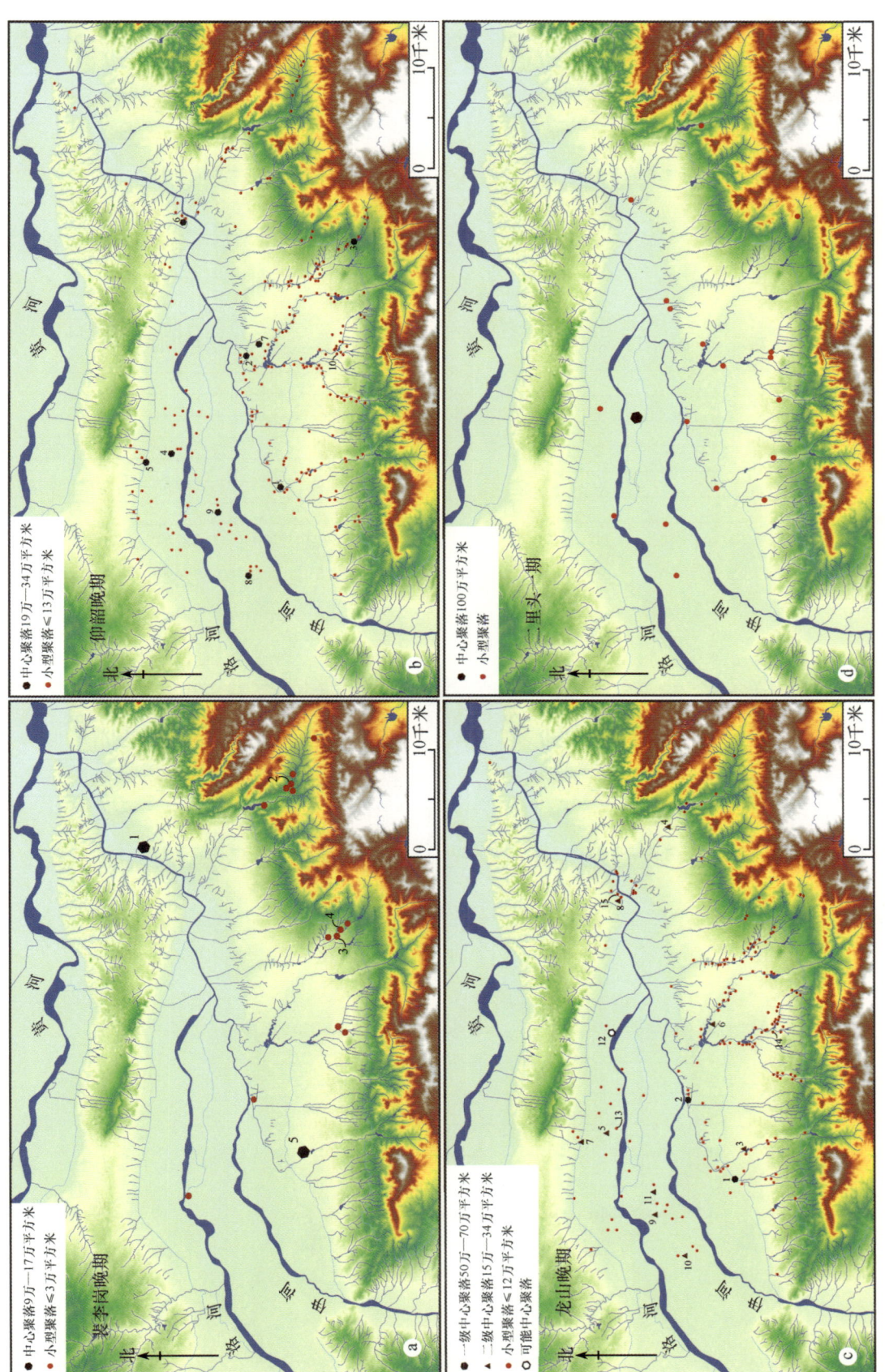

图4.1 裴李岗至二里头一期的聚落分布

a. 裴李岗晚期遗址：1. 瓦窑嘴 2. 铁生沟 3. 府店东 4. 府店东南 5. 西石桥 b. 仰韶中晚期遗址：1. 武屯东南 2. 苗湾C 3. 赵城 4. 景阳岗 5. 保庄西北 6. 寺沟 7. 东王河北 c. 龙山晚期遗址：1. 南寨上村东 2. 罗口东北 3. 陈家窑 4. 景阳岗 5. 寺沟西北 6. 盆窑寨西北 7. 保庄西北 8. 寺沟西南 9. 潘寨老寨东 10. 纲常 11. 金钟寺 12. 塔庄 13. 米沟东南 14. 灰嘴东 15. 寺沟东南 d. 二里头文化一期：中心遗址：二里头
8. 纲常 9. 金钟寺 10. 灰嘴东 c. 龙山晚期遗址：a. 裴李岗晚期（龙山早）

1210 洛阳盆地中东部先秦时期遗址

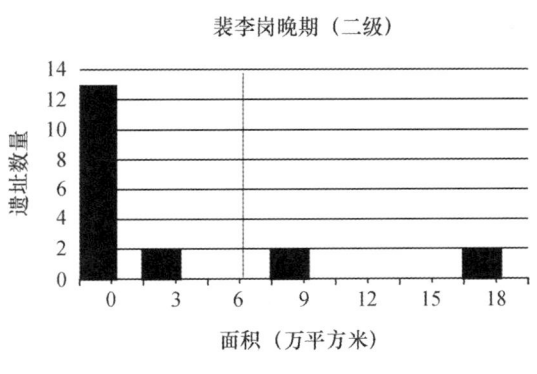

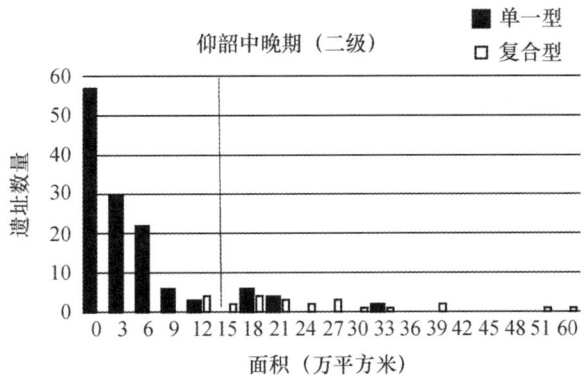

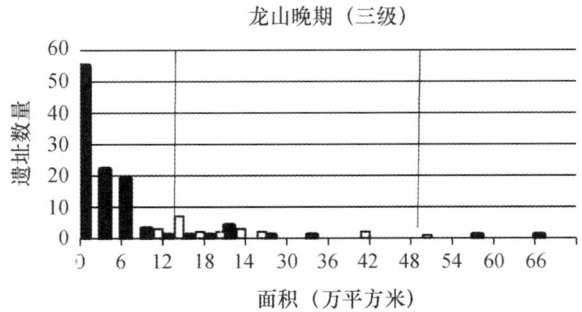

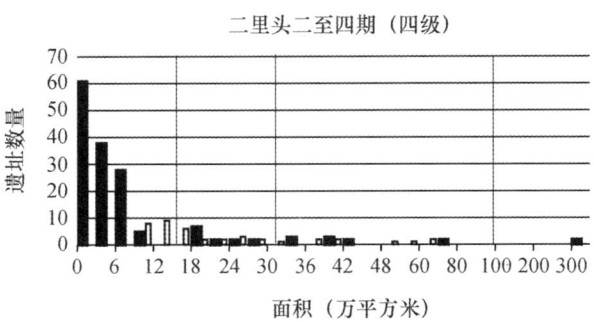

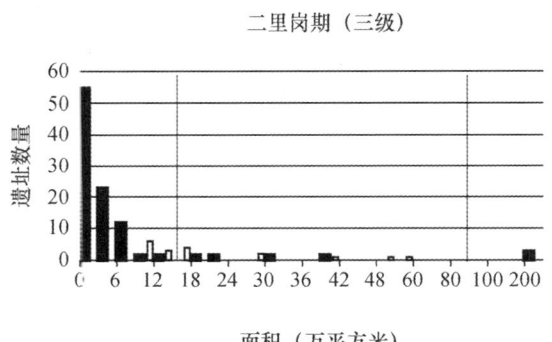

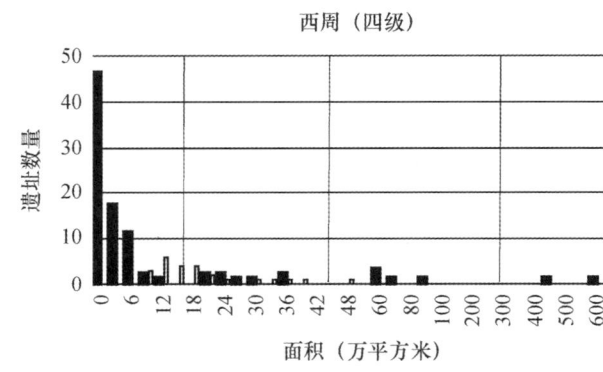

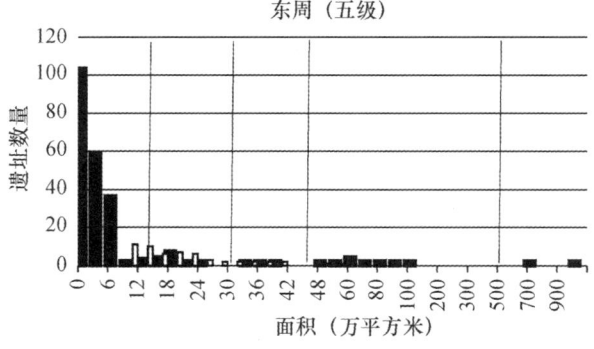

图4.2 从裴李岗晚期到东周的聚落等级变化

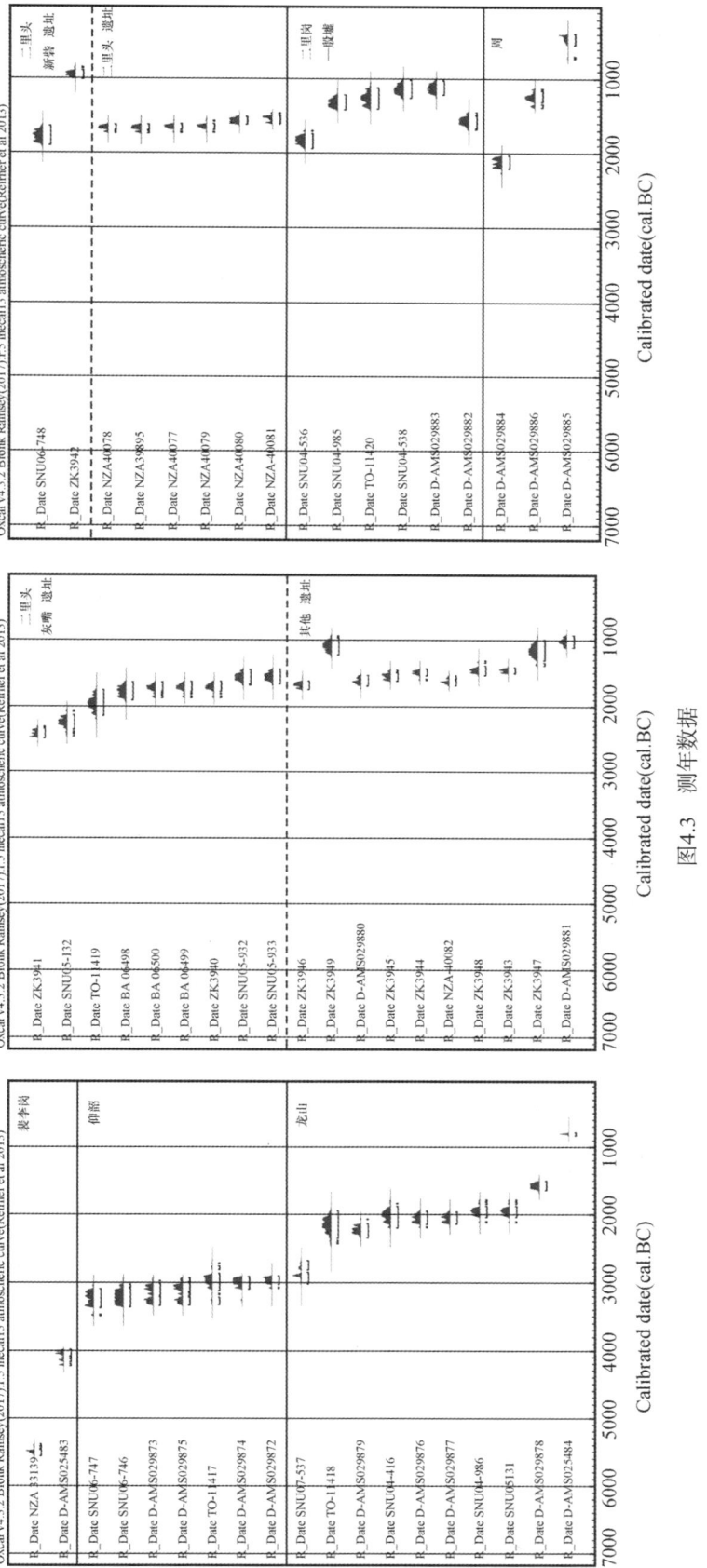

图4.3 测年数据

表4.1 伊洛地区裴李岗至东周AMS测年结果（N=55）*

序号	报告编号	原始编号	遗址名称	考古文化	实验室标本号	未校正 ^{14}C BP	校正后（Cal. BC）68.2%概率	校正后（Cal. BC）95.4%概率
裴李岗（N=2）								
313	Y124	00-124	府店东	裴李岗晚	NZA 33139	6521±35	5522 (68.2%) 5471	5557 (83.8%) 5463 5446 (4.6%) 5418 5410 (7.0%) 5380
308	Y118	00-118	府店东南	裴李岗晚	D-AMS025483	5256±26	4222 (6.3%) 4210 4154 (13.8%) 4132 4064 (22.9%) 4034 4024 (25.2%) 3993	4228 (10.8%) 4200 4170 (19.7%) 4126 4121 (5.9%) 4092 4082 (58.9%) 3982
仰韶（N=7）								
238	Y127	06-127E	灰嘴东	仰韶中晚	SNU06-747	4540±50	3362 (18.3%) 3320 3272 (2.0%) 3266 3236 (26.9%) 3169 3164 (21.0%) 3112	3491 (2.1%) 3470 3374 (93.3%) 3090
304	Y078	00-078	赵城西	仰韶早中	SNU06-746	4500±50	3338 (25.4%) 3264 3243 (12.7%) 3206 3195 (30.1%) 3103	3362 (89.5%) 3082 3068 (5.9%) 3026
390	Y050	98-050	羽林庄南	仰韶中晚	D-AMS029873	4454±32	3322 (34.6%) 3234 3171 (2.6%) 3163 3116 (13.9%) 3082 3067 (17.1%) 3027	3339 (44.1%) 3206 3196 (51.1%) 3012 2976 (0.1%) 2974
259	Y204	02-204	布村东南	仰韶晚	D-AMS029875	4443±36	3321 (14.3%) 3272 3267 (12.5%) 3235	3334 (35.0%) 3212 3191 (6.9%) 3152 3327 (6.7%) 3218 3176 (0.8%) 3160
420	Y019	98-019	嵕庄西	仰韶晚	TO-11417	4330±70	3082 (4.2%) 3068 3026 (64.0%) 2888	3121 (84.9%) 2862 2807 (2.7%) 2758 2718 (0.3%) 2709
238	Y127	06-127E	灰嘴东	仰韶中晚	D-AMS029874	4384±35	3078 (3.2%) 3072 3024 (65.0%) 2925	3096 (95.4%) 2909

续表

序号	报告编号	原始编号	遗址名称	考古文化	实验室标本号	未校正¹⁴C BP	校正后（Cal. BC） 68.2% 概率	校正后（Cal. BC） 95.4% 概率
421	Y018	98-018-H1	喂庄西南	仰韶中晚	D-AMS029872	4351±33	3011 (26.8%) 2976 2971 (41.4%) 2911	3084 (4.5%) 3066 3028 (90.9%) 2899
龙山（N=10）								
63	Y152	01-152	寺沟东南	龙山早	SNU04-537	4260±50	2921 (50.2%) 2864 2806 (18.0%) 2760	3016 (64.3%) 2848 2814 (31.1%) 2678
440	Y1003	97-1003	南石	龙山晚	TO-11418	3740±70	2278 (7.0%) 2251 2228 (1.8%) 2221 2210 (59.4%) 2033	2432 (0.4%) 2423 2402 (1.3%) 2380 2348 (93.7%) 1944
190	217	03-079	寨湾东北	龙山晚	D-AMS029879	3795±33	2286 (60.1%) 2198 2164 (8.1%) 2151	2345 (94.8%) 2134 2073 (0.6%) 2064
238	Y127	02-127	灰嘴东	龙山晚	SNU04-416	3640±60	2130 (15.9%) 2086 2050 (52.3%) 1926	2200 (95.1%) 1878 1837 (0.3%) 1831
413	Y022	98-022	罗口东北	龙山晚	D-AMS029876	3671±36	2132 (33.0%) 2082 2060 (26.5%) 2016 1996 (8.7%) 1980	2191 (1.4%) 2180 2142 (94.0%) 1946
409	Y032	98-032	坞罗南店	龙山晚	D-AMS029877	3667±30	2131 (32.1%) 2086 2051 (25.1%) 2014 1998 (11.0%) 1979	2137 (95.4%) 1956
344	Y069	00-069	马屯	龙山晚	SNU04-986	3590±40	2014 (9.1%) 1998 1979 (59.1%) 1892	2116 (1.7%) 2098 2039 (88.9%) 1874 1844 (2.9%) 1816 1798 (1.9%) 1779
250	Y196B	02-196	涧东村西北	龙山晚	SNU05131	3590±40	2014 (9.1%) 1998 1979 (59.1%) 1892	2116 (1.7%) 2098 2039 (88.9%) 1874 1844 (2.9%) 1816 1798 (1.9%) 1779
62	Y151	01-151-H1L6	寺沟南	龙山晚	D-AMS029878	3292±31	1612 (68.2%) 1531	1638 (95.4%) 1501
12	046	01-060	保庄西北	龙山晚	D-AMS025484	2625±26	811 (68.2%) 794	831 (95.4%) 786

续表

序号	报告编号	原始编号	遗址名称	考古文化	实验室标本号	未校正^{14}C BP	校正后（Cal. BC） 68.2% 概率	校正后（Cal BC） 95.4% 概率
二里头（N=27）								
238	Y127	05-127	灰嘴西	二里头三期	ZK3941	3925±25	2472 (31.1%) 2436 2420 (13.7%) 2404 2378 (23.4%) 2350	2484 (93.1%) 2336 2323 (2.3%) 2307
238	Y127	02-127	灰嘴西	二里头二期	SNU05-132	3800±40	2293 (56.9%) 2196 2171 (11.3%) 2146	2452 (2.0%) 2420 2405 (2.6%) 2378 2350 (89.0%) 2132 2082 (1.7%) 2059
238	Y127	00-127	灰嘴西	二里头	TO-11419	3600±70	2120 (6.2%) 2094 2041 (62.0%) 1880	2141 (95.4%) 1754
238	Y127	02-127E	灰嘴西	二里头	BA 06498	3455±45	1876 (17.7%) 1841 1821 (11.1%) 1796 1782 (26.4%) 1732 1719 (13.0%) 1693	1891 (95.4%) 1658
238	Y127	02-127E	灰嘴东	二里头	BA 06500	3425±35	1770 (68.2%) 1665	1876 (9.7%) 1840 1821 (4.6%) 1796 1782 (81.1%) 1633
238	Y127	02-127E	灰嘴东	二里头	BA 06499	3415±35	1752 (68.2%) 1662	1872 (6.0%) 1844 1814 (1.8%) 1800 1778 (87.6%) 1626
238	Y127	04-127	灰嘴西	二里头II	ZK3940	3410±35	1748 (68.2%) 1660	1871 (4.5%) 1844 1812 (1.0%) 1803 1776 (89.9%) 1622
238	Y127	04-127W	灰嘴西	二里头	SNU05-932	3280±50	1615 (68.2%) 1505	1681 (0.5%) 1676 1665 (94.9%) 1444
238	Y127	05-127W	灰嘴西	二里头	SNU05-933	3270±50	1612 (68.2%) 1502	1660 (95.4%) 1436
377	Y132	07-132	新后沟砖厂东	二里头	ZK-3946	3380±30	1692 (59.5%) 1636	1746 (95.4%) 1616
393	Y039	98-022	罗口	二里头	D-AMS029880	3335±29	1665 (53.8%) 1607 1582 (14.4%) 1560	1690 (95.4%) 1528

续表

序号	报告编号	原始编号	遗址名称	考古文化	实验室标本号	未校正 ^{14}C BP	校正后（Cal. BC）68.2% 概率	校正后（Cal. BC）95.4% 概率
249	Y196A	02-196	涧东村北	二里头二期	ZK3945	3260±30	1607 (19.7%) 1582 1560 (48.5%) 1500	1616 (87.8%) 1492 1481 (7.6%) 1454
394	Y037	98-037(Z2)	上庄南	二里头三期	ZK3944	3225±25	1515 (29.0%) 1490 1484 (39.2%) 1451	1600 (3.2%) 1585 1534 (92.2%) 1431
393	Y039	98-022	罗口	二里头	NZA-40082	3335±20	1661 (64.9%) 1610 1571 (3.3%) 1566	1686 (75.5%) 1600 1585 (19.9%) 1534
377	Y132	00-132	新后沟砖厂东	二里头三期	ZK3948	3175±40	1496 (23.8%) 1471 1464 (44.4%) 1419	1530 (91.7%) 1384 1340 (3.7%) 1311
394	Y037	98-037(Z3)	上庄南	二里头三期	ZK3943	3175±25	1495 (21.8%) 1476 1458 (46.4%) 1423	1500 (95.4%) 1412
361	Y083	00-083	回龙湾新村东	二里头二或三期	ZK3947	2950±60	1256 (1.7%) 1251 1231 (66.5%) 1056	1384 (3.7%) 1341 1308 (91.7%) 996
189	216	03-074	寨湾东南	二里头	ZK3949	2905±45	1190 (5.0%) 1178 1160 (6.5%) 1144 1130 (56.7%) 1014	1224 (93.9%) 974 956 (1.5%) 941
361	Y083	00-083	回龙湾新村东	二里头	D-AMS029881	2858±29	1070 (1.5%) 1066 1056 (62.7%) 975 953 (4.0%) 944	1116 (95.4%) 928
		04HXXAT10 H97坑底	新砦	二里头一期	SNU06-748	3460±50	1878 (18.9%) 1840 1826 (14.9%) 1793 1784 (24.6%) 1736 1716 (9.8%) 1695	1901 (95.4%) 1642
		04HXX-5 AT10④下，H1063	新砦	二里头一期	ZK3942	2795±25	978 (68.2%) 910	1012 (93.6%) 894 868 (1.8%) 854
78	090	05YLV	二里头	二里头二期	NZA 39895	3376±25	1691 (68.2%) 1631	1741 (16.7%) 1711 1699 (78.7%) 1618
78	090	03-035	二里头	二里头三期	NZA 40078	3374±20	1688 (68.2%) 1638	1738 (11.8%) 1714 1696 (83.6%) 1622

续表

序号	报告编号	原始编号	遗址名称	考古文化	实验室标本号	未校正¹⁴C BP	校正后（Cal.BC） 68.2%概率	校正后（Cal.BC） 95.4%概率
78	090	05YKV	二里头	二里头四期	NZA40077	3356±20	1681 (5.9%) 1676 1665 (62.3%) 1624	1732 (2.9%) 1718 1693 (92.5%) 1612
78	090	05YLV	二里头	二里头四期	NZA40079	3350±20	1665 (68.2%) 1618	1729 (1.2%) 1721 1692 (91.8%) 1609 1578 (2.3%) 1563
78	090	05YLV	二里头	二里头二期	NZA40080	3290±20	1610 (15.3%) 1594 1589 (52.9%) 1532	1618 (95.4%) 1512
78	090	05YLV	二里头	二里头	NZA-40081	3256±20	1600 (15.4%) 1585 1534 (52.8%) 1500	1611 (91.7%) 1496 1475 (3.7%) 1460

二里岗—殷墟（N=6）

序号	报告编号	原始编号	遗址名称	考古文化	实验室标本号	未校正¹⁴C BP	校正后（Cal.BC） 68.2%概率	校正后（Cal.BC） 95.4%概率
425	Y011	98-011	费窑西南	二里岗上	SNU04-536	3510±40	1890 (68.2%) 1771	1941 (93.9%) 1741 1710 (1.5%) 1700
388	Y043	98-043	天坡水库东北	二里岗、下	SNU04-985	3060±40	1392 (34.7%) 1336 1324 (33.5%) 1268	1418 (95.4%) 1218
388	Y043	98-043	天坡水库东北	二里岗上、下	TO-11420	3020±50	1385 (17.0%) 1340 1310 (48.5%) 1207 1201 (1.4%) 1196 1139 (1.3%) 1134	1409 (95.4%) 1122
324	Y058	00-058	杨寨西北	二里岗上、下	SNU04-538	2940±40	1215 (66.3%) 1083 1064 (1.9%) 1058	1260 (95.4%) 1018
315	Y086	00-086	颜良寨西南	二里岗上、下	D-AMS029883	2927±31	1193 (29.4%) 1142 1132 (34.2%) 1072 1066 (4.6%) 1056	1217 (95.4%) 1022
53	065	02-001	北窑东北	殷墟	D-AMS029882	3285±47	1614 (68.2%) 1510	1682 (0.8%) 1674 1666 (88.7%) 1490 1484 (5.9%) 1450

续表

序号	报告编号	原始编号	遗址名称	考古文化	实验室标本号	未校正^{14}C BP	校正后（Cal. BC） 68.2% 概率	校正后（Cal. BC） 95.4% 概率
周代（N=3）								
62	Y151	11-151	寺沟南	西周早、中	D-AMS029884	3726+31	2196 (18.8%) 2170 2148 (15.6%) 2125 2090 (33.8%) 2044	2206 (95.4%) 2029
257	Y199	07-199	老屯寨	西—东周	D-AMS029886	3010±30	1369 (3.6%) 1360 1295 (64.6%) 1209	1386 (12.2%) 1340 1310 (78.9%) 1156 1146 (4.4%) 1128 726 (0.5%) 720
63	Y152	11-152	寺沟东南	西周—春秋	D-AMS029885	2371±32	484 (68.2%) 396	704 (0.9%) 695 541 (94.0%) 386

* 除丁府店东（Y124，裴李岗晚期）的样品是木炭，其他均为炭化种子。

另外，在复合型遗址组中有14个相对较大（20万～68万平方米），其中一些也可能是中心聚落，但我们不确定其仰韶时期的实际面积。根据仰韶单一型遗址的数据，伊洛地区仰韶中晚期的遗址分布显示为一个二级聚落等级的区域系统（图4.1b、图4.2）。

仰韶时期的经济以粟黍的种植和猪的饲养为主[18]，但采集野生谷物（小麦族）和块根植物（如山药）也是生计策略的一部分[19]。一些遗址保存有仪式性的大型房屋建筑。例如，灰嘴东（10万平方米；图4.1b-10）的大房子可能是进行社区仪式的中心设施，包括饮用小米酒的宴饮活动[20]。这种以大房子为中心的村落布局常见于仰韶文化遗址。

根据最近发表的数据，仰韶文化在黄河流域持续了2000多年（约5000～2700 cal. BC）；在河南地区大致可以分为早、中、晚三期，半坡类型（5000～3900 cal. BC），庙底沟类型（4000～3100 cal. BC）和秦王寨类型（3700～2700 cal. BC）[21]。我们在调查区域的仰韶中期和晚期遗址中获得了7个测年数据。这些年代基本落在600年的范围里（3490～2860 cal. BC），与陶器分期的仰韶中、晚期相当吻合（图4.3，表4.1）。这些数据显示，伊洛地区在仰韶中晚期经历了非常强劲的人口增长，遗址分布显示二级的聚落等级体系已遍布伊洛的大部分地区。

三、龙山文化时期

调查区域共发现了211个龙山文化遗址，其中龙山早期61个、龙山晚期156个，另外25个遗址只能鉴定到龙山时期。与仰韶晚期（N=146）相比，龙山早期的遗址数量急剧减少，但从龙山早期到晚期，遗址数量增加了1.5倍，略高于仰韶晚期的遗址数量。

龙山早期的遗址往往相当小，单一型的面积通常不到10万平方米，有些遗址具有特殊遗迹现象。例如，宋湾东南（042，图4.1c-13）残留的龙山遗存虽然面积很小（6000平方米），但是发掘表明该遗址为仰韶晚期到龙山早期的环壕聚落[22]，因此当时的面积应该大得多。根据现有的资料，我们不能确定哪些遗址可能是龙山早期的中心聚落。

我们分析了132个龙山晚期遗址，包括110个单一型和22个复合型。在直方图中单一型遗址分布为三个群组：

（1）2个最大的遗址为一级中心聚落（50万～70万平方米；南寨上村东、高崖西）；

（2）9个中型遗址为二级中心聚落（15万～34万平方米；陈家窑、罗口东北、景阳岗、盆窑寨西南、保庄西北、寺沟南、潘寨老寨东、纲常、金钟寺）；

（3）99个遗址为小村庄（≤12万平方米）。

另外有12个较大的复合型遗址（15万～50万平方米），其中一些可能是中心聚落。根据单一型龙山遗址分布状态，可以观察到三级聚落等级，比仰韶时期要更加复杂（图4.1c，图4.2）。

在一些无法确定面积的遗址中发现有特殊遗迹。例如，塔庄（063）遗址（图4.1c-12）位于偃师商城南部；发掘商城时，在第Ⅱ号基址群附近发现有龙山晚期的陶质排水管道及相关的建筑遗迹和夯土基址,但是被二里岗时期的建筑基址严重破坏[23]。塔庄(063)可能是龙山时期的一个重要中心遗址,说明龙山晚期伊洛地区有些中心聚落已具备较规整的布局和设施,其社会复杂化程度显然高于仰韶晚期。另外,灰嘴东(Y127E,10万平方米;图4.1c-14)这一时期发展成为一个以生产石铲为主的手工业中心聚落[24]。石铲多用于挖土,应与农业生产有关;其专业化生产说明农业生产活动的增长。但这一时期人们对野生禾本科(如小麦族)和块根植物(包括山药、栝楼根、百合等)的利用仍然继续[25]。

河南龙山文化分为早期(庙底沟二期;公元前2900~前2600年)和晚期(王湾三期;公元前2600~前1900年)阶段[26]。我们从龙山遗址中获得了10个测年结果,其中一个龙山早期遗址,寺沟东南(Y152,图4.1c-15)年代为3016~2678 cal. BC;其他9个为龙山晚期,其中7个样本均落在2430~1780 cal. BC的范围内。这些年代与传统上接受的河南龙山文化早、晚期年代基本吻合,但最晚的年代显然超出了1900 cal. BC一百多年。另外两个异常年代(寺沟南,Y151,1638~1501 cal. BC;保庄西北,046,831~786 cal. BC;图4.1c-8、7)的出现,可能是由于后代遗存的混入造成。龙山早期的年代与仰韶晚期的年代部分重叠,或许意味着该地区人类居住的连续性。然而,显示在SPD图上,龙山早期和晚期之间的2600 cal. BC前后存在约200年的空缺(图4.4a,表4.1)。因为只有一个龙山早期的样本,这个现象是否反映历史真实尚不可知。今后还需要对更多龙山早期遗址的样本进行年代测试,以检验该地区是否在大约2600 cal. BC前后发生了人口极端稀少的情况。

四、二里头文化时期

伊洛地区二里头文化时期的遗址共记录207个,可分为四期。仅有19个遗址确定为一期,但遗址数量从二期(N=76)、三期(N=92)到四期(N=94)不断增加。有81个遗址无法确定到特定期别。这一时期最重要的事件是二里头大型区域中心的崛起[27]。其面积在二里头一期时已达到100万平方米,到二至四期时,发展到300万平方米[28]。在伊洛地区,二里头一期遗存较薄且稀少,常与二里头较晚阶段并存,导致难以估计一期的遗址面积(图4.1d)。因此,我们分析了二里头二至四期184个遗址的数据,其中包括144个单一型和40个复合型遗址。这一时期代表了该地区二里头文化发展的高峰期。

二里头单一型遗址的分布在直方图中聚为四组:

(1)二里头为主要区域中心(300万平方米);

(2)6个较大的中型遗址为第二级中心(33万~80万平方米;稍柴、金钟寺、高崖西、桂连凹南、罗圪垱、古城西);

(3)10个中型遗址为第三级中心(18万~29万平方米;罗口东北、西口孜、灰嘴、经周东、宫家窑、杨村北、南蔡庄西北、景阳岗、寺沟、纲常);

(4)127个小遗址为小村庄(≤12万平方米)。

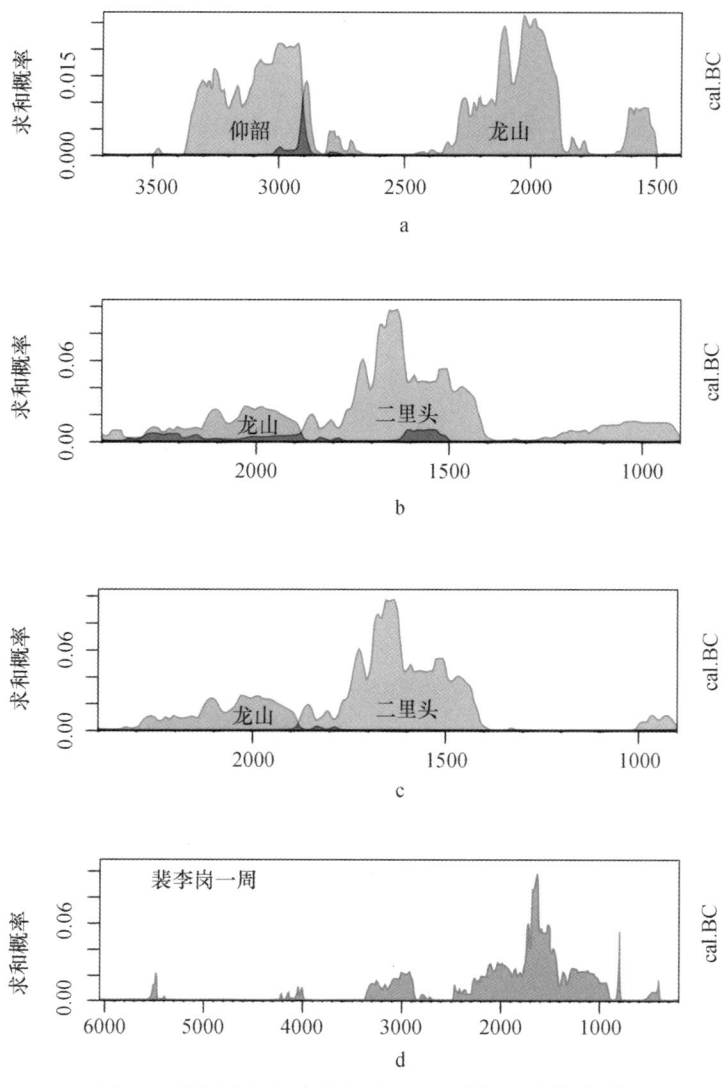

图4.4 利用求和概率分布（SPD）分析聚合^{14}C年代

a. 仰韶（N=7）和龙山（N=10）文化的年代的分布：3000~2900 cal. BC黑色阴影表示仰韶晚期和龙山早期年代重叠，同时在约2600 cal. BC介于龙山早期和晚期之间显示年代空缺　b. 龙山（N=10）和二里头（N=27）文化的年代分布：黑色阴影显示两个文化在2300~1800 cal. BC时期的重叠　c. 去除异常值之后龙山（N=8）和二里头（N=21）文化的年代分布：黑色阴影显示两个文化在1900~1800 cal. BC之间的重叠　d. 包括所有^{14}C年代（N=55）的SPD图像，显示从公元前6000到前200年间的波动

另外有15个较大复合型遗址（22万~80万平方米），其中一些也可能是二级或三级中心聚落。这个二至四期以二里头为中心的四级聚落等级结构的存在标志着一个国家级政治组织的出现（图4.2、图4.5a）。

二里头文化的年代序列是有争议的问题。最初的测年结果为1900~1500 cal. BC，但最近修改为1750~1530 cal. BC，其测年样本均来自二里头遗址[29]。我们从伊洛地区获得了25个测年，其中6个来自二里头遗址，9个来自灰嘴遗址，10个来自其他7个遗址。除二里头以外，其他为中、小型遗址；所有的测年样本均来自二里头文化二至四期的浮选样本。此外，我们还对二里头东南100多千米处的新密新砦遗址的两个二里头一期的浮选样本进行了测年。

二里头遗址的6个测年都集中在1741~1460 cal. BC，其起始年代与先前报道的该遗址年代

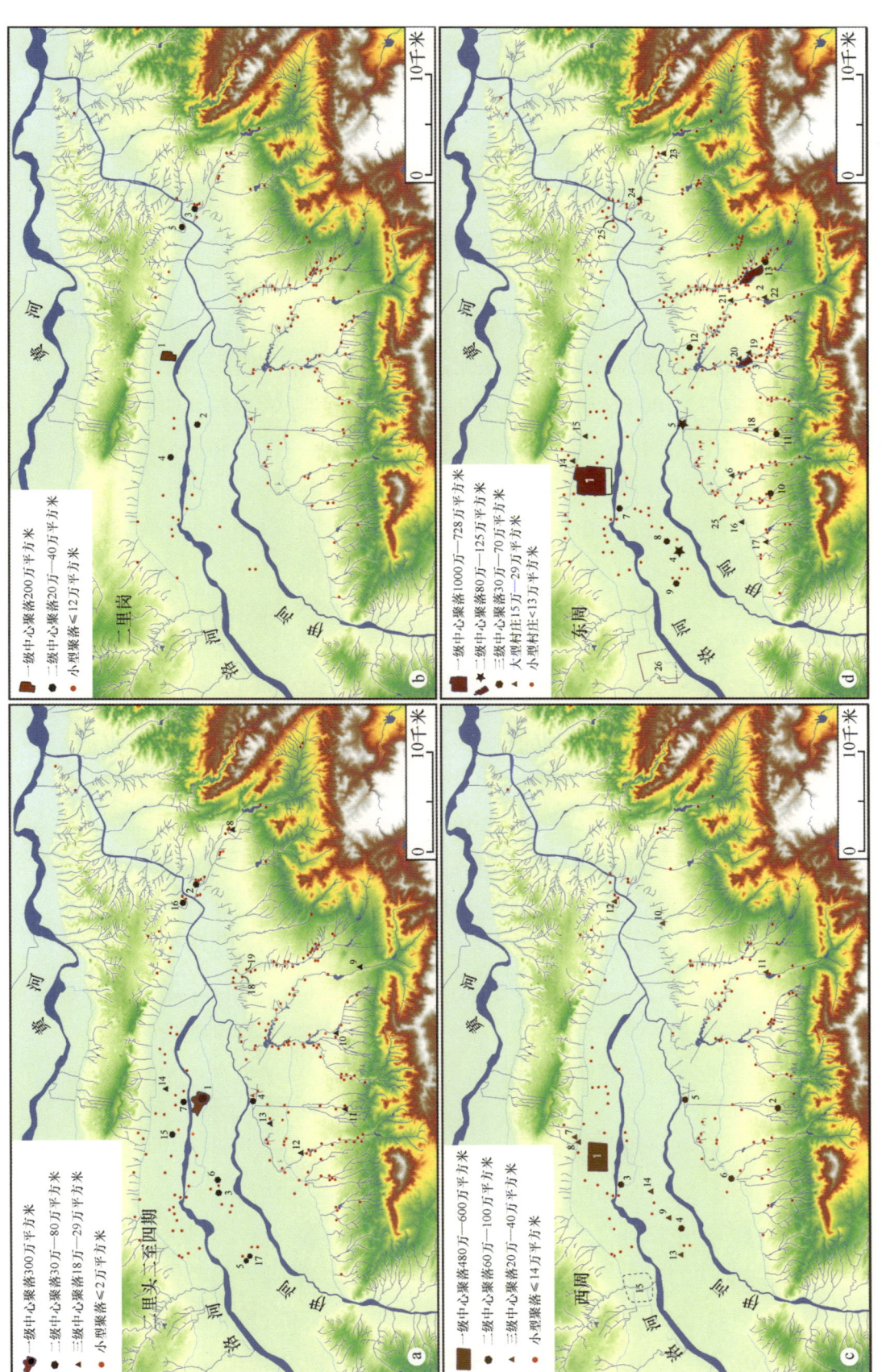

图4.5 二里头文化二至四期至东周时期聚落分布

a. 二里头文化二至四期遗址:1. 二里头(中心原点为1期范围,外圈为2—4期范围);2. 稍柴;3. 金钟寺;4. 高崖西;5. 桂连凹南;6. 罗圪垱;7. 古城西;8. 罗口东北;9. 西口孜;10. 灰嘴;11. 经周东;12. 官家窑;13. 纳常;14. 西周遗址;15. 景阳岗;16. 寺沟;17. 寺沟;b. 二里岗文化遗址:1. 偃师商城;2. 二里头;3. 稍柴;4. 穆庄;5. 莱湾东南;19. 南蔡庄西北;c. 西周遗址(洛邑和韩旗可能为先后关系):1. 韩旗城址;2. 滑国故城;3. 刘国故城;4. 穆庄;5. 南寨上村东;6. 西石垒;7. 孙家岗;8. 西石垒;9. 桂连凹南;10. 袁沟东;11. 经邑;12. 经周东;13. 纳常;14. 金钟寺;15. 洛邑;16. 寺沟;17. 刘沟东北;18. 吕桥东南;19. 郑窑南;20. 郑窑;d. 东周王城(东周王城和韩旗交替为主要城市);1. 韩旗城址;2. 滑国故城;3. 刘国故城;4. 穆庄;5. 南寨上村东;6. 西石垒;7. 孙家岗;8. 西石垒;9. 桂连凹南;10. 南罗;11. 经邑;12. 东王河北;13. 东王河北;14. 水库西;15. 石桥东北;16. 刘沟东北;17. 刘沟东北;18. 吕桥东南;19. 郑窑南;20. 郑窑;21. 王湾西北;22. 屯寨西北;23. 罗口东北;24. 清易镇东;25. 寺沟西;26. 东周王城一致，但其结束年代要晚于先前报道的年代范围（1750～1530 cal. BC）[30]。灰嘴（Y127）遗址（包括东址和西址）的9个测年分布范围为2485～1435 cal. BC，其中3个早于2000 cal. BC的异常值来自灰嘴西。其他地点的7个样本的年代范围为1765～1410 cal. BC。另外2个地点［回龙湾新村东（Y083）和寨湾东南（216）；图4.5a-18、19］的三个测年结果为异常值，均晚于1390 cal. BC。如果排除这5个异常值，其余来自灰嘴的6个测年和其他遗址的7个测年均落在1890～1410 cal. BC的范围内（表4.1）。SPD图像显示，无论包括或不包括这5个异常值，二里头年代范围与龙山晚期年代（公元前2430～前1780年）都有部分重叠（图4.4b，c）。这一现象意味着人类在这一地区居住的连续性，两组陶器类型可能有一段时期的共存关系。另外，伊洛地区二里头文化中小型聚落的年代分布范围明显比目前所知二里头中心聚落的年代范围要长[31]。同样值得注意的是，在二里头东南100多千米的新砦遗址的二里头一期遗存中获得的一个测年样本为1901～1642 cal. BC（SNU06-748），与伊洛地区二里头时期早段一致。但另一个新砦样本显示为异常值（1012～854 cal. BC；ZK3942）（图4.3，表4.1）。

6个二里头样本为异常值（早于公元前2000年和晚于公元前1400年，其中一个来自新砦）的情况可能有两种解释：

（1）伊洛地区的少数居民在公元前2000年以前就开始制造二里头风格陶器，例如在灰嘴，而且有些居民在公元前1400年后继续制作和使用这种陶器类型。

（2）早期种子（龙山期）或晚期种子（商代）混杂到二里头遗存中。

五、商（二里岗—殷墟文化）

伊洛地区共发现120个二里岗文化（商代早期）遗址，进一步分为二里岗下层（N=36）和二里岗上层（N=65）两个阶段，另外有33个遗址只能鉴定到二里岗时期。这一时期最重要的发展是偃师商城的兴起。这座位于二里头遗址东北6千米处的城址，一种观点认为是早商时期的政治和军事中心，是商人征服二里头夏都所建。另外，我们的调查还确定了60个属于殷墟文化（晚商）的遗址。

我们分析了111个二里岗文化遗址的聚落等级型态。其中94个单一型遗址在直方图中分布为三个集群：

（1）偃师商城为主要中心（200万平方米）；

（2）4个中型遗址二级中心（20万～40万平方米；二里头、稍柴、景阳岗、寺沟）；

（3）89个小村庄（≤12万平方米）。

有4个较大的多元文化遗址（27万～56万平方米），其中一些也可能是二级中心聚落（图4.2，图4.5b）。与二里头时期相比，二里岗时期的遗址数量、聚落等级和主要中心聚落的面积都明显下降，表明该地区政治重要性和人口密度总体衰落。这一时期正值偃师以东约100千米处的郑州商城崛起，应是政治中心从伊洛地区迁往郑州地区的结果。由于郑州商城此时是二里岗政治体系中最重要的中心，所以伊洛地区的遗址群是一个四级聚落等级系统一部分，代表一个国家。

伊洛地区聚落系统的衰退趋势持续到商代晚期的殷墟阶段，这时期遗址数量更少，均为多元文化遗址，无法确定是否有大型聚落。商代晚期伊洛地区的衰落显然与定都安阳殷墟有关。

根据以往郑州地区的测年样本，二里岗文化的年代为公元前1580～前1210年，可以分为二里岗下层（1580～1415 cal. BC）和二里岗上层（1429～1210 cal. BC）[32]。根据夏商周断代工程报告，偃师商城的^{14}C年代为1600～1260 cal. BC，与郑州的年代相呼应；殷墟文化的年代一般定为公元前1250～前1046年[33]。我们获得了5个二里岗遗址的测年和1个殷墟文化遗址的测年。其中，4个二里岗样品的年代范围为1420～1020 cal. BC，与二里岗上层到殷墟阶段的考古学年代一致，但是显然晚于偃师商城。费窑西南（Y011）样本（1941～1700 cal. BC）显然早于二里岗文化时期，但该遗址包含二里头二期遗存，因此这一异常值可能是由早期遗存的混合物造成的。北窑东北（065，1686～1450 cal. BC）的殷墟样品与二里头晚期同时。该遗址包含二里头四期遗存，因此测年样品可能也是与早期遗存混合（图4.3，表4.1）。值得注意的是，在我们的调查区域，二里头的年代范围（1890～1410 cal. BC）与二里岗的年代范围（1420～1020 cal. BC）基本衔接。

这些来自中小型遗址的资料说明，在大型区域中心（偃师商城）的人们使用了二里岗式陶器一段时间之后，一些中小型聚落原先使用二里头四期陶器的人群才开始使用二里岗式陶器。二里头遗址中四期的年代和偃师商城二里岗下层年代也有相当大的重叠，表明这两个中心遗址在同一时期曾各自使用不同类型的陶器。总之，以陶器风格的变化为代表的从二里头文化到二里岗文化的转变可能是一个漫长的过程。

六、西周和东周

在商代晚期之后，伊洛地区经历了又一次社会高度发展和人口快速增长的过程。遗址数量从商代晚期（N=60）到西周（N=138）（公元前1045～前771年）增加了一倍以上，同时在洛阳发现了一个非常大的城址，其中一处为西周早中期的位于瀍河两岸的大型聚落（600万平方米），可能为文献中所载的"洛邑（成周）"[34]；另一个为西周晚期[35]或两周之际[36]出现的城址（韩旗城址，480万平方米）[37]。这些变化在时间和空间上都与文献记载的西周早期周公在此洛邑（成周）和西周晚期周王室对"淮夷"采取军事行动相关[38]。我们分析了119个西周遗址，包括91个单一型和28个复合型。其中单一型遗址在直方图上显示为四级聚落等级的分布：

（1）瀍河两岸的大型聚落（600万平方米）和韩旗城址为主要区域中心（480万平方米）；

（2）5个二级中心（60万～100万平方米：经周东、孙家岗、穆庄、高崖西、南寨上村东）；

（3）8个三级中心（20万~40万平方米：保庄北、保庄西北、西石罢、南罗、屯寨西北、寺沟、纲常、金钟寺）；

（4）77个小村庄（≤14万平方米）。

另外，有19个相对较大的复合型遗址（19万~80万平方米），其中一些也可能是二级或三级中心聚落（图4.2，图4.5c）。

伊洛地区调查的范围里，社会发展和人口密度在东周时期（公元前770~前221年）达到了顶峰，表现为遗址数量大幅增加（N=294）和韩旗城面积扩大（728万平方米）[39]。我们分析了277个遗址，包括仅222个单一型遗址和55个复合型遗址。

直方图中的单一文化聚落分布显示了五级聚落等级结构：

（1）东周王城（约1000万平方米）和韩旗城址交替为主要城市中心（728万平方米）；

（2）4个大型聚落为二级中心（80万~125万平方米：滑国故城、刘国故城、穆庄、高崖西）；

（3）8个中型聚落为三级中心（30万~70万平方米：宫家窑、孙家岗、西石罢、桂连凹南、袁沟东、经周东、东王河北、颜良水库西）；

（4）11个次中型聚落为大村庄（15万~29万平方米：保庄北、石桥东北、刘家窑、刘沟东北、吕桥东南、郑窑南、郑窑、王湾西北、屯寨西北、罗口东北、清易镇东）；

（5）198个小型聚落为小村庄（<13万平方米）。

在复合型遗址中有35个较大的聚落（15万~80万平方米），其中一些也可能是不同层次的区域中心（图4.2，图4.5d）。这个前所未有的社会复杂程度，高密度人口，以及超大的东周王城和韩旗城的存在与文献记载的平王东迁和周王室公元前510年"城成周"的事件十分吻合。属于二级中心聚落的滑国故城和刘国故城是有城墙环绕的大型城址，它们的出现反映了一个新的分权型政治格局的产生：正如文献记载，当时东周王室逐渐失去其宗主国的霸权地位，而新兴的中小型政体间竞争加剧。

我们对3个周代遗址的样本进行了测年。其中寺沟东南（Y152）的年代（726~385 cal. BC；D-AMS029885，图4.5d-25）与东周年代一致，但其他2个为异常值（寺沟南，Y151：2206~2029 cal. BC；老屯寨，Y199：1386~1128 cal. BC），早于周代纪年（图4.3，表4.1）。这两个遗址均为复合型遗存；寺沟南有龙山晚期及二里头期的遗存，而老屯寨有殷墟期。因此，这些异常值可能是由于浮选样本中混合有早期遗存。

第四节　讨　　论

一、聚落形态和社会发展趋势

纵观伊洛地区聚落分布和AMS测年所反映的近6000年的历史进程，社会发展经历了数次波动。以下的讨论基于三个变量的综合分析：遗址数量、最大遗址面积和聚落等级，^{14}C测年结果主要代表中小型遗址。

1. 裴李岗文化

裴李岗晚期（5555~3980 cal. BC）伊洛地区出现最早的小型定居村落，但遗址数量少（17，包括瓦窑嘴）；可能有一个中心聚落（17，包括瓦窑嘴）；可能有两个中心聚落（9万~17万平方米）出现在伊洛河附近的平原地区，在伊洛平原形成局部地区的二级聚落等级。

2. 仰韶文化

早期遗址数量很少（20）、面积不大，与裴李岗晚期相比并无明显变化；但仰韶中晚期（3490~2860 cal. BC）出现第一次人口大幅度增长，表现为遗址数量明显增多（晚期至少146），10个中心遗址面积为19万~34万平方米，形成遍布于伊洛的大部分地区的二级聚落等级系统。

3. 龙山文化

龙山早期（3015~2680 cal. BC）为第一个衰落期，遗址数量减少（61），不见大型遗址。龙山晚期（2430~1780 cal. BC）为伊洛地区的第二次人口增长高峰，遗址数量明显增长（156），并出现两个一级中心聚落（50万~70万平方米）和9个二级中心聚落（15万~34万平方米），形成三级聚落等级。塔庄遗址出现的高等级建筑设施与聚落等级的发展是一致的。

4. 二里头文化

一期的遗址数量少（至少19），但此时二里头遗址已成为大型地区中心（100万平方米）。二至四期（多数遗址年代集中在1890~1410 cal. BC）为伊洛地区的第三次社会发展和人口增长高峰。二里头中心聚落扩大（300万平方米），出现6个二级中心聚落（33万~80万平方米）和10个三级中型中心聚落（18万~29万平方米），形成四级聚落等级。虽然二里头时期遗址总数（207）比龙山时期（211）略有减少，但多个大中型中心聚落和四级聚落等级的出现不仅反映了整个地区人口分布的聚合及人口密度的增长，也标志着国家的产生。这与二里头遗址考古发掘所揭示的阶层社会高度发展和都城形成的情况相吻合。

5. 商代（二里岗及殷墟文化，1600~1020 cal. BC）

二里头之后伊洛地区经历了一个逐渐失去政治中心地位的过程。总体来看二里岗下层（至少36）和上层（至少65）遗址都少于二里头四期（至少94），二里岗中心聚落面积缩小（偃师商城200万平方米），聚落等级减少为三级。至殷墟文化，遗址数量趋于减少（60），并缺少大型聚落。这些现象反映了商代伊洛地区的总体趋势为：人口密度减少，政治经济重要性降低。

6. 周代（1045～222 cal. BC）

伊洛地区先秦时期社会发展的最高峰阶段。西周和东周时期的遗址数量（分别为138、294）、中心聚落规模（分别为480万～600万、72万～1000万平方米）及聚落等级（分别为4级、5级）都远远超过之前的任何时代。这些聚落形态的变化与文献记载的周代政治变革历史基本吻合，此时伊洛地区重新成为古代王朝的政治经济中心。

总之，如图4.6所示，伊洛地区聚落形态的发展经历了数次波动，包括四次高潮和几次低谷阶段。经过从裴李岗到仰韶早期约2000年的缓慢发展，第一次高潮为仰韶晚期，其特点主要为人口密度的增加，二级聚落等级的社会组织结构遍布伊洛大部分地区。第二次高潮为龙山晚期，此时人口密度增加，社会组织结构更加复杂化，大致处于复杂酋邦社会。第三次高潮为二里头时期，不仅人口密度增加，而且社会组织结构发生质的飞跃，见证了国家产生的过程。第四次高潮为西周至东周，是早期王朝政治经济高度发展的结果。

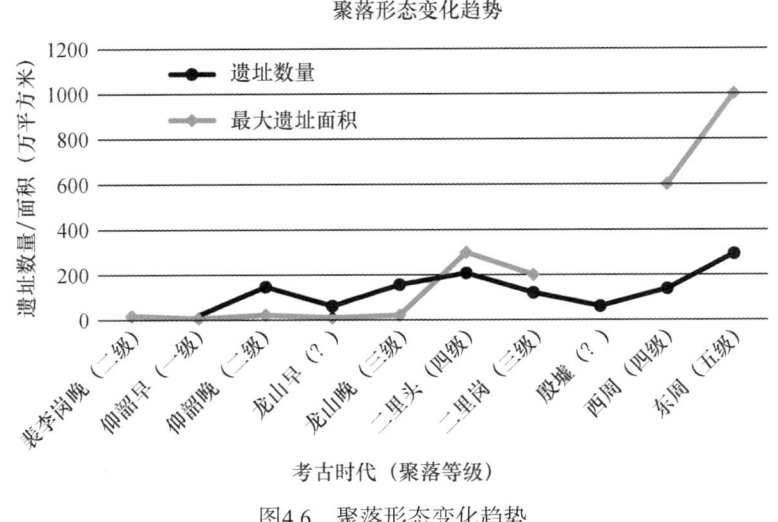

图4.6　聚落形态变化趋势

同时，我们可以观察到至少两次社会发展的低谷时期。第一次为龙山早期（约3000～2500 cal. BC），人口密度降低，这一时期正值中国北方全新世气候最适宜期结束，波动的干冷气候开始出现[40]。对黄土高原西部甘肃武都地区万象洞（位于洛阳以西约900千米）钟乳石的研究表明，夏季季风在5700～4920 cal. BP时期减弱，并在5400 cal. BP时出现极端减弱事件，导致降水量显著减少[41]。从洛阳附近的栾川（位于洛阳西南约150千米的山区）钟乳石资料中可以看到全新世河南西部也存在气候波动，但没有显示一个约3000 cal. BC的极端干旱事件[42]。因此未来的研究应该进一步检验这一中国北方普遍存在的气候波动对伊洛盆地自然环境影响的程度。第二次低谷期为商代晚期，是政治中心转移的结果。上述聚落形态波动也显示在综合了所有^{14}C年代的SPD图像上（图4.4-d）。第二、三次发展高潮（龙山晚期和二里头期）之间是否有一个低谷期，尚不明确。这一问题涉及二里头文化的起源和二里头国家形成过程，以下谨做初步探讨。

值得注意的是，气候变化并未以同样的方式影响社会形态。恶化的气候条件可能导致了龙山文化早期人口减少，但却见证了二里头文化的蓬勃发展。因此，应对外部压力的人类决策可能是决定社会发展或衰退的主要因素。

二、陶器的生产分配模式、考古学类型与人群的关系

由于测年样品的考古学年代是根据与浮选样本共存的陶器类型判断的，我们得到的^{14}C测年结果反映了陶器在某些遗址中使用的年代。伊洛地区龙山晚期遗址的年代（2430~1780 cal. BC）与二里头遗址大多数测年样品的年代（1890~1412 cal. BC）有明显重合（图4.4b、c；表4.1），反映了人口居住的连续性。一个地区陶器类型的发展变化在一定程度上与制陶工匠的技术传承，陶器的生产组织结构，以及产品的分配、交换范围有密切关系。因此，我们在讨论陶器类型的时空分布时，需要了解陶器的生产和分配模式。

对伊洛地区新石器时代至早期青铜时代三个重要遗址（二里头、灰嘴、稍柴）出土的陶器进行岩相和便携式X射线荧光仪（p-XRF）分析的结果显示，二里头中心聚落和周边主要二级或三级中心聚落之间没有广泛陶器产品交流。靠近洛河/伊洛河的二里头和稍柴的陶器中包含有以火山灰和硫化物–二氧化硅（Volcanic and Sulfide-silica）为特征的掺和料，而接近嵩山的灰嘴陶器的掺和料是以变质岩（闪石片麻岩和片岩）[Metamorphic（Amphibole Gneiss and Schist）]为特征。另外，灰嘴和稍柴遗址的陶器中都有细粒硅质碎屑和碳酸盐岩（Fine-grained Siliciclastic and Carbonate Sedimentary Lithic），具有嵩山的沉积岩特征。说明这三个遗址的陶器有各自的陶土和掺和料来源。另外，灰嘴遗址从仰韶、龙山到二里头时期的陶器显示出颇为一致的陶土成分和来源。这些结果说明，伊洛地区的陶器生产从新石器到二里头时期都显示为分散的多元模式，利用聚落附近的陶土和掺和料资源。这一模式并没有因二里头中心聚落的出现及伊洛地区政治结构变化而明显改变[43]。

伊洛地区的这种分散的小区域陶器生产模式可能影响了陶器类型分布的空间和时间关系。例如，二里头文化的起源是以二里头一期陶器的出现为标志，情况可能如下：如果当龙山晚期陶器仍然流行时，有些居民已开始制作和使用二里头类型陶器，那么有些二里头一期的遗址可能与龙山晚期遗址共存。二里头一期的遗址虽然数量少，但在调查区域内分布十分广泛（图4.1d），很可能是本地区发展的结果。在这种情况下，二里头一期遗址数量少的现象，可能不是这一时期人口减少的标志，而是反映了该地区陶器风格转变的过程。另外一个显示两个考古学文化^{14}C年代重叠的例子是二里头和二里岗之间的过渡：二里岗陶器在偃师商城出现的年代要早于周围的小型聚落。说明一种新的陶器风格已经在大型中心聚落开始流行，之后蔓延到较小的村落。偃师商城建造是一个有规划的过程：首先建造宫殿区，然后建内城，最后建外城[44]。那些使用二里岗类型陶器、建立偃师商城的人群在进入伊洛地区时显然是有组织的人口迁徙，他们很可能带着自己的陶工。

值得注意的是，上述两种情况的陶器类型过渡是以截然相反的方向发生，一是自下而上（从二里头一期的小型聚落到二里头中心聚落），一是自上而下（从二里岗的中心聚落到周边的小型聚落）。可见，陶器风格所代表的考古文化转型可能是漫长的、镶嵌式的、流动性的和多方向的过程。因此，我们不应该将陶器类型组合视为在一个固定的时空关系中代表一个特定人群的指示物。

三、二里头文化年代问题

二里头的年代也是一个重要问题。我们在伊洛地区调查过程中没有采集到二里头一期的浮选样本，因此缺少这一时期的测年。但大量来自该地区不同遗址的二里头二至四期测年数据多数集中在1890~1410 cal. BC范围内。因此，伊洛地区二里头一期的年代不应晚于1890 cal. BC，而四期的年代可能延续到1500 cal. BC之后，显示二里头文化年代的总跨度比以前估计的（1750~1530 cal. BC）要长。以前的二里头年代序列是参考了新砦遗址中新砦期的年代序列（1870~1720 cal. BC），这是根据新砦期为龙山晚期和二里头文化之间的过渡期的观点，认为二里头文化应晚于新砦期[45]。但新砦遗址位于伊洛地区之外，距二里头遗址100多千米，其间又有嵩山山脉相隔。而且在伊洛地区调查范围内，并没有发现有一个明确的新砦期遗存阶段。我们在伊洛地区观察到的陶器生产和分布呈现分散的小区域特征，应该具有普遍性。新砦地区的陶器序列应视为当地的发展系统，而伊洛地区的二里头文化也应有其本地的渊源和发展序列。因此，新砦和伊洛两地的考古学文化发展过程应分别对待。值得注意的是，我们的测年结果中，来自新砦二里头一期的年代达到1900 cal. BC。这些数据迫使我们重新考虑二里头文化的年代问题。

来自伊洛地区多个二里头文化遗址的测年数据表明，二里头类型陶器在该地区一些中小型聚落中的使用时间要长于这类陶器在二里头中心聚落的使用时间。二里头是一个政治经济中心，在其建立之前该地点没有龙山晚期的人类活动，而且在距今4000年前后有长期被洪水淹没的沉积现象[46]。因此二里头大型遗址在一期的突然出现，应是人口迁徙的结果。其人口显然来自其他地方，如灰嘴及伊洛地区内外的一些聚落。我们目前并没有证据确定伊洛地区使用二里头一期陶器的人群来自于新砦地区。在调查资料中，也没有看到伊洛地区的龙山晚期与二里头文化之间有另一种过渡文化阶段。因此，对伊洛地区二里头文化渊源的探索，应该包括本地的使用龙山文化陶器的人群，而不应依赖于新砦地区的龙山—新砦—二里头的陶器类型变化模式。

第五节 小 结

总之，伊洛地区调查结果为我们提供了至今最完整的6000年中该区域社会发展的时空关系资料，揭示了早期中国文明核心区从一个零星分布着小村落的新石器时代平等社会景观到集权的王朝统治中心的发展轨迹。这一进化过程是以人口密度的波动及复杂社会的兴衰为特征。人类活动和社会发展无疑受到了气候和环境变化的影响，但人类对各种外部挑战的应对策略最终决定了社会进化的轨迹。

在对该地区文明发展进程的探讨中仍存在大量未知数，其中最重要的问题与二里头文化有关。例如，如果从晚期龙山到二里头阶段的过渡发生在公元前1900年左右或之前，二里头中心聚落的出现是移民的结果，那么我们需要解释：

（1）是什么自然或社会力量驱动此时的人口迁移？

（2）这些移民来源于何处？

为了解答这些疑问，我们需要采取多学科的方法，包括重建环境和生态变化，人口的生物学分析，以及进一步研究陶器的生产和分配模式。最新建立的聚落形态数据为这些研究奠定了基础。

致谢：我们对参与了伊洛地区调查项目的中国、澳大利亚、美国和英国的众多考古学家、地质学家和技师表示最深切的感谢。特别是李润权、魏鸣、马萧林、艾琳·罗森（Arlene Rosen）、约翰·韦伯（John Webb）、安妮·福特（Anne Ford）、贝喜安（Sheahan Bestel）、廖永民、刘洪淼、王保仁、王法成、王宏章和二里头工作队的其他成员，以及中国社会科学院考古研究所河南第二工作队（偃师商城工作队），他们为调查和研究做出了巨大贡献。我们感谢澳大利亚研究理事会（Australian Research Council）、美国国家地理学会（National Geographic Society）、美国温纳−格伦基金会（The Wenner-Gren Foundation）、澳大利亚拉筹伯大学（La Trobe University）、美国哈佛大学（Harvard University）和中国社会科学院，没有这些研究机构提供的慷慨资助，这个项目是不可能实现的。

注　释

[1] 陈星灿、刘莉、李润权，等：《中国文明腹地的社会复杂化进程：伊洛河地区的聚落形态》，《考古学报》2003年第2期；Liu L, Chen X C, Lee Y K, et al. Settlement Patterns and Development of Social Complexity in the Yiluo Region, North China. Journal of Field Archaeology, 2002-2004, 29(1-2): 75-100; 中国社会科学院考古研究所二里头工作队：《河南洛阳盆地2001～2003年考古调查简报》，《考古》2005年第5期。

[2] Carneiro R. A Theory of the Origin of the State. Science, 1970, 169: 733-738.

[3] Feng Z D, An C B, Tang L, et al. Stratigraphic Evidence of a Megahumid Climate between 10,000 and 4000 Years B.P. in the Western Part of the Chinese Loess Plateau. Global and Planetary Change, 2004, 43: 145-155; Feng Z D, An C B, Wang H B. Holocene Climatic and Environmental Changes in the Arid and Semi-arid Areas of China: a Review. The Holocene, 2006, 16(1): 119-130; Ran M, Feng Z D. Holocene Moisture Variations across China and Driving Mechanisms: a Synthesis of Climatic Records. Quaternary International, 2013, 313/314: 179-193; Chen F H, Xu Q H, Chen J H, et al. East Asian Summer Monsoon Precipitation Variability since the Last Deglaciation. Scientific Reports, 2015, 5: 11186; Shi Y, Kong Z, Wang S, et al. Mid-Holocene Climates and Environments in China. Global and Planetary Change, 1993, 7: 219-233.

[4] Zhang J N, Xia Z K, Zhang X H, et al. Early–middle Holocene Ecological Change and Its Influence on Human Subsistence Strategies in the Luoyang Basin, North-central China. Quaternary Research, 2018, 89: 446-458.

[5] Rosen A M. The Role of Environmental Change in the Development of Complex Societies in China: a Study from the Huizui Site. Bulletin of the Indo-Pacific Prehistory Association, 2007, 27: 39-48; Rosen A M. The Impact of Environmental Change and Human Land Use on Alluvial Valleys in the Loess Plateau of China during the Middle Holocene. Geomorphology, 2008, 101: 298-307; Rosen A M. Macphail R, Liu L, et al. Rising Social Complexity, Agricultural Intensification, and the Earliest Rice Paddies on the Loess Plateau of Northern China. Quaternary International, 2017, 437: 50-59.

[6] Fish S K, Kowalewski S A. The Archaeology of Regions: A Case for Full-Coverage Survey. Washington, D.C.: Smithsonian Institution Press, 1990.

[7] 中美日照地区联合考古队：《鲁东南沿海地区系统考古调查报告》，文物出版社，2012年。

[8] Chifeng International Collaborative Archaeological Research Project. Settlement Patterns in the Chifeng Region. Pittsburgh: Center for Comparative Archaeology University of Pittsburgh, 2011.

[9] 中国社会科学院考古研究所、美国明尼苏达大学科技考古实验室中美洹河流域考古队：《洹河流域区域考古研究初步报告》，《考古》1998年第10期。

[10] Lee G A, Crawford G W, Liu L. Plants and People from the Early Neolithic to Shang Periods in North China. PNAS, 2007, 104(3): 1087-1092.

[11] Earle T K. The Evolution of Chiefdom//Earle T. Chiefdoms: Power, Economy, and Ideology. Cambridge: Cambridge University Press, 1991: 1-15; Flannery K V. The Ground Plans of Archaic States//Feinman G M, Marcus J. Archaic States. Santa: School of American Research Press, 1998: 15-58; Wright H T. Toward an Explanation of the Origin of the State//Hill J. Explanation of Prehistoric Change. Albuquerque: University of New Mexico Press, 1977: 215-230; Wright H T, Johnson G. Population, Exchange, and Early State Formation in Southwestern Iran. American Anthropologist, 1975, 77: 267-289.

[12] 陈星灿、刘莉、李润权，等：《中国文明腹地的社会复杂化进程：伊洛河地区的聚落形态》，《考古学报》2003年第2期。

[13] Ramsey C B. Development of the Radiocarbon Calibration Program. Radiocarbon, 2001, 43(2A): 355-363; Reimer P J, Bard E, Bayliss A. IntCal13 and Marine13 Radiocarbon Age Calibration Curves 0–50,000 Years Cal BP. Radiocarbon, 2013, 55(Nr 4): 1869-1887.

[14] Bevan A, Crema E, Silva F. Rcarbon v1.1.3: Methods for Calibrating and Analysing Radiocarbon Dates. 2018. https://CRAN.R-project.org/package=rcarbon.

[15] 巩义市文物保护管理所：《巩义市瓦窑嘴遗址第三次发掘报告》，《中原文物》1997年第1期；巩义市文物管理所：《河南巩义市瓦窑嘴新石器时代遗址试掘简报》，《考古》1996年第7期；郑州市文物工作队、巩义市文物管理所：《河南巩义市瓦窑嘴新石器时代遗址的发掘》，《考古》1999年第11期。

[16] Liu L, Chen X C, Lee Y K, et al. Settlement Patterns and Evelopment of Social Complexity in the Yiluo Region, North China. Journal of Field Archaeology, 2002-2004, 29(1-2): 75-100; Lee G A, Crawford G W, Liu L, et al. Plants and People from the Early Neolithic to Shang Periods in North China. PNAS, 2007, 104(3): 1087-1092; Liu L, Chen X C, Lee Y K, et al. Settlement Patterns and Development of Social Complexity in the Yiluo Region, North China. Journal of Field Archaeology, 2002-2004, 29(1-2): 75-100.

[17] 中国社会科学院考古研究所：《中国考古学·新石器卷》，中国社会科学出版社，2010年。

[18] Lee G A, Crawford G W., Liu L, et al. Plants and People from the Early Neolithic to Shang Periods in North China. PNAS, 2007, 104(3): 1087-1092.

[19] 刘莉、Maureece J. Levin、陈星灿，等：《河南偃师灰嘴遗址新石器时代和二里头文化时期工具残留物及微痕分析》，《中原文物》2018年第6期。

[20] 刘莉、王佳静、陈星灿，等：《仰韶文化大房子与宴饮传统：河南偃师灰嘴遗址F1地面和陶器残留物分析》，《中原文物》2018年第1期。

[21] 张雪莲、仇士华、钟建，等：《仰韶文化年代讨论》，《考古》2013年第11期。

[22] 中国社会科学院考古研究所洛阳汉魏城工作队内部资料。

[23] 中国社会科学院考古研究所：《偃师商城》，科学出版社，2013年。

[24] Liu L, Chen X C, Li B P. Non-state Crafts in the Early Chinese State: An Archaeological View from the Erlitou Hinterland. Bulletin of the Indo-Pacific Prehistory Association, 2007, 27: 93-102.

[25] 刘莉、Maureece J. Levin、陈星灿，等：《河南偃师灰嘴遗址新石器时代和二里头文化时期工具残留物及微痕分析》，《中原文物》2018年第6期。

[26] 中国社会科学院考古研究所：《中国考古学·新石器卷》，中国社会科学出版社，2010年。

[27] 中国社会科学院考古研究所：《偃师二里头》，中国大百科全书出版社，1999年；中国社会科学院考古研究所：《二里头（1999～2006）》，文物出版社，2014年。

[28] 许宏、陈国梁、赵海涛：《二里头遗址聚落形态的初步考察》，《考古》2004年第11期。

[29] 张雪莲、仇士华、蔡莲珍，等：《新砦—二里头—二里冈文化考古年代序列的建立与完善》，《考古》2007年第8期。

[30] 张雪莲、仇士华、蔡莲珍，等：《新砦—二里头—二里冈文化考古年代序列的建立与完善》，《考古》2007年第8期。

[31] 张雪莲、仇士华、蔡莲珍，等：《新砦—二里头—二里冈文化考古年代序列的建立与完善》，《考古》2007年第8期。

[32] 张雪莲、仇士华、蔡莲珍，等：《新砦—二里头—二里冈文化考古年代序列的建立与完善》，《考古》2007年第8期。

[33] 夏商周断代工程专家组：《夏商周断代工程1996—2000年阶段成果报告》，世界图书出版社，2000年。

[34] 叶万松、张剑、李德方：《西周洛邑城址考》，《华夏考古》1991年第2期。

[35] 刘富良：《洛阳西周陶器墓研究》，《考古与文物》1998年第3期；徐昭峰：《成周与王城考略》，《考古》2007年第11期。

[36] 梁云：《成周与王城考辨》，《考古与文物》2002年第5期。

[37] 中国社会科学院考古研究所洛阳汉魏城队：《汉魏洛阳故城城垣试掘》，《考古学报》1998年第3期。

[38] 徐昭峰：《成周与王城考略》，《考古》2007年第11期。

[39] 中国社会科学院考古研究所洛阳汉魏城队：《汉魏洛阳故城城垣试掘》，《考古学报》1998年第3期。

[40] Feng Z D, An C B, Wang H B. Holocene Climatic and Environmental Changes in the Arid and Semi-arid Areas of China: a Review. The Holocene, 2006, 16(1): 119-130.

[41] 白益军、张平中、高涛，等：《亚洲夏季风5400a BP极端减弱事件与文化演变》，《中国科学：地球科学》2017年第47卷第5期。

[42] Zhang N, Yang Y, Cheng H, et al. Timing and Duration of the East Asian Summer Monsoon Maximum during the Holocene Based on Stalagmite data from North China. The Holocene, 2018, 28(10): 1631-1641.

[43] Bonomo M F. Ceramic Production and Provenance in the Yiluo Basin (Henan, China): Geoarchaeological interpretations of utilitarian craft production in the Erlitou state. Archaeological Research in Asia, 2017, 14: 80-96.

[44] 中国社会科学院考古研究所：《偃师商城》，科学出版社，2013年。

[45] 张雪莲、仇士华、蔡莲珍，等：《新砦—二里头—二里冈文化考古年代序列的建立与完善》，《考古》2007年第8期。

[46] 张俊娜、夏正楷：《中原地区4 ka BP前后异常洪水事件的沉积证据》，《地理学报》2011年第66卷第5期。

第五章　伊洛地区复杂社会的演变：
地理信息系统基础上的人口和农业可耕地的分析[①]

伊洛盆地是中国早期国家起源的核心地带。本章以伊洛聚落调查项目获得的考古资料为基础，依据西方考古学中与人口规模估算、土地承载力、领地生产力相关的理论和方法，借助地理信息系统的有关模式，分析了伊洛地区从裴李岗时期到二里头时期的人口浮动情况，以及这种变化与社会复杂化的关系。

研究包括三个基本部分：

（1）人口规模的估计；

（2）在地理信息系统软件的辅助下重建研究区域土地承载量、领地生产力；

（3）阐述人口浮动和社会复杂化的交互作用。

研究发现：从仰韶晚期开始至二里头时期，伊洛地区的很多聚落有农业用地短缺的现象。如果排除聚落共存性的问题，可以推测出两个解决短缺的模式。

（1）再分配模式：即某些聚落食物的短缺可以用从其他聚落调配的形式来弥补；

（2）特殊资源模式：即农业用地短缺的聚落可以用特殊资源，如石器等手工业品，来换取食物。

研究认为，人口的增长和社会复杂化的加剧有密切联系。人口增长不一定会导致自然环境难以承载的生存压力，但会促发社会结构变革，以解决不断扩大的人口规模带来的各种问题，这就为社会上层运用不同策略获得和维护权力、建立更复杂的社会结构提供了机会。

第一节　研究基础、目的与方法

伊洛盆地北以邙岭，西以崤山和熊耳山，南以伏牛山，东南以嵩山为界。盆地内地貌景观由发源于山地的伊洛河众支流、河边冲积平原、高于河床10～70米的黄土阶地和山地组成。无霜期从3月一直持续到11月，年平均降水量620毫米，12月到次年2月是最干燥的季节，夏季季

[①] 本章由乔玉执笔。中文原文发表于《考古学报》2010年第4期。选入本报告后略有删减。文中遗址数量和年代的判断采用了中澳美伊洛河流域联合考古队早年调查数据，与本报告不一致之处，以本报告为准。

第五章 伊洛地区复杂社会的演变：地理信息系统基础上的人口和农业可耕地的分析

风从6月持续到8月，冬麦和玉米是目前主要的农作物[1]。全新世以来，本地区的气候和植被发生过一系列变化[2]，古植被的密度可能会比现在更稠密，古代居民可能更容易接近自然资源，如水、木材、野果和动物等[3]。

伊洛盆地为文献中记载的夏王朝的中心区域之一，是中国早期国家起源的核心地带，久已成为考古学家们关注的焦点[4]。对二里头遗址的调查和发掘工作已经持续了近60年，宫城、按中轴线布局的宫殿基址、高等级墓葬、手工作坊及青铜器、玉器和绿松石器等精美器物的发现都说明，该遗址是一个集政治、经济、宗教文化为一身的都邑性聚落[5]。然而，如何从宏观区域形态的角度探讨伊洛地区的社会复杂化进程仍是需要解决的问题。

1997年，由中国社会科学院考古研究所、澳大利亚拉筹伯大学（La Trobe University）等机构组成中澳美伊洛河流域联合考古队，由来自中国、澳大利亚、美国和英国等国各有专长的考古学家组成，开始了一个多学科国际合作考古项目，期望通过拉网式田野调查获得伊洛地区从新石器中期到早期国家形成期间的区域聚落形态变化资料，并综合地质考古调查、民族植物学的研究及石器和陶器的分析等内容，运用有关复杂社会出现及发展的理论，探究人口波动、环境变迁、土地开发利用程度、农业生产力水平、手工业生产专业化等因素与社会复杂化的关系问题[6]。

1997年1月到2002年6月，联合考古队沿伊洛地区的坞罗河、曹河、干沟河、马涧河和浏涧河5条小河谷，进行了6个季度拉网式调查，覆盖面积219平方千米（图5.1）。确定遗址194处。很多遗址包含不同时期遗存，本研究以上述调查资料为基础，但集中于对裴李岗到二里头时期遗址的研究（表5.1）。

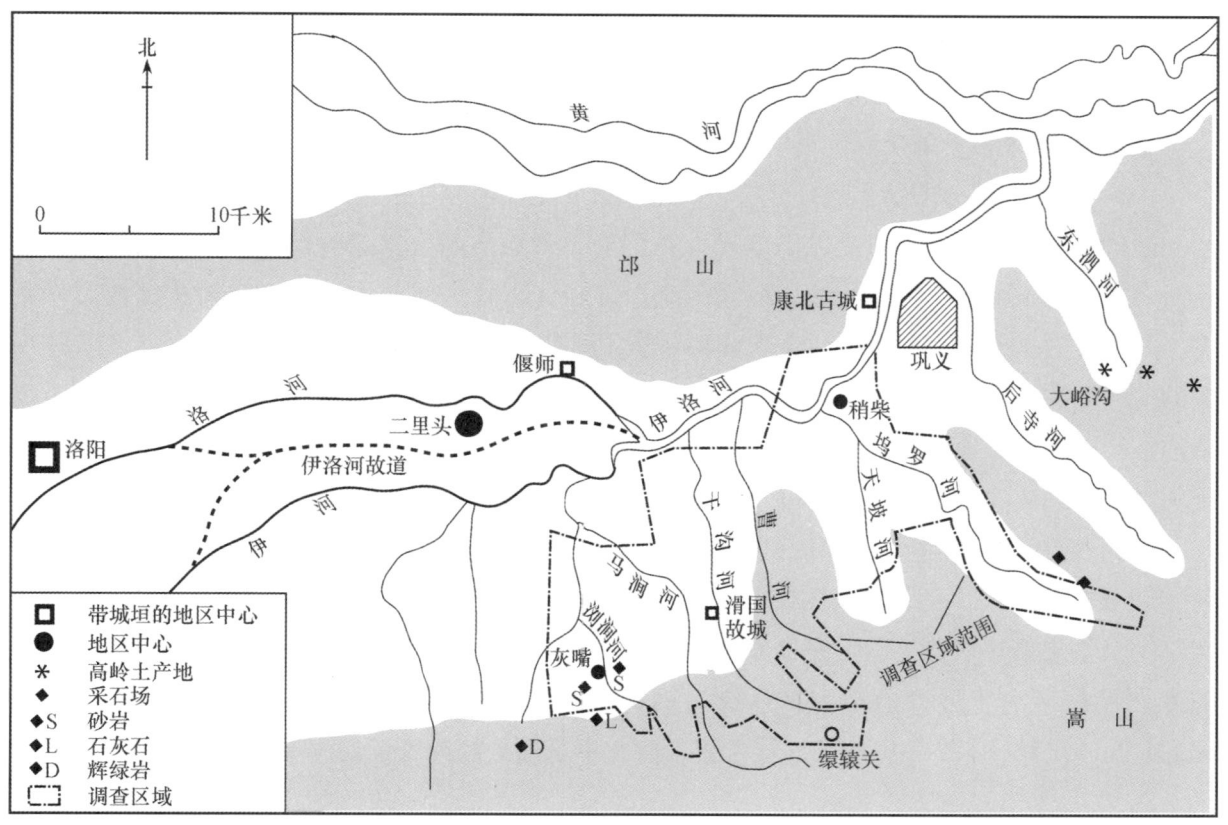

图5.1 伊洛地区的重要遗址及资源

表5.1 调查区域内裴李岗文化到二里头时期遗址分布情况

文化时期/地区	坞罗河	干沟河	曹河	马涧河	浏涧河	总数
裴李岗文化	4	1	0	0	2	7
仰韶早期	2	0	0	0	1	3
仰韶中期	5	5	0	3	1	14
仰韶晚期	13	14	3	12	3	45
仰韶文化（分期不确定）	0	3	0	1	6	10
龙山早期	2	7	0	1	1	11
龙山晚期	14	25	4	14	19	76
二里头一期	6	3	1	0	1	11
二里头二期	11	9	1	3	3	27
二里头三期	9	9	1	5	3	27
二里头四期	6	14	0	5	3	29
二里头文化（分期不确定）	6	8	0	0	1	15
合计	78	98	11	44	44	275

本章着重要解决的问题是：

（1）裴李岗到二里头时期研究区域内人口规模是如何变化的？

（2）人口压力是否在社会复杂化进程中起到了推动作用？

（3）在社会复杂化发展过程中，领地生产力和遗址人口数量的关系是什么？

这些问题的答案能够帮助我们更好地理解中原地区早期国家形成的过程和特征。

研究包括三部分：

（1）依据聚落面积对研究区域内各时期人口数量进行估计。

（2）在地理信息系统软件帮助下重建研究区域内各时期土地承载力和领地生产力。

（3）对前两部分的结果进行分析，讨论人口变化和社会复杂化之间的互动关系。

地理信息系统（GIS）是以电脑操作系统为平台对空间数据进行储存、描述、检索、显示、分析、运算的软件系统[7]。地理信息系统在分析处理问题中使用了空间数据与属性数据，并通过数据库管理系统将两者联系在一起共同管理、分析和应用，从而提供了认识地理现象的一种新的思维方法；它能进行有关空间数据的操作，如空间查询、检索、相邻分析以及复杂的空间分析等。地理信息系统强调空间分析，通过利用空间解析式模型来分析空间数据，地理信息系统的成功应用依赖于空间分析模型的研究与设计[8]。

大约在20世纪70年代地理信息系统被引入到西方考古学研究中[9]，主要用于分析遗物的空间分布规律[10]及其他制图统计方面的设计[11]。80年代，它被广泛应用于遗址位置预测[12]、文化遗产管理[13]、聚落形态分析[14]和其他空间数据的分析[15]；90年代以来，随着软件技术的发展，地理信息系统与重视研究人与环境关系的景观考古学（landscape archaeology）结合[16]，展现了其在考古学研究中更诱人的前景。我国考古学界对地理信息系统的应用始于20世纪90年代[17],许多中外合作的区域聚落调查项目,如河南颍河流域考古调查[18]、安阳考古调查[19]、伊洛河流域考古调查[20]、山东日照两城考古调查[21]和内蒙古赤峰半支箭河考古调查等都有GIS研究的参与[22]。在这些项目中,GIS主要用于制作数字化地图、建立遗址分布的数据库等基础性工作,以方便空间信息的检索和显示。本研究是对GIS运用的一种新的尝试。

第二节 人口数量估计及土地承载力和领地生产力的重建

一、人口数量估计

20世纪60年代以来,人口考古开始被广泛关注[23],人口数量估计是其中最重要的内容之一。目前最流行的史前人口数量估计方法是:把民族学研究和聚落考古学研究的成果有机地结合起来,首先根据民族学研究得出每间房屋居民数量、每个居民的平均居住面积或聚落内每公顷的平均居民数量,同时依据考古资料确认一个遗址中房屋总量(或居住总面积)或遗址总面积,然后根据以下的公式估计遗址的人口数量:

人口数量=每间房屋的居民数量×房屋的数量

人口数量=居住总面积/每个居民平均居住面积

人口数量=每公顷平均居民数量×遗址总公顷数

然而,大量民族学研究表明,每个居民的平均居住面积、每个房间居住的人口数量以及聚落内每公顷的平均人口数量在世界各地有明显的差异,甚至在同一地区内也有很大变化(表5.2~5.4)。正如柴尔德(V. G. Childe)在数十年前指出的:面积和人口的关系随环境因素和社会及心理因素的变化而变化[24]。

另外一种人口估计方法是以一个遗址的遗物数量为基础的,特纳尔(C. G. Turner)和罗夫格仁(L. Lofgren)在对美国西南地区史前普韦布洛印第安人的人口推测中,主要依据了每个人吃饭用碗的数量和房屋中出土碗的数量[25],测算出每个家庭平均5.3人。而库克(S. F. Cook)则是通过陶器的破碎率及遗址发现的陶器总量来推断一些遗址的人口数量[26]。

表5.2 民族学调查获得的世界不同地区人均居住面积

资料来源	地区	人均居住面积(平方米)
那罗尔(R. Naroll)[27]	世界范围内18个个案研究	10
莱布兰克(S. LeBlanc)[28]	伊朗	13.2
	伊朗	9.8
	伊朗	7.8
	秘鲁	12.8
卡斯尔百利(S. E. Casselberry)[29]	波兰	6
库克(S. F. Cook)[30]	美国加利福尼亚	1.86
	美国加利福尼亚	2.32

表5.3 美洲农业居民的家庭人口数量

资料来源	家庭人口数量（人）
斯图尔德（J. H. Steward）[31]	3.6～7.5
特纳尔（C. G. Turner）[32]	5.55
库克（S. F. Cook）[33]	4.5～7
哈维兰德（W. A. Haviland）[34]	5～6
克拉克（J. I. Clarke）[35]	2
卡拉斯科（P. Carrasco）[36]	5.6
卡拉斯科（P. Carrasco）[37]	5.4
努提尼（H. G. Nutini）[38]	5.5～7.5
努提尼（H. G. Nutini）[39]	5.5～6.5

引自：克尔伯（C. C. Kolb）文章[40]表1。

表5.4 西南亚地区农村人口密度

地区	人口密度（人/公顷）
沙哈巴德（Shahabad）30处聚落	106.8
马夫达斯特（Marv Dasht）110处聚落	147
陶兰中部（Central Tauran）13处聚落	52.3
德兹皮罗特地区（Dez Pilot）5处聚落	208.8
其他地区22处聚落	82.9 ± 58

引目：克拉莫尔（C. Kramer）文章[41]表2。

我国学者对史前聚落人口规模估算问题进行过有益的尝试。一般情况下，史前聚落中每间房屋的居民人数估计是以房屋的空间面积为基础的[42]。一些保存较好的房屋被用来作估算的标本，假设房屋中的遗物都在原来的位置未被移动，那么剩余的空间就是居民活动区域，由此就可以估计出一个房屋的人口数[43]。也有研究者利用墓葬资料做人口估计[44]。

国内外的相关研究，是我们进行伊洛地区史前人口估计的重要参考。

既然环境因素在人口研究中至关重要，最佳选择当然是以伊洛地区的一个遗址作人口数量估计的标本。遗憾的是，该地区还没有正式出版的资料来支持这种研究，我们只能选择与伊洛地区较接近的尉迟寺和姜寨两处遗址为研究标本。

安徽省蒙城县尉迟寺遗址总面积约10公顷。从1989年至1995年经过九次发掘揭露7000平方米[45]。2001年至2003年又进行了四次发掘，发掘面积3375平方米，对聚落的核心部位进行了全面揭露，目前围壕内所有残留的房屋均被揭露，完整地呈现了大汶口时期聚落的整体格局。

作者曾对该聚落的人口数量进行过专门分析。估算人口的标准有两个：一是适宜居住的10平方米以上房屋的数量和面积；二是与人口数量密切相关的陶器数量。估算结果是每间10平方米以上房屋的平均居住人数大致为3～4人，发掘揭露的这类房屋共58间，显示聚落人口为174～232人。考虑到部分房屋已经被破坏，聚落真正居住的人口可能会接近300人[46]。我们在此取一个保守一些的数字——280人作为该聚落的人口数。据发掘者介绍，遗址核心部分，即堌堆部分的面积约5公顷，则聚落的人口密度为56人/公顷。

陕西西安临潼姜寨遗址位于临河东岸的二级台地上，1972～1979年，共进行了11次大规模的科学发掘，揭露遗址面积5公顷。遗址按年代被分为五个不同的文化时期，代表了从公元前5000年到公元前3000年史前时期比较长的一个文化序列[47]。

姜寨一期（ca. BC 5000～4000）聚落的居住区大约2公顷，有壕沟环绕[48]，发现有120座保存完好的房屋基址。发掘者估计遗址内人口总数为500人[49]。然而，这个估计并没有考虑大型房屋和一些小型房屋的一些特殊功用，也忽略了一些房屋可能并不共存的问题。有学者把遗址内的房屋分为四种：大型房屋（面积大于60平方米）、中型房屋（面积20～40平方米）、小型房屋（面积10～20平方米）和一些特殊功用的更小型房屋（面积小于10平方米）。认为只有中型和小型房屋是用于居住的，大型房屋有公共场所的用途，而最小的房屋则是用于储存间或警卫房。有的研究参照民族学和墓葬的资料，重新对姜寨遗址的人口数量做了估计，认为姜寨文化一期的人口数量大约有100～125人[50]。我们认为这一估算较为合理，因此，姜寨一期聚落（2公顷）的人口密度大约是50～62.5人/公顷。我们可取其平均值56.25人/公顷。

参考上述两个遗址的人口密度，考虑到伊洛地区在自然景观、环境、气候、土壤等方面与尉迟寺和姜寨有诸多相似性，所以假设伊洛地区聚落的人口密度也与之相似，取整数值，可以设定为每公顷57人。需要指出的是，聚落人口密度在不同时期肯定是不同的，同时期不同等级聚落的人口密度肯定也有差别，鉴于目前难以对这些不同有更准确的表述，本研究中，我们只能将57人/公顷当作各时期所有聚落的人口密度标准。用各遗址的面积乘以这一人口密度值，便可以得出每个遗址的人口数量；用各时期遗址总面积值乘以此人口密度值，则可以得出各时期的人口总量。

二、重建研究区域内的土地承载力

"土地承载力（carrying capacity）"这一概念最初是20世纪30年代由西方动物学家提出的，20世纪50年代开始，考古学家日益重视环境因素和环境压力在人类社会发展中所起的作用，此概念被引入到考古学研究中，特指一个地区出产的食物能够养活的最大人口数量[51]。一些学者曾指出运用考古学资料推测古代土地承载力的局限性，如海登（B. Hayden）就提出过困扰这种推测的三个问题：第一，我们几乎不可能估算出一个地区的食物总量，采集狩猎的人群食物构成复杂，他们可利用的食物总量尤其难以推测；第二，在不同的技术水平下，开发食物资源的能力不同，土地承载力也就不同；第三，食物资源的种类多样，并有可再生性，这使得对土地可承载的"最大人口数量"推测困难重重[52]。虽然如此，土地承载力仍然是目前考古学研究中的重要概念，正如哈森（F. A. Hassan）所说，如果我们想重建古代人口模式，探讨人与环境的关系在人类社会发展过程发挥的作用，对土地承载力的研究就是必不可少的[53]。

伊洛盆地所在的黄河中游是旱作农业的重要起源地[54]，以粟为主要作物的旱作农业至少在新石器时代中期已经发展到了相当进步的阶段[55]，在很多已发掘的遗址中[56]，粟被断定为主要的农作物[57]。中国北方的几个新石器时代遗址的人骨 ^{13}C分析也证明仰韶文化时期将近58%的食物构成为粟,在龙山文化时期这个比例高达70%[58]。对伊洛项目1998~2000年度获得的植物化石样本和浮选样品的初步分析已经开展,粟也被认定为主要的作物[59]。因此,虽然狩猎采集和家畜饲养也可以提供食物补充,但粟无疑是伊洛地区裴李岗至二里头时期居民最主要的食物来源。本研究中,将研究区域内的土地承载力定义为:区域内全部可耕地的粟的年产量可供养的人口总数。

推测此土地承载力的数值需要以下数据:各时期内粟的单位面积产量、各时期粟的人均年消费量和研究区域内适合粟作农业的可耕地面积。计算公式为:

土地承载力=可耕地面积÷人均需要可耕地面积

人均需要可耕地面积=粟的人均年消费量÷粟的单位面积产量

获得史前时代粟单位面积产量的准确数值几乎是不可能的,我们只能参考对文献中记录的历史时期单位面积产量的研究和地方志的记载。

杨贵在其研究中推测,夏代粟的产量是每公顷300千克[60],他的研究主要以历史记载及一些民族学的研究结果为基础。《巩县志》记载,1933年粟的年均产量是375千克/公顷,在1952年之前,粟的年均产量从未超过750千克/公顷[61]。为了确定可供消耗的谷物数量,应该留出种子的数量,参考一些农民的经验和相关的研究[62],收获的15%应该是用作种子的。如果以最低的产量375千克/公顷作为参照,除去15%的种子,那么可供消耗的谷物产量应该是315千克/公顷。这与杨贵对夏代粟单位面积产量的推测颇为接近。因此,315千克/公顷应该是一个可以接受的二里头时期的粟单位面积产量推测值。石器是裴李岗时期到二里头时期最基本的农业工具,尽管种植粟的知识和技术在不断进步,但这种进步对产量的影响很难估计。研究区域内的气候、植被和自然景观等因素也会随着时间的推移不断发生变化,但我们同样很难量化这种变化对谷物产量的影响。因此,本研究把315千克/公顷设定为通用于从裴李岗到二里头各个时期的粟单位面积产量。

粟的人均年消费量可以从地方志中获得参考。据《巩县志》记载,当地14岁以上人口平均年消耗加工过的粮食245千克/人,14岁以下的儿童平均年消耗量是192千克/人,二者的平均值为219千克/人。需要注意的是,这个值是指加工过的谷物。为了得到未加工谷物消耗量的确切值,我们应该考虑加工粮食造成的消耗。一般来讲,加工后获得的谷物量是原谷物量的80%~90%,其平均值为85%。因此,219千克可食用谷物需要258千克原料谷物才能加工出来（219/0.85=258千克）。巩县居民的食物结构还包括蔬菜和肉类,但目前很多农村居民的食肉量还是相当少,这可能和史前居民食物构成相似[63],因此,本研究将258千克/人设定为史前居民粟的人均年消费量。

根据以上设定值,我们可以计算出裴李岗至二里头时期人均需要可耕地量为0.8公顷（258÷315）。即每人需要0.8公顷的可耕地才能产出足够养活自己粟。这里,土地轮耕制度是一个需要考虑到重要因素,文献记载,春秋战国时期土地轮耕方法已经流行[64]。本研究比较保守地设定从裴李岗时期到二里头时期所有的农业土地都施行一年轮耕政策,这样一个人每年实际所需要的土地就增加到了1.6公顷。

最后,我们需要设法获得研究区域内的可耕地总面积。

吉迪(Gidden Shelach)对内蒙古赤峰市阴河上游夏家店下层文化时期土地承载力的分析是利用中国考古学资料进行古代土地承载力推测的成功案例[65]。在估算研究区域内的可耕地面积时,他设定了海拔、坡度等要素,在纸地图上勾画出了阴河上游的可耕地范围。本研究借助地理信息系统软件的帮助,可以更方便准确地进行估算(图5.2)。

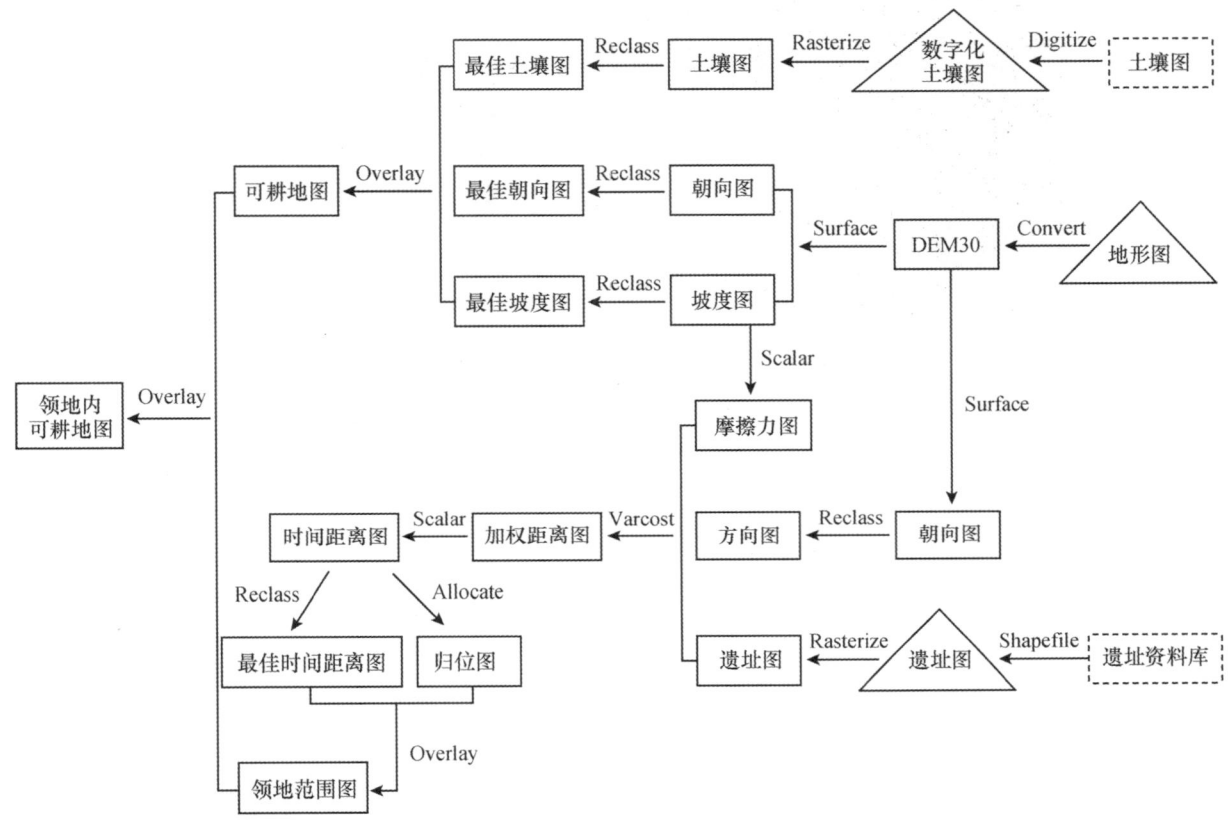

图5.2　地理信息系统计算伊洛地区土地生产流程图

注:虚线长方形框代表原始资料,实线的长方形框代表数字化的栅格图,三角形框代表数字化的矢量图,箭头上的文字代表GIS软件中的操作程序。

首先,我们需要建立调查区域的数字化高程模型(DEM)。我们选择的数字化底图是该区域的五万分之一地形图,数字化内容包括等高线和河流,因为在调查过程中使用GPS确定遗址的准确位置时使用的是UTM投影系统,地图数字化时也选择了此系统。数字化后的地图为矢量图(vector),每一条等高线都有高程值,而等高线之间的点则没有高程值。我们使用GIS软件将其转化为栅格式(raster)的数字化高程模型图(DEM30),在此图上,每一点(像素)都有高程值,形成没有空白的连续区域,便于进行各种运算。考虑到原始纸地图的比例尺、分析区域的面积和分析的目的等因素,在生成数字化高程模型时,我们选择了30米的分辨率,也就是说数字化高程模型上每一个像素的大小是30米×30米(图5.3)。

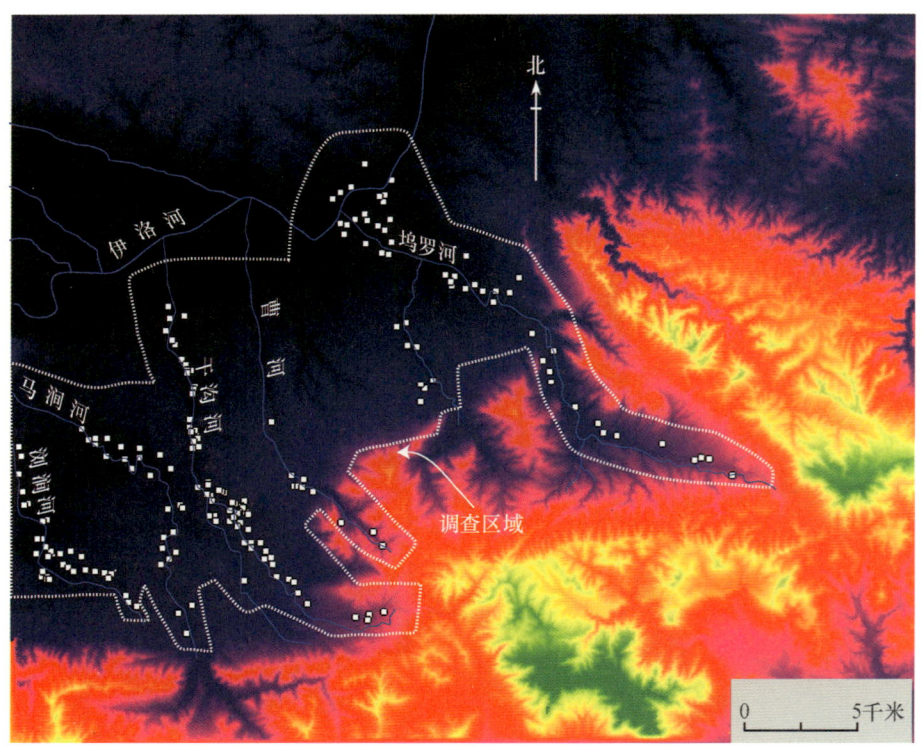

图5.3 伊洛地区数字化高程模型图（DEM30）及调查区域遗址分布

参考吉迪的研究，我们选择坡度、朝向和土壤类型作为确认可耕地要考虑的主要因素。为此，我们在DEM30的基础上生成了"坡度图"和"朝向图"两幅栅格图，并将研究区域的土壤类型图数字化，生成栅格图"土壤图"。

在"坡度图"上，每个像素有一个值，表示该位置的坡度。根据伊洛项目的田野调查，当地较陡峭的山地通常布满岩石，并且比较容易受到水蚀，很难用于耕种，现代耕地多在平缓的坡地或平地上，因此，我们设定0~20°是一个比较适合耕地的坡度。运用GIS软件的功能，我们可以将"坡度图"上的值归纳为两类：将所有>20°的值都重新赋值为0，将所有在0~20°范围间的值都重新赋值为1，这样就生成了一个新的栅格图——"最佳坡度图"。这是一个"二值图"（Boolean），图上只有0和1两个值，各用一种颜色表示。

"朝向图"上每个像素有一个值，表示该位置以正北为0°时的朝向。充足的日照是农作物生长的必要条件，确定可耕地范围时，需要将朝北背阴坡地的范围去除。考虑到研究区域的日照情况，我们设定最佳朝向为45°~225°，并运用GIS软件的功能，生成另一个二值图"最佳朝向图"，图上只有0和1两个值，所有0值区域代表朝向小于45°大于225°的范围，而所有1值区域代表朝向介于45°~225°之间。

"土壤图"中共有24个值，以24种颜色显示，代表研究区域内的24种土壤。这些土壤的pH值和肥力水平各不相同。比较肥沃、宜于耕种的棕黑色土覆盖了大部分地区，然而，还是有一些不适宜耕种的土壤，比如暴露的岩石、沙质层土壤、棕色黏土，以及黑棕色泥灰土等[66]。我们利用GIS软件的功能，将"土壤图"上的24个值分为两类，所有不适宜耕种的土壤的值都被重新赋值为0，所有适合耕种的土壤的值都被重新赋值为1，这样就产生了一个土壤的"二值图"——"最佳土壤图"。

最后，我们利用GIS软件的功能，将"最佳坡度图"、"最佳朝向图"和"最佳土壤图"相乘，得到一幅新的"二值图"——"可耕地图"。在三幅原图中赋值均为1的像素还会保持"1"的赋值（1×1×1＝1），在三幅图中任一幅内赋值为0，在"可耕地"图中就会被赋值为0（任何数乘以0值都为0）。换句话说，符合坡度、海拔和土壤种类全部三个条件的地域会被赋值为1，不符合其中任意一个条件的地域都会被赋值为0。GIS软件可以计算出"可耕地"图上赋值为1的地域的面积，也就是调查区域内适宜种植粟的可耕地的面积，这个值是29681.64公顷。用这个值除以上面得到的人均需要可耕地量1.6公顷/人，便可以得出研究区域土地承载力的值为18551人。也就是说，研究区域内所有可耕地每年出产的粟可以供养18551人。

三、重建各遗址的领地生产力

"领地生产力（catchment productivity）"指聚落领地范围内可提供的食物总量。斯蒂庞耐提斯（V. P. Steponaitis）在对墨西哥河流域史前农业居民的研究中提出，对于农业居民来说，领地生产力可以看成是聚落领地范围内可提供的农作物量[67]。本研究中的领地生产力指每个聚落领地范围内可以生产粟的可耕地面积。

估计每个遗址的领地生产力，首先要确定每个遗址的领地范围。目前确定此范围的方法主要有两种：一种是假设多数人都要在聚落中过夜[68]，领地范围的半径就由一天内往返路程的时间决定[69]。例如，如果白天的时间是10个小时，除去2小时准备食物的时间，按照每小时行走3千米计算，领地范围的半径应该不超过12千米（8小时的往返路程）[70]。另一种方法是以民族学资料为依据来估计领地范围的半径[71]。斯蒂庞耐提斯在其研究中就根据民族学资料以1千米、1.5千米和2千米作为领地范围的半径；而吉迪在他的研究中则以1.5千米和2千米为领地范围半径[72]。

根据伊洛项目的调查，该地区现代农村的耕地范围很少超过以村落为中心的1小时的步行距离，因此，本研究中采用了1小时的步行距离作为每个遗址领地范围的半径。为了估算在不同坡度上行走的速度，我们专门做了步行实验。实验是在有不同坡度的路面上行走，记录下行走的距离、坡度及所用的时间，这些数据经过统计软件的分析，可以得到下面的步行1米所需时间与坡度关系的公式：

$$Y = 0.0002 X^2 + 0.002 X + 0.6086 \quad (Y\text{为步行1米所需时间}, X\text{为坡度})$$

把这个公式运用到"坡度图"中，配合标示各时期遗址位置的栅格图"遗址图"，我们可以利用GIS软件计算的功能，获得从裴李岗至二里头各时期的栅格图"时间距离图"，图中每个像素的值是从距离其最近的遗址到这个像素所花费的时间。借助GIS软件的功能，我们还可以将"时间距离"图与标示各时期遗址位置的栅格图融合，得到各个时期的"归位图"，也就是将"时间距离"图上的每个像素归入与其最近的遗址,所有属于一个遗址的像素都会获得相同的值,以同一种颜色表示。某时期有多少个遗址,该时期的"归位图"上就会有多少个值,以不同的颜色显示。例如,裴李岗时期共有7处遗址,"时间距离图"上的像素就会按照就近归属的原则被分别归属到这7个遗址,该时期的"归位图"就会有7个值(1~7),以7种颜色表示,该图会呈现7个不同颜色的多边形,即泰森多边形。

如果我们将裴李岗时期"时间距离图"图中超过1小时的值重新赋值为0,少于1小时的值重新赋值为1,就会产生一个该时期的二值图"最佳时间距离图"。将此"最佳时间距离图"与该时期的"归位图"相乘,"归位图"中与"最佳时间距离图"中所有赋值为0的像素对应的像素的赋值都会变为0,与"最佳时间距离图"中所有赋值为1的像素对应的像素会保持原来的1~7的赋值,这样,我们就可以得到裴李岗时期的"领地范围图",图上7种颜色的不规则图形分别表示以1小时行走距离为标准的各遗址的领地范围。将此"领地范围图"与上面为计算土地承载力得到的二值图"可耕地图"相乘,则可以去除"领地范围图"中不适宜作耕地的部分,得到裴李岗时期的"领地内可耕地图",图上的7种颜色的不规则图形分别表示各遗址领地范围内的可耕地。GIS软件可以准确计算出每个遗址领地内的可耕地面积,即每个遗址的领地生产力。

用同样的方法,我们可以获得各个时期各遗址的领地生产力值。

第三节　裴李岗至二里头各时期的人口和土地利用[①]

根据上面得出的各项关键数值,我们可以获得研究区域内裴李岗至二里头各时期各遗址(本文仅分析坞罗河、曹河、干沟河三个流域)的一些重要数据,这包括各遗址的人口数量、领地生产力、必需耕地(供养聚落人口所需要的耕地面积)和土地利用率(必需土地占领地生产力的百分比)。在此基础上,可以对各时期的土地利用情况作初步描述和分析。

一、裴李岗文化时期

研究区域内共发现5个裴李岗文化晚期遗址,其中4个位于坞罗河流域的上游,1个位于干沟河流域(图5.4)。遗址面积从2000平方米到1公顷不等,总面积为38000平方米。遗址间并没有明显的等级差别,但有成组分布的现象。一组聚集于坞罗河流域。

---

① 本文中所采用的遗址面积的数据为调查初期所获,本文已先期发表,为尊重原文,表中涉及数字与报告正文不符之处,未作更改。另本研究仅选取三个流域,浏涧河及马涧河流域未选入本文,下文中遗址序号为包含另外两个流域的序号,插图及附表中遗址序号未进行更改,特此证明。

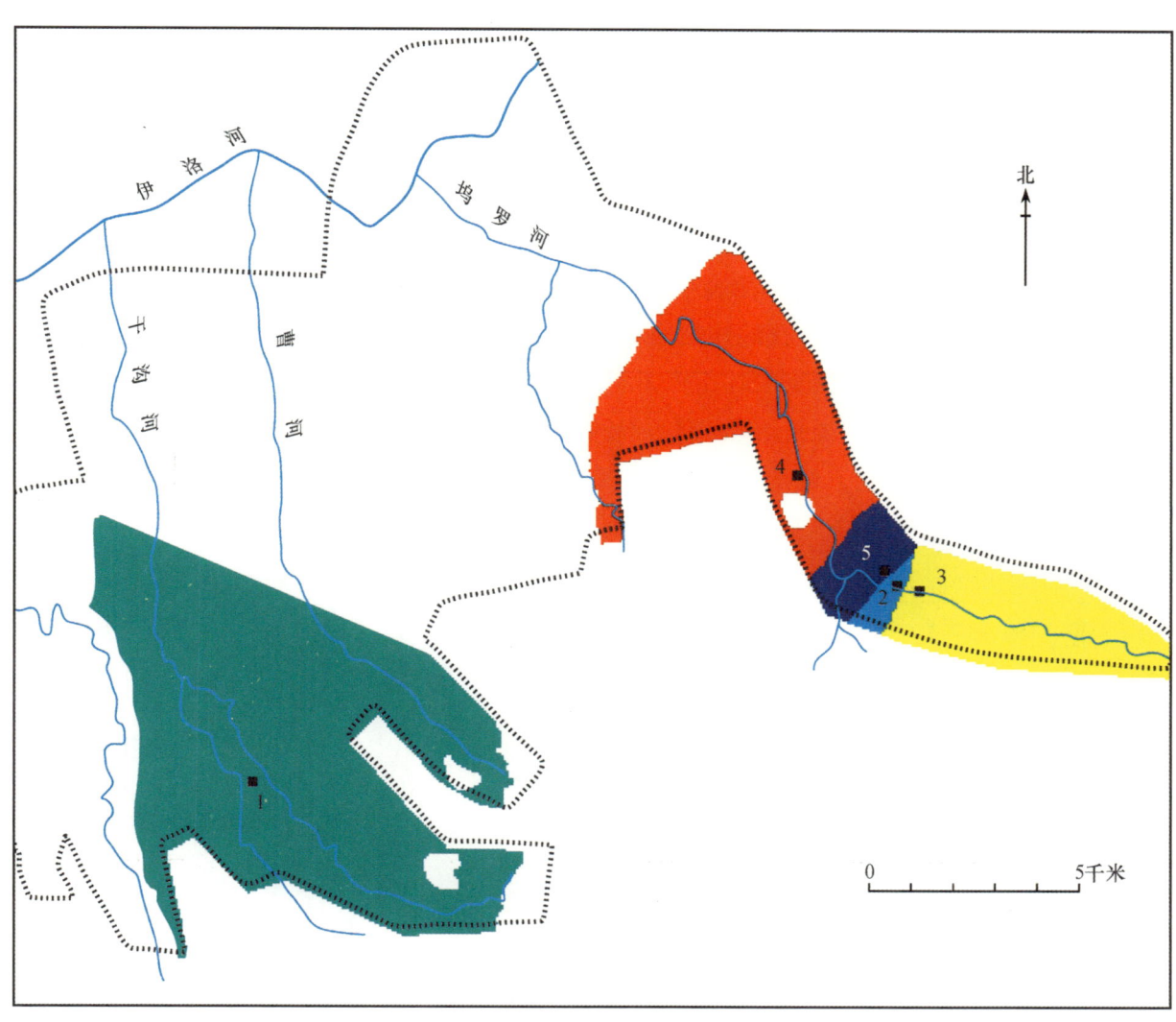

图5.4 裴李岗文化晚期遗址分布及领地生产力

表5.5 裴李岗文化晚期遗址面积、人口、领地生产力、必需耕地及土地利用率

序号	遗址名称	遗址编号	遗址面积（公顷）	人口数量	领地生产力（公顷）	必需耕地（公顷）	土地利用率
	干沟河流域		**0.5**	**28.5**	**8073.6**	**45.6**	**1%**
1	府店东	00-124	0.5	28.5	8073.6	45.6	1%
	坞罗河流域		**1.8**	**102.6**	**4308.6**	**164.16**	**4%**
2	铁生沟	98-029	0.2	11.4	114.3	18.24	16%
3	东山原	98-041	0.7	39.9	1329.6	63.84	5%
4	坞罗西坡	98-042	0.5	28.5	2480	45.6	2%
5	北营	98-044	0.4	22.8	384.7	36.48	9%
总计			2.3	131.1	12382.2	209.76	2%

由表5.5可知，本期，每一个聚落的领地生产力足以养活聚落内的居民，整个区域内的土地利用率也仅为2%。该时期的人口总数为131人。显然，裴李岗文化时期不存在环境压力，各聚落完全可以自给自足。

二、仰韶文化时期

(一)仰韶早期

研究区域内仅发现2个仰韶早期遗址,位于坞罗河流域(图5.5)。遗址面积从2000平方米到1公顷不等,没有出现等级分化的迹象。

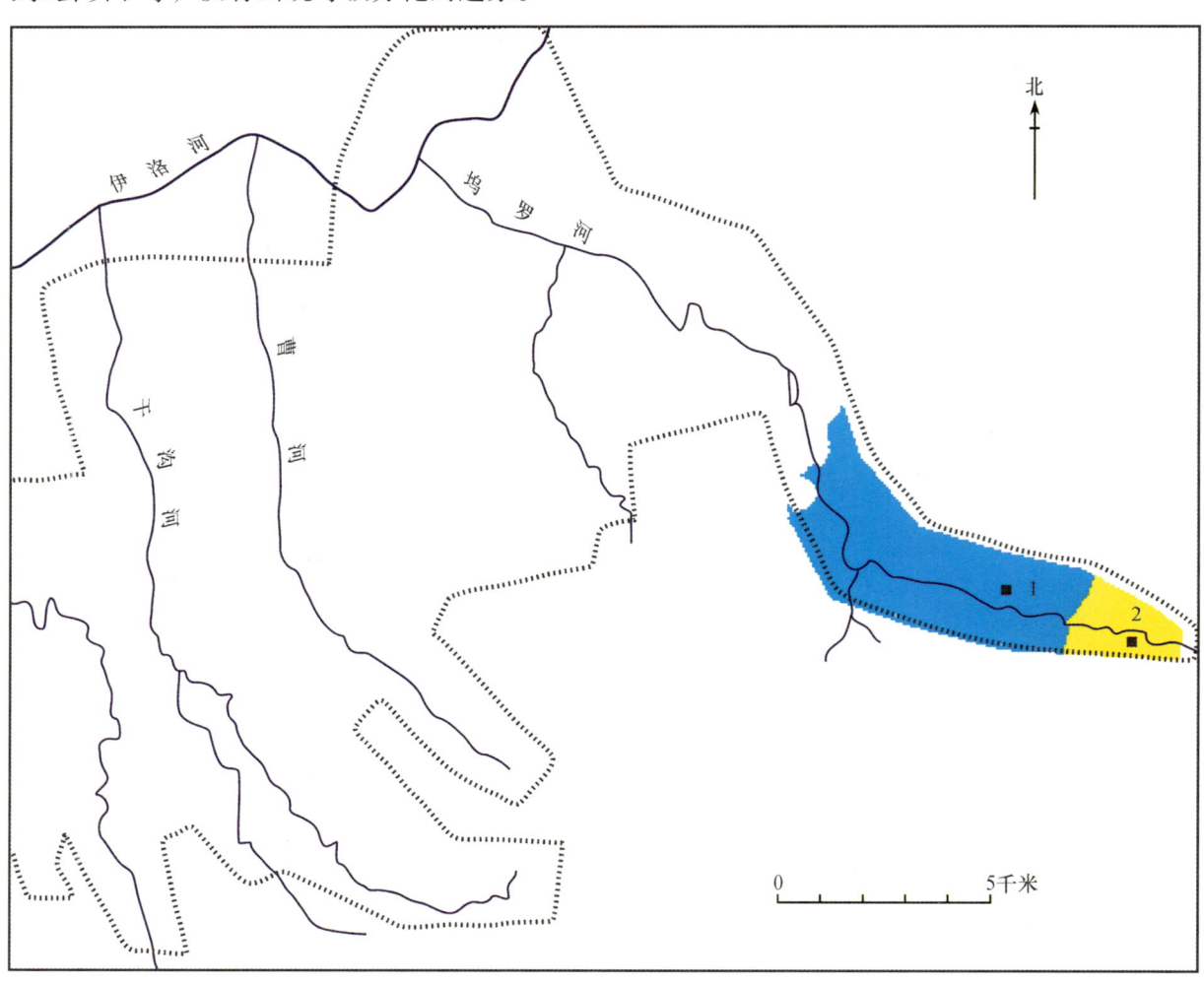

图5.5 仰韶文化早期遗址分布及领地生产力

表5.6 仰韶早期遗址面积、人口、领地生产力、必需耕地及土地利用率

序号	遗址名称	遗址编号	遗址面积(公顷)	人口数量	领地生产力(公顷)	必需耕地(公顷)	土地利用率
	坞罗河流域						
1	涉村东	98-035	0.2	11.4	1787.4	18.24	1%
2	大南沟	98-038	1.5	85.5	373.1	136.8	37%
总计			1.7	96.9	2160.5	155.04	7%

由表5.6可知，本期每一个聚落的领地生产力足以养活聚落内的居民，整个区域内的土地利用率仅为7%，比裴李岗文化略有提高。该时期人口总数为97人。显然，本期不存在环境压力，各聚落完全可以自给自足。

（二）仰韶中期

本期遗址的数量和面积有了显著的增长，共发现10个遗址，5个位于坞罗河流域，5个位于干沟河流域，总面积46公顷（图5.6）。

本期首次出现了聚落等级分化现象。干沟河流域的赵城遗址（20公顷）是其所在流域的中心性聚落，构成了两级聚落等级体系。

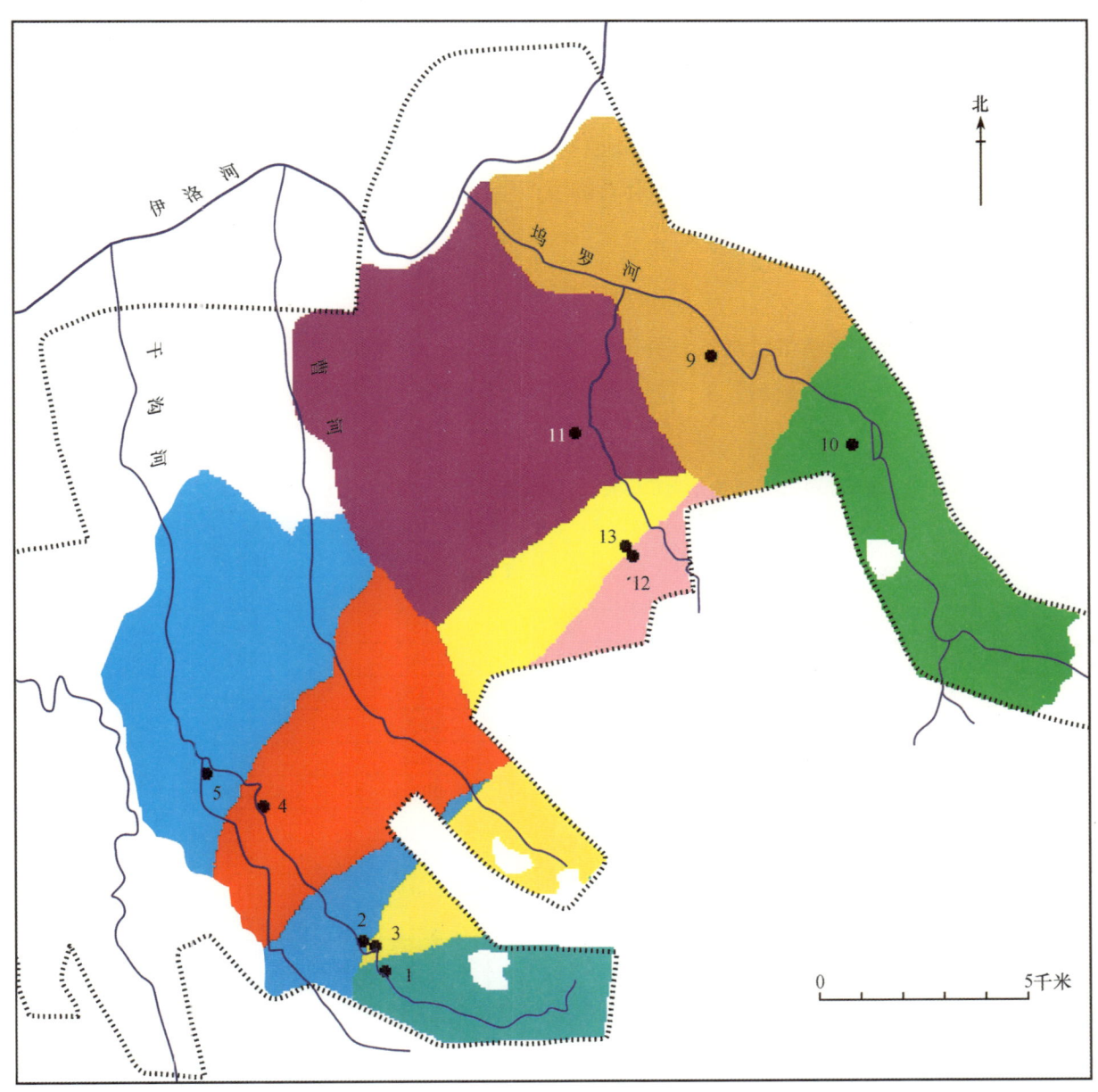

图5.6　仰韶文化中期遗址分布及领地生产力

表5.7　仰韶中期遗址面积、人口、领地生产力、必需耕地及土地利用率

序号	遗址名称	遗址编号	遗址面积（公顷）	人口数量	领地生产力（公顷）	必需耕地（公顷）	土地利用率
	干沟河流域		29	1653	7607.3	2644.8	**35%**
1	赵城	00-077	20	1140	942.8	1824	193%
2	赵城西	00-078	2.5	142.5	574.1	228	40%
3	赵城西南	00-079	1	57	749	91.2	12%
4	冯寨西北	00-090	2.5	142.5	2346.3	228	10%
5	三官庙	00-105	3	171	2995.1	273.6	9%
	坞罗河流域		21	1197	11295.9	1915.2	**15%**
9	喂庄	98-018	5.5	313.5	2780.8	501.6	18%
10	坞罗水库西	98-025	2	114	2092	182.4	9%
11	羽林庄南	98-050	1.5	85.5	3820.6	136.8	4%
12	堤东	98-052	4	228	481.3	364.8	76%
13	龙谷堆	98-053	4	228	986.6	364.8	37%
总计			46	2622	17768.6	4195.2	**24%**

由表5.7可知，所有一般性聚落的领地生产力均足以养活聚落内居民。区域内的土地利用率为24%，人口总数是2622人，仍然不会对环境产生压力。

（三）仰韶晚期

仰韶晚期的遗址数量继续增长，并达到第一次高峰。该时期共有遗址30个，13个位于坞罗河流域，14个位于干沟河流域，3个位于曹河流域（图5.7）。两级聚落等级体系继续存在并有一定发展。

表5.8　仰韶晚期遗址面积、人口、领地生产力、必需耕地及土地利用率

序号	遗址名称	遗址编号	遗址面积（公顷）	人口数量	领地生产力（公顷）	必需耕地（公顷）	土地利用率
	干沟河流域		44.56	2539.92	8324.9	4063.87	**49%**
1	南村寨	00-061	1	57	533.1	91.2	17%
2	桑沟南	00-066	4	228	315	364.8	116%
3	刘乐寨南	00-075	1	57	2508	91.2	4%
4	赵城	00-077	20	1140	972.3	1824	188%
6	冯寨西北	00-090	2.5	142.5	342.5	228	67%
7	顾家屯东	00-096	0.06	3.42	1253.6	5.472	0.4%
8	顾家屯南	00-098	0.8	45.6	397	72.96	18%
9	马屯西村	00-102	0.2	11.4	655.1	18.24	3%
10	三官庙北	00-104	0.75	42.75	291.6	68.4	23%
11	三官庙	00-105	3	171	61.5	273.6	445%
12	滑城河北	00-108	3	171	301.2	273.6	91%
13	邢村东	00-121	2	114	521.6	182.4	35%
14	半个寨	00-123	5.75	327.75	72.4	524.4	724%
15	桑沟五队北	00-126	0.5	28.5	100	45.6	46%
	曹河流域		7.25	413.25	2482.9	661.2	**27%**
16	曹河水库西	00-133	1	57	715.1	91.2	13%
17	曹闫	01-135	2.5	142.5	368.9	228	62%

续表

序号	遗址名称	遗址编号	遗址面积（公顷）	人口数量	领地生产力（公顷）	必需耕地（公顷）	土地利用率
18	北后沟西北	01-139	3.75	213.75	1398.9	342	24%
	坞罗河流域		**29.7**	**1692.9**	**11942.3**	**2708.64**	**23%**
5	东山原	98-041	0.7	39.9	1216.3	63.84	5%
22	稍柴	97-1001	5	285	2221.8	456	21%
23	喂庄西南	98-018	5.5	313.5	539.8	501.6	93%
24	喂庄西	98-019	0.2	11.4	769	18.24	2%
25	罗口东北	98-022	0.4	22.8	589.6	36.48	6%
26	喂庄东北	98-023	0.3	17.1	261.2	27.36	10%
27	坞罗水库西	98-025	2	114	922.7	182.4	20%
28	上庄	98-037	1	57	405.5	91.2	22%
29	上庄东南	98-039	0.4	22.8	327.2	36.48	11%
30	天坡村	98-049	1.2	68.4	757.6	109.44	14%
31	羽林庄南	98-050	1.5	85.5	1832	136.8	7%
32	堤东	98-052	4	228	461.7	364.8	79%
33	龙谷堆	98-053	4	228	511.8	364.8	71%
	总计		78.01	4446.57	21624	7114.51	33%

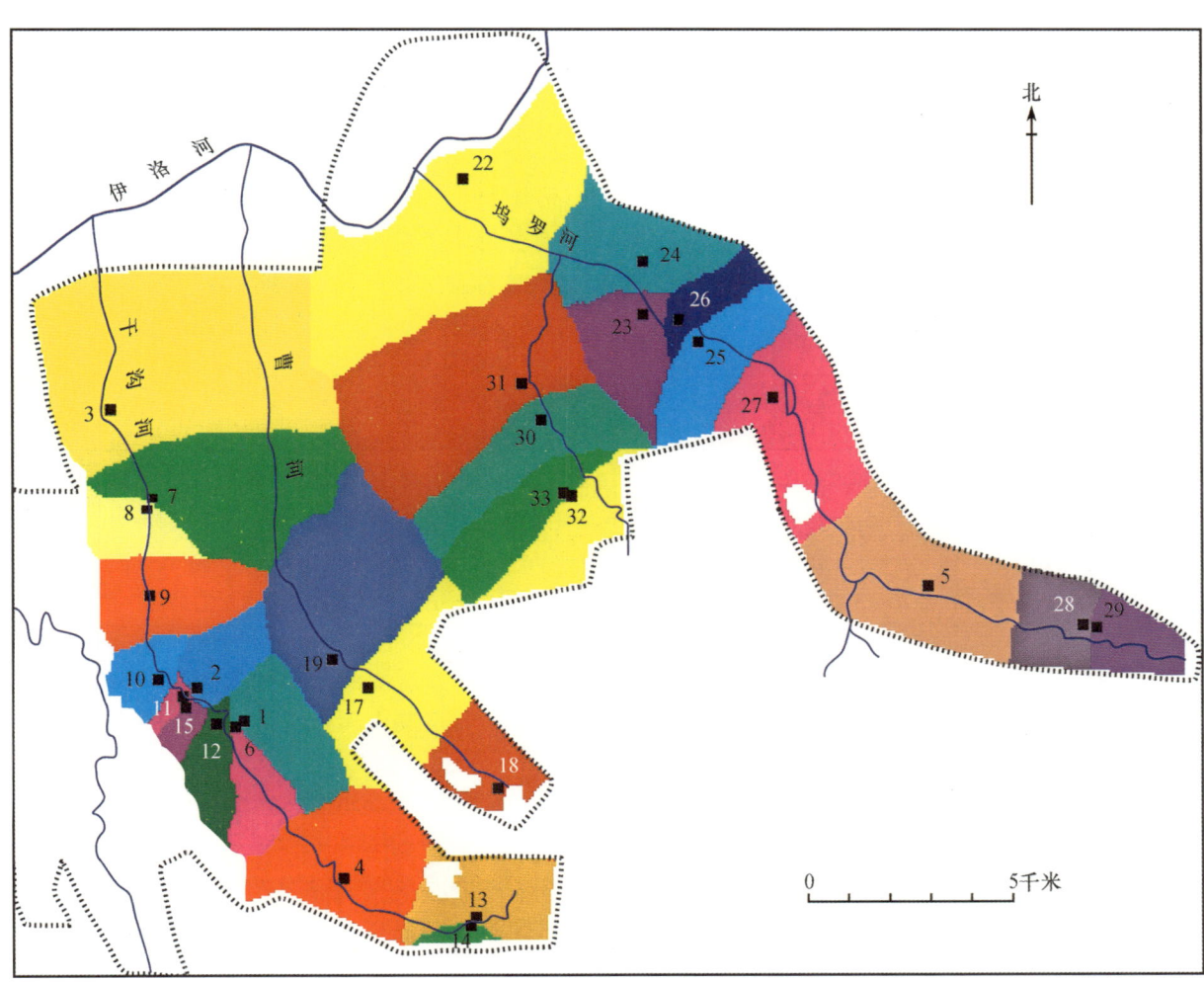

图5.7 仰韶文化晚期遗址分布及领地生产力

由表5.8可知，坞罗河流域，13个聚落都有足够的领地生产力来养活其居民，土地利用率仅为22%。曹河流域的3个聚落也都有足够的领地生产力来养活其居民，土地利用率为27%。这两个流域土地利用率均远低于整个区域值（33%）。

干沟河流域的14个遗址明显存在等级分化，有4个遗址出现农业用地短缺的现象。赵城遗址（20公顷）仍然是该流域的中心性聚落，领地生产力不足以养活其居民。另外三个面积较大的遗址也存在农业用地短缺的现象。整个流域的土地利用率为49%。

总体来说，在仰韶晚期，整个区域的土地足以供养区域内居民，土地利用率为33%。整个调查区域估计的人口总数为4447人，较中期明显提高。

三、龙山时期

（一）龙山早期

本期遗址共有9个，7个位于干沟河流域，2个在坞罗河流域，各遗址面积从0.3公顷到5.75公顷不等，等级分化不明显（图5.8）。

表5.9 龙山早期遗址面积、人口、领地生产力、必需耕地及土地利用率

序号	遗址名称	遗址编号	遗址面积（公顷）	人口数量	领地生产力（公顷）	必需耕地（公顷）	土地利用率
	坞罗河流域		4.3	245.1	9430.7	392.16	4%
1	喂庄东北	98-023	0.3	17.1	4860.3	27.36	1%
2	堤东	98-052	4	228	4570.4	364.8	8%
	干沟河流域		17.5	997.5	11005.6	1596	15%
3	刘乐寨南	00-075	1	57	4781.6	91.2	2%
4	三官庙	00-105	1	57	1375.7	91.2	7%
5	滑城河北	00-108	3	171	533	273.6	51%
6	滑城河东	00-112	0.75	42.75	1488.8	68.4	5%
7	颜良寨西	00-114	4	228	1597.2	364.8	23%
8	邢村东	00-121	2	114	1156.9	182.4	16%
9	半个寨	00-123	5.75	327.75	72.4	524.4	724%
总计			21.8	1242.6	20436.3	1988.16	10%

由表5.9可知，除了最大的遗址半个寨（Y123，5.75公顷）外，其余遗址均有足够领地生产力养活聚落人口，整个调查区域的土地利用率仅为10%。本期人口总量为1243人，较仰韶早期急剧降低。

（二）龙山晚期

龙山晚期，遗址数量剧增到43个，其中坞罗河流域14个，干沟河流域25个，曹河流域4个，遗址总面积108.96公顷（图5.9）。在这一时期区域聚落等级体系又重新建立起来。

第五章 伊洛地区复杂社会的演变：地理信息系统基础上的人口和农业可耕地的分析

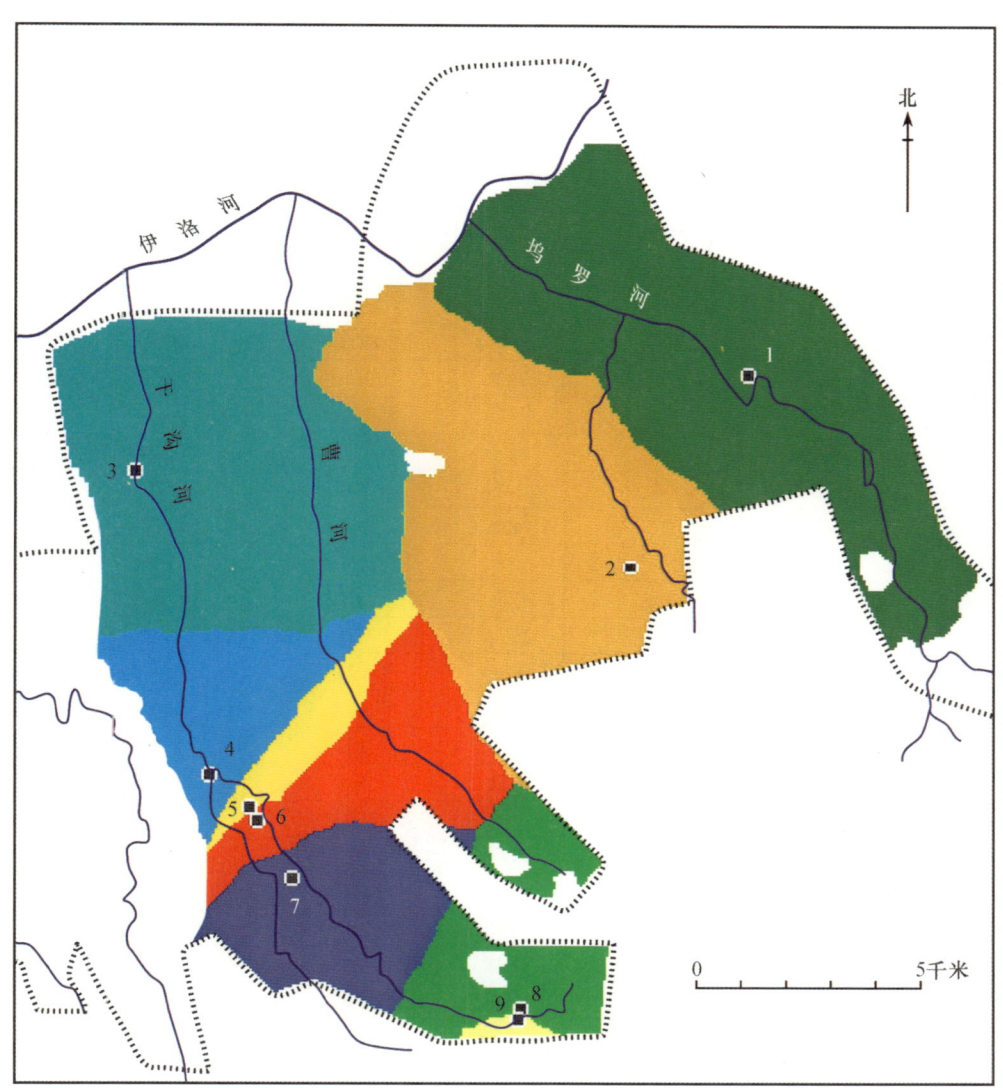

图5.8 龙山文化早期遗址分布及领地生产力

坞罗河流域罗口东北遗址（Y022，20公顷）明显是中心性遗址，领地内农业用地严重短缺。另两个大型遗址也有同样问题。其他聚落均有足够的农业用地，土地利用率是33%。

曹河流域的4个遗址均能自给，土地利用率为24%。

表5.10 龙山晚期遗址面积、人口、领地生产力、必需耕地及土地利用率

序号	遗址名称	遗址编号	遗址面积（公顷）	人口数量	领地生产力（公顷）	必需耕地（公顷）	土地利用率
	坞罗河流域		44.2	2519.4	12177.8	4031.04	33%
1	南石	97-1003	0.2	11.4	80.1	18.24	23%
2	罗口东北	98-022	20	1140	1013.5	1824	180%
3	坞罗南店	98-032	3	171	465.5	273.6	59%
4	寺院沟	98-034	1.5	85.5	221.7	136.8	62%
5	上庄东南	98-039	0.4	22.8	342.3	36.48	11%
6	涉村东南	98-040	0.4	22.8	703.6	36.48	5%
37	叶茂沟	01-144	7	399	321	638.4	199%
38	小南沟	01-146	6	342	320.7	547.2	171%

续表

序号	遗址名称	遗址编号	遗址面积（公顷）	人口数量	领地生产力（公顷）	必需耕地（公顷）	土地利用率
40	小訾店北	97-1004	0.2	11.4	19.3	18.24	95%
41	小訾店南	97-1005	0.5	28.5	1095.4	45.6	4%
42	喂庄	98-018	0.2	11.4	1470.1	18.24	1%
43	南石路南	98-046	0.2	11.4	2105	18.24	1%
44	双河	98-047	0.1	5.7	946.6	9.12	1%
45	金钟寺	98-054	0.5	28.5	1939.5	45.6	2%
	干沟河流域		62.76	3577.32	8271.3	5723.71	69%
7	南村寨南	00-060	0.5	28.5	281.6	45.6	16%
8	南村寨西南	00-063	1	57	188.5	91.2	48%
9	桑沟西北	00-067	1.5	85.5	172.8	136.8	79%
10	马屯	00-069	6	342	258.7	547.2	212%
11	马屯北	00-070	2.5	142.5	184.6	228	124%
12	念子庄西北	00-073	1	57	2686.1	91.2	3%
13	赵城	00-077	0.1	5.7	565.2	9.12	2%
14	小相西南	00-080	4.5	256.5	520.6	410.4	79%
15	颜良寨水库西	00-087	2	114	157.4	182.4	116%
16	冯寨西南	00-089	2.2	125.4	61.2	200.64	328%
17	冯寨西北	00-090	2.5	142.5	15.2	228	1500%
18	顾家屯东	00-096	0.06	3.42	820	5.472	1%
19	顾家屯南	00-098	0.8	45.6	223.7	72.96	33%
20	李家沟东	00-099	7.5	427.5	305.6	684	224%
21	孙家闸南	00-100	0.15	8.55	116.1	13.68	12%
22	马屯西村	00-102	0.2	11.4	135.3	18.24	13%
23	三官庙北	00-104	0.75	42.75	180.3	68.4	38%
24	三官庙	00-106	0.5	28.5	97.9	45.6	47%
25	滑城河西	00-109	3	171	47.1	273.6	581%
26	府西村北	00-110	13	741	179.2	1185.6	662%
27	滑城河东	00-112	0.75	42.75	42.9	68.4	159%
28	府北村北	00-113	0.5	28.5	92.2	45.6	49%
29	颜良寨西	00-114	4	228	345.1	364.8	106%
30	邢村东	00-121	2	114	521.6	182.4	35%
31	半个寨	00-123	5.75	327.75	72.4	524.4	724%
	曹河流域		6	342	2270.3	547.2	24%
33	新后沟	00-130	1	57	283	91.2	32%
34	新后沟东	00-131	1.5	85.5	1330.5	136.8	10%
35	南沟	00-134	1	57	406	91.2	22%
36	曹闸	01-135	2.5	142.5	250.8	228	91%
总计			108.96	6210.72	21585.9	9937.15	46%

干沟河流域的25个遗址聚集分布成三个遗址群，第一群包括10号～12号遗址及18号～22号遗址，其中20号遗址是这一群的中心性聚落；第二群包括7号～9号遗址、14号～17号遗址及23号～29号遗址，其中26号遗址是这一群的中心性聚落；第三群包括13号、30号和31号遗址，离前两个遗址群较远。20号和26号两处中心性聚落都存在农业用地短缺的问题。其余较大遗址也存在同样问题。这个流域的土地利用率为69%。

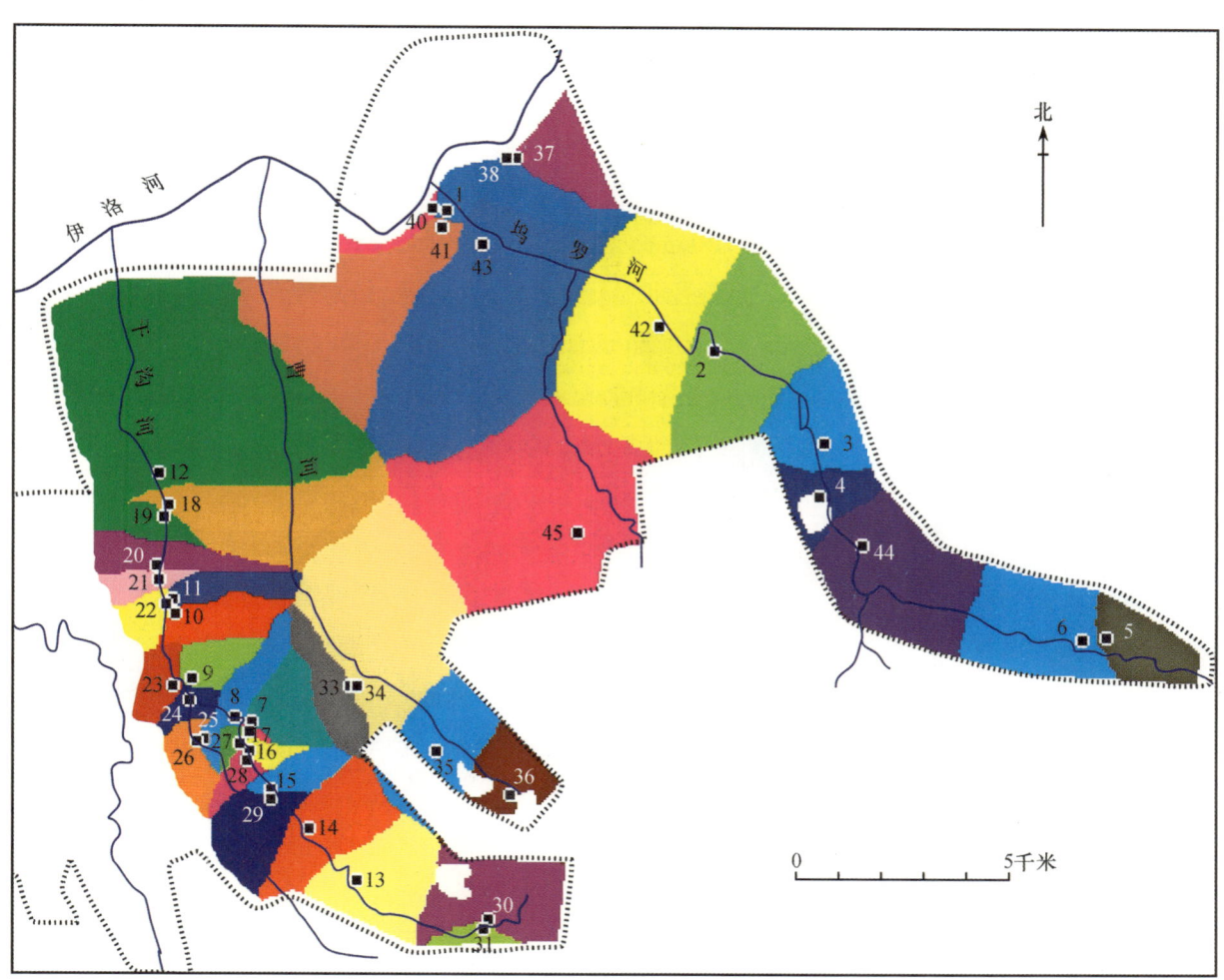

图5.9 龙山晚期遗址分布及领地生产力

总体来说，在龙山晚期整个调查区域的土地利用率增长到了46%，人口总数为6211人，达到了相当的高度。

四、二里头时期

（一）二里头一期

共发现二里头一期遗址10处，总面积119.8公顷，其中6个遗址位于坞罗河流域、干沟河流域3个、曹河流域1个（图5.10）。

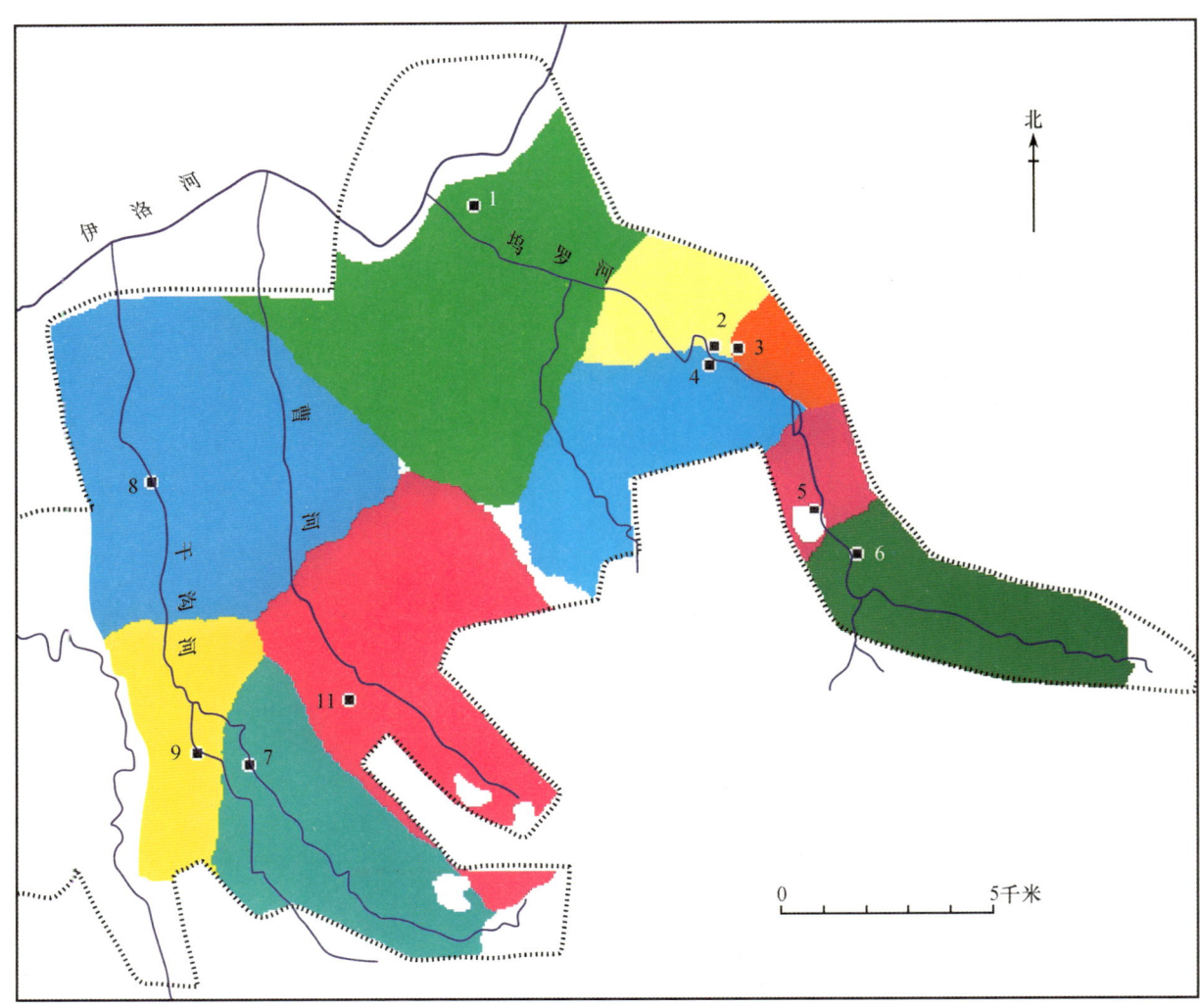

图5.10 二里头文化一期遗址分布及领地生产力

表5.11 二里头一期遗址面积、人口、领地生产力、必需耕地及土地利用率

序号	遗址名称	遗址编号	遗址面积（公顷）	人口数量	必需耕地（公顷）	领地生产力（公顷）	土地利用率
	坞罗河流域		86	4902	7843.2	9821.8	80%
1	稍柴	97-1001	60	3420	5472	4239.6	129%
2	喂庄东南	98-020	6	342	547.2	896	61%
3	喂庄	98-021	0.4	22.8	36.48	383.4	10%
4	罗口东北	98-022	18	1026	1641.6	1967.8	83%
5	寺院沟	98-034	1.5	85.5	136.8	531.3	26%
6	双河	98-047	0.1	5.7	9.12	1803.7	1%
	干沟河流域		8.25	470.25	752.4	11058.9	7%
7	冯寨西南	00-089	2	114	182.4	2331.2	8%
8	石家沟东北	00-093	4	228	364.8	5480.5	7%
9	府西村北	00-110	2.25	128.25	205.2	3247.2	6%
	曹河流域		0.5	28.5	45.6	3360.9	1%
10	新后沟	00-130	0.5	28.5	45.6	3360.9	1%
	总计		94.8	5400.75	24214.3	8641.2	36%

虽然遗址数量与龙山晚期相比急剧减少，但出现了面积达60公顷的稍柴这一大型中心性聚落，在整个区域内形成三级聚落等级体系，罗口东北（Y022）遗址（18公顷）为二级的地方中心聚落。除稍柴遗址外，所有的聚落都有足够的土地供应自己。区域内土地利用率为40%，人口总数为6826人，占区域土地承载率的36.7%。

（二）二里头二期

本期聚落数量有所增加，共发现21个遗址，总面积123公顷，其中坞罗河流域11个，曹河流域1个，干沟河流域9个（图5.11）。

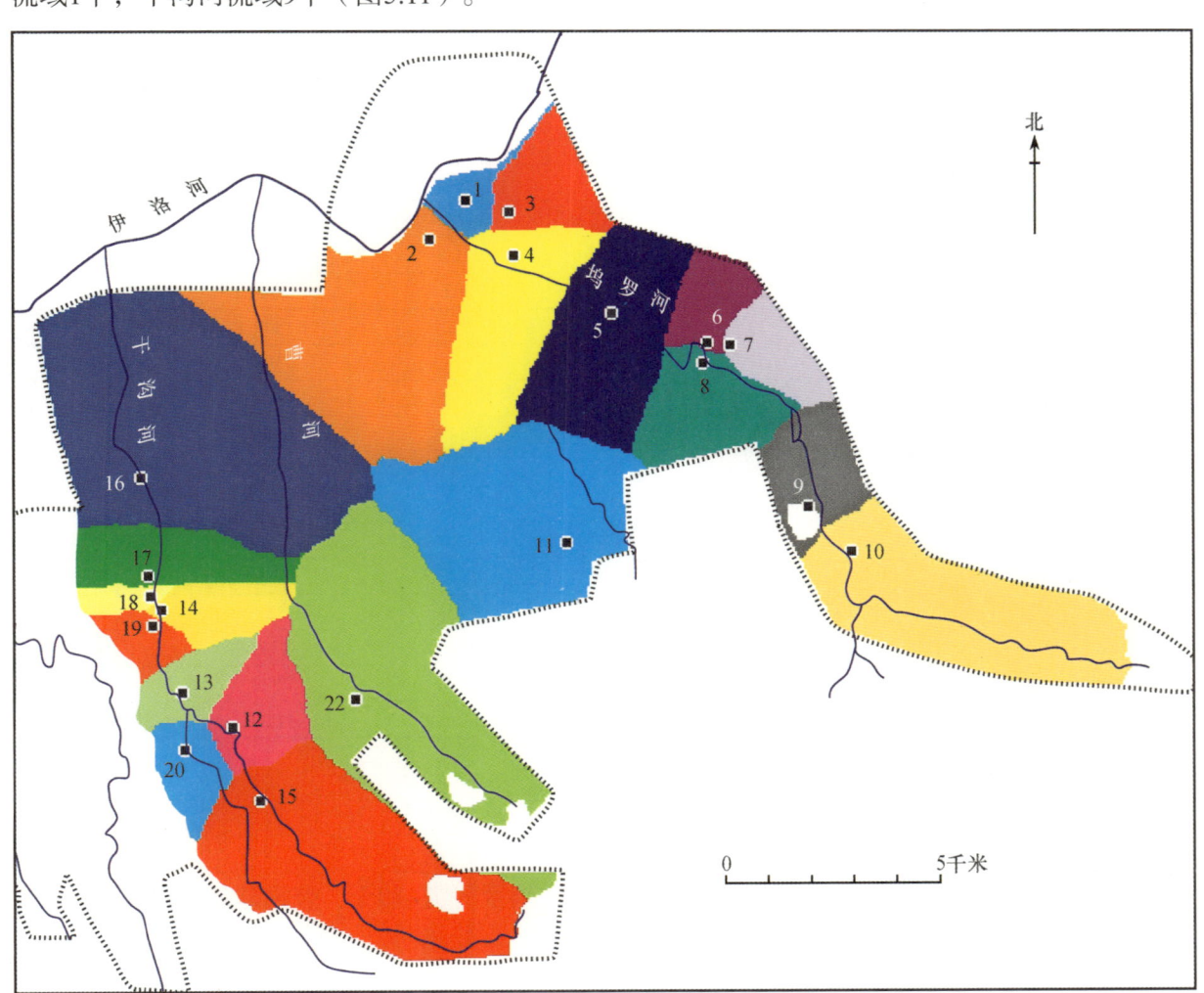

图5.11　二里头文化二期遗址分布及领地生产力

整个区域内仍然存在三级聚落等级分化现象。坞罗河流域的稍柴（Y1001）遗址（60公顷）仍为整个区域的中心聚落。罗口东北（Y022）遗址（18公顷）为坞罗河流域的二级中心聚落。除了这两个中心聚落和喂庄东南（Y020）遗址，坞罗河流域其余聚落都有足够的土地供养自己。但这个流域的土地利用率达到79%，意味着各聚落几乎要开垦所有的领地内土地才能够自给。

在干沟河流域，除了桑沟西（Y065）遗址（6公顷）这一该流域的地方中心聚落，其余聚落都有足够的农业用地供养自己，流域的土地利用率仅为27%。

本期整个区域的领地生产力是可以满足居民需要的，土地利用率为52%。这一时期的人口总量为7011人，继龙山文化晚期后又一次达到高峰。

表5.12 二里头二期遗址面积、人口、领地生产力、必需耕地及土地利用率

序号	遗址名称	遗址编号	遗址面积（公顷）	人口数量	必需耕地（公顷）	领地生产力（公顷）	土地利用率
	坞罗河流域		95.5	5443.5	8709.6	10997.8	79%
1	稍柴	97-1001	60	3420	5472	215.6	2538%
2	小訾店南	97-1005	2	114	182.4	2068.7	9%
3	电厂北	98-005	3.5	199.5	319.2	498.2	64%
4	电厂东南	98-008	1.5	85.5	136.8	1119.4	12%
5	费窑西南	98-011	2	114	182.4	1329.2	14%
6	喂庄东南	98-020	6	342	547.2	355.6	154%
7	喂庄	98-021	0.4	22.8	36.48	383.4	10%
8	罗口东北	98-022	18	1026	1641.6	720.4	228%
9	寺院沟	98-034	1.5	85.5	136.8	531.3	26%
10	双河	98-047	0.1	5.7	9.12	1803.7	1%
11	金钟寺	98-054	0.5	28.5	45.6	1972.3	2%
	干沟河流域		25.25	1439.25	2302.8	8394.1	27%
12	南村寨西南	00-062	2	114	182.4	542.5	34%
13	桑沟西	00-068	6	342	547.2	366.2	149%
14	马屯北	00-070	2.5	142.5	228	374.7	61%
15	颜良寨水库西	00-087	2	114	182.4	2129.7	9%
16	石家沟东北	00-093	4	228	364.8	3377.5	11%
17	李家沟东	00-099	5	285	456	872.6	52%
18	贾屯	00-101	0.5	28.5	45.6	145.1	31%
19	马屯西村南	00-103	1	57	91.2	249.9	36%
20	府西村北	00-110	2.25	128.25	205.2	335.9	61%
	曹河流域		2.25	128.25	205.2	2327.9	9%
22	新后沟东	00-132	2.25	128.25	205.2	2327.9	9%
总计			123	7011.25	21699.8	11217.6	52%

（三）二里头三期

本期聚落数量为19个，总面积113.45公顷，其中坞罗河流域9个，曹河流域1个，干沟河流域9个（图5.12），保持三级区域聚落等级分化。

稍柴（Y1001）遗址（60公顷）为整个区域的一级中心聚落，罗口东北（Y022）遗址（18公顷）是坞罗河流域的二级地方中心聚落，除了这两个中心聚落，坞罗河流域的其他聚落都有足够的土地供养自己，此流域的土地利用率为84%。

干沟河流域11号、12号和18号遗址及14号和15号遗址成组密集分布，遗址间的间距都不足200米。11号、14号、15号和17号遗址都存在农业用地短缺的问题，流域土地利用率为30%。

本期整个区域的土地利用率为52%，人口总量为6467人，占土地承载力的58%。

第五章 伊洛地区复杂社会的演变：地理信息系统基础上的人口和农业可耕地的分析

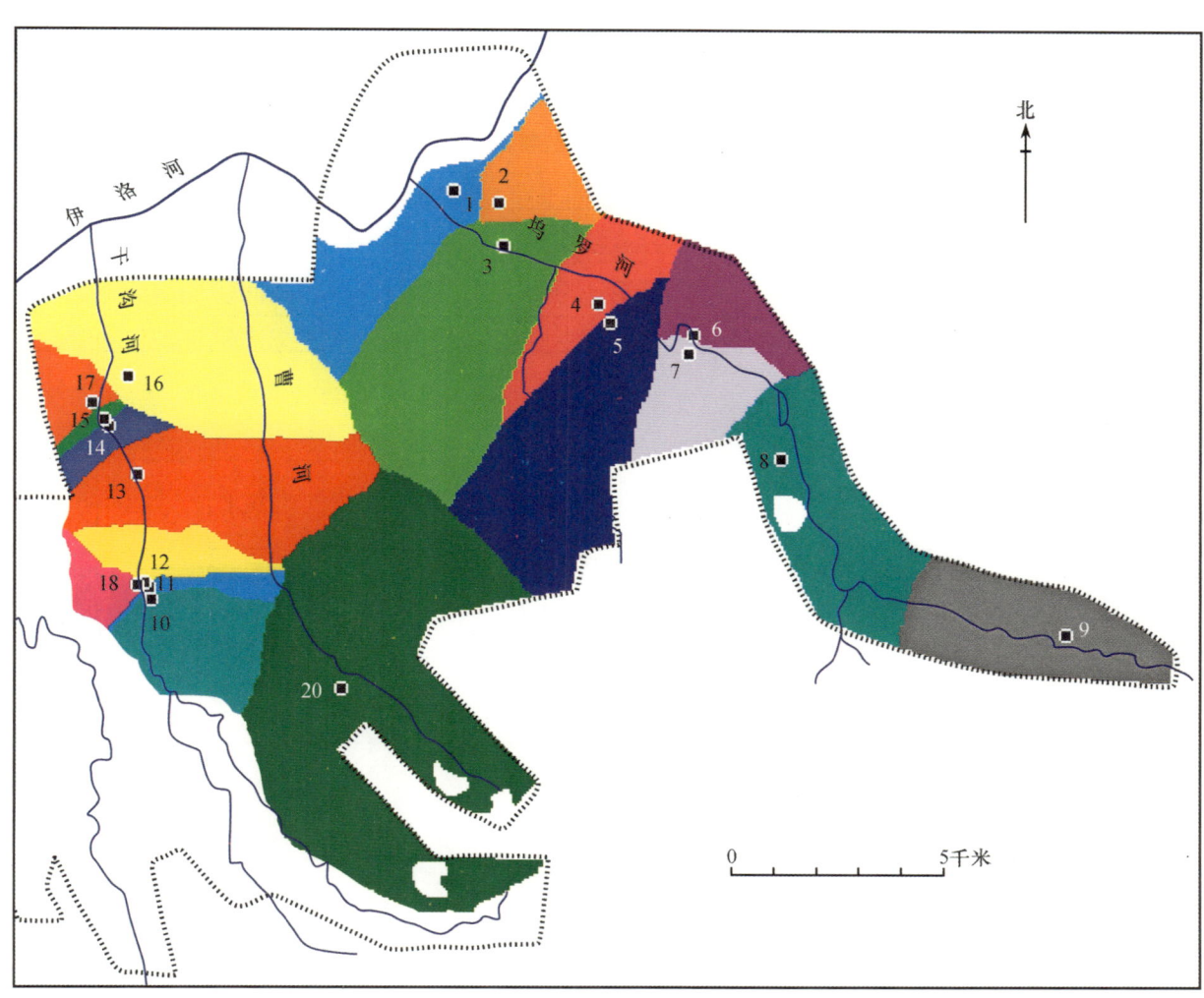

图5.12 二里头文化三期遗址分布及领地生产力

表5.13 二里头三期遗址面积、人口、领地生产力、必需耕地及土地利用率

序号	遗址名称	遗址编号	遗址面积（公顷）	人口数量	领地生产（公顷）	必需耕地（公顷）	土地利用率
	坞罗河流域		92.7	5283.9	10086.5	8454.24	84%
1	稍柴	97-1001	60	3420	1003.6	5472	545%
2	电厂北路东	98-005	3.5	199.5	498.2	319.2	64%
3	电厂东南	98-008	1.5	85.5	2133.9	136.8	6%
4	费窑东南	98-011	2	114	720.1	182.4	25%
5	费窑南	98-013	0.5	28.5	1836.9	45.6	2%
6	喂庄东南	98-020	6	342	597.1	547.2	92%
7	罗口东北	98-022	18	1026	653.4	1641.6	251%
8	坞罗西坡1	98-033	0.2	11.4	1398.8	18.24	1%
9	上庄	98-037	1	57	1244.5	91.2	7%
	干沟河流域		18.5	1054.5	5689.1	1687.2	30%
10	马屯北	00-070	2.5	142.5	804.9	228	28%
11	王闲	00-071	3	171	156.1	273.6	175%
12	罗彦庄西南	00-072	1	57	415.9	91.2	22%
13	念子庄西北	00-073	1	57	1544.9	91.2	6%
14	干沟猪场	00-074	6	342	194.3	547.2	282%

续表

序号	遗址名称	遗址编号	遗址面积（公顷）	人口数量	领地生产（公顷）	必需耕地（公顷）	土地利用率
15	刘乐寨南	00-075	1	57	64.1	91.2	142%
16	干沟南	00-076	0.5	28.5	2020.5	45.6	2%
17	回龙湾新村东	00-083	3	171	259.8	273.6	105%
18	贾屯	00-101	0.5	28.5	228.6	45.6	20%
	曹河流域		2.25	128.25	4157.7	205.2	5%
20	新后沟东	00-132	2.25	128.25	4157.7	205.2	5%
总计			113.45	6466.65	19933.3	10346.64	52%

（四）二里头四期

本期聚落总数21个，总面积103.85公顷，其中坞罗河流域6个，曹河流域1个，干沟河流域14个（图5.13），本期继续保持三级区域聚落等级分化体系。

坞罗河流域的稍柴（Y1001，60公顷）仍然是整个调查区域的一级中心聚落，随着周围小遗址的减少，它的领地生产力有了一定的增加，但仍然不能满足居民需要。坞罗河流域的其他聚落都有足够的可耕地，流域土地利用率为58%。

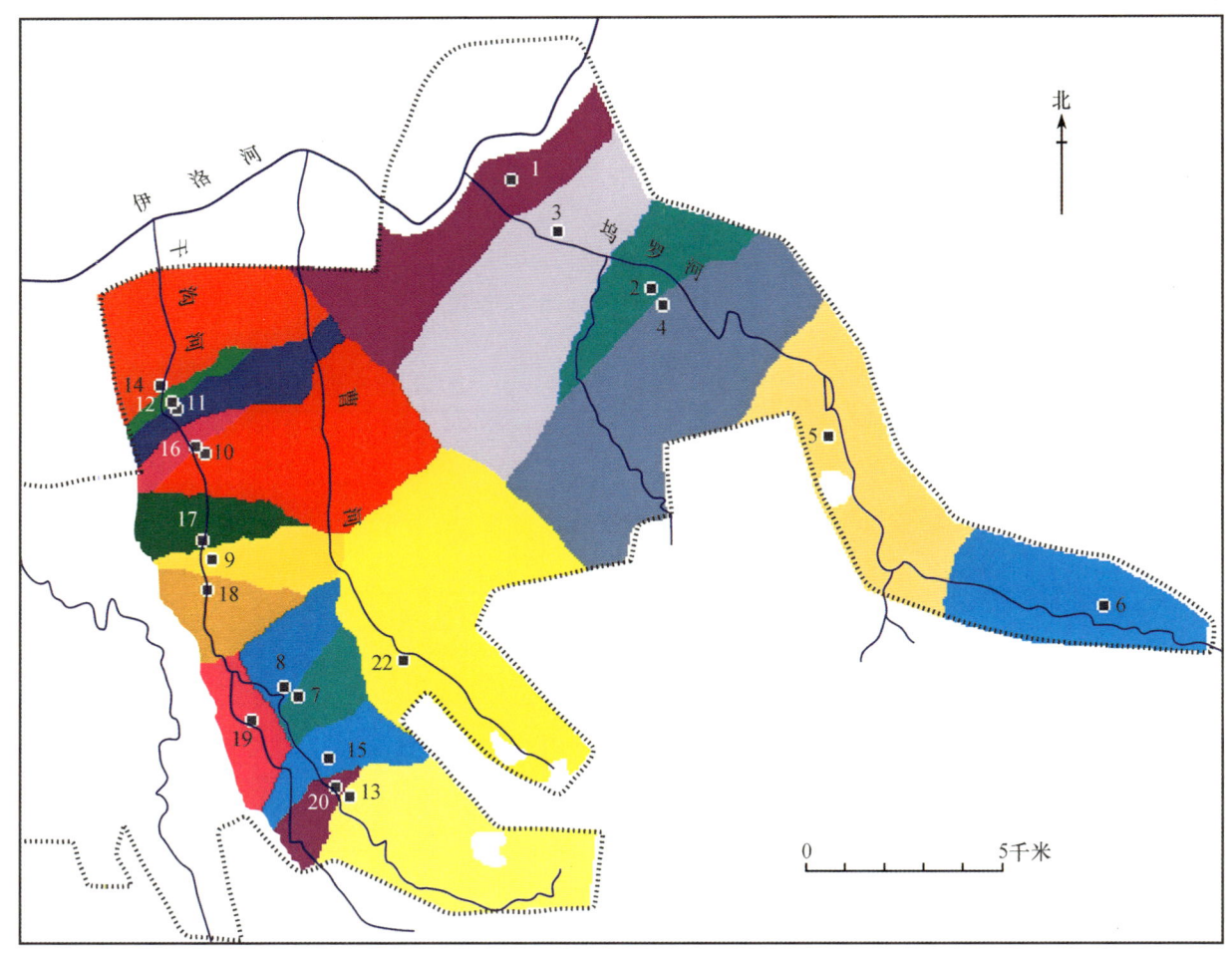

图5.13　二里头文化四期遗址分布及领地生产力

干沟河流域遗址面积均偏小，除2个较大遗址外，其余遗址均有足够的领地生产力，流域土地利用率是38%。

本期，整个区域的土地利用率为44%。区域人口总量有所降低，为5919人。

表5.14　二里头四期遗址面积、人口、领地生产力、必需耕地及土地利用率

序号	遗址名称	遗址编号	遗址面积（公顷）	人口数量	领地生产力（公顷）	必需耕地（公顷）	土地利用率
	坞罗河流域		65.2	3716.4	10281.4	5946.24	58%
1	稍柴	97-1001	60	3420	1412.5	5472	387%
2	电厂东南	98-008	1.5	85.5	2416.2	136.8	6%
3	费窑东南	98-011	2	114	767.5	182.4	24%
4	费窑南	98-013	0.5	28.5	2749.5	45.6	2%
5	坞罗西坡1	98-033	0.2	11.4	1691.2	18.24	1%
6	上庄	98-037	1	57	1244.5	91.2	7%
	干沟河流域		36.4	2074.8	8655.8	3319.68	38%
7	南村寨东南	00-061	1	57	342.5	91.2	27%
8	南村寨西南	00-062	2	114	388.8	182.4	47%
9	罗彦庄西南	00-072	1	57	463.5	91.2	20%
10	念子庄西北	00-073	1	57	1680.4	91.2	5%
11	干沟猪场	00-074	6	342	535.9	547.2	102%
12	刘乐寨南	00-075	1	57	119.2	91.2	77%
13	小相西南	00-080	4.5	256.5	1529.5	410.4	27%
14	回龙湾新村东	00-083	3	171	1254.1	273.6	22%
15	颜良寨西南	00-086	3	171	454.8	273.6	60%
16	石家沟东北	00-093	4	228	223.9	364.8	163%
17	李家沟东	00-099	5	285	477.1	456	96%
18	马屯西村南	00-103	1	57	482.6	91.2	19%
19	府西村东北	00-111	1.9	108.3	471.8	173.28	37%
20	小相西	00-115	2	114	231.7	182.4	79%
	曹河流域		2.25	128.25	2731.5	205.2	8%
22	新后沟东	00-132	2.25	128.25	2731.5	205.2	8%
总计			103.85	5919.45	21668.7	9471.12	44%

第四节　人口数量变化和资源再分配与伊洛地区社会复杂化进程

一、人口数量变化和伊洛地区社会复杂化进程

长期以来，人口压力被看成是社会复杂化发展进程中的首要动因[73]。卡内罗认为农业土地范围内的人口增长与国家政体的出现有密切联系[74]。杨[75]、吉布森[76]和阿丹姆斯[77]等学者对美索不达米亚地区文明化进程的研究中，以及桑德斯[78]对中美洲早期国家出现的研究中均提出人口的快速增长是社会发展的重要因素。哈森论述"土地承载力"这一概念时指出，人口数量应该低于土地承载力所能供养的水平，最大人口数量一般要保持在土地承载

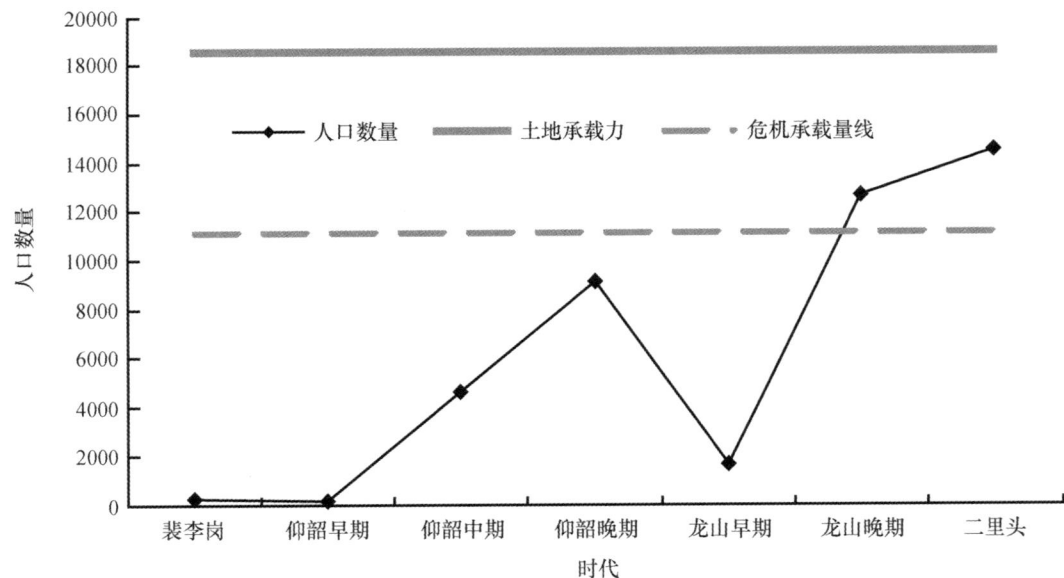

图5.14 裴李岗文化至二里头文化时期人口数量变化曲线

力的20%～60%之间，他把这种人口数量称作"最佳承载量"；人口数量若超过土地承载力的60%，则被称作"危机承载量"，人口就会对环境造成压力，导致资源短缺、环境恶化，引发包括社会复杂化等一系列问题[79]。

如图5.14所示，研究区域内的人口数量从裴李岗时期到二里头时期有很大的波动。第一次显著的增长是在仰韶中期，在仰韶晚期到达第一个高峰。然而，龙山早期人口却急剧下降，甚至低于仰韶中期。随后，龙山晚期人口急剧增长，超过仰韶晚期的最高峰。二里头时期人口数量（二里头四个时期人口的平均值）基本与龙山晚期持平。

仰韶中期出现人口数量的首次显著增长，同时也首次出现了二级区域聚落等级化体系。仰韶晚期，聚落等级化持续存在，人口数量也增加到一个更高的水平。龙山晚期，人口再次大量增长，二级区域聚落等级化体系也再次出现，二里头时期持续了龙山时期的高人口量，区域聚落形态形成了三级等级化体系、人口增长与社会复杂化的发展表现出了高度同步性，这是否意味着人口压力是促进社会等级化的首要动因呢？

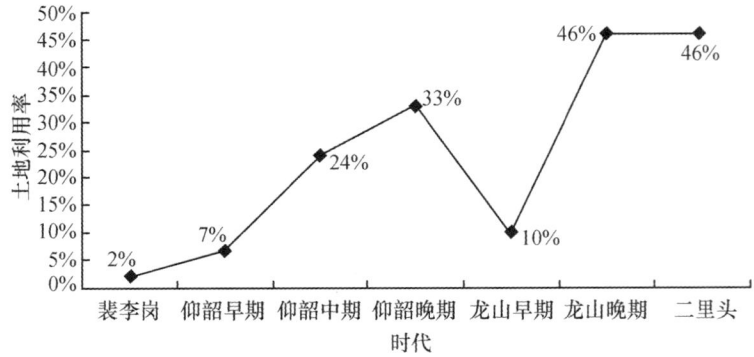

图5.15 裴李岗文化至二里头文化时期总土地利用率变化曲线图

土地利用率可以作为衡量人口压力的重要指标。由图5.15可以看出，虽然研究区域内的总土地利用率随人口的增长而增长，但在人口数量最多的龙山晚期和二里头时期，总土地利用率均为46%。也就是说，即使只计算各聚落领地内的可耕地面积，当时也只需要开垦一半的可耕地即可满足全部居民的食物需要，总土地利用率仍然低于哈森设定的60%的"危机承载量"标准，从整个研究区域的角度讲，不存在人口压力问题。

因此，仰韶时期人口增长与社会复杂化基本同步的现象并不支持人口压力是社会复杂化出现的首要动因这一推断。正如哈森所言，使用"人口压力"这一概念的主要误区就是把人口增长和人口压力混为一谈，人口数量的增长并不一定暗示着资源的短缺和饥荒的产生。人口的增长是受自然和文化因素调控的。过度的人口膨胀导致的经济问题只是人类社会自身调控失败的情况下才出现，而不是一种必然的趋势。过度的、不受控制的人口增长和生物的、文化的规则都是相悖的。当一个地区面临人口压力时，有效的社会调节机制能够在现有的技术和食物采集系统下更深程度地去开采地方资源或调配不同地区的资源，保持社会平稳发展[80]。

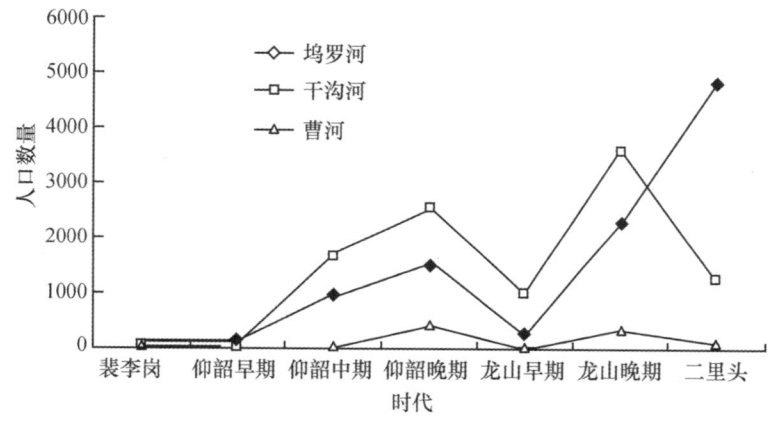

图5.16　各流域人口数量变化曲线对比图

仔细分析各流域的人口变动情况可以看出，研究区域内各流域的人口波动并不是完全同步的（图5.16）。在龙山文化晚期，坞罗河流域的人口总量少于干沟河流域，至二里头时期，坞罗河流域的人口数量急剧增长（从2291增长至4837人，增长了111.13%），成为全区域的人口聚集中心。其他两个流域的人口却呈现下降趋势（干沟河流域从3577下降至1260人，下降了66.77%；曹河流域从342降至103人，下降了69.88%。两流域共下降了65.22%）。正是在该时期，面积达60公顷的稍柴遗址出现在坞罗河下游与伊洛河道交汇处，成为整个区域内最大的中心性聚落。

对这种不同流域人口或增或减的幅度大致相当、特大型聚落出现的情况的一种解释是：这种人口数量变动不是自发形成的，而是某种权力机构有意调整的结果。如果从整个二里头文化的大背景下观察，稍柴聚落的出现应该看成是整个伊洛地区社会复杂化发展和早期国家形成进程中的一部分，相对于同时期的都邑性聚落二里头而言，稍柴应为附属的二级中心聚落，而且正如有学者指出的，它很可能是被二里头聚落控制的开采地方自然资源的地方中心聚落[81]。可见，在研究区域内社会复杂化过程中，人口数量的增加可能只是为社会上层操纵各种权利并建立更加复杂的社会结构提供更多的机会，但并不一定造成迫使社会复杂化的压力。如果操纵措施得当，人口增长会促进社会复杂化进程，并保持社会持续发展。

二、资源再分配和伊洛地区社会复杂化进程

裴李岗时期到仰韶早期，研究区域内聚落稀少，所有聚落的领地生产力都足以供养其居民。仰韶中期，聚落数量增加，而且出现面积达20公顷以上的大型中心性聚落，其领地生产力不足以供养本聚落人口。这种现象在仰韶晚期增多。龙山早期的聚落数量骤减，到龙山晚期，研究区域重新繁荣，并一直保持到二里头时期。很多大中型中心聚落均有领地生产力不足的情况。考虑到一些我们归入同一文化时期的遗址可能并没有共存过，估计实际上的领地生产力不足问题并不像本研究显示的那么严重，但可以肯定，这一问题是存在的，而且是需要对食物资源进行再分配来解决的。

与一般性聚落相比，中心性聚落承载着更多的功能，也会聚集更多人口，极易产生领地内耕地不足问题。这类聚落的产生和生存是社会复杂化发展的需要。推测这些中心性聚落的食物来源可能是由周围的小型聚落提供，在二里头时期有可能是以贡赋的形式提供。在中心性聚落控制下的食物资源再分配可以有效解决各领地生产力不足聚落的食物问题。

有些面积较小的非中心性遗址也存在领地生产力不足的问题，这可能与其特殊功能有关。如干沟河流域的半个寨遗址自仰韶晚期到龙山晚期均存在严重的领地生产力不足问题，即使将邻近的邢村东遗址的领地生产力考虑在内，土地利用率仍然超过百分之百。在仰韶晚期和龙山晚期，半个寨均不是流域的中心性聚落，但它是流域内最靠近南部山地的聚落，很可能拥有特殊资源，能够用以交换到其他聚落的食物资源维持生存。

第五节　本研究的局限性

和其他有关人口数量和领地生产力的研究一样[82]，本研究也存在一些局限性。

（1）本章研究最基本的前提是假设所有的同一时期的遗址都是共存的，但目前还没有可靠的方法来证明遗址的共存性。我们的研究是基于陶器类型学研究，二里头文化每期100年，在龙山文化早、晚期各为500年，仰韶文化早、中、晚各期约为500年，裴李岗时期约为1000年。每期的时间跨度越长，同期所有遗址共存的可能性越小，以共存为前提估算出的人口数量就会过大，而领地生产力会过小。

（2）很多聚落延续的时间很长，涵盖了多个文化阶段，仅仅通过地面的调查很难决定每个文化阶段的准确地域，涵盖多个文化阶段的聚落面积通常被假设为是不变的，这种假设往往会导致某种错误。例如，稍柴遗址在二里头文化四个时期的面积都被认为是60公顷。既然稍柴遗址人类活动出现在二里头一期，那么这个时期的聚落面积应该比后三期的小，人口数量

也少。

（3）人均消耗谷物的数量和每亩地产量的估算建立在县志资料的基础上，这和史前时期的状况肯定会有所不同，应该把它们看作是人均消耗和土地生产力的最高限。

（4）气候变化、谷物种植技术及知识在不同的文化时期应该是不断变化的，这些变化有可能影响谷物的产量。由于这种变化及其对产量的影响很难量化，本章假设在每个文化阶段谷物的生产力是相同的，这可能会高估每个文化阶段的产量。

尽管研究存在局限性，我们仍然可以通过以上的研究来更好地理解研究区域内人口数量、领地生产力和社会复杂化发展之间的关系。随着更精确的纪年及更多资料的发现，有些阐述可能会有所改变，但本章的研究毕竟是一种有益的尝试，其结果也会对深入认识伊洛地区社会复杂化过程中人口压力所扮演的角色有所帮助。

注　释

[1] 巩县志编纂委员会编：《巩县志》，中州古籍出版社，1991年，第69、70、257～265页。

[2] Ren G, Zhang L. A Preliminary Mapped Summary of Holocene Pollen Data for Northeast China. Quaternary Science Reviews, 1998, 17: 669-688.

[3] Zhao X. The Paleoclimate of China. Beijing: Geological Publishing House, 1992.

[4] 陈星灿：《中国史前考古学史研究（1895—1949）》，生活·读书·新知三联书店，1997年。

[5] 中国社会科学院考古研究所二里头工作队：《1981年河南偃师二里头墓葬发掘简报》，《考古》1984年第1期；中国社会科学院考古研究所二里头工作队：《偃师二里头遗址1980—1981年Ⅲ区发掘简报》，《考古》1984年第7期；中国社会科学院考古研究所二里头队：《1982年秋偃师二里头遗址九区发掘简报》，《考古》1985年第12期；中国社会科学院考古研究所二里头工作队：《二里头遗址田野工作的新进展》，《中国社会科学院古代文明研究中心通讯》2001年第1期；中国社会科学院考古研究所：《偃师二里头》，中国大百科全书出版社，1999年；Liu, L. Urbanization in China: Erlitou and its hinterland//Storey G R. Population and preindustrial cities: A Cross-cultural Perspective. University of Alabama Press, 2006.

[6] Liu L, Chen X C, Lee Y K, et al. Settlement Patterns and Development of social complexity in the Yiluo Region, North China. Journal of Field Archaeology, 2002-2004, 29(1/2): 75-100; Liu L, Chen X C. Settlement Archaeology and the Study of Social Complexity in China. The Review of Archaeology, 2001, 22(2): 4-21.

[7] Green S W. Approaching Archaeological Space: An Introduction to the Volume//Zubrow E B W. Interpreting Space: GIS and Archaeology. London & New York & Philadelphia: Taylor & Francis, 1990 :3-8.

[8] Green S W. Approaching Archaeological Space: An Introduction to the Volume//Zubrow E B W. Interpreting Space: GIS and Archaeology. London & New York & Philadelphia: Taylor & Francis, 1990 :3-8.

[9] Effland R W. Statistical Distribution Cartography and Computer Graphics//Upham S. Computer Graphics in Archaeology(No.15), Anthropological Research Papers. Tempe: Arizona State University, 1979: 17-29.

[10] Zimmerman L J. Prehistoric Locational Behavior: A Computer Simulation. Report No. 10, Office of the State Archaeologist. Lowa City: University of Iowa Press, 1977.

[11] Bove F J. Trend Surface Analysis and the Lowland Classic Maya Collapse. American Antiquity, 1981, 46: 93-112.

[12] Ebert J I, Kohler T A. The Theoretical and Methodological Basis of Archaeological Predictive Modelling. Chapter 4//BLM Predictive Modelling Draft. Bureau of Land Management, 1986.

［13］Kvamme K L. Geographic Information System in Regional Archaeological Research and Management//Schiffer M B. Archaeological Method and Theory(vol. 1). Tucson: University of Arizona Press, 1989: 139-203.

［14］Kvamme K L. GIS Algorithms and Their Effect on Regional Archaeological Analysis//Allen K M S, Green S W, Zubrow E B W. Interpreting Space: GIS and Archaeology. Taylor and Francis, 1990: 112-126.

［15］Clarke K C. Advances in Geographical Information Systems. Computers, Environment, and Urban Systems, 1986, 10: 175-184.

［16］Kvamme K L. A view from Across the Water: The North American Experience in Archaeological GIS//Stannic Z. Archaeology and Geographic Information Systems: A European Perspective. New York: Taylor & Francis, 1995.

［17］高立兵：《时空解释新手段——欧美考古GIS研究的历史、现状和未来》，《考古》1997年第7期。

［18］中国河南省文物考古研究所、美国密苏里州立大学人类学系：《河南颍河上游考古调查中运用GPS与GIS的初步报告》，《华夏考古》1998年第1期。

［19］Rapp G R, Jing Z C, et al. Anyang Project: Co-evolution of Human Societies and Landscapes. Annual Report for 1998-1999. Unpublished Report, 2000.

［20］Liu L, Chen X C, Lee Y K, et al. Settlement Patterns and Development of social complexity in the Yiluo Region, North China. Journal of Field Archaeology, 2002-2004, 29(1/2): 75-100.

［21］中美两城地区联合考古队：《山东日照市两城地区的考古调查》，《考古》1997年第4期。

［22］赤峰中美联合考古研究项目：《内蒙古东部（赤峰）区域考古调查阶段性报告》，科学出版社，2003年。

［23］Hassan F A. Demographic Archaeology//Schiffer M B. Advances in archaeological method and theory(vol. 1). New York: Academic Press, 1978: 49-103.

［24］Childe V G. Social Evolution. London: Watts Press, 1951.

［25］Turner C G, Lofgren L. Household Size of Prehistoric Western Pueblo Indians. Southwestern Journal of Anthropology, 1966, 22: 117-132.

［26］Cook S F. Can Pottery Residues be Used as An Index to Population? Contributions of the University of California Archaeological Research Facility, 1972, 14: 17-40.

［27］Naroll R. Floor Area and Settlement Population. American Antiquity, 1962, 27: 587-589.

［28］Leblanc S. An Addition to Naroll's Suggested Floor Area and Settlement Population Relationship. American Antiquity, 1971, 36: 210-211.

［29］Casselberry S E. Further Refinement of Formulae for Determining Population from Floor Area. World Archaeology, 1974, 6: 117-122.

［30］Cook S F. Prehistoric Demography. Mass: Addison-Wesley Publishing Reading, 1972.

［31］Steward J H. Ecological Aspects of Southwestern Society. Anthropos, 1937, 32: 87-104.

［32］Turner C G, Lofgren L. Household Size of Prehistoric Western Pueblo Indians. Southwestern Journal of Anthropology, 1966, 22: 117-132.

［33］Cook S F. Prehistoric Demography. Mass: Addison-Wesley Publishing Reading, 1972.

［34］Haviland W A. A New Population Estimate for Tikal, Guatemala. American Antiquity, 1969, 34: 429-433.

［35］Clarke J I. Population Geography. New York: Pergamon, 1965.

［36］Carrasco P. Family Structure in Sixteenth-century Tepoztlan//Manners R. Process and Pattern in Culture. Chicago: Aldine, 1964: 185.

［37］Carrasco P. Social Organization of Ancient Mexico//Bernal I. Handbook of Middle American Indians(vol. 10). Austin: University of Texas Press, 1971.

［38］Nutini H G. A Synoptic Comparison of Mesoamerican Marriage and Family Structure. Southwestern Journal of Anthropology, 1967, 23: 383-404.

［39］Nutini H G. San Bernardino Contla: Marriage and family structure in a Tlaxcalan municipio. Pittsburgh: University of Pittsburgh Press, 1968.

[40] Kolb C C. Demographic Estimates in Archaeology: Contributions from Ethnoarchaeology on Mesoamerican Peasants. Current Anthropology, 1985, 26: 581-599.

[41] Kramer C. 1978. Estimating Prehistoric Populations: An ethnoarchaeological Approach. Colloque International C.N.R.S, 1978, (580).

[42] 半坡博物馆、陕西省考古研究所、临潼县博物馆：《姜寨——新石器时代遗址发掘报告》，文物出版社，1988年，第68、69、352~357页。

[43] 中国社会科学院考古研究所：《蒙城尉迟寺——皖北新石器时代聚落遗存的发掘与研究》，科学出版社，2001年，第325~328页。

[44] 朱乃诚：《人口数量的分析与社会组织结构的复原》，《华夏考古》1994年第4期。

[45] 中国社会科学院考古研究所：《蒙城尉迟寺——皖北新石器时代聚落遗存的发掘与研究》，科学出版社，2001年，第1~6页。

[46] 乔玉：《尉迟寺遗址人口及相关问题》，《蒙城尉迟寺（二）》，科学出版社，2007年，第404~417页。

[47] 半坡博物馆、陕西省考古研究所、临潼县博物馆：《姜寨——新石器时代遗址发掘报告》，文物出版社，1988年，第1~14页。

[48] 半坡博物馆、陕西省考古研究所、临潼县博物馆：《姜寨——新石器时代遗址发掘报告》，文物出版社，1988年，第15页。

[49] 半坡博物馆、陕西省考古研究所、临潼县博物馆：《姜寨——新石器时代遗址发掘报告》，文物出版社，1988年，第68、69、352~357页。

[50] 赵春青：《也谈姜寨一期村落中的房屋与人口》，《考古与文物》1998年第5期。

[51] Hassan F A. Demographic Archaeology. New York & London: Academic Press, 1981: 164

[52] Hayden B. The Carrying Capacity Dilemma. American Antiquity, 1975, 30: 205-221.

[53] Hassan F A. Demographic Archaeology//Schiffer M B. Advances in Archaeological Method and Theory(vol. 1) New York: Academic Press, 1978: 49-103.

[54] 安志敏：《中国的史前农业》，《考古学报》1988年第4期。

[55] 佟伟华：《磁山遗址的原始农业遗存及其相关的问题》，《农业考古》1984年第1期。

[56] 丁清贤：《河南新石器时代农业考古的发现与研究》，《农业考古》1990年第1期。

[57] 任式楠：《我国新石器—铜石器并用时代农作物和其它食用植物遗存》，《史前研究》1989年第3~4期。

[58] 蔡莲珍、仇士华：《碳十三测定和古代食谱研究》，《考古》1984年第10期。

[59] Liu L, Chen X C, Lee Y K, et al. Settlement Patterns and Development of social complexity in the Yiluo Region, North China. Journal of Field Archaeology, 2002-2004, 29(1/2): 75-100.

[60] 杨贵：《对夏商周亩产量的推测》，《中国农史》1988年第2期。

[61] 巩县志编纂委员会编：《巩县志》，中州古籍出版社，1991年，第260页。

[62] Van Wersch H J. The agricultural Economy//Rapp G R. The Minnesota Messenia Expedition: Reconstructing a Bronze Age Environment. Minneapolis: University of Minnesota Press, 1972: 177-187.

[63] 巩县志编纂委员会编：《巩县志》，中州古籍出版社，1991年，第479页。

[64] 陈文华：《中国古代农业科技史图谱》，农业出版社，1991年，第126页。

[65] Shelach G. Leadership Strategies, Economic Activity, and Interregional Interaction: Social complexity in Northeast China. New York: Kluwer Academic, Plenum publishers, 1999: 121-138.

[66] 巩县志编纂委员会编：《巩县志》，中州古籍出版社，1991年，第99~104。

[67] Steponaitis V. P. Settlement Hierarchies and Political Complexity in Nonmarket Societies: The Formative Period of the Valley of Mexico. American anthropologist, 1981, 83: 320-363.

[68] Brumfiel E. Regional Growth in the Eastern Valley of Mexico: A test of the "Population Pressure" hypothesis//Flannery K V. The Early Mesoamerican Village. New York: Academic Press, 1976: 234-249.

[69] Vita-Finzi C, Higgs E S. Prehistoric Economy in the Mount Carmel Area of Palestine: Site Catchment Analysis.

Proceedings of the Prehistoric Society, 1970, 36: 1-37.

[70] Hassan F A. Demographic Archaeology. New York & London: Academic Press, 1981: 51-59.

[71] Chisolm M. Rural Settlement and Land Use: An Essay in Location. Chicago: Aldine, 1968: 131.

[72] Shelach G. Leadership Strategies, Economic Activity, and Interregional Interaction: Social complexity in Northeast China. New York: Kluwer Academic, Plenum publishers, 1999.

[73] F. A. Hassan, Demographic archaeology, Advances in archaeological method and theory, vol. 1. Edited by M. B. Schiffer, 49-103, New York, Academic Press, 1978.

[74] C. T. Carneiro, A theory of the origin of the state, Science 169: 733-738, 1970.

[75] C. T. Young, Population densities and early Mesopotamian urbanism, Man, settlement, and urbanism, Edited by P.J. Ucko, 827-842, London: Duckworth, 1972.

[76] M. Gibson, Population shift and the rise of Mesopotamian civilization, The explanation of culture change, Edited by C. Renfrew, 447-463, London: Duckworth, 1973.

[77] R. M. Adams, Demography and the urban "revolution" in low land Mesopotamia, Population growth: Anthropological implications, Edited by B. Spooner, 60- 63, Cambridge, MIT Press, 1972.

[78] W. T. Sanders, Chiefdom to state: Political evolution at Kaminaljuyu, Guatemala, Reconstructing complex societies: An archaeological colloquium, vol. No. 20. Edited by C. B. Moore, 97-113, Bulletin of the American Schools of Oriental Research, Supplement, 1974.

[79] F. A. Hassan, Demographic archaeology, Advances in archaeological method and theory, vol. 1. Edited by M. B. Schiffer, 49-103, New York, Academic Press, 1978.

[80] F. A. Hassan, Demographic archaeology, Advances in archaeological method and theory, vol. 1. Edited by M. B. Schiffer, 49-103, New York, Academic Press, 1978.

[81] 刘莉、陈星灿：《中国早期国家的形成：从二里头和二里岗时期的中心和边缘之间的关系谈起》，《古代文明》2002年第1卷。

[82] Shelach G. Leadership Strategies, Economic Activity, and Interregional Interaction: Social complexity in Northeast China. New York: Kluwer Academic, Plenum publishers, 1999.

第六章　伊洛地区调查遗址的植物考古分析[①]

第一节　样品研究方法与样品量

伊洛流域系统调查了1120平方千米的冲积平原和黄土阶地，记录了451个遗址。从91个遗址的167个遗迹单位中采集了堆积样品，获得181份浮选土样（表6.1）。采样率（样品数量/遗址数量）的比例从1%（殷墟文化）到44%（裴李岗文化时期）不等：仰韶文化采样率为11%，龙山文化为12%，二里头文化为8%，二里岗文化为8%，周代为3%。该地区汉代遗址的总数尚不清楚。虽然遗址通常埋藏在地表之下0.5~2.0米处，但在黄土阶地的垂直剖面中依旧可见相关遗迹，能够在这些位置采集到土样。

表6.1　伊洛地区已调查遗址中取样遗址的数量、浮选样品的数量、各阶段的土样体积

时期	调查遗址数量	浮选遗址数量	样本量（份）	采样单位数量（处）	土样量（升）	种数	种子数（颗）
裴李岗	16	7	17	12	169.50	9	69
仰韶	228	24	44	43	357.70	23	4215
龙山	211	26	37	36	323.65	32	22707
二里头	207	16	39	36	376.00	24	9583
二里岗	120	8	19	19	155.20	23	9273
周	435	11	22	19	208.50	23	1749
汉		3	3	3	19.00	12	141
合计		95	181	167	1616.55		47737

植物遗存往往与埋藏背景有关，因此我们集中采集同一单位的样本以求尽量降低遗迹背景不同对样品所带来的影响。大部分样品（90%）从灰坑的灰土层中采集。少数来自其他单位，其中包括采自房屋地面的5份土样（仰韶1、龙山2、二里头1、汉代1）、二里头文化灰沟内采集的1份和汉代窑炉中采集的1份（表6.1）。文化层是人工制品聚集的区域，对11处这类区域进行了采样，从大多数遗迹中采集了一份至少2升的样品，从少量遗迹中采集了2份样品。灰坑中的包含物通常来源于二次堆积（即充填了遗址上居民各种活动中产生的一般沉积物和垃圾）。因此，这些样品特别适合于在遗址内对比植物利用的基本规律。

[①] 本章由李炅娥（Gyoung-Ah Lee）、Gary W. Crawford、Rory C. Walsh、金河范（Habeom Kim）、Angelica Kneisly、李显洙（Hyunsoo Lee）、Brianna Kendrick、Maria Vaughn、竺君漪、方圆执笔，邓玲玲翻译。

在对早期26个遗址的前期研究中发现[1]，样品种类同样品体积呈正相关，也就是说，如果样品量较少的话，其中所包含的植物类别会更少，同时也会缺乏采集样品中稀缺的植物类别。我们将样品量增加7倍，土壤体积增加3倍（1616.55升）以期进行补救。但不同时期的样本量仍然存在不均等的情况（图6.1）。24个仰韶时期遗址中采集的样品量最多，共44份，体积为357.7升，汉代的2个遗址中获得的样品量最少（表6.1）。遗址中相对较小的样品采集量会限制我们对植物群共同性和差异性的解释，增量数据显示，样本的丰富程度并不直接同样品分量相对应，因而也缓解了我们的担忧。例如，种子密度的最大平均值来自龙山时期，此期采集的土样分量处于第三位，而土样分量最大的仰韶时期的平均种子密度仅排在第四位（图6.1-a，b）。最大的土样分量或样品数量不会导致该时期出现最多的植物类别，由此说明仰韶时期种子的多样性落后于之后样本量较小的时期（图6.2）。在样品之间进行比较，种子多样性（图6.3-a）或密度（图6.3-b）也与通过体积测量的样品体量无关。

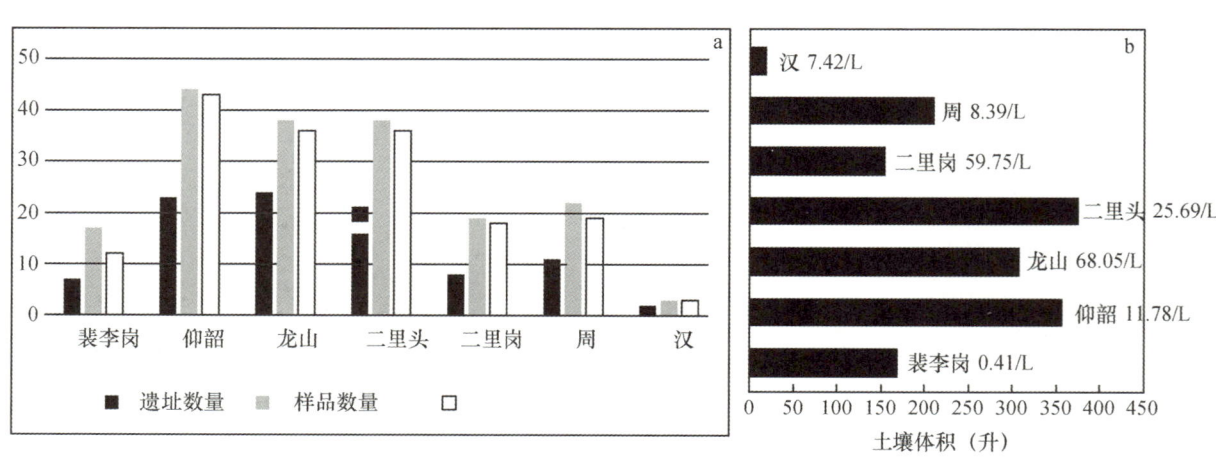

图6.1　每期样本量（a，左图）以及各期样品体积与种子密度（b，右图，种子数/土壤体积）

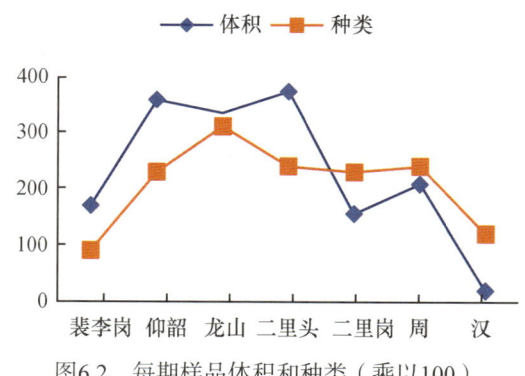

图6.2　每期样品体积和种类（乘以100）

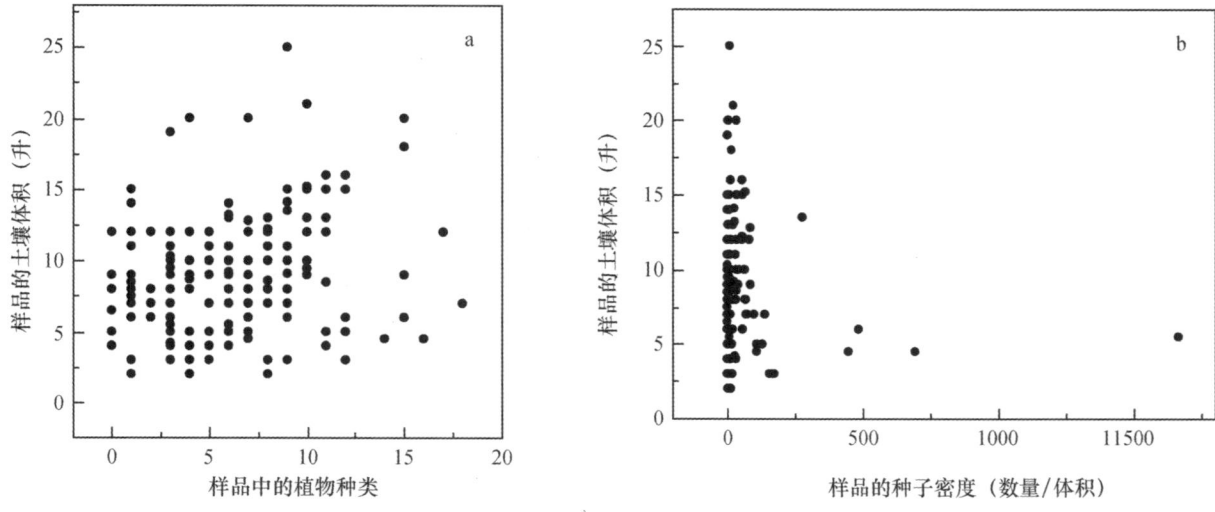

图6.3 根据土壤样品体积比较植物多样性（a，左图）和种子密度（b，右图）

a.植物多样性由每个样本中的植物种类代表　b.种类包括所有已鉴定的种子种类，一种普遍存在的、未识别的种子类型（附录1中未知类型1）和两种坚果类型，但不包括所有其他未知种子

第二节　分析方法

处理土壤样品采用两种浮选方法：1998～2001年的手工倾倒式浮选法以及2002～2011年使用的改良后的贝丘考古项目（SMAP）浮选仪浮选法[2]。在手动和机器浮选中，使用孔径0.2毫米的筛网采集轻浮物，使用孔径1毫米的筛网来采集重浮物。SMAP浮选仪是一个轻巧的柜式的聚氯乙烯（PVC）箱，采用金属框架支撑。将干燥的土壤样品缓慢放入充满水的箱子中，水溢出槽后流过孔径0.2毫米的筛网，则可获取漂浮或悬浮在水中的所有物质。在浮选槽中插入筛孔尺寸为1.0毫米的筛网用以获取由较稠密物质组成的重浮物，包括矿物、陶片、岩屑、重的碳化植物残留物（主要是木炭）以及骨渣。浮选完成一份样品后与将新样品倒入浮选槽之前需等待几分钟，继续让水流入0.2毫米的筛网中以确保没有任何物质从浮选槽底部的泥浆中再次循环回来。所有样品中，除了少量木炭碎片外，没有遗留任何植物残留物。将轻浮物和重浮物放入细枝棉或尼龙织物中，在阴凉处或室内晾干。

仅8份样品采集了重浮物。这8份样品的重浮物中均不含植物遗存，因此没有检查剩余样品中的重浮物。将干燥后的轻浮物通过一系列标准地质筛网进行筛选，网筛孔径分别为2、1、0.4和0.2毫米。体积超过2毫米的植物遗存可分为炭化种子、坚果壳、木炭、现代植物（如小型植物根系）和矿物颗粒，同时记录它们的重量。尺寸小于2毫米的浮选物中仅提取种子和可以识别的植物。

在6份土样中，选取2%～50%不等的分量，使用孔径0～2毫米网筛进行分选（表6.2）。除了两份样品之外，在大多数样品中没有发现任何可识别的种子残留物。例如，龙山晚期的张湾西北（11-210，H3[3]），使用0.2毫米孔径的网筛，在10%的样品中发现了5个野豆荚，而杨寨西（11-059，H2）的小米族（黍族）的一粒种子是在使用0.2毫米孔径网筛子分选时发现的。

当然，我们也不希望抽样筛选的结果会影响到对样品的总体成分和数量的判断。

采样的遗址中有四分之一无法准确到考古学文化的具体期段。在数量比较时，我们将每一个考古学文化的所有样品集中分析，而不再以详细期别来区分样品。

表6.2　部分分类样品

时代	遗址号	遗址名称	遗迹单位	样本量（升）	浮选样本重量（克）	0.2mm筛网筛选量（克）	完成量（%）	0.2 mm网筛获得种子概率/数量
裴李岗	11-124	府店东	H1	19	75.66	21.9	50.0	
龙山	11-060	保庄西北	H2	8	27.11	9.93	20.0	
龙山	11-210	张湾西北	H2	10	108.06	43.17	39.0	
龙山	11-210	张湾西北	H3	20	97.49	38.1	9.4	野生/5
龙山	11-087	颜良寨水库西	H3	10	65.6	24.8	23.9	
东周	11-059	杨寨西	H2	10	58.4	21.49	3.5	狗尾草/1

注：所有大于0.4毫米的部分都经过完全分类。

第三节　植物遗存的种类与多样性

共有33类可细分至种、属（或族）、少数能分入科的层面（表6.3）。一些非繁殖器官，如树枝、草茎碎片、草内颖/外稃（谷壳）、芽或块茎，大多都是碎片，其数量可以忽略不计。坚果遗骸仅存在于14份样本中；周代寺沟东南（11-152，Y152）是唯一一处保存有几乎完整的橡子果肉的遗址（照片组1）。尽管有些类似橡果，但这些坚果遗存实在太过残碎，无法正确识别它们的种属。

在本研究中，根据植物生态特征、生长习性和人类使用情况将遗存分为四类：栽培植物、旱地杂草、湿地杂草和食肉果类（表6.3）。除了4种驯化的类别（粟、黍、稻和小麦）之外，栽培类也包括具有模糊驯化状态的种类，如赤豆、大豆和紫苏。以前的研究发现，仅根据大小和形态不足以判定大豆和赤豆是否驯化[4]。这些豆科植物的野生种可以食用并且经常在农田内发现。紫苏属或紫苏很难根据种子形态来判定其驯化状态，并且其通常与小型紫苏非常相似。因此，我们无法进一步分辨这两者，而将之归入该地区原产且最终驯化的可食用植物类。

非驯化类或野生植物可进一步划细分为一年生草本植物、多年生草本植物、灌木丛杂草及具有很多柔软多汁组织的食肉水果等。根据它们的栖息地可进一步将杂草分为高地杂草和低地/湿地杂草。在我们的样本中，大多数高地杂草是在受到干扰的栖息地中繁殖的，包括农田及人类栖息地的周围。湿地杂草则大多常见于浅水体的边缘，包括今天的稻田。

除了上述群体外，目前大多数样本的种子无法进一步鉴定，我们将之统称为"未知"类。有些标本保留了可以判别种属的特征，但暂时尚未得出结论。这在所有植物考古学分析中都很常见，因为特定区域的植物群落很广泛，包含了数千种物种。对每一物种的正确识别需要可参考的样本，大多数时这些参考样品是缺乏的。很多样品包含无法识别和计数的碎种子。除了本

第六章 伊洛地区调查遗址的植物考古分析

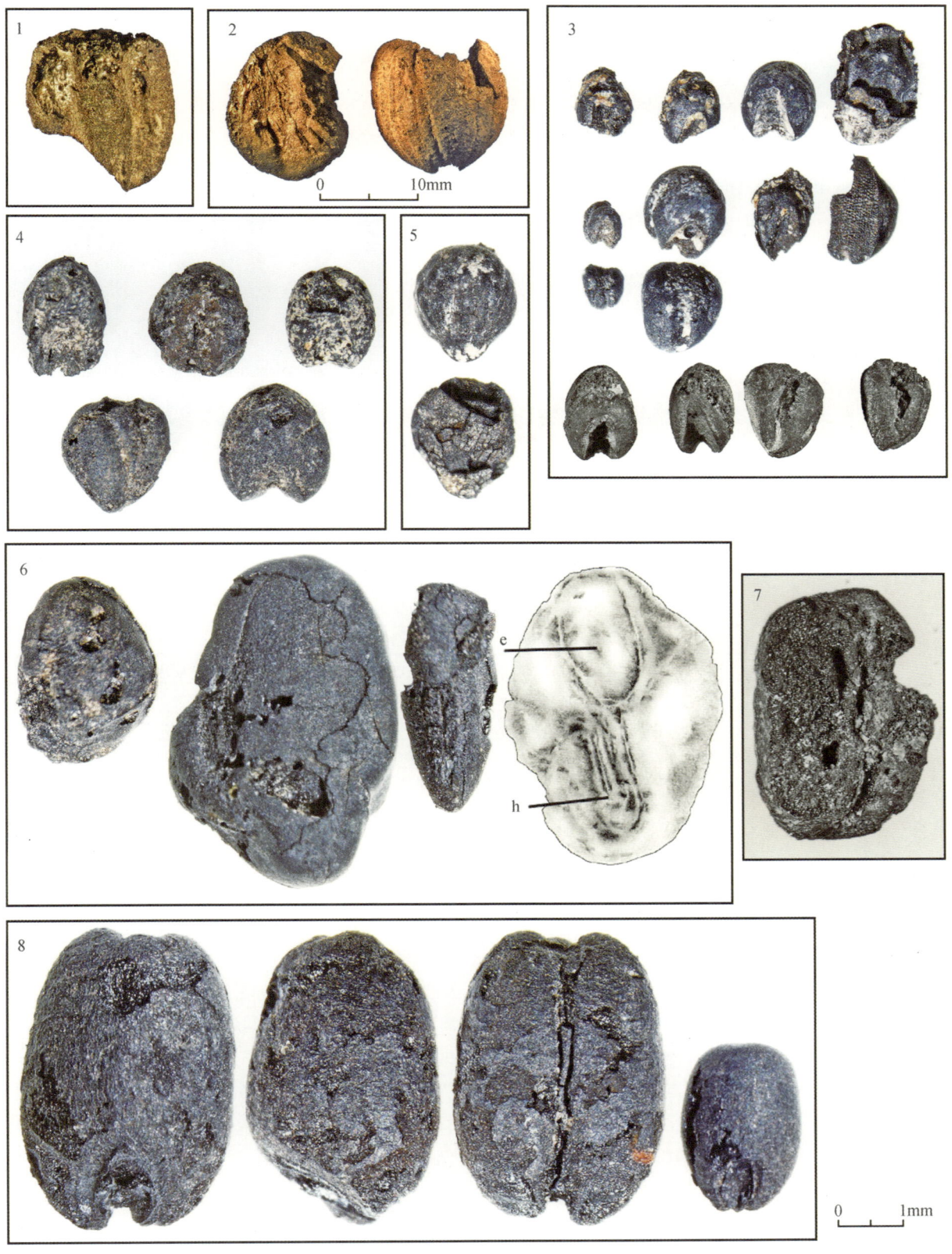

照片组1 可食用植物资源（标尺=除了栎之外皆为1毫米）

1. 稻属（*Oryza sativa*, rice）：来自二里头二至四期张湾西北（Y210）
2. 栎（*Quercus* sp., acorn）：来自西/东周寺沟东南（Y152），标尺 = 10mm
3. 粟（*Setaria italica*, foxtail millet）：第一行左起为第1、2件样品，来自裴李岗晚期坞罗西坡2（Y042）；第3件样品来自仰韶晚期的喂庄西（Y019）；第4件样品来自仰韶晚期的坞罗水库西（Y025）。第二和第三行的第1、2件样品来自二里头时期的稍柴（Y1001）；第二行的第3、4件样品来自二里岗上层时期的天坡水库东北（Y043）；第四行的样品来自二里头时期的新后沟砖厂东（Y132）

4. 黍（*Panicum miliaceum*, broomcorn millet）：上排依次是仰韶晚期的南瓦窑（Y156）、喂庄西南河南岸（Y018）和坞罗水库西1（Y025）采集的样品；下排是从仰韶晚期的坞罗水库西1（Y025）中采集的样品的左侧面和背部图片

5. 紫苏 or 石荠苧属（*Pellira frutescens or Mosla* sp., perilla or miniature beefsteak plant）：二里岗上层时期天坡水库东北（Y043）中采集的同一件样品的两面

6. 大豆（*Glycine max* ssp., soybean）：从左到右依次为龙山早期寺沟东南（Y152）、二里头时期的稍柴（Y1001）以及二里岗上层时期的天坡水库东北（Y403）。"e"和"h"代表考古样品中可见的胚根和种脐

7. 赤豆（*Vigna angularis* ssp, azuki）：东周时期杨寨西遗址（Y05）

8. 小麦（*Triticum aestivum*, wheat）：全部来自二里岗上层时期的天坡水库东北（Y043）

报告中标记为未知类型1的1件样品之外，未知类型通常使用一件或两件样本表示。即便如此，我们已经记录了很多未知类型及它们的特征，以待日后能够辨别时再将其加入数据库中。

表6.3　伊洛盆地发现的植物种类

种子类别	种属	通用名	科学名称
坚果（NUT）	壳斗科（Fagaceae）	栎属Oak	cf. *Quercus* sp.
栽培种（CULTIGENS）	禾本科（Poaceae）	黍Broomcorn millet	*Panicum miliaceum*
	禾本科	粟Foxtail millet	*Setaria italica* supsp. *italica*
		稻Rice	*Oryza sativa*
		小麦Bread wheat	*Triticum aestivum*
	豆科（Fabaceae）	大豆Soybean	*Glycine max* ssp.
	豆科	赤豆Azuki	*Vigna angularis* ssp.
	唇形科（Lamiaceae）	紫苏Beefsteak plant	*Perilla frutescens*
杂草（UFLAND WEEDS）	禾本科（Poaceae）	稗Barnyard grass	*Echinocloa crusgalli*
	禾本科	狗尾草Green foxtail Wild foxtail type grass	*Setaria viridis* cf. *Setaria* sp.
		黍属Panic grass Panic, manna grass or crabgrass	*Panicum* sp. *Panicum Glyceria*, or *Digitaria* sp.
		黍族Millet tribe	Paniceae
		牛筋草Goosegrass	*Eleusine indica*
		cf. Wheat tribe	cf. *Triticeae*
	十字花科Brassicaceae	芸薹属Mustard	*Brassica* sp.
	藜亚科Chenopodiaceae	藜属Chenopod	*Chenopodium* sp.
	蓼科Polygonaceae	蓼属Knotweed	*Polygonum* sp.
	豆科Fabaceae	豆茶决明Korean clever	*Chamaecrista nomame* or *Cassia nomane*
		草木樨属/胡枝子属 sweet clover or lespedeza	*Melilotus* or *Lespedenza* sp.
	大麻科Cannabaceae	葎草属Hop	*Humulus* sp.
	唇形科Lamiaceae	石荠苧属Minature beefsteak plant	*Molsa* sp.
	堇菜科cf. Violaceae	堇菜属cf. Viola	cf. *Viola* sp.

续表

种子类别	种属	通用名	科学名称
湿地杂草 （WETLAND WEEDS）	Cyperaceae 莎草科	藨草属Burlush	*Scirpus* sp.
		飘拂草属cf.Fimbry	*Fimbristylis* sp.
		莎草属Sedge	*Cyperus* sp.
	香蒲科cf.Typhaceae	香蒲属cf. Cattaii	cf. *Typha* sp.
鲜果 （FLESHY FRUITS）	Rosaceae 蔷薇科	悬钩子属Bramble	*Rubus*
		李属Plum	*Prunus* sp.
		其他蔷薇科other rose family	
	鼠李科Rhamnaceae	枣Jujuba	*Zizhiphus*

注：分类法参考《中国植物志》（FOC），必要时由种质资源信息中心（GRIN）提供现本次分类的参考。'cf'=可能。

一、栽 培 植 物

发现的47737粒种子中（表6.1），超过一半为驯化小米（27475粒），其中，粟的数量是黍的30倍以上，除裴李岗和周代外，排名第二（图6.4）。府店东南（11-114，Y118）一处裴李岗文化遗迹中发现了丰富的黍，AMS（加速器质谱）测年为仰韶早期（D-AMS 025484，4150～4100 cal. BC，在本文中所有校准日期为2σ范围），说明黍是从后段混入的。尽管其代表性较低，但比起山东地区[5]和朝鲜半岛[6]，黍在伊洛地区的记录中更为常见。通常来说，粟在东部较湿润的区域分布较广，通常黍在内陆较干旱的地区则更为常见[7]。根据对黍的植硅石的进一步辨认，研究者认为黍在灰嘴遗址中的使用应较炭化遗存所表现出的情况更为普遍[8]。该推论是否可以适用于史前时期的更多遗址尚需更多的研究，但我们推测黍在当时应该同粟一样得到了大量的使用。

粟通常是球形的，并且大多时候是膨化的。炭化实验表明，当谷物仍然紧紧包裹在壳（内稃、外稃和颖）内时，就容易膨化[9]。这说明，样品中的粟在烹饪前一直是未脱壳储存的。所有样品中大多数粟和黍都呈现出驯化小米的典型尺寸和形状。年代早的样品尺寸较之后期的小米平均略小，背面略微扁平，同该作物的祖先——狗尾草（*S. italica* ssp. *viridis*）相似，但

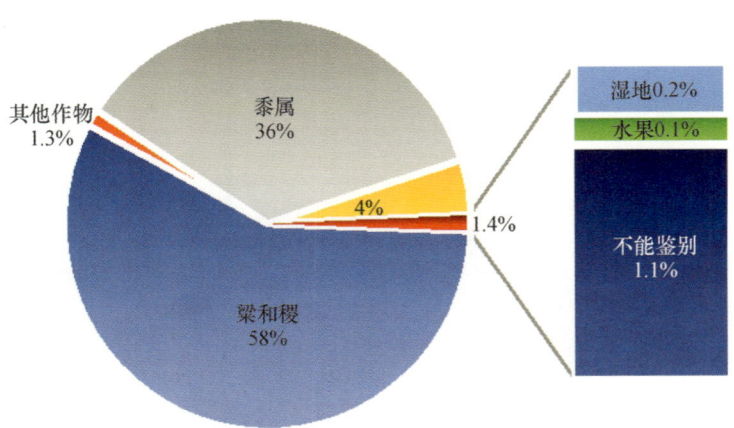

图6.4 所有样品中不同种子类别的比例

不完全相同。即使在一些后来的样品中，黍也显示出较小的尺寸以及稍微扁平化的特征。赵志军认为，兴隆沟遗址发现的新石器时代早期的黍也有相似的特征[10]。类似的谷物在龙山时期的山台寺和两城镇遗址中皆属常见物[11]。最近对粟的研究显示，由于某些谷物未成熟，即使在一个样本中也存在多样的尺寸变化[12]。这项研究进一步证实了我们的假设，即伊洛区域样品中的一些小米可能是未成熟果实的谷粒。

将所有时段综合起来看，驯化小麦、可能驯化的大豆、赤豆和紫苏仅占所有种子总数的1.3%（图6.4）。除了小米，小麦在作物类别中占比最高，它们主要发现于二里岗时期的遗存中（图6.5）。一直到很晚的阶段，东亚考古学中才记录了较为罕见的面包小麦这一类型[13]。从历史上看，小麦一直是伊洛地区的重要冬季作物，但其特殊性却引发了一个悬而未决的问题。在裴李岗晚期的西石桥东（01-010，76）和仰韶文化中期到晚期的赵城（05-077，Y077）中各发现了一粒小麦（附录6.1）。对赵城遗址发现的粟进行了AMS测年，证明它的年代为仰韶晚期（SNU 06-746，4500±50 uncal. BP，3362～3026 cal. BC）。但是，小麦标本的重量达不到测年的要求；保庄西北（11-060，046）龙山晚期灰坑中发现的小麦粒的时代为西周时期（D-AMS 025484，2625±26 uncal. BP，831～786 cal. BC）；也没有足够的二里头时期的小麦遗存可供测年，但来自天坡水库东北的小麦样品的直接年代说明二里岗时期已经存在小麦（98-043，Y043，TO-11420，3020±50 uncal. BP，1490～1122 cal. BC）；寺沟南（11-151，Y151）的小麦属于西周时期（11-152，D-AMS029885，2371±32 uncal. BP，726～386 cal. BC）。根据山东两城镇遗址的报道，小麦似乎是在龙山时期中国北部的其他地方引进的[14]。韩国西南部的中全新世遗址中发现了年代更早的炭化小麦[15]。Daechonri（대촌리）遗址小麦和大麦的两个^{14}C年代的变化范围为5430～4890 cal. BP，同相关木炭的年代符合（5460～4620 cal. BP）。

研究者认为4600～4200 cal. BP是中国北方广大地区小麦的快速适应期，从最初引入时在考古发现中的几无发现，到随后在考古记录中的分辨性出现了明显的提高[16]。伊洛区域

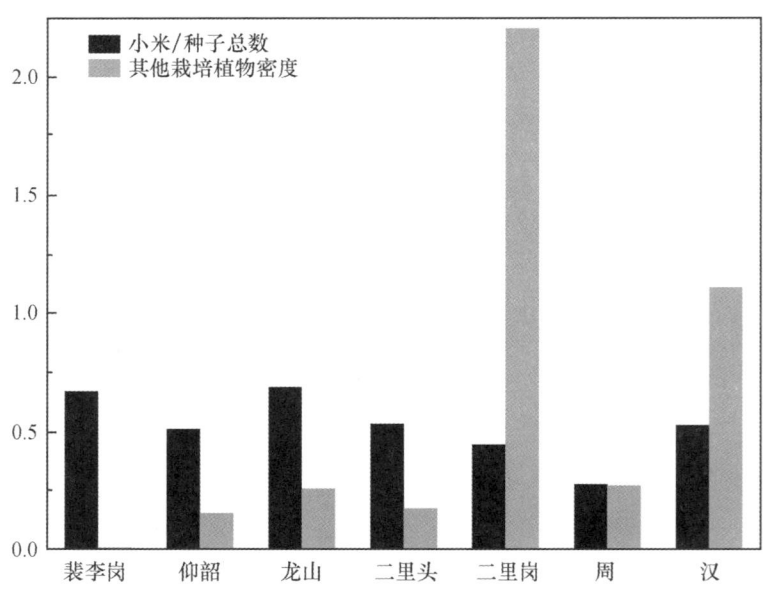

图6.5 不同时期小米在种子总数以及其他栽培植物密度（包括稻、小麦、大豆、赤豆和紫苏）中所占比例的变化

的例子和韩国发现的新石器时代小麦，可能是在小麦最初零星引入至东北亚地区时遗留下的罕见案例[17]。虽然我们现在还没有小麦年代的确切信息，但我们不能忽视小麦在二里岗文化时期之前引入该地区的可能性。

稻（*Oryza sativa*）是一种原产于华南地区的作物，华北最早发现的稻谷出土于黄河下游新石器时代早期的后李文化遗址[18]。长江以北最早出现的稻谷来自河南的贾湖遗址，年代可追溯到9000~7800 cal. BP[19]。在典型的裴李岗文化遗址中没有发现炭化稻遗存，河南唐户遗址的植硅石证据表明黄河中游的稻的传入可早至7800~4500 cal. BP[20]。中国东部地区，山东月庄遗址发现的炭化稻年代为7950~7800 cal. BP[21]，证明了黄河下游新石器时代早期的后李文化中存在种植稻谷和小米的农业。稻谷在龙山时期的山台寺遗址也十分罕见[22]，但在黄海沿岸龙山时期的两城镇遗址中却相对常见[23]。

虽然我们在之前的研究中公布了伊洛河谷发现的二里头时期（3900~3500 cal. BP）的稻谷，土壤微形态和植硅体的研究说明早至仰韶晚期（ca. 6600 cal. BP）已有稻田的存在[24]。最近的样本中新增了3粒仰韶晚期的稻谷粒，分别来自赵城（05-077，Y077）、喂庄西南（07-018，Y018），以及龙山时期的马屯新村（11-069，Y069，附录6.1）。我们在对灰嘴遗址（02-127，Y127）的研究中也发现了仰韶时期的稻谷，但尚未测定^{14}C年代。2004年，在灰嘴的田野发掘中发现的龙山时期稻谷的^{14}C年代为4060~3890 cal. BP（SNU05-132m，3800±40 uncal. BP，1681~1444 cal. BC），与二里头文化有关。二里头时期的多个遗址中经常发现稻谷遗存，包括新砦（04-HXX）、灰嘴（Y127）、张湾西北（11-210，Y210）、罗口（Y022）、稍柴（Y1001）、上庄南（Y037）、涧东（97-195）、景阳岗（041）、西口孜（07-201，Y201）和李家沟东（07-099，Y099）。

仅根据形态无法辨别稻谷样品属于湿地或旱地作物。伊洛地区的湿地杂草仅零星出现，数量仅占种子总数的0.2%。发现的一些莎草科植物，包括莎草属、飘拂草属和蔗草属，它们都是稻田常见的杂草。4粒小米族样品（2粒为龙山晚期，1粒为东周，1粒为汉代）同稗草（*Echinochloa crusgalli*）相似，稗草是稻田中常见杂草之一。植硅体、土壤形态及水稻和湿地野草之间的联系都指证了湿地水稻农业在伊洛区域农业体系中的存在，并且它的出现可能早至仰韶晚期。

大豆和赤豆是东亚地区长期以来栽培的主要豆类作物。《夏小正》和《史记》中提到黄河中游地区早在夏朝（ca. 2100~1600 BC）很可能就已经使用大豆了，周代时（ca. 1026~221 BC）[25]，将大豆称为一种作物，由此可见大豆在该地区有着悠久的历史。最近的研究表明，中国北部最早与小种子大豆有关的年代为9000~8600 cal. BP，中国确认出现大豆的年代为7000 cal. BP[26]。在笔者相关研究发布[27]之前，中国近30个遗址中发现了大豆种子，年代从7000BC到220AD（均未进行AMS测年）。伊洛地区的裴李岗文化遗址与贾湖遗址不同，并没有发现任何大豆。从仰韶及后段遗址的采集样品中，共鉴定出188个大豆样本（附录6.1）。炭化大豆种子的绝对测年结果表明，日本人工选择后产生的大尺寸种子的年代为5000 cal. BP（绳文时代中期），韩国则为3000 cal. BP（青铜时代早期），但伊洛盆地的种子大小类型的情况不太清楚。从汉代的遗迹中发现的二里岗期的大豆种子比早期的尺寸要大，长度上同日本和韩国样品差不多，但是总体尺寸上仍较两者小很多。但是，野生品种同考古发现的样品之间的尺寸差异不应过分解读。野生大豆生长在中国中北部地区，常常作为可食用的零食或是田间肥料使用[28]。尽管在韩国和日本，可以通过种子的尺寸将3000 cal. BP之后的驯化种子同野生种子区分开，但是尺寸不应该作为分辨驯化大豆的唯一参考指标[29]。虽然在人类有意识的控制下也可以培育出小尺寸的种子，但它们也可能是野生的。即便这些种子是野生的，但它们出现在几乎所有使用了浮选法的中国遗址中，说明其应该是人为植物群中的一个重要组成部分，并且为人类使用。如果这样，我们更倾向于不将伊洛地区的大豆归入野生（G. max ssp. soja）或驯化（G. max ssp. max），而是将其归于不进一步区分亚种的物种中。

紫苏（Perilla, beefstake plant, Perilla frutescens）是东亚重要的调味品和油料作物之一。我们的样本中发现了仰韶到二里头时期的近40粒紫苏或石荠苎属（Mosla sp.）的种子，另外还有唇形科的油料植物。即便在扫描电镜下也很难判断紫苏是野生还是驯化。考虑到紫苏的价值及中国紫苏遗存的多样性[30]，我们猜测它可能在很早的时候已经开始使用了。在我们的研究之前，少见史前和早段历史时期的文献中记载有紫苏[31]。

二、未驯化的植物

野生或未驯化的植物种类可以为我们提供像驯化种类一样的关于过去生业模式和农业体系的信息。基于它们的栖息地，本研究中将未驯化的种类归入两个类别：旱地种类和湿地种类。统计33个遗址所有时段的样品发现，湿地种类数量仅占全部种子的0.5%（表6.4）。19个遗址中发现了4个不同类别的莎草科瘦果，同一些芸薹属、莎草属、飘拂草属、藨草属相似（照片组2）。龙山时期的样品中此类植物遗存数量最多，特别是涧东村西北（02-196，Y196B）和颜良寨水库西（11-087，Y087）。发现稻谷遗存的12个遗址中，除了二里头时期的罗口（98-022，Y022）与上庄东南（98-039，Y039），以及汉代的罗口砖厂东北（98-017，Y017）之外，其他遗址内均发现了莎草科的植物遗存。

表6.4 全部种子密度和每期栽培植物/杂草的比率

年表	总种子密度					不详/野生比率				
	数量	范围	中位数	平均值	标准差	数量	范围	中位数	平均值	标准差
裴李岗	12	0～2.35	0.12	0.36	0.66	5	0～0.37	0.01	0.10	0.16
仰韶	43	0～446.67	2.00	16.85	69.00	36	0～1.54	0.16	0.28	0.37
龙山	36	0～1665.27	12.13	91.39	285.37	34	0～7.67	0.10	0.67	1.49
二里头	36	0～85.7	11.57	25.26	27.73	33	0.01～1.14	0.09	0.16	0.21
二里岗	18	1.67～693.33	35.87	91.72	161.24	18	0.02～6.85	0.14	0.60	1.58
周	19	0.29～40.89	3.85	8.20	12.09	19	0～0.29	0.04	0.09	0.10
汉	3	0.5～32.75	0.78	11.34	18.54	2	0.58～0.67	0.62	0.62	0.06

照片组2　湿地杂草

1. 莎草属（*Cyperus* sp., sedge）全部来自龙山晚期的涧东村西北（Y196B）
2. 飘拂草属（*Fimbrystlis* sp., fimbry）来自龙山晚期的涧东村西北（Y196B）
3. 其他 莎草科（other *Cyperaceae*, other sedge family）来自龙山晚期的涧东村西北（Y196B）

旱地生长的大多数野草属于黍属（稷亚科），也有可能是黍族，在全部样品中占36%。由于可塑性和跨类群的高交叉活力，仅根据种子很难区分黍族中的不同种。在种子长宽比的基础上，依据整体的形状、胚胎的尺寸形状及谷粒外壳的表面形态，可以将一些样品鉴定到种，其中包括狗尾草（*Setaria italica* ssp. *Viridis*）、稗属（*Echnicholoa crusgalli*）和牛筋草（*Eluesine indica*）（照片组3）。其他样品只能鉴定到属，包括狗尾草（*Setaria* sp.）、可能也有黍属（*Panicum* sp. 或 *P. Biscatum*）、黍属/马唐属/甜茅属（*Panicum, Digitaria, Glyceria* sp.）及其他小米族（*Paniceae*）。其中，狗尾草和黍由于有很高的遗传可塑性，因此有很多变种。黍中的一些成员的形态，特别是小而细长的种子和十分低的胚芽，同马唐属（*Digitaria* sp.）或是甜茅属（*Glyceria* sp.）相近。我们的样品中有很多这种类型的样品，暂时仅能将它们归入黍属/马唐属/甜茅属类。这些种子在仰韶晚期已经出现，在之后的时段内数量不断增加（表6.1）。如果它们是甜茅属或者马唐属，我们需要谨记在现在的稻田中该属的植物也十分常见。由于仰韶时期的稻谷植硅体的出现，这些杂草很可能同稻田有关系。

大多数黍族普遍适于旱地种植，在20世纪早期的中国东北地区常用作肥料[32]。有丰富小米的样品中同时也包含了多种黍属植物，为小米种植的农业生态提供了证据。两个小米族的草、稗草和牛筋草，也会生长在稻田中，两处历史时期的样品：东周时期的杨寨西（11-059，Y059）和汉代的罗口砖厂东北（98-017，Y017）都发现了稻谷。

除了黍族，最丰富的高地植物种类是藜属（lambsquarter，*Chenopodium* sp.，照片组4）。这种常见的一年生杂草类植物在所有时期均有出现（附录6.1）。我们样本中藜属种子的大小

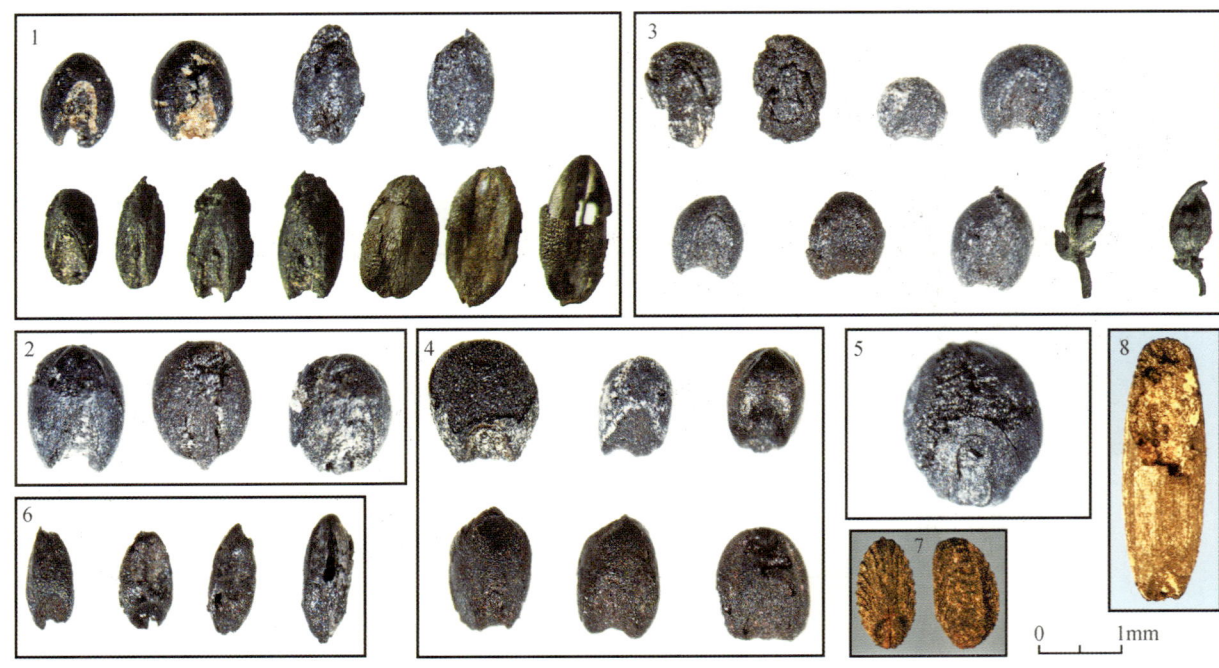

照片组3 禾本科杂草

1. 狗尾草（*Setaria viridis*, green foxtail）：上排第1、2件样品来自裴李岗晚期的坞罗西坡2（Y042）；第3、4件样品来自二里头时期的灰嘴（Y127）；下一排左起前4件来自仰韶中/晚期的赵城（Y077）；其余的外皮来自龙山晚期的涧东村西北（Y196B）
2. 粱属（other *Setaria* sp.）：所有都来自二里头时期的稍柴（Y1001）
3. 稷族（Paniceae, millet tribe）：上排的第1、2件样品来自二里头时期的稍柴（二里头期，Y1001）；上排的最后两件样品及下排左起的前3件样品来自二里头时期的灰嘴（Y027）；下排的其余样品是来自龙山晚期涧东村西北（Y196B）的小花
4. 黍属（*Panicum* sp., panic grass）：来自龙山晚期涧东村西北（Y196B）
5. 稗（*Echiincholoa crusgalli*, barnyard grass）：来自龙山时期的马屯新村（Y069）
6. 黍属/马唐属/甜茅属（Panic, Digitaria or Glyceria sp., Panic, digitaria or manna grass）：所有都来自二里岗上层时期的天坡水库东北（Y043）
7. 牛筋草（*Eleusine indica*, goosegrass）：来自龙山晚期的张湾西北（Y210）
8. 可能为小麦（麦类），采自龙山晚期马屯新村（11-069，Y069）

和形状的多样性表明了不同种的存在。一些种子截面观测，具有北美地区典型的薄外种皮的驯化藜属特征（*C. berlandieri*）[33]。伊洛样品中的许多标本在种皮上具有明显的细胞形态，同藜属的亚组——北美栽培种的纤维素相似。由此引出这种亚洲藜属国产化的关键问题。藜属在扰动区和旱地生长良好，今天在中国仍然用作绿植和淀粉粒来源。其中一种大型藜属，显然在中国"长期栽培"的[34]。事实上，台湾的高山族居民混种有一种藜属植物，称为藜（*Chenopodium album*），将之作为淀粉类食物的来源，栽种于小米田中[35]。

除了大豆属（*Glycine* sp.）之外，样品中至少有三种不同类型的野生豆科植物。有的样品中的豆科植物同决明子（山扁豆，也称作水皂角或番泻叶）类似[36]。在韩国和日本，这种植物是冲积扇上的重要植物[37]，叶子可以用作煮茶[38]。

绝大多数野生大豆可以归入三类草本豆类之中，甜苜蓿或胡枝子属（*Melilotus* or *Lespedeza* sp.，草木樨属/胡枝子属）。它们常见于东亚地区的旱地，20世纪初在中国东北地区常被用做田间肥料。

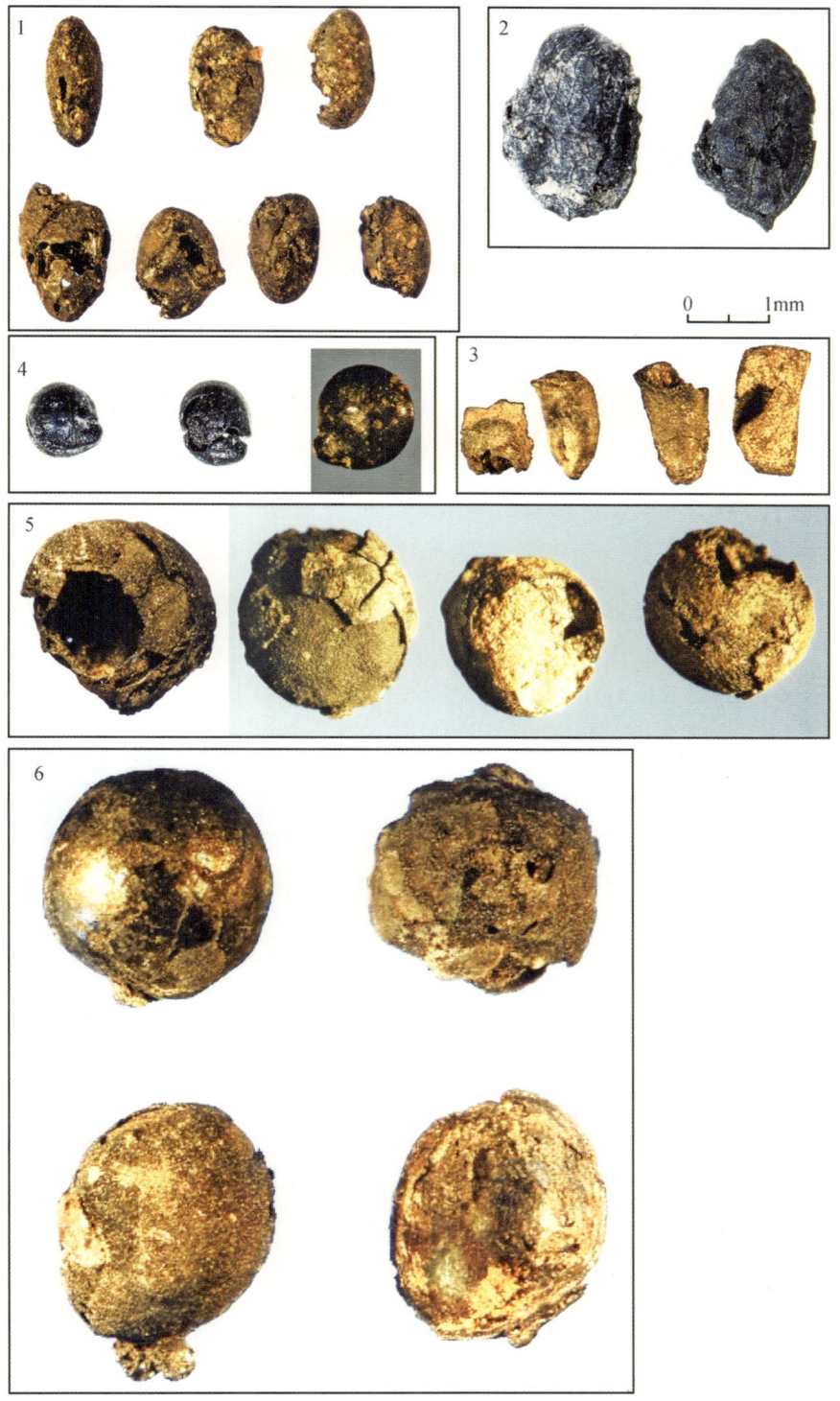

照片组4 其他高地杂草和水果

1. 草木樨属/胡枝子属（*Melilotus* or *Lespedeza* sp., sweet clover or lespedeza）：所有都来自龙山晚期的裴村B（119），箭头处为圆粒
2. 豆茶决明（*Chamaecrista nomame* or *Cassia nomane*, Korean clover）：来自二里岗上层时期的天坡水库东北（Y043）
3. 豆科（Fabaceae, other wild bean pod）：来自龙山晚期的涧东村西北（Y196B）
4. 藜属（*Chenopodium* sp., chenopod）：左起第一颗树是在龙山晚期罗口（Y022）发现的；最右边的树来自龙山晚期张湾西北（Y210）的11-210H3
5. 十字花科 芸薹属（Brassica family, cf. *Brasscia* sp., brassica）：最左边的来自龙山晚期的半个寨（Y123）；其余来自仰韶晚期的喂庄西（Y019）
6. 葎草属（*Humulus* sp., hop）：来自龙山晚期的颜良寨水库西（Y087）

其他草本山地杂草的种类包括芸薹属（*Brasscia* sp.）、蓼属（*Polygonum* sp.）、葎草属（*Humulus* sp.）、堇菜属（*Viola* sp.）等，但是在所有时期，皆很少见。这些种类的植物遗存仅在14个遗址中发现，年代从仰韶时代到周代。4粒葎草属的种子仅发现于龙山晚期的颜良寨水库西（11-087，Y087）。由于它们常在被扰动区域内发现，这些稀有的植物遗存很可能是意外混入房屋遗迹中的。在实验研究中发现了紫草科（Euphorbiaceae，大戟科），但是该鉴定尚未确证。茄科在中国北部的遗址中常见，但是在我们样品中，所有都是没有炭化的，因此也不能确定它们是否是古代样品。

肉质水果可以是草本植物或灌木。我们发现了可食用浆果、李子或大枣的种子，它们常生长在被扰动的区域内（照片组5）。这些水果可以生食，如果露天保存，不经炭化很少能在遗址中发现。虽然这些可食用水果遗存不经常发现，但通过人类学上的使用记录较高的保存概率，我们推测它们应该是日常饮食的重要补给。

除了上述已经鉴别的种类之外，目前还有1%的种子无法识别。他们中的大多数是可计数的，但失去了可供鉴定的关键特征。完整的种子中，有的类型在所有时间段反复出现，类似于伊洛地区常见的另一种湿地多年生植物——香蒲属（*Typha* sp.）。香蒲属植物在包涵所有阶段的24个遗址中发现。这些湿地种子同伊洛地区的水稻之间有明显的联系。另一个完整的未识别类型仅在一个地点中发现，即龙山晚期的涧东村西北（02-196，Y196B，照片组6）。类似于黍属/马唐属或玛纳粒，它们内含低胚胎，种子细长，但胚胎和种子的整体形状比较特殊。有趣的是，从二里头时期的涧东村（Y199）和二里岗上层时期的杨寨西北（Y058）中发现了一些编织的纤维。它们可能是用于制作篮子或垫子的绳索，可惜绳子的植物种类无法识别。

第四节　各阶段植物资源使用的变化

在定量分析方面，我们将相同遗迹背景中采集的多袋土壤样品中浮选得到的植物样品集中起来一同分析。我们的对比研究基于167份样品，除了1条灰沟、5座房屋基址、1座窑和9个文化层之外，大多样品来自灰坑。6份样品（44升）中没有发现种子遗存，它们是裴李岗时期的2件样品（北营，07-044，Y044；坞罗西坡2，07-042，Y042），仰韶时期的2件样品（西齐家窑东南，05-164，Y164；坞罗水库西1，98-025，Y025），龙山时期1件样品（齐家窑东北，02-166，Y166），以及二里头时期的1件样本（袁沟A，03-057，165)。灰沟与灰坑特征基本相同，只是灰沟的形状更长更大。同灰坑不同，文化层是遗物集聚的区域。不同类型的遗迹保留炭化植物遗存的概率不同，因此通常很难直接比较它们。但是，我们的大多数样品都来自同一种遗迹，即灰坑，由此我们可以将所有灰坑一同进行比较。

种子密度=种子数量/土壤体积，变化范围为0到1665.27（龙山时期南石遗址，97-1003，Y1003，F1，表6.4）。接下来的两个最丰富的样本来自从仰韶文化赵城（05-077，Y077，文化层，446.67/L）和二里岗上层时期的天坡水库东北（98-043，Y043，灰坑6层，693.33/L）。从

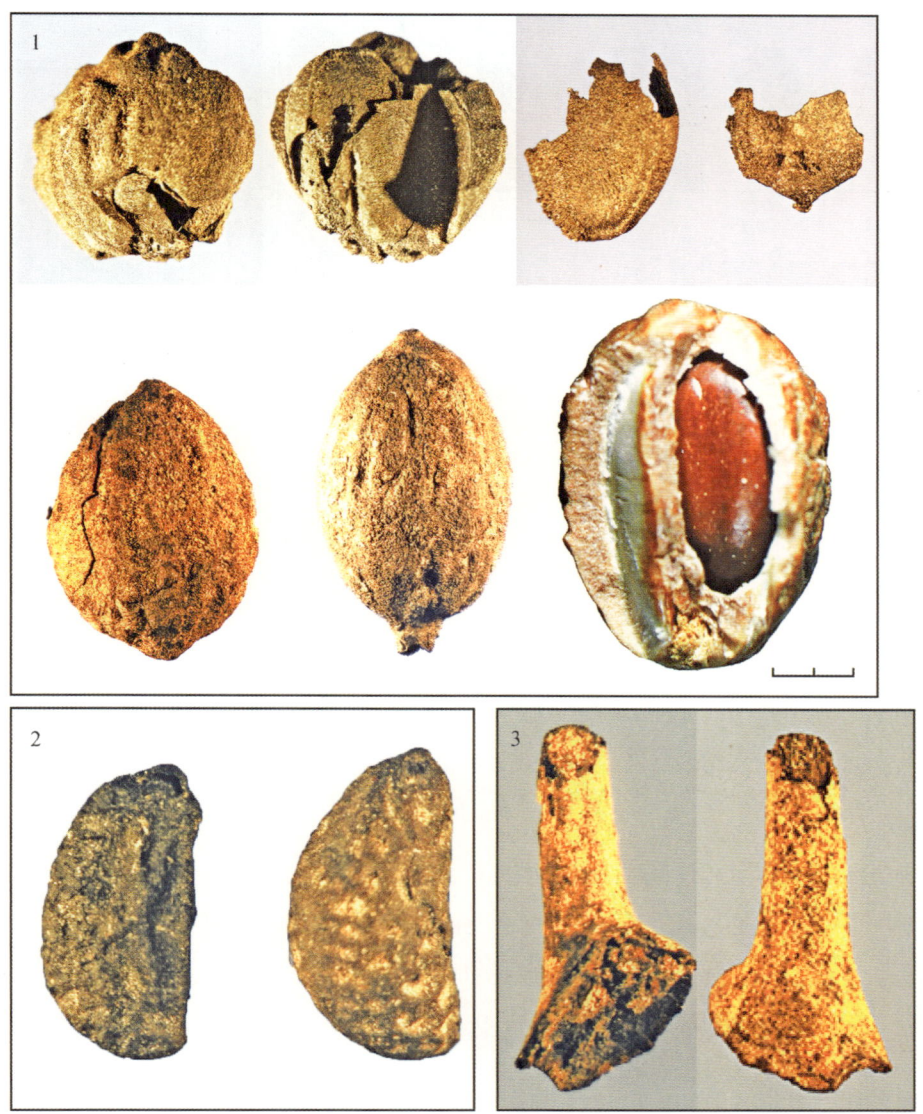

照片组5 肉果

1. 枣（*Zizhiphus* sp., jujuba）：上排是龙山晚期的张湾西北遗址（Y210）中发现的枣坑和种子；下排样品发现于东周时期寺沟东南遗址（Y152）的灰坑，左边发现于汉代罗口砖厂东北遗址（Y017）；现代的枣坑和种子同张湾西北遗址中发现的（上一排的第2件样品）相似（标尺=2毫米）
2. 悬钩子属（*Rubus* sp., bramble）：来自龙山晚期的涧东村西北遗址（Y196B，标尺=0.5毫米）
3. 蔷薇科 刺（Rosaceae thorn, rose family）：来自二里岗上层时期的天坡水库东北（Y043，98-043 H3 #51, Master #433，标尺=1.0毫米）

裴李岗到龙山时期，种子密度出现了明显的提升，这种现象可能与农业活动的增加有关。种子密度在后期的降低并不一定意味着农业重要性的降低，可能仅仅是样品数量太少的原因。周汉时期灰坑数量的减少表明，家庭垃圾和灰烬可能用作粪肥，致使种子保存下来的机会变小。出于同样的原因，龙山时期栽培物种与未驯化植物的比值出现增加的趋势，并在二里头及其后的时期内也表现出较小的比值。种类的多样性也表现出相同的模式。

除了二里岗时期的40%和周代的30%之外，在其他所有时段内小米样品数量占总数的一半

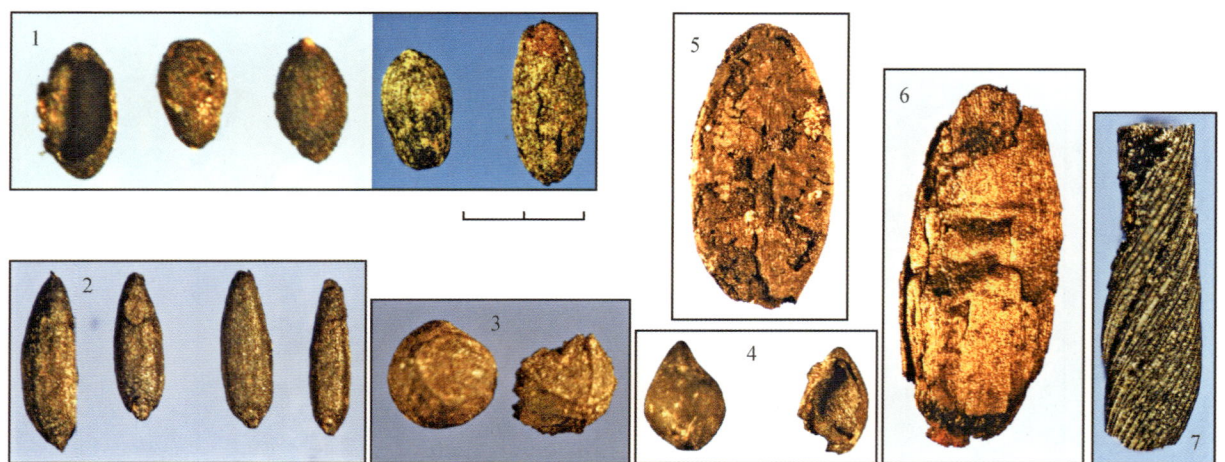

照片组6　未知植物遗存

1. 未知形式1（unknown type 1）：前3件来自龙山晚期涧东村西北（Y196B）；其余两件来自龙山晚期的颜良寨水库西（Y087），同香蒲属（*Typha* sp., cattaii）相似（标尺=0.5毫米）
2. 未知种子（unknown seeds）：来自龙山晚期涧东村西北（Y196B，标尺=1毫米）
3. 未知种子（unknown seed）：来自龙山晚期涧东村西北（Y196B，标尺=1毫米）
4. 未知种子（unknown seed）：来自龙山晚期涧东村西北（Y196B，标尺=1毫米）
5. 未知种子（unknown seed）：来自汉代罗口砖厂东北（Y017，标尺=2毫米）
6. 未知种属的芽：来自二里岗上层文化时期的天坡水库东北（Y043，标尺=2毫米）
7. 纤维片（a piece of fiber）：来自二里岗上层时期的杨寨西北（Y058，标尺=1毫米）

或以上。除去裴李岗时期，其他栽培植物仅有很少的数量。裴李岗晚期的西石桥（01-010，76）和仰韶中/晚期的赵城（05-077，Y077）中各发现了一粒小麦。由于没有确切的^{14}C年代数据，我们不能确定这些小麦是否是在新石器时代中期时传入伊洛地区的。小麦在3处龙山时代晚期的遗址中出现，分别为马屯新村（11-069，Y069）、保庄西北（11-060，046）和颜良寨水库西（11-087，Y087）。对保庄西北遗址的样品进行测年，年代偏晚（D-AMS025484，2625 ± 26 uncal. BP，831 ~ 786 cal. BC）。小麦在4000BP广泛分布于中国北部地区，它很可能是龙山时代晚期传入[39]。在其他的栽培植物之中，小麦的数量最多，近乎一半的小麦来自二里岗上层时期的天坡水库东北（98-043，Y043，附录6.1）。^{14}C测年数据表明，它属于二里岗时期（TO-11420，3020 ± 50 uncal. BP，1409 ~ 1122 cal. BC）。这种聚集情况的出现使得二里岗时期的其他栽培种的密度远比非二里岗时期高出许多（图6.5）。在调查的11处两周时期的遗址中，3处发现了小麦，它们大多数来自寺沟东南（11-152，Y152），且测定了^{14}C年代（D-AMS29885，2404 ± 47 uncal. BP，726 ~ 386 cal. BC）。

仰韶及以后阶段都发现了稻谷。仰韶中/晚期的赵城遗址和龙山晚期的马屯新村遗址发现了2粒稻谷。尽管现在还没有仰韶稻谷的^{14}C年代数据，但其他研究中发现了稻田和丰富的稻谷植硅体[40]。2002年灰嘴发现的稻谷年代是龙山时期（SNU04-416，3640 ± 60 uncal. BP，2200 ~ 1831 cal. BC）。5处二里头遗址中，每个遗址都发现了10粒以下的稻谷。5处遗址分别是张湾西北（11-210，Y210）、稍柴（97-1001，Y1001）、上庄南（98-037，Y037）、罗口（98-022，Y022）和灰嘴遗址（00-126，Y127）。

仰韶及以后阶段都发现了大豆属（*Glycine max* ssp.）植物。根据种子的长宽测量种子的尺寸，发现随着时间的推移种子尺寸不断增加，在二里头的样品中的豆科植物尺寸更大[41]。它的整体密度都比较低，全部时段的样品平均下来大体上每10升土壤中仅能发现1~4粒种子。两处东周时期的遗址，清易镇东2遗址（07-003，Y003）、杨寨西遗址（07-059，Y059）及汉代的吊桥寨东南遗址（07-216，Y216）中出土的谷粒用于鉴别的部分胚胎缺失，但根据谷粒的整体外形和质地，推测这4粒谷粒很可能是赤豆（azuki，*Vigna angularis* ssp.）。与韩国和日本不同[42]，赤豆在中国并不经常与大豆一起出土。这种差异说明这些豆科植物可能有着不同的起源。

种子密度同遗址面积无关（图6.6）。小于5000平方米的小型遗址中也发现大量的种子，密度变化范围从0 ~ 1665粒/升不等。除了2个仰韶中/晚期遗址，赵城（Y077）、羽林庄南（Y050）和龙山晚期的罗口遗址（Y022，图6.7），大部分种子密度25%左右的样本来自于小型遗址。与之前的评估不同，稻谷在不同等级的聚落中都有发现，包括小型遗址。小麦和湿地杂草也表现出同样的趋势。

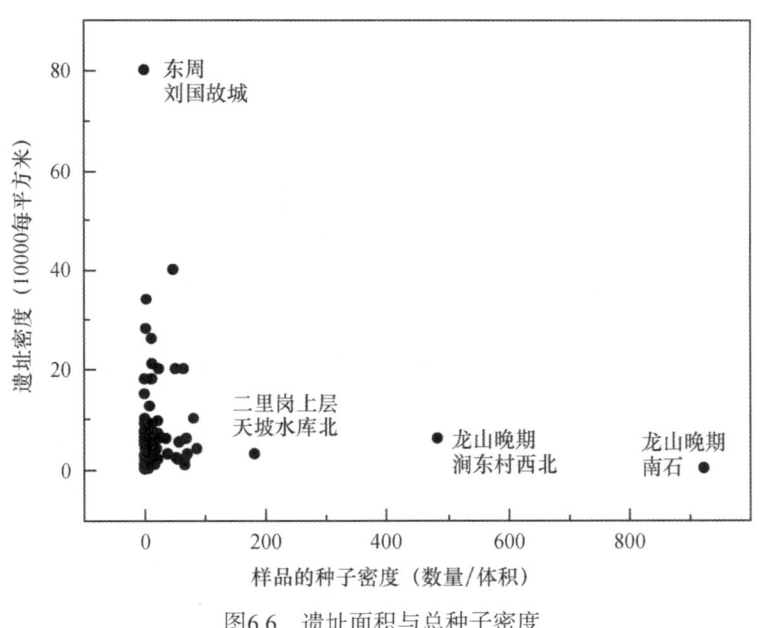

图6.6 遗址面积与总种子密度

所有阶段中，未驯化植物的数量都很多，特别是草本类黍族。大体上，小米和黍族杂草的密度一同提升（图6.8）。两处龙山晚期的遗址，涧东村西北（Y196B）和南石（Y1003）发现的栽培植物的比例比平均值高出许多，高地杂草密度则较低，反之亦然。黍族则常在小米附近生长，这种习性揭示了两者之间的联系。

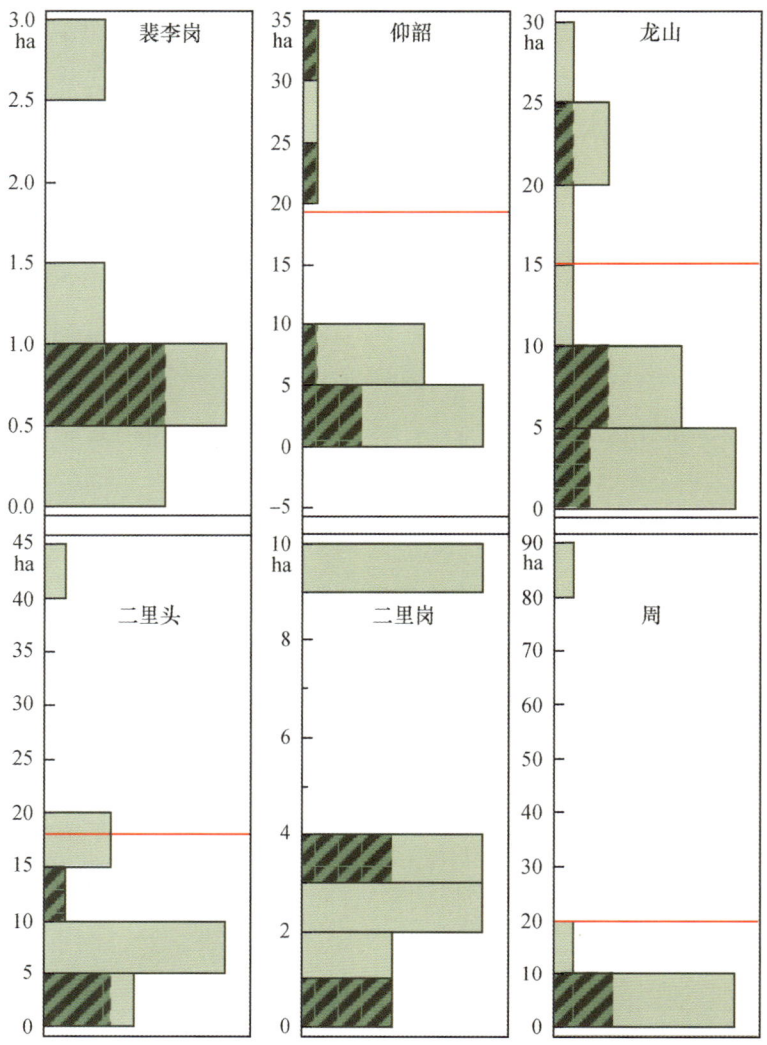

图6.7 不用时期的遗址面积与总种子密度

阴影样本表示具有上分位数（25%）的总种子密度的样本。红线下方是每期等级最低的遗址面积的大小。Y轴是以公顷为单位的遗址面积

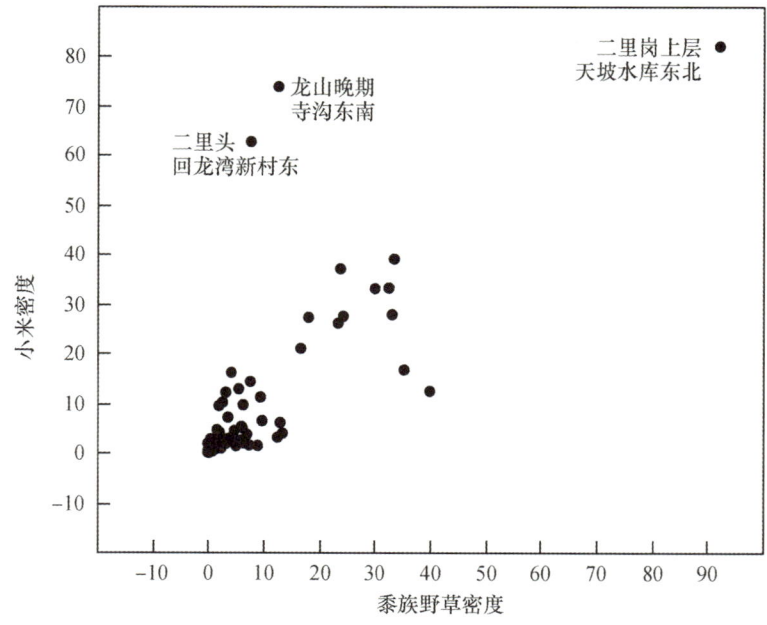

图6.8 小米密度与黍族杂草密度的相关性

第五节 结 语

伊洛流域考古调查项目探明了裴李岗至汉代植物资源利用模式的变化。大样品量中表现出很难简单描述的多种波动，这是由于植物遗存的保存情况和取样过程中的偏差导致的。当我们仅有从汉代的两个遗址中采集的3份样品时，除了说明该时期继承前段的作物种类外，很难再去准确推测汉代农业的详细状况。即便如此，我们还是通过大量的研究找到了如下的变化规律。

第一，在所有时间段内，小米都是主要的农业作物，它在样品中广泛出现且数量丰富。采样的91个遗址中，仅7个遗址未发现小米。不论是数量丰富程度还是与小米族中常见可耕种杂草的频繁联系，都证明了最晚从仰韶时代开始，小米得到了广泛的种植，并且在生业经济中扮演了十分重要的角色。与华北东部及韩国相比，伊洛地区黍的种植更多。尽管粟的数量多于黍，植硅体和炭化种子的比较结果也表明伊洛地区黍的种植更为广泛[43]。我们推测，黍的使用频率应该比它在炭化种子群中出现的频率更高，根源在于其保存情况的差异性或者说是烹饪方式的不同。

第二，两种引进作物水稻和小麦，仅在有限的遗址中发现，并且仅占种子总数的小部分，甚至到两周时期也是如此，至少，与二里岗时期的稻谷相比，小麦更多地出现于主食之中。从仰韶时期开始，稻谷就在此地区出现了。尽管我们没有稻谷的^{14}C年代，但是参照已经发现的水稻田和稻谷植硅石可以推知，稻谷从仰韶时期开始已经种植。稻谷在所有时段内的数量都比较少，总数只有46粒，不论是数量还是出现频率都无法同小米或是其他可食用野生植物相媲美。这种情况说明，在新石器时代，获取富含热量的主食并非是种植稻谷的原因。即使在二里头和之后时代中，伊洛地区小米的发现数量也超过了稻谷，这说明稻谷并非是当时的主食。根据其在伊洛盆地空间分布状况，可以通过社会环境来理解稻谷种植的重要性。9000 cal. BP时，贾湖遗址已经开始使用稻谷来酿酒[44]。两城镇龙山晚期的遗址中也发现了发酵稻谷的实例[45]。如果不考虑稻谷在华北地区出现的数量，在国家社会出现之前，稻谷似乎可以作为社会差异和礼仪出现的先兆。受体文化（北方地区作为权威物/仪式性用品）中的稻谷同供体文化中（南方地区作为主食）不同。相反，长江沿岸的华南地区没有出现社会、经济等级的发展[46]。使用稻谷本身并没有在中国北部的新石器时代社会中引发社会变化，长远来看，稻谷的出现，强化了社会趋势并改变了饮食文化和仪式行为。

第三，种子密度同遗址大小无关。大型聚落中拥有更多的居住者及更为复杂的社会，居民中包含了贵族群体。虽然拥有更多人口和更高社会地位居民的聚落可能会储存更多的食物，同时产生更多的废弃物，但我们的研究中没有发现这种情况。相反，我们推测小型的非中心性聚落主要由生产者和农田构成，在除草、收获和作物处理过程中则会产生更多的废弃物，这样一来则会造成更高的种子密度统计数据的出现。

致谢：我们感谢所有来自中澳美伊洛河流域考古队的帮助。特别要感谢在样品采集和浮选工作中帮助我们的人员，包括刘莉（斯坦福大学）、华翰维（密歇根大学）、贝喜安、艾琳·罗森（得克萨斯奥斯丁大学）、陈星灿、李永强、王宏章、王法成（中国社会科学院考古研究所）等。

注　释

[1] Lee G A, Crawford G W, Liu L, et al. Plants and People from the Early Neolithic to Shang periods in North China. PNAS, 2007, 104(3): 1087-1092.

[2] Watson P J. Excavation and Recovery of Biological Remains from Two Archaic Shell Middens in Western Kentucky. Presented at Symposium: The Research Potential of Shell Middens: Methodology. St. Louis: Washington University, 1976.

[3] 灰坑编号为采样中自编，遗址以年份加原遗址编号方式，与调查发现的遗址编号和遗迹编号不完全一致，下同。

[4] Lee G A, Crawford G W, Liu L, et al. Archaeological Soybean (Glycine max) in East Asia: Does Size Matter?. PLOS ONE, 2011, 6(11) doi: 10.1371/journal.pone.0026720; Lee G A. Archaeological Perspectives on Origins of Azuki (Vigna Angularis). The Holocene, 2013, 23(3): 453-459. First published on October 5, 2012, doi: 10.1177/0959683612460788.

[5] Crawford G W, Underhill A P, Zhao Z J, et al. Late Neolithic Plant Remains from Northern China: Preliminary Results from Liangchengzhen, Shandong. Current Anthropology, 2005, 46(2): 309-317.

[6] Crawford G W, Lee G A. Agricultural Origins in the Korean Peninsula. Antiquity, 2003, 77(295): 87-95; Lee G A, Crawford G W, Liu L, et al. Archaeological Soybean (Glycine max) in East Asia: does size matter?. PLOS ONE, 2011, 6(11) doi: 10.1371/journal.pone.0026720.

[7] Crawford G W, Underhill A P, Zhao Z J, et al. Late Neolithic Plant Remains from Northern China: Preliminary Results from Liangchengzhen, Shandong. Current Anthropology, 2005, 46(2): 309-317.

[8] Weisskopf A R, Lee G A. Phytolith Identification Criteria for Foxtail and Broomcorn Millets: A New Approach to Calculating Crop Ratios. Archaeological and Anthropological Sciences, 2016, (8): 29-42. Available online March 2014 issue. DOI: 10.1007/s12520-014-0190-7.

[9] Walsh R. Experiments on the Effects of Charring on Foxtail Millet (Setaria italica). Vegetation History and Archaeobotany, 2016, 26(4): 447-453.

[10] 赵志军：《从兴隆沟遗址浮选结果谈中国北方旱作农业起源问题》，《东亚古物（A卷）》，文物出版社，2004年，第188~199页。

[11] Crawford G W, Underhill A P, Zhao Z J, et al. Late Neolithic Plant Remains from Northern China: Preliminary Results from Liangchengzhen, Shandong. Current Anthropology, 2005, 46(2): 309-317.

[12] Walsh R. Experiments on the Effects of Charring on Foxtail Millet (Setaria italica). Vegetation History and Archaeobotany, 2016, 26(4): 447-453.

[13] Crawford G W. Prehistoric Plant Domestication in East Asia// Wesley C C, Watson P J. The Origins of Agriculture: An International Perspective. Washington: Smithsonian Institution Press, 1992: 7-38; Crawford G W, Lee G A. Agricultural Origins in the Korean Peninsula. Antiquity, 2003, 77(295): 87-95.

[14] Crawford G W, Underhill A P, Zhao Z J, et al. Late Neolithic Plant Remains from Northern China: Preliminary Results from Liangchengzhen, Shandong. Current Anthropology, 2005, 46(2): 309-317.

[15] Han C G, Koo J J, Kim G W. Date and Their Meanings of Carbonized Grains Collected from the Daecheon-ri Neolithic Site, Okcheon. Journal of Korean Neolithic Society, 2014, (28): 1-17; Lee G A. The Chulmun Period of Korea: Current Findings and Discourse on the Korean Neolithic Culture//Habu J, Lape P V, Olsen J W, et al. Handbook of East and Southeast Asian Archaeology. Springer International Publishing, 2017: 451-482.

[16] Barton L, An C B. An Evaluation of Competing Hypotheses for the Early Adoption of Wheat in East Asia. World Archaeology, 2014, (46): 775-798.

[17] Lee G A. The Spread of Domesticated Plant Resources in Prehistoric Northeast Asia//Hodos T. Routledge Handbook of Archaeology and Globalization. Taylor & Francis/Routledge Press, 2016: 394-412.

[18] 〔加〕Gary W. Crawford、陈雪香、栾丰实，等：《山东济南长清月庄遗址植物遗存的初步分析》，《江汉考古》2013年第2期。

[19] Zhang J Z, Wang X K. Notes on the Recent Discovery of Ancient Cultivated Rice at Jiahu, Henan Province: A New Theory Concerning the origin of Oryza Japonica in China. Antiquity, 1998, 72(278): 897-901.

[20] Zhang J P, Lu H Y, Gu W F, et al. Early Mixed Farming of Millet and Rice 7800 Years Ago in the Middle Yellow River region, China. PLoS One., 2012, 7(12): e52146.

[21] 〔加〕Gary W. Crawford、陈雪香、栾丰实，等：《山东济南长清月庄遗址植物遗存的初步分析》，《江汉考古》2013年第2期。

[22] Lee G A, Crawford G W, Liu L, et al. Plants and People from the Early Neolithic to Shang Periods in North China. Proceedings of the National Academy of Sciences, 2007, 104(3): 1087-1092.

[23] Crawford G W, Underhill A P, Zhao Z J, et al. Late Neolithic Plant Remains from Northern China: Preliminary Results from Liangchengzhen, Shandong. Current Anthropology, 2005, 46(2): 309-317.

[24] Rosen A M. The Role of Environmental Change in the Development of Complex Societies in China: A Study from the Huizui Site. Indo-Pacific Prehistory Association Bulletin, 2007, (27): 39-48; Rosen A. Macphail R, Liu L, et al. Rising Social Complexity, Agricultural Intensification, and the Earliest Rice Paddies on the Loess Plateau of Northern China. Quaternary International, 2015, 437(B): 50-59.

[25] Guo W T. On the Origin of Cultivated Soybean Problem. Studies in the History of Natural Science, 1996, 15: 326-333.

[26] Lee G A. Transition from Foraging to Farming in Prehistoric Korea. Current Anthropology, 2011, 52 (S4): S307-S329.

[27] Lee G A, Crawford G W, Liu L, et al. Plants and People from the Early Neolithic to Shang Periods in North China. PNAS, 2007, 104(3): 1087-1092.

[28] Theodore H, Singh R J. Taxonomy and Speciation//Wilcox J R. Soybeans: Improvement, Production, and Uses. Madison, WI: American Society of Agronomy(Issue 16), 1987: 23-48.

[29] Lee G A. Transition from Foraging to Farming in Prehistoric Korea. Current Anthropology, 2011, 52 (S4): S307-S329.

[30] Zeven A C, Zhukovsky P M. Dictionary of Cultivated Plants and their Centers of Diversity. Centre for Agricultural Publishing and Documentation, Wageningen, The Netherlands, 1975.

[31] Crawford G W. Prehistoric Plant Domestication in East Asia//Wesley C C, Watson P J. The Origins of Agriculture: An International Perspective. Washington: Smithsonian Institution Press, 1992: 28.

[32] King F H. Farmers of Forty Centuries: Permanent Agriculture in China, Korea, and Japan. Madison, WI: FH King, 1911.

[33] Smith B D. Chemopodium Berlandieri ssp. Jonesianum: Evidence for a Hopewellian Domesticate for Ash Cave, Ohio// Smith B D. Rivers of Change. Washington, DC: Smithsonian Institution Press, 1992: 103-131.

[34] Wu Z Y, Raven P H. Flora of China. St. Louis.: Missouri Botanical Garden, 1994.

[35] Fogg W H. Swidden Cultivation of Foxtail Millet by Taiwan Aborigines: A Cultural Analogue of the Domestication of Setaria Italica in China//Keightley D N. The Origins of Chinese Civilization. Berkeley: University of California Press, 1983: 95-115.

[36] Chen D, Zhang D, Larsen K.. Tribe CASSIEAE//Wu Z Y, Raven P H, Hon D Y. Flora of China: Fabaceae(vol. 10). Beijing: Science Press, 2009:27-34.

[37] Jarolímek I, Kolbek J. Plant Communities Dominated by Salix Gracilistyla in Korean Peninsula and Japan. Biologia, 2006, 61(1): 63-70.

[38] Hu S Y. Food Plants of China. Hong Kong: The Chinese University Press, 2005.

[39] Lee G A. The Spread of Domesticated Plant Resources in Prehistoric Northeast Asia//Hodos T. Routledge Handbook of Archaeology and Globalization. Taylor & Francis/Routledge Press, 2016: 394-412.

[40] Rosen A M. The Role of Environmental Change in the Development of Complex Societies in China: A Study from the Huizui Site. Indo-Pacific Prehistory Association Bulletin, 2007, (27): 39-48; Rosen A, Macphail R, Liu L, et al. Rising Social Complexity, Agricultural Intensification, and the Earliest Rice Paddies on the Loess Plateau of Northern China. Quaternary International, 2015, 437(B): 50-59.

[41] Lee G A, Crawford G W, Liu L, et al. Plants and People from the Early Neolithic to Shang Periods in North China. PNAS, 2007, 104(3): 1087-1092.

[42] Lee G A, Crawford G W, Liu L, et al. Plants and People from the Early Neolithic to Shang periods in North China. PNAS, 2007, 104(3): 1087-1092; Lee G A. Archaeological Perspectives on Origins of Azuki (Vigna angularis). The Holocene, 2013, 23(3): 453-459. First published on October 5, 2012, doi: 10.1177/0959683612460788.

[43] Weisskopf A R, Lee G A. Phytolith Identification Criteria for Foxtail and Broomcorn Millets: A New Approach to Calculating Crop Ratios. Archaeological and Anthropological Sciences, 2016, 8: 29-42. Available online March 2014 issue. DOI: 10.1007/s12520-014-0190-7.

[44] McGovern P E, Zhang Z Z, Tang J G, et al.. Fermented Beverages of Pre-and Proto-historic China. Proceedings of the National Academy of Sciences USA, 2004, 101: 17593-17598.

[45] McGovern P E, Underhill A P, Fang H, et al. Chemical Identification and Cultural Implications of a Mixed Fermented Beverage from Late Prehistoric China. Asian Perspective, 2005, 44(3): 249-275.

[46] Shelach-Lavi G. The Archaeology of Early China from Prehistory to the Han Dynasty. Cambridge: Cambridge University Press, 2015: 123.

附表6.1　伊洛盆地遗址的种子数量

分类法参考《中国植物志（FOC）》，必要时由种质资源信息中心（GRIN）提供现本次分类的参考

项目	1	2	3	4	5	6	7	8	9	10
时代	裴李岗晚期	裴李岗晚期	裴李岗晚期	裴李岗晚期	裴李岗晚期	裴李岗晚期	裴李岗晚期	裴李岗晚期	裴李岗晚期	裴李岗晚期
遗址原始编号	00-124	05-124	05-124	07-124	07-124	11-124	11-118	01-010	07-029	07-029
遗址正式编号	Y124	Y124	Y124	Y124	Y124	Y124	Y118	76	Y029	Y029
遗址名称	府店东	府店东	府店东	府店东	府店东	府店东	府店东南	西石桥东	铁生沟	铁生沟
采样遗迹	H1	H1 layer 1	H1 layer 1	H1	H1	H1	H1	Cultural layer	H1	H1
遗址面积（单位：万平方米）	0.5	0.5	0.5	0.5	0.5	0.5	0.5	2.7	0.2	0.2
样品量（单位：升）	7.0	9.0	9.0	11.0	8.0	19.0	20.0	8.0	9.0	9.0
浮选样品重量（单位：克）	–	–	–	–	1.9	75.7	9.3	–	–	0.6
木炭重量（单位：克）	–	*	*	0.00	0.51	0.01	0.01	0.00	0.01	0.34
种子总数（单位：颗）	2	1	1	1	0	5	47	1	1	1
粟（Foxtail millet）	2	1	1	1	–	1	–	1	–	–
黍（Broomcorn millet）	–	–	–	–	–	–	36	–	–	–
稻（Rice）	–	–	–	–	–	–	–	–	–	–
小麦（Wheat）	–	–	–	–	–	–	–	–	1	–
大豆（Glycine）	–	–	–	–	–	–	–	–	–	–
赤豆（Vigna）	–	–	–	–	–	–	–	–	–	–
黍属\马唐属\甜茅属（Panicum/Digitaria/Glyceria）	–	–	–	–	–	–	–	–	–	–
狗尾草（Green foxtail）	–	–	–	–	–	1	–	–	–	–
粟属（Other seteria）	–	–	–	–	–	–	–	–	–	–
黍属（Panic grass）	–	–	–	–	–	–	–	–	–	–
黍属马唐属（Panic/Digitaria）	–	–	–	–	–	–	–	–	–	–
稗属（Echinocloa）	–	–	–	–	–	–	–	–	–	–
黍族（Paniceae）	–	–	–	–	–	–	–	–	–	–
牛筋草（Eleusine indica）	–	–	–	–	–	–	–	1	–	–
禾本科不详（Unidentified grass）	–	–	–	–	–	–	–	–	–	–
山扁豆\豆茶决明（Cassia nomame）	–	–	–	–	–	–	–	–	–	–
草木樨属\胡枝子属（Melilotus/Lespedeza）	–	–	–	–	–	–	–	–	–	–
豆荚（Bean pods）	–	–	–	–	–	–	–	–	–	–
藜属（Chenopodium）	–	–	–	–	–	3	5	–	–	–
蓼属（Polygonum）	–	–	–	–	–	–	–	–	–	–
芸薹属（Brassica）	–	–	–	–	–	–	–	–	–	–
葎草属（Humulus）	–	–	–	–	–	–	–	–	–	–
堇菜属（Viola）	–	–	–	–	–	–	–	–	–	–
藨草属（Scirpus）	–	–	–	–	–	–	–	–	–	–
飘拂草属（cf. Fimbristylis）	–	–	–	–	–	–	–	–	–	–
莎草属（Cyperus）	–	–	–	–	–	–	–	–	–	–
莎草科其他（Other Cyperaceae）	–	–	–	–	–	–	–	–	–	–
悬钩子属（Rubus）	–	–	–	–	–	–	–	–	–	–
李（Prunus）	–	–	–	–	–	–	–	–	–	–
枣（Zizyphus）	–	–	–	–	–	–	–	–	–	–
蔷薇科（Rosaceae）	–	–	–	–	–	–	–	–	–	–
其他果实（Other fruits）	–	–	–	–	–	–	–	–	–	–
未知类型1（Unknown type 1）	–	–	–	–	–	–	2	–	–	–
未知（Unknown）	–	–	–	–	–	–	3	–	–	1
其他未知类型数量（N of other unknown types）	–	–	–	–	–	–	4	–	–	–
栎属（Quercus）	–	–	–	–	–	–	–	–	–	–
其他坚果（Other nut frag）	–	–	–	–	–	2	–	–	–	–

续表

种类	1	2	3	4	5	6	7	8	9	10	11
其他坚果（Other nut frag）	—	—	—	3	—	1	—	—	—	1	—
栎属（Quercus）	—	—	—	—	—	—	—	—	—	—	—
其他未知型数量（N of other unknown types）	—	—	—	—	—	—	—	—	—	—	2
未知（Unknown）	—	—	—	—	—	—	2	—	—	1	2
未知类型1（Unknown type 1）	—	—	—	—	—	—	—	—	—	—	—
其他果实（Other fruits）	—	—	—	—	—	—	—	—	—	—	—
蔷薇科（Rosaceae）	—	—	—	—	—	—	—	—	—	—	—
枣（Zizyphus）	—	—	—	—	—	—	—	—	—	—	—
李（Prunus）	—	—	—	—	—	—	—	—	—	—	—
悬钩子属（Rubus）	—	—	—	—	—	—	—	—	—	—	—
莎草科其他（Other Cyperaceae）	—	—	—	—	—	—	—	—	—	—	—
莎草属（Cyperus）	—	—	—	—	—	—	—	—	—	—	—
飘拂草属（cf. Fimbristylis）	—	—	—	—	—	—	—	—	—	—	—
藨草属（Scirupus）	—	—	—	—	—	—	—	—	—	—	—
堇菜属（Viola）	—	—	—	—	—	—	—	—	—	—	—
葎草属（Humulus）	—	—	—	—	—	—	—	—	—	—	—
芸薹属（Brasscia）	—	—	—	—	—	—	—	—	—	—	—
蓼属（Polygonum）	—	—	—	—	—	—	—	—	—	—	—
藜属（Chenopodium）	—	—	—	1	—	—	—	—	—	—	—
豆荚（Bean pods）	—	—	—	—	—	—	—	—	—	—	—
草木樨属\胡枝子属（Melilotus/Lespedeza）	—	—	—	—	—	—	—	—	—	—	—
山扁豆豆荚决明（Cassia nomame）	—	—	—	—	—	—	—	—	—	—	—
禾本科不详（Unidentified grass）	—	—	—	—	—	—	—	—	—	—	—
牛筋草（Eleusine indica）	—	—	—	—	—	—	—	—	—	—	—
黍族（Paniceae）	—	—	—	—	—	—	—	—	—	24	2
稗属（Echinocloa）	—	—	—	—	—	—	—	—	—	—	—
黍属\马唐属（Panic/Digitaria）	—	—	—	—	—	—	—	3	—	—	—
黍属（Panic grass）	—	1	—	—	—	—	—	—	—	—	—
粟属（Other seteria）	—	—	—	—	—	—	—	—	1	24	1
狗尾草（Green foxtail）	—	2	—	—	—	—	—	—	—	7	1
黍属\马唐属\甜茅属（Panicum/Digitaria/Glyceria）	—	—	—	—	—	—	—	—	—	8	3
赤豆（Vigna）	—	—	—	—	—	—	—	—	—	—	—
大豆（Glycine）	—	—	—	—	—	—	—	—	—	—	—
小麦（Wheat）	—	—	—	—	—	—	—	—	—	—	—
稻（Rice）	—	—	—	—	—	—	—	—	—	—	—
粟（Foxtail millet）	—	2	—	—	—	—	1	—	—	162	11
黍（Broomcorn millet）	—	—	—	—	—	—	—	—	—	2	—
种子总数（单位：颗）	0	5	1	0	0	0	3	3	1	228	20
木炭重量（单位：克）	0.00	—	0.01	0.00	0.00	—	0.01	—	—	—	1.02
浮选样品重量（单位：克）	—	—	1.3	1.5	—	1.6	0.6	2.6	0.8	—	3.2
样品量（单位：升）	8.0	6.0	12.0	8.0	7.5	12.0	7.0	14.0	8.0	9.2	7.0
遗址面积（单位：万平方米）	0.4	0.5	0.5	0.5	0.5	1	1	5.2	0.2	0.2	0.2
采样遗迹	Cultural layer	H1	layer	Cultural layer	Cultural layer	LY1	LY1	H1	Gound floor	H2	H1
遗址名称	北营	坞罗西坡2	坞罗西坡2	坞罗西坡2	坞罗西坡2	浏涧河	浏涧河	诸葛	水库北	喂庄西	喂庄西
遗址正式编号	Y044	Y042	Y042	Y042	Y042	Y187	Y187	178	Y019	Y019	Y019
遗址原始编号	07-044	98-042	07-042	07-042	07-042	07-187	07-187	07-052	07-019	98-019	07-019
时代	裴李岗晚期	裴李岗晚期	裴李岗晚期	裴李岗晚期	裴李岗晚期	裴李岗晚期	裴李岗晚期	裴李岗晚期	仰韶早中期	仰韶早期	仰韶晚期

续表

时代	仰韶中晚期	仰韶晚期	仰韶晚期	仰韶晚期	仰韶中期	仰韶晚期	仰韶中晚期	仰韶中晚期	仰韶晚期	仰韶中晚期	仰韶中晚期
遗址原始编号	98-018	07-018	07-018	05-164	05-164	98-050	98-050	07-050	05-077	05-077	05-077
遗址正式编号	Y018	Y018	Y018	Y164	Y164	Y050	Y050	Y050	Y077	Y077	Y077
遗址名称	喂庄西南河南岸	喂庄西南河南岸	喂庄西南河南岸	西茅窑东南	西茅窑东南	羽林庄南	羽林庄南	羽林庄南	赵城	赵城	赵城
采样遗迹	H1	H1	H2	H2	H1	H5	H4	H1	Cultural layer	H1 layer 1	H1 layer 2
遗址面积（单位：万平方米）	5.5	5.5	5.5	1	1	1.5	1.5	1.5	20	20	20
样品量（单位：升）	5.0	8.5	9.0	6.0	4.0	4.0	4.0	8.0	9.0	4.5	3.0
浮选样品重量（单位：克）	–	2.0	2.9	–	–	–	–	3.2	–	–	–
木炭重量（单位：克）	–	0.14	0.20	*	0.39	–	–	–	1.85	0.29	1.17
种子总数（单位：颗）	49	64	20	2	0	47	10	50	8	2010	1
黍（Broomcorn millet）	1	2	–	–	–	1	–	2	–	126	–
粟（Foxtail millet）	40	24	7	1	–	36	1	26	–	944	1
稻（Rice）	–	1	–	–	–	–	–	–	–	–	–
小麦（Wheat）	–	–	–	–	–	–	–	–	–	1	–
大豆（Glycine）	–	2	–	–	–	–	–	1	–	3	–
赤豆（Vigna）	–	–	–	–	–	–	–	–	–	–	–
黍属\马唐属\甜茅属（Panicum/Digitaria/Glyceria）	–	–	–	–	–	–	–	1	–	–	–
狗尾草（Green foxtail）	7	6	–	–	–	5	–	2	–	58	–
粟属（Other seteria）	–	7	7	–	–	–	1	9	–	121	–
黍属（Panic grass）	–	–	–	–	–	–	–	1	–	40	–
黍属\马唐属（Panic/Digitaria）	–	8	1	–	–	–	4	2	–	20	–
稗属（Echinocloa）	–	–	–	–	–	–	–	–	–	–	–
黍族（Paniceae）	1	9	4	1	–	–	2	6	1	677	–
牛筋草（Eleusine indica）	–	–	–	–	–	–	–	–	–	–	–
禾本科不详（Unidentified grass）	–	–	–	–	–	–	–	–	–	–	–
山扁豆\豆茶决明（Cassia nomame）	–	–	–	–	–	–	–	–	–	2	–
草木樨属\胡枝子属（Melilotus/Lespedeza）	–	–	–	–	–	–	1	–	–	–	–
豆荚（Bean pods）	–	–	–	–	–	–	–	–	–	–	–
藜属（Chenopodium）	–	1	–	–	–	–	–	–	–	6	–
蓼属（Polygonum）	–	–	–	–	–	–	–	–	–	–	–
芸薹属（Brasscia）	–	–	–	–	–	–	–	–	–	–	–
葎草属（Humulus）	–	–	–	–	–	–	–	–	–	–	–
堇菜属（Viola）	–	–	–	–	–	–	–	–	–	–	–
藨草属（Scirupus）	–	–	–	–	–	–	–	–	–	–	–
飘拂草属（cf. Fimbristylis）	–	–	–	–	–	–	–	–	–	–	–
莎草属（Cyperus）	–	–	–	–	–	–	–	–	–	–	–
莎草科其他（Other Cyperaceae）	–	–	1	–	–	–	–	–	–	2	–
悬钩子属（Rubus）	–	1	–	–	–	–	–	–	–	2	1
李（Prunus）	–	–	–	–	–	–	–	–	–	–	–
枣（Zizyphus）	–	–	–	–	–	–	–	–	–	–	–
蔷薇科（Rosaceae）	–	–	–	–	–	–	–	–	–	–	–
其他果实（Other fruits）	–	–	–	–	–	–	–	–	–	–	–
未知类型1（Unknown type 1）	–	–	–	–	–	–	–	–	–	1	–
未知（Unknown）	–	3	–	–	–	4	1	–	7	8	–
其他未知型数量（N of other unknown types）	–	3	–	–	–	–	–	–	–	7	–
栎属（Quercus）	–	–	–	–	–	–	–	–	–	–	–
其他坚果（Other nut frag）	–	1	–	–	–	–	–	–	–	–	–

续表

类别	C1	C2	C3	C4	C5	C6	C7	C8	C9	C10	C11
其他坚果（Other nut frag）	—	—	—	—	—	—	—	—	—	—	1
栎属（Quercus）	—	—	—	—	—	—	—	—	—	—	—
其他未知型数量（N of other unknown types）	7	—	—	—	—	2	—	—	—	—	—
未知（Unknown）	10	—	2	1	—	1	2	—	—	1	—
未知类型1（Unknown type 1）	15	—	—	—	—	—	—	—	—	2	—
其他果实（Other fruits）	—	—	—	—	—	—	—	—	—	—	—
蔷薇科（Rosaceae）	—	—	—	—	—	—	—	—	—	—	—
枣（Zizyphus）	—	—	—	—	—	—	—	—	—	—	—
李（Prunus）	—	—	—	—	—	—	—	—	—	—	—
悬钩子属（Rubus）	—	—	—	—	—	—	—	—	—	—	—
莎草科其他（Other Cyperaceae）	—	—	—	—	—	—	—	—	—	—	—
莎草属（Cyperus）	4	—	—	—	—	—	—	—	—	—	—
飘拂草属（cf. Fimbristylis）	—	—	—	—	—	—	—	—	—	—	—
藨草属（Scirupus）	—	—	—	—	—	—	—	—	—	—	—
堇菜属（Viola）	—	—	—	—	—	—	—	—	—	—	—
葎草属（Humulus）	—	—	—	—	—	—	—	—	—	—	—
芸薹属（Brasscia）	1	—	—	—	—	—	—	—	—	—	—
蓼属（Polygonum）	—	—	—	—	—	—	—	—	—	—	—
藜属（Chenopodium）	6	—	—	—	4	—	—	—	—	—	—
豆荚（Bean pods）	1	—	—	—	—	—	—	—	—	—	—
草木樨属\胡枝子属（Melilotus/Lespedeza）	7	—	—	—	—	—	—	—	—	—	—
山扁豆\豆茶决明（Cassia nomame）	1	—	—	—	—	—	—	—	—	—	—
禾本科不详（Unidentified grass）	1	—	—	—	—	—	—	—	—	—	—
牛筋草（Eleusine indica）	—	—	—	—	—	—	—	—	—	—	—
黍族（Paniceae）	261	2	12	—	3	3	—	3	13	—	3
稗属（Echinocloa）	—	—	—	—	—	—	—	—	—	—	—
黍属\马唐属（Panic/Digitaria）	29	1	—	—	1	—	—	—	1	—	—
黍属（Panic grass）	1	—	—	—	—	—	—	—	—	—	—
粟属（Other seteria）	76	1	—	—	2	—	—	1	2	—	6
狗尾草（Green foxtail）	14	—	1	9	—	13	—	—	—	1	1
黍属\马唐属\甜茅属（Panicum/Digitaria/Glyceria）	3	2	—	—	—	—	—	—	—	—	—
赤豆（Vigna）	—	—	—	—	—	—	—	—	—	—	—
大豆（Glycine）	13	4	—	—	—	—	—	—	—	1	2
小麦（Wheat）	—	—	—	—	—	—	—	—	—	—	—
稻（Rice）	2	—	—	—	—	—	—	—	—	—	—
粟（Foxtail millet）	246	66	82	1	2	50	—	12	25	—	22
黍（Broomcorn millet）	5	1	—	—	—	1	—	—	1	—	—
种子总数（单位：颗）	696	80	104	2	14	67	0	16	43	4	34
木炭重量（单位：克）	6.71	4.11	—	—	—	—	—	1.35	—	0.00	0.05
浮选样品重量（单位：克）	—	55.6	—	—	2.6	—	—	5.6	—	1.6	3.8
样品量（单位：升）	7.0	11.0	10.0	12.0	7.0	8.7	6.5	12.0	7.0	10.0	10.0
遗址面积（单位：万平方米）	20	20	20	20	1	2	2	0.4	2.5	2.5	7.5
采样遗迹	H2	H2	H1	H1	H2 Low	H1	H1	H1	H1	H1	H2
遗址名称	赵城	赵城	赵城	赵城	赵城西南	坞罗水库西1	坞罗水库西1	上庄东南	天坡村	天坡村	渭城河北
遗址正式编号	Y077	Y077	Y077	Y077	Y079	Y025	Y025	Y039	Y049	Y049	Y108
遗址原始编号	05-077	06-077	00-077	00-077	07-079	98-025	98-025	07-039	98-049	07-049	07-108
时代	仰韶中晚期	仰韶中晚期	仰韶晚期	仰韶晚期	仰韶晚期	仰韶晚期	仰韶晚期	仰韶晚期	仰韶晚期	仰韶晚期	仰韶晚期

续表

名称	裴村A	半个寨	秦沟五队北	南瓦窑	酒流沟水库西	酒流沟水库西	酒流沟水库西	布村东南	布村东南	北寨东南	宫家窑
其他坚果（Other nut frag）	–	–	–	–	–	–	–	–	–	–	–
栎属（Quercus）	–	–	–	–	–	–	–	–	–	–	–
其他未知型数量（N of other unknown types）	–	–	1	–	–	–	–	–	6	–	–
未知（Unknown）	–	–	1	–	2	–	–	–	6	1	1
未知类型1（Unknown type 1）	–	–	–	–	–	–	–	–	–	–	–
其他果实（Other fruits）	–	–	–	–	–	–	–	–	–	–	–
蔷薇科（Rosaceae）	–	–	–	–	–	–	–	–	–	–	–
枣（Zizyphus）	–	–	–	–	–	–	–	–	–	–	–
李（Prunus）	–	–	–	–	–	–	–	–	–	–	–
悬钩子属（Rubus）	–	–	–	–	–	–	–	–	–	–	–
莎草科其他（Other Cyperaceae）	–	–	–	–	–	–	–	–	–	–	–
莎草属（Cyperus）	–	–	–	–	–	–	–	–	–	–	–
飘拂草属（cf. Fimbristylis）	–	–	–	–	–	–	–	–	–	–	–
藨草属（Scirupus）	–	–	–	–	–	–	–	–	–	–	–
堇菜属（Viola）	–	–	–	–	–	–	–	–	–	–	–
葎草属（Humulus）	–	–	–	–	–	–	–	–	–	–	–
芸薹属（Brasscia）	–	–	–	–	–	–	–	–	–	–	–
蓼属（Polygonum）	–	–	–	–	–	–	–	–	–	–	–
藜属（Chenopodium）	–	1	6	–	2	–	–	–	8	1	3
豆荚（Bean pods）	–	–	–	–	–	–	–	–	–	–	–
草木樨属胡枝子属（Melilotus/Lespedeza）	–	–	–	–	1	–	–	–	9	–	–
山扁豆豆茶决明（Cassia nomame）	–	–	–	–	–	–	–	–	–	–	–
禾本科不详（Unidentified grass）	–	–	–	–	–	–	–	–	–	–	–
牛筋草（Eleusine indica）	–	–	–	–	–	–	–	–	–	–	–
黍族（Paniceae）	–	–	2	–	2	–	1	2	101	–	4
稗属（Echinocloa）	–	–	–	–	–	–	–	–	–	–	–
黍属马唐属（Panic/Digitaria）	–	2	–	–	1	–	–	1	###	–	2
黍属（Panic grass）	–	–	–	1	1	–	–	–	1	–	1
粟属（Other seteria）	–	–	1	–	–	–	–	4	50	1	–
狗尾草（Green foxtail）	–	–	1	–	9	–	–	–	17	–	–
黍属马唐属甜茅属（Panicum/Digitaria/Glyceria）	–	–	1	–	–	–	–	–	1	–	–
赤豆（Vigna）	–	–	–	–	–	–	–	–	–	–	–
大豆（Glycine）	–	–	–	–	–	–	–	–	5	–	–
小麦（Wheat）	–	–	–	–	–	–	–	–	–	–	–
稻（Rice）	–	–	–	–	–	–	–	–	–	–	–
粟（Foxtail millet）	2	–	23	1	8	4	8	9	119	–	6
黍（Broomcorn millet）	–	–	–	7	1	–	–	2	3	–	1
种子总数（单位：颗）	2	3	35	9	27	4	10	18	431	3	18
木炭重量（单位：克）	–	0.02	0.64	–	–	–	–	–	0.01	–	–
浮选样品重量（单位：克）	–	2.6	4.6	–	–	–	–	1.7	1.7	0.7	–
样品量（单位：升）	6.0	12.0	13.0	10.3	2.0	2.0	7.0	10.0	12.0	8.0	7.0
遗址面积（单位：万平方米）	6.2	5.75	0.5	0.1	34	34	34	4	4	9	28
采样遗迹	H	H1	H1	H1 layer 6-8	H lower layer	Adult deer spot	H upper layer	H1	H2	H1	H
遗址名称	裴村A	半个寨	秦沟五队北	南瓦窑	酒流沟水库西	酒流沟水库西	酒流沟水库西	布村东南	布村东南	北寨东南	宫家窑
遗址正式编号	118	Y123	Y126	Y156	159	159	159	Y204	Y204	Y218	183
遗址原始编号	03-009	07-123	07-126	01-156	03-044	03-044	03-044	07-204	07-204	07-218	03-025
时代	仰韶晚期	仰韶晚期	仰韶晚期	仰韶晚期	仰韶晚期	仰韶晚期	仰韶晚期	仰韶晚期	仰韶晚期	仰韶晚期	仰韶晚期

续表

项目	伏羲台	堤东	堤东	龙首堆	老周寨	东营茅东	东营茅东	寺沟东南	寺沟东南	寺沟东南	寺沟东南	高祖庙	罗口东北
时代	仰韶晚期	仰韶	仰韶	仰韶	仰韶	仰韶	仰韶	龙山早期	龙山早期	龙山早期	龙山早期	龙山早期	龙山晚期
遗址原始编号	—	07-052	07-052	07-053	07-200	07-202	07-202	01-152	01-152	01-152	01-152	07-167	98-022
遗址正式编号	—	Y052	Y052	Y053	Y200	Y202	Y202	Y152	Y152	Y152	Y152	Y167	Y022
采样遗迹	H	H1	H2	H1	H1	H1	H1	H1 layer 5	H1 outer layer 5	H2 layer 6	H3 layer 3	H1	H1
遗址面积（单位：万平方米）	—	4	4	0.15	6	5	5	4	4	4	4	2	20
样品量（单位：升）	5.0	12.0	7.0	9.0	15.0	8.0	8.0	12.0	12.0	13.5	8.0	9.0	10.0
浮选样品重量（单位：克）	—	1.5	1.7	5.6	1.7	—	—	—	—	—	—	0.6	—
木炭重量（单位：克）	—	—	*	—	—	0.61	0.00	—	—	—	—	—	—
种子总数（单位：颗）	10	15	16	1	1	18	21	33	184	3739	1	6	648
黍（Broomcorn millet）	—	—	—	—	—	3	3	2	5	56	—	—	4
粟（Foxtail millet）	3	2	13	—	1	11	11	16	152	3124	1	—	326
稻（Rice）	—	—	—	—	—	—	—	—	—	—	—	—	—
小麦（Wheat）	—	—	—	—	—	—	—	—	—	—	—	—	—
大豆（Glycine）	—	—	—	—	—	—	—	—	—	1	—	—	—
赤豆（Vigna）	—	—	—	—	—	—	—	—	—	—	—	—	—
黍属\马唐属\甜茅属（Panicum/Digitaria/Glyceria）	—	—	—	—	—	—	—	—	—	—	—	—	—
狗尾草（Green foxtail）	—	—	—	—	—	—	—	—	5	13	—	1	37
粟属（Other seteria）	1	5	1	—	—	—	—	3	8	78	—	—	82
黍属（Panic grass）	—	—	—	—	—	—	—	—	1	7	—	—	—
黍属\马唐属（Panic/Digitaria）	—	—	—	—	—	—	—	3	6	2	2	—	19
稗属（Echinocloa）	—	—	—	—	—	—	—	—	—	—	—	—	—
黍族（Paniceae）	5	7	2	1	—	1	1	2	2	453	—	2	163
牛筋草（Eleusine indica）	—	—	—	—	—	—	—	—	—	—	—	—	—
禾本科不详（Unidentified grass）	—	—	—	—	—	—	—	—	—	—	—	1	—
山扁豆豆荚决明（Cassia nomame）	—	—	—	—	—	—	—	—	—	—	—	—	—
草木樨属\胡枝子属（Melilotus/Lespedeza）	—	—	—	—	—	—	—	—	2	—	—	—	—
豆荚（Bean pods）	—	—	—	—	—	—	—	—	—	—	—	—	—
藜属（Chenopodium）	—	—	—	—	—	—	—	—	3	—	—	—	11
蓼属（Polygonum）	—	—	—	—	—	—	—	—	—	—	—	—	1
芸薹属（Brasscia）	—	—	—	—	—	—	—	—	—	—	—	—	—
葎草属（Humulus）	—	—	—	—	—	—	—	—	—	—	—	—	—
堇菜属（Viola）	—	1	—	—	—	—	—	—	2	—	—	—	—
麋草属（Scirpus）	—	—	—	—	—	—	—	—	—	—	—	—	—
飘拂草属（cf. Fimbristylis）	—	—	—	—	—	—	—	—	—	—	—	—	—
莎草属（Cyperus）	—	—	—	—	—	—	—	—	—	—	—	—	—
莎草科其他（Other Cyperaceae）	—	—	—	—	—	—	—	—	—	—	—	—	—
悬钩子属（Rubus）	—	—	—	—	—	—	—	—	—	—	—	—	—
李（Prunus）	—	—	—	—	—	—	—	—	—	—	—	—	—
枣（Zizyphus）	—	—	—	—	—	—	—	—	—	—	—	—	—
蔷薇科（Rosaceae）	—	—	—	—	—	—	—	—	—	—	—	—	—
其他果实（Other fruits）	—	—	—	—	—	—	—	—	—	—	—	—	—
未知类型1（Unknown type 1）	—	—	—	—	—	—	—	—	—	—	—	—	—
未知（Unknown）	1	—	—	—	—	—	—	8	6	3	—	2	5
其他未知型数量（N of other unknown types）	—	—	—	—	—	—	—	—	—	—	—	—	—
栎属（Quercus）	—	—	—	—	—	—	—	—	—	—	—	—	—
其他坚果（Other nut frag）	—	—	—	—	—	—	—	—	—	—	—	—	—

续表

种类												
其他坚果（Other nut frag）	–	–	–	–	–	–	–	–	–	–	–	–
栎属（Quercus）	–	–	–	–	–	–	–	–	–	–	–	–
其他未知型数量（N of other unknown types）	–	–	–	–	–	–	–	–	–	23	–	5
未知（Unknown）	3	2	–	3	1	–	4	1	–	23	–	5
未知类型1（Unknown type 1）	–	–	–	–	1	–	–	–	–	–	–	1
其他果实（Other fruits）	–	–	–	–	–	–	5	–	–	–	–	–
蔷薇科（Rosaceae）	–	–	–	–	–	–	–	–	–	–	–	–
枣（Zizyphus）	–	–	–	–	–	–	–	–	–	–	–	–
李（Prunus）	–	–	–	–	–	–	–	–	–	–	–	–
悬钩子属（Rubus）	–	–	–	–	–	–	–	–	–	1	–	–
莎草科其他（Other Cyperaceae）	–	–	–	–	–	–	–	–	–	1	–	–
莎草属（Cyperus）	–	–	–	–	–	–	–	–	–	–	–	5
飘拂草属（cf. Fimbristylis）	–	–	–	–	–	–	–	–	–	–	–	–
藨草属（Scirupus）	–	–	–	–	–	–	–	–	–	–	–	–
堇菜属（Viola）	–	–	–	–	–	–	–	–	–	–	–	–
葎草属（Humulus）	–	–	–	–	–	–	–	–	–	–	–	–
芸薹属（Brasscia）	–	–	–	–	–	–	–	–	–	–	–	–
蓼属（Polygonum）	–	–	–	–	–	–	–	–	–	–	–	–
藜属（Chenopodium）	9	–	–	–	–	–	–	–	–	71	–	19
豆荚（Bean pods）	–	–	–	–	–	–	–	–	–	5	–	–
草木樨属/胡枝子属（Melilotus/Lespedeza）	–	–	–	1	–	–	2	–	–	–	–	–
山扁豆/豆茶决明（Cassia nomame）	–	–	–	–	–	–	1	–	–	–	–	–
禾本科不详（Unidentified grass）	–	–	–	–	–	–	–	–	–	1	–	–
牛筋草（Eleusine indica）	–	–	–	–	–	–	–	–	–	–	–	–
黍族（Paniceae）	145	34	–	8	3	1	20	11	–	213	–	150
稗属（Echinocloa）	–	–	–	–	–	–	–	–	–	–	1	–
黍属/马唐属（Panic/Digitaria）	17	–	–	5	–	–	–	1	–	28	–	27
黍属（Panic grass）	–	–	–	–	–	–	4	–	–	4	–	–
粟属（Other seteria）	15	4	–	–	–	–	8	–	–	74	–	–
狗尾草（Green foxtail）	33	3	1	12	–	12	12	1	–	85	2	62
黍属/马唐属/甜茅属（Panicum/Digitaria/Glyceria）	–	–	–	–	–	–	1	–	–	–	–	–
赤豆（Vigna）	–	–	–	–	–	–	–	–	–	–	–	–
大豆（Glycine）	–	–	–	–	–	–	–	–	–	46	1	–
小麦（Wheat）	–	–	–	–	–	–	–	–	–	4	–	–
稻（Rice）	–	–	–	–	–	–	–	–	–	2	–	–
粟（Foxtail millet）	270	40	–	18	38	22	415	7	–	208	11	71
黍（Broomcorn millet）	4	–	2	2	2	1	39	–	–	8	–	3
种子总数（单位：颗）	496	83	3	49	57	24	511	21	–	774	14	344
木炭重量（单位：克）	–	–	–	–	–	–	–	–	–	–	–	–
浮选样品重量（单位：克）	–	–	–	–	–	–	–	–	–	164.2	–	–
样品量（单位：升）	7.0	8.0	7.0	4.0	3.0	3.0	3.0	2.0	9.0	9.0	4.0	6.0
遗址面积（单位：万平方米）	3	3	18	1.6	6	6	6	6	6	6	1	5.3
采样遗迹	H1	F1	H	H near an oven	H1	H2	H4	H5	H1	H1	H1	H upper layer
遗址名称	坞罗南店	坞罗南店	掘山	马寨	马屯新村	马屯新村	马屯新村	马屯新村	马屯新村	马屯新村	念子庄西北	寨弯东北
遗址正式编号	Y032	Y032	147	192	Y069	Y069	Y069	Y069	Y069	Y069	Y073	217
遗址原始编号	98-032	98-032	03-054	03-063	00-069	00-069	00-069	00-069	11-069	11-069	00-073	03-079
时代	龙山晚期	龙山晚期	龙山晚期	龙山晚期	龙山晚期	龙山晚期	龙山晚期	龙山晚期	龙山晚期	龙山晚期	龙山晚期	龙山晚期

续表

	贾屯	裴村B	邢村东	半个寨	高崖东北	寺沟南	寺沟南	西齐家窑东北	涧东村西北	老屯寨	张湾西北
其他坚果 (Other nut frag)	–	–	–	1	–	–	–	–	–	1	–
栎属 (Quercus)	–	–	–	–	–	–	–	–	–	–	–
其他未知型数量 (N of other unknown types)	–	–	–	–	–	–	–	–	7	–	–
未知 (Unknown)	–	–	1	–	–	1	–	–	68	1	–
未知类型1 (Unknown type 1)	–	–	–	–	–	–	–	–	19	–	–
其他果实 (Other fruits)	–	–	–	–	–	–	–	–	–	–	–
蔷薇科 (Rosaceae)	1	–	–	–	–	–	–	–	–	–	–
枣 (Zizyphus)	–	–	–	–	–	–	–	–	–	–	–
李 (Prunus)	–	–	–	–	–	–	–	–	–	–	–
悬钩子属 (Rubus)	1	–	–	–	–	–	–	–	5	–	–
莎草科其他 (Other Cyperaceae)	–	–	–	–	–	–	–	–	5	–	–
莎草属 (Cyperus)	–	–	1	–	–	–	–	–	4	–	–
飘拂草属 (cf. Fimbristylis)	–	–	–	–	–	–	–	–	42	–	–
藨草属 (Scirupus)	–	–	–	–	–	–	–	–	–	–	–
堇菜属 (Viola)	–	–	–	–	–	–	–	–	–	–	–
葎草属 (Humulus)	–	–	–	–	–	–	–	–	–	–	–
芸薹属 (Brasscia)	–	–	–	2	–	–	–	–	–	–	–
蓼属 (Polygonum)	–	–	–	–	–	–	–	–	2	–	–
藜属 (Chenopodium)	35	13	–	7	1	–	–	–	9	1	12
豆荚 (Bean pods)	–	–	–	–	–	–	–	–	–	–	–
草木樨属\胡枝子属 (Melilotus/Lespedeza)	–	13	1	–	1	–	–	–	1	–	–
山扁豆\豆茶决明 (Cassia nomame)	–	–	–	–	–	–	–	–	–	–	–
禾本科不详 (Unidentified grass)	–	1	–	–	–	–	–	–	–	–	–
牛筋草 (Eleusine indica)	–	–	–	–	–	–	–	–	–	–	–
黍族 (Paniceae)	7	–	48	13	1	38	11	–	1328	142	–
稗属 (Echinocloa)	–	–	–	–	–	1	–	–	–	–	–
黍属\马唐属 (Panic/Digitaria)	15	–	–	7	2	1	1	–	366	4	–
黍属 (Panic grass)	–	–	–	–	3	–	–	–	6	1	4
粟属 (Other seteria)	5	3	18	2	1	7	16	–	329	13	–
狗尾草 (Green foxtail)	3	–	3	8	2	4	7	–	368	15	2
黍属\马唐属\甜茅属 (Panicum/Digitaria/Glyceria)	–	–	–	–	–	–	–	–	–	–	–
赤豆 (Vigna)	–	–	–	–	–	–	–	–	–	–	–
大豆 (Glycine)	1	2	1	–	1	–	–	–	2	1	–
小麦 (Wheat)	–	–	–	–	–	–	–	–	–	–	–
稻 (Rice)	–	–	–	–	–	–	–	–	–	–	–
粟 (Foxtail millet)	11	3	29	16	37	312	7	–	441	48	16
黍 (Broomcorn millet)	6	–	1	–	10	3	2	–	–	3	–
种子总数（单位：颗）	85	35	103	55	60	366	44	0	2905	229	34
木炭重量（单位：克）	0.01	–	0.20	0.40	–	–	–	–	–	0.33	–
浮选样品重量（单位：克）	9.5	–	1.8	3.6	–	–	–	–	–	6.3	108.1
样品量（单位：升）	9.5	7.0	12.0	7.0	5.0	13.2	7.0	5.0	6.0	13.0	10.0
遗址面积（单位：万平方米）	6	4.1	2	5.75	26	4	4	5	6	6	20
采样遗迹	H1	H	H1	H2	H	H1 layer 6	H2 layer 3	H1	H1, NW corner	H1	H2
遗址名称	贾屯	裴村B	邢村东	半个寨	高崖东北	寺沟南	寺沟南	西齐家窑东北	涧东村西北	老屯寨	张湾西北
遗址正式编号	Y101	119	Y121	Y123	132	Y151	Y151	Y166	Y196B	Y199	Y210
遗址原始编号	07-101	03-010	07-121	07-123	03-048	01-151	01-151	02-166	02-196	07-199	11-210
时代	龙山晚期	龙山晚期	龙山晚期	龙山晚期	龙山晚期	龙山晚期	龙山晚期	龙山晚期	龙山晚期	龙山晚期	龙山晚期

续表

种类	1	2	3	4	5	6	7	8	9	10	11
其他坚果（Other nut frag）	3	-	-	-	-	-	-	1	-	-	-
栎属（Quercus）	-	-	-	-	-	-	-	1	-	-	-
其他未知类型数量（N of other unknown types）	1	-	-	-	3	1	2	-	-	1	2
未知（Unknown）	1	5	2	2	2	4	6	1	1	-	2
未知类型1（Unknown type 1）	-	-	-	-	1	-	20	-	-	1	-
其他果实（Other fruits）	-	-	-	-	-	-	-	-	-	-	-
蔷薇科（Rosaceae）	-	-	-	-	-	-	-	-	-	-	-
枣（Zizyphus）	1	-	-	-	-	-	-	-	-	-	-
李（Prunus）	2	-	-	-	-	-	-	-	-	-	-
悬钩子属（Rubus）	-	-	-	-	-	-	-	-	-	6	-
莎草科其他（Other Cyperaceae）	-	-	-	-	-	-	-	-	-	-	-
莎草属（Cyperus）	-	-	-	-	-	4	-	-	-	-	-
飘拂草属（cf. Fimbristylis）	1	-	-	-	-	-	19	-	-	-	-
藨草属（Scirupus）	-	-	-	-	-	-	-	-	-	-	-
堇菜属（Viola）	-	-	-	-	-	-	-	-	-	-	-
葎草属（Humulus）	-	-	-	-	-	-	-	4	-	-	-
芸薹属（Brasscia）	2	-	-	2	-	-	-	-	-	-	-
蓼属（Polygonum）	-	-	-	-	-	-	-	-	-	-	-
藜属（Chenopodium）	52	-	-	1	-	21	4	9	112	5	1
豆荚（Bean pods）	95	-	-	-	-	-	-	8	2	-	-
草木樨属胡枝子属（Melilotus/Lespedeza）	2	-	-	1	-	1	47	-	-	-	-
山扁豆豆茶决明（Cassia nomame）	-	-	-	-	-	-	-	-	-	-	-
禾本科不详（Unidentified grass）	-	-	-	-	2	-	-	-	-	-	-
牛筋草（Eleusine indica）	1	-	-	-	-	-	-	24	-	-	-
黍族（Paniceae）	-	186	28	17	39	101	70	33	58	49	3
稗属（Echinocloa）	-	-	-	-	-	-	-	-	-	-	-
黍属马唐属（Panic/Digitaria）	101	2	-	1	1	6	42	95	41	39	-
黍属（Panic grass）	-	-	1	-	-	3	15	-	-	-	-
粟属（Other seteria）	24	250	9	-	15	3	37	26	19	36	-
狗尾草（Green foxtail）	36	25	7	3	10	2	25	15	36	39	1
黍属马唐属甜茅属（Panicum/Digitaria/Glyceria）	-	-	-	10	-	1	1	-	-	-	-
赤豆（Vigna）	-	-	-	-	-	-	-	-	-	-	-
大豆（Glycine）	1	-	-	3	-	-	-	-	1	-	-
小麦（Wheat）	-	-	-	-	-	2	-	3	-	-	-
稻（Rice）	-	-	-	-	-	-	-	-	-	-	-
粟（Foxtail millet）	347	8458	499	9	5	5	36	28	55	48	5
黍（Broomcorn millet）	20	233	-	-	2	10	2	6	-	-	-
种子总数（单位：颗）	686	9159	546	38	86	156	270	284	355	224	12
木炭重量（单位：克）	1.00	-	-	0.06	-	0.01	0.85	-	-	0.06	-
浮选样品重量（单位：克）	97.5	-	-	13.3	16.5	27.1	49.7	46.1	65.6	136.8	1.8
样品量（单位：升）	20.0	5.5	5.0	7.0	7.0	8.0	18.0	13.0	10.0	25.0	3.0
遗址面积（单位：万平方米）	20	0.2	0.2	21	21	21	2	2	2	12.5	-
采样遗迹	H3	F1	H1	H1	H1	H2	H2	H2 (bag 2)	H3	H2	AT15 H123
遗址名称	张湾西北	南石	南石	保庄西北	保庄西北	保庄西北	颜良寨水库西	颜良寨水库西	颜良寨水库西	颜良寨水库西南	新砦
遗址正式编号	Y210	Y1003	Y1003	046	046	046	Y087	Y087	Y087	Y114	-
遗址原始编号	11-210	97-1003	97-1003	11-060	11-060	11-060	11-087	11-087	11-087	11-114	04HXX
时代	龙山晚期	龙山晚期	龙山晚期	龙山晚期	龙山晚期	龙山晚期	龙山晚期	龙山晚期	龙山晚期	龙山晚期	新砦

续表

分类	1	2	3	4	5	6	7	8	9	10	11
其他坚果（Other nut frag）	–	–	–	–	–	–	–	–	–	–	–
栎属（*Quercus*）	–	–	–	–	–	–	–	–	–	–	–
其他未知型数量（N of other unknown types）	–	–	–	2	1	1	–	–	–	–	–
未知（Unknown）	–	–	1	2	–	1	–	2	–	6	5
未知类型1（Unknown type 1）	–	–	–	1	–	–	3	–	–	–	–
其他果实（Other fruits）	–	–	–	–	–	–	–	–	–	2	–
蔷薇科（Rosaceae）	–	–	–	–	–	–	–	–	–	–	–
枣（*Zizyphus*）	–	–	–	–	–	–	–	–	–	–	–
李（*Prunus*）	–	–	–	–	–	–	–	–	–	–	–
悬钩子属（*Rubus*）	–	–	–	–	–	–	–	–	–	–	–
莎草科其他（Other Cyperaceae）	–	–	–	–	–	–	–	–	–	–	–
莎草属（*Cyperus*）	–	–	–	–	–	–	–	–	–	–	–
飘拂草属（cf. *Fimbristylis*）	–	–	–	–	–	–	–	–	–	–	–
藨草属（*Scirupus*）	1	–	1	–	–	–	–	–	–	–	–
堇菜属（*Viola*）	–	–	–	–	–	–	–	–	–	–	–
葎草属（*Humulus*）	–	–	–	–	–	–	–	–	–	–	–
芸薹属（*Brasscia*）	–	–	–	–	–	–	–	–	–	–	–
蓼属（*Polygonum*）	–	–	–	–	–	–	–	–	–	–	–
藜属（*Chenopodium*）	–	–	–	–	–	–	1	2	–	1	19
豆荚（Bean pods）	–	–	–	–	–	–	2	1	–	–	–
草木樨属/胡枝子属（*Melilotus/Lespedeza*）	–	–	–	–	–	–	2	–	–	–	–
山扁豆/豆茶决明（*Cassia nomame*）	–	–	–	–	–	–	–	–	–	–	–
禾本科不详（Unidentified grass）	–	–	–	–	–	–	–	–	–	–	–
牛筋草（*Eleusine indica*）	–	–	–	–	–	–	–	3	–	–	–
黍族（Paniceae）	2	–	1	3	3	–	28	12	33	200	377
稗属（*Echinocloa*）	–	–	–	–	–	–	–	–	–	–	–
黍属/马唐属（*Panic/Digitaria*）	–	–	3	–	1	–	3	–	–	2	9
黍属（Panic grass）	1	–	–	–	–	1	–	–	–	–	–
粟属（Other *seteria*）	–	–	–	–	–	–	13	–	9	42	103
狗尾草（Green foxtail）	–	–	1	–	–	–	17	8	22	35	45
黍属/马唐属/甜茅属（*Panicum/Digitaria/Glyceria*）	–	–	–	1	–	–	–	–	1	–	–
赤豆（*Vigna*）	–	–	–	–	–	–	–	–	–	–	–
大豆（*Glycine*）	–	–	–	1	–	–	3	–	–	–	–
小麦（Wheat）	–	–	–	–	–	–	–	–	–	–	–
稻（Rice）	–	1	1	6	–	1	–	–	–	–	–
粟（Foxtail millet）	2	32	9	2	1	2	12	10	52	368	520
黍（Broomcorn millet）	–	6	1	–	–	–	4	–	–	29	19
种子总数（单位：颗）	6	39	18	16	6	5	87	37	117	685	1097
木炭重量（单位：克）	*	0.04	–	0.16	0.00	*	0.00	–	0.90	–	–
浮选样品重量（单位：克）	2.6	0.6	18.0	3.6	0.8	0.6	3.5	22.9	585.0	–	–
样品量（单位：升）	8.0	8.0	9.0	8.0	9.0	9.0	12.0	10.0	11.0	12.2	12.8
遗址面积（单位：万平方米）	–	–	–	–	–	–	6	6	2.25	2.25	2.25
采样遗迹	AT9⑤轻样炭化物少	AT10 H97坑底	AT10④下	AT10④下 H106③	AT12⑥A探方北部	AT15⑥探方北隔梁	H3	H2	H1	H1 upper Layer5	H1 layer 7
遗址名称	新砦	新砦	新砦	新砦	新砦	新砦	涧东村西北	寺沟南	新后沟砖厂东	新后沟砖厂东	新后沟砖厂东
遗址正式编号							Y196B	Y151	Y132	Y132	Y132
遗址原始编号	04HXX	04HXX	04HXX	04HXX	04HXX	04HXX	07-196	11-151	07-132	00-132	00-132
时代	二里头一期	二里头一期	二里头一期	二里头一期	二里头一期	二里头一期	二里头二期	二里头二期	二里头三期	二里头四期	二里头三期

续表

植物名称	袁沟A	景阳岗	李家沟东	李家沟东	西口孜	西口孜	西口孜	张湾西北	稍柴	稍柴	稍柴	稍柴
其他坚果（Other nut frag）	-	-	-	-	-	-	-	1	-	-	-	-
栎属（Quercus）	-	-	-	-	-	-	-	-	-	-	-	-
其他未知型数量（N of other unknown types）	-	-	-	-	-	-	-	2	15	-	-	-
未知（Unknown）	-	2	-	-	1	-	7	-	2	20	8	7
未知类型1（Unknown type 1）	-	-	-	-	3	-	1	-	-	1	-	4
其他果实（Other fruits）	-	-	-	-	-	-	-	-	-	-	1	-
蔷薇科（Rosaceae）	-	-	-	-	-	-	-	-	-	-	-	-
枣（Zizyphus）	-	-	-	-	-	-	-	-	-	-	-	-
李（Prunus）	-	-	-	-	-	-	-	-	-	-	-	-
悬钩子属（Rubus）	-	-	-	-	-	-	-	-	-	-	-	-
莎草科其他（Other Cyperaceae）	-	-	-	-	4	-	-	-	2	-	-	-
莎草属（Cyperus）	-	-	-	-	-	-	-	-	-	-	-	-
飘拂草属（cf. Fimbristylis）	-	-	-	-	-	-	-	-	-	-	-	-
藨草属（Scirupus）	-	-	-	-	-	-	-	-	-	-	-	-
堇菜属（Viola）	-	-	1	-	-	-	1	-	3	-	-	-
葎草属（Humulus）	-	-	-	-	-	-	-	-	-	-	-	-
芸薹属（Brasscia）	-	-	-	-	-	-	-	-	-	-	-	-
蓼属（Polygonum）	-	-	-	-	-	-	-	6	-	-	-	-
藜属（Chenopodium）	-	2	16	-	63	27	75	7	63	-	-	-
豆荚（Bean pods）	-	-	-	2	1	-	-	60	-	-	-	-
草木樨属\胡枝子属（Melilotus/Lespedeza）	-	-	-	-	3	-	1	2	-	-	-	-
山扁豆豆茶决明（Cassia nomame）	-	-	-	-	-	-	-	-	-	-	-	-
禾本科不详（Unidentified grass）	-	-	-	-	-	-	-	-	-	-	-	-
牛筋草（Eleusine indica）	-	-	-	-	1	-	-	-	-	-	-	-
黍族（Paniceae）	-	18	65	20	41	21	12	253	52	245	125	-
稗属（Echinocloa）	-	-	-	-	-	-	-	-	-	-	-	-
黍属\马唐属（Panic/Digitaria）	-	1	10	-	1	-	10	20	4	2	-	-
黍属（Panic grass）	-	-	-	-	-	-	-	1	-	-	2	-
粟属（Other seteria）	-	-	28	5	26	11	9	97	4	42	26	-
狗尾草（Green foxtail）	-	11	30	-	2	-	-	32	16	21	22	-
黍属\马唐属\甜茅属（Panicum/Digitaria/Glyceria）	-	-	1	-	-	-	-	-	-	-	-	-
赤豆（Vigna）	-	-	-	-	-	-	-	-	-	-	-	-
大豆（Glycine）	-	-	2	1	-	-	-	1	1	1	4	-
小麦（Wheat）	-	-	-	-	-	-	-	3	3	-	-	-
稻（Rice）	-	-	-	-	-	-	-	3	1	-	4	-
粟（Foxtail millet）	-	6	45	13	36	29	15	451	109	226	315	-
黍（Broomcorn millet）	-	-	1	-	2	-	2	17	-	3	14	-
种子总数（单位：颗）	0	40	200	41	183	98	126	979	258	552	518	-
木炭重量（单位：克）	-	-	0.39	0.01	0.40	0.00	1.60	-	-	-	-	-
浮选样品重量（单位：克）	-	-	6.8	-	2.5	6.2	6.1	98.5	-	-	-	-
样品量（单位：升）	5.0	4.0	16.0	9.0	16.0	12.0	10.0	12.0	8.0	8.0	7.0	-
遗址面积（单位：万平方米）	7.2	5	9	9	18	18	18	10	40	40	40	-
采样遗迹	ash pit	ash pit	G1	H2	H1	H1	H2	H1	H1 pit layer A	H3	H4 layer 2	-
遗址名称	袁沟A	景阳岗	李家沟东	李家沟东	西口孜	西口孜	西口孜	张湾西北	稍柴	稍柴	稍柴	-
遗址正式编号	165	041	Y099	Y099	Y201	Y201	Y201	Y210	Y1001	Y1001	Y1001	-
遗址原始编号	03-057	03-055	07-099	11-099	07-201	07-201	07-201	11-210	97-1001	97-1001	97-1001	-
时代	二里头三四	二里头三四	二里头三四	二里头三四	二里头三四	二里头三四	二里头三四	二里头三四	二里头三四	二里头三四	二里头三四	-

续表

类别											
其他坚果 (Other nut frag)	—	—	—	—	—	—	—	—	—	—	—
栎属 (Quercus)	—	—	—	—	—	—	—	—	—	—	—
其他未知型数量 (N of other unknown types)	—	—	—	—	—	2	—	—	—	—	—
未知 (Unknown)	—	9	2	2	3	2	—	1	3	11	—
未知类型1 (Unknown type 1)	—	—	—	—	—	—	—	—	—	—	—
其他果实 (Other fruits)	—	—	—	—	1	—	—	—	—	—	—
蔷薇科 (Rosaceae)	—	—	—	—	—	—	—	—	—	—	—
枣 (Zizyphus)	—	—	2	—	—	—	—	—	—	—	—
李 (Prunus)	—	—	—	—	—	—	—	—	—	—	—
悬钩子属 (Rubus)	—	—	—	—	—	—	—	—	—	—	—
莎草科其他 (Other Cyperaceae)	—	—	—	—	—	—	—	—	—	—	—
莎草属 (Cyperus)	—	—	—	—	—	—	—	—	—	—	—
飘拂草属 (cf. Fimbristylis)	—	—	—	—	—	—	—	—	—	—	—
藨草属 (Scirupus)	—	—	—	—	—	—	—	—	—	—	—
堇菜属 (Viola)	—	—	—	—	—	—	—	—	—	—	—
葎草属 (Humulus)	—	—	—	—	—	—	—	—	—	—	—
芸薹属 (Brasscia)	—	—	—	—	—	—	—	—	—	—	—
蓼属 (Polygonum)	—	—	—	—	—	—	—	—	—	—	—
藜属 (Chenopodium)	—	4	48	—	—	2	—	—	2	2	—
豆荚 (Bean pods)	—	—	—	—	—	—	—	—	—	—	—
草木樨属\胡枝子属 (Melilotus/Lespedeza)	—	3	—	—	—	—	—	—	—	—	—
山扁豆\豆茶决明 (Cassia nomame)	—	—	—	—	—	—	—	—	—	—	—
禾本科不详 (Unidentified grass)	—	—	—	—	—	—	—	—	—	—	—
牛筋草 (Eleusine indica)	—	—	—	—	—	—	—	—	—	—	—
黍族 (Paniceae)	71	273	219	6	30	5	18	16	200	11	—
稗属 (Echinocloa)	—	—	—	—	—	—	—	—	—	—	—
黍属\马唐属 (Panic/Digitaria)	1	1	—	—	—	47	20	9	—	4	—
黍属 (Panic grass)	1	4	6	—	—	—	—	3	1	—	—
粟属 (Other seteria)	21	68	9	—	12	9	11	5	30	16	—
狗尾草 (Green foxtail)	19	20	22	7	12	11	—	13	30	—	—
黍属\马唐属\甜茅属 (Panicum/Digitaria/Glyceria)	—	—	1	—	—	2	—	—	—	—	—
赤豆 (Vigna)	—	—	—	—	—	—	—	—	—	—	—
大豆 (Glycine)	1	1	2	—	—	1	2	1	—	—	—
小麦 (Wheat)	—	—	—	—	—	—	—	—	—	—	—
稻 (Rice)	1	5	—	—	—	—	2	1	—	—	—
粟 (Foxtail millet)	223	637	328	88	438	28	52	72	259	24	5
黍 (Broomcorn millet)	4	—	18	—	1	—	3	6	1	—	—
种子总数(单位:颗)	342	1025	657	103	497	104	104	126	533	69	5
木炭重量(单位:克)	—	—	—	—	—	0.93	1.08	—	—	—	0.78
浮选样品重量(单位:克)	—	—	—	—	6.2	—	—	—	—	—	—
样品量(单位:升)	11.0	15.2	12.0	11.0	7.0	14.0	11.0	10.0	8.0	5.0	3.0
遗址面积(单位:万平方米)	40	40	40	40	3	2	2	2	2	7.5	7
采样遗迹	H4 lower layer 7	H4 layer 7	H5 layer 2	H6 layer 3a	H1	H1 (Z3)	H1	H2	H2	H lower layer	F3 layer 2R
遗址名称	稍柴	稍柴	稍柴	稍柴	回龙湾新村东	上庄南	上庄南	上庄南	罗口	聚湾东南	灰嘴
遗址正式编号	Y1001	Y1001	Y1001	Y1001	Y083	Y037	Y037	Y037	Y022	216	Y127
遗址原始编号	97-1001	97-1001	97-1001	97-1001	00-083	07-037	07-037	98-037	98-022	03-074	00-127
时代	二里头三四	二里头三四	二里头三四	二里头三四	二里头三四	二里头四期	二里头四期	二里头三四期	二里头三四期	二里头	二里头

续表

植物种类	1	2	3	4	5	6	7	8	9	10	11
其他坚果（Other nut frag）	—	—	—	—	—	—	—	—	—	—	—
栎属（Quercus）	—	—	—	—	—	—	—	—	—	—	—
其他未知型数量（N of other unknown types）	—	—	—	6	6	—	—	—	—	—	—
未知（Unknown）	2	2	1	6	6	—	—	2	4	10	4
未知类型1（Unknown type 1）	—	—	—	—	—	—	—	—	5	—	—
其他果实（Other fruits）	—	—	—	—	2	—	—	—	—	1	—
蔷薇科（Rosaceae）	—	—	—	—	—	—	—	—	—	—	—
枣（Zizyphus）	—	—	—	—	—	—	—	—	—	—	—
李（Prunus）	—	—	—	—	—	—	—	—	—	—	—
悬钩子属（Rubus）	—	—	—	—	—	—	—	—	2	—	—
莎草科其他（Other Cyperaceae）	—	—	—	—	—	—	—	—	1	—	—
莎草属（Cyperus）	—	—	—	—	—	—	—	—	—	—	—
飘拂草属（cf. Fimbristylis）	—	—	—	—	—	—	—	—	—	—	—
藨草属（Scirupus）	—	—	—	—	—	—	—	—	—	—	—
堇菜属（Viola）	—	—	—	—	—	—	—	—	—	—	—
葎草属（Humulus）	—	—	—	—	—	—	—	—	—	—	—
芸薹属（Brasscia）	—	—	—	—	—	—	—	—	—	—	—
蓼属（Polygonum）	—	—	—	—	—	—	—	—	—	—	—
藜属（Chenopodium）	—	13	—	—	2	1	—	—	—	—	—
豆荚（Bean pods）	—	—	—	2	—	—	—	—	—	—	—
草木樨属/胡枝子属（Melilotus/Lespedeza）	—	—	5	4	—	2	—	—	4	1	—
山扁豆/豆茶决明（Cassia nomame）	—	1	—	—	—	—	—	—	1	1	—
禾本科不详（Unidentified grass）	—	—	—	—	—	—	—	—	—	—	—
牛筋草（Eleusine indica）	—	—	—	—	—	—	—	—	—	—	—
黍族（Paniceae）	44	46	73	26	38	8	5	11	1711	217	76
稗属（Echinocloa）	—	—	—	—	—	—	—	—	—	—	—
黍属/马唐属（Panic/Digitaria）	3	—	—	1	7	—	—	2	36	25	4
黍属（Panic grass）	7	—	1	—	1	3	—	—	10	1	—
粟属（Other seteria）	15	8	20	22	15	2	3	—	25	51	23
狗尾草（Green foxtail）	22	10	17	6	7	—	3	1	92	34	24
黍属/马唐属/甜茅属（Panicum/Digitaria/Glyceria）	—	—	—	—	—	—	—	—	2	—	—
赤豆（Vigna）	—	—	—	—	—	—	—	—	—	—	—
大豆（Glycine）	1	—	1	2	9	—	—	—	1	7	—
小麦（Wheat）	—	—	—	—	—	—	—	—	29	1	87
稻（Rice）	1	—	1	—	—	—	—	—	1	3	—
粟（Foxtail millet）	268	35	174	42	338	2	10	28	1107	296	273
黍（Broomcorn millet）	6	2	5	1	—	—	—	—	30	—	1
种子总数（单位：颗）	369	119	297	113	427	15	23	42	3120	649	492
木炭重量（单位：克）	8.78	0.93	1.27	0.00	—	0.00	0.33	—	—	—	—
浮选样品重量（单位：克）	—	—	—	0.9	—	0.9	0.9	—	—	—	—
样品量（单位：升）	14.1	9.1	8.6	15.0	10.0	9.0	10.0	5.5	4.5	5.0	4.5
遗址面积（单位：万平方米）	7	7	7	6	2	2	2	3	3	3	3
采样遗迹	Sample 1&2 layer 4	Sample III layer 4	Sample II layer 5	H2	III	H1	H2	H5 high layer 4	H6 layer 6	H5 low layer 6	H6 layer 3
遗址名称	灰嘴	灰嘴	灰嘴	涧东村	费窑西南	费窑西南	费窑西南	天坡水库东北	天坡水库东北	天坡水库东北	天坡水库东北
遗址正式编号	Y127	Y127	Y127	Y195	Y011	Y011	Y011	Y043	Y043	Y043	Y043
遗址原始编号	00-127	00-127	00-127	07-195	98-011	07-011	07-011	98-043	98-043	98-043	98-043
时代	二里头	二里头	二里头	二里头	二里岗上层	二里岗上层	二里岗上层	二里岗上层	二里岗上层	二里岗上层	二里岗上层

续表

分类	Y043 / 98-043 / 天坡水库东北 / H6 layer 5	Y043 / 98-043 / 天坡水库东北 / H3	Y043 / 98-043 / 天坡水库东北 / H1	Y058 / 00-058 / 杨寨西北 / H	Y058 / 07-058 / 杨寨西北 / H1	Y058 / 07-058 / 杨寨西北 / H2	Y086 / 07-086 / 颜良寨西南 / H1	Y086 / 07-086 / 颜良寨西南 / H1	Y099 / 11-099 / 李家沟东 / H3	Y184 / 02-184 / 邢村西北 / H	Y198 / 07-198 / 屯寨西北 / H1
其他坚果（Other nut frag）	–	–	–	–	–	–	–	–	–	–	–
栎属（Quercus）	–	–	–	–	–	–	–	–	–	–	–
其他未知型数量（N of other unknown types）	–	–	–	–	–	–	–	–	–	–	–
未知（Unknown）	3	–	4	–	–	6	–	–	6	–	–
未知类型1（Unknown type 1）	–	–	–	–	8	–	–	–	–	–	–
其他果实（Other fruits）	–	–	–	–	–	–	–	–	–	–	–
蔷薇科（Rosaceae）	–	–	–	–	–	–	–	–	–	–	–
枣（Zizyphus）	–	–	–	–	1	–	–	–	–	–	–
李（Prunus）	–	–	–	–	–	–	–	–	–	–	–
悬钩子属（Rubus）	–	–	–	–	–	–	–	–	–	–	–
莎草科其他（Other Cyperaceae）	–	–	–	–	–	–	–	–	–	–	–
莎草属（Cyperus）	–	–	–	–	1	–	–	–	–	1	3
飘拂草属（cf. Fimbristylis）	–	–	–	–	–	–	–	–	–	–	–
藨草属（Scirupus）	–	–	–	–	–	–	–	–	–	–	–
堇菜属（Viola）	–	–	–	–	–	–	–	–	–	–	–
葎草属（Humulus）	–	–	–	–	–	–	–	–	–	–	–
芸薹属（Brasscia）	–	1	–	–	–	–	–	–	–	–	–
蓼属（Polygonum）	–	1	1	–	–	–	–	–	–	–	–
藜属（Chenopodium）	–	–	–	–	4	3	–	2	1	–	39
豆荚（Bean pods）	–	–	–	–	–	–	–	–	–	–	–
草木樨属/胡枝子属（Melilotus/Lespedeza）	–	4	2	–	21	1	–	–	–	2	3
山扁豆/豆茶决明（Cassia nomame）	–	–	–	–	–	–	–	–	–	–	–
禾本科不详（Unidentified grass）	–	–	–	–	–	–	–	–	–	–	–
牛筋草（Eleusine indica）	–	–	–	–	–	–	–	–	–	–	–
黍族（Paniceae）	3	190	107	121	312	11	4	–	8	20	312
稗属（Echinocloa）	–	–	–	–	–	–	–	–	–	–	–
黍属/马唐属（Panic/Digitaria）	–	2	–	7	35	1	–	8	7	23	67
黍属（Panic grass）	–	2	–	–	–	–	–	–	1	–	4
粟属（Other seteria）	–	21	19	–	190	5	–	2	2	–	133
狗尾草（Green foxtail）	1	38	16	102	69	11	–	–	1	6	50
黍属/马唐属/甜茅属（Panicum/Digitaria/Glyceria）	–	–	–	–	–	–	–	–	–	–	–
赤豆（Vigna）	–	–	–	–	–	–	–	–	–	–	–
大豆（Glycine）	–	1	–	–	10	–	–	–	3	–	4
小麦（Wheat）	–	16	39	92	14	–	2	–	5	–	4
稻（Rice）	–	–	1	–	–	–	–	–	–	–	–
粟（Foxtail millet）	115	188	335	587	178	13	4	26	7	32	220
黍（Broomcorn millet）	–	1	2	–	–	–	–	–	–	–	46
种子总数（单位：颗）	122	469	521	975	849	45	10	44	32	87	885
木炭重量（单位：克）	–	–	–	–	0.96	0.05	0.04	0.91	0.41	–	–
浮选样品重量（单位：克）	–	–	–	–	8.3	2.5	1.3	1.9	52.7	–	5.3
样品量（单位：升）	4.2	3.0	3.0	7.0	15.0	6.0	9.5	9.0	8.0	5.0	16.0
遗址面积（单位：万平方米）	3	3	3	0.9	0.9	0.9	3	3	9	1	2
采样遗迹	H6 layer 5	H3	H1	H	H1	H2	H1	H1	H3	H	H1
遗址名称	天坡水库东北	天坡水库东北	天坡水库东北	杨寨西北	杨寨西北	杨寨西北	颜良寨西南	颜良寨西南	李家沟东	邢村西北	屯寨西北
遗址正式编号	Y043	Y043	Y043	Y058	Y058	Y058	Y086	Y086	Y099	Y184	Y198
遗址原始编号	98-043	98-043	98-043	00-058	07-058	07-058	07-086	07-086	11-099	02-184	07-198
时代	二里岗上层	二里岗上层	二里岗上层	二里岗上层	二里岗上层	二里岗上层	二里岗上层	二里岗上层	二里岗上层	二里岗上层	二里岗上层

续表

种类	1	2	3	4	5	6	7	8	9	10	11	12	13
时代	殷墟	西周早中期	西周早中期	西周中期	西周/东周	西周/东周	东周	东周	东周	东周	东周	东周	东周
遗址原始编号	11-001	11-151	11-151	07-199	11-152	07-152	07-152	07-003	07-059	07-059	07-059	11-059	11-059
遗址正式编号	065	Y151	Y151	Y199	Y152	Y152	Y152	Y003	Y059	Y059	Y059	Y059	Y059
遗址名称	北窑东北	寺沟南	寺沟南	老屯寨	寺沟东南	寺沟东南	寺沟东南	清易镇东2	杨寨西	杨寨西	杨寨西	杨寨西	杨寨西
采样遗迹	H1	H1	H1	H2	H1	H1	H2	H1	H1	H2	H3	H1	H2
遗址面积（单位：万平方米）	9.5	6	6	6	6	6	6	15	3	3	3	3	3
样品量（单位：升）	21.0	6.0	5.0	8.0	10.0	9.0	9.0	7.0	15.0	7.0	13.0	8.0	9.0
浮选样品重量（单位：克）	57.8	14.6	18.8	3.3	—	—	7.4	1.3	—	1.8	2.4	69.6	24.4
木炭重量（单位：克）	—	0.21	—	0.00	—	0.23	0.10	0.04	0.00	0.58	0.82	0.06	0.13
种子总数（单位：颗）	466	125	41	187	46	368	49	3	41	10	51	10	42
粟（Foxtail millet）	167	85	18	89	5	128	11	1	10	3	13	5	7
黍（Broomcorn millet）	34	4	4	—	—	3	—	—	1	—	—	—	—
稻（Rice）	—	—	—	—	—	—	—	—	—	—	—	—	—
小麦（Wheat）	—	1	—	—	28	—	3	—	—	3	3	—	—
大豆（Glycine）	11	—	—	1	—	1	1	—	—	—	1	1	—
赤豆（Vigna）	—	—	—	—	—	—	—	1	—	2	—	—	—
黍属\马唐属\甜茅属（Panicum/Digitaria/Glyceria）	—	—	—	—	—	—	—	—	—	—	—	—	—
狗尾草（Green foxtail）	20	3	9	12	1	46	9	—	3	2	11	—	—
粟属（Other seteria）	50	4	—	36	1	26	2	1	7	2	1	—	8
黍属（Panic grass）	11	—	—	—	—	—	—	—	—	—	—	—	2
黍属马唐属（Panic/Digitaria）	29	2	—	3	—	4	—	—	6	—	—	—	4
稗属（Echinocloa）	—	—	—	—	—	—	—	—	—	—	—	—	—
黍族（Paniceae）	24	7	4	25	2	77	2	—	4	—	17	3	10
牛筋草（Eleusine indica）	—	—	—	—	—	—	—	—	—	—	—	—	—
禾本科不详（Unidentified grass）	—	—	—	—	—	—	—	—	—	—	—	—	—
山扁豆\豆茶决明（Cassia nomame）	—	—	—	—	—	—	—	—	—	—	—	—	—
草木樨属\胡枝子属（Melilotus/Lespedeza）	119	—	—	—	—	1	1	—	—	—	—	—	—
豆荚（Bean pods）	—	1	—	—	—	—	—	—	—	—	—	—	—
藜属（Chenopodium）	1	5	4	21	9	79	9	—	6	—	2	—	3
蓼属（Polygonum）	—	—	—	—	—	—	—	—	—	—	—	—	—
芸薹属（Brasscia）	—	—	—	—	—	—	—	—	—	—	—	—	—
葎草属（Humulus）	—	—	—	—	—	—	—	—	—	—	—	—	—
堇菜属（Viola）	—	—	—	—	—	—	—	1	—	—	—	—	—
藨草属（Scirupus）	—	—	—	—	—	—	—	—	—	—	—	—	—
飘拂草属（cf. Fimbristylis）	—	—	—	—	—	—	—	—	—	—	—	—	—
莎草属（Cyperus）	—	—	—	—	—	1	—	—	3	—	—	—	—
莎草科其他（Other Cyperaceae）	—	1	—	—	—	—	—	—	—	—	—	—	1
悬钩子属（Rubus）	—	—	1	—	—	—	—	—	—	—	—	—	—
李（Prunus）	—	—	—	—	—	—	—	—	—	—	—	—	—
枣（Zizyphus）	—	—	—	—	1	—	—	—	—	—	—	—	—
蔷薇科（Rosaceae）	—	—	—	—	—	—	—	—	—	—	—	—	—
其他果实（Other fruits）	—	—	—	—	—	—	—	—	—	—	—	—	—
未知类型1（Unknown type 1）	—	6	—	—	—	—	4	—	—	1	2	—	—
未知（Unknown）	—	6	—	1	—	—	2	6	—	—	1	1	7
其他未知型数量（N of other unknown types）	—	5	—	—	—	—	2	—	—	—	1	—	7
栎属（Quercus）	—	—	—	—	6	—	—	—	—	—	—	—	—
其他坚果（Other nut frag）	—	1	—	—	—	—	—	—	—	—	—	—	—

续表

种类	Y059 杨寨西 H2 东周	Y059 杨寨西 H3 东周	Y098 顾家屯南 H1 东周	Y101 贾屯 AL1 东周	Y108 渭城河北 H1 东周	Y126 枣沟五队北 H2 东周	Y190 刘国故城 H2 west part 东周	Y190 刘国故城 H2 west part 东周	Y190 刘国故城 H2 east part 东周	Y199 涧东村 H1 东周	Y017 罗口砖厂东北 Kiln 汉朝	Y017 罗口砖厂东北 H1 汉朝	Y216 吕桥寨东南 F1 汉朝
其他坚果（Other nut frag）	–	1	–	–	–	2	–	–	–	–	–	–	–
栎属（Quercus）	–	–	–	–	–	–	–	–	–	–	–	–	–
其他未知型数量（N of other unknown types）	2	–	2	–	–	–	–	–	–	5	2	–	–
未知（Unknown）	2	1	2	2	–	–	1	–	–	1	6	3	–
未知类型1（Unknown type 1）	–	–	–	–	–	–	–	–	–	–	5	5	–
其他果实（Other fruits）	–	–	–	–	–	–	–	–	–	–	–	–	–
蔷薇科（Rosaceae）	–	–	–	–	–	–	–	–	–	–	–	–	–
枣（Zizyphus）	–	–	–	–	–	–	–	–	–	–	3	1	–
李（Prunus）	–	–	–	–	–	–	–	–	–	–	–	–	–
悬钩子属（Rubus）	–	–	–	–	–	–	–	–	–	–	1	–	–
莎草科其他（Other Cyperaceae）	–	–	–	–	–	–	–	–	–	–	–	–	–
莎草属（Cyperus）	–	–	–	–	–	–	–	–	–	–	–	–	–
飘拂草属（cf. Fimbristylis）	–	–	–	–	–	–	–	–	–	–	–	–	–
藨草属（Scirupus）	–	–	–	–	–	–	–	–	–	–	–	–	–
堇菜属（Viola）	–	–	–	–	–	1	–	–	–	–	–	–	–
葎草属（Humulus）	–	–	–	–	–	–	–	–	–	–	–	–	–
芸薹属（Brasscia）	–	–	–	–	–	–	–	–	–	–	–	–	–
蓼属（Polygonum）	–	–	–	–	–	–	–	–	–	–	–	–	–
藜属（Chenopodium）	13	12	2	54	1	4	5	–	–	2	351	–	–
豆荚（Bean pods）	–	2	–	–	–	–	–	–	–	–	–	–	–
草木樨属\胡枝子属（Melilotus/Lespedeza）	–	–	–	–	–	–	1	–	–	–	–	–	–
山扁豆\豆茶决明（Cassia nomame）	–	–	–	–	–	–	–	–	–	–	–	–	–
禾本科不详（Unidentified grass）	–	–	–	–	–	–	–	–	–	–	–	–	–
牛筋草（Eleusine indica）	–	–	–	–	–	1	–	–	–	–	–	–	–
黍族（Paniceae）	8	19	3	4	–	–	–	–	–	–	23	27	–
稗属（Echinocloa）	1	–	–	–	–	1	–	–	–	–	–	1	–
黍属\马唐属（Panic/Digitaria）	–	21	–	–	–	1	–	–	–	–	24	2	–
黍属（Panic grass）	–	–	–	–	–	–	–	–	–	–	–	–	–
粟属（Other seteria）	–	2	–	–	–	–	–	–	–	–	37	2	–
狗尾草（Green foxtail）	29	–	–	2	–	2	–	–	–	–	22	4	1
黍属\马唐属\甜茅属（Panicum/Digitaria/Glyceria）	–	–	–	–	–	–	–	–	–	–	–	–	–
赤豆（Vigna）	–	–	–	–	–	–	–	–	–	–	–	–	1
大豆（Glycine）	–	4	–	–	–	–	–	–	–	–	7	7	1
小麦（Wheat）	1	–	–	–	–	–	–	–	–	–	–	3	1
稻（Rice）	–	–	–	–	–	–	–	–	–	–	7	–	–
粟（Foxtail millet）	10	16	3	2	–	1	–	–	–	51	69	2	3
黍（Broomcorn millet）	5	–	–	–	–	–	1	–	–	4	–	–	–
种子总数（单位：颗）	70	77	10	64	2	10	5	1	3	534	131	3	7
木炭重量（单位：克）	–	0.66	0.01	1.28	0.05	0.00	0.01	–	–	2.50	–	–	0.33
浮选样品重量（单位：克）	58.4	53.9	2.9	9.6	1.5	0.7	4.5	7.5	11.8	15.2	–	2.6	7.2
样品量（单位：升）	10.0	20.0	9.0	8.0	7.0	9.0	8.0	8.0	8.5	15.0	4.0	6.0	9.0
遗址面积（单位：万平方米）	3	3	0.8	6	7.5	0.5	80	80	80	6	2.5	2.5	10
采样遗迹	H2	H3	H1	AL1	H1	H2	H2 west part	H2 west part	H2 east part	H1	Kiln	H1	F1
遗址名称	杨寨西	杨寨西	顾家屯南	贾屯	渭城河北	枣沟五队北	刘国故城	刘国故城	刘国故城	涧东村	罗口砖厂东北	罗口砖厂东北	吕桥寨东南
遗址正式编号	Y059	Y059	Y098	Y101	Y108	Y126	Y190	Y190	Y190	Y199	Y017	Y017	Y216
遗址原始编号	11-059	11-059	07-098	07-101	07-108	07-126	06-190	06-190	06-190	07-195	98-017	07-017	07-216
时代	东周	东周	东周	东周	东周	东周	东周	东周	东周	东周	汉朝	汉朝	汉朝

第七章　灰嘴遗址石器加工原料的来源[①]

第一节　前　　言

灰嘴聚落的石器生产发生了很大的变化。仰韶时期，极少发现石器制作的证据，石片的原料来源于遗址附近河流中的河卵石，没有任何一种石料占主要地位，这说明灰嘴的仰韶居民使用本地石料制作石器，产品仅供自己使用。但是，从龙山晚期开始，灰嘴遗址成为了一处石器制作中心，它的主要产品是鲕状白云岩石铲，产品分布到遗址的周边区域[1]。

二里头文化时期，灰嘴的石器加工规模扩大，这同二里头文化的全面扩张有关。二里头文化是以手工业专业化、社会分层、大规模资源往来贸易网络和青铜冶铸为特征的复杂社会[2]。二里头文化中的青铜主要用于生产礼器和武器，而石器工业生产的石器则是为了满足日常生活的需要，因此也很重要。灰嘴遗址在生产不同种类的工具时明显表现出原料专门化的现象，即每一种石器主要使用一种岩石制作[3]（图7.1）：石铲使用鲕状白云岩，斧、锛、凿使用辉绿岩，刀由细云母砂岩制成，砺石由种类不一的砂岩制成。总之，灰嘴的主要石器种类为鲕状白云岩石铲，遗址中发现了大量的鲕状白云岩废料，包括石片和毛坯。

灰嘴遗址明显出现了原料专门化的现象，专门化的原因将通过以下几个方面进行阐释：首先，讨论周围区域的地质状况，包括富含石料的嵩山，这可以为解释灰嘴居民的原料选择提供整体的石料信息。接下来会讨论灰嘴遗址使用的原料的岩性，其中，重点关注原料的功能特性和开采的难易程度，以评估选择该原料的原因。最后，综合分析本地地质状况及石器原料的岩石学特性，为资源使用提供证据。

第二节　灰嘴地区的地质和地理情况

伊洛河南部的灰嘴遗址位于一处平坦的冲积平原上，该平原由再沉积的更新世和全新世风积黄土构成。隆起于第四纪沉积层上的是一些低矮的丘陵，包括低洼的三叠纪湖相砂岩和粉砂岩（图7.2，a、b），地势缓缓地（20°～30°）向北部下沉。

[①] 本章John Webb、Anne Ford、Justin Gorton执笔，邓玲玲翻译。

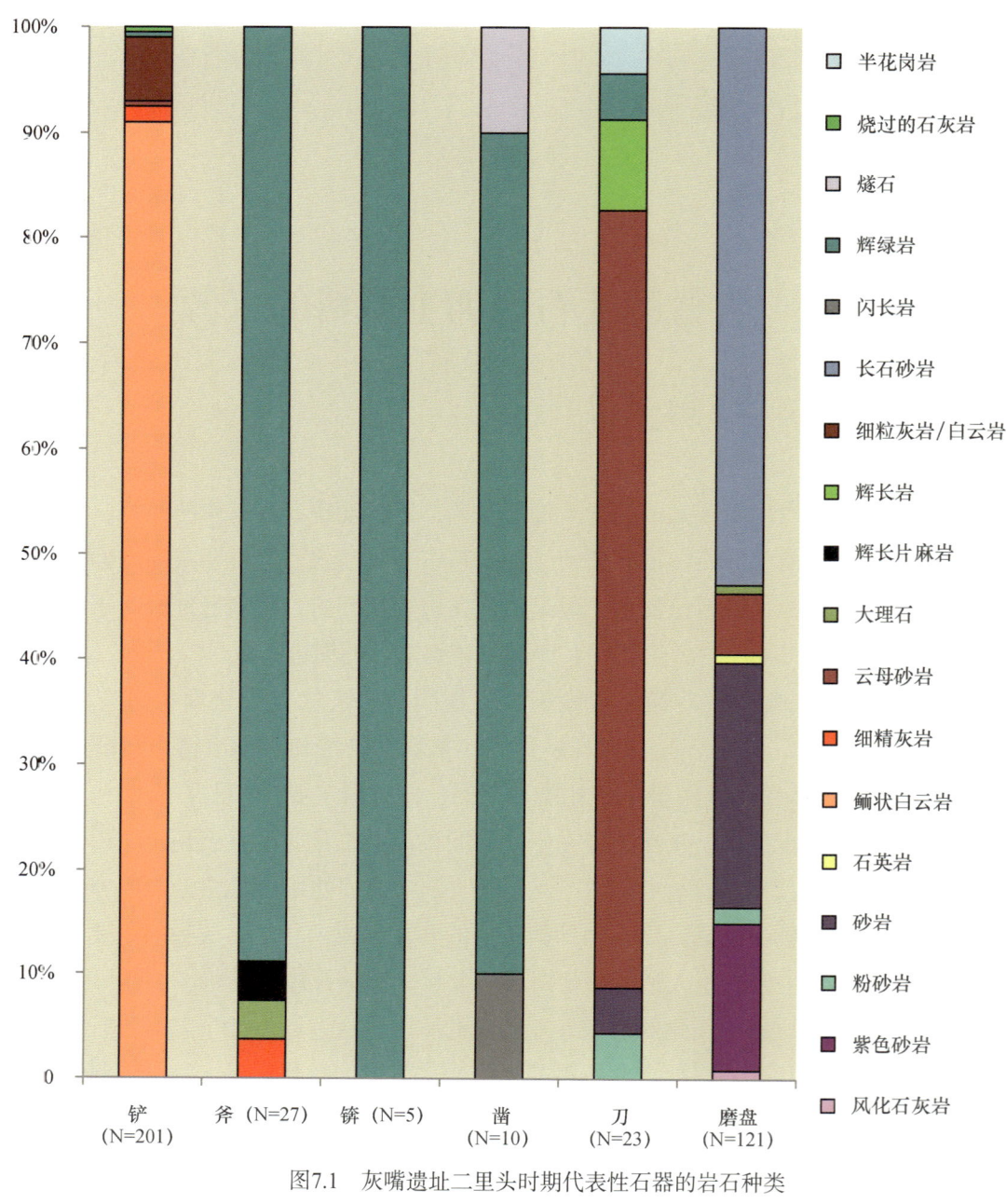

图7.1 灰嘴遗址二里头时期代表性石器的岩石种类
（包括1959年发掘品，2001年和2002年采集品）

嵩山北部寒武纪的地层可分为八个岩石组：早期和中期寒武纪主要以粉砂岩和石灰岩为主，在粉砂岩层中含有细砂岩夹层，例如：中寒武纪的张夏组。最晚期的岩石主要是碳酸盐矿物，包括了石灰岩和白云岩。

上寒武纪的凤山组组成了嵩山北麓，距离灰嘴遗址很近，由约150米厚的浅灰到深灰色的厚层大型细白云岩组成。凤山组最初的沉积为细颗粒、层压的石灰岩，有时候岩床为鲕粒灰岩。这些石灰岩大多白云岩化，其中包含了白云岩晶体形成了颗粒较大的粒状变晶结构，原有石灰岩颗粒的保存程度有所不同。大体上，白云岩化程度比较高且规整，保留了较少的石灰岩构造。凤山组顶部是部分硅化的地层，岩石表面中分散着风化形成的不规则形状的细石英（燧

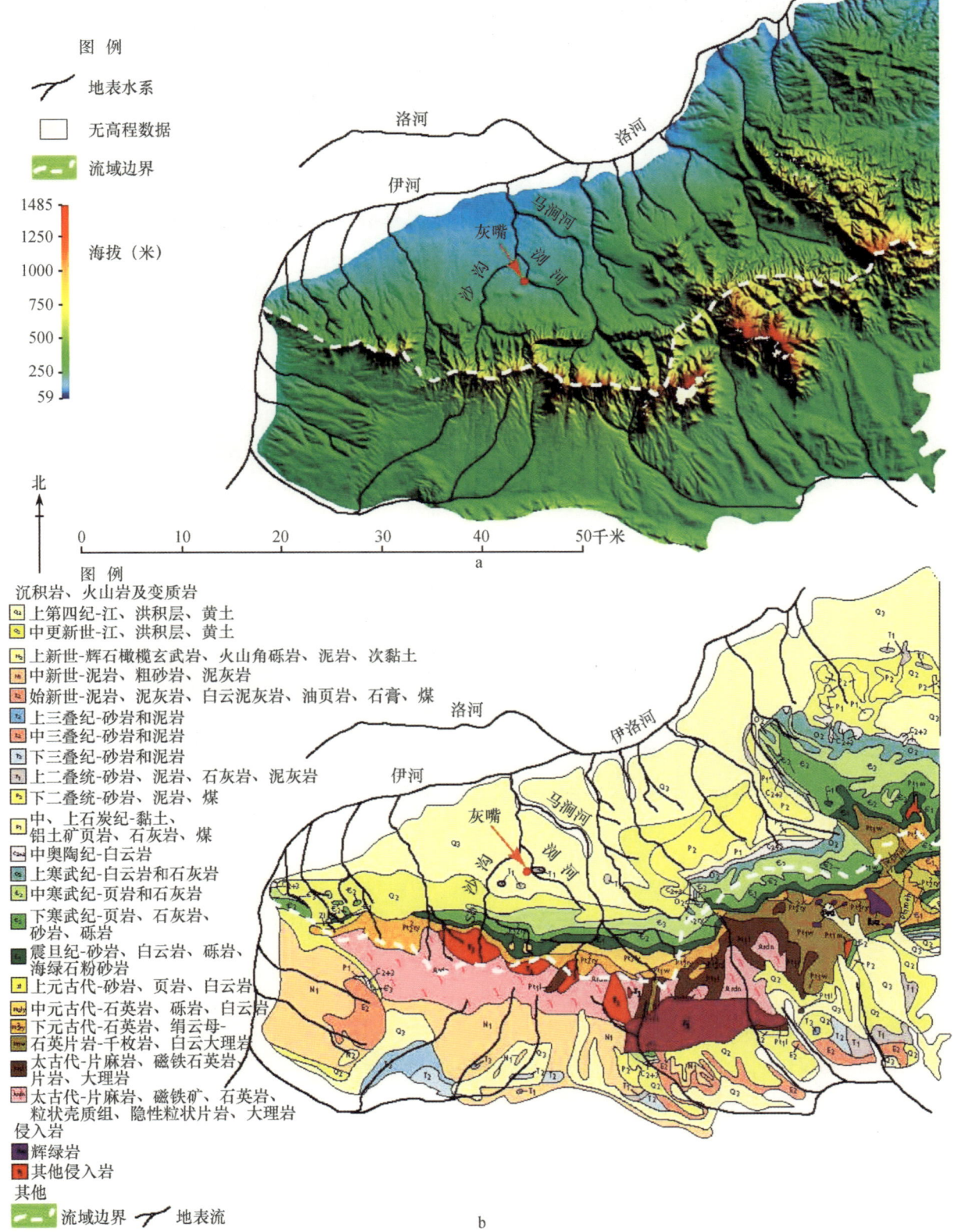

图7.2 灰嘴遗址附近地形及地质构造（河南省地矿局，1984年）
a.灰嘴遗址周边地形地势 b.灰嘴遗址所在区域（嵩山两侧）地质构造

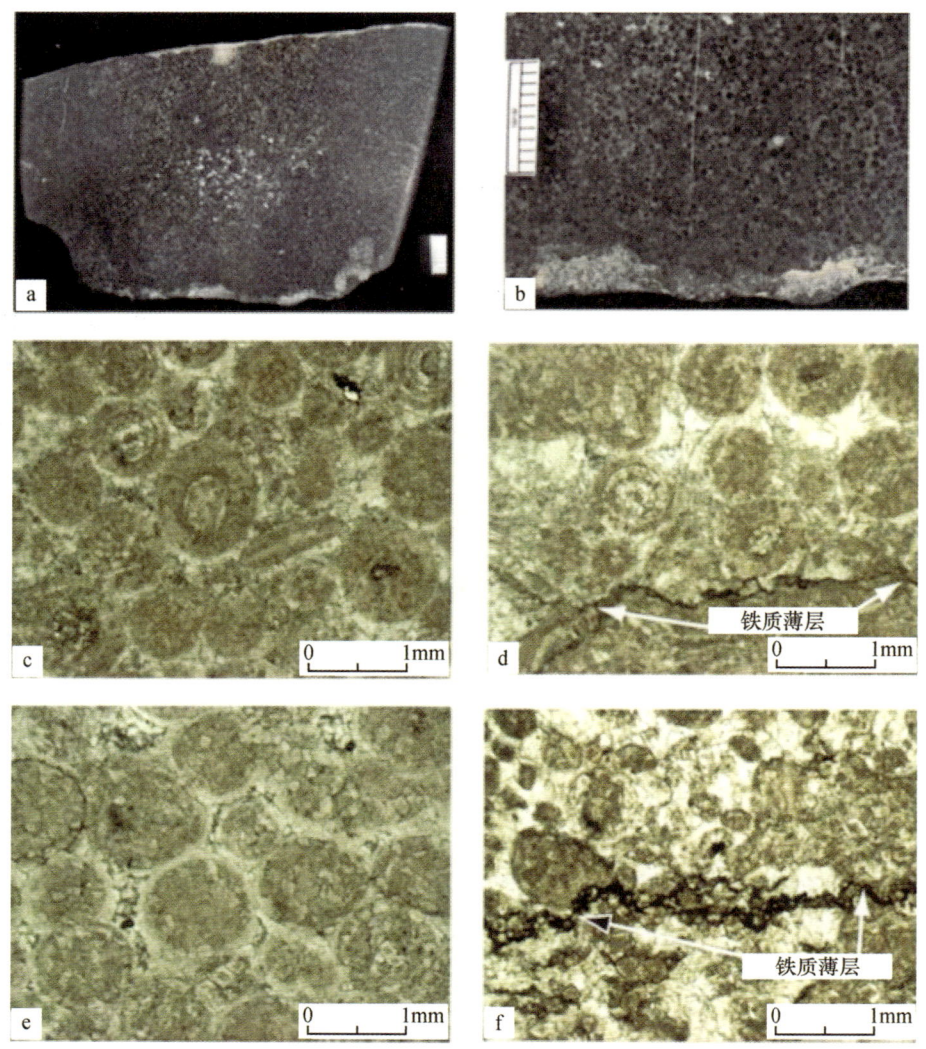

图7.3 石器显微照片

a、b. 鲕状白云岩石铲的抛光面；鲕粒就是灰白胶质内的深色圆点 c、d. 露头鲕状白云岩的显微照片；鲕粒大多是位于灰白胶质内的球体，有些是同心带状的；鲕粒和胶质被块状白云岩晶体所置换，有样本中间横穿一层含铁薄层 e、f. 白云岩石铲的显微照片；与露头的鲕状白云岩显示出很大的相似性，以及显示出轮廓鲜明的块状白云岩晶体置换了鲕粒岩

石）斑块。

在凤山组的下半部分清晰可见一块米色层叠的白云岩化的粉砂岩（泥灰岩），约10米厚，其下是15米厚的灰色鲕状白云岩（图7.4）；鲕粒很明显，很小，圆形，内部为深灰色（直径可达1毫米；图7.3 e，f）。这里还有两片薄床的鲕状白云岩，厚度小于1米，夹在粉砂岩的叠层内。鲕粒岩层整体小角度倾斜，呈现丘状地形，因米色粉砂岩而增强，后者遮盖住鲕粒地形。与位于自身上、下的白云岩相比，粉砂岩很容易风化，所以在山坡上形成了被草覆盖的台阶，缺少露头的岩石（图7.4，a、b）。粉砂岩下的鲕状白云岩总是出现在岩壳的下面，形成2～15米的高崖，岩床顶部则形成一处路面（图7.4，c），有时可作为山中的一处便捷的步行道。凤山组下是超过100米厚的上、中寒武纪的灰色鲕粒和细颗粒的大型石灰岩。嵩山东西向山脉最北端南侧的岩石露头靠近灰嘴遗址（图7.5）。

图7.4 地表鲕状白云岩和其叠压的粉砂岩的特性

a、b.在山体两侧，露头的鲕状白云岩形成小型崖面，而粉砂岩像草地一样，呈缓坡状 c.未经过开采的鲕状白云岩露头，在岩床一端呈现出自然路面的形态 d.历史上对鲕状白云岩的开采，请注意在开采面下碎石坡面 e.鲕状白云岩主要被开采矿床的岩面，叠压其上的粉砂岩包括很薄、分离的鲕状白云岩矿床；注意鲕状白云岩劈裂成薄石板的趋势 f.历史时期鲕状白云岩的开采；值得注意的是主要的矿床呈自然分层的状态

寒武纪地层之上是石炭纪的泥岩、铝质粉砂岩、石灰岩、砂岩和煤矿薄层，它们沉积于冲积扇、沼泽和湖泊环境下。随后是二叠纪的河流、沼泽和湖泊沉积，内含砂岩、泥岩和少量的煤。在灰嘴地区，由于被第四纪再沉积的黄土覆盖，石炭纪和二叠纪的沉积并不出露地表。

嵩山南部，寒武纪的地层覆盖在前寒武纪（太古代和原生代）基岩之上[4]（图7.2b）。基岩中是太古代的火成岩，及内含角闪片麻岩、石英岩、复片麻岩、片岩和大理石的变质程度高的复合岩体，内部有花岗岩和闪长岩侵入，伴随着少量伟晶岩。原生代的沉积包含了石英砂岩、砾岩、白云岩和粉砂岩，在变质作用下转变成为石英岩、白云大理岩、片岩、千枚岩和板岩。上原生代的花岗岩、花岗闪长岩和小浅层的辉绿岩侵入了原生代的地层。

在选取制作石器的原料之时，灰嘴的居民有多种石料可供选择。

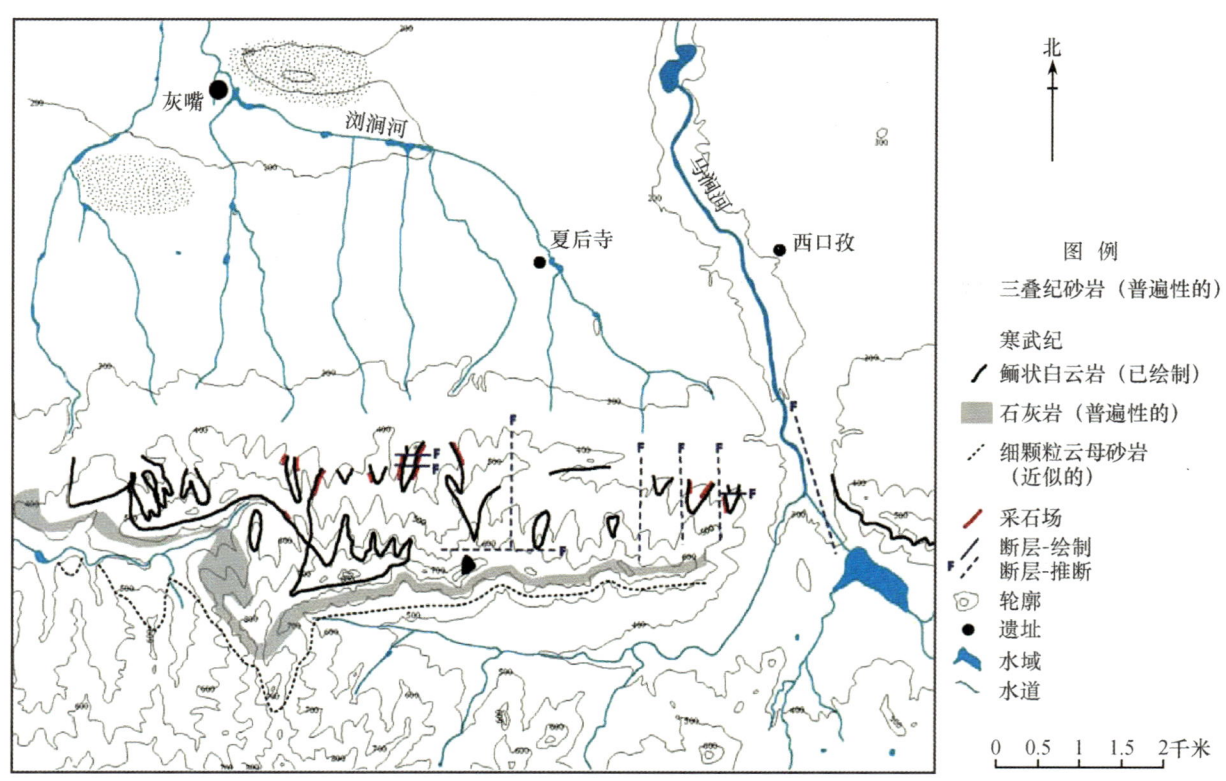

图7.5 灰嘴常见石器主要岩石来源分布
（根据现有研究绘制的鲕状白云岩分布图，仅显示现代化之前的采石场遗址）

第三节 灰嘴石器的岩石学

灰嘴遗址大约使用了25种不同种类的岩石，其中四类用量较大，它们是鲕状白云岩、辉绿岩、细云母砂岩和其他类型的砂岩（表7.1），另外，还使用了一定数量的细石灰岩和石灰岩。

表7.1 灰嘴遗址出土的所有石料中不同岩石类型的数量和比例

原料	成品工具数量	工具毛坯数量	石片（包括石核、石片和碎料）	合计
鲕状白云岩	22	321	15873	16216
细石灰岩/白云岩，石灰岩	22	66	383	471
其他砂岩	139	14	279	432
辉绿岩	82	45	38	165
云母细砂岩	59	24	60	143
泥岩	1	3	36	40
石灰/烧石灰石	1	2	36	39
石英	0	4	22	26
粉砂岩	6	1	15	22
石英岩	5	2	6	13
燧石	3	1	7	11
白云石/方解石晶体	0	0	10	10
大理石	4	2	1	7

续表

原料	成品工具数量	工具毛坯数量	石片（包括石核、石片和碎料）	合计
片岩	0	0	6	6
细晶岩	1	4	0	5
页岩	2	2	1	5
流纹岩	4	0	0	4
砾岩	0	0	2	2
闪长岩	2	0	0	2
闪长片麻岩	1	1	0	2
辉长岩	1	1	0	2
辉长岩片麻岩	2	0	0	2
玉?	0	2	0	2
泥岩	0	0	2	2
绿松石	2	0	0	2
硅质黏土岩	1	0	0	1
花岗片麻岩	0	1	0	1
辉岩	1	0	0	1
页岩/泥板岩	0	1	0	1
硅质岩	0	1	0	1
总计	361	498	16777	17636

一、鲕状白云岩

鲕状白云岩石铲表现出特有的细点状外观，在经过打磨的表面上特别明显（图7.3a，b）。当地人将有这种外观的岩石称为"小米石灰岩"，使用鲕状白云岩制作的石铲十分容易分辨。

嵩山北麓的凤山组中发现了鲕状白云岩的岩床。如上文所述，岩床叠压在一块米色层叠的泥灰岩下（图7.5），该岩床很可能是灰嘴遗址中鲕状白云岩石铲的石料来源，两者的石料几乎一模一样（比较图7.3c，d和图7.3e，f）。两者内部都包含了深灰色的、圆形、中到粗粒的鲕粒（直径为0.5～1毫米），位于白色胶质内部，经常呈同心式叠层。有些情况下，鲕粒的颜色更浅且包含了清晰的粗粒无定向晶体。小的鲕粒晶体（0.2毫米）可能同棘皮动物和三叶虫化石残片一同出现。鲕粒、化石和胶质原本由方解石组成，现在已经全部被中粒大小相对规整的大块白云石晶体置换，但鲕粒依旧可见。

灰嘴制作鲕状白云岩石铲的区域发现了一件使用米色泥灰岩制作的石刀毛坯，以及一些泥灰岩质地的小碎片和石片，证实了米色泥灰岩下的鲕状白云岩是制作石铲的原料。凤山组中鲕状白云岩的其他岩床一般含有细小、更致密的鲕粒，但缺乏上部的泥灰岩。

嵩山北部山脚下（图7.4d-f）的一些鲕状白云岩岩床已经经过开采，这些地点同灰嘴之间的距离大约是4千米。直到50年前，当地村民还在使用这些采石场的石材搭建房基，这些地点可能在更早的阶段已经开始使用。

有两个因素使得泥灰岩下的鲕状白云岩特别适合开采。首先，叠压在鲕状白云岩之上的泥灰岩比较松软，风化之后经常露出其下的鲕状白云岩岩床顶部，为石料的开采提供了一处开阔的路面；白云岩中自然生成的水平层状结构便于薄石板的开采。破裂面上经常出现一层很薄的红紫色的含铁层（图7.4d），这在鲕状白云岩石坯两面都能见到（图7.4e），说明人们使用白云岩的自然节理来控制石坯的厚度。

其次，鲕状白云岩的机械特性十分适合且易于制作石铲。它均匀的交织晶体结构使得岩石在加工时可以均匀且可预见性地破裂。此外，鲕状白云岩相对坚硬，在使用中不容易损坏[5]。白云岩是一种硬度较低的矿物（硬度3.5~4），使用坚硬的岩石可以容易地打磨出平滑的高抛光面以及锋利的刃缘，在挖掘黄土时也能有效地发挥作用。但它硬度较低，容易刮坏，一旦受到更硬的岩石的打击，白云岩工具的薄刃会很快碎裂。

综上，鲕状白云岩的易开采及功能特性解释了为何其在嵩山北麓露头岩石中占有量不到5%，但却成了90%以上的灰嘴石器的原料来源（表7.1）。

细白云岩，在嵩山北麓的储量十分丰富，是一小部分石铲的石料来源（图7.1）。颜色从灰色到奶油棕色不等，一般比较均匀，外观很结实，有些样本表现出特殊的长条状或者半圆形的点状物，说明这些矿物着床在原生石灰岩里。细白云岩含有交织白云岩晶体，因颗粒大小不同存在一些变体，它们在物理特性上与鲕状白云岩很相似。灰嘴遗址较少使用细白云岩制作石器的原因可能是由于这种岩石露头部分不是很平坦；相较细白云岩，鲕状白云岩更容易开采。在溯源方面，细白云岩制品没有特殊岩性，可能从嵩山北侧的任意地点开采。

二、辉绿岩

灰嘴遗址发现的辉绿岩一般为含有灰色到深绿色不等（偶尔呈棕红色）中粒结构的侵入火成岩。包含交织长条状的长度达0.6毫米的斜长石条纹，同时还有刺状的阳起石晶体及绿泥石颗粒、绿帘石及丰富的浑浊体，所有矿物都包含在细粒结构的黏土基质中。斜长石和阳起石的数量不定，在一些样本中，斜长石板条被拉长，形成鬣刺结构（明显的双晶结构）。辉绿岩的绿片岩化程度较低，这也是绿泥石和绿帘石存在的原因。

辉绿岩用于制作木器加工工具（斧、锛、凿；图7.1），这些工具对于刃缘的强度及抗外力的要求较高。1959年的发掘中在二里头时期的地层中发现了一件辉绿岩石斧。辉绿岩的硬度相对较高（硬度为5~6.5），交织晶体结构规整，因此这种岩石很坚硬，在使用中不容易破碎，非常适合制作磨制刃缘的工具。辉绿岩打磨平滑后也可以制作坚固锐利的刃缘，这种刃缘易于重新打磨锐利。

灰嘴的大多数辉绿岩工具石坯使用水蚀鹅卵石制作，鹅卵石的来源不确定。由于附近的浏涧河全部流经寒武纪碳酸岩和第三纪砂岩（图7.2b），因此河中的砾石中不见辉绿岩。这种岩石可能来自于距离灰嘴遗址西北2千米的沙沟中（图7.2a）。现有的研究表明，辉绿岩鹅卵石采自于灰嘴以西3.5千米的沙沟里的砾石岩床。沙沟的源头位于前寒武纪的基层，大概包括露头的辉绿岩，尽管在地图上尚无标识（图7.2b）。砾石也可能来自于伊河和（或）马涧河，这两条河分别位于灰嘴遗址以北10千米和以东6千米。河流的上游流经大面积的前寒武纪岩矿（图7.2b），那里很可能也包含露头的辉绿岩矿。

选择鹅卵石作为工具石坯的原料减少了加工过程中的消耗，因为不论是形状还是尺寸，天然鹅卵石和工具成品之间的差异都很小，仅需要将侧缘修整成方形作为刃部就可以使用[6]。选择鹅卵石作为原料是十分有效的，在河流的搬运过程中，内有裂隙的鹅卵石十分容易破碎，因此保留下来的完整鹅卵石内部基本不会出现严重的裂缝。

三、细云母砂岩

灰嘴的细云母砂岩呈绿色或棕色，颗粒均匀，包含的矿物以石英颗粒为主，也含有平行于岩床的少量特殊的白云母片。另外，它还含有同石英颗粒大小相近的方解石颗粒，褐色的海绿石圆球、氯化黑云母片及少量的管状化石碎片分散在其周围。由于石英和方解石颗粒的充分发育，砂岩固结良好。

云母砂岩很可能从嵩山东西向山脉最北边山峰南侧底部的中寒武纪张夏组中开采（图7.5）。该地区的张夏组基层包括15米厚的红棕色及绿色粉砂岩断面，岩床中有8层细云母砂岩夹层，厚度可达20厘米。砂岩岩床总是平行叠压并在叠层周围劈裂成薄片。这些细云母砂岩的剖面同灰嘴发现的很相似，灰嘴发现的一些云母砂岩质地的工具中也包含了红棕色和绿色的粉砂岩薄层。另外，灰嘴发现了未加工的细云母砂岩石板也指向该石材应为本地来源。

砂岩岩床在该地区的其他早、中寒武纪岩石中也有发现，但同灰嘴所使用的云母砂岩的矿物颗粒大小及内含化石的特征不符。张夏组的砂岩岩床距离灰嘴不到6千米（图7.5），但由于有一处山脊阻挡，从灰嘴到露出地表的砂岩之间的距离增加到8千米。

灰嘴使用云母砂岩生产薄的长方形或半圆形的石刀和石镰（图7.1）。工具毛坯的尺寸和厚薄已经十分合适，在制作过程中仅仅需要修整刃部使之锋利并具有斜角即可[7]。工具的器身通常会微微打磨或磨光以制作光滑的表面。制作磨盘时偶尔也会使用云母砂岩（图7.1）。

云母砂岩的两个特性使之特别适合制作刀和镰。其一，白云母片同岩床平行的构造使得云母砂岩可以容易地剥离成均匀的石板，其厚度同工具的要求匹配，这样一来，当在采石场将石料初步加工为石斧和石镰的毛坯时，就能更为高效，减少时间的消耗。其二，细粒均匀良好的构造及以石英（硬度可达7）矿物为主的成分保证了云母砂岩质地工具的锋利刃缘具有良好的耐切削能力[8]。

四、其他砂岩

除上述细云母石英砂岩之外，中粒和粗粒的其他种类的砂岩在灰嘴也有大量出现（表7.1）。这些砂岩主要由石英组成，粗粒砂岩同时也含有大量的风化长石颗粒。砂岩的颜色多变，有紫色、栗色、浅灰色或奶油色等。粗粒长石砂岩的颜色较浅，颗粒较小的砂岩中的含铁薄层及其内部石英颗粒上覆盖的铁质层使其常呈现出紫色或红色。

灰嘴是一处生产磨制石器工具的遗址，需要大量的磨料，而砂岩正是合适的选择[9]。砂岩磨料的形状为保存原料形状的岩石以及磨盘（图7.1）。粗粒砂岩很可能用于石器的初步打磨，细粒砂岩则用于器表磨平及锐化石器刃缘[10]。最后的抛光需要使用更细的介质，比如有机物或细粒黏土/粉砂；稀少的砂岩质地的磨盘可能也是一种磨光的工具（图7.1）。

灰嘴用于制作磨石的砂岩可能来自附近两座含有下三叠纪砂岩的小山（图7.2a，b）。小山西南距灰嘴约1.5千米，出产白色中粒到粗粒的长石砂岩。而小山的东北部，距离其中一个发掘地点不到500米的东北部的山丘主要由细粒紫色的铁质石英砂岩组成。地表出露的岩石都有采石的迹象，但大多数应该是近现代开采的。山坡处杂乱分布着一些大的砂岩岩石和鹅卵石，可以十分容易地运到灰嘴。灰嘴已经发现了与之尺寸相同的未加工的鹅卵石和岩石[11]。

五、细石灰岩和石灰

灰色细石灰岩经常被加工为工具，主要产品为石铲[12]，此外还发现了一件石斧（图7.1）。较之白云岩，硬度相近的细石灰岩的晶体颗粒更小且颗粒不太均匀，岩石内部的裂隙情况难以预测，因此不适合制作工具。

石灰岩的形状大多数不太规则，常表现为白色的粉末状外观，可用于生产石灰。石灰通过加热石灰岩而得，在加热过程中，石灰岩中的方解石（$CaCO_3$）会转变为石灰[氢氧化钙$Ca(OH)_2$]。氢氧化钙能很快从大气中吸收二氧化碳，并还原成呈白色、粉末状的石灰石，并在此过程中不断变硬，这是可以使用白压碎石灰的原因。压碎的石灰可以用来涂抹房屋地面，这是石灰在灰嘴使用的方式之一。

发掘中出土了大量白色白垩块（表7.1）。使用X射线衍射法对其进行矿物学分析，发现它们大多数由方解石构成，是加热石灰岩得到的石灰还原后生成的粉末状的石灰石。然而，其中一件是通过加热白云石得到的，它是含有方解石和水菱镁石的混合物。加热过程中，白云石[$CaMg(CO_3)_2$]变成氢氧化钙和氢氧化镁的混合物，后来又吸收二氧化碳形成了碳酸钙（方解石）和碳酸镁（水菱镁矿）。

石灰有时候使用不合格或损坏的石灰岩工具生产；一件石灰岩石铲出现了白色粉末状的外观，为上述观点提供了极好的证据（图7.1）。

嵩山东—西向山脊的最北端的南侧有很多石灰岩出露（图7.5）。遗址发现的石灰岩块和工具并无特殊之处，可能来自该区域的任何一个地点。如细云母砂岩（岩矿位置也在山脊的南侧，图7.5），从灰嘴到石灰岩出露地点的距离至少有8千米。尽管白云岩岩矿的距离更近，但石灰岩才是生产石灰的最佳材料，使用白云岩生产的石灰的品质较差。

六、细粒硅酸岩（燧石、硅质粉砂岩、流纹岩）

燧石、硅质粉砂岩和流纹岩，都属于晶体颗粒十分小的硅酸岩类，在灰嘴发现得不多，但却很重要（表7.1）。由于颗粒尺寸都极小，且缺乏特殊的特征，我们很难将三者区分开来（尽管流纹岩多为红色）。

灰嘴的燧石和硅化粉砂岩虽然在颜色上差别比较大，但大多数在灰色到黑色的范围内。燧石用于制作凿和箭头，而硅化粉砂岩则用于制作刀（图7.1）。有的硅化粉砂岩质地石刀的原始石料呈板状，意味着这些石料应该是从粉砂岩出露处开采。尽管燧石和粉砂岩在灰嘴附近都有发现，但是质量较差，不太可能是原料的来源。凤山组的上层处的燧石体积小且多孔隙，同灰嘴附近更新世沙砾岩床中的燧石鹅卵石一样。该区域的粉砂岩没有硅化，也不适合制作工具。

灰嘴的红色流纹岩多发现在仰韶时期的遗存中。有的岩石已经经过加工，其上有切割和锯的痕迹。遗物中有一件手镯残片，说明仰韶时期的灰嘴居民们也使用红色流纹岩制作装饰品，这些装饰品很可能是为居民自己所使用。红色流纹岩制作的成品仅在龙山和二里头时期发现，包括1件凿、1件抛光的直径为10毫米的球及1件箭头。红色流纹岩颗粒细小，多不含斑晶。同时还发现了少量灰色的熔灰流纹岩，其特征是岩体内部含有扁平的浮石碎片（浆屑）。

除了仰韶时期的流纹岩工具外，灰嘴遗址没有发现使用非常细粒的硅质岩石制作器物的证据。这很可能是因为这些岩石是外来材料，成品直接由其他地区传入，流纹岩在嵩山并未发现，它必然是外来的。

七、大　理　石

大理石在灰嘴遗址是一种罕见的原料（表7.1），用于生产包括1件斧和1件磨盘在内的小部分工具，另外，也用于制作如手镯（发现1件）和石板（发现1件）类的装饰用品。大理石在颜色（白、绿和棕色）和晶体颗粒大小（细粒至中粒）上比较多样；有的样品是页片状的。不同的大理石种类及仅发现成品的现象说明这些岩石是外来的，且来自不只一处地点。大理石在嵩山南部的前寒武纪地层中出现（图7.2）。

使用大理石制作的罕见器物应为贵族使用的或具有等级的器物。在新石器时期，大理石在中国中部地区既可以制作贵族用品[13]，也用于生产日常生活用品[14]。甘肃的师赵村和西山坪遗址分别发现了磨棒和研钵，年代为新石器时代和青铜时代早期[15]。

二里头的中心城市遗址使用大理石制作如镰和镞之类的生活用品[16]，但对于那些没有玉器和青铜器之类等级物品的地区中心遗址来说，大理石也可能用作贵族物品。在二里岗晚期（商代），人们喜欢使用白玉般的白色石头和大理石来制作贵族或仪式使用的工具，这可能与仅供贵族阶层使用的白陶的地位类似[17]。

八、其他变质岩（片麻岩、石英岩、片岩、板岩）

灰嘴也发现了一些其他的变质岩类的岩石，但数量较少（表7.1）。变质程度高的变质岩，如片麻岩和石英岩，在灰嘴仅以成品的形式出现。片麻岩用于制作石斧，而石英岩则用于制作石锤及磨棒（图7.1）。变质程度低的变质岩，如片岩和板岩，质地较软，不适合制作石器工具。发现了两件用板岩制作的石斧毛坯，但在制作完成之前就已经破裂了，这表明了原料的易碎特性。

低档和高档的变质岩在嵩山南部基岩都有发现，石英岩卵石在距离灰嘴5千米的马涧河中有发现。

九、石英

石英残片数量少，质地差，为乳白色脉状石英。这种岩石可能在南部的前寒武纪基底处出现。

十、中粒、粗粒的火成岩（闪长岩、半花岗岩、辉长岩、花岗岩）

极少量的火成岩（除流纹岩之外）被用于制作工具，工具种类包括凿（闪长岩）和刀（半花岗岩和辉长岩，图7.1）。所有材料都具有坚固的晶体结构，使用这些岩料制作的工具都具有锋利的可长期使用的刃缘，在使用过程中可以承受大的力度。

半花岗岩卵石在灰嘴发掘中的出现说明这种原料来自河流的沙砾之中，很可能产自马涧河。这条河流距离灰嘴不到5千米，流经的地区包括了出产半花岗岩的嵩山南部前寒武纪基底（图7.1b）。

十一、结晶方解石和白云石（包括石笋）

在石器中发现了几件白云石和方解石裂纹残片（表7.1）。这些矿物都有很好的菱形解理（3处裂面方向角为120°），因此大块晶体被打击后会碎裂为菱形的碎块。另外，有的方解石晶体呈现出典型的石笋构造，带有呈放射束状排列的颜色带和长条形的晶体。

方解石和白云石晶体可以从寒武纪碳酸盐岩脉中获得。石笋物质可能源自本地，在嵩山北部发现过小型的洞穴。

十二、绿松石和玉石？

灰嘴发现了两件绿松石珠和两件质量差的疑似玉器物，颜色为深棕和绿色。玉和绿松石用于制作高等级或贵族用品。灰嘴没有制作这些物品的证据，但在二里头的城市中心发现了绿松石作坊[18]。绿松石物品可能仅在二里头生产，然后再分配到不同地区的贵族阶层。二里头的贵族墓葬和灰坑中发现了玉器，比如玉珠，但是否开展玉器生产目前还不清楚[19]。二里头的绿松石和玉的来源还未找到。

第四节　决定灰嘴石料选择的若干因素

至少有三个主要因素决定了灰嘴的原料选择：距离石料的远近，原料的功能（机械）特性及开采的难易程度。

灰嘴使用的五种主要石料（鲕状白云岩、辉绿岩、细云母砂岩、其他砂岩和细石灰岩）都可以在距离遗址8千米以内的区域获得。可能最重要的因素是需要挨近砂岩岩矿。因为砂岩是灰嘴打磨石器时使用的主要材料，稳定且大量的砂岩资源十分重要。灰嘴距离砂岩山丘的距离为500米到1.5千米，这样可以获得丰富的磨料资源。

然而，距离原材料的远近并非是原料选择中的唯一决定因素。有证据表明原料专业化的存在，石器的功能组中很明显存在占有主要地位的石料（图7.1）。另外，嵩山很多可利用的石材在灰嘴中都没有使用。原料的特性对于原料的选择必然产生了影响。

原料性质可分为两种主要类别：功能（机械）和开采难易程度。灰嘴石器的所有功能性组群都同某一类特定的岩石相联系。木器工具（斧、锛和凿）要求原料可以抗外力并提供坚固的锋利刃部。辉绿岩坚固的特性使之适合制作这类石器，辉绿岩质地的木器工具通过抛光可以得到锋利高效的刃部，在使用过程中也易于重新打磨锋利。承担低强度工作的工具，如用于挖黄土的石铲，则可以使用硬度较低的石料，如鲕状白云石。这种原料可以轻易地打磨和抛光，使得制作过程相对较快捷及高效。鲕状白云岩不如辉绿岩那么坚硬牢固，但是在挖掘黄土方面，硬度并非是一个重要的考虑对象。

除了原料的功能（机械）特性之外，工具石坯获取的效率也是原料选择中的一个重要因素。选择同成品形状相近的原料，则可减少处理原料的时间和劳动，因此可以提高石器生产的整体效率。

灰嘴的岩石来自于地表出露的岩石及河流沙砾。鲕状白云岩（石铲原料）和细云母砂岩（石刀原料）经开采的原料都是顺着自然解理分开即得的薄石板，其厚度同最终产品的厚度已经十分相近。这对于鲕状白云岩来说特别重要。细白云岩虽然也有同鲕状白云岩相似的机械特性，且同灰嘴的距离更近，矿产也更丰富，但由于细白云岩的露头处没有形成一个易于石料开采的路面，因此在灰嘴中仅用于制作一小部分石铲。

辉绿岩从河卵石中获取，在尺寸和形状上同最后产品（斧、锛、凿）很接近，不需要太多的加工。另外，河卵石有很好的内部硬度，因为内部有裂隙的河卵石在河流搬运过程中会碎裂开，很难保存完整。

除了主要的原料种类外，灰嘴较少使用其他岩石，且大多仅发现成品。这些岩石可能是从其他生产石器的遗址"进口"的产品；也可能是出于质量和价值考量的通过有针对性的采购获得，或者是偶然获得的原料进行加工实验留下。

综上所述，灰嘴遗址的原料选择反映了距离原料的远近、功能特性及岩石开采是否适用于工具制造等因素。灰嘴石器的制造者基于以上因素对于原料选择做出了有效的决策。

致谢：我们十分感谢伊洛考古队的各位成员：刘莉、陈星灿、魏鸣、李昊娥、艾琳·罗森、李永强、谢礼晔、魏兴涛、王法成、王宏章、杨军锋、贝喜安、杰弗里·休伊特、利兹·基尔帕特里克及查尔斯·哈特利（贺成砺）。我们还要特别感谢许国伟和卡梅伦·凯恩斯提供的地理地质信息，感谢这方面的专家戴尔·欧文先生为我们拍摄了白云岩石铲的照片。该项目得到了澳大利亚研究理事会的发现项目资助（DP0450025）。

注　释

[1] Liu L, Chen X C, Lee Y K, et al. Settlement Patterns and Development of Social Complexity in the Yiluo Region, North China. Journal of Field Archaeology, 2002-2004. 29(1-2): 75-100; Liu L, Chen X C. Non-state Crafts in the Early Chinese State: An Archaeological View from the Erlitou Hinterland. Indo-Pacific Prehistory Association Bulletin, 2007, (27): 93-102.

[2] Liu L, Chen X C. State Formation in Early China. London: Duckworth, 2003; Liu L. Urbanization in China: Erlitou and Its hinterland//Storey G. Urbanism in the Preindustrial World: Cross-Cultural Approaches. Tuscaloosa: University of Alabama Press, 2006: 161-189.

[3] Ford A. Stone Tool Production-Distribution Systems during the Early Bronze Age at Huizui, China. Unpublished Master's Thesis, Melbourne: La Trobe University, 2007; Webb J, Ford A, Gorton J. Influences on Selection of Lithic Raw Material Sources at Huizui, A Neolithic/Early Bronze Age site in Northern China. Indo-Pacific Prehistory Association Bulletin, 2007, (27): 76-86.

[4] Bureau of Geology and Mineral Resources of Henan Province. Regional Geology of Henan Province. Beijing: Geological Publishing House, 1984; Meyerhoff A A, Kamen-Kaye M, Chen C, et al. China: Stratigraphy, Paleogeography and Tectonics. Dordrecht: Kluwer Academic Publishers, 1991.

[5] Garber J. Archaeology at Cerros, Belize, Central America (Volume 2). Dallas: Southern Methodist University Press, 1989: 15.

[6] Ford A. States and Stones: Ground Stone Tool Production at Huizui, China. Honours dissertation, Archaeology Program, Melbourne: La Trobe University, 2001: 58; Ford A. Ground Stone Tool Production at Huizui, China: An Analysis of a Manufacturing Site in the Yiluo River Basin. Indo-Pacific Prehistory Association Bulletin, 2004, (24): 73.

[7] Ford A. States and Stones: Ground Stone Tool Production at Huizui, China. Honours dissertation, Archaeology Program, Melbourne: La Trobe University, 2001: 60.

[8] 谢礼晔：《微痕分析在磨制石器功能研究中的初步尝试——二里头遗址石斧和石刀的微痕分析》，中国社会科学院研究生论文，2005年；《二里头遗址石斧和石刀的微痕分析——微痕分析在磨制石器功能研究中的初

步尝试》，《中国早期青铜文化——二里头文化研究专题》，科学出版社，2008年。

[9] Ford A. States and Stones: Ground Stone Tool Production at Huizui, China. Honours dissertation, Archaeology Program, Melbourne: La Trobe University, 2001; Ford A. Ground Stone Tool Production at Huizui, China: An Analysis of a Manufacturing Site in the Yiluo River Basin. Indo-Pacific Prehistory Association Bulletin, 2004, 24: 71-78; Ford A. Stone Tool Production-Distribution Systems during the Early Bronze Age at Huizui, China. Unpublished Master's Thesis, Melbourne: La Trobe University, 2007.

[10] Owen D. When to call a Spade a Spade: An Exercise in Experimental Archaeology on an Ancient Chinese Stone Tool. B.A. Honours thesis, Archaeology Program, Melbourne: La Trobe University, 2006.

[11] Ford A. States and Stones: Ground Stone Tool Production at Huizui, China. Honours dissertation, Archaeology Program, Melbourne: La Trobe University, 2001: 45.

[12] Ford A. Stone Tool Production-Distribution Systems during the Early Bronze Age at Huizui, China. Unpublished Master's Thesis, Melbourne: La Trobe University, 2007.

[13] Liu L. Ancestor Worship: An Archaeological Investigation of Ritual Activities in Neolithic North China. Journal of East Asian Archaeology, 2000, (2): 149.

[14] 中国社会科学院考古研究所：《师赵村与西山坪》，中国大百科全书出版社，1999年。

[15] 中国社会科学院考古研究所：《师赵村与西山坪》，中国大百科全书出版社，1999年。

[16] 中国社会科学院考古研究所：《偃师二里头——1959年～1979年考古发掘报告》，中国大百科全书出版社，1999年，第401页。

[17] Yang M L. A Study of the Jade Ge-Dagger. The Journal of Chinese Jade. San Francisco: S. Bernstein & Co., 1996: 64-113.

[18] Liu L, Xu H. Rethinking Erlitou: Legend, History and Chinese Archaeology. Antiquity, 2007, 81: 886-901.

[19] Childs-Johnson E. Symbolic Jades of the Erlitou Period: A Xia Royal Tradition. Archives of Asian Art, 1995, (48): 64.

第八章　中国早期国家非国有手工业：二里头畿内的考古学分析[①]

第一节　国有手工业与非国有手工业

自从柴尔德首次提出手工业专业化是城市革命的重要组成部分之后[1]，很多研究者尝试建立手工业专业化同文明/国家的出现之间的联系[2]。考古学家提出了三种通用模式来描述不同形式的手工业专业化：

（1）贵族控制下的附属的专业化，主要生产具有地位象征意义的权威物；

（2）没有贵族参与的独立的专业化，主要生产普通民众所需的日常用品；

（3）身份是贵族的专业手工匠，为高等级贵族生产权威物品[3]。

对于手工业专业化的绝大部分研究集中在第一和第三种，其目的是为了强调在社会政治进程中的贵族行为，很少有学者以社会变化进程中独立的非贵族手工业生产的政治功能为研究目标[4]。这种情况在中国考古学界也存在，大部分的研究同国家控制的手工业有关，例如二里头政治中心、郑州和安阳的青铜礼器[5]。为了全面地了解中国早期国家的形成过程，这种局面需要改变。

有人提出，中国早期国家可以被描述为疆域国家，这些国家往往表现出特殊的手工业生产特征，特别是在涉及国家的权威物方面[6]。根据炊格尔的理论，疆域国家更倾向于拥有两个层次的手工业生产模式：其一，贵族手工作坊，在宫殿区或附近生产具有象征意义的特殊产品，同时，宫殿区周围和低等级中心聚落的手工匠人生产国家所需次一级贵族物品；其二，农民使用本地资源生产日常用品以满足自己和邻居所需，但手工业生产仅是农民的副业而已[7]。上述假设还需进一步论证。

对于早期中国的考古学研究主要集中于大型的城市中心，因为这些地区更容易识别出社会高度分层的证据。这些研究多倾向于揭示城市中高等级贵族的主要物质遗存，忽略与前者同样重要的低等级贵族和普通人的活动。与前文所言研究方法不同，我们的考古研究项目将以伊洛地区的灰嘴遗址为研究对象，获得以二里头为中心的最早国家腹地社会政治进程的信息。

---

① 本章由刘莉、陈星灿、李宝平执笔，邓玲玲翻译。

以伊洛平原的区域性调查为基础，二里头核心地区的聚落形态展现出高度集中的政治体系[8]，以及可以通过二里头遗址出土物质遗存表现出的分层社会[9]。灰嘴遗址是仰韶和龙山时期（c. 5000-2000 BC）的一个区域中心，在公元前2千纪的早段成为二里头国家的次级中心，其后一直到东周时期此处才重新有聚落出现。灰嘴遗址是石器工具的生产地，主要产品是白云岩质地的石铲，石铲在附近区域皆有流通[10]。我们认为灰嘴遗址有独特的研究价值，可以在三个方面提供重要的参考信息：其一，研究一个遗址中出现的长时段的社会政治变化；其二，研究本区域内聚落之间的关系；其三，研究日用品生产和流通中的手工业专业化程度。

本研究具有若干特殊性，这些特殊性长期被中国考古学家所忽视。本研究的对象包含日用品和权威物，它们的生产地区远离政治中心，主要消费群体是普通人或者低级贵族。灰嘴遗址的情况同政治中心高等级权威物品的生产形成了鲜明的对比，提供了一个探究二里头国家政治经济的新视角。

为了解二里头国家的区域社会形态，本章将重点介绍伊洛地区石铲和白陶的生产和分配，证明从事非国有手工业生产的匠人在早期国家的社会政治结构中发挥了重要的作用。

第二节　灰嘴遗址的石器作坊

灰嘴遗址位于河南省偃师市灰嘴村的东部和西北部。现存遗址被一条未知年代的大冲沟分为东、西两部分，我们将其称为灰嘴东区和灰嘴西区（图8.1）。仰韶和龙山晚期的居民最初在灰嘴东区生活；到了二里头时期，人们的居住区域从东区扩展到西区；东周时期聚落面积又收缩到灰嘴东区。整个遗址的面积为25万平方米，不同文化阶段遗址的面积有所不同。土壤的侵蚀和现代密集的农业活动彻底改变了灰嘴的地表景观，特别是地表的高程。为了将原有的坡地变为适于农耕的梯田，超过1米厚的表土在近几十年中被陆续移走，许多考古遗存遭到破坏。现在保留的遗址区域，特别是仰韶和龙山时期的遗迹，较之原有面积缩小了很多。东周时期的遗存仅有少部分被发现，其中包括水井和墓葬，大部分的周代遗存被自然或人类活动所破坏[11]。

灰嘴遗址在20世纪50年代由河南考古工作者首次发掘，2002~2006年伊洛河流域联合考古队在此继续发掘，总发掘面积为665平方米。探方分布于灰嘴东、西两区，地层深度近4米，揭露了仰韶、龙山至二里头时期的遗存。20世纪50年代，考古工作者根据地表可见的大量毛坯，认为灰嘴是一处石器制作点。为了确认灰嘴手工业生产的发展及专业化水平，我们在田野工作中采用了一系列方法，包括密集调查法、洛阳铲探查法和田野发掘法。

仰韶期遗存分布区现存6万平方米（图8.1），同原本的聚落面积大体相近，较之后段遗存保存完整。我们研究的初步成果表明，仰韶期发现的石片很少，使用多种岩石制作，其中没有一种岩石特别占优势。这说明，灰嘴的仰韶人群使用周围可用的石料生产石器，且主要是为了满足自身的使用需要。

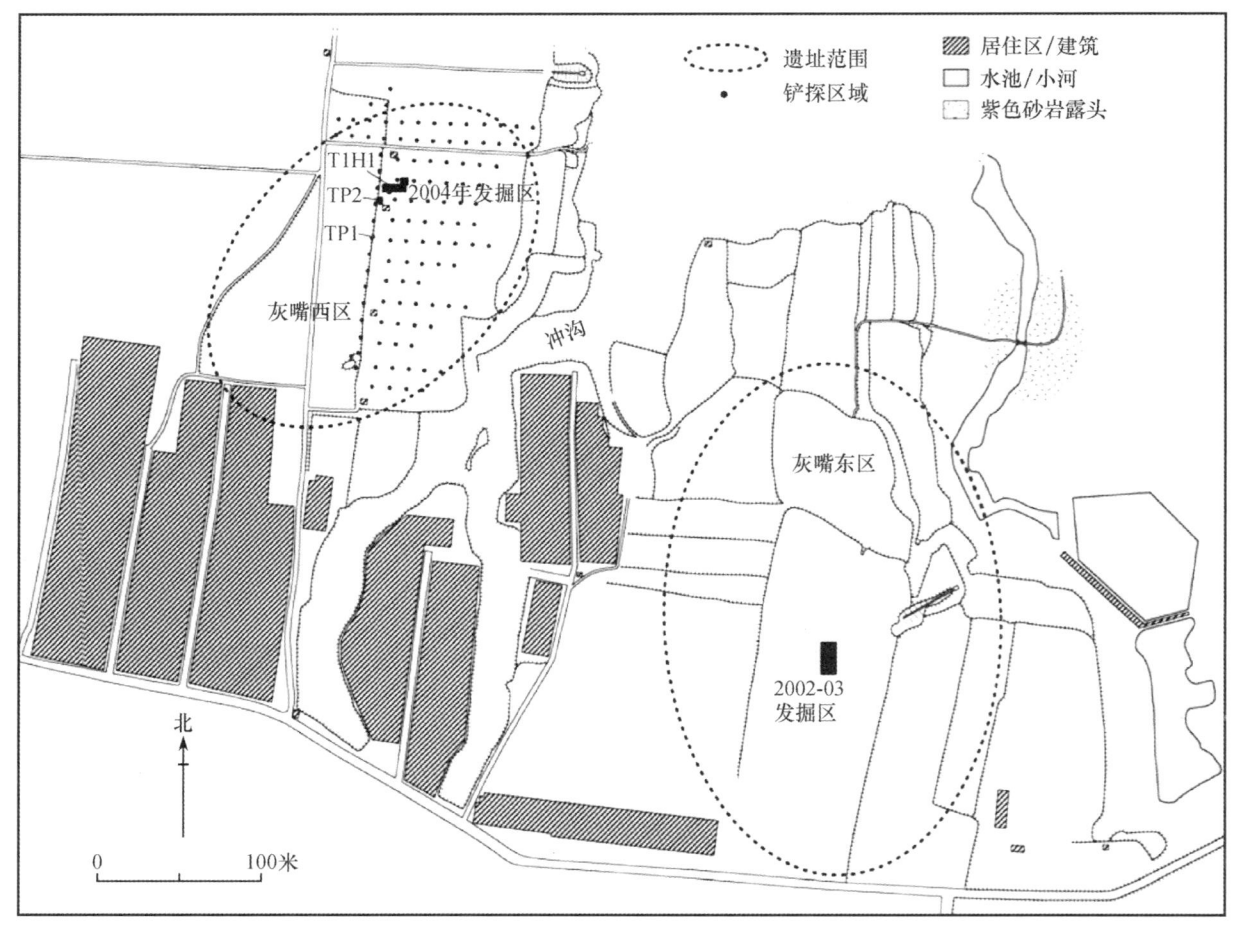

图8.1 灰嘴遗址发掘地点（2002—2004年）

龙山时期遗存的分布区现存3万平方米，遗存分布区域内发现了大量的石片和毛坯，有的高度集中出土于特定的区域。以灰坑H100和H101为例，灰坑中出土了大量的毛坯和数千件石片，石片尺寸很小，大多数长度在5毫米以下。毛坯和石片的质地主要是白云岩，毛坯的形状和石片的材质同发现的石铲很符合。灰坑中的石器遗物很可能是附近石器作坊生产过程中的废弃物。这些灰坑中还发现了很多日常废弃物，如动物骨骼、陶器碎片、植物遗存和工具。灰坑附近发现了水井、房屋和墓葬，说明石器作坊分布在居住区内部，很可能是以家庭为单位进行生产。很明显，从龙山晚期开始，灰嘴成了一个石器的生产地点，主要生产白云岩的石铲。遗憾的是，我们无法确认石器生产区域的原始面积，但通过石器遗存在龙山时期遗迹上的分布可以看出，手工业专业化很可能是由社会群体中大部分人实施的。

二里头阶段，石器生产继续开展，生产区域扩大到灰嘴东、西两区（图8.1）。上文提到，灰嘴东区大多数二里头时期的遗存已经被破坏了，我们无法估计遗址的原始面积。由于遗址的上层堆积为现代的农业活动所破坏，现在地表调查过程中采集的石制品很可能来自被扰动的龙山及二里头时期的遗存。但是，这也不能帮助我们确定灰嘴东区遗址的原始区域范围。灰嘴西区的二里头遗存扰动较少，我们估计其分布范围约有3万平方米。在此区域内，探孔、梯田断面和探沟中普遍发现了石片和毛坯，这说明石器生产在灰嘴西区二里头时期的遗存分布范围内广泛存在。

灰嘴人群使用不同的原材料生产不同种类的石器工具，主要包括白云岩质的铲，辉绿岩质的斧、锛、凿，云母细砂岩质的刀和镰及砂岩质的磨盘和砺石。2000年的调查在灰嘴西区地表采集了94件毛坯和半成品，其中白云岩占绝大多数，达78%[12]（图8.2A）。根据对2004年发掘的灰坑T1H1（2-4单位）中出土的111件浮选重样标本中石制品的分析，白云岩石片的重量高达92%（图8.2B）。在毛坯和石片中出现如此高比例的白云岩，同1959年灰嘴发掘的二里头时期石质工具出土情况形成了鲜明的对比。1959年发现的石铲（大多数为鲕状白云岩）仅仅占石器总数的22%（图8.2C）。

灰嘴西区同东区的情况很相似，发掘的生活遗迹（如房屋、水井、墓葬和灰坑）中出土了大量的动物骨骼、陶片和炭化植物遗存及石片和毛坯。我们注意到白云岩、砂岩毛坯、石片高度集中于三个地点。根据它们的埋藏形式，地点一（TP1）是石匠的工作场所；地点二（TP2）是一处靠近房屋墙壁的垃圾坑；地点三（T1H1）也是一处垃圾坑，可能位于院子中。TP1和TP2皆属于二里头文化二期，二者间距25米，可能对应的是两处作坊之间的距离（图8.1）。

以上所言二里头时期遗存情况同龙山时期十分相似，这说明二里头时期的石器生产持续了龙山时期的模式：即以家庭为单位进行；手工业专业化在群体内部广泛存在；主要的产品是白云岩石铲；石铲不仅仅供应本地使用，也用于贸易和物品交换。

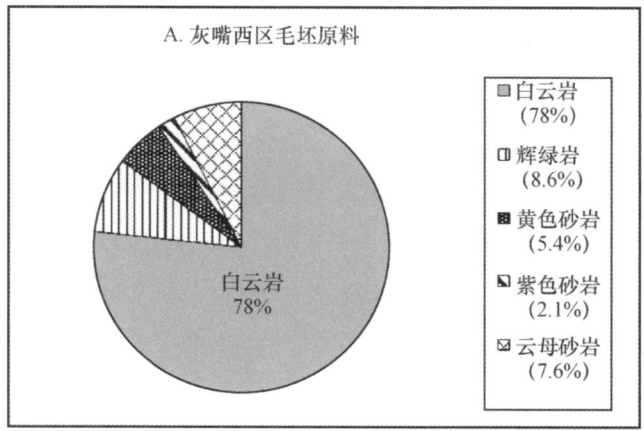

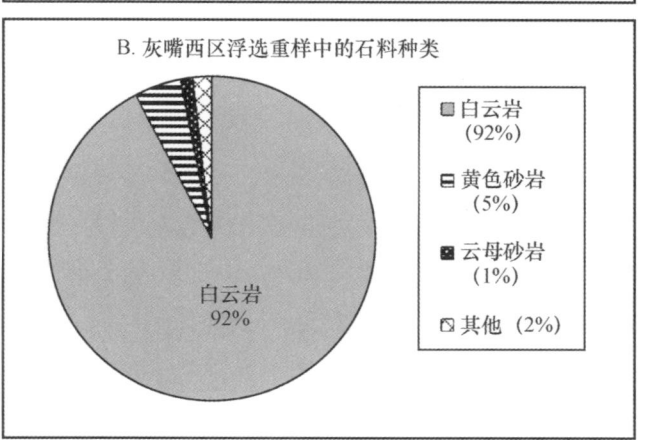

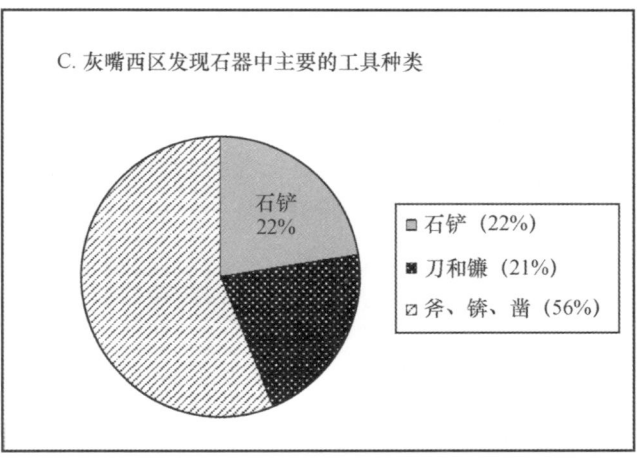

图8.2 白云岩毛坯、浮选重样和白云岩石铲在工具中的比例
A. 地表调查采集白云岩毛坯的比例（总数：94） B. 111件浮选重样中白云岩石片的比例（总重量：6654.8克） C. 灰嘴遗址出土的二里头时期工具中白云岩石铲的比例（总数量：72）

第三节　石器原料的获取

灰嘴遗址制作石器的三种原料为鲕状白云岩、白云岩和石灰岩，其中，鲕状白云岩的使用最多。灰嘴的大部分毛坯和半成品石铲都呈长方形，长10~40厘米，宽6~15厘米，厚2~4厘米。原料从嵩山白云岩露天矿获得，此地南距灰嘴约4~5千米。鲕状白云岩的露出部分呈薄层构造，沿山脉的北麓分布[13]。在硬度方面，白云岩并非制作石质工具的好材料。但是，这种石料即使在石器时代的技术条件下（没有金属工具和爆破技术）也十分容易开采。另外，白云岩露出部分的薄层构造让人们可以更容易获得适于制作薄、长石铲的厚度适中的石片。因此当时的人们选择白云岩作为制作石铲的原料是十分合理的。

在我们调查的区域，白云岩料的分布范围东西横跨12千米，在山脉的山脚下分布着4个二里头时期的遗址，它们是寨湾、灰嘴、夏后寺和西口孜。这些遗址相互之间距离2.5~4.5千米左右，同附近的白云岩矿的距离相近，在3~5千米左右（图8.3）。我们的调查团队已经从4个遗址中发现了相同器形的白云岩毛坯。在这4个遗址中，仅灰嘴遗址发现有从龙山时期一直延续到二里头时期的工具制造的明确证据。寨湾遗址的使用时间同灰嘴遗址相似，可能也从龙山至二里头时期一直生产石铲。如果我们的调查数据是可靠的，石铲生产中心的数量从龙山时期的2处提升至二里头时期的4处，区域的石铲产量得到了很大的提高。此结论在今后还需继续验证。

伊洛盆地地域分布广大，很多遗址并不靠近石料资源，延伸12千米的鲕状白云岩也并非随处可得的原材料。由于我们还没有对整个嵩山北麓进行调查，很难估计具体有多少个生产石质工具的遗址。鲕状白云岩矿层在嵩山北麓的早寒武纪沉积中出现，它的西部在寨湾西南几千米

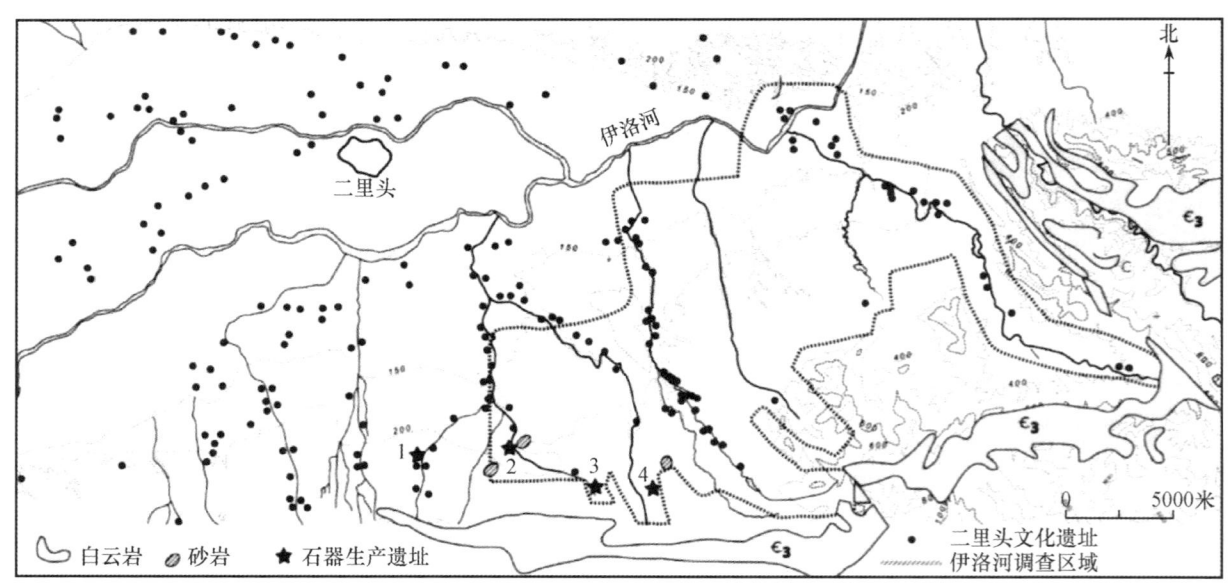

图8.3　二里头文化遗址在伊洛区域的分布
1.寨湾　2.灰嘴　3.夏后寺　4.西口孜

处结束，东部延伸数千米进入嵩山山脉。然而，并不是所有的鲕状白云岩矿都能够成为石质工具的原料，吸引开采者定居，还有很多其他的因素决定着一个地点能否成为石质工具的生产中心。

考虑到石匠大多数是由农民兼职承担，石料很重且难以远距离运输，一个稳定的石器生产团体应该是：① 在石匠聚落的附近拥有一定规模的农田以供应足够的农产品；② 同石料产地的距离需要控制在1天来回的路程之内；③ 靠近制作砺石所需的砂岩矿产。在伊洛盆地的系统区域调查中[14]，我们并没有发现多少适合石器生产的遗址。但我们计划今后注意寻找这类地点。

我们的调查发现了一些关于原料开采过程的有趣现象。西口孜遗址南面不到100米的山麓上发现了一个古采石场，遗址面积为1500平方米，名为九龙角水库西（Y223），遗址发现了石球、1件非本地材质的石锤和很多鲕状白云岩石片。这里应该是石匠在获得石材后对石材进行粗加工的地点。在上文提到的4个石铲制作遗址和鲕状白云岩矿之间没有发现其他的遗址，说明岩矿资源直接由生产团体拥有。居址同岩矿间3~5千米的距离十分适合工匠在一天之内完成对原料获取的程序。获取工作内容包括：走到岩石矿区，开采石料，初步打制及搬运粗坯回家。我们在灰嘴遗址的发掘仅发现少数大型的石片[15]，这进一步证实了石料的初步打制在采石场附近已经完成的假设，当然，该假设在今后需进一步验证。

生产群体可以直接从山体获得原料，说明这些群体对于岩石出露区域已经形成了控制。4个石铲生产聚落间等距离的分布也说明他们之间存在着一种竞争关系。灰嘴可能同周围遗址间存在对原料控制和产品贸易上的竞争。这种假设需要通过对其余3个遗址的发掘得到验证，看同样的生产过程是否在其他3个遗址中也存在。

一、鲕状白云岩石铲的分配

灰嘴64%的石铲使用鲕状白云岩制作，其余36%由细白云岩、粉砂岩和云母细砂岩和细砂岩制作。鲕状白云岩是主要原料，但并非唯一的原料。与之相对应，石器集中区域，比如04T1H1，发现的主要石质工具都是由鲕状白云岩制作的，这说明鲕状白云岩是专门用于制作"出口石铲"的专用原料。这种现象有助于我们辨识生产灰嘴石铲的地区分布情况。

遗憾的是，由于考古报告中很少报道制作普通工具的石料，因此尽管已知工具的制作地点，也很难追踪有关石制品的分布范围。为了调查鲕状白云岩石铲的分布范围，我们测试了7个二里头时期遗址的石器，包括灰嘴在内，在伊洛和郑州地区，东西分布约200千米（图8.1）。

若能将所有遗址的鲕状白云岩石铲在石器中的比例进行分析，则可观察石质工具群体中原料的比例同生产中心的距离之间的关系。但是由于无法获取所有遗址完整的石制品信息，我们的采样不够系统，这阻碍了进一步的数据统计分析工作。

鲕状白云岩石铲在距离灰嘴遗址100千米的二里头文化时期遗址——郑窑遗址中也有发现，该遗址位于伊洛盆地的西部（图8.4）。鲕状白云岩质地的石铲在二里头遗址发现的石铲中仅占24%，相较于其他遗址比例较低（表8.1）。这些数据可能说明二里头城市人口成分的多元性，实用的工具也来自不同地区。另一种解释为，二里头遗址作为当时的政治和经济中心，可能从周围拥有制作石铲原料的地区获得进贡的物品和劳动力。二里头遗址的工具群中，一小部分应该是从灰嘴遗址获得的。

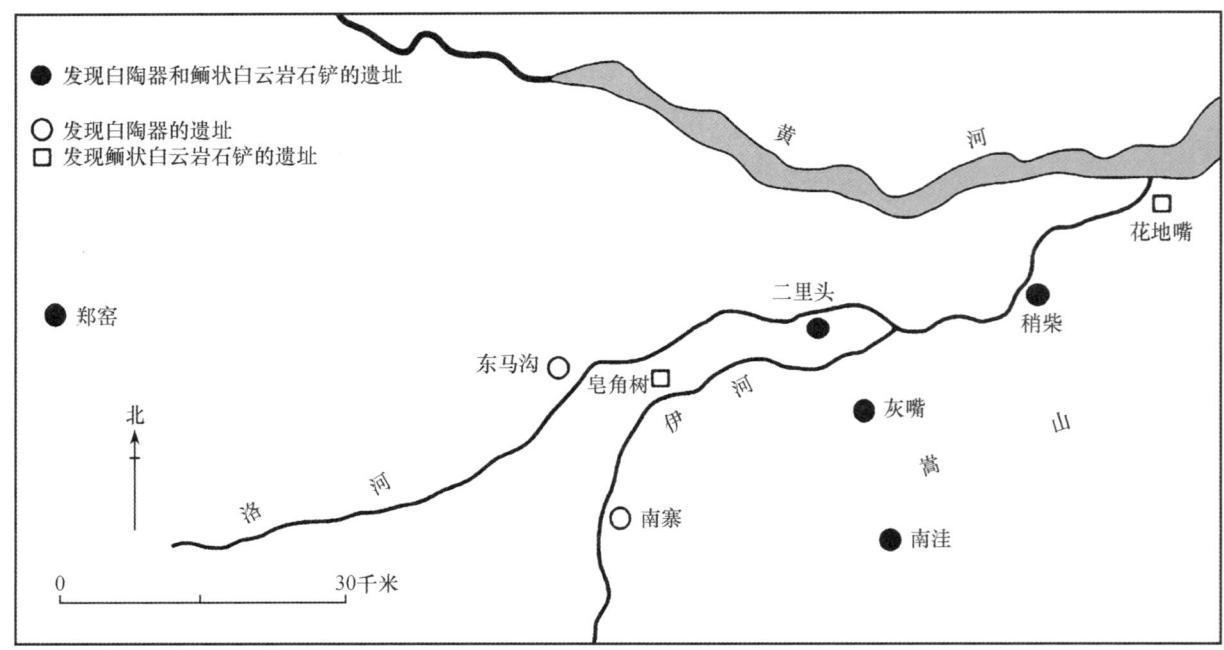

图8.4　伊洛地区发现白陶和鲕状白云岩石铲的二里头文化遗址的地理位置

鲕状白云岩石铲和其他物资在区域流通网络中的分配是一个十分复杂的问题，为了了解贸易模式的更多信息，原料和人工制品的微量元素分析十分必要。

表8.1　伊洛和郑州地区8个二里头文化遗址的白云岩制品统计表

遗址	所有材质石铲的数量	鲕状灰岩石铲的数量（鲕状灰岩在全部材质中比例）	距离灰嘴遗址距离	资料来源
偃师灰嘴	11	7（64%）		河南省文物考古研究所，1990
偃师二里头	41	10（24%）	西北15千米	谢礼晔整理数据
巩义稍柴*	23	5（22%）	东北20千米	河南省文物考古研究所，1993
巩义花地嘴	14	2（14%）	东北35千米	John Webb，2006
洛阳皂角树	检测6（报导16）	6（100%）	西30千米	John Webb，2006
渑池郑窑	24	3（12.5%）	西100千米	河南省文物考古研究所，1987
登封南洼	检测9（总数不详）	5（56%）	嵩山南侧20千米	John Webb，2006
郑州洛达庙	检测34（报导47）	0（0%）	嵩山东缘70千米	河南省文物考古研究所，1989

*稍柴石铲包括了二里头和二里岗时期，根据现有材料，两个时期的石铲尚无法区分开。

二、白陶的生产和分配

灰嘴西区的居住区内发现了白陶片，它是白陶权威物存在的证据。在二里头时期，白陶是一种酒礼器，是等级的象征，经常在二里头的高等级墓葬或次级中心的较低等级贵族墓葬中发现。河南西部至少有7个二里头文化的遗址发现了白陶片，它们是：二里头、灰嘴、巩义稍柴、伊川南寨、登封南洼、洛阳东马沟和渑池郑窑。这些遗址属于二里头国家的一级或二级中心，分布在距离二里头遗址100千米的范围内（图8.4）。我们过去认为白陶是在靠近陶土资源的地点制作的，二里头城市中心的贵族可能在控制白陶的分配上发挥了重要的作用[16]。

不同遗址发现的白陶器有共同的器形特征，但这些遗址都没有发现生产白陶器的证据，白陶的产地始终未知。在南洼遗址，考古学家发现了许多白陶制作的器物，除礼仪用器，还发现了日用品，例如网坠和纺轮[17]。另外，南洼遗址地下1米处广泛分布有厚达30～40厘米的白色土壤，一些考古学家认为这些土壤就是制作白陶的原料。如果此推断为真，那么南洼遗址可能就是白陶器的生产中心，为二里头遗址提供白陶器皿[18]，至今在南洼遗址还没有发现陶器生产的证据，以上推论还需进一步讨论。

陶器的成分分析是研究陶器产地的重要手段。为了调查白陶产地，对来自南洼（14件）、灰嘴（7件，其中2件来自同一器物，由此共6种器物）、二里头（9件）和南寨遗址（2件）的共32件白陶片样本进行成分分析。这项工作在昆士兰大学进行，使用ICP-MS（电感耦合等离子体质谱仪）对样品进行分析，对40种微量元素的常规测量中，大部分可以达到相对标准偏差为0.5%～3%的可重复性[19]。微量元素在黏土和陶器中的浓度低于1000ppm。同硅和铝等其他陶土主要构成元素相比，微量元素在黏土中的出现实际上是"偶然"的，他们的含量很大程度上源于母岩的成分和地质历史。因此，微量元素在进行化学分组及辨别不用原料制作的陶器中十分有效。南洼遗址的14件陶片中，6件小的样品有相同的颜色和质地，很可能来自同一件陶器，因此并不符合测试目的。由于白陶片的稀缺，我们依旧将其纳入测试范围。这6件陶片有着十分相似的元素含量，与其他南洼遗址的陶片不同，可单独作为一个亚群（图8.5）。测试的结果说明，这些陶片很可能属于同一件陶器，或者是使用同一批陶土制作的几件器物。尽管我们不能在上述两个结论中确定一个，但也有助于我们认识ICP-MS方法在确定陶片元素含量上的高精度及在判断白陶器的化学同质性上的作用。

需要强调的是，南洼遗址的14片陶片可能仅仅来自9件陶器。因此，当同灰嘴、二里头和南寨遗址的陶片对比时，40种微量元素的分析结果表现出有限的变化性。比较其他三个遗址，南洼在元素组成的二元分布图上表现出更小的范围（图8.5）。以上的观察有如下阐释。

南洼白陶器的原料来源有限，意味着制作地点少。南洼白陶的微量元素特征证明了考古学家关于这些白陶器是本地生产的推论，南洼遗址是一处白陶器的生产中心。

灰嘴、二里头和南寨遗址的很多白陶器落在南洼白陶微量元素分布区之外，它们应该并非南洼的产品。南洼遗址并非二里头时期白陶的唯一生产者和供应者。

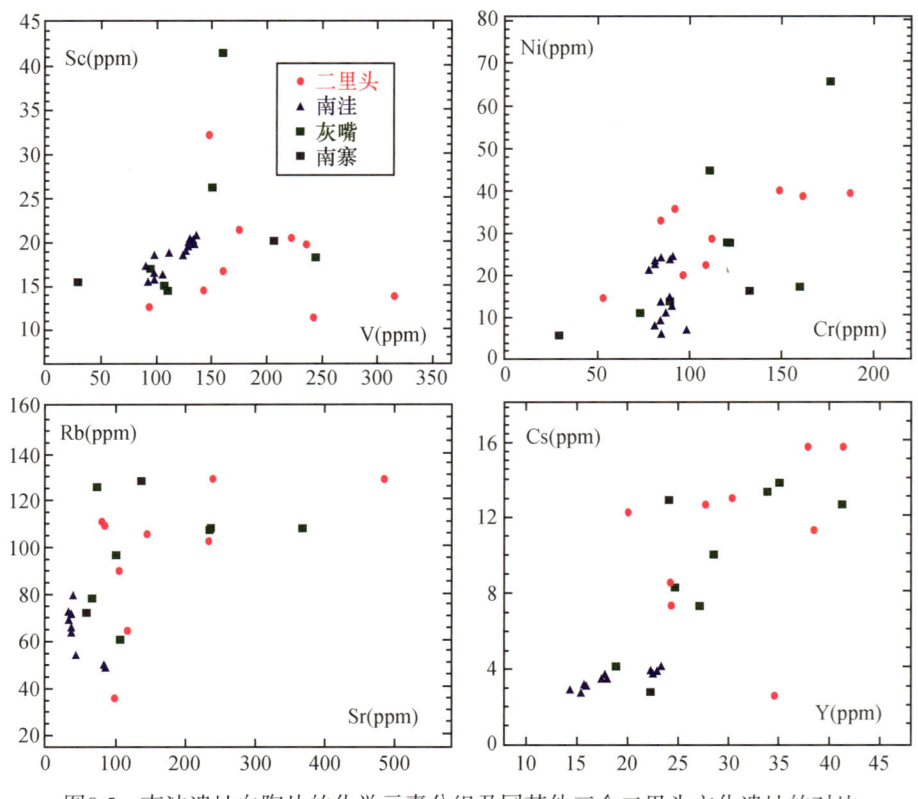

图8.5 南洼遗址白陶片的化学元素分组及同其他三个二里头文化遗址的对比

比较南洼白陶的集中分布状态，以上三个遗址的白陶片的微量元素组成要分散得多，超出南洼的分布区域。这说明它们的原料来源更加多元，这三个遗址的白陶很可能来自不同的生产地。

超过半个世纪的考古发掘，二里头遗址也没有发现白陶生产的证据。在灰嘴和南寨遗址也都没有类似迹象的出现（南寨遗址主要遗迹为墓葬，还未发现生活区）。鉴于上述情况和1~3部分的微量元素分析结果，白陶的生产地点应有多个，位于二里头城市中心之外，南洼遗址就是其中之一。灰嘴、二里头和南寨遗址的白陶器非本地生产。

有一些灰嘴、二里头和南寨遗址的白陶器落在南洼白陶样本的分布范围，说明这三个遗址中的一些白陶来自南洼。尽管有一部分相互重合，但灰嘴和南寨遗址的样本分布区间同二里头遗址有所不同。即使二里头是一个分配中心，灰嘴和南寨很可能不仅从二里头遗址获得白陶，而且是直接从其他有待发现的类似南洼的白陶产地获取。

南洼白陶在分布图上的集中可能会因为样本尺寸过小而产生偏差。将来对更多遗址白陶样本进行更为系统取样，有望取得更好的化学分组结果。

综上所述，白陶产品的分配模式可能是分散的而非集权式的，可以通过地区内贵族阶层之间的交往实现。尽管白陶是二里头国家腹地交换网络的一部分，二里头城市中心应该不可能完全垄断白陶的生产和分配。

有几个遗址同时拥有白陶器和鲕状白云岩石铲，这一现象表明，二里头腹地存在区域交换网络，进行日常用品和权威物（石器和贵族陶器）贸易。在这些遗址中，皂角树（100%）和南洼遗址（56%）的鲕状白云岩石铲在各自石铲总数中的比例很大。由于南洼生产白陶，而灰嘴生产白云岩石铲，这两个遗址的人群很可能会直接交易他们的产品。

包括灰嘴遗址在内的当地的贵族群体，可以通过交换网络，使用如鲕状白云岩石铲等物品来获取权力、地位和财富。石铲在灰嘴产量超过内需，灰嘴人用石铲换取其他商品，如日用品和珍贵产品等，十分合理。灰嘴的一些人可能会使用白陶来实现他们进入地区贵族圈的目的。这种假设，需要伊洛地区更多遗址白陶和石质工具的微量元素分析方能进一步证实。

第四节 结 论

我们关于石铲的生产和分配的研究及二里头腹地白陶的分析为检验上文提及的炊格尔关于疆域国家手工业生产的模式提供了机会。根据这些数据，我们看到一个具有多方面和多层次的手工业生产体系，而不是炊格尔提出的两极化双层体系。

在二里头时期，国家手工业体系可能已经控制绝大部分具有地位象征性的珍贵物品，如铜礼器，它们的分配被严格限制在高等级贵族群体中，主要发现于二里头城市中心。这些为国家统治群体提供财富和正统性的产品，很少提供给更广阔地域内其他贵族群体。本地的下层贵族通过市场和交换权威物，如仪式中使用的白陶酒礼器等物品，积极参与到权利获取的机制中来。这些白陶礼器是后来铜礼器的原型[20]，在二里头时期，它们同与自己具有相同形状的青铜器一直共存。截至目前，仅南洼遗址被证明为白陶的生产地，是否有其他遗址参与白陶生产尚未可知。本项目正在不断推进，我们正在二里头核心区域寻找生产白陶器的其他遗址。

在石铲的生产方面，产品虽为日用品，但原料并非任何聚落可得，而有的社会群体希望通过聚落位置的优势控制原料。生产很可能以家庭为单位进行，产品不仅可以满足生产者及周围人群的日常需要，还能帮助个人通过贸易获得更高的社会地位和财富。

鲕状白云岩石铲和白陶各自在距离其产地100千米外的地区发现，可以说明二里头腹地贸易网络的存在（图8.4）。通过这些网络，贵族用品和日用品都可以流通，为二里头腹地低等级贵族和普通人创造了获得权力、威望和财富的机会。

考古证据表明二里头核心区域存在一个高度集中的政治体系，二里头遗址代表了一个高度发展的等级社会。一些权威物品，包括白陶器，很可能通过二里头的高级贵族实现再分配。然而，我们的研究也指出了二里头政治经济结构中的一个横向分布的权利关系网。在腹地制作贵族和非贵族器物的独立手工匠人并非仅仅是中心城市贵族的附属，他们也在积极地使用自己的原材料资源和手工技艺寻求社会地位和财富。

在二里头核心地区的国家形成过程中，社会各阶层之间存在有许多利益竞争。我们对于非国有手工业专业化的研究为今后这一领域的探索打开了一扇窗口。

致谢：该项目得到了澳大利亚研究理事会发现项目资助（DP0450025）。十分感谢伊洛河流域联合考古队成员约翰·韦伯、艾琳·罗森、魏鸣、李润权、李永强、谢礼晔、王法成、王宏章、杨军锋、张朋峰、安妮·福特、希恩·比斯特、杰弗里·休伊特、利兹·基尔帕特里克和查尔斯·哈特利（贺成砺）等人员参加了从2002年开始的灰嘴遗址的发掘和区域调查工作。此外我们也向马萧林、许宏、韩国河、朱君孝、张松林、史家珍、袁广阔和托马斯·巴特利等同仁表示感谢，他们慷慨地提供许多资料和帮助。我们对本章中的任何不完善之处负责。

注　释

[1] Childe V G. *Man Makes Himself*. London: Watts and Co, 1936; Childe V G. The Urban Revolution. *Town Planning Review*, 1950, 21(1): 3-17.

[2] Adams R M. *The Evolution of Urban Society: Early Mesopotamia and Prehispanic Mexico*. Chicago: Aldine, 1966; Bagley R. Shang Ritual Bronzes: Casting Technique and Vessel Design. *Archives of Asian Art*, 1990, 43: 6-20; Chang K C. *Shang Civilization*. New Haven: Yale University Press, 1980.

[3] Brumfiel E, Earle T. Specialization, Exchange, and Complex Societies: An Introduction//Brumfiel E, Earle T. *Specialization, Exchange, and Complex Societies*. Cambridge: Cambridge University Press, 1987: 1-9; Costin C L. Craft Production Systems//Feinman G M, Price T D. *Archaeology at the Millennium: A Sourcebook*. New York: Kluwer Academic/Plenum Publishers, 2001: 273-328.

[4] Schortman E M, Urban P A. Modeling the Roles of Craft Production in Ancient Political Economies. *Journal of Archaeological Research*, 2004, 12(2): 185-226.

[5] Bagley R. Shang Ritual Bronzes: Casting Technique and Vessel Design. *Archives of Asian Art*, 1990, 43: 6-20; Bagley R. Shang Archaeology. //Loewe M, Shaughnessy E. *The Cambridge History of Ancient China*. Cambridge: Cambridge University Press, 1999: 124-231; Liu L. The Products of Minds as Well as of Hands: Pro-duction of Prestige Goods in the Neolithic and Early State Periods of China. *Asian Perspectives*, 2003, 42(1): 1-40; Liu L, Chen X C. *State Formation in Early China*. London: Duckworth, 2003.

[6] Liu L, Chen X C. *State Formation in Early China*. London: Duckworth, 2003; Trigger B. Shang Political Organization: A Comparative Approach. *Journal of East Asian Archaeology*, 1999, 1(1-4): 43-62; Trigger B. *Understanding Early Civilizations: A Comparative Study*. Cambridge: Cambridge University Press, 2003.

[7] Trigger B. *Understanding Early Civilizations: A Comparative Study*. Cambridge: Cambridge University Press, 2003: 368-374.

[8] 中国社会科学院考古研究所二里头工作队：《河南洛阳盆地2001～2003年考古调查简报》，《考古》2005年第5期；Liu L, Chen X C, Lee Y K, et al. Settlement Patterns and Development of Social Complexity in the Yiluo Region, North China. *Journal of Field Archaeology*, 2002-2004, 29(1-2): 75-100;许宏、陈国梁、赵海涛：《二里头遗址聚落形态的初步考察》，《考古》2004年第11期。

[9] 中国社会科学院考古研究所二里头工作队：《河南偃师二里头遗址宫城及宫殿区外围道路的勘察与发掘》，《考古》2004年第11期；中国社会科学院考古研究所二里头工作队：《河南洛阳盆地2001～2003年考古调查简报》，《考古》2005年第5期；中国社会科学院考古研究所二里头工作队：《河南偃师二里头遗址中心区的考古新发现》，《考古》2005年第7期；中国社会科学院考古研究所：《偃师二里头》，中国大百科全书出版社，1999年。

[10] Liu L, Chen X C, Lee Y K, et al. Settlement Patterns and Development of Social Complexity in the Yiluo Region, North China. *Journal of Field Archaeology*, 2002-2004, 29(1-2): 75-100.

[11] 中国社会科学院考古研究所河南一队：《河南偃师灰嘴遗址东周墓发掘简报》，《考古》2004年第12期。

[12] Ford A. *States and Stones: Ground Stone Tool Production at Huizui, China*. Honours Thesis. Department of Archaeology, Melbourne: La Trobe University, 2001.

[13] Webb J, Ford A, Gorton J. Influences on Selection of Lithic Raw Material Sources at Huizui, A Neolithic Early Bronze Age Site in Northern China. *Bulletin of the Indo-Pacific Prehistory Association*, 2007, 27: 76-86.

[14] 中国社会科学院考古研究所二里头工作队：《河南洛阳盆地2001～2003年考古调查简报》，《考古》2005年第5期；Liu L, Chen X C, Lee Y K, et al. Settlement Patterns and Development of Social Complexity in the Yiluo Region, North China. *Journal of Field Archaeology*, 2002-2004, 29(1-2): 75-100.

[15] Chen X C. *Lithic Production of Early States in China: An Examination of the Development of Craft Specialization. Workshop on Early Chinese Civilization*. Vancouver: The University of British Columbia, 2005.

[16] Liu L, Chen X C. *State Formation in Early China*. London: Duckworth, 2003.

[17] 郑州大学历史学院考古系、郑州市文物考古研究所：《河南登封南洼遗址2014年试发掘简报》，《中原文物》2006年第3期。

[18] 郑州大学历史学院考古系、郑州市文物考古研究院：《登封南洼2004～2006年二里头文化聚落发掘简报》，《中原文物》2011年第6期。

[19] Li B P, Zhao J X, Collerson K D, et al. Application of ICP-MS Trace Element Analysis in Study of Ancient Chinese Ceramics. *Chinese Science Bulletin*, 2003, 48(12): 1219-1224; Li B P, Zhao J X, Greig A, et al. Characterisation of Chinese Tang Sancai from Gongxian and Yaozhou Kilns Using ICP-MS Trace Element and TIMS Sr-Nd Isotopic Analysis. *Journal of Archaeological Science*, 2006, 33(1): 56-62.

[20] Liu L. The Products of Minds as well as of Hands: Production of Prestige Goods in the Neolithic and Early State Periods of China. *Asian Perspectives*, 2003, 42(1): 1-40.

第九章　伊洛河流域灰嘴遗址的土壤微形态、化学和磁化率研究：以典型仰韶地层序列为主[①]

第一节　前　言

2005年，在河南省伊洛地区的灰嘴遗址周围开展了两个季度的田野工作，对裴李岗、仰韶、龙山和二里头时期的地质考古学样品进行了微观地层学分析[1]（表9.1、图9.1）。这项微观地层学研究是跨学科团队伊洛河流域联合考古队调查项目（2003—2006）的组成部分，主要目的是研究地质考古学、植物遗存、聚落形态、手工业专业化及中国文明在黄土高原地区的崛起过程[2]。

利用土壤微形态、化学和磁化率的方法对灰嘴的微观地层进行分析，目的是认识当地的自然土壤和沉积物，进而识别人类活动遗存，如灰坑内的包含物、"白灰面"地层序列及令人费解的近河土壤沉积物堆积的一些背景。本章主要关注典型的仰韶地层序列和几个灰坑（图9.2），也对其他沉积物给出了初步的解释，以便在考古和景观背景下更准确地了解仰韶地层序列。

第二节　样品和方法

2005年初，中国社会科学院考古研究所采集的一系列样本送至伦敦学院大学，通过土壤微形态的方法[3]进行综合分析。2005年11月在伊洛河流域联合考古队的协助下，Macphail优化了采样策略，重新开展了的新的田野取样工作。

前后，共获得了44件未受干扰的整块石料（图9.3）和37件块状样本以资研究。经与合作研究者讨论，最终选择了31件薄片和25件大块样品进行分析（表9.1），以解决相关考古学问题。

本章所使用研究方法的全部细节已有文章介绍[4]。总的来说，采用了土壤微形态学（包括微探针X射线分析）与烧失量测量（LOI在375℃）、磷酸盐分馏（包括无机和有机磷）、磁化率（%χconv）、重金属铜（Cu）、铅（Pb）、锌（Zn）成分分析相结合[5]的方法。

[①]　本章由Richard I. Macphail、John Crowther执笔，邓玲玲翻译。

第九章 伊洛河流域灰嘴遗址的土壤微形态、化学和磁化率研究：以典型仰韶地层序列为主

表9.1 灰嘴土壤微形态（薄片）以及块状样品初步分析

遗址编号	量化分析（见表9.2）	时代和单位	切片号：相对深度，初步解释
齐家窑		裴李岗地层和灰坑	
05HYQGS2	43	地基A2&Bt？地平	M43：0~75毫米，厚黄土A2层，基本不见生物痕迹和炭屑
05HYQH1	44	H1下部近壁处	M44：0~75毫米，黄土（A2、Bt和钙质Btk层），填充物含烧土、陶片、木炭、骨头和磷酸盐，为生活垃圾
府店		裴李岗灰土	M34：参考样品，含有木灰、灰（部分风化）、烧骨、土块和烧土
灰嘴		仰韶F1堆积序列	
05HYEHF1		第9层：黏土	M19A：0~75毫米，由植物回火的黄土构成的泥浆抹灰层（由于土壤氧化和中度燃烧而呈红色）
05HYEHF1	19/8	第8层：活动面	M19A：0~75毫米（M19B）：2层钙华板，有植硅体和植物残留、染色黄土和包含物（碳酸盐含量高，没有磁化率增强现象），矿物学分析表明含有石英、绿泥岩、氧化铁/氢氧化铁，与黄土中的包含物一致
05HYEHF1		第7层上部：活动面处理层	M19B：75~150毫米，泥质抹灰层由包含植物的黄土回火而成，或燃烧植物的回火土坯
05HYEHF1		第6a和6b层：活动面中的最上层和中层	M18A：10~85毫米，2~3层钙华板，在中间层（6b）和最上层（6a）之间有非常薄的（含木炭）细粉尘黏土表面层
05HYEHF1		第6c层：活动面的最下层	M18B：85~140毫米，2层钙华板
05HYEHF1		第6d层：活动面处理层	M18B：140~170毫米，由植物回火的黄土构成的泥浆抹灰层
05HYEHF1		第5层：淡黄色黄土层/活动面堆积层	可能是混合灰白色的A2水平层土壤和烧毁的，参见下表M17A
05HYEHF1	17/4a	第4a层：黑灰填土	M17A：0~55毫米，混合A2水平层土壤和烧毁的涂抹层形成的堆积层（磁化率增强）
05HYEHF1		第4b层：活动面	M17B：95~105毫米，钙华板层（三层中的底层）
05HYEHF1	17/3a	第3a层：深褐色活动面处理层	M17B：105~115毫米，用黄土建造的泥浆抹灰层，由黄土的熟化和黏土形成的深色纹理（没有腐殖质增加的充分证据）
05HYEHF1		第3b层	M17B：115~165毫米用干净黄土建造的土坯地基
05HYEHF1	16/3a	第3a层：褐色活动面处理层（横向延续7/3a）	没有人为沉积或腐殖土形成的明显迹象
05HYEHF1	16/3b	第3b层：活动面填土	没有人为沉积或腐殖土形成的明显迹象
05HYEHF1		第2层：活动面	M16A：0~5毫米，底板有单块泥灰岩建成；M16B：5~75毫米，由黄土（土坯）制成的泥浆抹灰过火层地面处理薄面，建于富含磷酸盐和层化率增强的土层上
05HYEHF1	16/1	第1层：扰土层	M16B：80~155毫米，所在地土壤，同上
05HYHF1		活动面碎块样品	M1：三个钙华板碎片（活动面）
05HYHF1		活动面	M2：0~30毫米，活动面由开采的钙华板建造：30~35毫米，由干净的黄土制成的植物回火"泥浆抹灰"活动面处理层表面
05HYEH3		龙山灰坑	
05HYEH3S1	10	灰坑	M31A：0~75毫米，灰坑（挖掘？）填土分层包含当地土壤、木灰和植物残留，此外，可能还有谷类和植物的废弃物及垫土以及湿润环境下形成的人类食物获取的钙铁的磷酸盐
05HYEH3S2	11	灰坑	M31B：75~150毫米，同上

续表

遗址编号	量化分析（见表9.2）	时代和单位	切片号：相对深度，初步解释
05HYEH3		灰层下的填土	M32：0~75毫米，底层（挖掘？）填土为扰乱的地层和表层土壤、从上倾倒的生活堆积、潮湿环境下形成的钙铁锰磷酸盐
05HYEH4		龙山灰坑	
05HYH4S1	12	含草木灰和木炭的系列薄层	M22A：0~75毫米，与H3填土相似，但是包含强烈燃烧后的材料，垫土中似乎包含更多细小的人类遗留物（更脏）
05HYH4S2	13	含草木灰和木炭的系列薄层	M22B：75~150毫米，同上
		GS2中的全新世、仰韶和龙山堆积序	（见下页）
		龙山冲积层	M38A：0~55毫米，晶体构造预示着人类在泥泞的条件踩踏形成的沉积物，含有许多细小的人类活动遗留物
05HYEGS2	38b	垂直取样的龙山冲积物	M38A：55~75毫米，同下；M38B：75~150毫米，颗粒较大的、粗糙的、潮湿的人为沉积物
05HYEGS2	39a	仰韶土壤的沉积物序列	M39A：0~75毫米，被铁锰染色的淤积物，细小的人类遗留物（可能有后沉积的磷酸盐富集物，包括铁、锰）；M39（计划）：同上，并有微探针证实
05HYEGS2	39b	仰韶土壤沉积物序列中的砂砾沉积	M39B：75~150毫米，包括夹杂有疏松的泥浆块、有机物碎屑（75~100毫米），还有富含砾石的填土；含烧泥土块、碳酸钙和钙华板的土壤，夹杂有木炭、沙粒、骨渣和磷酸盐结节（100~150毫米）；M39：底部0~75毫米，同样序列
05HYEGS2	40	晚更新世/早全新世沉积土	M40A：0~75毫米，土壤最上部见有砾石（0~15毫米，截面？，见下文）；M40B：75~150毫米，晚更新世/早全新世（？）冲积的灰黏土，由沉积黄土形成，见有被铁染色的根孔，不含人工物
05HYEGS2		层状全新世（仰韶？）冲积层截断晚更新世/早全新世土壤	M30：0~75毫米，细碎的粉质冲积层与晚更新世/早全新世冲积的黏土共同组成，见有被铁染色根孔，不含人工物
		二里头土壤、灰坑和路土	
04HYHT4J1	4	保存较好的表层	M4：（仅碎块），被截断的底层土，有被踩踏和水淹的迹象
05HYHWTer2 H2	8、9（6、7）	H2堆积	M8：0~75毫米，富含磷酸盐的灰坑沉积物，含有强烈燃烧的物质（玻璃化二氧化硅渣）、木灰、植物加工和人类排泄物
T3H22	15	二里头三期灰土堆积	M15：（仅碎块）土壤、涂抹和污染都会导致灰嘴遗址磷酸盐浓度和磁化率偏高
05HYHWTer2 L1	37	二里头路土	M37：0~75毫米，潮湿和干燥条件下形成的质密的、分层的路土踩踏面，含有许多细小的人为遗留物

第九章 伊洛河流域灰嘴遗址的土壤微形态、化学和磁化率研究：以典型仰韶地层序列为主

表9.2 灰嘴化学（除去磷酸盐分解）和磁化率数据

样品	简述	失水率 LOI (%)	pH 1:2.5 水	碳酸盐 § (est,%)	磷酸盐-P† (毫克/克)	Pb$ (毫克/克)	Zn$ (毫克/克)	Cu$ (毫克/克)	χ (10⁻⁸ SI)	χ max (10⁻⁸ SI)	χ conv¶ (%)
裴李岗地层和灰坑（齐家箐：05HYQ和05HYQGS2）											
43	房基A2&Bt?	1.08	8.6	5	0.871				23.8	298	7.99*
44	灰坑1	1.30	8.2	2	1.26				34.8	355	9.80*
仰韶活动面和建筑堆积											
17/4a	活动面：4a层	1.26	8.5	5	2.46				53.0	877	6.04*
17/3a	活动面：3a层	0.782	8.8	>10	1.30	18.4	40.6	14.8	20.3	880	2.31
16/3a	活动面：3a层	0.984	8.8	5	1.25				18.0	1000	1.80
16/3b	活动面：3b层	1.09	8.7	5	1.29				22.3	911	2.45
16/1	地面处理层：1层	1.44	8.7	>10	3.13*	17.0	68.2	25.6	37.8	522	7.24*
龙山灰坑											
10	灰坑	2.25	8.6	5	7.24**				27.4	144	19.0**
11	灰坑	2.13	8.7	>10	4.98*				16.4	179	9.16*
12	灰坑	2.37	9.6	>10	5.21**				59.6	256	23.3***
13	灰坑	1.99	9.6	>10	5.94**				68.7	294	23.4***
GS2中仰韶（Y）和龙山（L）堆积序列（05HYEGS2）											
38a	冲积土（L）	1.76	9.4	>10	1.25	24.4	75.1	22.5	12.1	433	2.79
38b	土壤（L）	1.08	9.6	>10	1.90	20.0	60.0	20.0	9.7	269	3.61
39a	基底土壤（Y）	1.14	9.6	>10	3.59*	16.7	42.6	14.8	19.7	447	4.41
39b	底层砾石（Y）	1.25	9.4	>10	0.801	16.6	47.6	16.6	9.8	390	2.51
40	底层冲积土	1.04	9.1	5	1.07	18.8	50.1	18.8	10.3	542	1.90
二里头土壤、灰坑、"道路"和活动面											
4	地表层	1.08	8.3	>10	1.32				28.1	576	4.88
6	灰坑	3.44	8.2	2	6.89**				103	309	33.3***

续表

样品	简述	失水率 LOI (%)	pH 1:2.5 水	碳酸盐§ (est,%)	磷酸盐-P† (毫克/克)	Pb§ (毫克/克)	Zn§ (毫克/克)	Cu§ (毫克/克)	χ (10^{-8} SI)	χ max (10^{-8} SI)	χ conv¶ (%)
7	灰坑	2.43	8.4	5	5.40**				192	462	41.6***
8	灰坑	2.76	8.3	2	7.12**				56.6	255	22.2***
9	灰坑	2.84	8.2	5	5.55**				99.4	331	30.0***
37	"道路"	1.61	8.6	5	3.54*				140	744	18.8**
14	灰坑上层	1.98	8.6	>10	11.6***				164	406	40.4***
15	灰坑上层	1.51	8.7	>10*	13.3***				142	279	50.9***

碳酸盐：* 粗体突出显示的碳酸盐含量高于其他样品记录的>10%；** 基于该样品的不溶性酸残留物测定（AIR =32.4%）。

磷酸盐：以粗体突出显示的数字显示磷酸盐富集的迹象：* = 丰富（2.50～4.99毫克/克），** = 非常丰富（5.00～9.99 mg g^{-1}），*** = 极其丰富（≥10.0 mg g^{-1}），磷酸盐分馏数据列于表9.3中；

重金属（铅Pb、锌Zn和铜Cu）：所分析的样品均未显示出明显的富集迹象。χ：以粗体突出显示磁化率增强的迹象：* = 增强（conv=5.00%～9.99%），** = 强烈增强（conv=10.0%～19.9%），*** = 非常强烈增强（conv ≥20.0%）。

图9.1 采样点位置

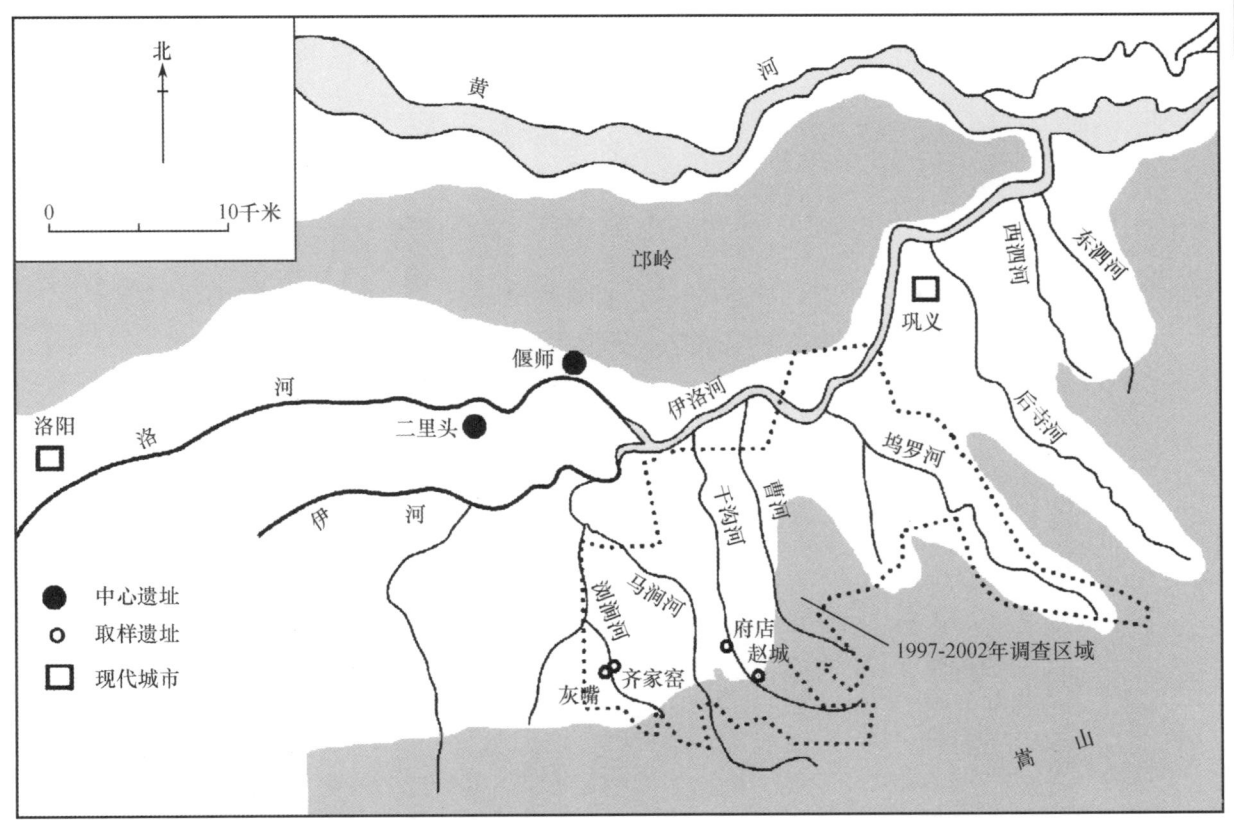

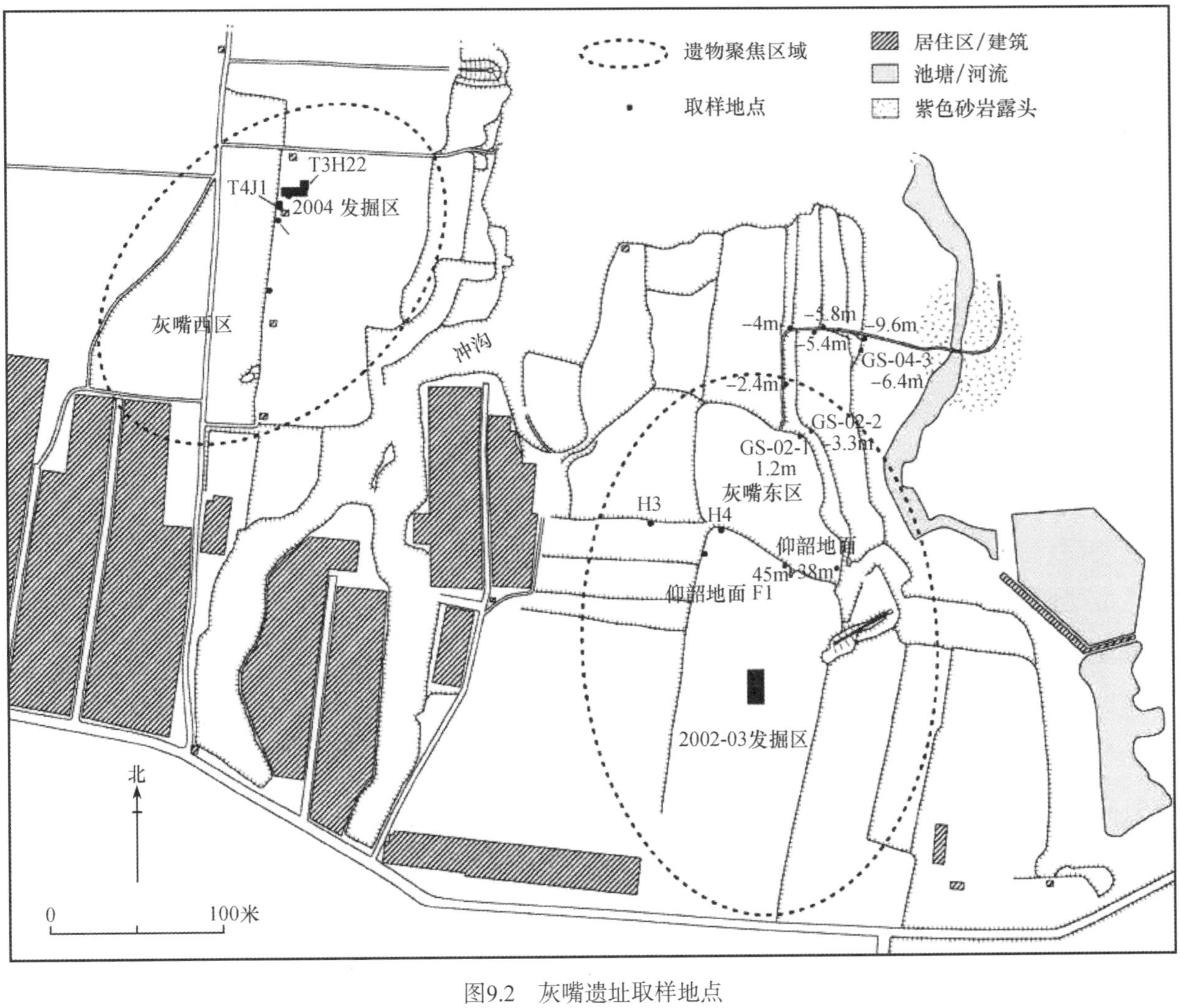

图9.2 灰嘴遗址取样地点

第三节 结论和讨论

表9.1、表9.2和图9.3~图9.11中所列结果是对所研究对象的初步解释（表9.1）。

图9.3 灰嘴仰韶F1堆积序列 05HYEHF1

地表抬升和预制表面（第1，3，5和7层）；土层（第2，4，6和8层）以及烧土块（第9层）；样本M16~M19。注意生物作用和均质化的上部沉积（第11层）和可能的垂直墙或分区（白色箭头）

一、后沉积效应

几千年来，灰嘴及其周围的土壤和地表景观受到人类活动的极大影响。而GS2的晚更新世/早全新世冲积土（样品40）是无菌样品对比的一个很好的例子。正如预期一样，这种"天然"土壤具有较低的烧量（有机物的部分），同时，磷酸盐浓度低，磁化率也极低。它的主要特征是大型块状结构及铁染色的孔洞（根系残留下的通道）[6]。随后二价碳酸钙的形成也对该土壤造成了影响。后者被认为是碳酸钙和其他碱性盐类对考古土壤进行普遍污染的结果，这些碱性盐使得整个遗址出现了非常高的pH值（最大pH值为9.6，见表9.2）。至少从仰韶时期开始，灰嘴出现的碱性沉积都与此有关（见下文）；同时，还应考虑昆虫和小型哺乳动物等的掏洞行为带来的影响（见第11层，图9.3）。

图9.4 15厘米长的灌入块（M18）显微影像

样本第5层是掺和了植物的土块，也是一处预制表面（APS）；第6层是一系列内含化石的凝灰岩土层（TFL），内含开采而来的凝灰岩石板。底部石板及其上叠压的厚石板说明此处存在自然形成的水平向分隔。凝灰岩是在碳酸钙泉水中形成的一种石灰岩种类

图9.5 14厘米长的土块（M19）显微影像

样品的第7层土块是地表抬升沉积（AGR）和掺和植物的预置表面土块（APS）；第8层是一系列含有化石的凝灰岩土层（TFL），凝灰岩石片表现出自然形成的水平向分隔；第9层是火烧过的土块残骸（BDD）

图9.6 薄片M19B显微影像

（第7层）出现掺和植物（PT）和深色土块预制表面（APS）的无效假象，涂抹泥灰的土层和（第8层）凝灰岩土层（TFL）包含了化石特征。宽度是～5厘米

图9.7 M18A切片显微影像

凝灰岩土层（第6层）包含了黄土颗粒和植物化石，同时现出水平向的破裂（HC），这是板状凝灰岩自然形成的水平向分离，在一处破裂（淤泥）的底部覆盖着含有丰富细颗粒木炭的黄土淤泥——见文章。宽度是～5厘米

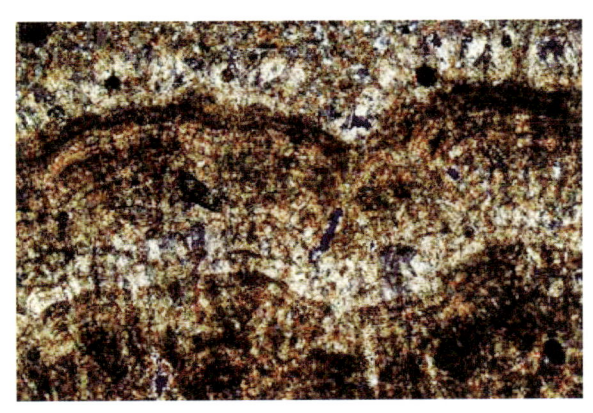

图9.8　M1切片显微影像

图面碎片化的样本；凝灰岩中生物化学生长模式的具体情况。交叉偏光（XPL），宽度是～2.3毫米

图9.9　M18A切片显微影像

（6b层）通过胶质方解石（方解石）在一个不纯净的微晶灰岩含量高且含有粉砂尺寸的石英（黄土）的微亮晶灰岩基质（凝灰岩）中形成的植物假形及化石遗存（XPL，宽度是～4.6毫米）

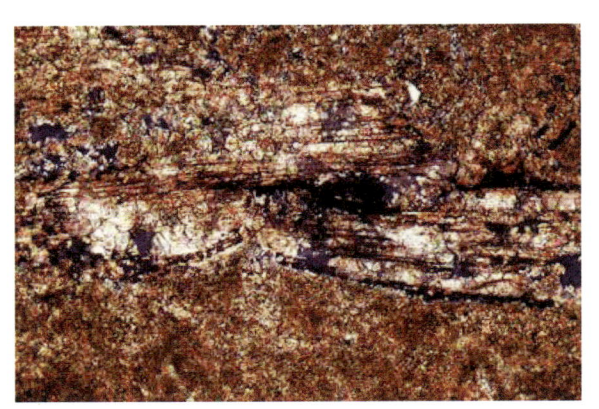

图9.10　M18A切片显微影像

黑色的植物组织，嵌在方解凝灰岩中，是天然地包含植物碎片的证据（XPL，宽度是～1.06毫米）

图9.11　M18B1切片显微影像

掺和了植物的涂抹了泥灰的黄土，在预制地面上形成（箭头指出植物掺和料的空洞假形）；基质的稠密特征是由于涂泥过程中导致的土壤熟化（XPL，宽度～4.6毫米）

二、本地土壤

对齐家窑遗址土壤（裴李岗灰坑；样品43）的野外调查和土壤微形态的观察以及灰嘴遗址仰韶时期灰坑下的土壤（观察样品M32）的研究皆表明，在阔叶林地下的粉砂质黏土中存在着典型的铁和黏土稀少的上层土壤A2以及黏土和铁相对含量较多的下层土壤Bw／B（t）。这些底层土壤通常也含有二价碳酸钙〔B（t）k／Ck层〕。

在赵城遗址，更新世古土壤的特征是含有明显的碳酸盐结节。黄土高原典型的全新世（及早期）古土壤，主要是风积粉砂层[7]，伴随淋滤和黏土移动以及深层的二价碳酸盐形成，最后形成薄层湿润淋溶土[8]或正常的（含钙）淋溶土[9]。

三、裴李岗时期

府店遗址[10]灰坑填土和灰坑沉积物中含有本地表土和底土,此外还发现骨骼、烧骨、灰烬、木炭、陶器、烧土和磷酸盐物质,皆为人类活动的废弃物(表9.1,M34、M43、M44)。灰坑中有细颗粒土壤移动的证据,由灰的风化和钾的分解造成,这与欧洲新石器时代灰坑的情况一致[11]。

四、灰嘴遗址使用时期

重点介绍GS2(M39-40)的非本地土壤沉积物和05HYEHF1的地层序列(图9.3;M16A~M19B)。

(一)仰韶堆积序列(05HYEHF1)

在05HYEHF1的构造序列中,我们对第1~11层进行了调查(图9.3)。此地层序列多由在预制表面上铺设的四层或更多白灰层组成(表9.1和表9.2)。第1层由2毫米厚的生活土壤(或地面垃圾)组成,其上的白灰层(第2层)正下方铺设有松软层土壤。这种土壤似乎是抹平土层和预处理面,由"干净"的黄土制成。白色层(第2层)由3厘米厚的含化石的凝灰岩石板构成。事实上,第2、4、6、8层都是由单层或多层2~3厘米厚的凝灰岩板构成,表现出天然的水平劈缝(见图9.4、图9.5)。对于其中一个样品(第8层,表9.2)的分析显示其含有大量的碳酸钙矿物(67.6%碳酸盐),只是成分不纯(酸性难溶解的残留物占32.4%;主要是淤泥和黏土),同时,没有出现任何磷酸盐的富集或磁化率增强的迹象。土壤微形态学表明淤泥和黏土存在于黄土中。硫化物的出现也表明其可能是天然的水成层潜育土。对于灰嘴F1地面序列和F4地面的化学元素和矿物学分析发现,它们富含方解石、石英、亚氯酸盐、伊利石和氧化铁/氢氧化铁,与黄土边缘地带沉积形成的凝灰岩一致[12]。

1. 凝灰岩建筑材料

凝灰岩(参见石灰华)在含有大量溶解碳酸钙的泉水中形成,这些碳酸钙沉淀为微晶灰岩含量高的类似石灰岩沉积物。它们通常在藻类、地衣和苔藓周围形成,并以微亮晶灰岩和亮晶石灰岩大小的方解石的形式产生出植物的假象,有的形态也反映出细菌和藻类的存在[13](图9.8、图9.9)。凝灰岩中还常常包含植物和土壤,就如灰嘴遗址凝灰岩石板中发现的那样(图9.10)。灰嘴遗址附近发现的第四纪凝灰岩,同黄土的风化和富含碳酸钙的Bk深层下层水平面、区域内的碳酸盐结核和泉水环境中的凝灰岩的形成基本一致[14]。在白色层中无处不在的化石痕迹，包括植物、有机残骸、土壤碎屑、黄土（见上文的块状分析）和碳酸盐结核，证实了它们是经开采而得的凝灰岩石板[15]（图9.8c）。虽然在这些地层中偶尔留下了中型动物的打洞痕迹，但化石证据不能被误认为是次生沉积出现和二价碳酸钙的形成，因为这些特征不会跨越凝灰岩各层之间的界限（图9.4、图9.5）。

凝灰岩（层状形成的凝灰岩）自然分解的特性可能是促使人们开采石材的原因。显而易见，凝灰岩板也可以用于制造墙壁或隔墙（图9.3），如图9.3所示。没有发现任何化学的、矿物学的和微形态学的证据可证明燃烧的存在，另外天然凝灰岩的构成也证明所调查的白色层都不是使用烧石灰制作的。

2. F1的建筑堆积（05HYEHF1第2~9层）

没有证据表明使用时期的堆积之间存在遗迹，哪怕是人类或动物在活动时的踩踏遗留[16]，这意味着每一个活动面都被清扫或者覆盖[17]。第6层（图9.7）内发现了一个罕见的富含细小炭粒的淤泥沉积例子，但这可能并不重要。

第2和4b层之间的3b层并非人类活动堆积，而是由"干净"黄土制作的内含未燃烧植物的土坯（涂层）组成（样本16/3b，见图9.6、图9.11）。掺和了植物的土坯和泥砖中，植物因加热大部分消失，热处理后的土坯，提升了房屋的建设水平[18]，可参考仰韶时期烧过的涂抹层（M33）。我们原本认为4a层下的深色土层（3a）内含腐殖质，但它既非腐殖的，也没有人为干扰的迹象（表9.2，样本16/3a，17/3a）。它仅由"干净"的黄土组成，深色是在制作另一泥浆涂抹层时产生的，湿润的土壤中的黏土颗粒分离，并填充到孔隙之中，从而使其呈现出深红色（图9.4和图9.9）[19]。泥浆面在许多地方都有出现，例如土耳其的恰塔休克遗址（Çatalhöyük），来自土耳其和印度的民族志实例也是例证[20]。地面下的泥浆层（第6层和第8层，M18B和M19B）同掺和了植物的土坯遗留相似（图9.9）。建造序列中的第5层在野外又被称为淡黄色黏土。在薄片中，这是一个很明显的水平倾倒层，主要由当地黄土土壤的A2层部分即浅色土壤组成（见上文）。

第9层覆盖在第8层上，由红烧土（经过适度烤烧，表9.1）的大颗粒和生物作用下未经燃烧的泥土（M18A）小颗粒组成。红烧土可能与第10层下烧过的抹泥墙有关（图9.3和图9.5）。这些碎屑在干净的地层表面之上。堆积物的出现可能意味着建筑被火烧毁，与英国汉普郡的巴斯特（Butser）古农场所进行的实验或在伦敦发现的遗迹类似，而该遗迹经历了布迪卡（Boudicca）在公元59~60年间的反抗活动[21]。但是，对于中国的新石器时代，研究者们认为火烧土墙（变硬）是出于建筑加固的目的[22]。

（二）龙山时期

1. 05HYEH3

与灰嘴其他的遗迹相比，灰坑H3填土（样品10和11）中腐殖质的含量是中度的，且富含或极富含磷酸盐。它们显示出增强或强烈增强的磁化率。在薄片（M31A和M31B）中，它们的特征主要在于草木灰层沉积，内含烧土颗粒、偶尔出现的炭屑和层积的植硅体，同时也包括铰接的植硅体（例如，产生于植物加工和"席子"的倾倒物）。（目前尚未就05HYEHF1序列中此层的使用方式达成共识，但如果它们是生活遗迹的同时又是"干净的"，则可能是由于被垫土覆盖的结果）。草木灰可以从大的菱形方解石晶体和木炭中识别出来[23]。人类（？）的粪便碎片、骨骼、陶片和可能的铁-钙-磷染色非晶体的存在表明此处倾倒了厨余和厕所排弃物。这些土层很少发现生物活动，可能是因为灰烬的碱性成分含量很高，对蚯蚓等生物有害，同时也可能因为堆积的分层特征与05HYEH3一致，是偶发性的积水环境。在考古资料中，沟渠、采石场等地区短暂的水生沉积物并不常见。

2. 05HYEH4

化学成分上，该灰坑填土与灰坑05HYEH3类似，但磁化率更高（样品12和13）。在以薄截面模式（M22A和M22B）测试的150毫米的样品中，发现了多层草木灰，混合有土壤、清晰的植硅体，以及棕色的被有机物染色的植硅体。此外填土中可能还来自"垫土"，但似乎比05HYEH3中的"垫土"更"脏"。可识别的植硅石包含草梗、莎草和芦苇[24]。沉积物也受到了二价铁染色和小动物掘挖的影响，再次表明填土堆积可能在积水环境下形成。

（三）仰韶和龙山时期（2005HYEGS2的土壤沉积序列）

GS2的剖面包括现代扰动面，其下有2.30米厚的堆积（表9.1）；罗森曾研究过这种地质剖面以及其他类似海拔地区的情况[25]。简言之，在0.20～0.45米处，主要为包含龙山时期陶片的层层覆盖的铁染色层，样品38a和38b以及M38A和38B中检测了这些土层。约2.00米处，细颗粒轻微铁染色的沉积物覆盖在沙砾层上的细颗粒浅色淋滤层上。沙砾层包含了仰韶时期的陶器（样品39a和39b，分别为M39A，M39B，M39base和M39plan）。显然这些砾石隔断了可能为原生的晚更新世/早全新世冲积土，在这两层和下层堆积垂直相间处提取了样品（样品40，M40A和M40B），此外还采集了层状冲积土和冲积层之间的横向连接处的对照样品（M30），间距为0.40米。这些土壤和沉积物的特征总结参见表9.2。最底层的灰色冲积层中发现植物根系残留，此层内没有发现人类活动痕迹，与仰韶砾石层和覆盖在它之上的粉砂质泥浆不同。后者含有陶片、砂粒或砾石大小的火烧过的涂料、碳酸盐结核、凝灰岩、骨骼、木炭和人为的磷酸盐结核[26]。由于沉积后磷酸盐的流失和地下水的运动[27]，化学成分中少见磷酸盐，除了样品39a（表9.2），二价磷酸盐旁边聚集着明显的二价铁和二价锰（微探针分析）。但是，在此序列中没有重金属浓度增高的现象。

对于探孔中采集的龙山时期的样品（M38A和M38B）进行分析，其中薄板状的沉积物（38a）明显存在于大量异质沉积物（38b）之上。后者含有大量的涂料碎块和烧过的涂块（有的夹杂木炭、炭屑、骨渣和粪化石），存在二价磷酸铁染色的情况，颜色非常深，含有灰层的黏土空隙填充物和涂层的出现证明了在涝渍条件下该沉积物曾经发生过剧烈扰动。覆盖层和明显呈薄片状的39b层同样富含人类活动遗留物（涂料、烧过的涂料、骨骼、粪化石、木炭、磷酸盐染色的富含木炭的土壤），但它们的体积较小，以砂或粗砂的形态存在。此外，偶尔出现细小植物碎片，包括"软"组织，很可能是地层序列中出现高有机物含量的原因。然而，在干燥时，明显呈薄片状的"地层"形成了晶体状结构。由于潮湿土壤的熟化和扰动，纹理状特征出现，表明可能在涝渍地区形成了人类踩踏面，是人为形成的沉积物。

（四）二里头时期

我们对水井旁边的土层（样品4）、5个灰坑的沉积物（样品6~9、14、15）和一条"路土"（样品37）进行了分析。除水井旁的土壤外，所有沉积物都富含磷酸盐（样品15中最大浓度为13.3mg/g，灰嘴遗址中发现的最高检测值），大幅增加的磁化率，这些现象是存人类活动存在的标识性指标。

井下的土壤似乎主要是一种失去顶端的底土材料（M4，仅有碎片），除了一些富含扬尘的黏土填充物外，几乎没有人类活动的迹象。最后可能是由于踩踏和水的溢出引起了土壤塌陷。

灰坑填土（M8）是一个由土壤、涂料、烧过的涂料、骨骼、粪化石等共同组成的混合填充物，其中含有非常丰富的草木灰和炭化的植物遗存，包括小米[28]、一些硅化物碎片（多见气泡），较高的磁化率说明存在经过相对高温燃烧的植硅石（样品6~9）。这些包含物说明此处倾倒了加工后的食物（谷物？）、厨余垃圾和厕所的排弃物（粪便）。这不仅与英国事前时代晚期中发现的富含灰的非典型沉积不同[29]，与龙山时期的灰坑相比，灰含量也较少（见表9.2中估计的碳酸盐含量）。M15以草木灰为主（发现"白灰层"），并且残存有炭化的树皮；焦化的土壤、涂层是磷酸盐比例高和磁化率信号强烈的原因。

道路堆积非常质密，虽然它包括粗烧涂层，但主要是人类活动留下的细砂和中等粒度的砂粒、贝壳、木炭、骨骼、灼烧后骨骼及可能的磷酸化骨富集集聚体（粪化石），这些遗物致使磷酸盐和磁化率信号存在（样本37）。质密分层是踩踏面的典型特征，炭化的有机物和水平分布的氧化植物残骸留下的平面空隙形成了路土层间的夹层。从遗迹表面的实验和分析结果来看，这种堆积是在相对干燥的条件下人类踩踏后形成的活动面，在英国，这种现象主要发现于房层内的结构中[30]。但是，路土层内其他土层的观察结果却显示出含灰层的黏土的平整及黏土孔隙的填充是在通路依旧泥泞的状态下完成的[31]。

第四节 结 论

2005年的田野工作后，虽然对灰嘴及其周围地区的31个薄切片和25个块状样本进行了研究，但野外分析仍处于初始阶段，需谨慎对待。

将土壤微形态（同微探针）与有机物含量、磷酸盐分馏、磁化率（包括χmax）、重金属铜、铅、锌的研究结合起来进行分析，初步了解了裴李岗至二里头时期土壤和沉积物的微观地层。由此得到了一个虽有限但广泛的数据集，使得本章能够对仰韶地层序列的结构起源有所了解。

仰韶地层序列中，使用本地"干净"黄土掺和植物制作土坯，然后使用土坯建筑地面，并在每个"白灰面"下方制作"深红色"的泥浆涂抹层。"白灰面"并非烧石灰层，而是由单层和多层凝灰岩石板建造，这些凝灰岩石板可能开采自本地沿泉水线一线沉积的凝灰岩岩石。石板的尺寸似乎皆超过3～4米，其开采和运输的实现说明当时存在着高度的社会组织。但是，至今尚未发现任何采石场。

仰韶时期的活动面（只有地面上的遗迹）至今没有发现，那么，该地面若非具有仪式用途[32]，就是已经被清扫或用垫土覆盖。整个数据库还提供了对遗址的遗迹和景观史的间断观察，包括对河流系统的控制及在积水环境中人为活动的土壤及沉积物的"非现场"累积的信息。

致谢：我们非常感谢在灰嘴工作的同仁——斯坦福大学的刘莉、澳大利亚拉筹伯大学的约翰·韦伯（John Webb）、中国社会科学院考古研究所的陈星灿及伦敦大学学院艾琳·罗森（Arlene Rosen）等人员的合作和共同探讨，感谢澳大利亚研究理事会对这项研究的资助。我们还十分感谢约翰·韦伯（拉筹伯大学）允许引用他的矿物学数据，感谢李炅娥（Gyoung-Ah Lee）和魏鸣（拉筹伯大学）在实地考察期间提供的帮助，Paul Goldberg（波士顿大学考古系）对一些切片的分析及Chris Hayward（剑桥大学地质系）对样品的观察。

注 释

[1] Liu L, Chen X C, Lee Y K, et al. Settlement Patterns and Developing of Social Complexity in the Yiluo Region, North China. Journal of Field Archaeology, 2002-2004, 29: 75-100.

[2] Liu L, Chen X C, Lee Y K, et al. Settlement Patterns and Developing of Social Complexity in the Yiluo Region, North China. Journal of Field Archaeology, 2002-2004, 29: 75-100.

[3] 研究20～30μm厚的切片中未受干扰的土壤和沉积物。Courty M A, Goldberg P, Macphail R I. Soils and Micromorphology in Archaeology. Cambridge: Cambridge University Press, 1989.

[4] Goldberg P, Macphail R I. Practical and Theoretical Geoarchaeology. Oxford: Blackwell Publishing, 2006; Macphail R I, Crowther J. Tower of London Moat: Sediment Micromorphology, Particle Size, Chemistry and Magnetic Properties//Keevil G. Tower of London Moat Excavation, 1 Historic Royal Palaces Monograph. Oxford: Oxford Archaeology, 2004: 41-43, 48-50, 78-79, 82-83, 155, 183-186, 202-204, 271-284.

[5] Bethell P H, Máté I. The Use of Soil Phosphate Analysis in Archaeology: A Critique//Henderson J. Scientific Analysis in Archaeology, 19. Oxford: Oxford University Committee, 1989: 1-29; Courty M A, Goldberg P, Macphail R I. Soils and Micromorphology in Archaeology. Cambridge: Cambridge University Press, 1989; Crowther J. Potential Magnetic Susceptibility and Fractional Conversion Studies of Archaeological Soils and Sediments. Archaeometry, 2003, 45: 685-701; Crowther J, Barker P. Magnetic Susceptibility: Distinguishing Anthropogenic Effects from the Natural. Archaeological Prospection, 1995, 2: 207-215; Stoops G. Guidelines for Analysis and Description of Soil and Regolith Thin Sections. Madison, Wisconsin: Soil Science Society of America, Inc, 2003.

[6] Bouma J, Fox C A, Miedema R. Micromorphology of Hydromorphic Soils: Applications for Soil Genesis and Land Evaluation//Douglas L A. Soil Micromorphology: A Basic and Applied Science, 19 Developments in Soil Science. Amsterdam: Elsevier, 1990: 257-278.

[7] Duchaufour P. Pedology. London: Allen and Unwin, 1982.

[8] Soil Survey Staff. Soil Taxonomy. Washington D. C.: U. S. Department of Agriculture, U. S. Government Printing Office, 1999.

[9] FAO-Unesco. Soil Map of the World. Rome: FAO, 1988.

[10] Liu L, Chen X C, Lee Y K, et al. Settlement Patterns and Developing of Social Complexity in the Yiluo Region, North China. Journal of Field Archaeology, 2002-2004, 29: 75-100, Fig.3.

[11] Courty M A, Fedoroff N. Micromorphology of a Holocene Dwelling. Proceedings Nordic Archaeometry, PACT 7, 1982: 257-277; Slager S, Van der Wetering H T J. Soil Formation in Archaeological Pits and Adjacent Loess Soils in Southern Germany. Journal of Archaeological Science, 1977, 4: 259-267.

[12] Webb J, Ford A, Gorton J. Influences on Selection of Lithic Raw Material Sources at Huizui, a Neolithic/Early Bronze Age Site in Northern China. Bulletin of the Indo-Pacific Prehistory Association, 2007, (27): 76-86.

[13] Courty M A, Goldberg P, Macphail R I. Soils and Micromorphology in Archaeology. Cambridge: Cambridge University Press, 1989: 99, Figure 6.9b.

[14] Avery B W. Soils of the British Isles. Wallingford: CAB International, 1990: 187-188.

[15] 参见俄罗斯Kostenki地区黄土覆盖区的第四纪类似凝灰岩的地层。
Goldberg P. Boston University, pers. comm., 2006; Holliday V T, Hoffecker J, Goldberg P, et al. Geoarchaeology of the Kostenki-Borshchevo sites, Don River Valley, Russia. Geoarchaeology, 2007, 22: 181-228.

[16] Macphail R I, Crowther J. Tower of London Moat: Sediment Micromorphology, Particle Size, Chemistry and Magnetic Properties//Keevil G. Tower of London Moat Excavation, 1 Historic Royal Palaces Monograph. Oxford: Oxford Archaeology, 2004: 41-43, 48-50, 78-79, 82-83, 155, 183-186, 202-204, 271-284.

[17] Goldberg P, Macphail R I. Practical and Theoretical Geoarchaeology. Oxford: Blackwell Publishing, 2006; Macphail R I, Courty M A, Hather J, et al. The Soil Micromorphological Evidence of Domestic Occupation and Stabling Activities//Maggi R. Arene Candide: A Functional and Environmental Assessment of the Holocene Sequence (Excavations Bernabò Brea-Cardini 1940-50). Roma: Memorie dell'Istituto Italiano di Paleontologia Umana, 1997: 53-88; Matthews W, French C A I, Lawrence T, et al. Multiple Surfaces: The Micromorphology//Hodder I. On the Surface: Çatalhöyük 1993-95. Cambridge: McDonald Institute for Archaeological Research and British Institute of Archaeology at Ankara. 1996: 301-342; Matthews W, Hastorf C A, Ergenekon B. Ethnoarchaeology: Studies in Local Villages Aimed at Understanding Aspects of the Neolithic Site//Hodder I. Towards Reflexive Method in Archaeology: the Example at Çatalhöyük. Cambridge: McDonald Institute for Archaeological Research and British Institute of Archaeology at Ankara, 2000: 177-188.

[18] Courty M A, Goldberg P, Macphail R I. Soils and Micromorphology in Archaeology. Cambridge: Cambridge University Press, 1989; Goldberg P, Macphail R I. Practical and Theoretical Geoarchaeology. Oxford: Blackwell Publishing, 2006.

[19] Goldberg P, Macphail R I. Practical and Theoretical Geoarchaeology. Oxford: Blackwell Publishing, 2006.

[20] Boivin N L. Life Rhythm's and Floor Sequences: Excavating Time in Rural Rajasthan and Neolithic Çatalhöyük. World Archaeology, 1999, (31): 367-388.

[21] Goldberg P, Macphail R I. Practical and Theoretical Geoarchaeology. Oxford: Blackwell Publishing, 2006: Figures 11.9 and 12.8; Macphail R I, Crowther J. Tower of London Moat: Sediment Micromorphology, Particle size, Chemistry and Magnetic Properties//Keevil G. Tower of London Moat Excavation, 1 Historic Royal Palaces Monograph. Oxford: Oxford Archaeology, 2004: 41-43, 48-50, 78-79, 82-83, 155, 183-186, 202-204 and 271-284.

[22] Liu L, Chen X C, Lee Y K, et al. Settlement Patterns and Developing of Social Complexity in the Yiluo Region, North China. Journal of Field Archaeology, 2002-2004, 29: 75-100.

[23] Courty M A, Goldberg P, Macphail R I. Soils and Micromorphology in Archaeology. Cambridge: Cambridge University Press, 1989.

[24] Rosen A M. The Role of Environmental Change in the Development of Complex Societies in China: A Study from the Huizui Site. Bulletin of the Indo-Pacific Prehistory Association, 2007, (27): 39-48.

[25] Rosen A M. The Role of Environmental Change in the Development of Complex Societies in China: A Study from the Huizui Site. Bulletin of the Indo-Pacific Prehistory Association, 2007, (27):39-48.

[26] 例如含有植硅体的磷酸盐结核，可广泛地称为"粪便"。Goldberg P, Macphail R I. Practical and Theoretical Geoarchaeology. Oxford: Blackwell Publishing, 2006: 206.

[27] Thirly M, Galbois J, Schmitt J M. Unusual Phosphate Concretions Related to Groundwater Flow in a Continental Environment. Journal of Sedimentary Research, 2006, (76): 866-877.

[28] 遗址上发现的植硅体证据。Rosen A M. The Role of Environmental Change in the Development of Complex Societies in China: A Study from the Huizui Site. Bulletin of the Indo-Pacific Prehistory Association, 2007, (27): 39-48.

[29] Macphail R I. Soils and Microstratigraphy: A Soil Micromorphological and Micro-chemical Approach//Lawson A J. Potterne 1982-5: Animal Husbandry in Later Prehistoric Wiltshire, 17 Archaeology Report. Salisbury: Wessex Archaeology, 2000: 47-70; Macphail R I, Crowther J, Battlesbury H. Ampshire: Soil Micromorphology and Chemistry (W4896). Unpublished report. Salisbury: Wessex Archaeology, 2002.

[30] Goldberg P, Macphail R I. Practical and Theoretical Geoarchaeology. Oxford: Blackwell Publishing, 2006; Macphail R I, Crowther J. Tower of London Moat: Sediment Micromorphology, Particle Size, Chemistry and Magnetic Properties//Keevil G. Tower of London Moat Excavation, 1 Historic Royal Palaces Monograph. Oxford: Oxford Archaeology, 2004.

[31] Rentzel P, Narten G B. Zur Entstehung von Gehniveaus in sandig-lehmigen Ablagerungen -Experimente und archäologische Befunde (Activity surfaces in sandy-loamy deposits - experiments and archaeological examples), Jahresbericht 1999. Basel: Archäologische Bodenforschung des Kantons Basel-Stadt, 2000: 107-127.

[32] Liu L, Chen X C. Lee Y K, et al. Settlement Patterns and Developing of Social Complexity in the Yiluo Region, North China. Journal of Field Archaeology, 2002-2004, 29: 75-100.

CHAPTER 4 RISE AND FALL OF COMPLEX SOCIETIES IN THR YILUO REGION, NORTH CHINA: THE SPATIAL AND TEMPORAL CHANGES[①]

1. INTRODUCTION

The Yiluo River region has been regarded as a core area of Chinese civilization in the Yellow River valley, associated with the process of early state formation and the emergence of the first dynasties of ancient China (Liu and Chen, 2003). Decades of archaeological investigations have revealed rich material remains from several large Bronze Age urban centers in the region. The discovery of the Erlitou site, in particular, has attracted a great deal of attention and generated intense debates in regard to its historical affiliation with the first Chinese dynasty, Xia (Liu and Chen, 2003; Liu and Xu, 2007). However, we know much less about the regional development throughout the Neolithic and Bronze Ages, developments that involve not only large regional centers, but also medium and small settlements. In order to understand the regional-scale social processes, a fine-grained analysis of changes in settlement patterns through time over the entire region was urgently needed. The Yiluo regional survey project, therefore, was designed to address these issues. This project was conducted by two teams (the China-Australia-U.S Yiluo Region Collaborative Archaeological Team and the Erlitou Archaeology Team of Institute of Archaeology, Chinese Academy of Social Sciences), which carried out systematic full-coverage surveys from 1997 to 2007. The preliminary results from these surveys have been published in independent reports previously (Chen et al., 2003; Liu et al., 2002-2004; Xu et al., 2005). This paper aims to integrate the data generated by the two teams, and to present a coherent analysis of the settlement patterns in the entire Yiluo region.

---

① This chapter is written by Liu Li, Chen Xingcan, Henry T. Wright, Xu Hong, Li Yongqiang, Chen Guoliang, Zhao Haitao, Habeom Kim, Gyoung-Ah Lee during writing and editing archaeological report. The English version is post on *Quaternary International*, 2019(521): 4-15. Because this part has not been corrected with the latest data, some data are not consistent with the research part of this book.

2. REGIONAL SETTING

The Yiluo River valley is a vast fertile alluvial basin. The Yi and Luo rivers flow from SW to NE through the basin and join together forming a single channel, known as the Yiluo River, before emptying into the Yellow River. The basin is bound on the north by the Mangling hills, which separate the Yiluo Plain from the Yellow River, and is surrounded by mountain ranges on the other three sides including the Xiaoshan, Xiong'er, Funiu, and Songshan mountains running W-E, 500–2000 m in altitude. Despite these natural barriers, this basin is effectively connected by its rivers to adjoining regions in all directions. The basin's fertile land has ensured high agricultural yields that can support a high population density. The advantages of these geographical features appear to have been appreciated by imperial rulers throughout recorded Chinese history; at least ten dynasties established their capitals in the basin (Zhao and Xu, 1986).

North China experienced a warm-moist Mid-Holocene Climatic Optimum event (ca. 6000–3000 cal. BC), providing favorable conditions for the flourishing of Neolithic communities. However, this time period was also characterized by periodical fluctuations. Also, an episode of unstable cold-dry climate began around 2000 cal. BC during the Late Holocene (Chen et al., 2015; Feng et al., 2004; Feng et al., 2006; Ran and Feng, 2013; Shi et al., 1993). The palynological and lithological analyses of the sediments suggest that vegetation shifted from broad-leaved deciduous forest (9230–8850 cal. BP) to steppe-meadow vegetation (8850–7550 cal. BP), and then to steppe with sparse trees (7550–6920 cal. BP) in the Luoyang basin (J. Zhang et al., 2018). A geoarchaeological investigation in the Yiluo area has revealed a sequence of landscape changes related to human land use during the Mid-Holocene, beginning with a stable landscape, soil development and high-water tables in the Early Mid-Holocene, with limited human impact from the early Neolithic Peiligang populations. Subsequently, there was a rapid shift to episodes of hillslope erosion and increased valley alluviation in the later Mid-Holocene (ca. 7300–4100 cal. BP), indicative of intensive landscape management. This change coincides with more intensified millet agriculture and the first appearance of rice paddies during the middle and late Yangshao period. After ca. 4000 cal. BP, Holocene valley incision in some catchments led to narrowing floodplains, and the disappearance of the valley wetland deposits. This change corresponds with a period of drier climatic conditions in North China as the result of weakened summer monsoons. These seemingly unfavorable climatic conditions, however, correlated with the development of the Erlitou culture, which was the first state-level social organization in the region (Rosen, 2007, 2008; Rosen et al., 2017). It is clear that the interplay between climatic conditions and human activities is one of the key factors for understanding social development, a topic which will be further discussed later.

3. MATERIAL AND METHODS

Settlement pattern archaeology aims to comprehend the factors that determined the arrangement of sites in a region (Chang, 1968; Fish and Kowalewski, 1990). Settlement archaeology, based on systematic regional surveys, has facilitated the understanding of social processes in many regions around the world. This approach has also been proven successful in China, as exemplified by a number of survey projects in southeast Shandong (Fang et al., 2012), Chifeng in Inner Mongolia (Chifeng International Collaborative Archaeological Research Project, 2011), and the Huan River valley in Anyang, Henan (Tang and Jing, 1998). The Yiluo regional survey project has recorded 456 sites dating from the Paleolithic to Bronze Ages within an area of 1183 km^3, providing a relatively complete picture of changing sociopolitical landscapes in the region (Zhongguo Shehui Kexueyuan Kaogu Yanjiusuo and China-Australia-U.S. Cooperative Archaeological Team in Yiluo Region, in press). During the surveys, flotation samples, mostly from ash pits, were also collected for archaeobotanical analysis (Lee et al., 2007). Fifty-five charred plant specimens from flotation samples, dating to the Neolithic and Bronze Ages, were AMS-dated in order to check the absolute chronology in the region. AMS dates were calibrated using OxCal v.3.2 (Ramsey, 2001), based on IntCal 13 atmospheric curve (Reimer et al., 2013) (Table S1). All calibrate dates indicate a 1 sigma range). Then summed probability distributions (SPDs) were used to aggregate AMS dates to show the patterns of continuity and discontinuity of absolute dates among chronological periods. SPDs were generated using 'rcarbon' R package (Bevan et al., 2018).

Measuring the degree of regional social complexity requires a quantitative approach. We use three variables to analyze the social development process of the Yiluo area, including (1) the number of sites, (2) the largest site area, and (3) the levels of settlement hierarchy. The number of sites can reflect the population density while the size of the largest central settlement and the levels of settlement hierarchy indicate not only population density, but also social complexity and social organization. It has been suggested that when two to three levels of settlement hierarchy are observed in a region, the social organizations may be described as simple to complex chiefdoms; and when a regional system exhibits a four or more tiers of settlement hierarchy, it is likely to indicate the formation of a state (Earle, 1991; Flannery, 1998; Wright, 1977; Wright and Johnson, 1975).

Determining site boundaries and documenting site sizes were crucial in the surveys. We tentatively subscribe to a criterion of at least 3–5 diagnostic sherds from the same archaeological period, found within an area of 100 m square, as the minimal definition of a site. This is only, however, a heuristic criterion and other contextual factors (e.g., formation processes and micro-landscapes) are also taken into consideration. In most cases, we used archaeological features to verify the existence of sites. Hand-held Global Positioning Systems were used to confirm the actual surveyed locations on maps. Site boundaries were determined after a larger area was covered and artifacts were securely dated. Pottery sherds gathered from the surveys were used as the primary phase markers in our study, based on an established local ceramic sequence [for more details about survey methods see (Liu, et al., 2002-2004)].

In the Yiluo region, sites are characterized by containing either a single archaeological cultural period (single component) or multiple cultural periods (multicomponent). A majority of sites found are multicomponent with different occupation areas. This situation makes it difficult to estimate site size for each archaeological period. Three methods were used to record site size of multicomponent sites due to various depositional conditions: (1) the site size for each cultural period was identified; (2) one size was recorded for the entire site; and (3) sizes for certain periods were recorded, but for other periods they remain unclear. In many cases, for the site hierarchy analysis, we only include the sites whose sizes were recorded. Sites equal to or less than 9 ha are treated as single component settlements, since they are classified as small villages at the lowest tier of the settlement hierarchy. Larger sites may represent regional centers; therefore, the sites larger than 9 ha are classified into two categories: single component and multicomponent. Some large multicomponent settlements recorded with one size are also analyzed as single component cases, as they appear to have been continuously occupied for a long period of time with relatively similar material distribution for each period. In addition, when some sites were recorded with two sizes, a core area of material distribution and a maximum area of distribution (e.g., Erlitou, 300 ha and 540 ha, respectively; and Jinzhongsi, 34 ha and 83 ha, respectively), we use the size of the core area for this analysis. The above-mentioned criteria help us, to some extent, to avoid underestimating or overestimating site sizes, given the complexity of depositional conditions in this region. Site hierarchy analysis is based on the tendency of site-size clusters observable in histograms. The distributions of both types of site category (single component and multicomponent) are shown in histograms, but the determination of settlement hierarchy is based on the single component sites.

At some large multicomponent sites, the sizes of important early settlements are unclear, as they were partially destroyed by later occupations or recent development. In this situation, we will rely on the artifacts and features unearthed to discuss the nature of these early remains.

4. THE RESULTS

The settlement pattern analysis in this paper is based on the information of 451 Neolithic and the Bronze Age sites in the Yiluo survey database (Table 1), with a time span of nearly 6000 years. The archaeological cultures covered here include late Peiligang, Yangshao, Longshan, Erlitou, Erligang, Yinxu, Western Zhou, and Eastern Zhou. We will present analyses of settlement distribution and associated AMS dates in each cultural period.

4.1 The Peiligang period

A total of 16 sites were identified as the late Peiligang culture based on the ceramic typology. All sites are small (0.2–9 ha), located in various topographic settings, ranging from mountainous slopes, loess tablelands, to floodplains. Some small sites in the mountainous areas may have been seasonal settlements, whereas larger sites in the river valley are more likely to have been sedentary villages (Liu, et al., 2002-2004). Prior to our survey, a late Peiligang site at Wayaozui (17 ha; Figure 4.1a-1) in the southwestern part of Gongyi township was excavated in the 1990s (Gongyishi Wenwu Baohu Guanlisuo, 1996, 1997; Zhengzhou Wenwu Gongzuodui and Gongyishi Wenwu Guanlisuo, 1999). The site is situated outside our survey area and it no longer exists, due to residential developments after the excavations. Therefore, we are unable to verify its size. If the published information is correct, Wayaozui would account for the largest known Peiligang settlement in the Yiluo region. In addition, Xishiqiao (9 ha; Figure. 4.1a-5) is much larger than the rest sites (0.2-2.5 ha). Therefore, these two settlements may have formed regional centers in a two-tiered settlement hierarchy, but a large part of the region was sparsely occupied by very small settlements (Figures 4.1, 4.2).

Peiligang people practiced a broad-spectrum subsistence economy, characterized by hunting, wild plant foraging, and millet farming. Carbonized plant remains and starch analysis of grinding stones from the Tieshenggou site (Figure 4.1a-2) indicates that people collected and processed domesticated and wild cereals, acorns, beans, and tubers for food (Bestel, 2012; Lee, et al., 2007; Liu, et al., 2002-2004).

The Peiligang culture (excluding the Jiahu site) has been previously dated to ca. 6200–5000 cal. BC, which come from charcoal at sites outside the Yiluo region (Zhongguo Shehui Kexueyuan Kaogu Yanjiusuo, 2010:804-805). Two AMS dates were obtained from Peiligang sites in our survey. The date from Fudian E (Figure 4.1a-3) (5557–5380 cal. BC; NZA 33139; from charcoal) falls into the late Peiligang period, while the date from Fudian SE (Figure 4.1a-4) (4228–3982 cal. BC; D-AMS025483; from foxtail millet) seems contemporaneous with the early part of the Yangshao period (Figure 4.3; Table S4.1). These two sites are situated about 500 m apart, both containing pottery remains similar in typology. The AMS date on charcoal from Fudian E may be slightly earlier than the real age of the site due to an old-wood effect. The date from Fudian SE may suggest that the Peiligang style pottery continued to be in circulation to the early Yangshao period. More Peiligang dates need to be obtained in the future.

CHAPTER 4 RISE AND FALL OF COMPLEX SOCIETIES IN THR YILUO REGION, NORTH CHINA: THE SPATIAL AND TEMPORAL CHANGES

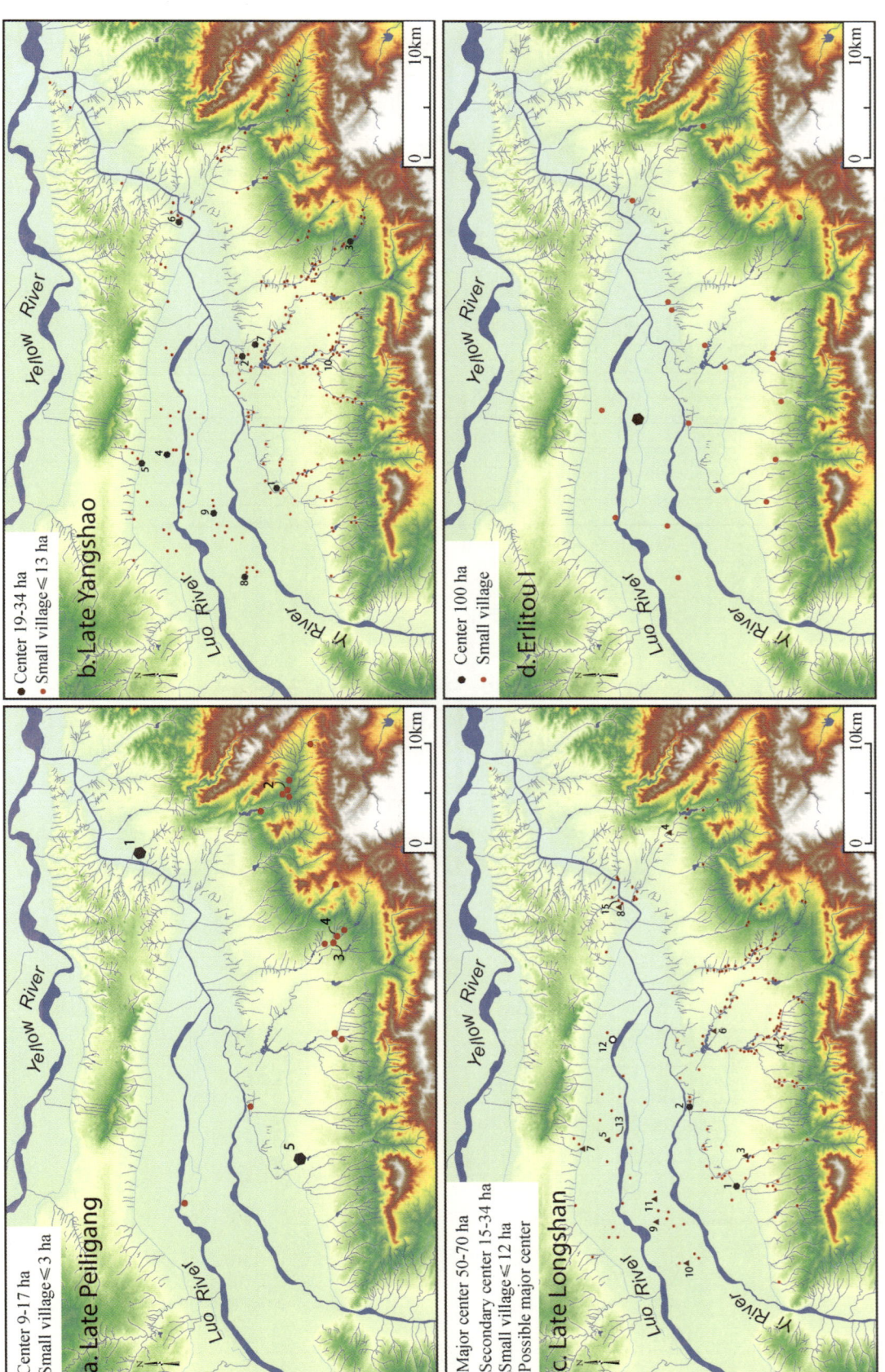

Figure 4.1 Settlement distribution from Peiligang to Erlitou I

a. Peiligang settlements: 1. Wayaozui; 2. Tieshenggou; 3. Fudian E; 4. Fudian SE; 5. Xishiqiao.
b. Mid-Late Yangshao settlements: 1. Wutun SE; 2. Miaowan; 3. Zhaocheng; 4. Jingyanggang; 5. Baozhuang NW; 6: Sigou; 7. Dongwanghe N; 8. Gangchang; 9. Jinzhongsi; 10. Huizui E.
c. Late Longshan settlements: 1. Nanzhaishangcun E; 2. Gaoya W; 3. Chenjiayao; 4. Luokou NE; 5. Jingyanggang; 6. Penyaozhai SW; 7. Baozhuang NW; 8. Sigou S; 9. Panzhailaozhai E; 10. Gangchang; 11. Jinzhongsi; 12. Tazhuang; 13. Songwan SE (Early Longshan); 14. Huizui E; 15. Sigou SE.
d. Erlitou I central settlement: Erlitou.

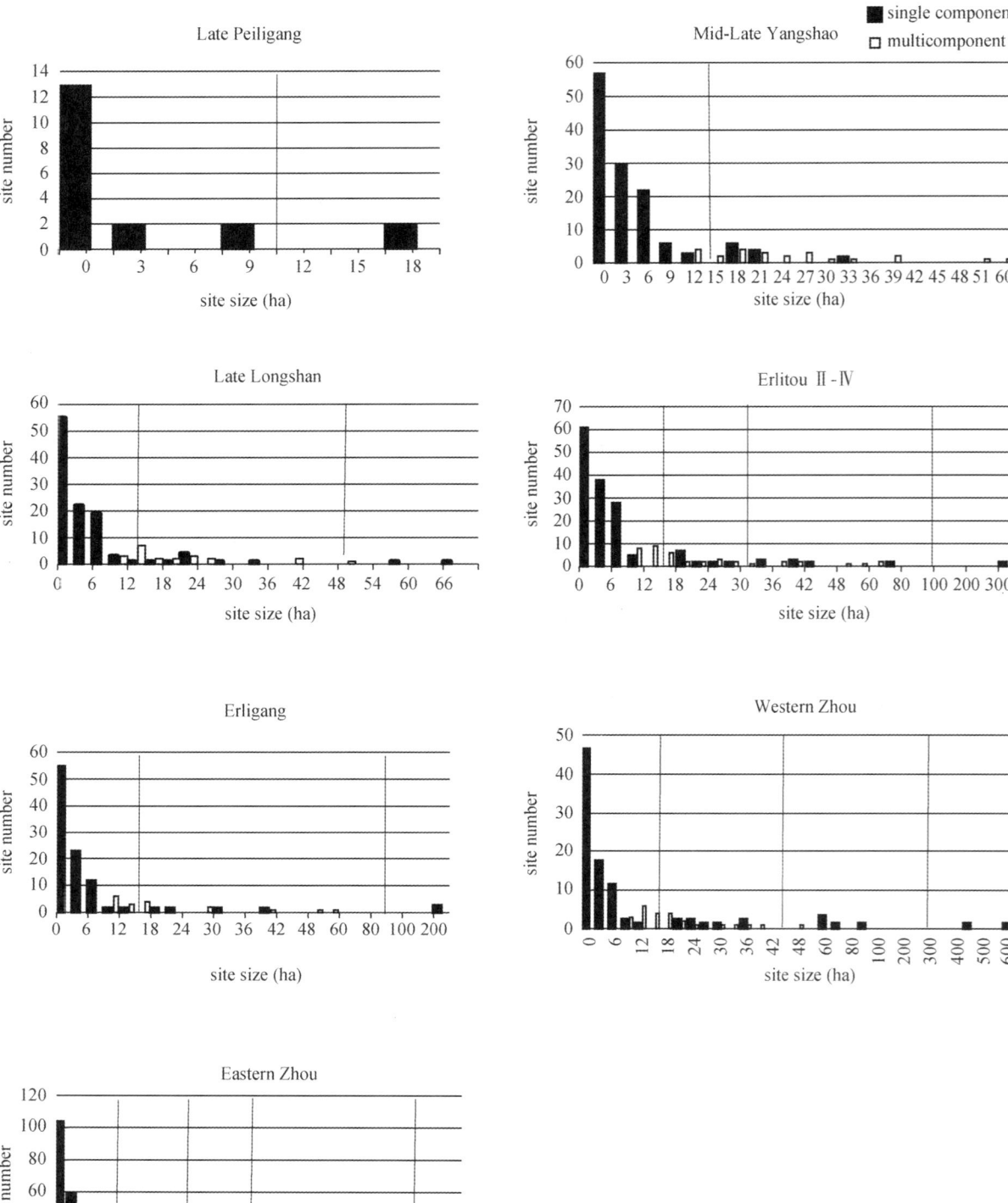

Figure 4.2 Settlement hierarchy from major periods

CHAPTER 4 RISE AND FALL OF COMPLEX SOCIETIES IN THE YILUO REGION, NORTH CHINA: THE SPATIAL AND TEMPORAL CHANGES

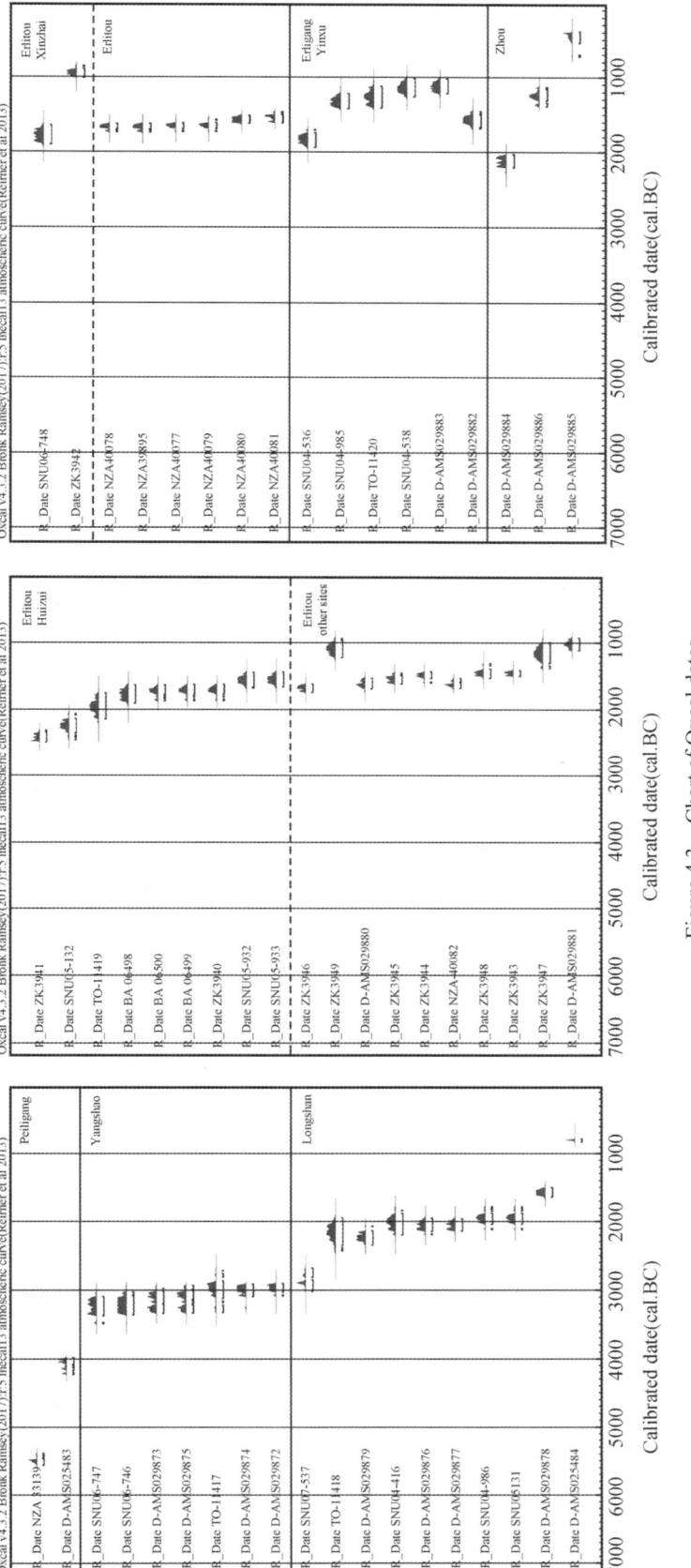

Figure 4.3 Chart of Oxcal dates

Table 4.1 AMS dates from the Yiluo region: Peiligang – Eastern Zhou
(all samples are charred seeds except a wood charcoal from Fudian E)

Serial #	Report #	Original #	Site name	Culture	Lab #	^{14}C BP	Cal. BC 68.2% probability	Cal. BC 95.4% probability	Cal. 95.4% BC range
PLG (n=2)									
313	Y124	00-124	Fudian E	Late PLG	NZA 33139	6521 ± 35	5522 (68.2%) 5471	5557 (83.8%) 5463 5446 (4.6%) 5418 5410 (7.0%) 5380	5557-5380
308	Y118	00-118	Fudian SE	Late PLG	D-AMS025483	5256 ± 26	4222 (6.3%) 4210 4154 (13.8%) 4132 4064 (22.9%) 4034 4024 (25.2%) 3993	4228 (10.8%) 4200 4170 (19.7%) 4126 4121 (5.9%) 4092 4082 (58.9%) 3982	4228-3982
YS (n=7)									
238	Y127	06-127E	Huizui E	Mid-late Yangshao	SNU06-747	4540 ± 50	3362 (18.3%) 3320 3272 (2.0%) 3266 3236 (26.9%) 3169 3164 (21.0%) 3112	3491 (2.1%) 3470 3374 (93.3%) 3090	3491-3090
304	Y078	00-078	Zhaocheng W	Early-mid Yangshao	SNU06-746	4500 ± 50	3338 (25.4%) 3264 3243 (12.7%) 3206 3195 (30.1%) 3103	3362 (89.5%) 3082 3068 (5.9%) 3026	3362-3026
390	Y050	98-050	Yulinzhuang S	Mid-late Yangshao	D-AMS029873	4454+32	3322 (34.6%) 3234 3171 (2.6%) 3163 3116 (13.9%) 3082 3067 (17.1%) 3027	3339 (44.1%) 3206 3196 (51.1%) 3012 2976 (0.1%) 2974	3339-2974
259	Y204	02-204	Bucun SE	Late Yangshao	D-AMS029875	4443+36	3321 (14.3%) 3272 3267 (12.5%) 3235	3334 (35.0%) 3212 3191 (6.9%) 3152	3334-3152
420	Y019	98-019	Weizhuang W	Late Yangshao	TO-11417	4330 ± 70	3082 (4.2%) 3068 3026 (64.0%) 2888	3327 (6.7%) 3218 3176 (0.8%) 3160 3121 (84.9%) 2862 2807 (2.7%) 2758 2718 (0.3%) 2709	3327-2709

CHAPTER 4 RISE AND FALL OF COMPLEX SOCIETIES IN THR YILUO REGION, NORTH CHINA: THE SPATIAL AND TEMPORAL CHANGES

(continued)

Serial #	Report #	Original #	Site name	Culture	Lab #	^{14}C BP	Cal. BC 68.2% probability	Cal. BC 95.4% probability	Cal. 95.4% BC range
238	Y127	06-127E	Huizui E	Mid-late Yangshao	D-AMS029874	4384 ± 35	3078 (3.2%) 3072 3024 (65.0%) 2925	3096 (95.4%) 2909	3096-2909
421	Y018	98-018	Weizhuang SW	Mid-late Yangshao	D-AMS029872	4351±33	3011 (26.8%) 2976 2971 (41.4%) 2911	3084 (4.5%) 3066 3028 (90.9%) 2899	3084-2899
Longshan (n=10)									
63	Y152	01-152	Sigou SE	Early Longshan	SNU04-537	4260 ± 50	2921 (50.2%) 2864 2806 (18.0%) 2760	3016 (64.3%) 2848 2814 (31.1%) 2678	3016-2678
440	Y1003	97-1003	Nanshi	Late Longshan	TO-11418	3740 ± 70	2278 (7.0%) 2251 2228 (1.8%) 2221 2210 (59.4%) 2033	2432 (0.4%) 2423 2402 (1.3%) 2380 2348 (93.7%) 1944	2432-1944
190	217	03-079	Zhaiwan NE	Late Longshan	D-AMS029879	3795 ± 33	2286 (60.1%) 2198 2164 (8.1%) 2151	2345 (94.8%) 2134 2073 (0.6%) 2064	2345-2064
238	Y127	02-127	Huizui E	Late Longshan	SNU04-416	3640 ± 60	2130 (15.9%) 2086 2050 (52.3%) 1926	2200 (95.1%) 1878 1837 (0.3%) 1831	2200-1831
413	Y022	98-022	Luokou NE	Late Longshan	D-AMS029876	3671 ± 36	2132 (33.0%) 2082 2060 (26.5%) 2016 1996 (8.7%) 1980	2191 (1.4%) 2180 2142 (94.0%) 1946	2191-1946
409	Y032	98-032	Wuluo Nandian	Late Longshan	D-AMS029877	3667 ± 30	2131 (32.1%) 2086 2051 (25.1%) 2014 1998 (11.0%) 1979	2137 (95.4%) 1956	2137-1956
344	Y069	00-069	Matun	Late Longshan	SNU04-986	3590 ± 40	2014 (9.1%) 1998 1979 (59.1%) 1892	2116 (1.7%) 2098 2039 (88.9%) 1874 1844 (2.9%) 1816 1798 (1.9%) 1779	2116-1779
250	Y196B	02-196	Jiandongcun NW	Late Longshan	SNU05131	3590 ± 40	2014 (9.1%) 1998 1979 (59.1%) 1892	2116 (1.7%) 2098 2039 (88.9%) 1874 1844 (2.9%) 1816 1798 (1.9%) 1779	2116-1779
62	Y151	01-151	Sigou S	Late Longshan	D-AMS029878	3292 ± 31	1612 (68.2%) 1531	1638 (95.4%) 1501	1638-1501
12	046	01-060	Baozhuang NW	Late Longshan	D-AMS025484	2625 ± 26	811 (68.2%) 794	831 (95.4%) 786	831-786

洛阳盆地中东部先秦时期遗址

(continued)

Serial #	Report #	Original #	Site name	Culture	Lab #	^{14}C BP	Cal. BC 68.2% probability	Cal. BC 95.4% probability	Cal. 95.4% BC range
ELT (n=27)									
238	Y127	05-127W	Huizui W	Erlitou III	ZK3941	3925 ± 25	2472 (31.1%) 2436 2420 (13.7%) 2404 2378 (23.4%) 2350	2484 (93.1%) 2336 2323 (2.3%) 2307	2484-2307
238	Y127	02-127W	Huizui W	Erlitou II	SNU05-132	3800 ± 40	2293 (56.9%) 2196 2171 (11.3%) 2146	2452 (2.0%) 2420 2405 (2.6%) 2378 2350 (89.0%) 2132 2082 (1.7%) 2059	2452-2059
238	Y127	00-127W	Huizui W	Erlitou	TO-11419	3600 ± 70	2120 (6.2%) 2094 2041 (62.0%) 1880	2141 (95.4%) 1754	2141-1745
238	Y127	02-127E	Huizui E	Erlitou	BA 06498	3455 ± 45	1876 (17.7%) 1841 1821 (11.1%) 1796 1782 (26.4%) 1732 1719 (13.0%) 1693	1891 (95.4%) 1658	1891-1658
238	Y127	02-127E	Huizui E	Erlitou	BA 06500	3425 ± 35	1770 (68.2%) 1665	1876 (9.7%) 1840 1821 (4.6%) 1796 1782 (81.1%) 1633	1876-1633
238	Y127	02-127E	Huizui E	Erlitou	BA 06499	3415 ± 35	1752 (68.2%) 1662	1872 (6.0%) 1844 1814 (1.8%) 1800 1778 (87.6%) 1626	1872-1626
238	Y127	04-127W	Huizui W	Erlitou II	ZK3940	3410 ± 35	1748 (68.2%) 1660	1871 (4.5%) 1844 1812 (1.0%) 1803 1776 (89.9%) 1622	1871-1622
238	Y127	04-127W	Huizui W	Erlitou	SNU05-932	3280 ± 50	1615 (68.2%) 1505	1681 (0.5%) 1676 1665 (94.9%) 1444	1681-1444
238	Y127	05-127W	Huizui W	Erlitou	SNU05-933	3270 ± 50	1612 (68.2%) 1502	1660 (95.4%) 1436	1666-1436
377	Y132	07-132	Xinhougou Zhuanchang E	Erlitou	ZK-3946	3380 ± 30	1731 (8.7%) 1720 1692 (59.5%) 1636	1746 (95.4%) 1616	1766-1616
393	Y039	98-022	Luokou	Erlitou	D-AMS029880	3335 ± 29	1665 (53.8%) 1607 1582 (14.4%) 1560	1690 (95.4%) 1528	1690-1528

CHAPTER 4 RISE AND FALL OF COMPLEX SOCIETIES IN THR YILUO REGION, NORTH CHINA: THE SPATIAL AND TEMPORAL CHANGES

(continued)

Serial #	Report #	Original #	Site name	Culture	Lab #	^{14}C BP	Cal. BC 68.2% probability	Cal. BC 95.4% probability	Cal. 95.4% BC range
249	Y196A	02-196	Jiandongcun N	Erlitou II	ZK3945	3260 ± 30	1607 (19.7%) 1582 1560 (48.5%) 1500	1616 (87.8%) 1492 1481 (7.6%) 1454	1616-1454
394	Y037	98-037	Shangzhuang S	Erlitou III	ZK3944	3225 ± 25	1515 (29.0%) 1490 1484 (39.2%) 1451	1600 (3.2%) 1585 1534 (92.2%) 1431	1600-1431
393	Y039	98-022	Luokou	Erlitou	NZA-40082	3335 ± 20	1661 (64.9%) 1610 1571 (3.3%) 1566	1686 (75.5%) 1600 1585 (19.9%) 1534	1686-1534
377	Y132	00-132	Xinhougou Zhuanchang E	Erlitou III	ZK3948	3175 ± 40	1496 (23.8%) 1471 1464 (44.4%) 1419	1530 (91.7%) 1384 1340 (3.7%) 1311	1530-1311
394	Y037	98-037	Shangzhuang S	Erlitou III	ZK3943	3175 ± 25	1495 (21.8%) 1476 1458 (46.4%) 1423	1500 (95.4%) 1412	1500-1412
361	Y083	00-083	Huilongwan Xincun E	Erlitou II/III	ZK3947	2950 ± 60	1256 (1.7%) 1251 1231 (66.5%) 1056	1384 (3.7%) 1341 1308 (91.7%) 996	1384-996
189	216	03-074	Zhaiwan SE	Erlitou	ZK3949	2905 ± 45	1190 (5.0%) 1178 1160 (6.5%) 1144 1130 (56.7%) 1014	1224 (93.9%) 974 956 (1.5%) 941	1224-941
361	Y083	00-083	Huilongwan Xincun E	Erlitou	D-AMS029881	2858 ± 29	1070 (1.5%) 1066 1056 (62.7%) 975 953 (4.0%) 944	1116 (95.4%) 928	1116-928
		04HXX AT10 H97 坑底	Xinzhai	Erlitou I	SNU06-748	3460 ± 50	1878 (18.9%) 1840 1826 (14.9%) 1793 1784 (24.6%) 1736 1716 (9.8%) 1695	1901 (95.4%) 1642	1901-1642
		04HXX-5 AT10④, H106③	Xinzhai	Erlitou I	ZK3942	2795 ± 25	978 (68.2%) 910	1012 (93.6%) 894 868 (1.8%) 854	1012-854
78	090	05YLV	Erlitou	Erlitou II	NZA 39895	3376 ± 25	1691 (68.2%) 1631	1741 (16.7%) 1711 1699 (78.7%) 1618	1741-1618
78	090	03-035	Erlitou	Erlitou III	NZA 40078	3374 ± 20	1688 (68.2%) 1638	1738 (11.8%) 1714 1696 (83.6%) 1622	1738-1622

Serial #	Report #	Original #	Site name	Culture	Lab #	^{14}C BP	Cal. BC 68.2% probability	Cal. BC 95.4% probability	Cal. 95.4% BC range
78	090	05YKV	Erlitou	Erlitou IV	NZA40077	3356 ± 20	1681 (5.9%) 1676 1665 (62.3%) 1624	1732 (2.9%) 1718 1693 (92.5%) 1612	1732-1612
78	090	05YLV	Erlitou	Erlitou IV	NZA 40079	3350 ± 20	1665 (68.2%) 1618	1729 (1.2%) 1721 1692 (91.8%) 1609 1578 (2.3%) 1563	1729-1563
78	090	05YLV	Erlitou	Erlitou II	NZA 40080	3290 ± 20	1610 (15.3%) 1594 1589 (52.9%) 1532	1618 (95.4%) 1512	1618-1512
78	090	05YLV	Erlitou	Erlitou	NZA-40081	3256 ± 20	1600 (15.4%) 1585 1534 (52.8%) 1500	1611 (91.7%) 1496 1475 (3.7%) 1460	1611-1460

ELG-YX (n=6)

Serial #	Report #	Original #	Site name	Culture	Lab #	^{14}C BP	Cal. BC 68.2% probability	Cal. BC 95.4% probability	Cal. 95.4% BC range
425	Y011	98-011	Feiyao SW	Upper Erligang	SNU04-536	3510 ± 40	1890 (68.2%) 1771	1941 (93.9%) 1741 1710 (1.5%) 1700	1941-1700
388	Y043	98-043	Tianposhuiku NE	Erligang	SNU04-985	3060 ± 40	1392 (34.7%) 1336 1324 (33.5%) 1268	1418 (95.4%) 1218	1418-1218
388	Y043	98-043	Tianposhuiku NE	Erligang	TO-11420	3020 ± 50	1385 (17.0%) 1340 1310 (48.5%) 1207 1201 (1.4%) 1196 1139 (1.3%) 1134	1409 (95.4%) 1122	1409-1122
324	Y058	00-058	Yangzhai NW	Erligang	SNU04-538	2940 ± 40	1215 (66.3%) 1083 1064 (1.9%) 1058	1260 (95.4%) 1018	1260-1018
315	Y086	00-086	Yanliangzhai SW	Erligang	D-AMS029883	2927 ± 31	1193 (29.4%) 1142 1132 (34.2%) 1072 1066 (4.6%) 1056	1217 (95.4%) 1022	1217-1022
53	065	02-001	Beiyao NE	Yinxu	D-AMS029882	3285 ± 47	1614 (68.2%) 1510	1682 (0.8%) 1674 1666 (88.7%) 1490 1484 (5.9%) 1450	1686-1450

Zhou (n=3)

Serial #	Report #	Original #	Site name	Culture	Lab #	^{14}C BP	Cal. BC 68.2% probability	Cal. BC 95.4% probability	Cal. 95.4% BC range
62	Y151	11-151	Sigou S	Early-mid W. Zhou	D-AMS029884	3726+31	2196 (18.8%) 2170 2148 (15.6%) 2125 2090 (33.8%) 2044	2206 (95.4%) 2029	2206-2029

(continued)

CHAPTER 4 RISE AND FALL OF COMPLEX SOCIETIES IN THR YILUO REGION, NORTH CHINA: THE SPATIAL AND TEMPORAL CHANGES

(continued)

Serial #	Report #	Original #	Site name	Culture	Lab #	^{14}C BP	Cal. BC 68.2% probability	Cal. BC 95.4% probability	Cal. 95.4% BC range
257	Y199	07-199	Laotunzhai	W-E Zhou	D-AMS029886	3010 ± 30	1369 (3.6%) 1360 1295 (64.6%) 1209	1386 (12.2%) 1340 1310 (78.9%) 1156 1146 (4.4%) 1128	1386–1128
63	Y152	11-152	Sigou SE	W-E Zhou	D-AMS029885	2371 ± 32	484 (68.2%) 396	726 (0.5%) 720 704 (0.9%) 695 541 (94.0%) 386	726–386

4.2 The Yangshao period

The Yiluo regional survey recorded a total of 228 Yangshao sites, rather densely distributed over the entire region. All, except for 54 sites, can be further ascribed to the early, middle, and late phases, based on pottery typology. Early Yangshao sites are scarce (n=20), but the number increased considerably in the middle (n=77) and the late (n=146) phases. Six single-component early Yangshao sites are less than 6 ha in size, indicating a very low population density similar to the Peiligang period. We analyzed 142 clearly dated and measured middle and late Yangshao sites, including 95 single component and 47 multicomponent sites. The single component sites tend to form two clusters in the histogram for settlement hierarchy: (1) ten relatively large sites as regional centers (19–34 ha), and (2) 85 sites as small villages (≤ 13 ha). Some of the 14 relatively large multicomponent sites (20–68 ha) may have also functioned as regional centers, but it is hard to pinpoint the actual areas of the Yangshao occupations. The data indicates that a two-tiered settlement hierarchy emerged by the middle and late Yangshao period (Figures 1b, 2).

The Yangshao period is characterized by more intensive millet farming (Lee, et al., 2007) and pig domestication, but collecting wild cereals (Triticeae) and tubers (such as yam *Dioscorea polystachya*) was also a part of subsistence strategies (Liu et al., 2018a). Some sites also exhibit complex features in settlement layout. For example, Huizui E (10 ha; Figure 4.1b-10) has revealed several large house foundations, which may have functioned as central facilities for community ceremonies, such as feasting involving consumption of millet-based alcoholic beverages (Liu et al., 2018b).

Based on recent publications, the Yangshao culture lasted over 2000 years in the Yellow River region, generally dating to the period 5000–2700 cal. BC. It can be further divided into early, middle and late phases in Henan, represented by the Banpo phase (ca. 5000–3900 cal. BC), Miaodigou phase (ca. 4000–3100 cal. BC), and Qinwangzhai phase (ca. 3700–2700 cal. BC) (Zhang et al., 2013). We obtained seven AMS dates from middle and late Yangshao sites in our survey area. These dates fall into a range of 600 years (3490–2900 cal. BC), which seems to match well with the ceramic chronology (Figure 4.3; Table S4.1). Our settlement data indicates that the Yiluo region experienced very strong population growth during the middle and late Yangshao periods, and a two-tiered settlement system spread over a large part of the region (Figure 4.3).

4.3 The Longshan period

The survey area revealed a total of 211 Longshan sites, including 61 early- and 156 late- phase examples. The remaining (25) can only be assigned generally to the Longshan culture. The early Longshan period seems to have experienced a sharp reduction in site number as compared to the late

Yangshao (146), but from the middle to the late Longshan, the number nearly tripled, being slightly higher than that of the late Yangshao.

The early Longshan sites tend to be small, generally less than 10 ha in area; but some sites show special features. Songwan SE (Figure 4.1c-13), for example, is a small site with a remaining area of 0.6 ha; but based on an early excavation, the site appears to have been surrounded by moats, suggesting a much bigger original site size.

We analyzed 132 late Longshan sites for settlement hierarchy, including 110 single component and 22 multicomponent sites. Three clusters emerged from the histogram of site sizes: (1) two large sites as major centers (50–70 ha), (2) nine medium sites as secondary centers (15–34 ha), and (3) 99 sites as small villages (≤ 12 ha). Some of the 12 multicomponent sites (15–50 ha) may have also functioned as regional centers. The settlement data suggests a three-tiered settlement hierarchy, which is more complex than the Yangshao period (Figures 4.1c, 2).

Some sites have revealed special features and artifacts, consistent with the development of high levels of social complexity. Tazhuang (size unclear; Figure 4.1c-12), for example, was found at the location where Yanshi Shang City was built during the Erligang period. Excavations at Tazhuang revealed Longshan drainage pipes associated with large architectural features and rammed-earth foundations (Zhongguo Shehui Kexueyuan Kaogu Yanjiusuo, 2013: 119, 310), which were largely destroyed by the later construction of the Yanshi Shang City. These Longshan architectural facilities suggest the presence of a high ranking, large settlement, possibly a major center. Also, Huizui E (10 ha; Figure 4.1c-14) grew to a craft production center for making stone spades, suggesting the development of craft specialization in the region (Liu et al., 2007). The specialized manufacture of spades, mostly soil-working tools, may point to increased control of agricultural activities in the region, although wild cereals (Triticeae) and tubers (yam; root of snakegourd, *Trichosanthes kirilowii*; and lily, *Lilium* sp.) were continuously collected (Liu, et al., 2018a).

The Longshan culture in Henan is generally divided into the early (Miaodigou II; 2900–2600 cal. BC) and late (Wangwan III; 2600–1900 cal BC) phases (Zhongguo Shehui Kexueyuan Kaogu Yanjiusuo, 2010). We obtained ten AMS dates from the Longshan sites, including one from the early and nine from the late phases. The early Longshan sample from Sigou SE (Figure 4.1c-15) dates to 3016–2678 cal. BC, while seven samples from the late Longshan sites ranges from 2430 to 1780 cal. BC. These dates are relatively consistent with the conventional Longshan chronology in Henan. Two outliers from late Longshan sites of Sigou S (Figure 4.1c-8; 1638–1501 cal BC; D-AMS029878) and Baozhuang NW (Figure 4.1c-7; 831–786 cal. BC; D-AMS025484) may result from samples relocated from later contexts (Figure 4.3; Table S4.1). The early Longshan date partially overlaps with the late Yangshao dates, perhaps suggesting a continuity of human occupation in the region. However, a gap of about 200 years at ca. 2600 cal BC between the early and late Longshan periods is shown on the SPD graph (Figure 4.4a). This observation needs to be tested with a larger sample size from early Longshan sites to see whether an episode of depopulation, indeed, occurred at this time in the region.

4.4 The Erlitou period

A total of 207 sites date to the Erlitou period, which is further divided into four phases according to the pottery typology. Only 19 sites are assigned to ELT Phase I (Figure 4.1d), but sites increased

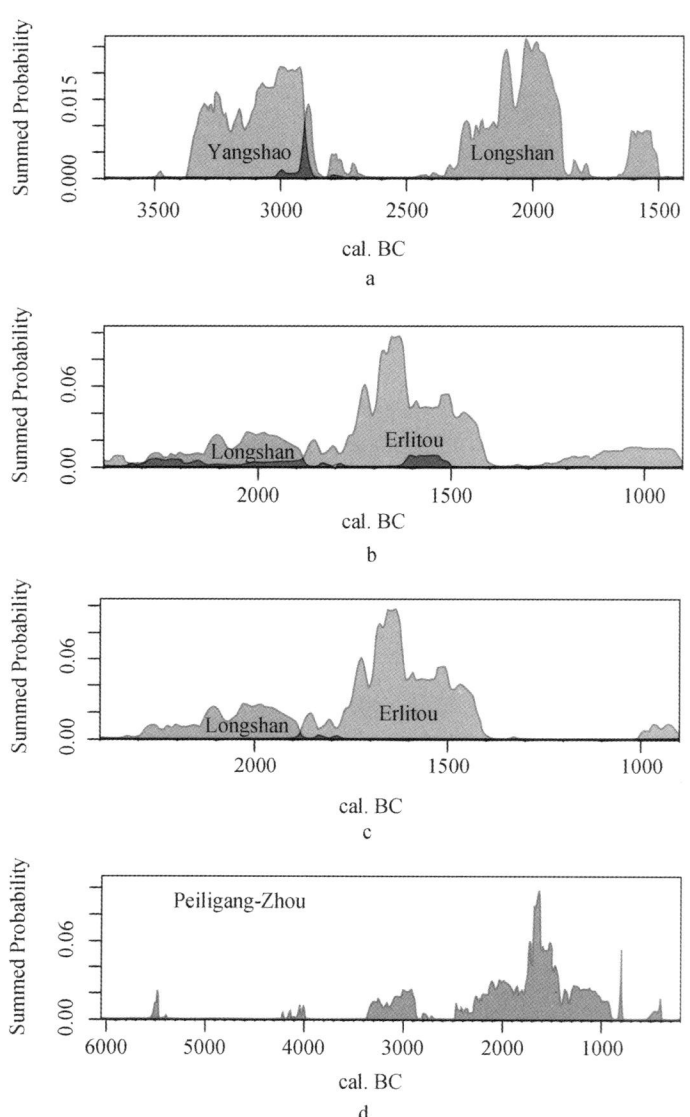

Figure 4.4　AMS dates analyzed with the summed probability distributions (SPD) method

a. The overlay of the SPD of Yangshao (n=7) and Longshan dates (n=10), showing the overlap of the two periods between ca. 3000 and 2900 cal. BC in dark shade, also a gap at ca. 2600 cal. BC between early Longshan and late Longshan.

b. The overlay of the SPD of Longshan (n=10) and Erlitou dates (n=27), showing the overlap of the two periods between ca. 2300 and 1800 cal. BC in dark shade.

c. The overlay of the SPD of Longshan (n=8) and Erlitou (n=21) dates after removal of outliers, showing the overlap of the two periods between 1900 and 1800 cal. BC in dark shade.

d. The SPD of all 14C dates (n=55), showing fluctuations from 6000 to 200 cal. BC.

in number continuously from Phase II (n=76), Phase III (n=92), to Phase IV (n=94). Eighty-one sites cannot be assigned to a specific phase. The emergence of the Bronze Age Erlitou urban center was the most significant event during this time period, characterized by the presence of palatial complex, elite burials, and the production of prestige items, such as bronze ritual vessels and turquoise objects (Zhongguo Shehui Kexueyuan Kaogu Yanjiusuo, 1999, 2014). This urban center measured 100 ha in site size during Phase I, and reached 300 ha during Phases II-IV during the peak of the Erlitou culture development (Xu et al., 2004). Erlitou Phase I deposits are thin and scarce, and often occur together with those of later phases, so it is difficult to estimate the site hierarchy in Phase I. Therefore, we analyzed 184 sites from Phase II-IV, including 144 single component and 40 multicomponent sites. The distribution of the single-component sites appears to cluster into four groups in the histogram: (1) the primary center at Erlitou (300 ha), (2) six secondary centers (33–80 ha), (3) ten tertiary centers (18–29 ha), and (4) 127 small villages (≤12 ha). Some of the 15 relatively large multicomponent sites (22–80 ha) may have also functioned as regional centers. This four-tiered settlement hierarchy centered in Erlitou II-IV times marks the beginning of a state-level political organization (Figures 2, 5a).

Specialized craft production developed to a new height, exemplified by the emergence of at least four stone spade manufacturing centers near the Songshan Mountains (Liu, et al., 2007). This development suggests a higher degree of the organization of agriculture in order to cultivate more land and support a larger population in the region.

The chronology of the Erlitou culture has been a matter of changing interpretations. It was first dated to 1900–1500 cal. BC, but recently revised to 1750–1530 cal. BC, all based on samples from the Erlitou site (Zhang et al., 2007). We obtained 25 AMS dates from the Yiluo region, including six from the Erlitou site, nine from the Huizui site, and ten from other sites. All sites except for Erlitou are medium or small settlements, and all samples were collected from deposits dating to Phases II-IV based on pottery chronology. In addition, we also dated two samples from Erlitou Phase I deposits at the Xinzhai site in Xinmi, which is more than 100 km southeast of the Erlitou site.

All six dates from the Erlitou site are concentrated within a range of 1740–1460 cal. BC. The beginning date of this range is consistent with the previously reported chronology of the site, but its ending date is later (1750–1535 cal. BC) (Zhang, et al., 2007). The nine dates from Huizui spread out widely (2485–1440 cal. BC), with three samples earlier than 2000 cal. BC. Seven samples from other sites fall into a range of 1765–1410 cal. BC. Three outlier dates from Huilongwan Xincun E and Zhaiwan SE (Figure 4.5a-18,19) are later than 1390 cal. BC. Beside the six outliers, 13 samples (six from Huizui and seven from other sites) all fall into a range of 1890–1410 cal. BC (Figure 4.3; Table S1). The SPD analysis shows that the late Longshan and Erlitou AMS dates overlap considerably with and without inclusion of the outliers (Figure 4b, c), suggesting a continuous occupation in the region, and these two types of pottery may have coexisted for a while. Also, medium and small settlements

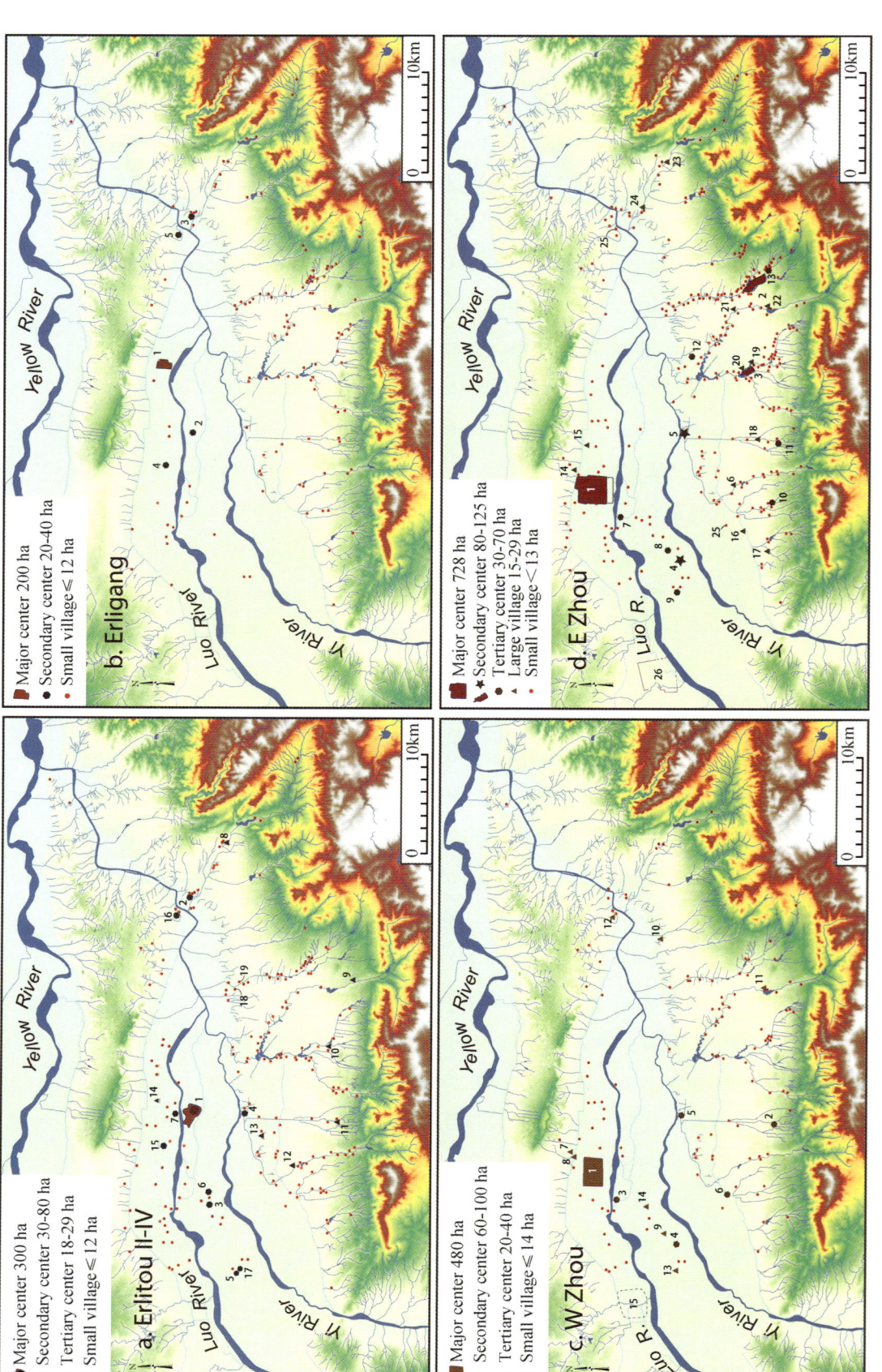

Figure 4.5 Settlement distribution from Erlitou II-IV to Eastern Zhou

a. Erlitou II-IV settlements: 1. Erlitou (central dot: Erlitou Phase I, outer area: Phases II-IV); 2. Shaochai; 3. Jinzhongsi; 4. Gaoya W; 5. Guilianwa S; 6. Luogedang; 7. Gucheng W; 8. Luokou NE; 9. Xikouzi; 10. Huizui; 11. Jingzhou E; 12. Gongjiayao; 13. Yangcun N; 14. Nancaizhuang NW; 15. Jingyanggang; 16. Sigou; 17. Gangchang; 18. Huilongwan Xincun E; 19. Zhaiwan SE.
b. Erligang settlements: 1. Yanshi Shang City; 2. Erlitou; 3. Shaochai; 4. Jingyanggang; 5. Sigou.
c. Western Zhou settlements: 1. Hanqi city; 2. Jingzhou E; 3. Sunjiagang; 4. Muzhuang; 5. Gaoya W; 6. Nanzhaishangcun E; 7. Baozhuang NW; 8. Baozhuang N; 9. Xishiba; 10. Nanluo; 11. Tunzhai NW; 12. Sigou; 13. Gangchang; 14. Jinzhongsi; 15. Luoyi (Chengzhou) (Luoyi and Hanqi existed successively).
d. Eastern Zhou settlements: 1. Hanqi city; 2. Huaguo Gucheng; 3. Liuguo Gucheng; 4. Muzhuang; 5. Gaoya W; 6. Gongjiayao; 7. Sunjiagang; 8. Xishiba; 9. Guilianwa S; 10. Yuangou E; 11. Jingzhou E; 12. Dongwanghe N; 13. Yanliangshuiku W; 14. Baozhuang N; 15. Shiqiao NE; 16. Liujiayao; 17. Lugou NE; 18. Luqiao SE; 19. Zhengyao S; 20. Zhengyao; 21. Wangwan NW; 22. Tunzhai NW; 23. Luokou NE; 24. Qingyizhen E; 25. Sigou W; 26. E. Zhou Wangcheng (E. Zhou Wangcheng and Hanqi were major urban centers successively).

show a wider margin in dates than the Erlitou urban center in both ours and previously published data (Zhang, et al., 2007). It is also notable that one sample from the Erlitou Phase I deposit at the Xinzhai site, located more than 100 km southeast of Erlitou, dates to 1901–1642 cal. BC (SNU06-748), which is consistent with the early part of the Erlitou period in the Yiluo region. The other Xinzhai sample, however, is an outlier date (1012–854 cal. BC; ZK3942) (Figure 4.3; Table S1).

Six outliers in the Erlitou dates (pre-2000 cal. BC or post-1400 cal. BC) may reflect two possibilities: (1) Erlitou-style pottery emerged among some settlements in the Yiluo region when the late Longshan-style vessels were still in circulation, and some people continued to make the Erlitou-style pottery after 1400 cal. BC. (2) Seeds dated were those relocated from either earlier (Longshan) or later contexts (Shang) rather than those *in situ* from the Erlitou deposits.

4.5 The Shang period (Erligang-Yinxu)

A total of 120 sites have been identified as the Erligang culture, commonly regarded as the early Shang period, which are further divided into Lower (n=36) and Upper (n=65) phases. Thirty-three sites can only be assigned to the Erligang period. The most significant development of this time was the rise of the Yanshi Shang City, a walled urban center built at a location only 6 km northeast of Erlitou (Zhongguo Shehui Kexueyuan Kaogu Yanjiusuo, 2013). It has been commonly interpreted as a political and military center of the early Shang dynasty, whose people conquered the Xia capital at Erlitou (Liu and Chen, 2003). Sixty sites of the Yinxu phase (the Late Shang dynasty) have also been found.

We analyzed 111 Erligang sites, including 94 single components. These sites tend to group into three clusters in the histogram: (1) the major center at Yanshi Shang City (200 ha), (2) four secondary centers (20–40 ha), and (3) 89 small villages (≤12 ha). Some of the four relatively large multicomponent sites (27–56 ha) may have also functioned as secondary centers in the region (Figures 2, 5b). The data, during the period from Erlitou to Erligang, show a clear trend of decrease in site number, site hierarchy, and size of the major center, implying an overall decline in political importance and population density in the Yiluo region. This event was parallel to the rise of the contemporaneous Zhengzhou Shang City (ca. 1300 ha or larger), about 100 km east of Yanshi, indicating that the political center moved from the Yiluo region to the Zhengzhou area. Since Zhengzhou was the paramount center for the Erligang political system, the Yiluo sites are part of a four-level settlement hierarchy, representing a state.

This downturn in scale of the settlement system continued to the Yinxu phase, indicated by fewer sites and the lack of large settlements as regional centers. The Yiluo region was no longer a political center at this time, a situation in a sharp contrast to the very large Shang capital city that flourished at Yinxu in the modern city of Anyang, northern Henan, some 250 km northeast.

The Erligang culture has been dated to 1580–1210 cal. BC, which is further divided to the Lower (1580–1415 cal. BC) and Upper (1429–1210 cal. BC) phases, based on the samples from the Zhengzhou area (Zhang, et al., 2007). The ^{14}C dates from Yanshi Shang City fall into a range of 1600–1260 cal. BC, largely echoing that of the Zhengzhou dates. The chronology of the Yinxu phase is reported as 1250–1046 cal. BC (Xia Shang Zhou Chronology Project Team, 2000). We obtained five AMS dates from Erligang deposits and one from a Yinxu deposit in the Yiluo region. Of them, four Erligang samples fall into a range of 1420–1020 cal. BC, consistent with a period from the Upper Erligang to the Yinxu phase. The other two dates are outliers, probably affected by the deposits mixed with earlier materials. It is notable that in our survey record, the date range of most Erlitou sites (1890–1410 cal. BC) and that of Erligang sites (1420–1020 cal. BC) are sequentially connected (Figure 4.3; Table S1). These dates from our survey, derived from medium and small sites, suggest that replacement of the Erlitou IV pottery with Erligang pottery occurred in some medium and small settlements long after people at the large regional center (Yanshi Shang City) already adopted the Erligang style pottery. There is also a considerable overlapping in ^{14}C dates between Erlitou IV at Erlitou and Lower Erligang at Yanshi Shang City, suggesting the coexistence of two pottery styles at these central settlements. Taken together, the transition from Erlitou culture to Erligang culture, represented by the change of pottery styles, may have been a long process.

4.6 Western and Eastern Zhou

The Yiluo region experienced another episode of rapid social development and population growth during the Zhou period. The sites are more than double in number from the late Shang (n=60) to the Western Zhou (n=138) (1045–771 cal. BC), accompanied by the emergence of two very large walled urban centers. One is located on both sides of the Chan River (600 ha), probably was the "Luoyi (Chengzhou)" recorded in ancient texts (Ye et al., 1991), and the other is at the Hanqi City (Figure 4.5c-1) (Zhongguo Shehui Kexueyuan Luoyang Hanweicheng Dui, 1998), which was built in late Western Zhou or the transition between Western and Eastern Zhou (Liang, 2002; Liu, 1998; Xu, 2007). These changes correlated, in time and space, with the construction of Luoyi (Chengzhou) by the Duke of Zhou in the early Western Zhou era and the Zhou court involved in the conflict with *Huaiyi* in late Western Zhou, based on textual records (Xu, 2007). We analyzed 119 Western Zhou sites, including 91 single-component cases, revealing a four-tiered settlement hierarchy: (1) two major centers on the Chan River (600 ha) and at the Hanqi City (480 ha), (2) five secondary centers (60–100 ha), (3) eight tertiary centers (20–40 ha), and (4) 77 small villages (≤14 ha). Some of the 19 relatively large multicomponent sites (19–80 ha) may have also functioned as secondary or tertiary centers (Figures 2, 5c).

The Yiluo region reached its highest level of social development and population density during the Eastern Zhou period (770–221 cal BC), as indicated by the marked increase in site number (n=294) and the much enlarged Hanqi walled city (728 ha; Figure 4.5d-1) (Zhongguo Shehui Kexueyuan Luoyang Hanweicheng Dui, 1998). We analyzed 277 sites, including 222 single-component ones. The site distribution in the histogram shows a five-tiered settlement hierarchy: (1) two primary urban center at the Eastern Zhou Wangcheng (1000 ha) and Hanqi City (728 ha), (2) four secondary centers (80–125 ha), (3) eight tertiary centers (30–70 ha), (4) 11 large villages (15–29 ha), and (5) 198 small villages (<13 ha). Some of the 35 relatively large multicomponent sites (15–80 ha) may have also functioned as regional centers at different levels (Figures 2, 5d). This unprecedented level of social complexity, the high population density, and the presence of very large Eastern Zhou Wangcheng and Hanqi City correlated with establishment of the Eastern capital city at Luoyang on 510 BC by the Zhou court, as recorded in ancient texts. Two secondary centers at Huaguo Gucheng and Liuguo Gucheng (Figure 4.5d-2,3) were large, fortified cities, and their developments reflected a decentralized political landscape at the time, when the Eastern Zhou court was losing its hegemonic power and inter-polity competition among smaller states intensified in the region (Hsu, 1965; Lewis, 1999).

We dated three samples from the Zhou sites. One sample from Sigou SE (Figure 4.5d-25) (726–385 cal. BC; D-AMS029885) is consistent with the Eastern Zhou chronology, but the other two appear to be outliers, which are too early for the Zhou period (Figure 4.3; Table S4.1). The samples were probably affected by a mixture with earlier deposits at these sites.

5. DISCUSSION

5.1 General trend of sociopolitical and population fluctuations

Settlement data and AMS dates indicate the Yiluo region experienced several episodes of sociopolitical and population fluctuations throughout the 6,000 years of occupation, as judged by the three criteria: number of sites, size of the largest site, and level of settlement hierarchy (Figure 4.6). In the following summary of each period, the AMS dates for the prehistoric period in our database represent mostly small and medium sites.

(1) Late Peiligang culture (5555–3980 cal. BC): for the first time, small sedentary villages, with a mixed farming and foraging subsistence strategies, appeared in the region. Population density was likely very low (17 small sites). Two central settlements (9–17 ha) possibly developed near rivers, forming a two-tiered settlement hierarchy in some areas of the region.

(2) Yangshao culture: population density was likely also low during the early Yangshao (20 small sites), and no significant changes are observable from late Peiligang to the Early Yangshao transition.

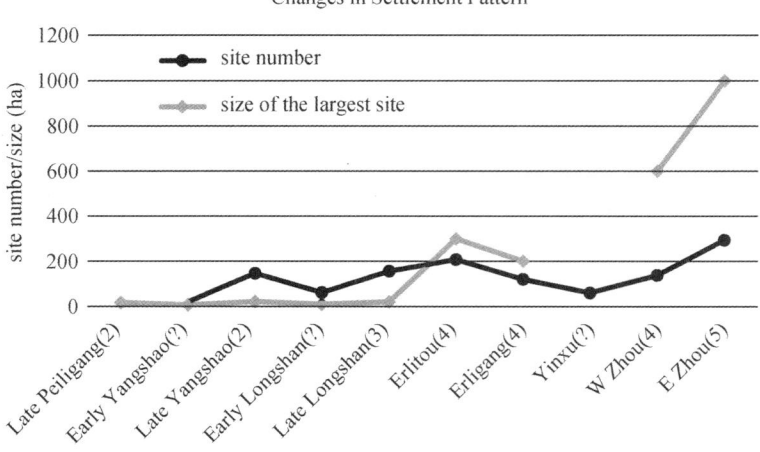

Figure 4.6 Changing settlement patterns from Peiligang to Eastern Zhou

The first episode of population increase happened in the middle and late Yangshao period (3490–2860 cal. BC). This is indicated by the dramatic increase in site number (at least 146 late Yangshao sites) and the emergence of ten central settlements (19–34 ha), forming a two-tiered settlement hierarchy over large part of the region.

(3) Longshan culture: The early Longshan period (3015–2680 cal. BC) suffered dramatic decline in site number (61) and absence of large settlements, suggesting a population downturn. This was followed by the second peak of population growth during late Longshan (2430–1780 cal. BC), showing a significant increase in site number (156), and the presence of two primary centers (50–70 ha) and nine secondary centers (15–34 ha), altogether forming a three-tiered settlement hierarchy, possibly representing a complex chiefdom system. The presence of high-ranking architectural facilities at Tazhuang is consistent with the development in settlement hierarchy.

(4) Erlitou culture: The number of sites in Phase I was low (at least 19), but the Erlitou site *per se* had become a large regional center (100 ha). Phases II-IV (most sites dating to 1890–1410 cal. BC) account for the third peak of social development and population growth in the region. This change is characterized by expansion of the Erlitou urban center (300 ha), as well as the emergence of six secondary centers (33–80 ha) and ten tertiary centers (18–29 ha). The formation of a four-tiered settlement hierarchy indicates a state level of social organization.

(5) Erligang and Yinxu periods (1600–1020 cal. BC): After the Erlitou period the region gradually lost its status as the primary sociopolitical center, with attendant decline in population density. In general, there are fewer sites in the Lower Erligang (at least 36) and Upper Erligang (at least 65) phases than in the Erlitou phase IV (at least 94). Given the overlapping AMS dates between Erlitou IV and Lower Erligang, the population decline may have occurred around Upper Erligang phase (ca. 1400 cal. BC). The primary regional center was smaller (Yanshi Shang City 200 ha), and the settlement

CHAPTER 4 RISE AND FALL OF COMPLEX SOCIETIES IN THR YILUO REGION, NORTH CHINA: THE SPATIAL AND TEMPORAL CHANGES

hierarchy also reduced to three levels. During the Yinxu period, the sites continued to drop in number (60), and large settlements were lacking.

(6) Zhou period (1045–222 cal. BC): The region witnessed the highest peak of social development in the pre-Qin period. From the Western Zhou to Eastern Zhou, the numbers of sites (138, 294), the sizes of the primary regional centers (480–600 ha, 728–1000 ha), and the levels of settlement hierarchy (4, 5) all reached the unprecedented levels. These changes in the settlement patterns are consistent with the history of political changes in the Zhou Dynasty. At this time, the Yiluo area re-emerged as a political center in the early dynastic era.

In short, as shown in Figure 4.6, settlement patterns in the Yiluo region exhibit several episodes of fluctuation in social evolution. After some 2000 years of slow development from Peiligang to early Yangshao, the first highpoint was the late Yangshao, characterized by an increase in population density and formation of two-tiered societies spread over the entire region. The second climax was the late Longshan, characterized by a marked increase in population density and a higher level of social complexity, representing the emergence of a complex chiefdom organization. The third peak was the Erlitou period; not only did the population density increase, but also the social structure demonstrated a qualitative transformation, marking the initial instance of state formation. The fourth peak was the Zhou dynasty, which was the result of the high political and economic development of a historical dynasty.

In the meantime, we observe two episodes of sociopolitical downturn, with low population density (Figure 4.6). The first was in the early Longshan period around 3000–2500 cal. BC, correlating with the beginning of the post Holocene climatic optimum period, characterized by fluctuating cool and dry conditions (Feng, et al., 2006). The stalactite data from Wanxiang cave (about 900 km west of Luoyang), in the western loess plateau of Gansu, has revealed a period of summer monsoon weakening in 5700–4920 cal BP, with an event of extreme weakening at 5400 cal. BP, causing significant reduction in precipitation (Bai et al., 2017). A study of stalagmite data from Dongshiya and Laomu caves in Luanchuan (in the mountainous region, about 150 km southwest of Luoyang) has revealed climatic fluctuations throughout the Holocene in western Henan, although it has not found an abrupt event around 3000–2500 cal. BC (N. Zhang et al., 2018). Future research needs to investigate to what extent this general climatic fluctuation around 3000 cal. BC affected the Yiluo basin. The second decline occurred in the late Shang dynasty, with low population density and lack of regional centers, due to the political center's move to other regions. Whether or not there is population decline between the late Longshan and the Erlitou is not clear. This particular issue concerns the origin of the Erlitou culture and the formation of the Erlitou state, which is further discussed below. These fluctuations in settlement pattern also mirror the SPD graph of all AMS dates (Figure 4.4d).

It is interesting to note that different phrases of climatic change may correlate with contrary trends in social formation; for example, deteriorated climatic conditions may have led to decline of population in the early Longshan culture, but have later entailed the flourishing of the Erlitou culture. Human decisions in response to external pressures may have played a determining role in social development or decline.

5.2 Pottery production, archaeological culture, and population

Since the archaeological chronology of the flotation samples, from which seeds were dated, is judged by the associated pottery types, the AMS dating results measure the age of pottery used in certain sites. The date ranges from late Longshan sites (2430–1780 cal. BC) clearly overlaps with that from most samples of Erlitou sites (1890–1410 cal. BC), possibly reflecting the continuity of human habitation in the region (Figure 4.4b, c). The development of a pottery type in a region is closely related to the technological inheritance of craftsmen, and the organizational structure of pottery manufacture and distribution. Therefore, when discussing the temporal and spatial distribution of pottery types, we need to understand the production and distribution patterns of pottery.

The results of Petrographic and portable X-ray fluorescence (p-XRF) analyses performed on pottery sherds (n=56) unearthed from three sites in the Yiluo region (Erlitou, Huizui, and Shaochai; for locations see Figure 4.5a-1,2,10) show a pattern of localized pottery production during the Erlitou period, characterized by (1) volcanic and sulfide-silica "Luo River" inclusion signature seen at Erlitou and Shaochai, (2) a metamorphic (amphibole gneiss and schist) signature seen almost exclusively in sherds from Huizui, and (3) a predominantly fine-grained siliciclastic and carbonate sedimentary lithic "Songshan Mountains" signature observed among sherds at both Huizui and Shaochai. Present evidence shows that there is little exchange of pottery products between the three sites, which represent regional centers at three levels of settlement hierarchy. In addition, the persistence of local production signatures throughout the Yangshao, Longshan, and Erlitou periods at Huizui suggests that systems of localized ceramic production and procurement within the Yiluo basin were not significantly altered in response to processes of urbanism and regional sociopolitical integration characterizing formation of the Erlitou state (Bonomo, 2017).

Such a pattern of localized pottery production in the Yiluo region may have affected the spatial and temporal relationships of pottery types used to define archaeological cultures. In terms of the origin of the Erlitou culture, which is signaled by the emergence of Erlitou Phase I pottery, a possible scenario is as follows. If, when the late Longshan pottery was still commonly in circulation, some residents also began to make and use the Erlitou type pottery in the Yiluo region, then some Erlitou I remains may coexist with late Longshan sites. Erlitou Phase I sites are few, but widely distributed over the survey area (Figure 4.1d), probably as a result of local development. Therefore, the presence of a small number of the Erlitou Phase I sites may not be a sign of population decline during this period, but rather a process of changing pottery styles in the region. Another archaeological cultural transition associated with overlapping ^{14}C dates is the one between Erlitou and Erligang, with the occurrence of the Erligang pottery at Yanshi Shang City being much earlier than those at small settlements. In this case, a new pottery style appears to have started in a large fortified center before spreading to smaller settlements. Yanshi Shang City was a planned center, which was built in a sequence from the palatial central complex, to the inner city, and finally to the outer city (Liu and Chen, 2003; Zhongguo Shehui Kexueyuan Kaogu Yanjiusuo, 2013). It is most likely that the Erligang population was moved from the east to the Yiluo region with their potters while establishing the fortification.

It is interesting to note that the transitional processes in these two cases appear to have happened in opposite directions, either bottom-up (from small to large sites for Erlitou I) or top-down (from large to small site for Lower Erligang). Transitions in archaeological culture indicated by pottery styles may have involved a mosaic of fluid and multidirectional processes over a long period of time; therefore, we should not regard a pottery assemblage as representing a population in a fixed block of time and space.

5.3 Chronology of the Erlitou culture

The chronology of the Erlitou culture has been one of the most crucial factors for understanding early dynastic history of China. We were unable to collect flotation samples from Erlitou I deposits during the surveys, but a large number of Erlitou II-IV dates from different sites fall in the range of 1890–1410 cal. BC, thus Erlitou phase I should not be later than 1890 cal. BC, while Erlitou Phase IV may have continued for some time after 1500 cal. BC. The total span of the Erlitou culture period would have been longer than previously estimated (1750–1530 cal. BC). The beginning time of the Erlitou culture was previously determined on the basis of the pottery chronological sequence of the Xinzhai period at the Xinzhai site (1870–1720 cal. BC), following the idea that the Xinzhai period was the transitional phase between the late Longshan and the Erlitou cultures. Therefore, assuming this idea to be true, the Erlitou culture must have been later than the Xinzhai phase (Zhang, et al., 2007). However, the Xinzhai site is located outside the Yiluo area, more than 100 km away from the Erlitou site, with the Songshan Mts. situated between the two regions. Within the Yiluo survey area, no stratigraphic layer of Xinzhai materials has been identified. Therefore, the pottery sequence in the Xinzhai area should be regarded as a local development, and the Erlitou culture in the Yiluo region should also have had its local origins and developmental sequence. Given the localized nature of pottery production described above, the growth of the archaeological cultures in the two regions should be treated separately. It is worth noting that in our data, an AMS date from the Erlitou Phase I deposit at Xinzhai was a relatively early 1900 cal. BC. These lines of new data, therefore, forces us to reconsider the age of the Erlitou culture.

Our data indicates that the Erlitou style pottery assemblage existed for a longer period of time at some medium and small settlements in the Yiluo region than at the Erlitou urban center itself. Since the Erlitou settlement was developed rapidly as a political and economic center without a previous occupation during the late Longshan period, its sudden appearance as the largest site in the region during Phase I is likely to have been the result of the migration of the surrounding populations. The sources of these populations, however, are unclear and need further study. At present, evidence is lacking to suggest either that the Erlitou I population in the Yiluo region originated from Xinzhai, or that an archaeologically transitional phase occurred between the late Longshan and Erlitou I in our survey area. In addition, the remains of the Longshan drainage system and large rammed-earth foundations found underneath the Yanshi Shang City also point to prior emergence of a sophisticated social system in the region, before the Erlitou culture. Therefore, ongoing exploration of the Erlitou culture's origins should take consideration of the local population who used Longshan style pottery in the core area of the Erlitou culture – the Yiluo region – rather than rely on the ceramic typological sequence of Longshan-Xinzhai-Erlitou characteristic of the Xinzhai area.

6. CONCLUSION

The results of the Yiluo regional survey project provide us with the most comprehensive data yet for comprehending the spatial and temporal relationships of settlement distribution during a 6000-year history. It demonstrates a developmental trajectory from a landscape dotted with scattered, small, and egalitarian Neolithic Many questions still remain to be answered, and some of the most significant issues are related to the Erlitou culture. If the transition from the late Longshan to Erlitou Phases I occurred around or before 1900 BC, and the emergence of the Erlitou urban center was the result of population migration, then we need to answer the following questions: (1) what natural or social forces drove the population movement at this time? (2) Where did these migrants come from? To address these issues, we need to take an interdisciplinary approach, including reconstruction of environmental and ecological changes, biological analyses of ancient human remains, and further study of pottery productions and distributions. The newly established settlement data has laid the foundation for more in-depth research in the future.

Acknowledgements: Our deepest appreciation goes to numerous archaeologists and geologists from China, Australia, the US, and UK, who participated in the Yiluo regional survey project. In particular, Yun

Kuen Lee, Arlene Rosen, Ming Wei, Xiaolin Ma, John Webb, Facheng Wang, and Hongzhang Wang made great contributions to the surveys and researches. This project would not be possible without the generous funding that has been provided by the Australian Research Council, the National Geographic Society, the Wenner-Gren Foundation, La Trobe University, and Harvard University.

REFERENCES

Bai, Y., Zhang, P., Gao, T., Yu, R., Zhou, P. and Cheng, H., 2017. Yazhou Xiajifeng 5400a BP jiduan jianruo shijian yu wenhua yanbian (Asian summer monsson 5400a BP extreme weakening event and cultural change). Scientia Sinica Terrae 47 (5), 554-566.

Bestel, S., 2012. An Archaeobotanical Analysis of Late Palaeolithic, Peiligang and Yangshao Sites in Henan and Shanxi Provinces, North China. Monash University, PhD dissertation. Melbourne.

Bevan, A., Crema, E. and Silva, F., 2018. rcarbon v1.1.3 : Methods for calibrating and analysing radiocarbon dateshttps://CRAN.R-project.org/package=rcarbon.

Bonomo, M.F., 2017. Ceramic production and provenance in the Yiluo Basin (Henan, China): Geoarchaeological interpretations of utilitarian craft production in the Erlitou state. Archaeological Research in Asia 14, 80-96.

Chang, K.-c., 1968. Settlement Archaeology. National Press, Palo Alto, California.

Chen, F., Xu, Q., Chen, J., Birks, H.J.B., Liu, J. and Zhang, S., 2015. East Asian summer monsoon precipitation variability since the last deglaciation. Scientific Reports 5, 11186.

Chen, X., Liu, L., Lee, Y.K., Wright, H. and Rosen, A., 2003. Zhongguo wenming fudi de shehui fuzahua jincheng: Yiluohe diqu de juluo xingtai yanjiu (Development of social complexity in the heartland of Chinese civilization: Yiluo region settlement patterns). Kaogu Xuebao 2, 161-218.

Chifeng International Collaborative Archaeological Research Project, 2011. Settlement Patterns in the Chifeng Region. Center for Comparative Archaeology University of Pittsburgh, Pittsburgh.

Earle, T.K., 1991. The evolution of chiefdom. In: T. Earle (Ed.) Chiefdoms: Power, Economy, and Ideology, Cambridge University Press, Cambridge, pp. 1-15.

Fang, H., Underhill, A., Feinman, G., Nicholas, L., Luan, F., Yu, H. and Cai, F., 2012. Archaeological Report of Regiona Systematic Survey in the Southeast Shandong. Wenwu Press, Beijing.

Feng, Z.D., An, C.B., Tang, L. and Jull, A.J.T., 2004. Stratigraphic evidence of a megahumid climate between 10,000 and 4000 years B.P. in the western part of the Chinese Loess Plateau. Global and Planetary Change 43, 145–155.

Feng, Z.D., An, C.B. and Wang, H.B., 2006. Holocene climatic and environmental changes in the arid and semi-arid areas of China: a review. The Holocene 16 (1), 119-130.

Fish, S.K. and Kowalewski, S.A., 1990. The Archaeology of Regions: A Case for Full-Coverage Survey. Smithsonian Institution Press, Washington, D.C.

Flannery, K.V., 1998. The ground plans of archaic states. In: G. M. Feinman and J. Marcus (Eds.), Archaic states, School of American Research Press, Santa Fe, pp. 15-58.

Gongyishi Wenwu Baohu Guanlisuo, 1996. Henan Gongyi shi Wayaozui xinshiqi shidai yizhi shijue jianbao (Preliminary report of testing excavation at the Wayaozui Neolithic site in Gongyi city, Henan). Kaogu 7, 12-16,94.

Gongyishi Wenwu Baohu Guanlisuo, 1997. Gongyi shi Wayaozui yizhi disanci fajue baogao (Report of the third excavation season at the Wayaozui site in Gongyi city). Zhongyuan Wenwu 1, 41-52.

Hsu, C.-y., 1965. Ancient China in Transition: An analysis of Social Mobility, 722-222 B.C. Stanford University Press, Stanford.

Lee, G.-A., Crawford, G.W., Liu, L. and Chen, X., 2007. Plants and people from the early Neolithic to Shang periods in North China. Proceedings of the National Academy of Sciences 104 (3), 1087-1092.

Lewis, E.M., 1999. Warring States: political history. In: M. Loewe and E. Shaughnessy (Eds.), The Cambridge History of Ancient China: From the Origins of Civilization to 221 BC, Cambridge University Press, Cambridge, pp. 587-650.

Liang, Y., 2002. Chengzhou yu Wangcheng kaobian (On Chengzhou and Wangcheng). kaogu yu Wenwu 5, 51-55.

Liu, F., 1998. Luoyang Xizhou taoqi mu yanjiu (On the pottery-burials of Western Zhou in Luoyang). kaogu yu Wenwu 3, 44-68.

Liu, L. and Chen, X., 2003. State Formation in Early China. Duckworth, London.

Liu, L., Chen, X., Lee, Y.K., Wright, H. and Rosen, A., 2002-2004. Settlement patterns and development of social complexity in the Yiluo region, north China. Journal of Field Archaeology 29 (1-2), 75-100.

Liu, L., Chen, X. and Li, B., 2007. Non-state crafts in the early Chinese state: An archaeological view from the Erlitou hinterland. Bulletin of the Indo-Pacific Prehistory Association 27, 93-102.

Liu, L., Maureece, J.L., Chen, X. and Li, Y., 2018a. Henan Yanshi Huizui yizhi xinshiqi shidai he Erlitou wenhua shiqi gongju canliuwu ji wenhen fenxi (Analyses of residues and use-wear on tools of the Neolithic and Erlitou periods at Huizui in Yanshi, Henan). Zhongyuan Wenwu 6, 82-97.

Liu, L., Wang, J., Chen, X., Li, Y. and Zhao, H., 2018b. Yangshao wenhua dafangzi yu yanyin chuantong: Henan Yanshi Huizui yizhi F1 dimian he taoqi canliuwu fenxi (Large houses and feasting tradition of the Yangshao Culture: Starch and phytolith analyses of the residues from oottery vessels and floors of House No.1 at Huizui in Yanshi, Henan). Zhongyuan Wenwu 1, 32-43.

Liu, L. and Xu, H., 2007. Rethinking Erlitou: Legend, history and Chinese archaeology. Antiquity 81, 886-901.

Ramsey, C.B., 2001. Development of the radiocarbon calibration program. Radiocarbon 43 (2A), 355-363.

Ran, M. and Feng, Z.D., 2013. Holocene moisture variations across China and driving mechanisms: a synthesis of climatic records. Quaternary International 313/314, 179-193.

Reimer, P.J., Bard, E. and Bayliss, A., 2013. IntCal13 and Marine13 radiocarbon age calibration curves 0–50,000 years Cal BP. Radiocarbon 55 (Nr 4), 1869-1887.

Rosen, A.M., 2007. The role of environmental change in the development of complex societies in china: a study from the Huizui site. Bulletin of the Indo-Pacific Prehistory Association 27, 39-48.

Rosen, A.M., 2008. The impact of environmental change and human land use on alluvial valleys in the Loess Plateau of China during the Middle Holocene. Geomorphology 101, 298-307.

Rosen, A.M., Macphail, R., Liu, L., Chen, X. and Weisskopf, A., 2017. Rising social complexity, agricultural intensification, and the earliest rice paddies on the Loess Plateau of northern China. Quaternary International 437, 50-59.

Shi, Y., Kong, Z., Wang, S., Tang, L., Wang, F., Yao, T., Zhao, X., Zhang, P. and Shi, S., 1993. Mid-Holocene climates and environments in China. Global and Planetary Change 7, 219-233.

Tang, J. and Jing, Z., 1998. Huanhe liuyu quyu kaogu yanjiu chubu baogao (Preliminary report of regional survey in the Huan River valley). Kaogu 10, 13-22.

Wright, H.T., 1977. Toward an explanation of the origin of the state. In: J. Hill (Ed.) Explanation of Prehistoric Change, University of New Mexico Press, Albuquerque, pp. 215-230.

Wright, H.T. and Johnson, G., 1975. Population, exchange, and early state formation in southwestern Iran. American Anthropologist 77, 267-289.

Xia Shang Zhou Chronology Project Team, 2000. Xia Shang Zhou Duandai Gongcheng 1996-2000 Nian Jieduan Chengguo Baogao. Shijie Tushu Press, Beijing.

Xu, H., Chen, G. and Zhao, H., 2004. Erlitou yizhi juluo xingtai de chubu kaocha (Preliminary investigation of settlement patterns of the Erlitou site). Kaogu 11, 23-31.

Xu, H., Guoliang, C. and Haitao, Z., 2005. Henan Luoyang pendi 2001-2003 nian kaogu diaocha jianbao (Report of the 2001-2003 archaeological survey in the Luoyang basin, Henan). Kaogu 5, 18-37.

Xu, S., 2007. Chengzhou yu Wangcheng luekao (On Chengzhou and Wangcheng). Kaogu 11, 62-70.

Ye, W., Zhang, J. and Li, D., 1991. Xizhou Luoyi chengzhi kao (On the city Luoyi of Western Zhou). Huaxia Kaogu 2, 70-76.

Zhang, J., Xia, Z., Zhang, X., Storozum, M.J., Huang, X., Han, J., Xu, H., Zhao, H., Cui, Y., Dodson, J. and Dong, G., 2018. Early–middle Holocene ecological change and its influence on human subsistence strategies in the Luoyang Basin, north-central China. Quaternary Research 89, 446-458.

Zhang, N., Yang, Y., Cheng, H., Zhao, J., Yang, X., Liang, S., Nie, X., Zhang, Y. and Edwards, R.L., 2018. Timing and duration of the East Asian summer monsoon maximum during the Holocene based on stalagmite data from North China. The Holocene 28 (10), 1631-1641.

Zhang, X., Chou, S., Zhong, J., Lu, X. and al., e., 2013. Yangshao wenhua niandai taolun (Discussion on the Yangshao chronology). Kaogu 11, 84-104.

Zhang, X., Qiu, S., Cai, L., Bo, G., Wang, J. and Zhong, J., 2007. Xinzhai-Erlitou-Erligang wenhua kaogu niandai xulie de jianli yu wanshan (The establishment of the Xinzhai-Erlitou-Erligang cultural chronological sequence). Kaogu 8, 74-89.

Zhao, Z. and Xu, D., 1986. Gudai Luoyang de wu da chengzhi (Five urban sites in ancient Luoyang). In: Association of Ancient Capitals (Ed.) Zhongguo Gudu Yanjiu (Studies of Ancient Capitals in China), 2, Zhejiang Renmin Press, Hangzhou, pp. 107-120.

Zhengzhou Wenwu Gongzuodui and Gongyishi Wenwu Guanlisuo, 1999. Henan Gongyishi Wayaozui xinshiqi shidai yizhi d fajue (Excavations of the Neolithic site at Wayaozui in Gongyi, Henan). Kaogu 11, 13-20.

Zhongguo Shehui Kexueyuan Kaogu Yanjiusuo, 1999. Yanshi Erlitou. Zhongguo Dabaikequanshu Press, Beijing.

Zhongguo Shehui Kexueyuan Kaogu Yanjiusuo, 2010. Zhongguo Kaoguxue: Xinshiqi Juan (Cinese Archaeology: The Neolithic Volume). Zhongguo Shehui Kexue Press, Beijing.

Zhongguo Shehui Kexueyuan Kaogu Yanjiusuo, 2013. Yanshi Shangcheng (Yanshi Shang City). Kexue Press, Beijing.

Zhongguo Shehui Kexueyuan Kaogu Yanjiusuo, 2014. Erlitou: 1999-2006. Wenwu Press, Beijing.

Zhongguo Shehui Kexueyuan Kaogu Yanjiusuo and China-Australia-U.S. Cooperative Archaeological Team in Yiluo Region, in press. Luoyang Pendi Zhong-Dongbu Diqu Xianqin Shiqi Yizhi Diaoch Baogao (Report of Regional Survey of Pre-Qin sites in Eastern-Central Luoyang Basin). Kexue Press, Beijing.

Zhongguo Shehui Kexueyuan Luoyang Hanweicheng Dui, 1998. Han Wei Luoyang gucheng chengyuan shijue (Test excavation of the Han and Wei ancient city in Luoyang). Kaogu Xuebao 3, 361-388.

CHAPTER 5   DEVELOPMENT OF COMPLEX SOCIETIES IN THE YILUO REGION: A GIS BASED POPULATION AND AGRICULTURAL AREA ANALYSIS[①]

1. INTRODUCTION

The Yiluo River valley is a vast fertile alluvial basin bounded by the Mangling hills to the north, the Xiao and Xiong'er Mountains in the west, the Funiu Mountains in the south and the Songshan Mountains in the southeast. The research area is situated in the eastern part of the Yiluo valley, from where the highlands of the Songshan Mountains descend to the Yiluo plains (Fig. 5.1). (Gongxian County Chronicle Editorial Board 1991:43, 69-70, Liu et al. 2002-2004).

According to ancient texts, the Yiluo basin witnessed the birth of the Xia dynasty – the first dynasty in China. Thus this significant region has long been the focus of Chinese archaeologists who regard the pursuit of the origins of early state or civilization in China as their mission (Chen 1997). Surveys and excavations at the famous Erlitou site over the past 40 years have yielded much information suggesting that this settlement, covering an area of 300 ha, was the largest settlement of Erlitou period not only in the Yiluo basin but anywhere in China. Furthermore, the palace/temple complex, residential areas, burials, and craft workshops producing bronze, ceramic, and bone objects demonstrate that this site was a political, economic and ritual central (Erlitou Working Team 1984a, b,1985, 2001, Institute of Archaeology 1999, Liu 2006). However, it is only in recent years that several archaeological projects have been launched to systematically study the social developmental trajectory of this significant region. Among them is the Yiluo Project, an international collaborative and interdisciplinary archaeological program involving archaeologists from Australia, China, America and England (Liu et al. 2002-2004, Liu and Chen 2001).

[①]   This chapter is written by Qiao Yu, Chinese version post on *Acta Archaeologica Sinica*, English version post on *Indo-Pacific Prehistory Association Bulletin*, 2007(27) :61-75. with some slightly changes. Previous investigation data (number of sites and some judgement) are used in this chapter. If there are differences between this chapter and this report, the latter one holds more reference value.

CHAPTER 5 DEVELOPMENT OF COMPLEX SOCIETIES IN THE YILUO REGION: A GIS BASED POPULATION AND AGRICULTURAL AREA ANALYSIS

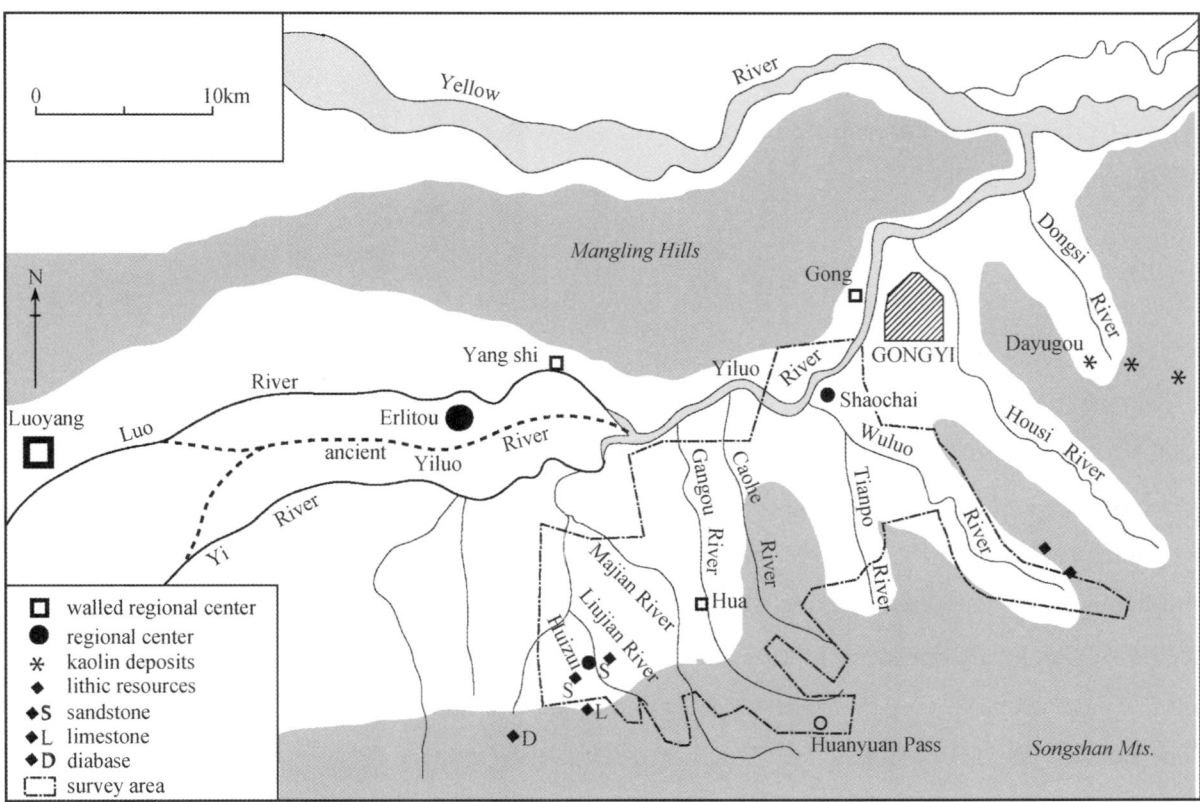

Figure 5.1 Important sites and resources in the Yiluo River valley

During the first six field seasons from January 1997 to June 2002, full-coverage surveys were conducted over the alluvial plains and loess tableland along five small river valleys in the Yiluo region: the Wuluo, the Caohe, the Gangou, the Majian, and the Liujian river valleys (Fig. 1). A total area of about 219 km^2 was surveyed, and 194 sites dating from the late Peiligang to the Zhou period were recorded.

The 6000 years of time span covered by these sites includes six archaeological periods, which are further partitioned into phases:

1. Late Peiligang (ca. 6000-5000 B.C.).

2. Yangshao, subdivided into Early (ca. 5000-4000 B.C.), Middle (ca. 4000-3500 B.C.), and Late (ca. 3500-3000 B.C.) phases.

3. Longshan, subdivided into Early (ca. 3000-2500 B.C.), and Late (ca. 2500-2000 B.C.) phases.

4. Erlitou (ca. 1900-1500 B.C.), subdivided into four phases, I-IV, approximately 100 years for each phase.

5. Shang, subdivided into Early Shang or Erligang (ca. 1600-1300 B.C.), and Late Shang or Yinxu (ca. 1300-1046 B.C.) phases.

6. Zhou, subdivided into Western Zhou (1046-771 B.C.) and Eastern Zhou (771-206 B.C.) phases.

Based on data from the project, I constructed a GIS based study detailing population fluctuation and development of social complexity in the Yiluo area. The basic framework of my study consists of three parts: an estimation of population size; the reconstruction of carrying capacity and catchment productivity; and the interpretation of interaction between the population fluctuation and the development of complex society.

2. ESTIMATION OF POPULATION SIZE

Population size and density in prehistoric China is difficult to estimate, as most sites have only been partially excavated and little systematic research has been undertaken in regards to population size based on archaeological evidence. To estimate the population of the Yiluo region I have to refer to Chinese research on population size of other Neolithic sites: Yuchisi (Institute of Archaeology 2001) and Jiangzhai (Banpo Museum 1989). Both settlements are almost completely excavated, and exemplify good preservation of houses, many of which are full of artefacts of everyday use. Rich and reliable data can be derived from the two sites to estimate the relationship between population size and floor area, as well as settlement size. The average density of the two sites, that is 57 people/ha (Banpo Museum 1989:68-69, 352-357, Institute of Archaeology 2001:325-328, Zhao 1998, Zhu 1994) is taken as the population density in my study.

3. HOW MANY AGRICULTURAL HECTARES DID A PERSON NEED?

According to the records for Gongyi County, in 1933 the average annual yield of millet was 375 kg/ha (Gongxian County Chronicle Editorial Board 1991:260). To determine the quantity of grain available for consumption, an allowance needs to be made for grain put aside for seed. After referring to experienced peasants and some related research (Van Wersch 1972), 15% of the harvest is normally used for seed. If adopting the lowest production of 375 kg/ha, and taking the 15% seeds into account, the new estimation of the total consumable millet production is 315 kg/ha.

Another factor to be considered in this context is the grain consumption for each person. The records for Gongyi County is a good reference for this estimation. According to this record, the average annual consumption of processed grain for each person was about 245 kg (Gongxian County Chronicle Editorial Board 1991:479). For children up to 14 years, the average annual consumption is 192 kg. An average of 219 kg/person thus is assumed to be the annual consumption value.

To determine the value of consumption of raw millet, the milling efficiency is also considered. Using the traditional milling techniques and assuming consumer acceptance of the resulting product, this efficiency can be placed between 80-90%. Assuming an average milling efficiency of 85%, I obtain a grain equivalent of 258 kg (219/0.85), which may be an acceptable calculation of the annual consumption of raw millet per person.

From the above results, necessary agricultural land that can efficiently support a person in this region can be calculated according to the following formulation:

Agricultural area per person needs (ha) = annual consumption of grain per person (kg) / yield of grain (kg) per ha.

The result is that each person needs 0.8 ha for one year to support himself/herself. However, fallow land is also an important factor that needs to be considered. According to several ancient texts, fallow land was very common in the Spring and Autumn period (770-221 BC) (Chen 1991:126). In this study, I use a more conservative figure, one-year fallow after one year of crop for all the agricultural lands. Thus the actual land a person needs increases to 1.6 ha, and this value is applied to calculate the carrying capacity of the surveyed area and catchment productivity of each site.

4. GIS-BASED ANALYSIS OF CARRYING CAPACITY AND CATCHMENT PRODUCTIVITY

Carrying capacity represents an upper limit for population growth within an area. First developed by zoologists in the 1930s, this concept has been widely applied and debated by anthropologists and archaeologists since the 1950s (Hassan 1981:164). Hassan points out that human populations tend to subsist at levels below their maximum carrying capacity, maintaining their numbers at a level that is 20-60% of the maximum population size possible. This optimum carrying capacity level is a successful response to periodic, unpredictable fluctuations in the available yields of utilizable resources.

Two GIS programs – IDRISI and CARTARLINX provide effective methods to conduct my study in the surveyed region.

As millet is the only food resource considered in my research, the carrying capacity can be defined as the total population that could be supported by the available millet field in the surveyed area. Similarly, the catchment productivity here is the available millet field within the catchment of a site.

I obtained the digitalized contour line map made by Mr. Jianguo Liu of the Institute of Archaeology, Chinese Academy of Social Science, and established a referenced database of each cultural period in the Yiluo project. I also digitalized the site distribution map, soil map, and river map of the Yiluo region. Below is a cartographic model that illustrates the process of my GIS analysis (Fig. 5.2). Several factors need to be taken into consideration for the estimation of carrying capacity, including slope, aspect, friction, elevation, and soil type, which can affect the land use pattern.

A digital contour map of the surveyed area is the basic database. It was digitised from four

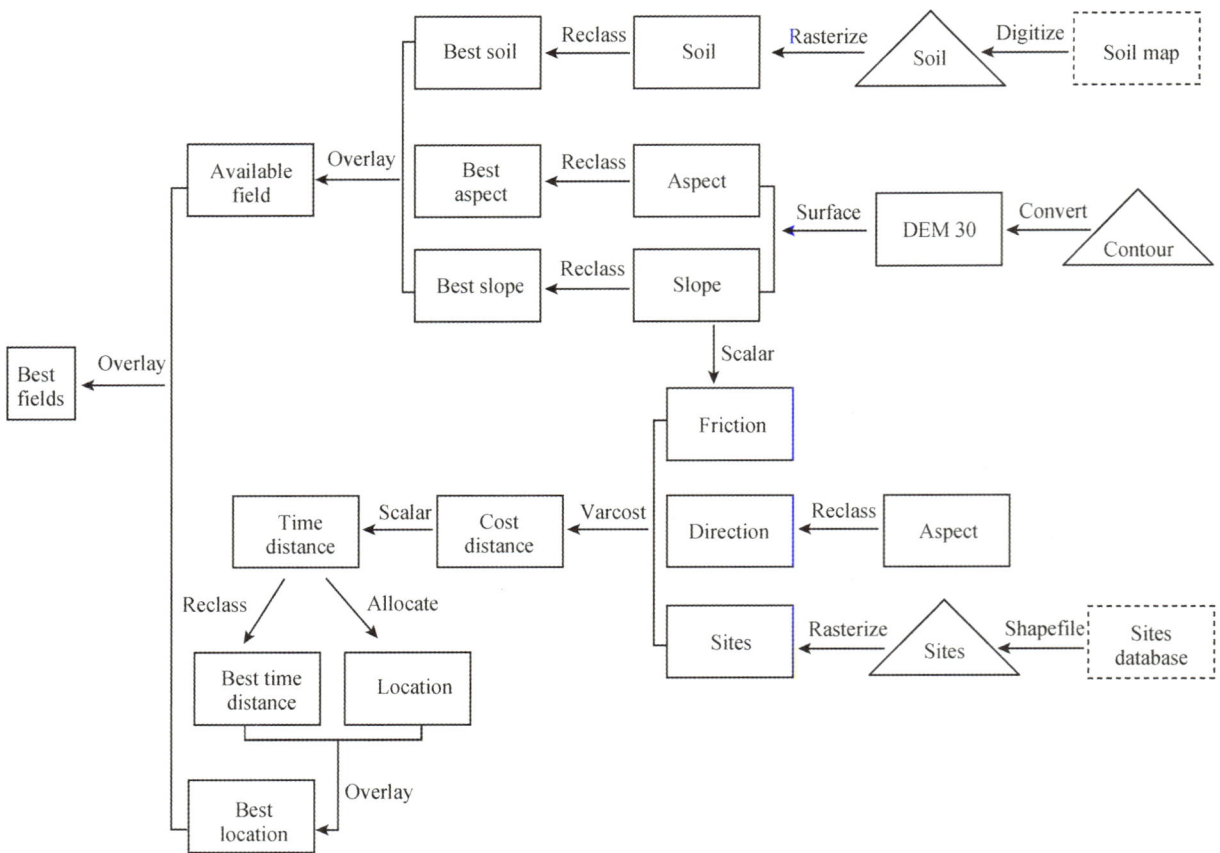

Figure 5.2 Cartographic model of the Gongyi GIS Analysis

topographic maps at a scale of 1:50,000, and configured to Universal Transverse Mercature (UTM) projection. Once digitised, the contour layer had to be transformed into an analytical surface – a Digital Elevation Model (DEM).

This process was completed using IDRIS 32. A common method of creating a DEM is by digitising contour lines from a topographic map on a vector platform and then converting that vector to raster format. Considering the aims of the analysis and the scales of the digital map, a resolution of 30, which means each pixel in the DEM map represents 30 m * 30 m, was chosen to proceed. In the image of DEM30, several layers can be added to express other information within this image, such as the layers of sites, rivers, the survey area, boundaries etc. (Fig. 5.3).

Two other raster images – slope and aspect, were produced from the DEM30 with the Surface Module, which can produce slope gradient, aspect, and analytical hill shade images from a surface model. It was assumed that the slopes between 0-20 degrees were the best for millet field since steep slopes are usually covered with rocks, are exposed to water erosion, and are difficult to cultivate. By Reclassing the values in the slope image, a Boolean image – "the Best Slope" was generated. This image has only two values: 0, representing those areas with slopes greater than 20 degrees; and 1, representing those areas with slopes less than 20 degrees. It is assumed that the best aspects when

CHAPTER 5 DEVELOPMENT OF COMPLEX SOCIETIES IN THE YILUO REGION: A GIS BASED POPULATION AND AGRICULTURAL AREA ANALYSIS

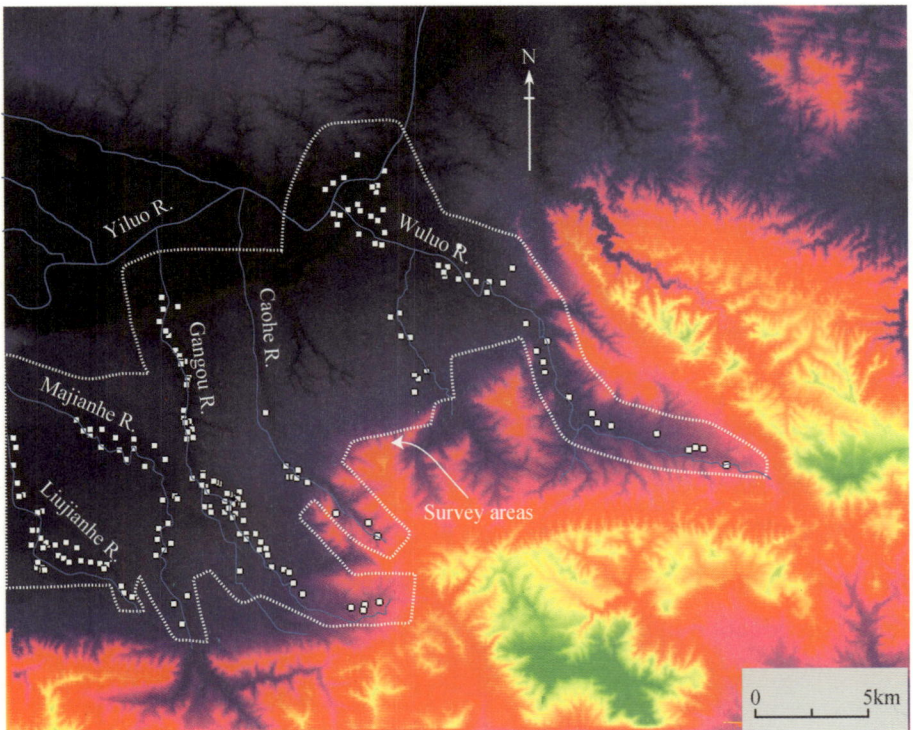

Figure 5.3 The site distribution and the survey areas in the Yiluo Project

considering available sunlight is 45-225 degree, so another Boolean image – "the Best Aspect", was produced by Reclassing the values in the aspect image. In the "Best Aspects image", value 0 represents the area with the aspects <45 or >225 degrees, and the value 1 represents the areas with the aspects between 45-225 degrees. Also considered was the elevation suitable for cultivation.

I digitalized the soil maps of the surveyed region using the CARTALINX software and converted it into a Raster image. From the ethnohistoric record of the Gongyi and Yanshi regions, the information on soil distribution, soil depth, the balance of PH value, natural plant productivity, and agricultural productivity in the total of 24 soil types in the study area can be determined. Most of the soils in the study area are kinds of dark brown soil that are fertile and suitable for agriculture (Gongxian County Chronicle Editorial Board 1991:99-104). However, there are still several soils that are unsuitable for agriculture, such as some kinds of sandy brown loam, and dark brown marl.

The Reclass module was applied again to give a new value 0 to all the soils unsuitable to agriculture, and a value of 1 to all the soils suitable to agriculture. Another Boolean image – "Best Soil" was produced.

Finally, the OVERLAY module was applied to multiply the three Boolean images: Best Slope * Best Aspect * Best Soil, and this operation produced a new Boolean image – Available field. In this image, those areas that have a value of 1 in all the three images (the areas suitable for agriculture) keep their value in the new Boolean image (1 * 1 = 1). Those areas that have a value of 0 in any of the three images (areas not suitable for agriculture either for slope, aspect or soil type) will get a value 0 in the new image (1 * 0 = 0; 0 * 0 = 0).

The surveyed region does not include all the area in the digital map, so the boundary of the surveyed area is considered as the boundary to calculate the carrying capacity. Applying the Area module in IDRISI to the data, a total carrying capacity of 29,681.64 ha was calculated from the image of Available Field within the surveyed region. As defined above, this means that there are 29,681.64 ha land suitable for millet agriculture within the surveyed area. This could support 18,551 persons (1.6 ha/person) whose subsistence was based mainly on millet. It needs to be pointed out that millet was not the only staple in this region during prehistoric and historic times. An archaeobotanical study of plant remains from the survey area reveals that millet was the dominant crop, while rice, soybean and wheat gradually added to people's diet over time (Lee et al. 2007). However, since it is difficult to estimate the proportion of each crop in the subsistence system, we simply use the data from millet to calculate the total agricultural production in this study.

The first thing required before estimation of the catchment productivity of each site is to decide the boundary of each site's catchment. Two methods have been employed in previous studies of catchment size. One is based on the assumption that the majority of the people will tend to spend their nights in their settlement, so the radius of a catchment was decided by the time for a return trip within a day (cf. Brumfiel 1976, Vita-Finzi and Higgs 1970). The other method simply takes the ethnographic record as reference, and assumes a radius for a catchment (Chisolm 1968:131). It was assumed that agriculturalists would walk only a certain maximum distance to reach their fields, and that this maximum distance was the same for all sites of a given period. While one hour's walking distance is assumed to be the radius of the catchment area of each site in this study, travel through varying slopes, frictions and different walking speeds have been taken into consideration.

The friction of walking will be an important factor in deciding the catchment boundary. In the Cost Analysis module of IDRISI, friction is a value greater than 1 by which you multiply the base cost of movement in order to arrive at the actual cost of movement. Slope is the only friction considered here. Since the topography of the study area is complex, the costs for walking upslope and downslope are different.

To estimate the effect of friction on walking in different slopes, a walking experiment was conducted with the assistance of my colleagues. People walked on a road with different slopes and recorded the length, degree and walking time of each slope. Processing the data by the statistic software SPPS, we gain the following formula of the relationship between time and slope:

$Y = 0.0002 * X^2 + 0.002 * X + 0.6086$

In this formula, Y is the time for walking one metre; X is the degree of slope. Downslope is considered as minimum X value.

Another experiment in the Gongyi region arrived at similar results. Applying this formula to the "Slope" image, a new image – "Friction" was produced. In this image each pixel has a friction value based on the slope of the pixel. Another "Direction" image was produced from the "Aspect" to inform the computer the location of upslope and downslope.

Detailed databases including the accurate UTM value of each site have been established, and they have been imported into ARCVIEW in order to convert them into SHAPEFILE – a spatial referenced file, in which a vector point image of the "Sites" was produced. These vector "Sites" images were then converted into raster "Sites" images to determine the start point for the computer calculation of the Cost distance. By combining the three images: Friction, Direction, and raster Sites with the Varcost module of IDRISI, the Cost distance surface of each site in different period can be computed while taking into account directionally-dependent frictional effects of slope.

The Cost distance is a kind of isotropic cost that means movement in space incurs a cost. This is a function of the standard (or base) costs associated with movement, and is modified by the frictions and forces that impede or facilitate movement. In this "Cost distance" image, each cell has the value of the Cost distance from the nearest site to this cell.

In the analysis discussed above, the distance to agricultural land was identified as one hour. Thus, the values in Cost distance image should be transformed into a time value. According to the walking experiment, the average walking speed of the four participants on smooth road is 1.5 m per second. Since the resolution in DEM image is 30, the standard (or base) cost to walk through one flat pixel is 20 seconds. Hence, a "Time Distance" image can be produced by multiplying 20 seconds and dividing by 3600 seconds in the "Cost Distance" image. In this image, the value of each pixel is the number of hours it takes for travel from the nearest site to this pixel. Giving the values over 1 hour a new value 0, and values less than 1 hour a new value 1, a Boolean image of "Best Time" was obtained.

In order to determine the catchment of each site, I applied another module of IDRISI – Allocate to get a new image "Location". Allocate assigns each cell to the nearest of a set of designated features. It is used as a follow-on to the DISTANCE, COST or VARCOST modules. In the output of all these three modules, the distance of each cell to the nearest feature is indicated, but not the name of the feature itself. The Allocate function designates names to these features. Each cell will therefore end up with one of the identifiers of the original feature from which the distance was calculated. In the "Location" images, each site will have its own Thiessen polygon around the site, which indicates the catchment of this site.

The Overlay module was applied to multiply the "Location" images of different periods with the Boolean image "Best Time". The "Best Location" images are then obtained, in which the Thiessen polygons of each site is constrained within the radius of one hour.

The last step was to multiply the Best location images with the Available Field image (derived above) by applying the Overlay module. This produces the "Best Field" images, in which polygons of different colours represent the areas suitable for agriculture within the catchments of the different sites (Figs. 5.4 to 5.13). The area of each Thiessen polygon can be computed automatically. Tables 5.1 to 5.10 (after the text) show site sizes, estimated populations, catchment productivities (CP), necessary fields (NF) and land-use ratios (NF/CP) for the sites in each period.

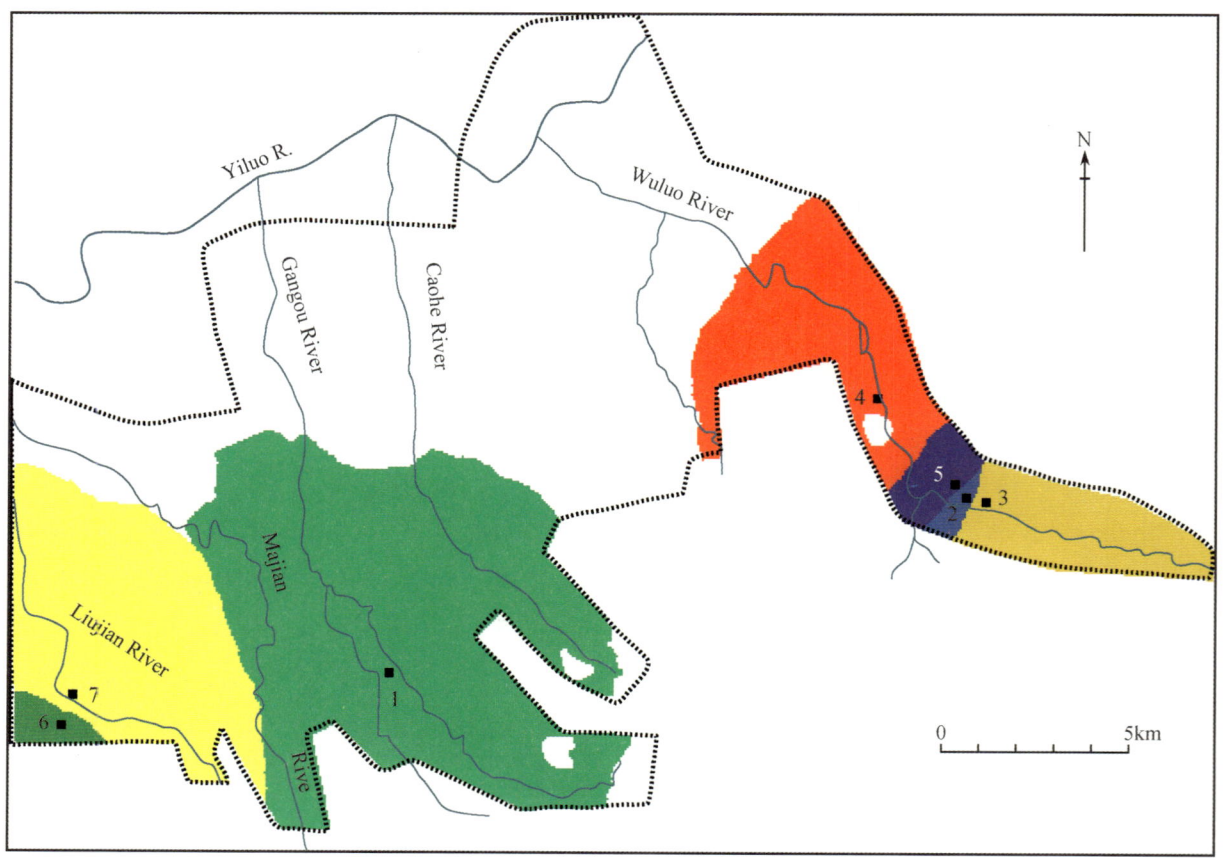

Figure 5.4　Late Peiligang Period

5. DISCUSSION AND CONCLUSION: POPULATION SIZE AND THE DEVELOPMENT OF SOCIAL COMPLEXITY

As Fig. 5.14 displays, population size of the study area fluctuated dramatically from the Peiligang to the Erlitou period. The first noticeable increase took place in the middle Yangshao phase reaching a peak in the late Yangshao phase. However, a sharp decline occurred in the early Longshan phase, when the population fell below that of the middle Yangshao phase. A dramatic population increase followed this decline and the population reached a higher point than the Late Yangshao in the late Longshan phase – this is the first time that the optimum carrying capacity was exceeded (67.4% of the carrying capacity). Another large-scale increase of the population size occurred in the Erlitou period when the population reached its maximum, well above the optimum carrying capacity (78% of the carrying capacity).

CHAPTER 5 DEVELOPMENT OF COMPLEX SOCIETIES IN THE YILUO REGION: A GIS BASED POPULATION AND AGRICULTURAL AREA ANALYSIS

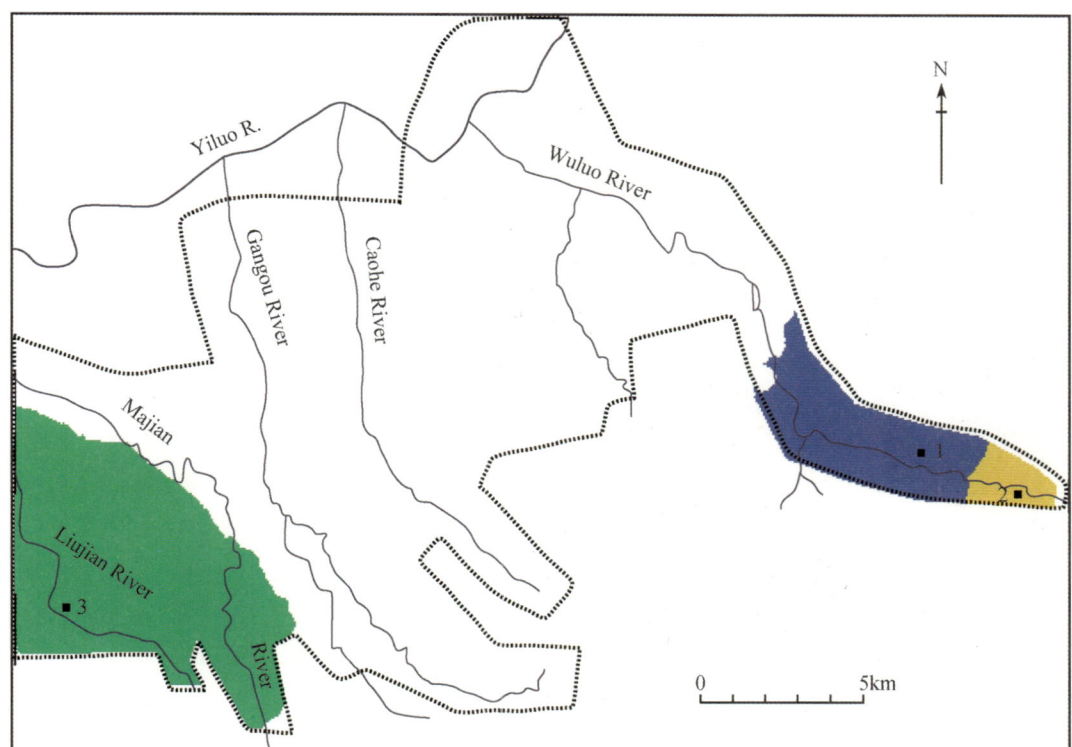

Figure 5.5 Early Yangshao Period

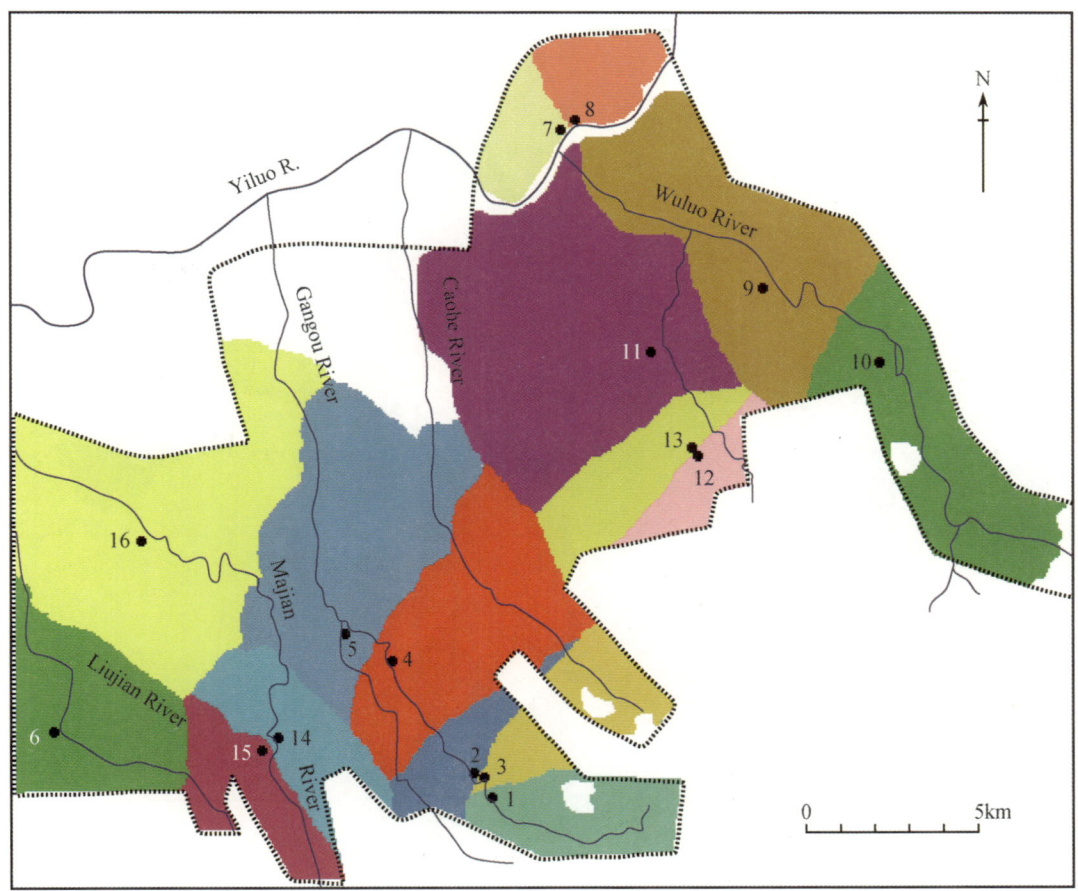

Figure 5.6 Middle Yangshao Period

1386 洛阳盆地中东部先秦时期遗址

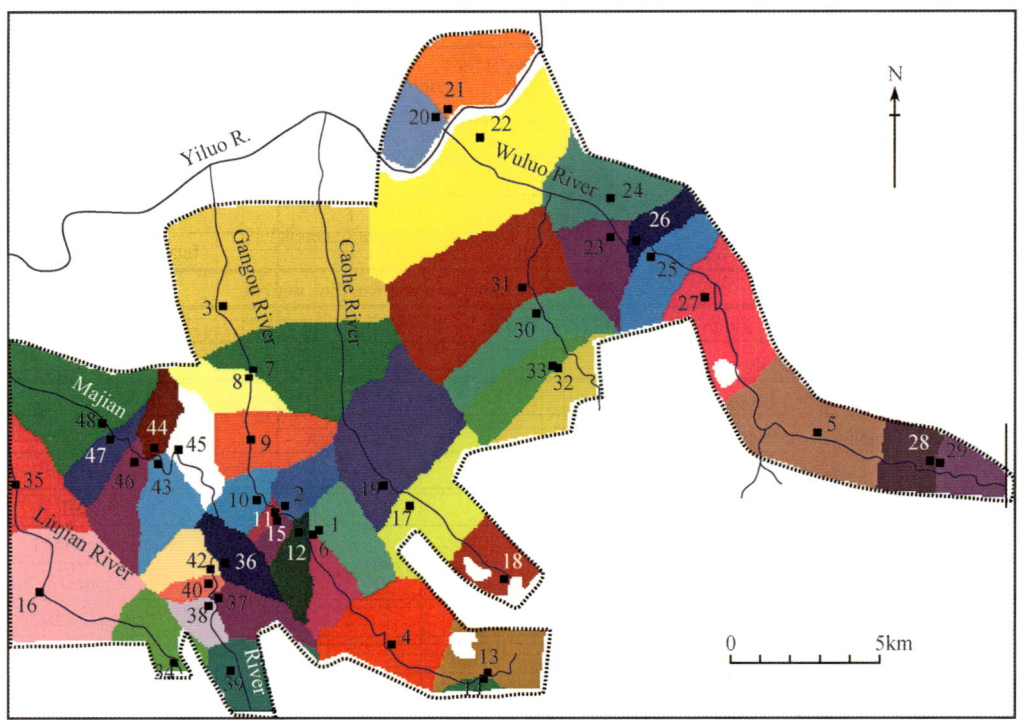

Figure 5.7 Late Yangshao Period

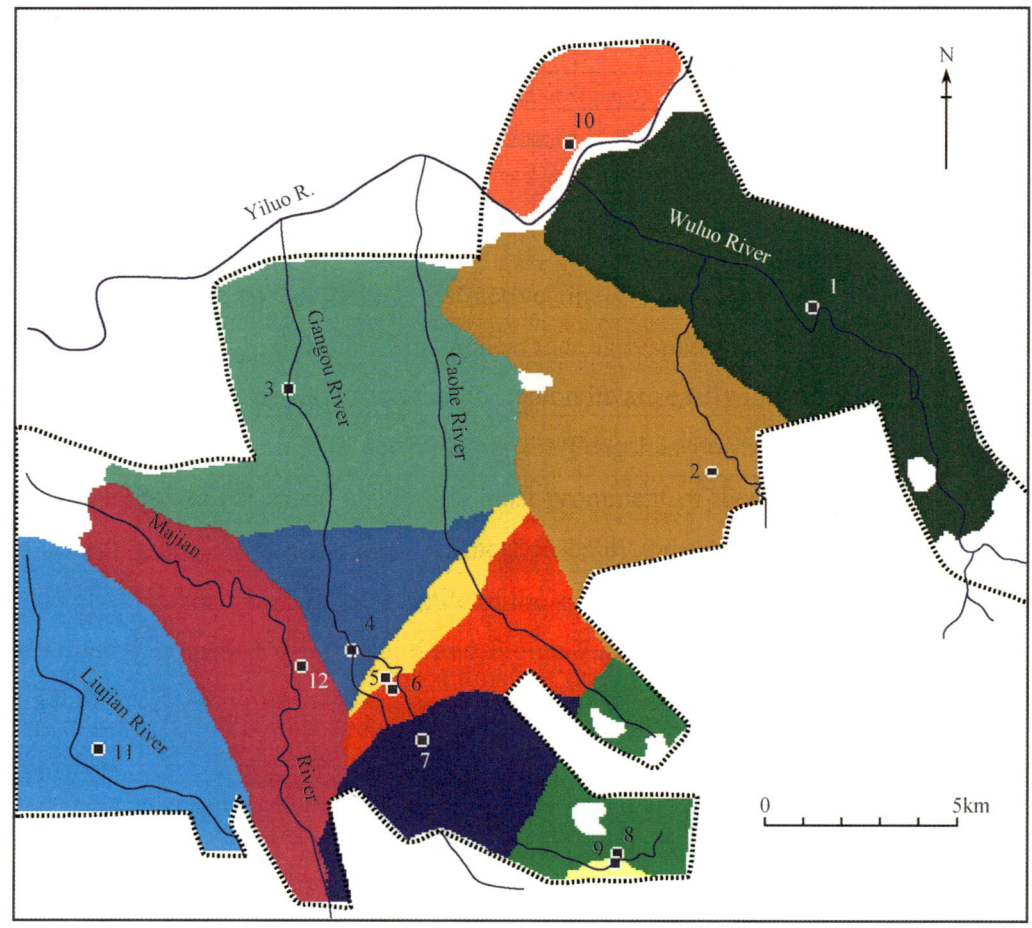

Figure 5.8 Early Longshan Period

CHAPTER 5 DEVELOPMENT OF COMPLEX SOCIETIES IN THE YILUO REGION: A GIS BASED POPULATION AND AGRICULTURAL AREA ANALYSIS

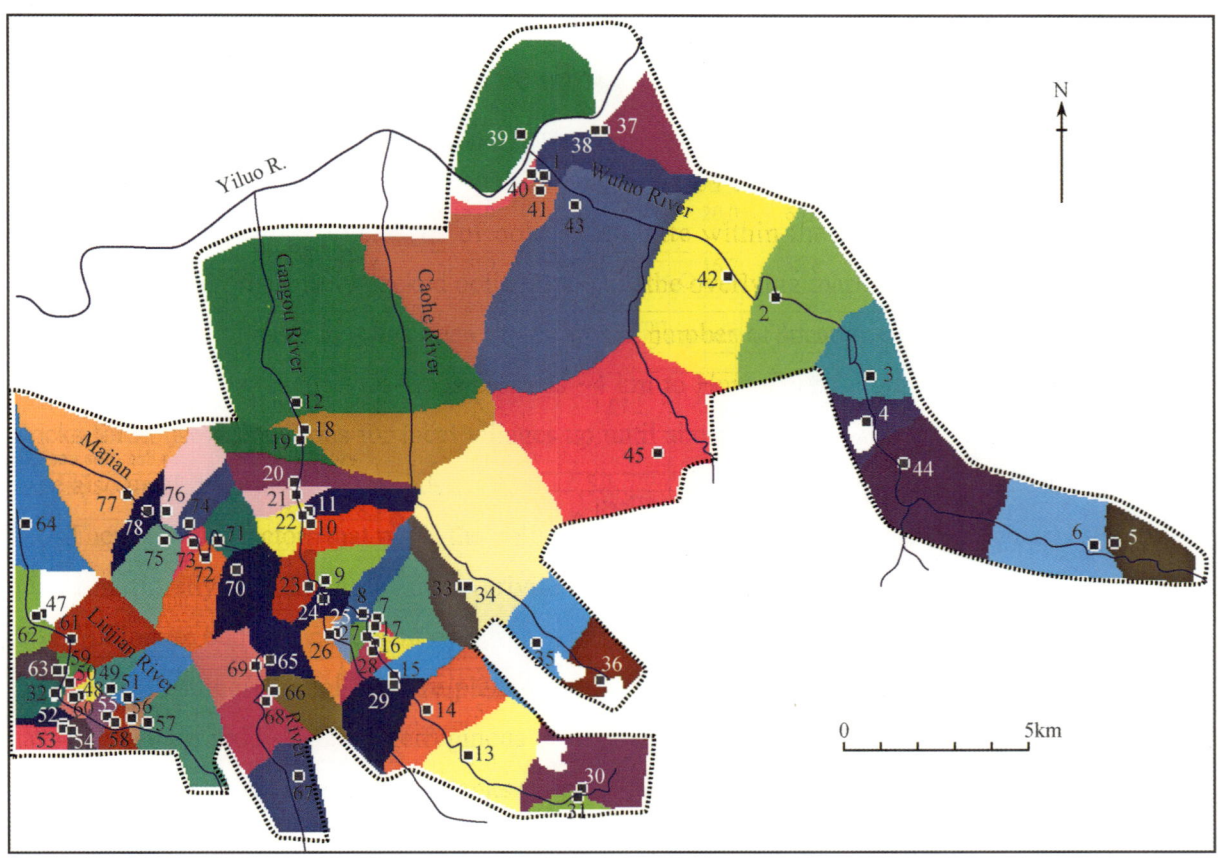

Figure 5.9 Late Longshan Period

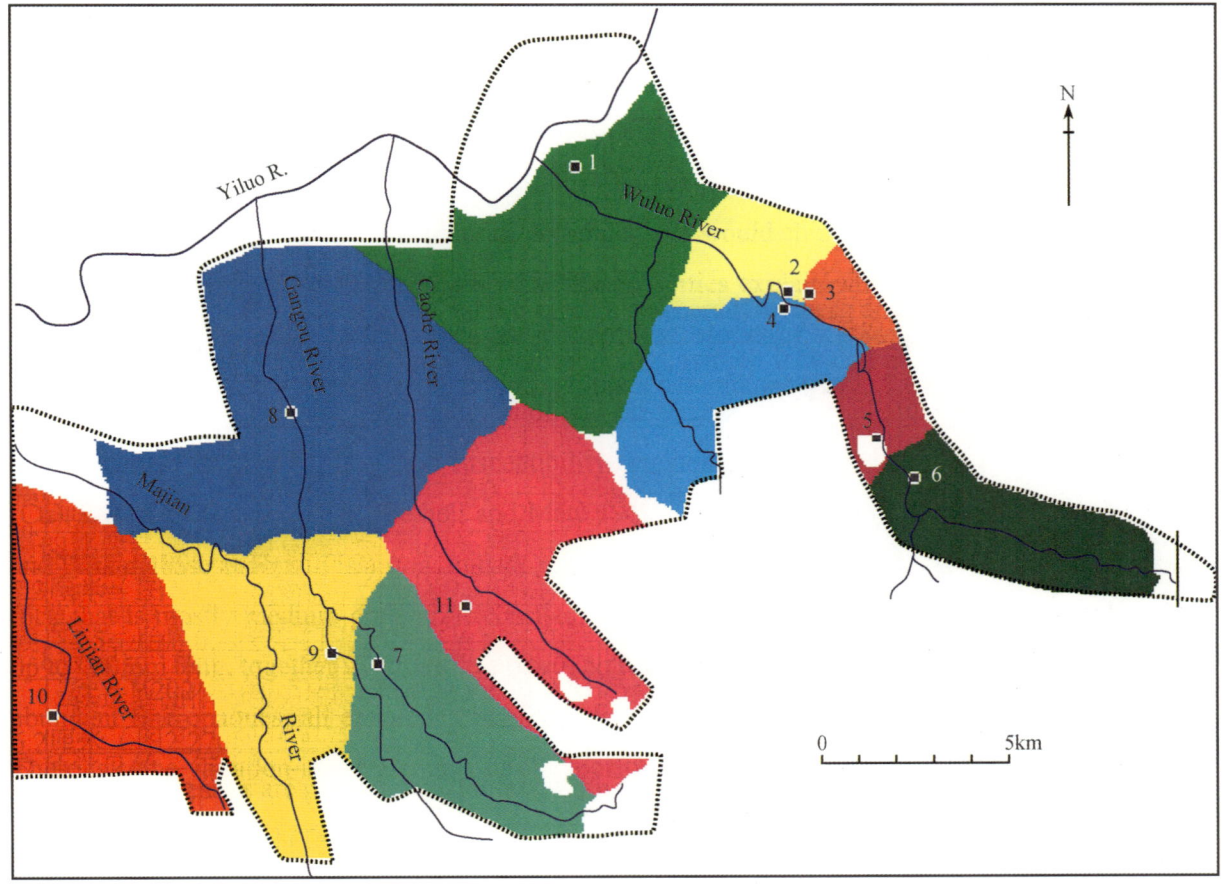

Figure 5.10 Erlitou I

1388　洛阳盆地中东部先秦时期遗址

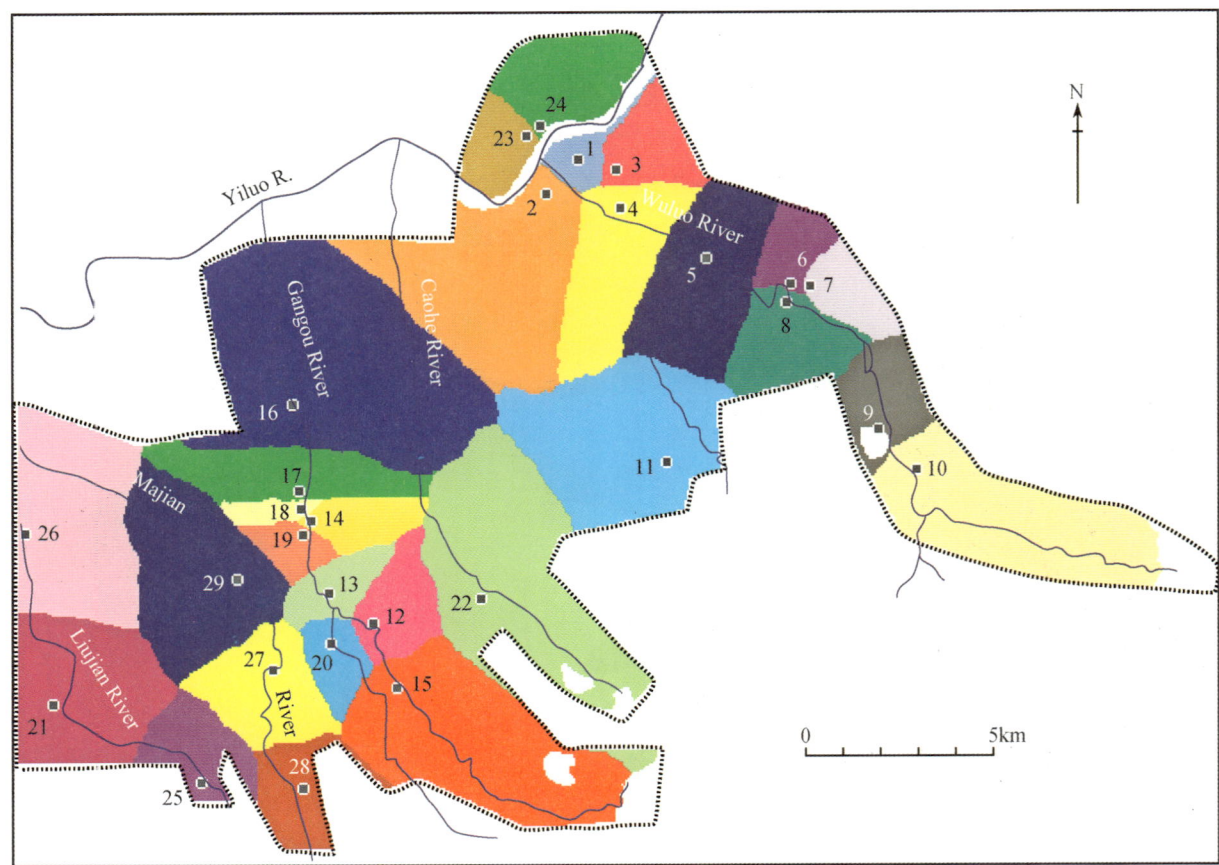

Figure 5.11　Erlitou II

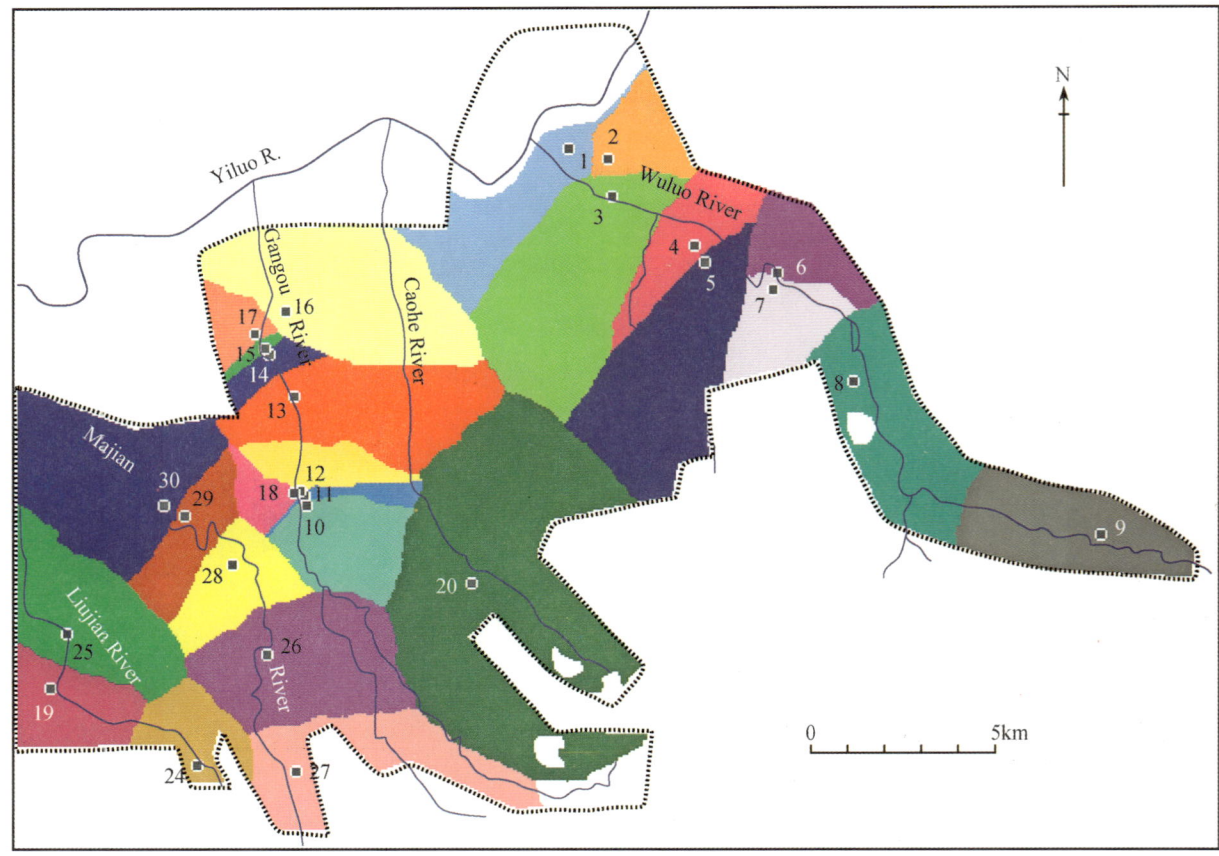

Figure 5.12　Erlitou III

CHAPTER 5 DEVELOPMENT OF COMPLEX SOCIETIES IN THE YILUO REGION: A GIS BASED POPULATION AND AGRICULTURAL AREA ANALYSIS

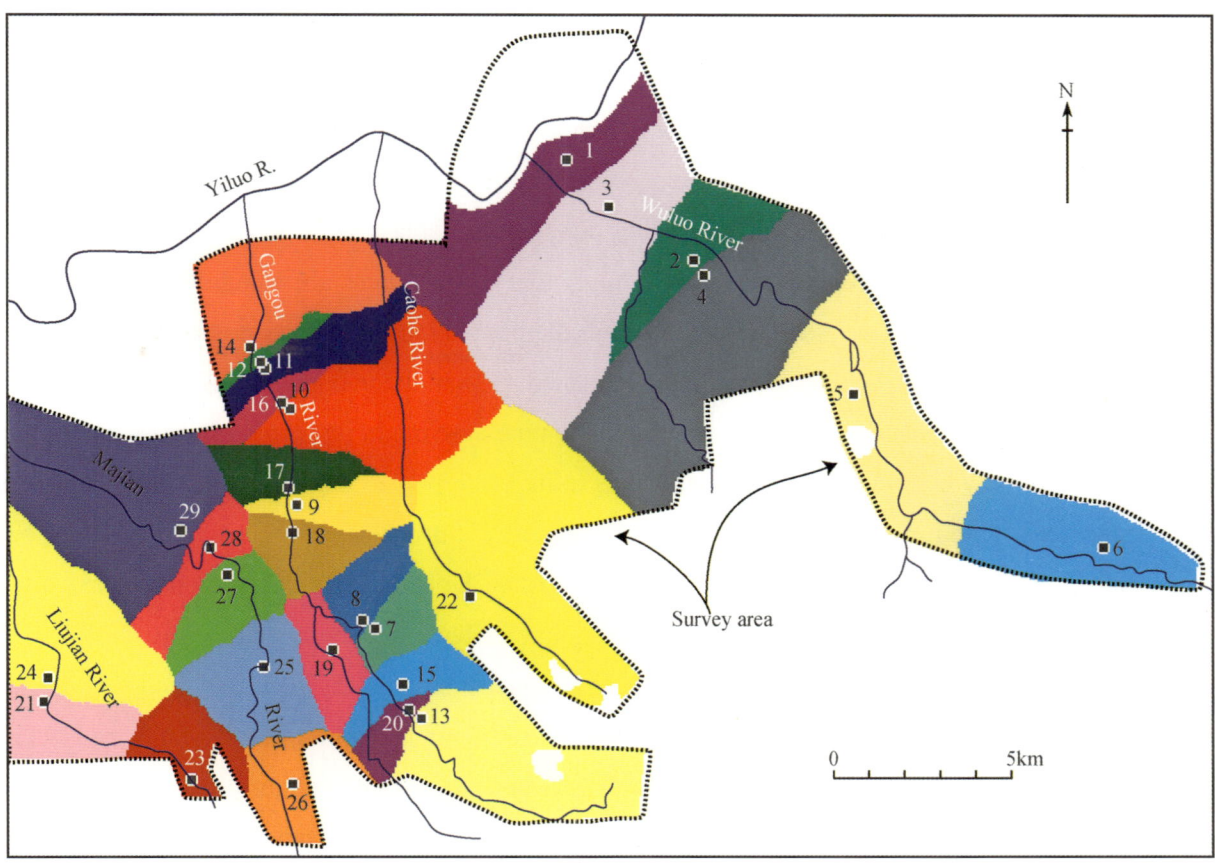

Figure 5.13　Erlitou IV

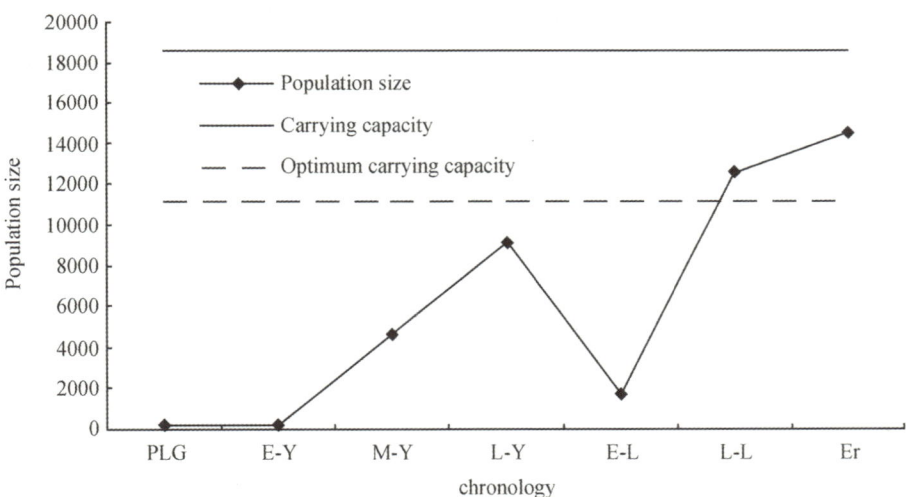

Figure 5.14　Fluctuations of population size through time

Significantly, the increase of population size coincided with the initiation of social complexity. The middle Yangshao phase witnessed both the first noticeable population increase and the emergence of a two-tiered settlement hierarchy system, indicating a more complex social structure. After that, the settlement hierarchy system spurred the population to a high level in the late Yangshao phase, and kept it at a relatively high level in the late Longshan phase, although the most marked population decline happened in the early Longshan phase.

The results, however, do not support any assumption that "population pressure" was the prime mover for the initiation of social complexity. As Hassan argued, one of the major weaknesses of the population pressure concept lies in confusing population increase with population pressure. An increase in population size does not necessarily imply that the resources are being depleted and that famine is around the corner (Hassan, 1978). Though the population kept increasing from the middle Yangshao to the late Yangshao phases, it still only reached 33 % of the maximun carrying capacity and was not likely to introduce survival pressures. Population increase might just provide more chances for elites to intentionally manipulate different strategies to maintain power and establish a more complex social structure. This initial population increase apparently did not cause siginificant pressure on resource, which may lead the societies towards complexity. The archaeological data shows that two-tiered hierarchy systems developed long before any significant level of population pressure.

Population size exceeded the optimum carrying capacity limit in the Erlitou period and might have caused environmental pressure. But the three-tiered settlement hierarchy system had been maintained during the whole Erlitou phases and population size declined slightly from Erlitou II to Erlitou IV. This seems to support Hassan's argument that when an area is facing population pressure, instead of being forced to develop a more complex social structure, the societies might have a chance to adjust the population size to a level of safety and might conduct a more intensive exploration for local resources under existing technology and food-gatherings systems (Hassan, 1978).

From the Peiligang to the early Yangshao period, all of the sites had enough catchment productivity (or enough agricultural land within a catchment), to support their own residents (Tables 5.1-5.2; Figs 5.4-5.5). However, a dramatic change started at the late Yangshao period. Twelve of the 48 sites were short of agricultural lands within their catchment territories, while the total land-use ratio was only 49% (Table 5.4; Fig 5.7). This imbalance in land-use ratio among sites continued in the later periods. This should be regarded as a new land-use pattern which has a close relationship with the development of social complexity. I employ three models to explain the shortage of agricultural land for some sites.

The "tribute" model, which proposes that the food shortage of a site will be met up by tribute from the other sites, could be applied to explain the shortfall of the central sites in a settlement hierarchy system. A two-tiered settlement hierarchy emerged in the middle Yangshao period and developed into a three-tiered settlement hierarchy in the Erlitou period. After the middle Yangshao phase, most of the central sites no longer had enough agricultural lands within their catchments to support their populations. Gathering tribute from the surrounding low-level sites is an important strategy for survival.

The "special resources" model proposes that sites short of agricultural land might have had special resources which could be used for the exchange of food. The special resources included both natural resources, such as stone material for making tools, wood, mine, animal, clay for pottery production etc., and technical resources, such as some special method of craft production. This model can be employed to explain the shortfall in agricultural land at some relatively small low-level sites as well as at some high-level sites such as Xikouzi NW, dating to the Erlitou Phases II-IV, which shows a severe land shortage (Tables 5.8-5.10; Figures 5.11-5.13).

The two models would not always operate separately. On the contrary, they often co-operated in an economic system which developed political central control but lacked a diversified market economy. Liu and Chen's sophisticated interpretation of the complex economic system of early states on the Central Plains area (Liu and Chen 2003) provides one way of understanding the economic system in this study area, especially during the Erlitou period. According to their study, the high-level local central sites were usually the centers of craft specialization and located near natural resources. For example, the Huizui site, a local center in the Liujian valley, was also a center for stone tools manufacture (Henan Cultural Bureau 1961, Ford 2001, Liu and Chen 2003; Liu et al. this volume). On the other hand, special resources might also be part of tribute paid by low-level sites, which might not always be able to freely exchange their products.

Although some river valleys suffered from a shortage of agricultural land in some periods, the surveyed area as a whole had enough cultivatable land in all the ten chronological phases. In other words, the shortage at some sites could always be made up by other sites within the region. Noticeably, from the Erlitou phase II, the population size in the surveyed area fluctuated around the optimum carrying capacity, which indicates that in an ideal situation, this region might have had little crop surplus to support the capital settlement of the Erlitou polity – the Erlitou site or other regions. This implies that the redistribution of food in the form of tribute might have primarily occurred at the local level, and food itself was not the main tribute item which regional centers in the study area submitted to the capital.

A noticeable fact demonstrated by the archaeological data is that the shortage of catchment productivity did not coincide with the emergence of settlement hierarchy. In the middle Yangshao period, when the two-tiered settlement hierarchy first formed in the study area, the Zhaocheng site (20 ha) as a local center suffered a shortage of agricultural land, while the other two local centers (Huizui and Beizhai SE) had enough agricultural land to support themselves (Table 5.3; Fig 5.6). In the late Yangshao, the Huizui site still had enough agricultural land to be self-sufficient, though its land-use ratio increased from 56% to 75% (Table 5.4; Fig 5.7). It was in the late Longshan period, when several small sites of less than 1 ha (sites No.48, 52, 59, 60) emerged nearby, that the Huizui site began to suffer a catchment productivity shortfall (Table 5.6; Fig 5.9), and was likely to be supported by those small sites. Thus, it appears that the tribute model might have been established after a hierarchy system had been developed.

In spite of some limitations, the GIS-based research still can help us obtain a better understanding of the general relationship between population size, catchment productivity and development of social complexity in an area that was part of the heartland of early states in China. Although some specific interpretation may change as more data and finer chronological controls become available, the analytical methods employed here have shown great potential for application in future studies.

Table 5.1 The site size (SS), estimated population, catchment productivity (CP), necessary field (NF), and the Land-use ratio in the Late Peiligang period

Id	SITE NAME	SITE No	Phase	SS(ha)	Population	CP (ha)	NF (ha)	Land-use ratio
	Gaogou River			0.5	28.5	8073.6	45.6	1%
1	Fudian E	00-124	P	0.5	28.5	8073.6	45.6	1%
	Wuluo River			1.8	102.6	4308.6	164.16	4%
2	Tieshenggou	98-029	P	0.2	11.4	114.3	18.24	16%
3	Dongshanyuan	98-041	P	0.7	39.9	1329.6	63.84	5%
4	Wuluoxipo	98-042	P	0.5	28.5	2480	45.6	2%
5	Beiying	98-044	P	0.4	22.8	384.7	36.48	9%
	Liujian River			1.5	85.5	3893.3	136.8	4%
6	Shuangquan SW	02-171	P	0.5	28.5	223.8	45.6	20%
7	Liujuanhe Shuike E	02-187	P	1	57	3669.5	91.2	2%
Total				3.8	216.6	16275.5	346.56	2%

Table 5.2 The site size (SS), estimated population, catchment productivity (CP), necessary field (NF), and Land-use ratio in the Early Yangshao phase

ID	SITE NAME	SITE No	PHASE	SS (ha)	Population	CP (ha)	NF (ha)	Land-use ratio
	Wuluo River			1.7	96.9	2160.5	155.04	7%
1	Shecun E	98-035	E-Y	0.2	11.4	1787.4	18.24	1%
2	Danangou	98-038	E-Y	1.5	85.5	373.1	136.8	37%
	Liujian River			1	57	4917.8	91.2	2%
3	Liujuanhe Shuiku E	02-187	E-Y	1	57	4917.8	91.2	2%
Total				2.7	153.9	7078.3	246.24	3%

Table 5.3 The site size (SS), estimated population, catchment productivity (CP), necessary field (NF), and Land-use ratio in the Middle Yangshao phase

ID	SITE NAME	SITE No	PHASE	SS (ha)	Population	CP (ha)	NF (ha)	Land-useratio
	Gangou River			29	1653	7607.3	2644.8	35%
1	Zhaocheng	00-077	M-Y	20	1140	942.8	1824	193%
2	Zhaocheng W	00-078	M-Y	2.5	142.5	574.1	228	40%
3	Zhaocheng SW	00-079	M-Y	1	57	749	91.2	12%
4	Fengzhai NW	00-090	M-Y	2.5	142.5	2346.3	228	10%
5	Sanguanmiao	00-105	M-Y	3	171	2995.1	273.6	9%
	Liujian River			10	570	1632.7	912	56%

(continued)

ID	SITE NAME	SITE No	PHASE	SS (ha)	Population	CP (ha)	NF (ha)	Land-use ratio
6	Huizui	00-127	M-Y	10	570	1632.7	912	56%
	Majian River			21	1197	5757.9	1915.2	33%
14	Laotunzhai	02-199	M-Y	6	342	998.1	547.2	55%
15	Laozhouzhai	02-200	M-Y	6	342	855.1	547.2	64%
16	Beizhai SE	02-218	M-Y	9	513	3904.7	820.8	21%
	Wuluo River			21	1197	11295.9	1915.2	15%
7	Sigou SE	01-152	M-Y	3	171	517.3	273.6	53%
8	Shijiazhuang SW	01-153	M-Y	1	57	617.3	91.2	15%
9	Weizhuang	98-018	M-Y	5.5	313.5	2780.8	501.6	18%
10	Wuluo Shuiku W	98-025	M-Y	2	114	2092	182.4	9%
11	Yulinzhuang S	98-050	M-Y	1.5	85.5	3820.6	136.8	4%
12	Didong	98-052	M-Y	4	228	481.3	364.8	76%
13	Longgudui	98-053	M-Y	4	228	986.6	364.8	37%
Total				81	4617	26293.8	7387.2	28%

Table 5.4 The site size (SS), estimated population, catchment productivity (CP), necessary field (NF), and Land-use ratio in the Late Yangshao phase

ID	SITE NAME	SITE No	PHASE	SS (ha)	Population	CP (ha)	NF (ha)	Land-use ratio
	Gangou River			44.56	2539.92	8324.9	4063.87	49%
1	Nancunzhai SE	00-061	L-Y	1	57	533.1	91.2	17%
2	Sanggou S	00-066	L-Y	4	228	315	364.8	116%
3	Liulezhai S	00-075	L-Y	1	57	2508	91.2	4%
4	Zhaocheng	00-077	L-Y	20	1140	972.3	1824	188%
6	Fengzhai NW	00-090	L-Y	2.5	142.5	342.5	228	67%
7	Gujiatun E	00-096	L-Y	0.06	3.42	1253.6	5.472	0%
8	Gujiatun S	00-098	L-Y	0.8	45.6	397	72.96	18%
9	Matun Xicun	00-102	L-Y	0.2	11.4	655.1	18.24	3%
10	Sanguanmiao N	00-104	L-Y	0.75	42.75	291.6	68.4	23%
11	Sanguanmiao	00-105	L-Y	3	171	61.5	273.6	445%
12	Huachenghe N	00-108	L-Y	3	171	301.2	273.6	91%
13	Xingcun E	00-121	L-Y	2	114	521.6	182.4	35%
14	Bangezhai	00-123	L-Y	5.75	327.75	72.4	524.4	724%
15	Sanggouwudui N	00-126	L-Y	0.5	28.5	100	45.6	46%
	Caohe River			7.25	413.25	2482.9	661.2	27%
17	Caohe Shuiku W	00-133	L-Y	1	57	715.1	91.2	13%
18	Caomer	01-135	L-Y	2.5	142.5	368.9	228	62%
19	Beihougou NW	01-139	L-Y	3.75	213.75	1398.9	342	24%
	Wuluo River			29.7	1692.9	11942.3	2708.64	23%
5	Dongshanyuan	98-041	L-Y	0.7	39.9	1216.3	63.84	5%
20	Sigou S	01-151	L-Y	0.5	28.5	375.3	45.6	12%
21	Sigou SE	01-152	L-Y	3	171	750.8	273.6	36%
22	Shaochai	97-1001	L-Y	5	285	2221.8	456	21%
23	Weizhuang	98-018	L-Y	5.5	313.5	539.8	501.6	93%
24	Weizhuang W	98-019	L-Y	0.2	11.4	769	18.24	2%

(continued)

ID	SITE NAME	SITE No	PHASE	SS (ha)	Population	CP (ha)	NF (ha)	Land-use ratio
25	Luokou NE	98-022	L-Y	0.4	22.8	589.6	36.48	6%
26	Weizhuang NE	98-023	L-Y	0.3	17.1	261.2	27.36	10%
27	Wuluoshuiku W1	98-025	L-Y	2	114	922.7	182.4	20%
28	Shangzhuang	98-037	L-Y	1	57	405.5	91.2	22%
29	Shangzhuang SE	98-039	L-Y	0.4	22.8	327.2	36.48	11%
30	Tianpocun	98-049	L-Y	1.2	68.4	757.6	109.44	14%
31	Yulinzhuang S	98-050	L-Y	1.5	85.5	1832	136.8	7%
32	Didong	98-052	L-Y	4	228	461.7	364.8	79%
33	Longgudui	98-053	L-Y	4	228	511.8	364.8	71%
	Liujian River			11	627	1608.5	1003.2	53%
16	Huizui	00-127	L-Y	10	570	1219.3	912	75%
34	Jiulong Shuiku	02-183	L-Y	1	57	389.2	91.2	23%
35	Zhengcun W	02-194	L-Y	1.5	85.5	562.8	136.8	24%
	Majian River			65.5	3733.5	4748.1	5973.6	79%
36	Xinzhai N	02-197	L-Y	5	285	357.1	456	128%
37	Laotunzhai	02-199	L-Y	6	342	351.3	547.2	156%
38	Laozhouzhai	02-200	L-Y	6	342	188.1	547.2	291%
39	Dongguanmao E	02-202	L-Y	5	285	388.2	456	117%
40	Bucun SE	02-204	L-Y	4	228	117.5	3648	310%
42	Bucun E	02-206	L-Y	1	57	305.3	91.2	30%
43	Nan Wujiawan SE	02-213	L-Y	4.5	256.5	469.8	410.4	87%
44	Bei Wujiawan	02-214	L-Y	6	342	252.9	547.2	216%
45	Jintun E	02-215	L-Y	1	57	419.9	91.2	22%
46	Diaoqiaozhai SE	02-216	L-Y	8	456	477.6	729.6	153%
47	Beizhai SE	02-218	L-Y	9	513	310.9	820.8	264%
48	Beizhai N	02-219	L-Y	10	570	1109.5	912	82%
Total				159.5	9092.07	29669.5	14547.3	49%

Table 5.5 The site size (SS), estimated population, catchment productivity (CP), necessary field (NF), and Land-use ratio in the Early Longshan phase

ID	SITE NAME	SITE No	PHASE	SS (ha)	Population	CP (ha)	NF (ha)	Land-use ratio
	Wuluo River			4.3	245.1	9430.7	392.16	4%
1	Weizhuang NE	98-023	E-L	0.3	17.1	4860.3	27.36	1%
2	Didong	98-052	E-L	4	228	4570.4	364.8	8%
	Gangou River			17.5	997.5	11005.6	1596	15%
3	Liulezhai S	00-075	E-L	1	57	4781.6	91.2	2%
4	Sanguanmiao	00-105	E-L	1	57	1375.7	91.2	7%
5	Huachenghe N	00-108	E-L	3	171	533	273.6	51%
6	Huachenghe E	00-112	E-L	0.75	42.75	1488.8	68.4	5%
7	Yanliangzhai W	00-114	E-L	4	228	1597.2	364.8	23%
8	Xingcun E	00-121	E-L	2	114	1156.9	182.4	16%
9	Bangezhai	00-123	E-L	5.75	327.75	72.4	524.4	724%
10	Sigou SE	01-152	E-L	4	228	1134.6	364.8	32%

(continued)

ID	SITE NAME	SITE No	PHASE	SS (ha)	Population	CP (ha)	NF (ha)	Land-use ratio
	Liujian River			2	114	2876.6	182.4	6%
11	Gaozumiao	02-167	E-L	2	114	2876.6	182.4	6%
	Majian River			1	57	2962.7	91.2	3%
12	Mahe N	02-207	E-L	1	57	2962.7	91.2	3%
Total				28.8	1641.6	27410.2	2626.56	10%

Table 5.6 The site size (SS), estimated population, catchment productivity (CP), necessary field (NF), and Land-use ratio in the Late Longshan phase

ID	SITE NAME	SITE No	Phase	SS (ha)	Population	CP (ha)	NF (ha)	Land-use ratio
	Wuluo River			44.2	2519.4	12177.8	4031.04	33%
1	Nanshi	97-1003	L-L	0.2	11.4	80.1	18.24	23%
2	Luokou NE	98-022	L-L	20	1140	1013.5	1824	180%
3	Wulu Nandian	98-032	L-L	3	171	465.5	273.6	59%
4	Siyuangou	98-034	L-L	1.5	85.5	221.7	136.8	62%
5	Shangzhuang SE	98-039	L-L	0.4	22.8	342.3	36.48	11%
6	Shecun SE	98-040	L-L	0.4	22.8	703.6	36.48	5%
37	Yemaogou	01-144	L-L	7	399	321	638.4	199%
38	Donggou N	01-146	L-L	6	342	320.7	547.2	171%
39	Sigou S	01-151	L-L	4	228	1133.5	364.8	32%
40	Xiaocidian N	97-1004	L	0.2	11.4	19.3	18.24	95%
41	Xiaocidian S	97-1005	L	0.5	28.5	1095.4	45.6	4%
42	Weizhuang	98-018	L	0.2	11.4	1470.1	18.24	1%
43	Nanshi lunan	98-046	L	0.2	11.4	2105	18.24	1%
44	Shuanghe	98-047	L	0.1	5.7	946.6	9.12	1%
45	Jinzhongsi	98-054	M-L	0.5	28.5	1939.5	45.6	2%
	Gangou River			62.76	3577.32	8271.3	5723.71	69%
7	Naicunzhai S	00-060	L-L	0.5	28.5	281.6	45.6	16%
8	Nancunzhai S	00-063	L-L	1	57	188.5	91.2	48%
9	Sanggou NW	00-067	L-L	1.5	85.5	172.8	136.8	79%
10	Matun	00-069	L-L	6	342	258.7	547.2	212%
11	Matun N	00-070	L-L	2.5	142.5	184.6	228	124%
12	Nianzizhuang NW	00-073	L-L	1	57	2686.1	91.2	3%
13	zhaocheng	00-077	L-L	0.1	5.7	565.2	9.12	2%
14	Xiaoxiang SW	00-080	L-L	4.5	256.5	520.6	410.4	79%
15	YLZ shuiku W	00-087	L-L	2	114	157.4	182.4	116%
16	Fengzhai SW	00-089	L-L	2.2	125.4	61.2	200.64	328%
17	Fengzhai NW	00-090	L-L	2.5	142.5	15.2	228	1500%
18	Gujiatun E	00-096	L-L	0.06	3.42	820	5.472	1%
19	Gujiatun S	00-098	L-L	0.8	45.6	223.7	72.96	33%
20	Lijiagou E	00-099	L-L	7.5	427.5	305.6	684	224%
21	Sunjiamer S	00-100	L-L	0.15	8.55	116.1	13.68	12%
22	Matun Xicun	00-102	L-L	0.2	11.4	135.3	18.24	13%
23	Sanguanmiao N	00-104	L-L	0.75	42.75	180.3	68.4	38%
24	Sanguanmiao	00-106	L-L	0.5	28.5	97.9	45.6	47%

(continued)

ID	SITE NAME	SITE No	Phase	SS (ha)	Population	CP (ha)	NF (ha)	Land-use ratio
25	Huachenghe W	00-109	L-L	3	171	47.1	273.6	581%
26	Fuxicun N	00-110	L-L	13	741	179.2	1185.6	662%
27	Huachenghe E	00-112	L-L	0.75	42.75	42.9	68.4	159%
28	Fubeicun N	00-113	L-L	0.5	28.5	92.2	45.6	49%
29	Yanliangzhai W	00-114	L-L	4	228	345.1	364.8	106%
30	Xingcun E	00-121	L-L	2	114	521.6	182.4	35%
31	Bangezhai	00-123	L-L	5.5	327.75	72.4	524.4	724%
	Caohe River			6	342	2270.3	547.2	24%
33	Xinhougou	00-130	L-L	1	57	283	91.2	32%
34	Xinhougou E	00-131	L-L	1.5	85.5	1330.5	136.8	10%
35	Nangou	00-134	L-L	1	57	406	91.2	22%
36	Caomer	01-135	L-L	2.5	142.5	250.8	228	91%
	Liujian River			46	2622	2625.4	4195.2	160%
32	Huizui	00-127	L-L	10	570	112.5	912	811%
47	Zhengyao	01-140	L-L	0.5	28.5	150.2	45.6	30%
4	Xiqijiayao SE	02-164	L-L	0.5	28.5	32.3	45.6	141%
49	Lucun	02-168	L-L	1	57	87.7	91.2	104%
50	Xiqijiayao NW	02-166	L-L	5	285	20.9	456	2182%
51	Lucun NE	02-169	L-L	1.5	85.5	210.2	136.8	65%
52	Quanzhai W	02-170	L-L	0.5	28.5	41.9	45.6	109%
53	Suangquan SW	02-171	L-L	0.5	28.5	75	45.6	61%
54	Suangquan N	02-172	L-L	1	57	59.4	91.2	154%
55	Lucun	02-177	L-L	0.5	28.5	67.8	45.6	67%
56	Rencai SW	02-178	L-L	0.5	28.5	50.3	45.6	91%
57	Rencai SE	02-179	L-L	3	171	468.1	273.6	58%
58	Lucun S	02-186	L-L	1	57	74.5	91.2	122%
59	Xiqijiayao NW	02-188	L-L	1	57	41.1	91.2	222%
60	Liujuanhe Shuike E	02-187	L-L	1	57	40.9	91.2	223%
61	Zhengyao S	02-189	L-L	3	171	426	273.6	64%
62	Liuguo Gucheng	02-190	L	0.5	28.5	162.8	45.6	28%
63	Huizui N	02-192	L	3	171	68.7	273.6	398%
64	Jiandongcun NW	02-196	L-L	12	684	435.1	1094.4	252%
	Majian River			60.5	3448.5	4182.7	5517.6	132%
65	Xinzhai N	02-197	L-L	5	285	211.6	456	216%
66	Tunzhai NW	02-198	L-L	2	114	228.5	182.4	80%
67	Xikouzi NW	02-201	L-L	2	114	396.7	182.4	46%
68	Laotunzhai	02-199	L-L	6	342	338.9	547.2	161%
69	Bucun E	02-206	L-L	1	57	270.4	91.2	34%
70	Zhangwan N	02-210	L-L	20	1140	316.4	1824	576%
71	Linxiaozhai	02-211	L-L	2	114	188.5	182.4	97%
72	Linxiaozhai SW	02-212	L-L	1	57	343.5	91.2	27%
73	Nan Wujiawan SE	02-213	L-L	4.5	256.5	56.7	410.4	724%
74	Bei Wujiawan	02-214	L-L	8	456	145.2	729.6	502%
75	Diaoqiaozhai SE	02-216	L-L	4	228	312.1	364.8	117%
76	Qiuhe W	02-221	L-L	2	114	256.6	182.4	71%

(continued)

ID	SITE NAME	SITE No	Phase	SS (ha)	Population	CP (ha)	NF (ha)	Land-use ratio
77	Beizhai N	02-219	L-L	2	114	964.4	182.4	19%
78	Fenghuangtai S	02-220	L-L	1	57	153.2	91.2	60%
Total				219.5	12509.2	29527.5	20014.8	68%

Table 5.7 The site size (SS), estimated population, catchment productivity (CP), necessary field (NF), and land-use ratio in the Erlitou phase I

ID	SITE NAME	SITE No	PHASE	SS (ha)	Population	NF (ha)	CP (ha)	Land-use ratio
	Wuluo River			86	4902	7843.2	9821.8	80%
1	Shaochai	97-1001	EI	60	3420	5472	4239.6	129%
2	Weizhuang SE	98-020	EI	6	342	547.2	896	61%
3	Weizhuang	98-021	EI	0.4	22.8	36.48	383.4	10%
4	Luokou NE	98-022	EI	18	1026	1641.6	1967.8	83%
5	Siyuangou	98-034	EI	1.5	85.5	136.8	531.3	26%
6	Shuanghe	98-047	EI	0.1	5.7	9.12	1803.7	1%
	Gangou River			8.25	470.25	752.4	11058.9	7%
7	Fengzhai SW	00-089	EI	2	114	182.4	2331.2	8%
8	Shijiagou NE	00-093	EI	4	228	364.8	5480.5	7%
9	Fuxicun N	00-110	EI	2.25	128.25	205.2	3247.2	6%
	Liujian River			25	1425	2280	3244.2	70%
10	Huizui	00-127	EI	25	1425	2280	3244.2	70%
	Caohe River			0.5	28.5	45.6	3360.9	1%
11	Xinhougou	00-130	EI	0.5	28.5	45.6	3360.9	1%
Total				119.8	6825.75	10921.2	27485.5	40%

Table 5.8 The site size (SS), estimated population, catchment productivity (CP), necessary field (NF), and land-use ratio in the Erlitou phase II

ID	SITE NAME	SITE No	PHASE	SS (ha)	Population	NF (ha)	CP (ha)	Land-used ratio
	Wuluo River			95.5	5443.5	8709.6	10997.8	79%
1	Shaochai	97-1001	EII	60	3420	5472	215.6	2538%
2	Xiaocidian S	97-1005	EII	2	114	182.4	2068.7	9%
3	Dianchang N	98-005	EII	3.5	199.5	319.2	498.2	64%
4	Dianchang SE	98-008	EII	1.5	85.5	136.8	1119.4	12%
5	Feiyao SE	98-011	EII	2	114	182.4	1329.2	14%
6	Weizhuang SE	98-020	EII	6	342	547.2	355.6	154%
7	Weizhuang	98-021	EII	0.4	22.8	36.48	383.4	10%
8	Luokou NE	98-022	EII	18	1026	1641.6	720.4	228%
9	Siyuangou	98-034	EII	1.5	85.5	136.8	531.3	26%
10	Shuanghe	98-047	EII	0.1	5.7	9.12	1803.7	1%
11	Jinzhongsi	98-054	EII	0.5	28.5	45.6	1972.3	2%
	Gangou River			25.25	1439.25	2302.8	8394.1	27%
12	Nancunzhai SW	00-062	EII	2	114	182.4	542.5	34%
13	Sangou W	00-068	EII	6	342	547.2	366.2	149%
14	Matun N	00-070	EII	2.5	142.5	228	374.7	61%

(continued)

ID	SITE NAME	SITE No	PHASE	SS (ha)	Population	NF (ha)	CP (ha)	Land-used ratio
15	YLZ shuiku W	00-087	EII	2	114	182.4	2129.7	9%
16	Shijiagou NE	00-093	EII	4	228	364.8	3377.5	11%
17	Lijiagou E	00-099	EII	5	285	456	872.6	52%
18	Jiatun	00-101	EII	0.5	28.5	45.6	145.1	31%
19	Matun Xicun S	00-103	EII	1	57	91.2	249.9	36%
20	Fuxicun N	00-110	EII	2.25	128.25	205.2	335.9	61%
	Caohe River			2.25	128.25	205.2	2327.9	9%
22	Xinhougou YC E	00-132	EII	2.25	128.25	205.2	2327.9	9%
23	Sigou S	01-151	EII	0.5	28.5	45.6	329.5	14%
24	Sigou SE	01-152	EII	2	114	182.4	745.9	24%
	Liujian River			41	2337	3739.2	3550.9	105%
21	Huizui	00-127	EII	25	1425	2280	1394.2	164%
25	Xiahousi	02-182	EII	4	228	364.8	533.6	68%
26	Jianxicun NW	02-196	EII	12	684	1094.4	1623.1	67%
	Majian River			38	2166	3465.6	2959.1	117%
27	Xinzhai N	02-197	EII	10	570	912	864	106%
28	Xikouzi NW	02-201	EII	18	1026	1641.6	504.7	325%
29	Zhangwan N	02-210	EII	10	570	912	1590.4	57%
Total				204.5	11656.5	18650.4	29305.2	64%

Table 5.9 The site size (SS), estimated population, catchment productivity (CP), necessary field (NF), and land-use ratio in the Erlitou phase III

ID	SITE NAME	SITE No	PHASE	SS (ha)	Population	CP (ha)	NF (ha)	Land-use ratio
	Wuluo River			92.7	5283.9	10086.5	8454.24	84%
1	Shaochai	97-1001	EIII	60	3420	1003.6	5472	545%
2	Dianchang Beilu E	98-005	EIII	3.5	199.5	498.2	319.2	64%
3	Dianchang SE	98-008	EIII	1.5	85.5	2133.9	136.8	6%
4	Feiyao SE	98-011	EIII	2	114	720.1	182.4	25%
5	Feiyao S2	98-013	EIII	0.5	28.5	1836.9	45.6	2%
6	Weizhuang SE	98-020	EIII	6	342	597.1	547.2	92%
7	Luokou NE	98-022	EIII	18	1026	653.4	1641.6	251%
8	Wuluoxipo 1	98-033	EIII	0.2	11.4	1398.8	18.24	1%
9	Shangzhuang	98-037	EIII	1	57	1244.5	91.2	7%
	Gangou River			18.5	1054.5	5689.1	1687.2	30%
10	Matun N	00-070	EIII	2.5	142.5	804.9	228	28%
11	Wangmer	00-071	EIII	3	171	156.1	273.6	175%
12	Luoyanzhuang SW	00-072	EIII	1	57	415.9	91.2	22%
13	Nianzizhuang NW	00-073	EIII	1	57	1544.9	91.2	6%
14	Gangou zhuchang	00-074	EIII	6	342	194.3	547.2	282%
15	Liulezhai S	00-075	EIII	1	57	64.1	91.2	142%
16	Gangounan	00-076	EIII	0.5	28.5	2020.5	45.6	2%
17	Huilongwan Xincun E	00-083	EIII	3	171	259.8	273.6	105%
18	Jiatun	00-101	EIII	0.5	28.5	228.6	45.6	20%

CHAPTER 5   DEVELOPMENT OF COMPLEX SOCIETIES IN THE YILUO REGION: A GIS BASED POPULATION AND AGRICULTURAL AREA ANALYSIS

(continued)

ID	SITE NAME	SITE No	PHASE	SS (ha)	Population	CP (ha)	NF (ha)	Land-use ratio
	Caohe River			2.25	128.25	4157.7	205.2	5%
20	Xinhougou YC E	00-132	EIII	2.25	128.25	4157.7	205.2	5%
	Liujian River			32	1824	2524.5	2918.4	116%
19	Huizui	00-127	EIII	25	1425	678.6	2280	336%
24	Xiahousi	02-182	EIII	4	228	514	364.8	71%
25	Zhengyao S	02-189	EIII	3	171	1331.9	273.6	21%
	Majian River			43	2451	5808.4	3921.6	68%
26	Xinzhai N	02-197	EIII	10	570	1661.4	912	55%
27	Xikouzi NW	02-201	EIII	18	1026	1110.6	1641.6	148%
28	Zhangwan N	02-210	EIII	10	570	694.2	912	131%
29	Bei Wujiawan	02-214	EIII	3	171	583	273.6	47%
30	Qiuhe W	02-221	EIII	2	114	1759.2	182.4	10%
Total				188.45	10741.65	28266.2	17186.6	61%

Table 5.10   The site size (SS), estimated population, catchment productivity (CP), necessary field (NF), and Land-use ratio in the Erlitou phase IV

ID	SITE NAME	SITE No	PHASE	SS (ha)	Population	CP (ha)	NF (ha)	Land-use ratio
	Wuluo River			65.2	3716.4	10281.4	5946.24	58%
1	Shaochai	97-1001	EIV	60	3420	1412.5	5472	387%
2	Dianchang SE	98-008	EIV	1.5	85.5	2416.2	136.8	6%
3	Feiyao SE	98-011	EIV	2	114	767.5	182.4	24%
4	Feiyao S2	98-013	EIV	0.5	28.5	2749.5	45.6	2%
5	Wuluoxipo 1	98-033	EIV	0.2	11.4	1691.2	18.24	1%
6	Shangzhuang	98-037	EIV	1	57	1244.5	91.2	7%
	Gangou River			36.4	2074.8	8655.8	3319.68	38%
7	Nancunzhai SE	00-061	EIV	1	57	342.5	91.2	27%
8	Nancunzhai SW	00-062	EIV	2	114	388.8	182.4	47%
9	Luoyanzhuang SW	00-072	EIV	1	57	463.5	91.2	20%
10	Nianzizhuang NW	00-073	EIV	1	57	1680.4	91.2	5%
11	Gangou zhuchang	00-074	EIV	6	342	535.9	547.2	102%
12	Liulezhai S	00-075	EIV	1	57	119.2	91.2	77%
13	Xiaoxiang SW	00-080	EIV	4.5	256.5	1529.5	410.4	27%
14	Huilongwan Xincun E	00-083	EIV	3	171	1254.1	273.6	22%
15	Yanliangzhai SW	00-086	EIV	3	171	454.8	273.6	60%
16	Shijiagou NE	00-093	EIV	4	228	223.9	364.8	163%
17	Lijiagou E	00-099	EIV	5	285	477.1	456	96%
18	Matun Xicun S	00-103	EIV	1	57	482.6	91.2	19%
19	Fuxicun NE	00-111	EIV	1.9	108.3	471.8	173.28	37%
20	Xiaoxiang W	00-115	EIV	2	114	231.7	182.4	79%
	Caohe River			2.25	128.25	2731.5	205.2	8%
22	Xinhougou YC E	00-132	EIV	2.25	128.25	2731.5	205.2	8%
	Liujian River			32	1824	2430.7	2918.4	120%
21	Huizui	00-127	EIV	25	1425	551.8	2280	413%
23	Xiahousi	02-182	EIV	4	228	523.5	364.8	70%

(continued)

ID	SITE NAME	SITE No	PHASE	SS (ha)	Population	CP (ha)	NF (ha)	Land-use ratio
24	Huizui N	02-192	EIV	3	171	1355.4	273.6	20%
	Majian River			43	2451	4447.7	3921.6	88%
25	Xinzhai N	02-197	EIV	10	570	881.2	912	103%
26	Xikouzi NW	02-201	EIV	18	1026	511.8	1641.6	321%
27	Zhangwan N	02-210	EIV	10	570	539.8	912	169%
28	Linxiaozhai	02-211	EIV	2	114	459.2	182.4	40%
29	Bei Wujiawan	02-214	EIV	3	171	2055.7	273.6	13%
Total				178.8	10194.5	28547.1	16311.1	57%

REFERENCES

Banpo Museum. 1989. Jiangzhai--xinshiqi shidai yizhi fajue baogao (Report on the excavation of a Neolithic site --Jiangzai). Beijing: Wenwu Press.

Brumfiel, E. 1976. "Regional growth in the Eastern Valley of Mexico: A test of the "Population Pressure" hypothesis," in The Early Mesoamerican village. Edited by K. V. Flannery, pp. 234-249. New York: Academic Press.

Chen, W. 1991. Zhongguo gudai nongye keji shi tupu (The illustrations of the history of ancient Chinese agricultural technology). Beijing: Nongye press.

Chen, X. 1997. Zhongguo shiqian kaoguxueshi yanjiu (A study of the history of the prehistoric archaeology of China). Beijing: Sanlian Press.

Chisolm, M. 1968. Rural settlement and Land use: An essay in location. Chicago: Aldine.

Erlitou Working Team, IACASS. 1984a. 1981 nian Henan Yanshi Erlitou muzang fajue jianbao (Brief report on the excavation of burials at the Erlitou site in Yanshi, Henan in 1981). Kaogu 1:37-40.

—. 1984b. Yanshi Erlitou yizhi 1980-1981 nian III qu fajue jianbao (Brief report on the excavation at section III of the Erlitou site in Yanshi). Kaogu 7:582-590.

—. 1985. 1982 nian qiu Yanshi Erlitou yizhi jiuqu fajue jianbao (Brief report on the excavation at Section Nine of the Erlitou site in Yanshi). Kaogu 12:1085-1093.

—. 2001. Erlitou yizhi tianye gongzuo de xinjinzhan (New progress in the Fieldwork at the Erlitou site). Zhongguo shehui kexueyuan gudai wenming yanjiu zhongxin tongxun 1:32-34.

Ford, A. 2001. States and Stones: Ground Stone Tool Production at Huizui, China.

Gongxian County Chronicle Editorial Board. Editor. 1991. Gongxian zhi. Zhengzhou: Zhongzhou Guji Press.

Hassan, F. A. 1978. "Demographic archaeology," in Advances in archaeological method and theory, vol. 1. Edited by M. B. Schiffer, pp. 49-103. New York: Academic Press.

Hassan, F.A. 1981. Demographic Archaeology. New York & London.

Henan Cultural Bureau. 1961. Henan Yanshi xian Huizui Shangdai yizhi de diaocha (survey of the Shang site at Huizui in Yanshi). Kaogu 2:99-100.

Honours Thesis, La Trobe University, Melbourne.

Institute of Archaeology, C. 1999. Yanshi Erlitou. Beijing: Zhongguo Dabaikequanshu Press.

—. 2001. Mengcheng yuchisi--wanbei xinshiqi shidai juluo yicun de fajue yu yanjiu. Beijing: Science press.

Lee, G-A, G. W. Crawford, L. Liu and X. Chen. 2007. Plants and people from the early Neolithic to Shang periods in North China. PNAS 104(3): 1087-1092.

Liu, L. 2006. Urbanization in China: Erlitou and its hinterland. In Urbanism in the Preindustrial World: Cross-Cultural Approaches. Edited by G. Storey, pp. 161-189. Tuscaloosa: University of Alabama Press.

Liu, L., and Xingcan Chen. 2001. Settlement archaeology and the study of social complexity in China. The Review of Archaeology 22:4-21

Liu, L. and X. Chen. 2003. State Formation in Early China. London: Duckworth.

Liu, L., X. Chen, Y. K. Lee, H. Wright and A. Rosen. 2002-2004. Settlement patterns and development of social complexity in the Yiluo region, north China. Journal of Field Archaeology 29(1-2): 75-100.

Van Wersch, H. J. 1972. "The agricultural economy," in The Minnesota Messenia Expedition: Reconstructing a Bronze age Environment. Edited by G. R. Rapp, pp. 177-187. Minneapolis: University of Minnesota Press.

Vita-Finzi, C., and E. S. Higgs. 1970. Prehistoric economy in the Mount Carmel Area of Palestine: Site catchment analysis. Proceedings of the Prehistoric Society 36:1-37.

Zhao, C. 1998. Ye tan jiangzai yiqi cunluo zhong de fangwu yu renkou (Another analysis on the houses and population in the settlement of Jiangzai period I. kaogu yu wenwu 5:49-55.

Zhu, N. 1994. Renkou shuliang de fenxi yu shehui zuzhi jiegou de fuyuan (Analysis of population size and the reconstruction of the structure of social organization). Huaxia kaogu 4:46-52.

CHAPTER 6 ARCHAEOBOTANICAL ANALYSIS ON SITES SURVEYED IN THE YILUO REGION (1998-2011)[1]

1. SAMPLE SURVEY METHOD AND SAMPLE SIZE

The Yiluo team systematically surveyed 1120 km^2 of alluvial plains and loess terraces, documenting 451 sites. Sediment samples were collected from 167 features in 91 sites, yielding 181 soil samples for flotation (Table 6.1). Proportions of sites sampled versus documented vary from 1% (Yinxu) to 44% (Peiligang): 11% of the Yangshao, 12% of the Longshan, 8% of the Erlitou, 8% of the Erligang and 3% of the Zhou periods. We do not know a total number of the Han sites found in the region. Sites are often buried 0.5–2.0 m below the surface, but archaeological features visible in vertical cuts of the loess terraces enabled the collection of soil samples from them.

Table 6.1 Numbers of sites sampled among sites surveyed, numbers of floated samples, soil volumes per period in the Yiluo region

Period	N of sites surveyed	N of sites floated	N of samples	N of features	Vol. liters	N of taxa	Seed counts
Peiligang	16	7	17	12	169.50	9	69
Yangshao	228	24	44	43	357.70	23	4215
Longshan	211	26	37	36	333.65	32	22707
Erlitou	207	16	39	36	376.00	24	9583
Erligang	120	8	19	19	155.20	23	9273
Zhou	435	11	22	19	208.50	23	1749
Han		3	3	3	19.00	12	141
ALL		95	181	167	1616.55		47737

Assemblages of plant remains tend to vary by context, so we focus on the same type of context for sampling to minimize the impact of contextual variation. A majority of samples (90%) were collected pits filled with ash (ash pit), while a small number represents other contexts, including five samples from house floors (Yangshao 1, Longshan 2, Erlitou 1, Han 1), one from an Erlitou period

---

[1] This chapter is written by Gyoung-Ah Lee, Gary W. Crawford, Rory C. Walsh, Habeom Kim, Angelica Kneisly, Hyunsoo Lee, Brianna Kendrick, Maria Vauhn, Zhu Junyi, and Fang Yuan.

ash ditch, and one from a kiln of the Han period (Appendix 6.1). Cultural layers indicate areas with artifact concentrations, which are hard to define otherwise; 11 such areas were sampled. One bag of sample of at least 2 liters was collected from most features, except for a few yielding two samples. Pit fills normally represent secondary deposition (i.e., infill of general sediment and refuse resulting from a variety of activities by the site occupants). Thus, such samples are ideal for intersite comparisons of a general nature of plant use.

In our earlier pilot study on 26 sites (Lee et al. 2007), we found the number of taxa in the samples exhibit a positive correlation with sample volume; that is, small samples tend to contain fewer plant taxa and few or no examples of plants that are rare in the collection as a whole. We increased our sample size by seven times in sample numbers and over three times in soil volumes (1,616.55 liters) to remedy this problem. We still have unequal number of sample sizes across the periods (Fig 6.1). We collected the largest number of samples (44) and volumes (357.7 liters) from the 24 Yangshao period sites, while the Han period yielded the least number of samples with small volumes from two sites (Table 6.1). The relatively small sample amount from each site can limit interpretations of similarities and differences among the plant assemblages. Our expanded data shows we can ease such a concern as both the abundance and richness of the samples are not correspondent to the sample size. For example, the highest average of the seed density came from the Longshan period, which is the third in the number of soil volumes, while the average seed density of the Yangshao context with the highest volume is ranked only the fourth (Fig. 6.1-a, b). The highest volume of soils or the number of samples do not generate the highest diversity of taxa by period, showing the Yangshao falls behind the later periods with smaller sample sizes in seed diversity (Fig. 6.2). In comparison among individual samples, seed diversity (Fig.6.3-a) or density (Fig. 6.3-b) also does not correlate to the sample size measured by volume.

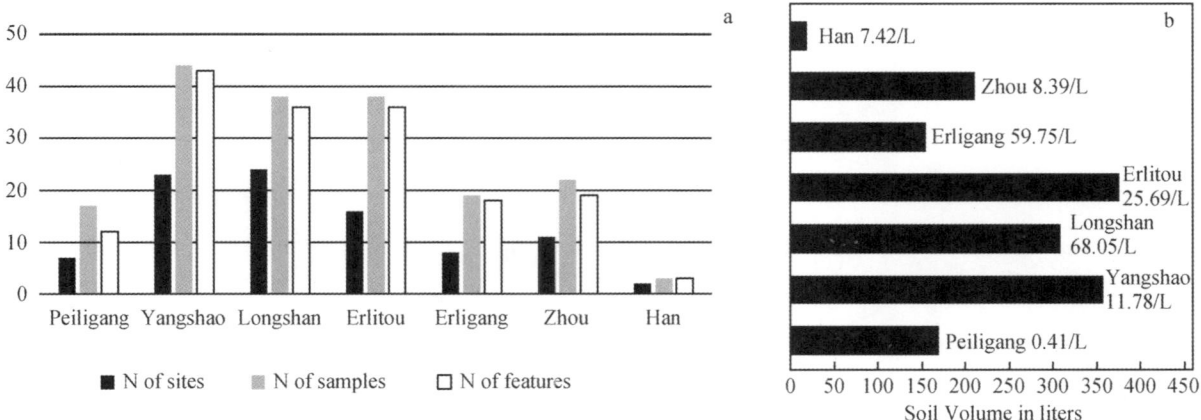

Figure 6.1 Sample sizes by periods (a) and sample volumes and seed density (seed No/soil liters) per period (b)

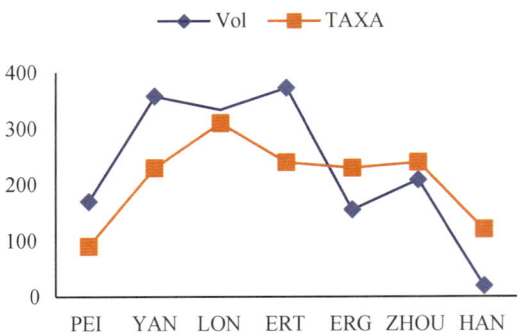

Figure 6.2 Sample volumes and number of taxa multiplied by 100 by periods

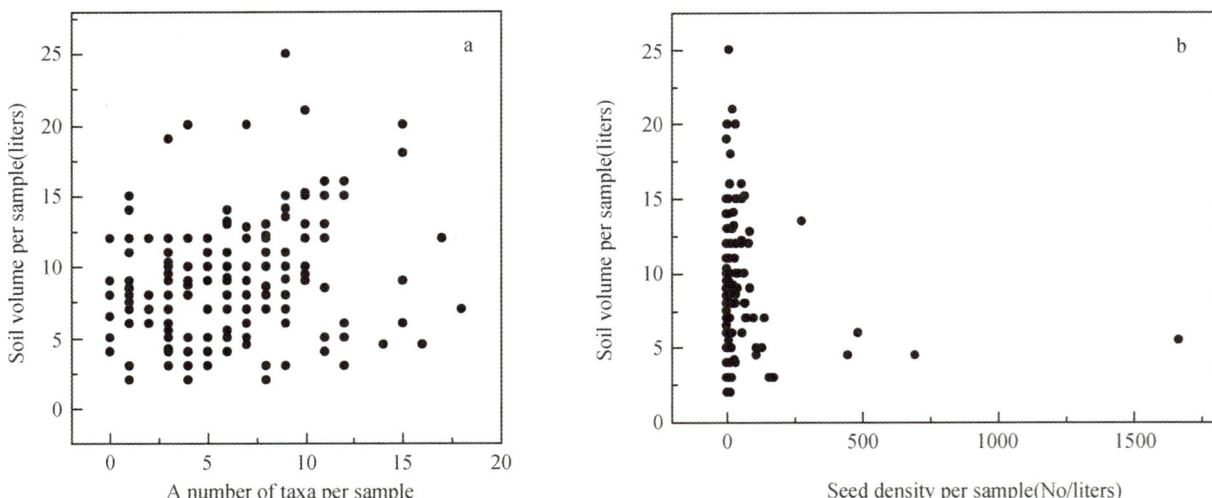

Figure 6.3 Comparison of plant diversity (a) and seed density (b) by soil sample volume. Plant diversity is represented by a number of taxa per sample. Taxa in (b) include all identified seed taxa, one ubiquitous, unidentified seed type (unknown type 1 in Appendix 1), and two nut types but excludes all other unknown seeds

2. ANALYTICAL METHODS

Two flotation methods were used to process soil samples: a manual decanting method in 1998-2001 and a modified Shell Mound Archaeology Project (SMAP)-style apparatus in 2002-11 (Watson 1976). In both manual and mechanic flotation, light fractions were collected with a 0.2-mm sieve, while heavy fractions were recovered in a 1-mm mesh. The SMAP apparatus is a light, rectangular PVC box supported on a metal frame stand. Dry soil samples were slowly placed in the water-filled box. The water overflows into a trough and into a 0.2 mm sieve that traps any material floating or suspended in the water. A screen with a mesh size 1.0 mm inserted in the flotation tank traps the heavy fraction comprised of denser material, including mineral, potsherds, lithics, heavy, carbonized plant remains (mostly charcoal), and bone. After finishing one element and before pouring a new one into a flotation tank, water continued to flow into a 0.2 mm sieve for a few minutes to ensure that nothing

CHAPTER 6 ARCHAEOBOTANICAL ANALYSIS ON SITES SURVEYED IN THE YILUO REGION (1998–2011)

was recirculating from the mud settled at the bottom of the tank. In all sample elements, no plant remains were left behind except for a few charcoal fragments. Both light and heavy fractions were entrapped in fine cotton or nylon fabrics and dried in the shade or inside.

Except for eight samples, only light fractions have been examined. The eight heavy fractions contained no plant remains, so none of the remaining heavy fractions was examined. Dried light fractions were sieved through a stack of standard geological screens with mesh sizes of 2 mm, 1mm, 0.4 mm, and 0.2 mm. Plant remains over 2 mm in their smallest dimension were sorted thoroughly into their constituent components of charred seeds and nutshell, charcoal, modern plant material such as rootlets, and mineral particles, and their weights are recorded. Only seeds and identifiable plant parts were extracted from the fractions less than 2 mm.

Six samples were sorted through 2% to 50% of subsample weights in 0.2 mm sieve (Table 6.2). The portions in 0.2 mm sieve did not show any identifiable seed remains in most samples except for the two. For example, five wild bean pods were found in 10% of sample in 0.2 mm sieves from the Late Longshan Zhanwan NW Site (张湾西北, 11-210, ash pit 3), while one seed of millet-tribe (Paniceae) was identified in sorted portions of 0.2mm sieve subsample from the Yangzhai W (杨寨西, 11-059, ash pit 2). And thus, we do not expect incomplete portion of samples would affect the overall composition and quantity of the samples.

About a quarter of sites sampled in this study cannot be identified to the subphase of each cultural period. In the quantitative comparison, therefore, we lumped all samples of each period together without further separating them into subphases.

Table 6.2 Samples partially sorted*

Period	Site code	Site name	Feature	Soil vol. L	Floated sample g.	0.2mm g	% completed	Taxa/N of Seeds in 0.2 mm
Peiligang	11-124	Fu Dian E	H1	19	75.66	21.9	50.0	
Longshan	11-060	Baozhuang NW	H2	8	27.11	9.93	20.0	
Longshan	11-210	Zhangwan NW	H2	10	108.06	43.17	39.0	
Longshan	11-210	Zhangwan NW	H3	20	97.49	38.1	9.4	Wild bean pod/5
Longshan	11-087	Yanliangzhai Shuiku W	H3	10	65.6	24.8	23.9	
E Zhou	11-059	Yangzhai W	H2	10	58.4	21.49	3.5	Paniceae/1

* All portions larger than 0.4 mm were sorted completely.

3. COMPOSITIONS AND DIVERSITY OF PLANT REMAINS

A total of 33 of taxa were identified mostly into the species, genus, or tribe (族) level and a few at least into the family level (Table 6.3). Some non-reproductive organs, such as twigs, grass-stem fragments, grass lemma/palea (chaff), buds or tubers are mostly fragmentary in negligible quantities to be identified. Nut remains are present only in 14 samples in total; the Zhou-period Sigou SE (寺沟东南, 11-152, Y152) is the only site shows well preserved almost complete pieces of acorn meat (Photo Group 1). Other nut remains are too fragmentary to securely identify their taxa, although some resemble acorn.

In this report plant remains are grouped into four categories by their ecological characteristics, growth habits, and human usage: cultigens, upland weeds, wetland weeds, and fleshy fruits (Table 6.3). Beyond four domesticated taxa, such as foxtail millet, broomcorn millet, rice, and wheat, the 'cultigen' category includes taxa with ambiguous status of domestication, including azuki, soybean, and beefsteak plant. Earlier studies demonstrate the size and morphology alone are not a sufficient indicator of domestication of soybean and azuki (Lee 2013; Lee et al. 2011). The wild counterparts of these legumes are edible and often found in farming fields. Perilla or beefsteak plant is hard to identify its domestication status based on the seed morphology alone, and it is often very similar to minature beefsteak plant. And thus, we did not further identify these two, and lump into the crop category as the edible plants that are native to the region and were eventually domesticated.

Non-domesticated taxa or wild are further divided into the weeds of herbacious annual or perennial grass or bushes and fresh fruits with largely soft succulent tissues. Their habitats further divide weeds into those growing uplands and lowlands/wetlands. In our samples most upland weeds are those florific in disturbed habitats, including farming fields and near human habitats. Wetland weeds are mostly common at the edge of the shallow water bodies, including rice paddy fields today.

Besides these groups, most samples have seeds that cannot be further identified at this moment, which are collectively labeled as 'unknown' taxa. Some specimens have features that could permit them to be identified but as yet they are not identified. This is common in all archaeobotanical analyses because floras of particular regions are extensive and includes thousands of species. Proper identification requires reference specimens and these are not always available. Most samples also have seed fragments that cannot be identified and counted. Unknown types are usually represented by one or two specimens except one, which is labeled as unknown type 1 in this report. Nevertheless, many unknown types are documented and characteristics recorded so that they may be identified and added

CHAPTER 6 ARCHAEOBOTANICAL ANALYSIS ON SITES SURVEYED IN THE YILUO REGION (1998–2011)

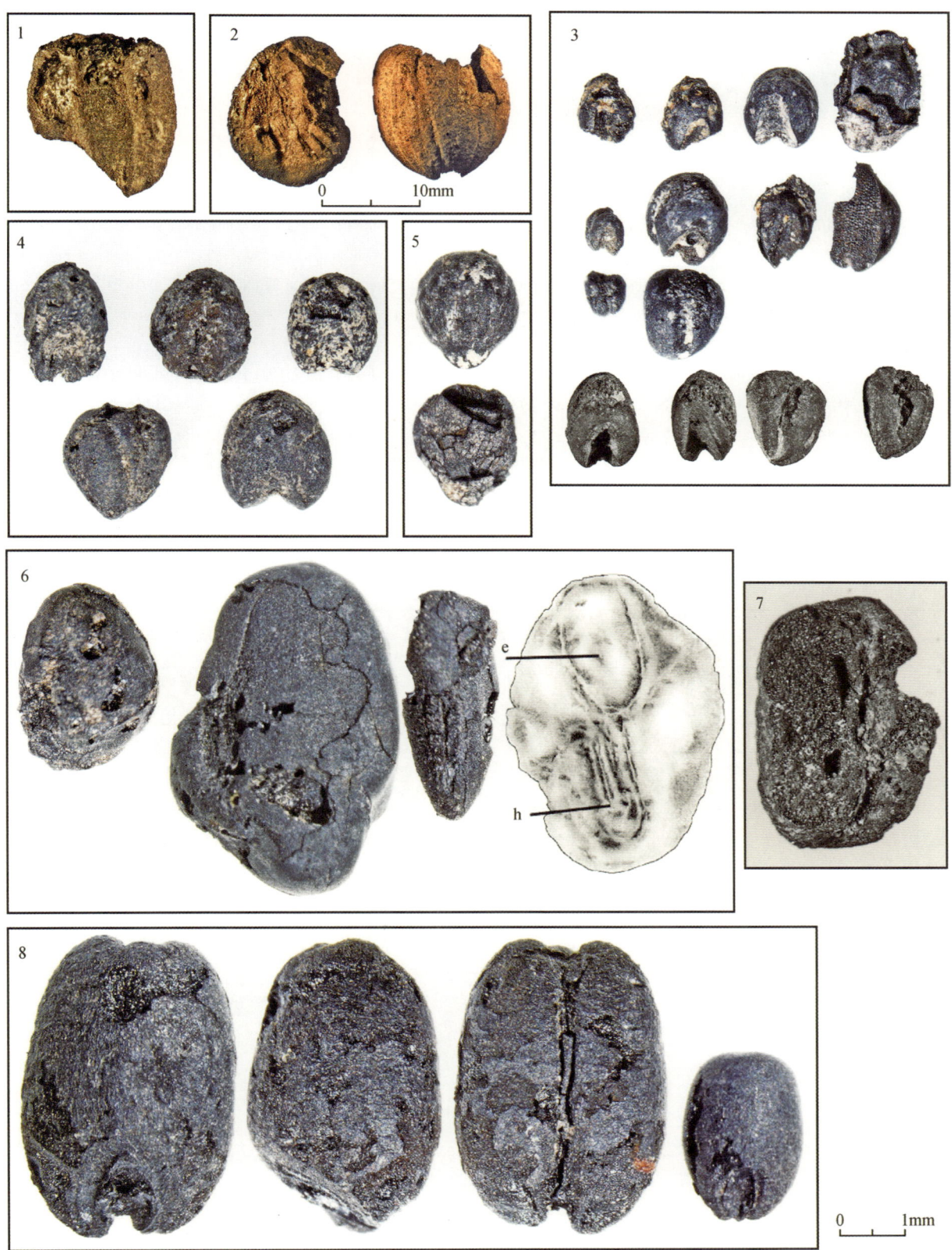

Photo Group 1 Edible plant resources
Scale= 1 mm for all others except for acorn.

1. 稻属 (*Oryza sativa*, rice), 二里头二至四期, 张湾西北 (Y210).

2. 栎 (*Quercus* sp., acorn), 西/东周, 寺沟东南 (Y152). Scale = 10 mm.

3. 粟 (*Setaria italica*, foxtail millet). The 1st row from the left shows the 1st & 2nd specimens from the Late Peiligang Wuluo Xipo 2 site (裴李岗晚期，坞罗西坡2，Y042), the 3rd specimen from the Late Yangshao Weizhuang W site (仰韶晚期，喂庄西，Y019), and the 4th specimen from the Late Yangshao Wuluo Shuiku W site (仰韶晚期，坞罗水库西，Y025). The 1st & 2nd specimens of 2nd & 3rd rows are from the Erlitou Shaochai site (二里头期，稍柴，Y1001). The 3rd & 4th specimens of the 2nd row are from the Upper Erligang Tianposhuiku NE (二里岗上层，天坡水库东北，Y043). The 4th row shows specimens from the Erlitou Xinhougou Zhuanchang site (新后沟砖厂东，Y132).

4. 黍 (*Panicum miliaceum*, broomcorn millet). The upper row shows specimens from the Late Yangshao Nanwayao (南瓦窑, Y156), the Late Yangshao Weizhuang SW (喂庄西南河南岸, Y018), and the Late Yangshao Wuluo Shuiku W1 (坞罗水库西1,Y025). The specimen in the lower row shows the lateral (left) and dorsal side of the specimen from the Late Yangshao Wuluo Shuiku W1 (坞罗水库西1,Y025).

5. 紫苏 or 石荠苎属 (*Pellira frutescens* or *Mosla* sp., perilla or miniature beefsteak plant) Two sides of the same specimen from the Upper Erligang Tianposhuiku NE (天坡水库东北, Y043).

6. 大豆 (*Glycine max* ssp., soybean). From left to right, the Early Longshan Sigou SE (寺沟东南,Y152), the Erlitou Shaochai (稍柴, Y1001), and the Upper Erligang Tianposhuiku NE (天坡水库东北, Y043). The 'e' and 'h' indicates embryonic radicle (胚根) and hilum (种脐) which are visible in archaeological specimens.

7. 赤豆 (*Vigna angularis* ssp., azuki). Easter Zhou Yangzhai W site (杨寨西, Y059).

8. 小麦 (*Triticum aestivum*, wheat). All from the Upper Erligang Tianposhuiku NE (二里岗上层 天坡水库东北, Y043).

to the database at a later date.

Table 6.3 Plant taxa recovered in the Yiluo basin

Seed category	Family	Common name	Scientific name
NUT	Fagaceae	Oak栎属	cf. *Quercus* sp.
CULTIGENS	Poaceae	Broomcorn millet黍	*Panicum miliaceum*
	禾本科	Foxtail millet粟	*Setaria italica* supsp. *italica*
		Rice稻	*Oryza sativa*
		Bread wheat小麦	*Triticum aestivum*
	Fabaceae	Soybean 大豆	*Glycine max* ssp.
	豆科	Azuki赤豆	*Vigna angularis* ssp.
	Lamiaceae	Beefsteak plant紫苏	*Perilla frutescens*
UPLAND WEEDS	Poaceae	Barnyard grass稗	*Echinocloa crusgalli*
	禾本科	Green foxtail狗尾草	*Setaria viridis*
		Wild foxtail type grasslian黍属	cf. *Setaria* sp.
		Panic grass黍属	*Panicum* sp.
		Panic, manna grass or crabgrass	*Panicum, Glyceria*, or *Digitaria* sp.
		Millet tribe 黍族	Paniceae
		Goosegrass 牛筋草	*Eleusine indica*
		cf. Wheat tribe	cf. Triticeae
	Brassicaceae十字花科	Mustard 芸薹属	*Brassica* sp.
	Chenopodiaceae藜亚科	Chenopod藜属	*Chenopodium* sp.
	Polygonaceae蓼科	Knotweed蓼属	*Polygonum* sp.
	Fabaceae豆科	Korean clover豆茶决明	*Chamaecrista nomame* or *Cassia nomane*
		sweet clover or lespedeza 草木樨属/胡枝子属	*Melilotus* or *Lespedenza* sp.
		Unidentified bean pod	
	Cannabaceae 大麻科	Hop 葎草属	*Humulus* sp.
	Lamiaceae唇形科	Minature beefsteak plant石荠苎属	*Molsa* sp.
	cf. Violaceae堇菜科	cf. *Viola*堇菜属	cf. *Viola* sp.

(continued)

Seed category	Family	Common name	Scientific name
WETLAND WEEDS	Cyperaceae 莎草科	Burlush 藨草属	*Scirpus* sp.
		cf.Fimbry 飄拂草属	*Fimbristylis* sp.
		Sedge 莎草属	*Cyperus* sp.
	cf.Typhaceae香蒲科	cf. Cattaii香蒲属	cf. *Typha* sp.
FLESHY FRUITS	Rosaceae 薔薇科	Bramble 悬钩子属	*Rubus* sp.
		Plum 李属	*Prunus* sp.
		other rose family	
	Rhamnaceae鼠李科	Jujuba 枣	*Zizhiphus* sp.

* Taxonomy follows the Flora of China (FOC) while the Germplasm Resources Information Center (GRIN) informs current taxonomy when necessary. 'cf' = possibly.

3.1 Cultigens

Among a total of 47,737 seeds found (Table 6.1), more than half are domesticated millets (27,475) and foxtail outnumberes broomcorn more than 30 times, which ranks second except for the Peiligang and Zhou period (Fig. 6.4). An abundance of broomcorn millet in one Peiligang feature in Fudian SE (府店东南, 11-114, Y-118) yielded an AMS date of the Early Yangshao period (D-AMS 025484, 4150–4100 cal. BC. All calibrated dates in this report indicate 2 σ ranges), indicating their relocation from the later period. Despite its low representation, broomcorn millet is significantly more common in the Yiluo record than in the regions farther east such as Shandong (Crawford et al. 2005) and the Korean Peninsula (Crawford and Lee 2003; Lee 2011). Foxtail millet was traditionally more common in the wetter eastern areas, and broomcorn millet was more common in the drier interior areas (Crawford et al. 2005). With an improved identification of broomcorn phytolith, Weisskopf and Lee (2016) suggest broomcorn millet might have been more common than its representation in charred remains in the Huizui site. It needs further study to confirm whether this practice can be extended to the prehistoric period but we suspect broomcorn millet probably used substantially as much as foxtail millet.

Foxtail millet grains are typically spherical and mostly popped. Charring experiment indicates that popping occurred when grains are still wrapped tightly in husks (palea, lemma, and glumes) (Walsh 2016). This may indicate foxtail millets in our samples were burnt while they were stored without hulling till the time for cooking. Most foxtail and broomcorn millets throughout the sequence show typical sizes and shapes of domesticated millets. The earliest examples in our sample are slightly smaller than later millet on average, and the dorsal face is slightly flattened, a trait similar, but not identical, to green foxtail grass (*S. italica* ssp. *viridis,* 狗尾草), the ancestor of the crop. Broomcorn millet even in some later samples show smaller sizes and slightly flattened too. Zhao (2006) notes that the Early Neolithic broomcorn millet from Xinglongou has similar characteristics. Similar grains are common in the Longshan period Shantaisi and Liangchengzhen sites (Crawford et al. 2005). A recent study on modern foxtail millet shows a wide size range even in one specimen due to an immaturity of some grains (Walsh et al. 2016). This study further confirms our hypothesis on some small millets among the Yiluo samples may be grains from immature fruit.

Other crops, including domesticated wheat and possibly cultivated soybean, azuki and beefsteak plant, only comprise 1.3 % of all seeds, if all the periods are lumped together (Fig. 6.4). Besides millets, wheat counts the most among the crop category, mostly from the Erligang context (Fig. 6.5). It is a very small variety of bread wheat that is the only type documented in the archaeological record of East Asia until very late (Crawford and Lee 2003; Crawford 1992). Historically, wheat has been a crucial winter crop in the Yiluo region but its antiquity puts into an unsolved question. One wheat grain each was found in Late Peiligang Xishiqiao E (西石桥东, 01-010, 76) and Middle to Late Yangshao Zhaocheng site (赵城, 05-077, Y077) (Appendix 1). The Zhaocheng site has one AMS date on foxtail millet, confirming its association to the Late Yangshao period (SNU 06-746, 4500±50 uncal. BP, 3362–3026 cal. BC.). However, neither of wheat specimens weighs enough for dating. Wheat grains from the Late Longshan pit at the Baozhuang NW site (保庄西北, 11-060, 046) is dated to the Western Zhou (D-AMS 025484, 2625±26 uncal. BP, 831–786 cal. BC). The Erlitou period does not yield enough wheat remains to be dated, but the Erligang context shows a firm association of wheat to that period with a direct date on wheat from the Tianposhuiku NE site (天坡水库东北, 98-043,Y043, TO-11420, 3020±50 uncal. BP, 1490–1122 cal. BC). Wheat from the Sigou SE site (寺沟南, 11-151, Y151) also shows it's in place to the Western Zhou period (11-152, D-AMS029885, 2371±32 uncal. BP, 726–386 cal. BC). Wheat appears to be developing elsewhere in North China by the Longshan period, as reported in the Liangchengzhen site in Shandong (Crawford et al, 2005). An even earlier record of charred wheat was found in Middle Holocene site in southwestern Korea (Han, Koo, and Kim 2014; Lee 2017). Two direct dates on each grain of wheat and barley at the Daechonri site range from 5430–4890 cal. BP, matching those on charcoal in association (5460–4620 cal. BP),

Barton and An (2014) suggest that the appearance of wheat from 4600 to 4200 cal. BP in a vast strip of northern China may represent a period of swift adoption (resulting in enhanced visibility in archaeological records) sometime after the initial introduction (not yet visible archaeologically). The Yiluo example and the Neolithic Korean presence of wheat are possibly a rare survival of the initial, sporadic introduction to northeast Asia (Lee 2016). Although we have not yet had a correctly associated direct date on wheat, we cannot downplay a possibility of wheat introduction to the region earlier than the Erligang period.

Rice (*Oryza sativa*) is a crop native to South China and its earliest confirmed presence in North China is in the lower Huanghe Early Neolithic Houli culture (Crawford, Chen, Luan, and Wang 2013). The earliest presence of rice north of the Yangzi River is from the Jiahu site in Henan, dating as early as 9000–7800 cal. BP (Zhang and Wang 1998). No charred grains of rice were found in typical Peiligang cultural sites, but phytolith evidence at the Tanghu site in Henan indicates the arrival of rice in the middle Huanghe as early as 7800–4500 cal. BP (Zhang et al. 2012). Further east, the Early Neolithic Houli culture revealed the incorporation of rice into millet farming in the lower Huanghe, as supported by a direct date on charred rice grains at the Yuezhuang site in Shandong (7950–7800 cal. BP) (Crawford, Chen, Luan, and Wang 2013). Rice is also a rare crop at the Longshan period Shantaisi site (Lee et al. 2007), but it is relatively common at the Longshan site of Liangchengzhen on the east coast (Crawford et al. 2005).

Although our earlier work reports rice from the Erlitou period (3900–3500 cal. BP) in the Yiluo valley (Lee et al. 2007), studies on soil micromorphology and phytolith indicates wet paddy farming as early as the Late Yangshao period (ca. 6600 cal. BP) (Rosen 2007; Rosen et al. 2015). The current expanded samples yield three rice grains from two Late Yangshao contexts, including the Zhaocheng site (赵城, 05-077, Y077) and Weizhuang SW (喂庄西南河南岸, 07-018, Y018), and one Longshan site at Matun (马屯新村, 11-069, Y069) (Appendix 1). Our ongoing study on the Huizui site (灰嘴, 02-127, Y127) reveals the Yangshao rice but no carbon date is available yet. Instead, rice grains from the Late Longshan Huizui in 2004 field season is directly dated to 4060–3890 cal. BP (SNU 05-132m 3800±40 uncal. BP, 1681–1444 cal. BC), which is rather associated to the Erlitou period. By the Erlitou period, rice was more frequently found in several sites, including the Xinzhai (新砦, 04-HXX), Huizui, Zhanwan NW (张湾西北, 11-210, Y210), Luokou (罗口, 98-022, Y022), Shaochai (稍柴, 97-1001, Y1001), Shangzhuang S (上庄南, 98-037, Y037), Jingyanggang (景阳岗，97-195，041), Xikouzi (西口孜，07-201，Y201) and Lijiagou E (李家沟东，07-099，Y099).

It is impossible to identify whether it was a wetland or dryland crop only based on rice morphology. Wet land weeds in the Yiluo region are sporadically found, only 0.2% of the total number of seeds. Some of the sedge family identified, including genera *Cyperus*, possible *Fimbristylis*, and *scirpus*, are common ruderal weeds in rice paddy fields. Four millet tribe grains from two Late Longshan, one Eastern Zhou, and one Han sample resemble barnyard grass (*Echinochloa crusgalli*), which is one of the most ubiquitous rice farming weeds. Evidence from phytoliths, soil morphology, and the association of rice and wetland weeds all point to wet rice farming was incorporated into Yiluo agricultural regime, possibly as early as the Late Yangshao.

Soybean and azuki have been key bean crops throughout history in East Asia. The *Xiaxiaozheng* and *Shijing* texts mention soybean in the middle Huanghe from possibly as early as the Xia Dynasty (ca. 2100–1600 B.C.) and refer to soybean as a crop during the Zhou period (ca. 1026–226 B.C.) (Guo 1996), so the crop has a deep history in the region. Recent studies show an early association of small-seeded soybean is as old as 9000–8600 cal. BP in northern China and 7,000 cal. BP in China (Lee et al. 2011). Piror to Lee et al. (2007) publication, soybean seeds have been reported from nearly 30 other sites in China in contexts dating from 7000 B.C. to A.D. 220 (none are AMS-dated). In the Yiluo region, Peiligang sites do not yield any soybean in contrast to the contemporaneous Jiahu site. From the Yangshao and later period sites, a total of 188 soybean specimens were identified in our samples (Appendix 6.1). Direct dates on charred soybean seeds indicate selection resulted in large seed sizes in Japan by 5000 cal BP (Middle Jomon) and in Korea by 3000 cal BP (Early Bonze) but a sign of size selection in the Yiluo basin is less clear. Soybean seeds from the Erligang through Han contexts are larger than the earlier ones, similar in length to the large Korean and Japanese specimens but the overall size are still significantly smaller than them. However, the size difference between the wild and archaeological specimens should not be overemphasized. Wild soybean grows throughout northcentral China and often used as edible snacks and also field fertilizer (Hymowitz and Singh 1987). Although seed size can distinguish domesticated from wild soybean in collections postdating 3000 BP in Korea and in Japan, size should not be the sole distinguishing trait of domesticated soybean (Lee et al. 2011). Small seeds could be from purposefully managed populations, but they may also be wild. Even if they are wild, their representation in nearly all Chinese sites at which flotation has been conducted suggests that they were a component of anthropogenic plant communities and people exploited them. Nevertheless, we prefer not to classify the Yiluo soybean as either wild (*G. max* ssp. *soja*) or domesticated (*G. max* ssp. *max*), by referring it to species level without further distinguishing the subspecies level.

Perilla (or beefstake plant, 紫苏, *Perilla frutescens*) is one of the key condiment and oil crops in East Asia. From the Yangshao to the Erlitou contexts in our samples, 40 seeds are identified into either perilla or mosla (*Mosla* sp.), another oil plant of the mint family (唇形科). It is hard to distinguish Perilla (or beefstake plant, 紫苏) is one of the key condiment and oil crops in East Asia. From the Yangshao to the Erlitou contexts in our samples 40 seeds are identified into either Perilla or Mosla (*Mosla* sp., 石荠苎属), another oil plant of the mint family. It is hard to distinguish whether perilla is wild or domesticated even with scanning electron microscopic observation. We hypothesize perilla may have been used early, considering its value and genetic diversity in China (Zeven and Zhukovsky 1975). Prior to our study, little prehistoric and early historic Chinese references to this plant exist (Crawford 1992a: 28).

3.2 Non-domesticated plant

Wild or non-domesticated plant taxa can be informative to past subsistence patterns and farming regimes as much as domesticated taxa. Non-domesticated taxa in this study can be grouped as two categories based on habitats, upland vs. wetland taxa. Counting all periods together, wetland taxa consist of only 0.5% of all seeds from 33 sites (Fig. 6.4). Nineteen sites revealed sedge family (莎草科) achenes of four different types, which resemble some species of genera *Carex*, *Cyperus*, *Fimbristylis*, and *Scirpus* (芸薹属, 莎草属, 飘拂草属, 蔗草属) (Photo group 2). Longshan samples

CHAPTER 6 ARCHAEOBOTANICAL ANALYSIS ON SITES SURVEYED IN THE YILUO REGION (1998-2011)

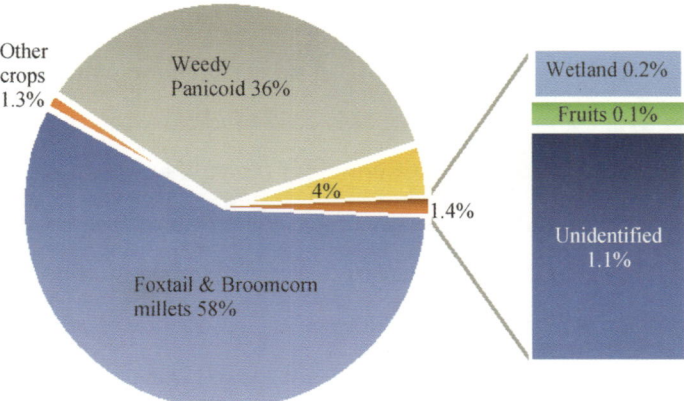

Figure 6.4　Proportions of seed cateories in all samples

show the most of these taxa, particularly the Jiandongcun NW (涧东村西北, 02-196, Y196B) and Yanliangzhai Shuiku W (颜良寨水库西, 11-087, Y087) sites. Among 12 sites that yielded rice remains, sedge is also found except for three sites: Luokou (罗口, 98-022, Y022) and Shangzhuang S (上庄东南, 98-037, Y0349) of the Erlitou period and Luokou Zhuanchang NE (罗口砖厂东北, 98-017, Y017) of the Han period. No wetland seed is found in Huizui from samples collected during the survey in 2000, but our ongoing study confirms the presence of wetland seeds from the samples from other field seasons. This combination may reflect a wet paddy habitat, considering sedges are common weeds in rice fields.

Photo Group 2　Wetland weeds

1. 莎草属 (*Cyperus* sp., sedge). All from the Late Longshan Jiandongcun NW (涧东村西北, Y196B).
2. 飘拂草属 (*Fimbrystlis* sp., fimbry) from the Late Longshan Jiandongcun NW (涧东村西北, Y196B).
3. 其他莎草科 (other *Cyperaceae*, other sedge family) from the Late Longshan Jiandongcun NW (涧东村西北, Y196B).

The most numerous upland weeds are panicoid grasses (subfamily Panicoideae, 稷亚科), probably Paniceae (millet tribe, 黍族), consisting of 36% of all seeds in the entire samples (Fig. 6.4). Due to plasticity and high cross-fertalization across taxa, it is hard to identify the species level of Paniceae only based on seeds. On the basis of the seed length-to-width ratios, the overall shape, the embryo size and shape, and the surface patterns of hulls attached to grains, some of them can be discerned into species level, including green foxtail (*Setaria italica* ssp. *viridis*, 狗尾草), barnyard grass (*Echnichloa crusgalli*, 稗属), and goosegrass (*Eluesine indica*, 牛筋草) (Photo group 3). All others are only identified to the genus level, including weedy foxtail (*Setaria* sp.), possible panic grass (*Panicum* sp. Possibly *P. biscatum* 黍属), panic/manna/or digitaria (*Panicum*, *Digitaria* or *Glyceria* sp., 黍属/马唐属/甜茅属), and other types of millet tribe (Paniceae). Among them *Setaria* and *Panicum* are extremely variable genus with a very high genetic plasticity. The morphology of some members of *Panicum*, particularly tiny elongated seeds with a

Photo Group 3 Poaceae weeds

1. 狗尾草 (*Setaria viridis*, green forxtail). The upper row shows the 1st and 2nd specimens from the Late Peiligang Wuluo Xipo 2 (裴李岗晚期, 坞罗西坡2, Y042) and the 3rd and 4th specimens from the Erlitou Huizui site (二里头期, 灰嘴, Y127). In the lower row, the first four from the left are from the Middle/Late Yangshao Zhaocheng site (仰韶中晚期, 赵城, Y077) and the rest in husks from the Late Longshan Jiandongcun NW (涧东村西北, Y196B).

2. 粱属 (other *Setaria* sp.). All from the Erlitou Shaochai site (二里头期, 稍柴, Y1001).

3. 稷族 (Paniceae, millet tribe). The 1st and 2nd specimens of the upper row are from the Erlitou Shaochai site (二里头期, 稍柴, Y1001). The last two of the upper row and the first three from the left of the lower lows are from the Erlitou Huizui (二里头期, 灰嘴, Y027) site. The rest of the lower row are florets from the Late Longshan Jiandongcun NW site (涧东村西北, Y196B).

4. 黍属 (*Panicum* sp., panic grass) from the Late Longshan Jiandongcun NW (涧东村西北, Y196B).

5. 稗 (*Echincholoa crusgalli*, barnyard grass) from the Late Longshan Matun site (马屯新村, Y069).

6. 黍属/马唐属/甜茅属 (*Panic, Digitaria* or *Glyceria* sp., Panic, digitaria or manna grass). All from the Upper Erligang Tianposhuiku N Site (二里岗二层, 天坡水库东北, Y043).

7. 牛筋草 (*Eleusine indica*, goosegrass) from the Late Longshan Zhangwan NW (龙山晚期, 张湾西北, Y210).

very low embryo, is similar to digitaria (*Digitaria* sp.) or manna grass (*Glyceria* sp.). Our samples contain a large number of these specimens that we can only classify as a Panicum-Glyceria-Digitaria type at the moment. These seeds are in samples as old as the Late Yangshao and increase in its frequency throughout the time (Table 1). If they are manna grass or digitaria, it is important to consider that the genus is common in rice paddy fields today. Considering the presence of rice phytoliths from the Yangshao period, these weeds might have been associated with paddy fields.

Most Paniceae taxa are common arable weeds in dry fields and were also used as field fertilizer in Northeast China in the early 20th century (King 1909). Samples with abundant millets also show diverse Panicoid weeds, indication millet farming agroecology. Two millet tribe grasses, that is, barnyard grass and goosegrass, can also grow in rice paddy fields, which we found two historical samples which also have rice: Yangzhai W (杨寨西, 11-059, Y059) of the Eastern Zhou period and Luokou Zhuanchang NE (罗口砖厂东北, 98-017, Y017) of the Han period.

Except for Paniceae, the most abundant upland taxa are chonopod (or lambsquarter, *Chenopodium* sp., 藜属) (Photo group 4). This common annual weedy plant is represented in all periods (Appendix 6.1, see page 1287). The variation in size and shape of chenopod seeds in our samples indicates that different species are represented. In particular, some seeds have truncated margins, typical of thin testa domesticated chenopod (*C. berlandieri*) in North America (Smith 1992). Many of the specimens in the Yiluo samples have a distinct cellular pattern on the testa similar to the North American cultigen that is in the Cellulata subsection of *Chenopodium*, so it raises a critical question of the domestic ability of this Asian chenopod. Chenopod grows well in disturbed areas and dry fields and is still used in China today as a source of greens and starchy grain. One species, *Chenopodium giganteum*, has apparently been "long cultivated in China" (Wu and Raven 1994). Indeed, highland indigenous people in Taiwan intermixed a chenopod, said to be *Chenopodium album* as a crop in millet fields for starchy food (Fog 1983).

Beside genus soybean (*Glycine* sp.), we found at least three different types of wild legumes in our samples. A few samples yield legumes similar to Korean clover (*Chamaecrista nomame*, also known as *Cassia nomame* or *Senna nomame* (Chen, Zhang and Larson 2009). The plant is also a significant component of alluvial communities in Korea and Japan (Jarolímek and Kolbek 2006). The leaves are used for brewing a tea (Hu 2005: 149).

A majority of wild beans can be only identified one of the three herbacious beans, that is, sweet clover or lespedeza (*Melilotus* or *Lespedeza* sp., 草木樨属/胡枝子属). They are common in dry fields throughout East Asia and were used as field fertilizer in Northeast China in the early 20th century (King 1911). Several samples have broken pods, clearly showing convex contours with seeds inside (Photo group 4).

Other upland weedy herbacious taxa include possible mustard (*Brassica* sp., 芸薹属), knot weed (*Polygonum* sp., 蓼属), hop (*Humulus* sp., 葎草属), and Viola (*Viola* sp., 堇菜属), but their presence

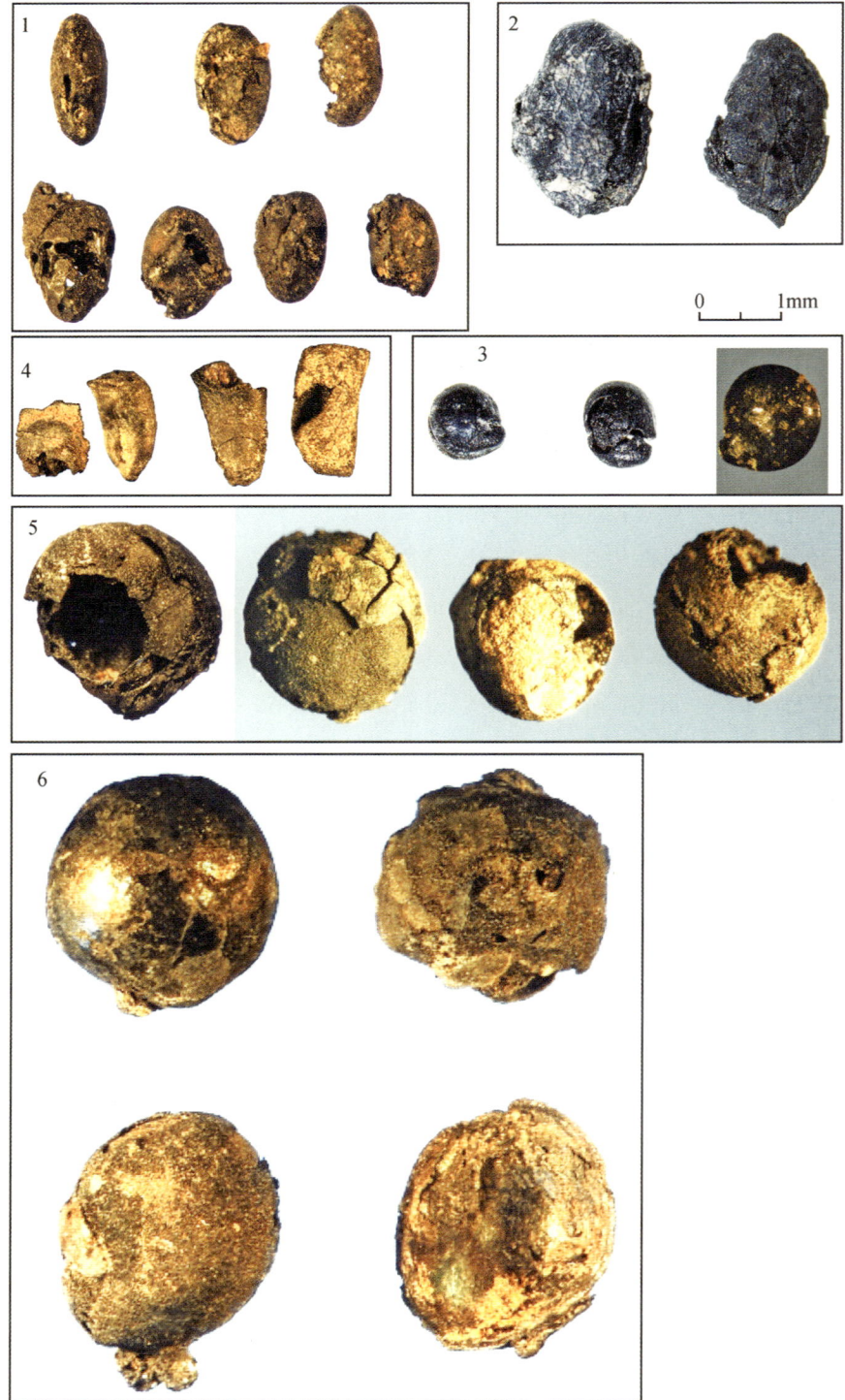

Photo Group 4　Other upland weeds & fruits

1. 草木樨属/胡枝子属 (*Melilotus* or *Lespedeza* sp., sweet clover or lespedeza). All from the Late Longshan Peicun B site (龙山晚期 裴村B, 119). Arrow pointing a circular hilum.
2. 豆茶决明 (*Chamaecrista nomame* or *Cassia nomane*, Korean clover) from the Upper Erligang Tianposhuiku NE (天坡水库东北, Y043).
3. 豆科 (Fabaceae, other wild bean pod) from the Late Longshan Jiandongcun NW (涧东村西北, Y196B). #63 02-196.
4. 藜属 (*Chenopodium* sp., chenopod). The first tree from the left are recovered from the Late Longshan Luokou site (龙山晚期 罗口, Y022) and the far right one is from 11-210 H3 from the Late Longshan Zhangwan NW (龙山晚期 张湾西北, Y210).
5. 十字花科 芸薹属 (Brassica family, cf. *Brasscia* sp., brassica). Far left from the Late Longshan Bangezhai site (龙山晚期 半个寨, Y123) and the rest from the Late Yangshao Weizhuang W (仰韶晚期 喂庄西, Y019).
6. 葎草属 (*Humulus* sp., hop) from the Late Longshan Yanliangzhai Shuiku W (龙山晚期 颜良寨水库西, Y087).

is rare across the periods. A few of these species are found only from 14 sites, dating from the Yangshao to Zhou periods. Four seeds of hop are found only in the Late Longshan Yanliangzhai Shuiku W (颜良寨水库西, 11-087, Y087) site. Considering their abundance in disturbed areas, these rare species probably represent an accidental inclusion into households. Our pilot study (Lee et al. 2007) reported Borage family (Euphorbiaceae, 大戟科), but their identification cannot be confirmed. Nightsade family (茄科) is common in other northern Chinese site (Crawford et al. 2006) but our sample shows all are uncharred, and thus cannot confirm their antiquity.

Fleshy fruits can be either herbaceous or bush (Photo group 5). Taxa we identified are seeds of edible berries, plums or jujuba which commonly grow in disturbed areas. As these fruits can be consumed raw, their presentation in open sites are rare without a chance of carbonization. We hypothesize these edible fruits were important supplement of daily diet, despite its low representation, considering the ethnographic use record and biased preservation rate.

Besides all these identified taxa, about 1% of all seeds cannot be identified at this moment. Most of them are countable but lost an identifiable feature. Among intact ones, some types are reoccurring throughout the period, which resemble cattail (*Typha* sp., 香蒲属), another wetland perennial common in the Yiluo region. These specimens are present in 24 sites from every period examined. These wetland seeds show a clear association to rice in the Yiluo region. Another intact type unidentified is found abundantly only one site, Late Longshan Jiandongcun NW site (涧东村西北, 02-196, Y196B) (Photo group 6). Similar to panic/digitalis or manna grains, they have a low embryo in the elongate seed but the overall shape of embryo and seeds are distinctive. Interestingly, a few pieces of twisted fibers are found from the Erlitou Jiandongcun site (Y199) and the Upper Erligang Yangzhai NW (Y058). They were probably ramnent of cords for basketly or mat but the taxa of the cord is not identifiable.

4. CHANGES IN PLANT RESOURCE UTILIZATION THROUGH TIME

For quantitative analysis, we combined flotation samples from the same features which multiple bags of soils were collected. As a result, our comparison is based on 167 samples, mostly coming from ash pits except for one ash ditch, five house foundations, one kiln, and nine culultal layers. Six samples (44 liters) yield no seed remains, including two Peiligang samples (Beiying, 北营, 07-044, Y044; Wuluo Xipo 2, 坞罗西坡 2, 07-042, Y042), two Yangshao samples (W Qijiayao SE, 西齐家窑东南, 05-164, Y164; Wuluo Shuiku W1, 坞罗水库西1, 98-025, Y025), one Longshan sample (Xiqijiayao NW, 西齐家窑东北, 02-166, Y166), and one Erlitou sample (Yuangou A, 袁沟A, 03-057, 165). An ash ditch is basically same as an ash pit, just a more elongate and larger. Cultural

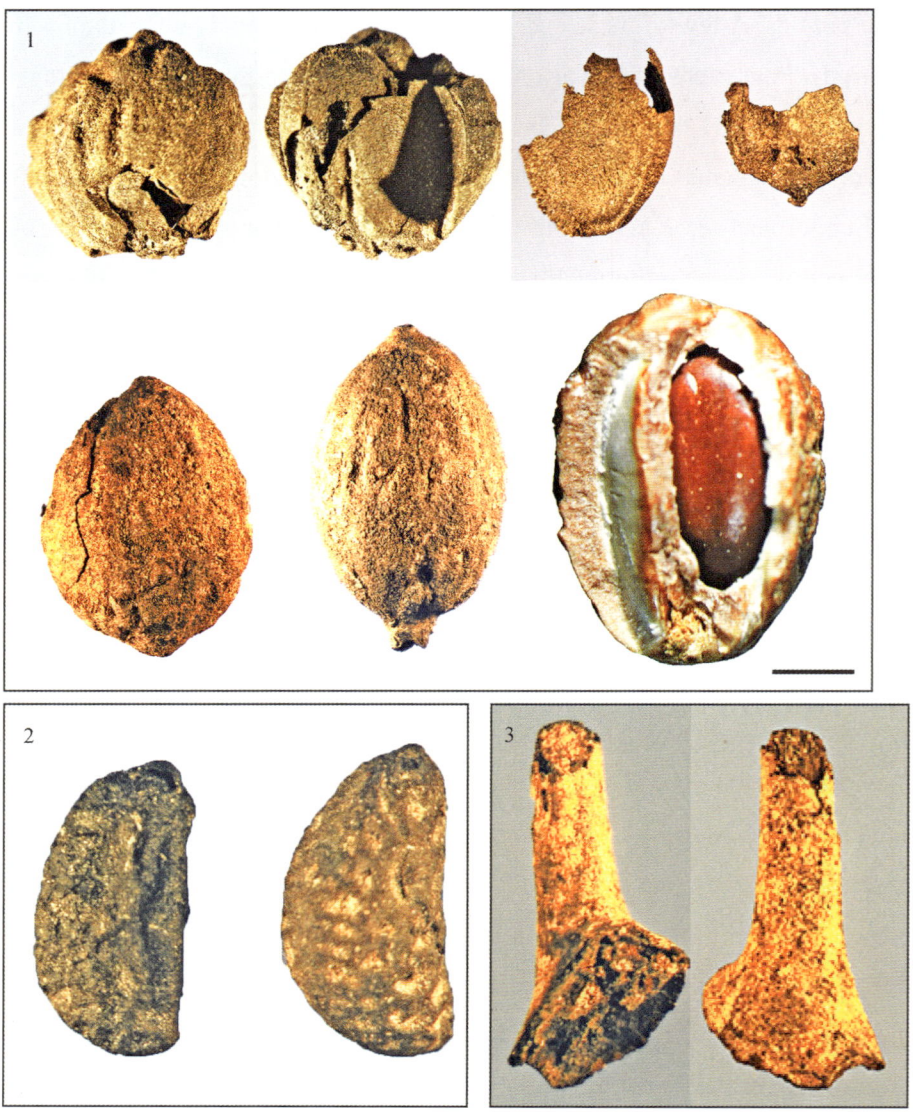

Photo Group 5　Fleshy fruits

1. 枣 (*Zizhiphus* sp., jujuba). The upper row shows the jujuba pit and seeds from the Late Longshan Zhangwan NW (龙山晚期 张湾西北, Y210). The lower row shows the pits from the Easter Zhou Sigou SE (东周 寺沟东南, Y152) and the Han Luokou Zhuanchang NE (汉朝 罗口砖厂东北, Y017) from the left. The modern jujuba pit and seed inside resemble those from the Zhangwan NW (2nd one of the upper row). Scale=2 mm.
2. 悬钩子属 (*Rubus* sp., bramble) from the Late Longshan Jiandongcun NW (涧东村西北, Y196B). Scale=0.5 mm.
3. 蔷薇科 刺 (Rosaceae thorn, rose family) from the Upper Erligang Tianposhuiku NE (二里岗上层 天坡水库东北, Y043). =98-043 H3 #51, Master #433. Scale=1.0 mm.

layers indicate spots with artifact concentrations but does not resemble ash pits. Different types of features have a different chance of retaining charred plant remains, so it is usually hard to compare them directly. However, most of our samples came from one type of feature, ash pits, and thus we will compare all features together.

Seed densities, calculated by seed number divided by soil volume, shows a wide range from 0 to 1,665.27 (Longshan period Nanshi 南石, 97-1003, Y1003, house foundation 1) (Table 6.4). The next

CHAPTER 6 ARCHAEOBOTANICAL ANALYSIS ON SITES SURVEYED IN THE YILUO REGION (1998–2011)

Photo Group 6　Unknown plant remains

1. 未知形式 1 (unknown type 1). The first three are from the Late Longshan Jiandongcun NW (涧东村西北，Y196B) and the rest two are from the Yanliangzhai Shuiku W (龙山晚期 颜良寨水库西，Y087). Some similar to 香蒲属 (*Typha* sp., cattaii). Scale=0.5 mm.
2. 未知种子 (unknown seeds) from the Late Longshan Jiandongcun NW (涧东村西北，Y196B). Scale=1 mm.
3. 未知种子 (unknown seed) from the Late Longshan Jiandongcun NW (涧东村西北，Y196B). Scale=1 mm.
4. 未知种子 (unknown seed) from the Late Longshan Jiandongcun NW (涧东村西北，Y196B). Scale=1 mm.
5. 未知种子 (unknown seed) from the Han Luokou Zhuanchang NE site (汉，罗口砖厂东北，Y017). Scale=2 mm.
6. A bud from the unknown taxa from the Upper Erligang Tianposhuiku NE site (二里岗上层 天坡水库东北，Y043). Scale=2 mm.
7. 纤维片 (a piece of fiber) from the Yangzhai NW site (二里岗上层 杨寨西北，Y058). Scale=1 mm.

two richest samples are recovered from the Yangshao Zhaocheng site (赵城, 05-077, Y077, cultural layer, 446.67/L) and the Upper Erligang Tianposhuiku NE (天坡水库东北, 98-043, Y 043, ash pit 6 layer 6, 693.33/L). From the Peiligang to the Longshan periods, total seed densities increased dramatically, probably related to the increasing farming activity. A decrease in seed densities in the later periods does not necessarily mean the decrease in agricultural importance but merely the artifact of smaller sample sizes. Also decreasing ash pits in Zhou and Han periods indicate household waste and ash may have been contributed to manures, causing a smaller chance of seed preservation. At the same token, the cultigens-to-non-domesticates taxa ratios increased through the Longshan period, but again showing smaller values in the Erlitou period onward. Taxa diversity is also showing the same pattern.

Table 6.4 Total seed density and ratios of cultigens divided by weeds per period*

Chronology	Total Seed density					Cultigen/Wild Ratios				
	N	Range	Median	Mean	Std	N	Range	Median	Mean	Std
Peiligang	12	0 to 2.35	0.12	0.36	0.66	5	0 to 0.37	0.01	0.10	0.16
Yangshao	43	0 to 446.67	2.00	16.85	69.00	36	0 to 1.54	0.16	0.28	0.37
Longshan	36	0 to 1665.27	12.13	91.39	285.37	34	0 to 7.67	0.10	0.67	1.49
Erlitou	36	0 to 85.7	11.57	25.26	27.73	33	0.01 to 1.14	0.09	0.16	0.21
Erligang	18	1.67 to 693.33	35.87	91.72	161.24	18	0.02 to 6.85	0.14	0.60	1.58
Zhou	19	0.29 to 40.89	3.85	8.20	12.09	19	0 to 0.29	0.04	0.09	0.10
Han	3	0.5 to 32.75	0.78	11.34	18.54	2	0.58 to 0.67	0.62	0.62	0.06

* Std= standard diviation.

Millets, combining foxtail and broomcorn, consistently show a high proportion per a total number of seeds (Fig. 6.5). Millets are ubiquitous, appearing all sites except for save: three Peiligang sites (Xishiqiao E, Tieshenggou, Beiying), one Yangshao (Longgudui), one Longshan (Xiqijiayao NW),

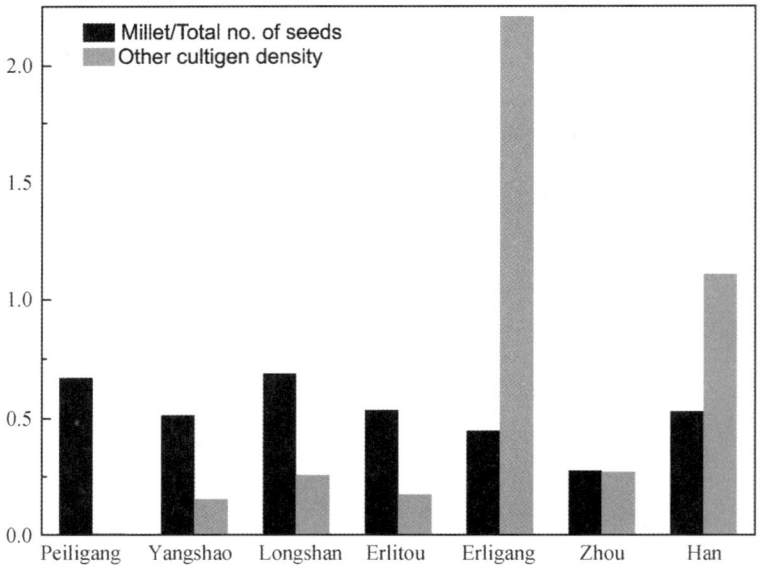

Figure 6.5 Changes in millet proportions per a total number of seeds and densities of other cultigens, including rice, wheat, sobyean, azuki and perilla, through time

one Erlitou (Yuangou A), and one Zhou site (Huachenghe N).

Millet proportions are 50% or higher in all periods except for the Erligang (40%) and Zhou (30%) samples. Except for the Peiligang period, other cultigens are present in a small amount. One grain of wheat was found each from the Late Peiligang Xishiqiao E (西石桥, 01-010, 76) site and the Middle/Late Yangshao Zhaocheng site (赵城, 05-077, Y077). Without a direct date on grains, we cannot confirm whether wheat was introduced to the Yiluo region to this early or Middle Neolithic period. Wheat was found in three Late Longshan sites, including the Matun (马屯新村, 11-069, Y069), Baozhuang NW (保庄西北, 11-060, Y046), and Yanliangzhai Shuiku W (颜良寨水库西, 11-087, Y087). We dated specimens from Baozhuang NW, yielding a later date (D-AMS025484, 2625±26 uncal. BP, 831–786 cal. BC). It is likely that wheat was introduced to the region by the Late Longshan, considering its wide spread across northern China by 4000 BP (Lee 2016). Among other cultigens, wheat counts the highest number (345) and about a half of them came from the Upper Erligang Tianposhuiku NE (天坡水库东, 98-043, Y043) site (Appendix 6.1). A direct date on wheat shows the Erligang affiliation (TO-11420, 3020±50 uncal. BP, 1409–1122 cal. BC). This concentration makes the other cultigen density of the Erligang period much higher than any other period (Fig. 6.5). Among 11 Zhou sites examined, three yielded wheat and most of them came from Sigou SE (寺沟东南, 11-152, Y152) with a direct date (D-AMS29885, 2404±47 uncal. BP, 726–386 cal. BC).

Rice is present from the Yangshao period onward. Two grains of rice were found the Middle/Late Yangshao Zhaocheng and Late Longshan Matun sites. Although we have no direct date on Yangshao rice, other studies indicated presence of rice paddy fields and abundant rice phytoliths (Rosen 2007; Rosen et al. 2015). Rice grains from the Huizui site in 2002 is dated to the Longshan period (SNU04-416, 3640±60 uncal. BP, 2200–1831 cal. BC). Five Erlitou sites yielded less than 10 rice grains per site, including Zhanwan NW (张湾西北, 11-210, Y210), Shaochai (稍柴, 97-1001，Y1001), Shangzhuang S (上庄南, 98-037, Y037), Luokou (罗口, 98-022, Y022), and Huizui (灰嘴, 00-126, Y127). Only one site each yielded rice from Erligang (Tianposhuiku NE，天坡水库东北, 98-043, Y043), Zhou (Yangzhai W, 杨寨西, 11-059, Y059) and Han period (Luokou Zhuanchang NE, 罗口砖厂东北, 98-017, Y017).

Soybean genus (*Glycine max* ssp.) is present from the Yangshao period onward. The size, measured by the seed length and width, increases through time, showing larger legumes in the Erlitou samples (Lee et al. 2007). Its overall density is very low, equivalent to only 1 to 4 grains per 10 liters of samples overall throughout the period. Four grains are possibly azuki (*Vigna angularis* ssp., 赤豆), considering tis overall shape and texture, although it is missing a diagnostic embryo part from the two Eastern Zhou Qingyizhen 2 (清易镇东2, 07-003, Y003) and Yangzhai W (杨寨西, 07-059, Y059) as well as the Han Diaoqiaozhai SE site (吊桥寨东南, 07-216, Y216). Unlike Korea and Japan (Lee et al. 2007, Lee 2013), azuki is not found frequently with soybean in China. Such a difference may indicate separate origins of these common legumes.

Seed densities do not correlate to the size of the site (Fig. 6.6). Smaller sites with less than 5,000 sq. meters show the widest range of seed densities from 0 to 1665/liter. Most samples with a total seed density in the upper quantile (25%) came from the lower settlement tiers, that is, small sites, except

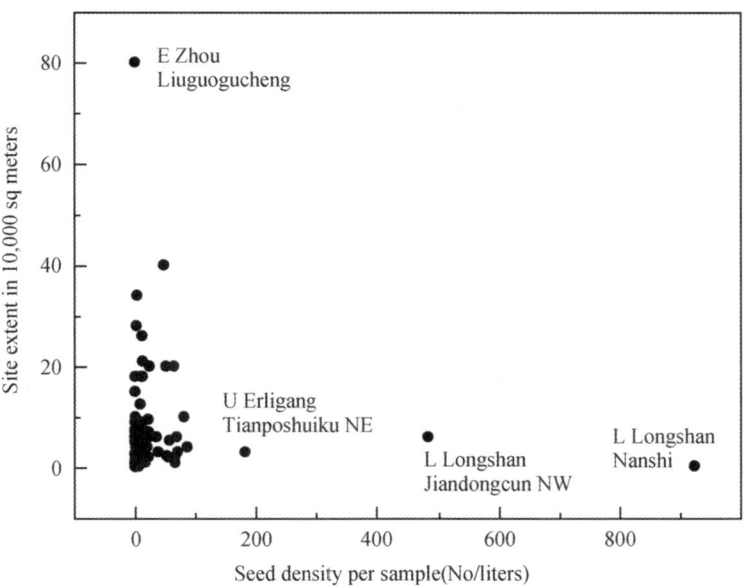

Figure 6.6 Total seed densities by site extents

for the two Middle/Late Yangshao sites, Zhaocheng (赵城, Y077) and Yulinzhuang S (羽林庄南, Y050) and the Late Longshan Luokou (罗口, Y022) site (Fig. 6.7). Unlike our earlier assessment, rice was found through all settlement tiers, including smaller sites. Wheat and wetland weeds show the same trends.

Quantities of non-domesticates, particularly weedy Pinaceae taxa, are high throughout the periods. In general, both millets and Pinaceae weeds increase their densities together (Fig.6.8). Two Late Longshan sites, Jiandongcun NW (涧东村西北, Y196B) Nanshi (南石, Y1003), are exception as either they show the much higher than average cultigen density with a lower upland weed density or vice versa. Pinaceae are common weeds growing together with millet, and this may explain the correlation.

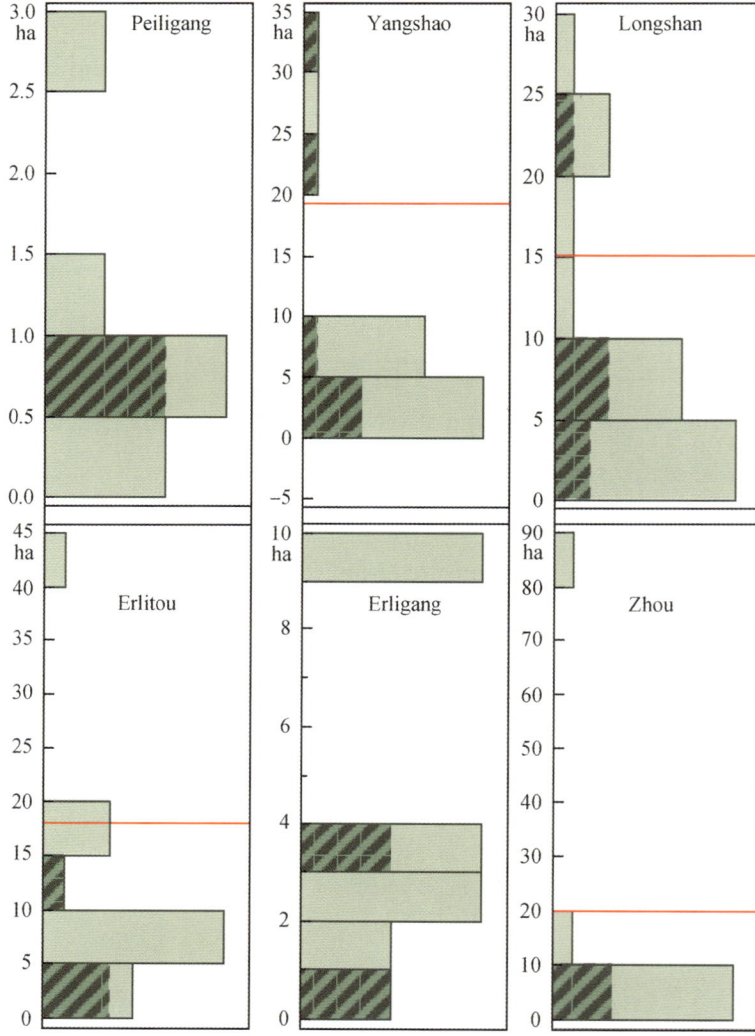

Figure 6.7 Total seed densities by site sizes in each period. Hatched samples represent those with total seed densities of the upper quantile (25%). Below the red lines are the sizes of the lowest settlement tiers in each period. Y axis is site sizes in hectare

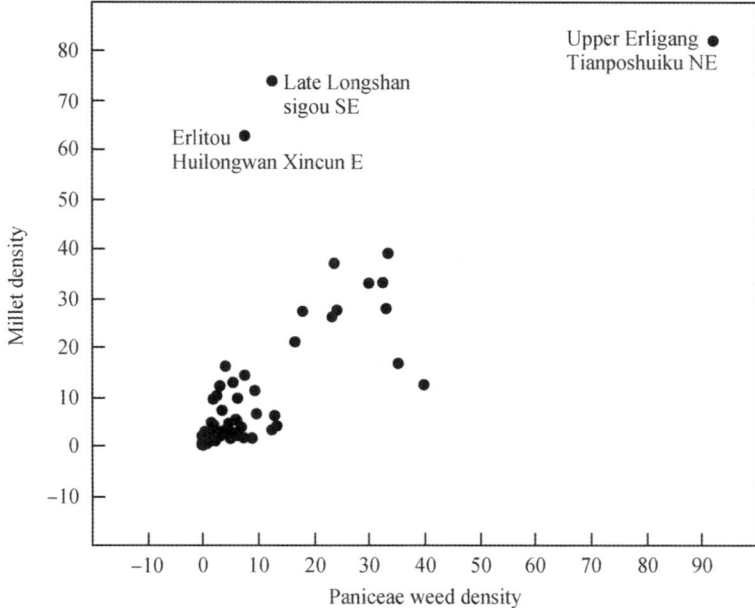

Figure 6.8   Correlation between millet density and *paniceae* weed density. Two outliers, Jiandongcun NW (Y196B) Nanshi (Y1003), are excluded in this bivariate plot

5. SUMMARY

The archaeobotanical project in the Yiluo survey region illustrates changing patterns of plant resource use from the Late Peiligang to Han periods. A large sample size shows many variations that is hard to simplify, affected by differences in plant preservation and sampling bias. Nevertheless, we are able to find the following trends from this extensive study. As we analyzed only three samples from two sites, we cannot speculate the nature of agriculture during the Han period with a certainty except for that continuing practice of multiple cropping's of cultigens from the previous periods.

Firstly, Millets are dominant staples throughout the period, considering the overall abundance and frequency in our samples. Millets are absent only seven sites among 91 sites examined. Not just abundance but its frequent association with common arable weeds of millet tribe indicate intensity of millet farming and importance in subsistence at least from the Yangshao period. Compared to eastern North China and Korea, the Yiluo region shows more percentage of broomcorn millets. Although foxtail millet is much more abundant than broomcorn, comparison of phytolith and charred seeds indicates a possibility of more broomcorn millet in the Yiluo region (Weisskopf and Lee 2015). We hypothesize broomcorn millet was probably used more frequently than it appeared in charred seed assemblages, possibly due to differences in preservation or culinary methods.

Secondly, two introduced crops, rice and wheat, consist only of small portions of all seeds only in a limited number of sites even to the Zhou period. At least, wheat may have been incorporated to the staple more than rice from the Erligang period. Rice was found from the Yangshao period onward in our region. Although we do not have a direct date on rice, considering the evidence of wet paddy fields and rice phytolith, we can speculate rice was incorporated into farming from the Yangshao period. Throughout the period, rice is minimal crop, counting only 46 in total, that is, its amount and frequency (a total of 46 grains) did not measure up to those of millets and/or edible wild plants. This pattern implies that calorific staple is not the reason for rice farming there during the Neolithic period. Even in the Erlitou and later periods, rice is outnumbered by millets in the Yiluo region, indicating that rice was not a staple. Its spatial distribution in the Yiluo basin suggests that the importance of rice farming can be understood in social contexts. Rice might have been a special occasion such as ritual offering or a luxury food for elites. Rice is fermented to alcohol as early as 9000 cal. BP site at Jiahu (McGovern et al. 2004). Late Longshan example of rice fermentation came from the Liangchengzhen (McGovern et al. 2005). Regardless how sporadic findings of rice is in North China, rice seems a harbinger of signaling social differentiation and ritualization well before the rise of state-level societies. Rice was contextualized in the recipient culture (as a prestigious/ritual item in the north) differently from the donor (as a stable in the south). On the contrary, South China along the Yangzi River provides very little evidence to support the development of social, economic hierarchies (Shelach-Lavi 2015: 123). Rice adoption itself did not trigger social changes in the northern Neolithic societies per se but it was a part of the regalia that fortified social trends and that changed both food culture and ceremonial practice in the long run.

Thirdly, seed densities do not correlate to the size of the site. A larger settlement represents a larger number of inhabitants and more complex structural patterns, including elite residence. More populations and higher status residences could have caused more food storage and waste residue, but our study does not show the case. On the other hand, we may speculate smaller non-center settlements may represent a producer, agricultural farmlands, which may cause more waste from weeding, harvest and crop processing, resulting higher seed densities in most cases.

Acknowledgements: We appreciate all the helps from the Yiluo archaeology team. Particularly, we appreicte the crews who helped sample collection or flotation, including Li Liu (Stanford University), Henry Wright (University of Michigan), Sheahan Bestel, Arlene Rosen (University of Texas Austin), Xingcan Chen, Yongqiang Lee, Hongzhang Wang and Facheng Wang (Chinese Academy of Social Sciences Institute of Archaeology).

REFERENCES

An, Cheng-Bang, Weimiao Dong, Hu Li, Yufeng Chen & Loukas Barton 2013. Correspondence regarding "Origins and spread of wheat in China" by Dodson, J.R., Zhou, X., Zhao, K., Sun, N., Atahan, P. (2013). Quaternary Science Reviews

72: 108-111.

Barton, Loukas, and An, Cheng-Bang. 2014. An evaluation of competing hypotheses for the early adoption of wheat in East Asia. World Archaeology 46: 775-798.

Chen, D., D. Zhang and K. Larsen 2009. Tribe CASSIEAE. In Flora of China: Fabaceae, edited by Z. Y. Wu, P. H. Raven and D. Y. Hon, pp. 27-34. vol. 10. Science Press, Beijing.

Crawford, Gary W. 1992. XX In: The Origins of Agriculture: An International Perspective, Cowan C. Wesley and Watson, Patty J. (eds), Smithsonian Institution Press, Washington, DC, pp. 7-38.

Crawford, Gary W., Xuexiang Chen (陈雪香), Feng Shi Luan (栾丰实), and J. Wang (王建华). 2013. A preliminary analysis of plant remains assemblage from the Yuezhuang site, Changqing district, Jinan, Shandong province (山东济南长清月庄遗址植物遗存的初步分析). Jianghan Kaogu 2013.2 (127): 107-113.

Crawford, Gary W., Anne P. Underhill, Zhijun Zhao, Gyoung-Ah Lee, Gary Feinman, Linda Nicholas, Fengshi Luan, Haiguang Yu, Hui Fang, and Fengshu Cai. 2005. Late Neolithic plant remains from northern China: preliminary results from Liangchengzhen, Shandong. Current Anthropology 46(2): 309-317.

Fogg, Wayne H. 1983. Swidden cultivation of foxtail millet by Taiwan aborigines: a cultural analogue of the domestication of Setaria italica in China. In: The Origins of Chinese Civilization, Keightley David N. (ed.) University of California Press, Berkeley. pp 95-115.

Guo, W. T. 1996. On the origin of cultivated soybean problem. Studies in the History of Natural Science 15:326-333.

Han, Chang-Gyun, Ja-jin Koo & Guen-wan Kim. 2014. Date and their meanings of carbonized grains collected from the Daecheon-ri Neolithic site, Okcheon. Journal of Korean Neolithic Society 28: 1-17.

Hu, Shiu-ying (胡秀英). 2005. Food plants of China. The Chinese University Press, Hong Kong.

Hymowitz Theodore and Ram Janam Singh. 1987. Taxonomy and speciation. In: Soybeans: Improvement, Production, and Uses. J. R. Wilcox (ed.) American Society of Agronomy, Madison, WI, Issue 16. pp 23-48.

Jarolímek, Ivan and Jiří Kolbek 2006. Plant communities dominated by Salix gracilistyla in Korean Peninsula and Japan. Biologia 61(1):63-70.

King, Franklin H. 1911. Farmers of Forty Centuries: Permanent Agriculture in China, Korea, and Japan. FH King, Madison, WI.

Lee, Gyoung-Ah 2011. Transition from foraging to farming in prehistoric Korea. Current Anthropology 52 (S4): S307-S329.

Lee, Gyoung-Ah 2016. The spread of domesticated plant resources in prehistoric northeast Asia. In Routledge Handbook of Archaeology and Globalization, T. Hodos (ed.). Taylor & Francis/Routledge Press, pp. 394-412.

Lee, Gyoung-Ah 2017. The Chulmun period of Korea: current findings and discourse on the Korean Neolithic culture. In Handbook of East and Southeast Asian Archaeology, J. Habu, P. Lape, J. Olsen, and J. Zhichun (eds). Springer International Publishing, pp. 451-482.

Lee, Gyoung-Ah, Gary W. Crawford G, Li Liu, Yuka Sasaki, and Xuexiang Chen. 2011. Archaeological soybean (Glycine max) in East Asia: does size matter? PLoS ONE 6(11) doi: 10.1371/journal.pone.0026720.

Lee, Gyoung-Ah 2013. Archaeological perspectives on origins of azuki (Vigna angularis). The Holocene 23(3): 453-459. First published on October 5, 2012, doi: 10.1177/0959683612460788.

Lee, Gyoung-Ah, Gary W. Crawford, Li Liu, and Xuexiang Chen. Plants and People from the Early Neolithic to Shang periods in North China. PNAS 104(3): 1087-1092.

McGovern, Patrick E., Zuzhong Zhang, Jigen Tang, Zhiqing Zhang, Gretchen R. Hall, Robert A. Moreau, Alberto Nuñez, Eric D. Butrym, Michael P. Richards, Chen-shan Wang, Guansheng Cheng, Zhijun Zhao and Changsui Wang. 2004. Fermented beverages of pre-and proto-historic China. Proceedings of the National Academy of Sciences USA 101: 17593-17598.

McGovern, Patrick E., Anne P. Underhill, Hui Fang, Fengshi Luan, Gretchen R. Hall, Haiguang Yu, Wang CS, Fengshu Cai, Zhijun Zhao, and Gary M. Feinman. 2005. Chemical identification and cultural implications of a mixed fermented beverage from late prehistoric China. Asian Perspective 44(3): 249-275.

Rosen, A. M. 2007. The role of environmental change in the development of complex societies in China: a study forms the Huizui site. Indo-Pacific Prehistory Association Bulletin 27: 39-48.

Rosen, A., Richard Macphail, Li Liu, Xingcan Chen, and Alison Weisskopf. 2015. Rising social complexity, agricultural intensification, and the earliest rice paddies on the Loess Plateau of northern China. Quaternary International 437(B): 50-59.

Shelach-Lavi, Gideon. 2015. The archaeology of early China From prehistory to the Han Dynasty. Cambridge: Cambridge Universtiy Press.

Smith, Bruce D. 1992. Chenopodium berlandieri ssp. jonesianum: Evidence for a Hopewellian Domesticate for Ash Cave, Ohio. In: Rivers of Change. Bruce D. Smith (ed.). Smithsonian Institution Press, Washington, DC, pp. 103-131.

Walsh, Rory. 2016. Experiments on the effects of charring on foxtail millet (Setaria italica). Vegetation History and Archaeobotany 26(4): 447-453.

Walsh, Rory, Gyoung-Ah Lee, Li Liu, and Xingcan Chen. 2016. Millet grain morphometry as a tool for social inference: a case study from the Yiluo basin, China. The Holocene 26 (11): 1778-1787.

Weisskopf, Alice R and Gyoung-Ah Lee. 2016. Phytolith identification criteria for foxtail and broomcorn millets: a new approach to calculating crop ratios. Archaeological and Anthropological Sciences 8: 29-42. Available online March 2014 issue. DOI: 10.1007/s12520-014-0190-7.

Wu, Zhengyi (吴征镒) and Peter H. Raven. 1994. Flora of China. Missouri Botanical Garden, St. Louis.

Zeven, A. C. and P. M. Zhukovsky.1975. Dictionary of Cultivated Plants and their Centers of Diversity. Centre for Agricultural Publishing and Documentation, Wageningen, The Netherlands.

Zhang, Juzhong and Xiangkun Wang. 1998. Notes on the recent discovery of ancient cultivated rice at Jiahu, Henan Province: a new theory concerning the origin of Oryza japonica in China. Antiquity 72:897-901.

Zhang, Jianping, Houyuan Lu, Wanfa Gu, Naiqin Wu, Kunshu Zhou, Yayi Hu, Yingjun Xin & Can Wang. 2012. Early mixed farming of millet and rice 7800 years ago in the Middle Yellow River region, China. Proceedings of the National Academy of Sciences USA 7: e52146.

Zhao Zhijun. 2006. Antiquities of Eastern Asia Archaeology, 188-199.

Zhao, Zhijun. 2009. Eastward spread of wheat into China: new data and new issues. Chinese Archaeology 9: 1-9.

CHAPTER 7 RAW MATERIAL SOURCES UTILISED IN STONE TOOL PRODUCTION AT HUIZUI[1]

1. INTRODUCTION

The nature of stone tool production changed substantially during the occupation of Huizui. In the Yangshao period, evidence for stone tool manufacture is minimal; flakes were made from cobbles available in the nearby river, with no dominant lithology, suggesting that the Yangshao population at Huizui accessed raw material locally and opportunistically to produce stone tools for their own uses. However, starting from the late Longshan period, the site became a stone tool production centre, whose major product, oolitic dolomite spades, was distributed to the surrounding areas (Liu et al. 2004; Liu and Chen 2007).

During the Erlitou period, lithic manufacture at Huizui expanded in scope again. This has been linked to the overall expansion of the Erlitou culture, which was a complex society with craft specialisation, social stratification, extensive resource exchange networks and bronze metallurgy (Liu and Chen 2003; Liu 2006). The Erlitou culture used bronze mainly for ritual objects and weapons, so lithic industries, which produced stone tools for everyday utilitarian purposes, remained important. At Huizui, raw material specialisation became evident in the manufacture of several different types of tools, each of which was made from predominantly one lithology (Ford 2007, 2009; Webb et al. 2007) (Figure 7.1): spades (91%) from oolitic dolomite; axes (89%), adzes (100%) and chisels (80%) from diabase, knives (74%) from fine micaceous sandstone, and grinding slabs (90%) from several other varieties of sandstone, including violet and feldspathic. Overall, stone tool production at Huizui was dominated by oolitic dolomite spades, with large quantities of oolitic dolomite manufacturing debris, including flakes and tool blanks, found on site (Ford 2009).

Raw material specialisation is therefore highly evident at Huizui. Reasons for this specialisation will be sought below. Firstly, the geology of the surrounding region will be described, including the

---

[1] This chapter is written by John Webb, Anne Ford and Justin Gorton, post on *Indo-Pacific Prehistory Association Bulletin*, 2007(27) : 76-86.

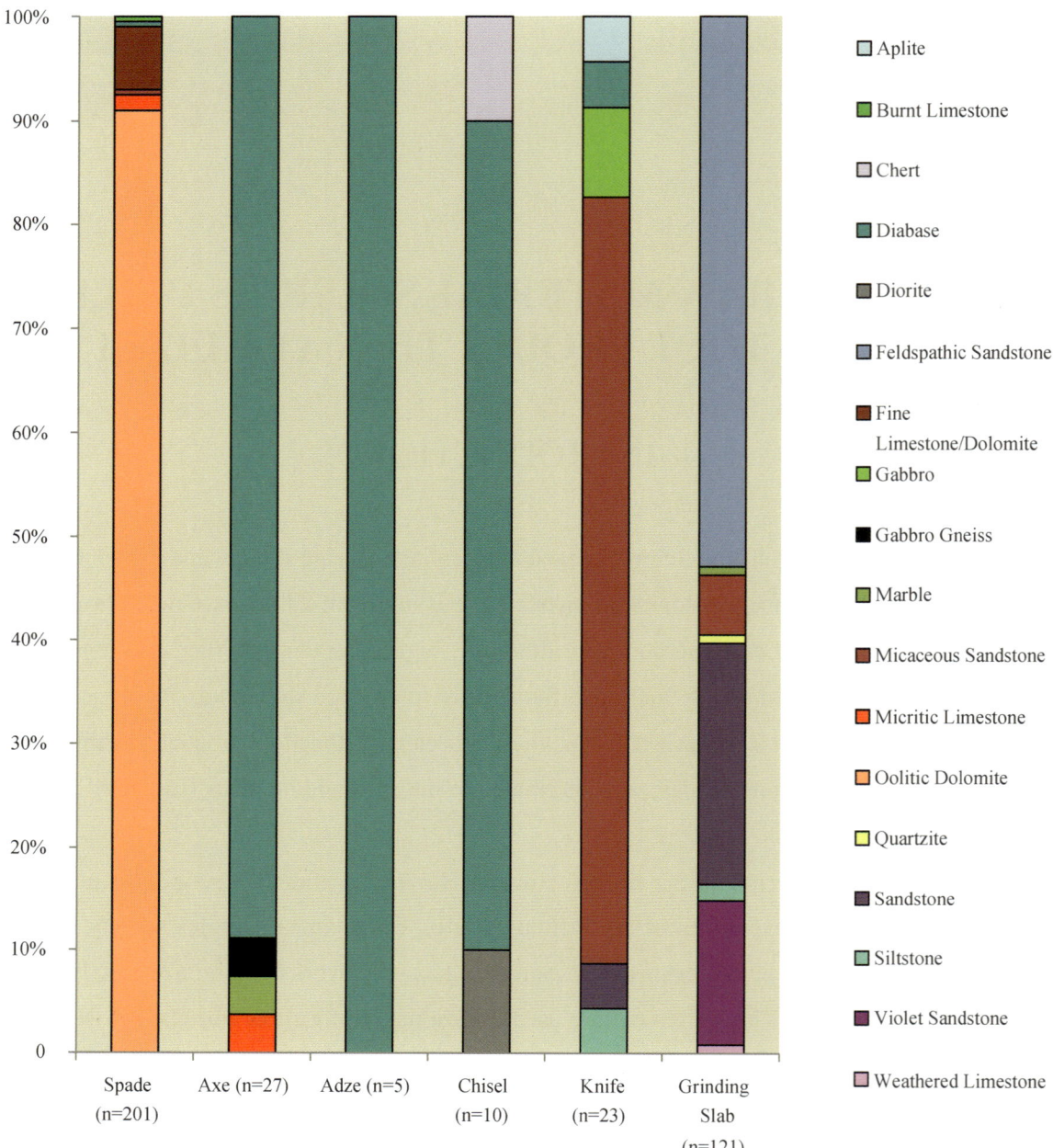

Figure 7.1 Lithologies of stone tools dating to the Erlitou period at Huizui; representative sample of overall assemblage from the site (collected during surveys in 2001 and 2002, and excavations in 1959)

lithic-rich Song Mountains, in order to provide an overview of the lithic landscape from which the people of Huizui could select their raw material. The lithologies of the raw materials chosen for use at Huizui will then be discussed in detail, with particular attention paid to the functional and extractive properties of the raw materials to assess possible reasons for selection. Evidence for sources used will also be discussed by relating the local geology to the petrographic characteristics of the lithologies used for tool manufacture.

2. GEOLOGY AND GEOMORPHOLOGY OF THE HUIZUI AREA

Huizui lies south of the Yiluo River on a flat alluvial plain composed of redeposited Pleistocene and Holocene wind-blown loess. Protruding through these Quaternary deposits are several low hills composed of Lower Triassic fluvial and lacustrine sandstone and siltstone (Figure 7.2 a, b), dipping shallowly (20°-30°) to the north.

The Cambrian strata of the northern Song Mountains are divided into eight formations. The lower Early and Middle Cambrian units are dominated by siltstones and limestones; within the siltstone sequences are thin interbeds of fine sandstone, e.g. in the Middle Cambrian *Zhangxia* Formation. The upper formations consist largely of carbonates, both limestone and dolomite.

The uppermost unit, the Upper Cambrian *Fengshan* Formation, forms the northern slopes of the Song Mountains, closest to Huizui, and is composed of ~150m of light to dark grey mostly thick-bedded, massive, fine-grained dolomite. Originally the *Fengshan* Formation was deposited as limestones, which were predominantly fine-grained, laminated and stromatolitic, with occasional beds of oolitic grainstone. These limestones have been pervasively dolomitized and now consist of coarse mosaics of dolomite crystals, with varying degrees of preservation of the original limestone grains. Most commonly, the dolomitization is comparatively coarse and uniform, and preserves relatively little of the limestone fabric. Towards the top of the *Fengshan* Formation is a partly silicified layer, in which scattered irregularly shaped patches of fine-grained quartz (chert) weather out in relief on the rock surfaces.

In the lower part of the *Fengshan* Formation is a readily distinguishable unit comprising a beige laminated dolomitic siltstone (marl), ~10m thick, overlying about 15m of grey oolitic dolomite (Figure 7.4); the oolites are evident as tiny, spherical, dark grey bodies (up to 1 mm in diameter; Figure 7.3e, f). There are also two thin beds of oolitic dolomite, less than 1m thick, within the laminated siltstone itself. The oolitic beds show overall low angle hummocky topography, enhanced by the beige siltstone, which drapes the topography. The siltstone weathers much more readily than the overlying and underlying dolomites, so on the hillsides it forms a grass-covered step that lacks rock outcrop (Figure 7.4a, b). The oolitic dolomite beneath the siltstone frequently outcrops as a 2-15m high cliff; the top of the bed forms a pavement (Figure 7.4c) that is sometimes used as a convenient location for walking tracks through the mountains.

Underlying the *Fengshan* Formation are over 100m of Upper and Middle Cambrian grey oolitic and fine-grained massive limestones. These lithologies outcrop on the southern (but not northern) flanks of the northernmost E-W ridge of the Song Mountains near Huizui (Figure 7.5).

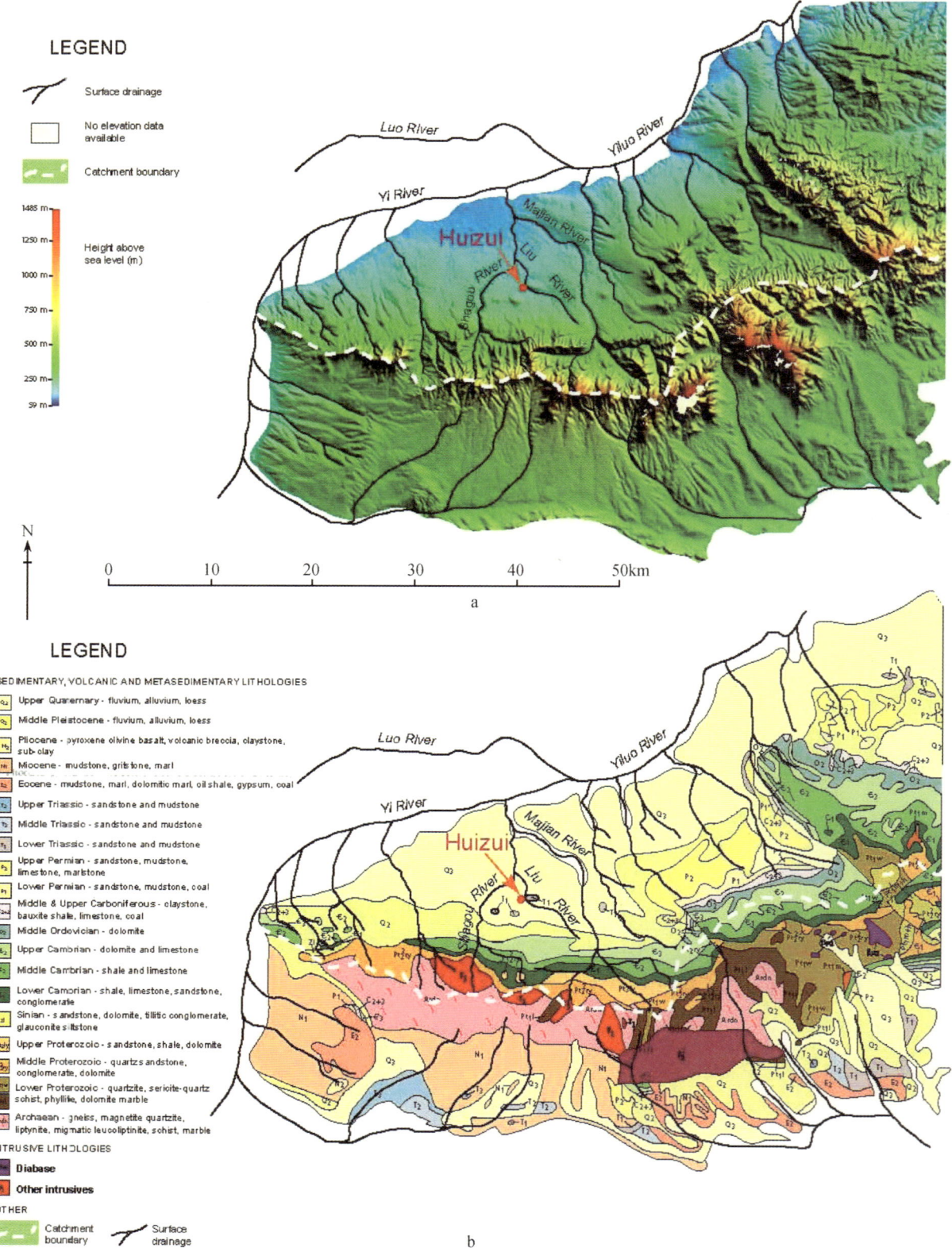

Figure 7.2 from Bureau of Geology and Mineral Resources of Henan Province, 1984
(a) Topographic setting of Huizui. (b) Regional geology of area around Huizui, particularly the Song Mountains

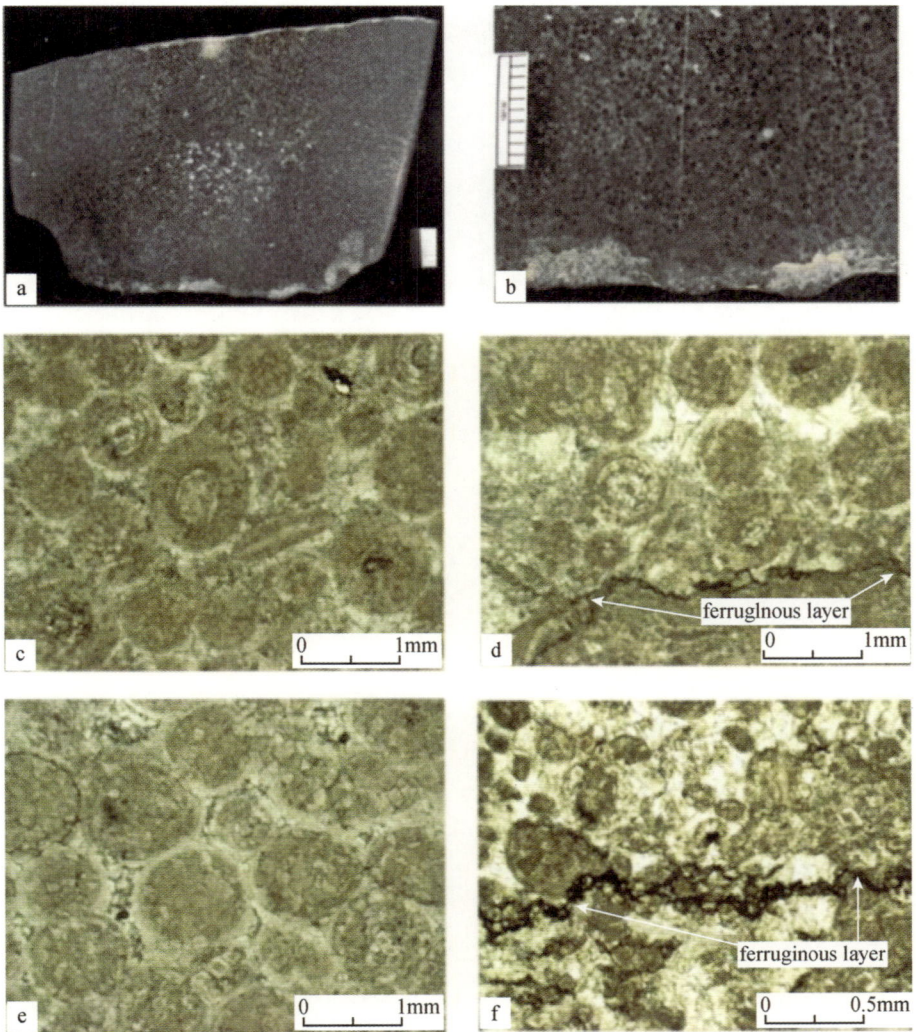

Figure 7.3 (a, b) Polished surface of oolitic dolomite spade; oolites appear as dark spots embedded in pale cement. (c, d) Photomicrographs of oolitic dolomite from outcrop; oolites appear as mostly circular bodies, some concentrically banded, within pale cement; oolites and cement replaced by blocky crystals of dolomite, sample traversed by thin bedding-parallel ferruginous layer. (e, f) Photomicrographs of oolitic dolomite from spade; note strong similarities to oolitic dolomite from outcrop, and well-marked outlines of blocky dolomite crystals replacing oolites

Overlying the Cambrian strata is a thin-bedded Carboniferous sequence of claystone, bauxitic siltstone, limestone, sandstone and coal, deposited in alluvial fan, swamp, or lacustrine environments. Succeeding this are Permian river, swamp and lake sediments consisting of sandstone, mudstone, and minor coal. In the Huizui area the Carboniferous and Permian sediments do not outcrop because they are covered by Quaternary redeposited loess.

In the southern Song Mountains, the Cambrian strata overlie a Precambrian (Archaean and Proterozoic) basement (Figure 7.2b; BGMR of Henan Province 1984; Meyerhoff et al. 1991). Within the basement are Archaean igneous and high-grade metamorphic complexes consisting of hornblende gneiss, quartzite, migmatite, schist and marble, which have been intruded by granites and diorites, with

Figure 7.4 Outcrop characteristics of oolitic dolomite and overlying siltstone. (a, b) In hillsides oolitic dolomite forms small cliff; siltstone occurs as grassy, less steep slope. (c) Unquarried outcrop of oolitic dolomite, showing natural pavement at top of bed. (d) Premodern quarry in oolitic dolomite; note rubble slope below quarry. (e) Quarried pavement of main bed of oolitic dolomite, with overlying siltstone containing a thin separate bed of oolitic dolomite; note tendency of oolitic dolomite to split into thin slabs. (f) Premodern quarry in oolitic dolomite; note thin-bedded nature of main (lower) bed

very minor pegmatite. The Proterozoic deposits comprise quartz sandstone, conglomerate, dolomite and siltstone, which have been metamorphosed in places to quartzite, dolomite marble, schist, phyllite and slate. Upper Proterozoic granites, granodiorites and minor shallow-level diabases intrude these Proterozoic strata.

The occupants of Huizui therefore had a wide variety of lithologies to choose from when selecting raw material for the production of stone tools.

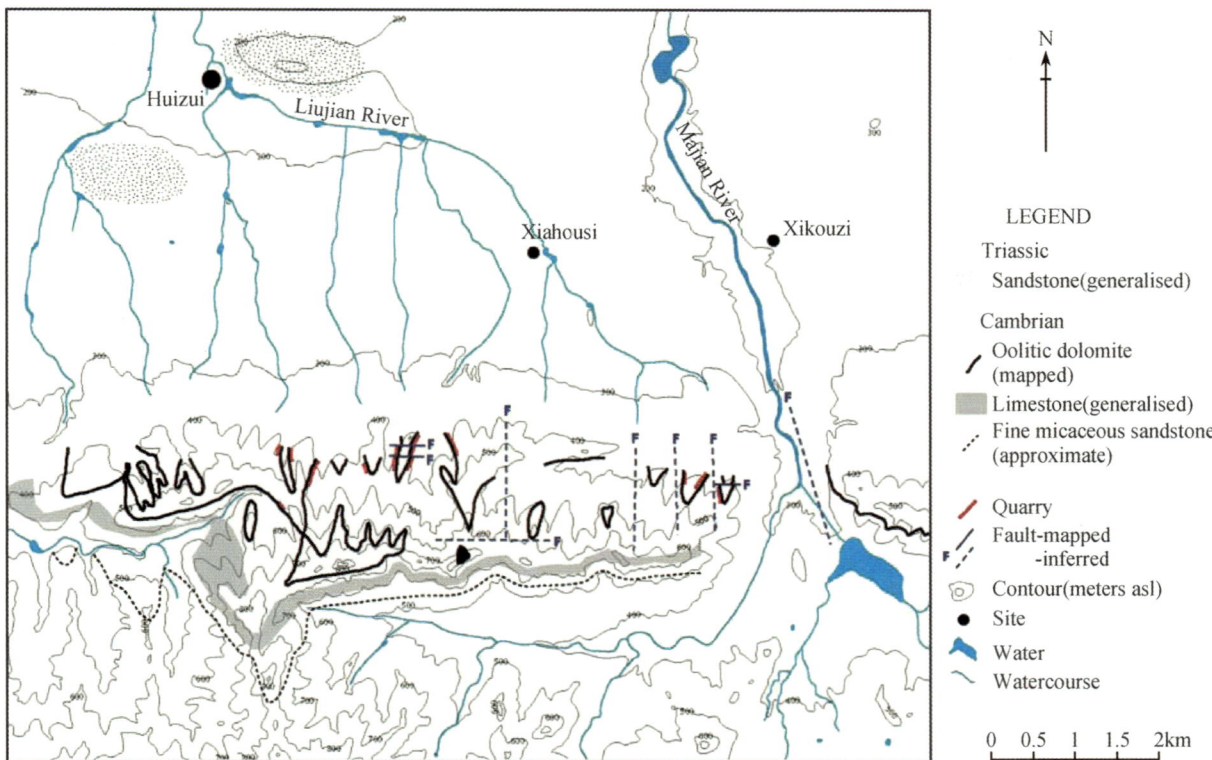

Figure 7.5 Distribution of most of the common rock types used for artefact manufacture at Huizui. Distribution of oolitic dolomite based on mapping carried out during the present study; sites of premodern quarries shown

3. LITHOLOGIES OF STONE TOOLS PRESENT AT HUIZUI

Approximately 29 different lithologies have been identified from the excavations at Huizui. Of these, five were present in large quantities (oolitic dolomite, fine limestone/dolomite/limestone, diabase, micaceous sandstone and other types of sandstone; Table 7.1). Please note that the assemblage figures are updated from Webb et al. 2007 as the current data includes substantial additional excavated and survey material from 2002.

Table 7.1 Number and proportion of different rock types within all lithic material (tools, blanks, flakes and indeterminate pieces) recovered from Huizui survey and excavations and identified by authors

Raw material	Finished Tools (n)	Tool Blanks (n)	Manufacturing Debris (inc. cores, flakes and angular fragments) (n)	Total (n)
Oolitic Dolomite	22	321	15873	16216
Fine Limestone/Dolomite, Limestone	22	66	383	471
Other Sandstones	139	14	279	432
Diabase	82	45	38	165
Micaceous Fine Sandstone	59	24	60	143
Marl	1	3	36	40
Lime/Burnt Limestone	1	2	36	39
Quartz	0	4	22	26

				(continued)
Raw material	Finished Tools (n)	Tool Blanks (n)	Manufacturing Debris (inc. cores, flakes and angular fragments) (n)	Total (n)
Siltstone	6	1	15	22
Quartzite	5	2	6	13
Chert	3	1	7	11
Dolomite/Calcite Crystal	0	0	10	10
Marble	4	2	1	7
Schist	0	0	6	6
Aplite	1	4	0	5
Slate	2	2	1	5
Rhyolite	4	0	0	4
Conglomerate	0	0	2	2
Diorite	2	0	0	2
Diorite gneiss	1	1	0	2
Gabbro	1	1	0	2
Gabbro gneiss	2	0	0	2
Jade?	0	2	0	2
Mudstone	0	0	2	2
Turquoise	2	0	0	2
Argillite	1	0	0	1
Granite gneiss	0	1	0	1
Pyroxenite	1	0	0	1
Shale	0	1	0	1
Siliceous Rock	0	1	0	1
Total	361	498	16777	17636

3.1 Oolitic dolomite

The oolitic dolomite spades have a distinctive finely spotted appearance, particularly evident on polished surfaces (Figure 7.3a, b). This appearance is responsible for the local name of "millet limestone", and means that spades made of oolitic dolomite are easily identifiable.

A few beds of oolitic dolomite occur within the Fengshan Formation on the northern flanks of the Song Mountains. As described above, the most prominent of these lies directly beneath a beige laminated marl (Figure 7.5), and this bed was most probably the source of the oolitic dolomite used to produce spades at Huizui. The oolitic dolomite of the spades is almost identical to the oolitic dolomite beneath the marl (compare Figure 7.3c, d and Figure 7.3e, f). Both consist of dark grey, spherical, mostly medium to large oolites (0.5-1mm in diameter), often concentrically laminated, embedded in a white cement. In some samples, the oolites are lighter in colour and composed of clear, coarse, randomly oriented crystals. Smaller oolites (0.2mm) may be present, along with minor amounts of echinoderm and trilobite fossil fragments. The oolites, fossils and intervening cement were originally composed of calcite, but have all been replaced by medium-sized, relatively uniform blocky dolomite crystals; the oolites are still visible despite the replacement.

The presence at Huizui of a single knife tool blank made from beige marl, as well as indeterminate tool blanks, fragments and flakes of this lithology within areas used for oolitic dolomite spade manufacture, confirms that the oolitic dolomite bed beneath the beige marl was quarried to produce the spades. The other beds of oolitic dolomite within the Fengshan Formation generally contain smaller, more densely packed oolites and lack the overlying marl.

The oolitic dolomite bed has been quarried at a number of locations in the northern foothills of the Song Mountains (Figures 4d-f), as close as ~4 km to Huizui. These quarries were used to supply blocks for house foundations for local villages up until about 50 years ago, and it is possible that they were also used in earlier time periods.

There are two factors that make the oolitic dolomite bed beneath the marl particularly suitable for quarrying. Firstly, weathering of the overlying relatively soft marl frequently exposes the top of the oolitic dolomite bed as a pavement open for extraction; this can be easily broken into thin slabs using the natural bedding-parallel fracture planes within the dolomite. The surfaces of the fractures often have a very thin reddish-purple ferruginous coating (Figure 7.4d), which is also visible on both sides of many of the oolitic dolomite tool blanks (Figure 7.4e), showing that the natural fracture planes were used to control the desired thickness of the tool blank.

Secondly, the mechanical properties of the oolitic dolomite mean that it was easy to work and suitable for use as spades. The homogenous structure of interlocking crystals means that oolitic dolomite will generally break evenly and predictably when being worked, and that it is relatively strong and tough, and therefore less likely to break during use (Garber 1989: 15). Furthermore, dolomite is a soft material (hardness 3.5-4) that is easily ground by harder rocks to give very smooth, high polished faces and sharp edges, effective for working loess soils. However, its softness means that it is readily scratched, and the thin edges of dolomite tools would chip if struck against harder rocks.

Taken together, the extractive and functional properties explain why the oolitic dolomite, which makes up <5% of the dolomite outcrops on the northern slopes of the Song Mountains, accounts for >90% of the dolomite/limestone material in the Huizui assemblage (Table 7.1).

3.2 Diabase

The diabase at Huizui is a grey to dark green (occasionally brownish red) intrusive basic igneous rock that is mostly medium-grained. It consists of interlocking elongated sericitised plagioclase laths up to 0.6 mm long, together with needle-like actinolite crystals and grains of chlorite, epidote and often abundant fine opaques, all embedded in a very fine-grained matrix that is generally altered to clay. There is some variation in the amounts of plagioclase and actinolite present, and the plagioclase laths may be highly elongate and spinifex-textured (strongly interlocking) in some samples. The diabase has undergone low-grade greenschist metamorphism, accounting for the presence of chlorite and epidote.

Diabase was used to produce mostly woodworking tools (axes, adzes and chisels; Figure 7.1) that require strong edge-holding capabilities and the ability to withstand large amounts of force. A single diabase knife was also identified from the Erlitou layers of the 1959 excavation. Diabase is very suitable for ground-edge tools, as its uniform texture of interlocking crystals of relatively hard minerals (hardness 5-6.5) means that it is relatively strong and tough, and therefore unlikely to break during use. Diabase also grinds smoothly to create strong, sharp working edges, which are easily resharpened.

Most of the diabase tool blanks present at Huizui are made from waterworn cobbles. The source of the cobbles is uncertain; gravels in the nearby Liujian River lack diabase as this river runs entirely through Cambrian carbonates and Triassic sandstones (Figure 7.2b). The diabase cobbles may have been derived from the Shagou River, which runs as close as 2 km to Huizui to the northwest (Figure 7.2a); during the present study diabase cobbles were collected from gravel beds in this river about 3.5 km to the west of Huizui. The headwaters of the Shagou River lie in Precambrian basement, which presumably contains diabase outcrops, although none are mapped (Figure 7.2b). The gravels could also have been sourced from the Yi and/or Majian Rivers, which lie respectively 10 km or more to the north and 6 km or more to the east of Huizui; the upper reaches of both rivers run through extensive areas of Precambrian rocks (Figure 7.2b), which are likely to contain diabase outcrops.

Selecting river cobbles as tool blanks minimised the amount of reduction required, as there is little change in size and shape between the natural cobble and the finished tool. Only the lateral margins were squared and the working edge created before the tool was ready to use (Ford 2001: 58; 2004: 73). Waterworn cobbles are also an effective choice of raw material, as any fractures inherent within a cobble are likely to have resulted in breakage during fluvial transport; thus, intact cobbles probably lack serious flaws.

3.3 Fine micaceous sandstone

The fine-grained micaceous sandstone at Huizui is green or brown, even-grained and composed predominantly of quartz grains, with a small but distinctive component of muscovite flakes aligned parallel to bedding. It also contains calcite grains similar in size to the quartz grains, scattered rounded pellets of brownish glauconite, flakes of chloritised biotite, and occasional tubular fossil fragments. The sandstone is well-cemented by overgrowths on the quartz and calcite grains.

The micaceous sandstone was most probably quarried from outcrops of the Middle Cambrian Zhangxia Formation at the base of the steep southern flanks of the northernmost E-W ridge of the Song Mountains (Figure 7.5). The basal part of the Zhangxia Formation in this area contains a 15m section of thick red-brown and green siltstone with as many as eight thin interbeds of fine micaceous sandstone up to 20 cm thick. The sandstone beds are often plane laminated and split into thin sheets along the laminations. Thin section examination shows they are very similar to the micaceous sandstone found at Huizui, and a small number of micaceous sandstone tools contain thin laminae of red-brown and green siltstone. Furthermore, the presence of slabs of unmodified fine micaceous sandstone at Huizui shows that this raw material was available locally.

Sandstone beds are present in other Early and Middle Cambrian formations in the area, but all differ in grain size and/or fossil content from the micaceous sandstone used at Huizui. The sandstone beds in the Zhangxia Formation lie within 6 km of Huizui (Figure 7.5), but because a high ridge separates Huizui from the outcrops, a journey of at least 8 km would have been required to reach them.

Micaceous sandstone was utilised at Huizui to produce thin, rectangular or semi-circular knives and sickles (Figure 7.1). The tool blanks were already close to ideal size and thickness, so during manufacture only the edges were trimmed to create the shape and to bevel the working edge (Ford 2001: 60). The body of the tool generally received only a light grinding or polishing to smooth the surface. Micaceous sandstone was also used in small amounts as grinding slabs (Figure 7.1).

There are two factors that make the micaceous sandstone particularly suitable for production of knives and sickles. Firstly, the presence of muscovite flakes aligned parallel to bedding means that beds of micaceous sandstone could be broken readily into even sheets of appropriate thickness for tool production at the quarry site, thus making the initial reduction of the knife and sickle tool blanks more efficient and less time-consuming. Secondly, the fine, even, well-cemented texture and the predominant quartzose mineralogy (quartz is tough with a hardness of 7) meant that tools of micaceous sandstone take a moderately sharp edge that is resistant to chipping (Xie 2005).

3.4 Other varieties of sandstone

Apart from the fine-grained micaceous sandstone already discussed, fine, medium and coarse-grained varieties of sandstone are found in large amounts at Huizui (Table 7.1). These sandstones are composed predominantly of quartz, although the coarser-grained ones generally have a substantial component of weathered feldspar grains. The colour varies considerably, from violet or maroon to pale grey or cream; the coarse-grained feldspathic sandstones tend to be lighter-coloured, whereas the finer-grained varieties often have a violet or reddish colour due to the presence of ferruginous laminae and ferruginous coatings on the quartz grains.

At a ground stone tool manufacturing site like Huizui, large amounts of abrasive material are required, and this was supplied by these sandstones (Ford 2001, 2004, 2007, 2009), which are present both as blocks of raw material and as grinding slabs (Figure 7.1). The coarser sandstones were probably used for initial grinding of the stone tools, with the finer sandstones employed to smooth surfaces and sharpen edges (Owen 2006). Final polishing would have required an even finer medium, most likely an organic product or very fine clay/silt sediment; rare grinding slabs made of siltstone (Figure 7.1) may also have been used for this purpose.

The sandstone at Huizui used for grinding stones was likely sourced from two hills of Lower Triassic sandstones located nearby (Figure 7.2a, b), which was confirmed by thin-section analysis comparing these sources to artefactual material from Huizui (Ford 2009). The hill ~1.5 km to the southwest of Huizui is composed of white, medium-coarse grained, feldspathic sandstone, whilst the hill to the northeast, which lies within 500 metres of one of the excavation sites, is composed predominantly of fine-grained quartzose ferruginous violet-coloured sandstone. Both outcrops show evidence for quarrying, although much of it appears to be sub-modern; in addition, large sandstone boulders and cobbles litter the hillsides, and could have been easily transported to Huizui. Similar sized cobbles and boulders have been found at Huizui in their natural state (Ford 2001: 45).

3.5 Fine-grained limestone and lime

Fine-grained dolomite, which is very abundant in the northern slopes of the Song Mountains, was used to manufacture a small proportion of spades. This lithology is grey to cream-brown in colour and generally uniform and massive in appearance, although some samples show distinctive elongate or subcircular spots that represent burrows in the original limestone when it was deposited. The fine-grained dolomite is composed of interlocking dolomite crystals, with some variation in grain size, and probably has similar mechanical properties to oolitic dolomite. Its limited use at Huizui compared to oolitic dolomite may be attributed to the fact that it does not outcrop as pavements; the oolitic dolomite is far easier to extract. In terms of sourcing, the fine dolomite artefacts are not lithologically distinctive and could have been quarried almost anywhere on the northern flanks of the Song Mountains.

Fine-grained grey limestone occurs occasionally as tools, predominantly as spades (Figure 7.1). Fine-grained limestone is finer and less even grained than dolomite (although much the same hardness), and so may fracture more unpredictably, making it less suitable for tool manufacture.

Limestone is more commonly present as irregular pieces, often with a white, chalky appearance; these were used in lime production. Lime is produced by heating limestone; this converts the calcite ($CaCO_3$) of the limestone to lime (calcium hydroxide; $Ca(OH)_2$). Lime absorbs carbon dioxide from the atmosphere to form a white, chalky variety of limestone, hardening in the process; this is the basis for crushed lime, used as mortar. Crushed lime is also suitable for making house floors, and this was one of its uses at Huizui.

A large number of white, chalky blocks were found in the excavations (Table 7.1). Mineralogical analysis using X-ray diffraction showed that most of these are composed of calcite, so they represent limestone blocks that were heated to form lime and have since reverted to chalky limestone. However, one piece represents heated dolomite, as it is made up of a mixture of calcite and hydromagnesite. Heating converts dolomite ($CaMg(CO_3)_2$) to a mixture of calcium hydroxide and magnesium hydroxide; these then absorb carbon dioxide to form calcite and magnesium carbonate (hydromagnesite) respectively.

Lime was occasionally produced from defective/broken limestone tools; one limestone spade has a white, chalky appearance giving clear evidence of burning (Figure 7.1).

Limestone outcrops extensively on the southern flanks of the northernmost E-W ridge of the Song Mountains (Figure 7.5). The limestone pieces and tools found in the excavations are not distinctive and could have been sourced from anywhere in this area. Just like the fine micaceous sandstone, which also outcrops on the southern flanks of this ridge (Figure 7.5), a journey of at least eight km would have been required to reach the limestone outcrops from Huizui. Although dolomite is present much closer, limestone is strongly preferred for lime manufacture, because lime made from dolomite has inferior properties.

3.6 Very fine-grained siliceous rocks (chert, silicified siltstone, rhyolite)

Chert and rhyolite are both very fine-grained siliceous lithologies, although with very different geological origins. These materials occur in small but significant numbers in the Huizui assemblages (Table 7.1). The very fine grain size and lack of distinctive features often makes these materials hard to distinguish from each other, although the rhyolite pieces are often a distinctive red colour.

Chert at Huizui varies in colour but is mostly grey or black, and is used to produce chisels and arrowheads. Although chert is found close to Huizui, it is low quality and unlikely to be the source material. Chert concretions within the upper part of the Fengshan Formation are small and porous, as are the chert cobbles present within Pleistocene gravel beds near Huizui.

Red rhyolite artefacts include a fragment of bracelet dating to the Yangshao period, indicating that red rhyolite was used to made ornaments. During the Erlitou and Longshan periods, tools included a chisel, a small polished ball 10 mm in diameter and an arrowhead. The red rhyolite is very fine grained and often lacks phenocrysts. A few pieces of grey ignimbritic rhyolite are also present, which are identified by their characteristic flattened pumice fragments (fiamme).

Apart from the Yangshao rhyolite tools, there is no evidence for manufacture of very fine-grained siliceous materials on site at Huizui, so it is likely that these lithologies were exotic materials, with tools being brought to Huizui as finished products. Rhyolite is not recorded from the Song Mountains, so it is almost certainly exotic.

3.7 Marble

Marble is a rare raw material at Huizui (Table 7.1) and was used to produce a small number of tools, including an axe and grinding slab, as well as more decorative items like a bracelet and a stone slab. The marble varies substantially in colour (white, green and brown) and grain size (fine to medium); some samples are foliated. The variety of marble types and its presence only as finished tools suggests that this lithology is exotic and probably sourced from more than one location. Marble is present within the Precambrian basement of the southern Song Mountains (Figure 7.2).

The rarity of items made from marble may indicate that these were elite or status goods. During the Neolithic, marble was used in central China for both elite items (Liu 2000: 149) and utilitarian items (Institute of Archaeology 1999a). This included grinding slabs and mortars, which were found at the site Shizhaocun and Xishanping in Gansu Province, which date to the Neolithic and Early Bronze Age periods respectively (Institute of Archaeology 1999a).

Marble was used for utilitarian purposes such as sickles and adzes at the urban centre site of Erlitou (Institute of Archaeology 1999b: 401), but may have been an elite item at the regional centres that did not have access to other status items such as jade and bronze. During the later Erligang period (Shang dynasty), white stones such as white jade and marble, were preferred for use in elite or ritual stone tools and may have been associated with the same status as the white kaolin pottery which was used by elite classes (Yang 1996: 72).

3.8 Other metamorphic rocks (gneiss, quartzite, schist, slate)

A variety of other metamorphic rocks are present at Huizui, but in small numbers (Table 7.1). The higher-grade metamorphics, such as gneiss and quartzite, were found mostly in finished tool form at Huizui. Gneiss was used to make an axe, chisel and a spade tool blank. Quartzite was used for hammerstones and grinding slabs (Figure 7.1). The lower grade metamorphic rocks, such as schist and slate, are much softer raw materials and do not feature significantly in stone tool production. Slate was used for two knife tool blanks but these were broken prior to completion, showing the fragile nature of the raw material, as well as one finished arrowhead.

Both low and high grade metamorphic rocks are present in the Precambrian basement in the southern Song Mountains, and quartzite cobbles are found in Majian River gravels within five km of Huizui.

3.9 Quartz

The few quartz fragments present are poor quality, milky vein quartz. This lithology probably occurs in the Precambrian basement to the south.

3.10 Medium and coarse-grained igneous rocks (diorite, aplite, gabbro, granite)

The very small amount of igneous rock material (apart from rhyolite) present was used to make a few tools, including a chisel (diorite) and knives (aplite and gabbro; Figure 7.1). All of these materials have a strong crystalline structure, so tools manufactured from these lithologies have sharp, durable working edges, and can withstand large amounts of force during use.

The presence of aplite cobbles within the Huizui excavations suggests that this raw material was obtained from river gravels, possibly from the Majian River; this flows within 5 km of Huizui, and drains an area in the Precambrian basement in the southern Song Mountains where aplite occurs (Figure 7.1b).

3.11 Crystalline calcite and dolomite (including stalagmite)

Within the assemblage are several dolomite and calcite cleavage fragments (Table 7.1). Both these minerals have perfect rhombohedral cleavage (3 cleavage directions at ~120°), so large crystals that are struck will break into rhombohedral fragments. In addition there are a few pieces of crystalline calcite that display typical stalagmite fabrics: colour banding and/or elongate crystals often arranged in radiating sheaves.

The calcite and dolomite crystals could have been derived locally from veins within the Cambrian carbonate sequence. The stalagmite material could also be local, as small caves are known within the northern Song Mountains.

3.12 Turquoise and jade?

Two turquoise beads and two pieces of possible poor quality jade, patterned dark brown and green in colour, were excavated at Huizui. Both jade and turquoise were used to produce high status or elite items. There is no evidence for the manufacture of these items at Huizui, but there was a turquoise workshop at the urban centre of Erlitou (Liu and Xu 2007). Turquoise items may have been produced only in Erlitou and redistributed to regional elites. It is not clear if jade was also manufactured in Erlitou, although jade items, including small beads, have been recovered from elite graves and pits at this site (Childs-Johnson 1995: 64). The sources of the turquoise and jade recovered from Erlitou have not yet been identified.

4. FACTORS DETERMINING THE CHOICE OF RAW MATERIALS AT HUIZUI

From a review of the raw material selections made at Huizui, there appear to be at least three major factors determining the choices made: proximity to source, and functional (mechanical) and extractive raw material properties.

The five main lithologies used at Huizui (oolitic dolomite, diabase, fine micaceous sandstone, other varieties of sandstone and fine limestone) can all be sourced within eight kilometres of the site. Perhaps the most important factor was the proximity to sources of sandstone for grinding. As sandstone was the main abrasive used in ground stone tool production at Huizui, the ready availability of large quantities of this raw material was extremely important. Huizui is located 500 m to 1.5 km away from sandstone hills which provided an abundant source of abrasive material.

However, proximity to source is not the only factor in raw material selection. There is also clear evidence of raw material specialisation, whereby larger functional groups of stone tools are clearly associated with a dominant lithology (Figure 7.1). Furthermore, there are many lithologies available within the Song Mountains that were not utilised at Huizui. Properties of the raw materials themselves must therefore have had an impact in raw material selection.

Raw material properties can be divided into two main categories: functional (mechanical) and extractive. As suggested above, all of the functional groups of stone tools at Huizui are linked with a particular lithology. Woodworking tools (axes, adzes and chisels) require a raw material that can withstand force and provide a strong, sharp working edge. Diabase was selected to produce these tools as it is strong and tough, and can be polished to a sharp and efficient working edge which is easily resharpened. Tools which were required for lower impact duties, such as spades used for digging loess, were made from softer raw materials, in this case oolitic dolomite. This raw material can be ground and polished easily, thus making manufacture relatively quick and efficient. Oolitic dolomite is not as strong or durable as diabase, but for digging loess, those properties were not an important consideration.

Apart from functional (mechanical) properties of raw materials, the efficiency of extraction of the original tool blank is also an important factor in determining raw material selection. By choosing raw materials which are already close to the desired finished product, the time and effort required to reduce the raw material is minimised, thus increasing the efficiency of the overall production of the stone tool.

The lithologies used at Huizui were both quarried from outcrop and obtained from river gravels. The oolitic dolomite and fine micaceous sandstone were quarried in areas where these raw materials split along natural cleavage plans into thin slabs, already close to the desired thickness of the final product (spades and knives respectively). This was probably particularly important for oolitic dolomite; fine-grained dolomite has similar mechanical properties to oolitic dolomite, is much more common and occurs closer to Huizui, but does not outcrop as exposed pavements that can be easily quarried as thin slabs, and as a result was used to manufacture only a small proportion of spades.

Diabase was obtained as river cobbles, which are close in size and shape to the desired end-product (finished axes/adzes/chisels), with minimal shaping required. Furthermore, river gravels represent an effective test of internal toughness, as any major flaws will cause fracturing during fluvial transport.

Apart from the dominant raw material types, the other lithologies recorded at Huizui were all used in very small amounts, and many are finished tools. These lithologies probably represent a combination of imported finished tools from other stone tool production sites, targeted procurement due to perceptions of quality or value, and experimentation with raw materials acquired opportunistically.

In summary, it would appear that the choice of raw materials used at Huizui was a reflection of proximity to source, functional properties and efficiency of extraction of tool blanks. The stone tool producers at Huizui were making cost efficient decisions about raw material selection based on these factors.

Acknowledgements: We are thankful to the members of the Yiluo Archaeology Team, Li Liu, Xingcan Chen, Ming Wei, Gyoung-Ah Lee, Arlene Rosen, Li Yongqiang, Xie Liye, Wei Xingtao, Wang Facheng, Wang Hongzhang, Yang Junfeng, Sheahan Bestel, Geoffrey Hewitt, Liz Kilpatrick, and Charles Hartley. We are also grateful to Guowei Xu and Cameron Cairns, who provided geological information and expertise, and Dale Owen, who provided photographs of dolomite spades. This project was supported by a Discovery Project grant from the Australian Research Council (DP0450025).

REFERENCES

Bureau of Geology and Mineral Resources of Henan Province, 1984. *Regional Geology of Henan Province*. Geological Publishing House, Beijing.

Childs-Johnson, E. 1995. Symbolic Jades of the Erlitou Period: A Xia Royal Tradition. *Archives of Asian Art* 48: 64-92.

Cochrane, G., G. Quick and D. Spencer-Jones. 1995. *Introducing Victorian Geology*. Geological Society of Australia, Melbourne.

Ford, A., 2001. *States and Stones: Ground Stone Tool Production at Huizui, China.* Honours dissertation, Archaeology Program, La Trobe University, Melbourne.

Ford, A., 2004. Ground Stone Tool Production at Huizui, China: An Analysis of a Manufacturing Site in the Yiluo River

Basin. *Indo-Pacific Prehistory Association Bulletin* 24: 71-78.

Ford, A. 2007. Stone Tool Production-Distribution Systems during the *Early Bronze Age at Huizui, China*. Unpublished Masters Thesis, La Trobe University, Melbourne.

Ford, A. 2009. Stone Tool Production-Distribution Systems at Huizui, China. *Internet Archaeology 26: Proceedings of the Implement Petrology Conference*. http://intarch.ac.uk/journal/issue26/ford_index.html.

Garber, J. 1989. *Archaeology at Cerros, Belize, Central America, Volume 2*. Southern Methodist University Press, Dallas.

Gorton, J. 2003. *Cambrian Sediments in the Songshan Range, Henan Province, China and* their *Archaeological Significance*. Honours dissertation, Department of Earth Sciences, La Trobe University, Melbourne.

Institute of Archaeology, Chinese Academy of Social Sciences. 1999a. *Shizhaocun and Xishanping*. China Publishing House, Beijing.

Institute of Archaeology, Chinese Academy of Social Sciences. 1999b. *Yanshi Erlitou*. Zhongguo Dabaikequanshu Press, Beijing.

Liu, L., 2000. Ancestor Worship: An Archaeological Investigation of Ritual Activities in Neolithic North China. *Journal of East Asian Archaeology* 2: 129-164.

Liu, L., 2006. Urbanization in China: Erlitou and its hinterland. In *Urbanism in the* Preindustrial *World: Cross-Cultural Approaches*. G. Storey, pp. 161-189. Tuscaloosa: University of Alabama Press.

Liu, L. and X. Chen. 2003. *State Formation in Early China*. London: Duckworth.

Liu, L. and X. Chen. 2007. Non-state crafts in the early Chinese state: An archaeological view from the Erlitou hinterland. *Indo-Pacific Prehistory Association Bulletin*.

Liu, L. and H. Xu. 2007. Rethinking Erlitou: legend, history and Chinese archaeology. *Antiquity* 81: 886-901.

Liu, L., X. Chen, Y. Lee, H. Wright and A. Rosen. 2004. Settlement Patterns and Development of Social Complexity in the Yiluo Region, North China. *Journal of Field Archaeology* 29(1-2): 75-100.

Meng, X., M. Ge and M. E. Tucker. 1997. Sequence stratigraphy, sea-level changes and depositional systems in the Cambro-Ordovician of the North China carbonate platform. *Sedimentary Geology* 114: 189-222.

Meyerhoff, A. A., M. Kamen-Kaye, C. Chen and I. Taner. 1991. *China: Stratigraphy, Paleogeography and Tectonics*. Kluwer Academic Publishers, Dordrecht.

Owen, D., 2006. *When to call a spade a spade: an exercise in experimental archaeology on an ancient Chinese stone tool*. B.A. Honours thesis, Archaeology Program, La Trobe University.

Webb, J., A. Ford and J. Gorton. 2007. Influences on selection of lithic raw material sources at Huizui, a Neolithic/Early Bronze Age site in Northern China, *Indo-Pacific Prehistory Association Bulletin* 27: 76-86.

Xie, L., 2005. *A Preliminary Study of Functional Analysis in Ground Stone Tools: Usewear analysis of stone axes and knives from Erlitou*. Masters Dissertation, Graduate *School*, Chinese Academy of Social Sciences, Beijing.

Yang, Mei-Li.1996. A Study of the Jade Ge-Dagger. In *the Journal of Chinese Jade, edited* by S. Bernstein, pp. 64-113. S. Bernstein & Co., San Francisco.

Zhu, X., 1989. *Chinese Sedimentary Basins*. Elsevier Scientific Publications, Amsterdam.

CHAPTER 8   NON-STATE CRAFTS IN THE EARLY CHINESE STATE: AN ARCHAEOLOGICAL VIEW FROM THE ERLITOU HINTERLAND①

1. INTRODUCTION: STATE CRAFTS VS. NON-STATE CRAFTS

Since Gordon Childe (1936; 1950) first pointed out that craft specialization was a major component of the urban revolution, many studies have attempted to demonstrate a close link between the development of craft specialization and the emergence of civilization/state (e.g., Adams 1966; Chang 1980). Three general models have been put forward by archaeologists to characterize different forms of craft specialization; these are, (1) attached specialization under elite supervision, for making primarily prestige items used as status symbols; (2) independent specialization without elite involvement, for making utilitarian goods demanded by the general public; and (3) manufacture by embedded specialists who are themselves members of elite groups and who make prestige items for inner circles of the elite (Brumfiel and Earle 1987; Costin 2001). It is not surprising to see that most studies of craft production in state-level societies focus on the first and third categories, to illustrate elite behaviours in the sociopolitical process, while few investigations have particularly targeted the political function of independent nonelite craft production during the process of social change (Schortman and Urban 2004). A similar situation also can be seen in Chinese archaeology, in that most studies are related to state-sponsored crafts, such as bronze ritual items, in the political centres of Erlitou, Zhengzhou and Anyang (Bagley 1990, 1999; Li 2003; Liu 2003; Liu and Chen 2003). This situation needs to be changed, because it has prevented us from gaining a fuller understanding the formation of early states in China.

It has been suggested that early states in China can be described as territorial states, which often show particular characteristics in craft production, particularly with state involved prestige items (Liu and Chen 2003; Trigger 1999, 2003). In general, territorial states tend to have two tiers of craft

---

① This chapter is written by Liu Li, Chen Xingcan and Li Baoping, post on *Indo-Pacific Prehistory Association Bulletin*, 2007(27) : 93-102.

production. On the one hand, royal workshops produced specialised products with high symbolic significance at or near the royal court, and craftsmen around the court and provincial centres produced less valuable luxury goods required by the state. On the other hand, farmers used locally available materials to manufacture utilitarian goods for themselves and their neighbours, mostly on a part-time basis (Trigger 2003: 368-374). However, this proposition needs to be tested.

Archaeological studies of early states in China have traditionally focused on large urban centres, where most indicators of a highly stratified society are easily observable. These studies tend to reveal mainly material remains of the urban high elite, but neglect the activities of the lesser elite and commoners in the surrounding areas, which are equally important for understanding the social formation at the regional level. In contrast to these traditional approaches, our recent archaeological project, focused on the Huizui site in the Yiluo region, aims to obtain some insights into the sociopolitical process in the hinterland of the earliest state, centred at Erlitou.

Based on regional surveys in the Yiluo basin, settlement patterns in the Erlitou core area show a highly centralized political system (Erlitou Working Team 2005; Liu et al. 2002-2004; Xu et al. 2004), and material remains uncovered from the Erlitou site indicate a well developed hierarchical society (Erlitou Working Team 2004, 2005; Institute of Archaeology 1999). Huizui appears to have been a regional centre during the Yangshao and Longshan periods (c. 5000-2000 BC), and then to have become a secondary centre of the Erlitou state during the early part of the second millennium BC, followed by settlement in the Eastern Zhou. This site was a stone tool production locus, whose major products, dolomite spades, appear to have been distributed to the surrounding areas (Liu et al.2002-2004). Huizui therefore provides a unique opportunity for investigating (1) a long-term sociopolitical change at one settlement, (2) inter-settlement relationships in the region, and (3) craft specialization in relation to the production and distribution of utilitarian goods.

This study is unique in several aspects, which have long been neglected by Chinese archaeologists in general. The products under study in this project were both utilitarian and prestige items, their production occurred away from the major political centre, and their primary consumers were commoners and lesser elites across the region. These factors manifest a sharp contrast to the circumstances of high prestige items produced at the urban centres, providing a new perspective on the political economy of the Erlitou state.

In order to understand the regional social formation of the Erlitou state, in this paper we will focus on the production and distribution of spades and white pottery around the Yiluo region. We will demonstrate that craftsmen engaged in non-state craft production in regional communities played a significant role in the sociopolitical fabric of the early state.

2. HUIZUI STONE WORKSHOPS

The Huizui site is located in areas east and northwest of the modern village of Huizui in Yanshi county, Henan province. As the existing site is separated by a wide gully whose time of formation is unclear, we refer to the two areas of the site as Huizui East and Huizui West (Figure 8.1). The Yangshao and late Longshan people first occupied the site at Huizui East, then the Erlitou people extended their residence to both Huizui East and West, and finally the Eastern Zhou people resided again at Huizui East. The entire site measures about 25 ha, but the occupation area for each cultural phase varied. Soil erosion and modern intensive agricultural practices, particularly land levelling, have dramatically changed the Huizui landscape. Much topsoil, more than 1 m in thickness, has been removed in the past decades, in order to transform the original sloping land into modern terraces for farming. As a result, a large quantity of archaeological deposits have been destroyed, and the remaining occupation areas, particularly for the Longshan and Erlitou periods, are likely to be much smaller than their original sizes. Few remains of Eastern Zhou have been found, including only water wells and

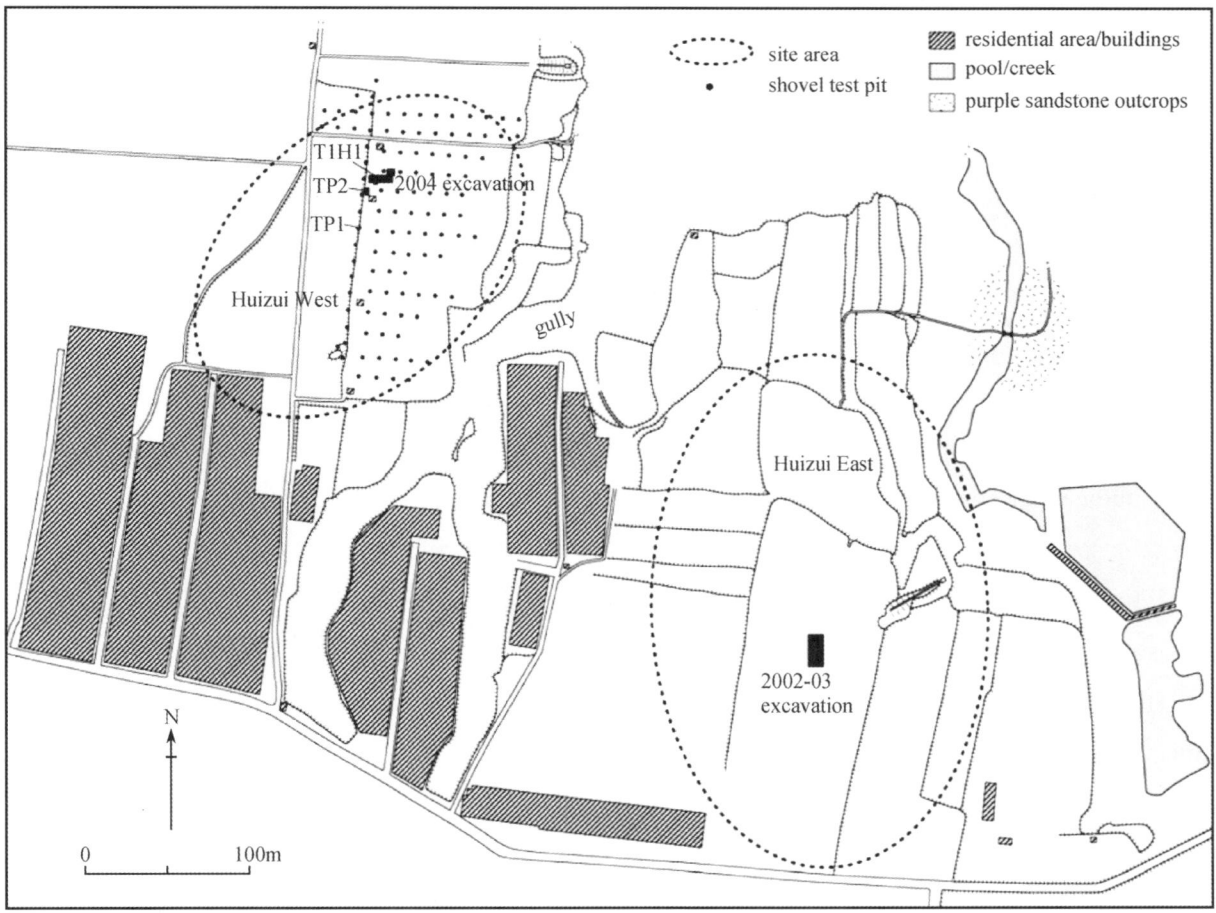

Figure 8.1 Map of Huizui and location of excavation areas

burials, suggesting that most Zhou deposits have been eroded by nature or removed by humans (Henan 1st Team 2004).

Huizui was excavated first in the 1950s by Henan archaeologists, and then in 2002-2006 by our Yiluo team. A total area of 665 sq. m at both Huizui East and West has been excavated, revealing deposits up to 4 m in thickness and dating to a long period from Yangshao, through late Longshan, to Erlitou. Archaeologists have identified Hui zui as a locus of stone tool manufacture since the 1950s, as suggested by abundant blanks readily visible on the ground surface. In order to determine the development of craft production and the level of specialisation at Huizui, we have employed several methods in our fieldwork; these include intensive survey, shovel tests, and excavation.

The remaining Yangshao occupation area is about 6 ha (Figure 8.1), which is perhaps fairly close to the original settlement size, as the Yangshao deposits appear to have been the least disturbed, compared to those of the later cultures. The preliminary results of our study show that flakes recovered from the Yangshao deposits are scarce and made of diverse rock types, none of which is particularly dominant. This suggests that the Yangshao population at Huizui produced stone artefacts, using various lithic materials available in the nearby areas, perhaps mainly for their own uses.

The remaining site size for the Longshan period measured about 3 ha. Within this area numerous flakes and blanks were found, sometimes in high concentrations. In two ash pits (H100, H101), for example, many blanks and a few thousand flakes were unearthed; the flakes are small in size, mostly under 5 mm in length. They are predominantly of dolomite, among several other rock types, and the shapes and material of blanks match the stone spades uncovered at the site. The lithic debris in these pits is likely to have been the manufacturing waste associated with nearby lithic workshops. These pits associated with lithic debris also yielded various kinds of domestic refuse, such as animal bones, pottery sherds, plant remains, and tools. They are also found in close proximity to such features as water wells, houses, and burials, indicating that lithic workshops were located within the residential area, and the production was likely operated at the household level. It is quite clear that, starting from the late Longshan period, Huizui became a stone tool production locus, particularly for making dolomite spades. Unfortunately, we are unable to determine the original size of the lithic manufacturing area; but the distribution of lithic production debris over the entire remaining Longshan occupation area suggests that the craft specialisation was most likely practiced by a large part of the community.

During the Erlitou period, lithic manufacture continued, and the production area extended to both Huizui East and West (Figure 8.1). For the reasons mentioned above, most Erlitou deposits at Huizui East have been destroyed, causing difficulties in estimating the site size. Since the upper deposits of the site were destroyed by recent agricultural activities, it is quite possible that many of those stone artefacts collected from ground survey were derived from disturbed Longshan and Erlitou deposits. This inference, however, does not help us to determine the original site sizes at Huizui East. At Huizui

West, the Erlitou deposits are less disturbed, so we estimate an area of 3 ha for the Erlitou occupation. In this area, lithic flakes and blanks were recovered from shovel tests, terrace cuts and excavation trenches situated over the remaining site, confirming that lithic manufacture was carried out over the entire occupation area.

Huizui people appear to have produced various types of tools using different raw materials. These mainly include spades made of dolomite; axes, adzes and chisels made of diabase; knives and sickles made of micaceous fine sandstone; and grinding slabs made of sandstone. Ninety-four blanks and semi-finished tools collected on the surface at Huizui West during the 2000 survey show a pattern in which dolomite is the dominant material (78% by number), followed by much smaller proportions of other materials (Ford 2001) (Figure 8.2A). Dolomite flakes account for an even higher proportion (92% by weight) of lithic materials from heavy fractions of 111 flotation samples obtained from a pit (T1H1 spits 2-4) in the 2004 excavation (Figure 8.2B). Such high ratios of dolomite in blanks and flakes are in sharp contrast to the corresponding ratios seen in the finished tool assemblage from the 1959 excavation, in which spades (mostly made of oolitic dolomite) only account for 22% of the major tool types dating to the Erlitou period (Figure 8.2C).

At Huizui West, similar to Huizui East, excavations have revealed domestic features (such as houses, water wells, burials, and ash pits) filled with animal bones, pottery sherds, charred plant remains, as well as blanks and flakes. We have identified three locations with high concentrations of dolomite and sandstone blanks and flakes.

Based on their depositional forms, the first locale at TP1 was the workplace of a stonemason, the second one at TP2 was a debris dump, perhaps next to a house wall, and the third one at T1H1 was also a debris dump, probably in a courtyard. TP1 and TP2 appear to have been contemporary (Erlitou phase II), and were spaced about 25 m apart, a length perhaps indicating the distance between two households/workshops (Figure 8.1).

These remains from the Erlitou deposits show a similar pattern that is also observable in the Longshan occupation area at Huizui, suggesting that lithic manufacture occurred continuously within household settings during the Erlitou period; craft specialisation was practiced at the community level, and the major products were dolomite spades, not only for local use but also for trade and exchange.

3. LITHIC RAW MATERIAL PROCUREMENT

Three types of lithics for making spades have been identified from the Huizui lithic assemblage: oolitic dolomite, dolomite and limestone. The first type is the most dominant in quantity. At Huizui most stone blanks and semifinished spades are rectangular in shape, ranging roughly 10-40 cm long,

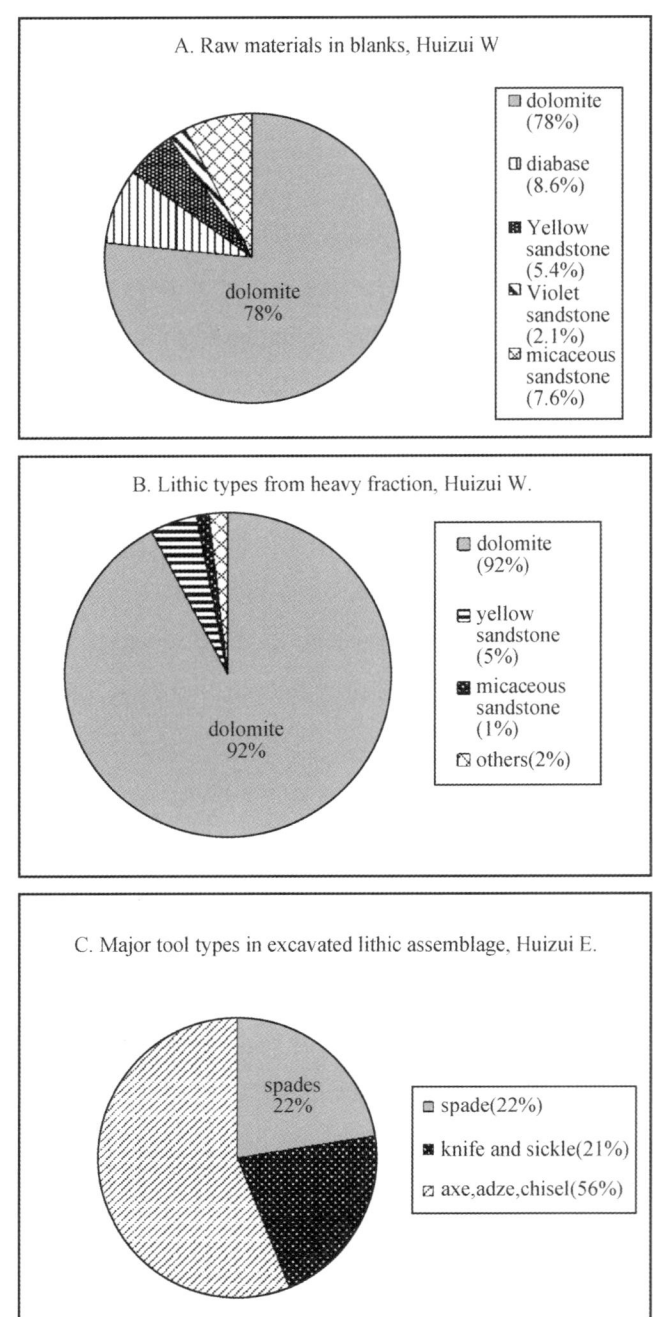

Figure 8.2 Ratio of raw materials in blanks, lithic types from heavy fraction, major tool types in Huizui
A. Ratio of dolomite blanks from surface survey (total number: 94); B. ratio of dolomite in lithic flakes from 111 heavy fraction samples (total weight: 6654.8 g); C. ratio of spades made of mainly dolomite from excavated tools (total number:72), Huizui, Erlitou period

6-15 cm wide, and 2-4 cm thick. The raw materials were quarried from dolomite outcrops along the Songshan Mountains, about 4-5 km to the south of Huizui. The outcrops of oolitic dolomite show thin-bedded formation, distributed along the northern side of the mountain ranges (see John Webb's paper in this volume). Dolomite has no advantages, in terms of its hardness, for making stone tools. But it was easily quarried with Stone Age technology before use of metal tools or explosives, and its thin-bedded formation on the outcrops provides the right thickness for fabricating into thin and long spades. Therefore it makes perfect sense that ancient people choose this raw material for making spades.

Correlating with the distribution of dolomite outcrops about 12 km E-W in our survey area, there are four Erlitou sites located near the foothills of the mountain ranges, including Zhaiwan, Huizui, Xiahousi, and Xikouzi. These sites are spaced 2.5-4.5 km apart from one another, and all with similar distances (3-5 km) to the nearby dolomite outcrops (Figure 8.3). Our survey team has found dolomite blanks of similar forms from all four sites. Among these four sites, only Huizui shows clear evidence of tool manufacture from the Longshan to Erlitou periods. Zhaiwan has a similar occupation span as Huizui, and may have also produced spades in the Longshan and Erlitou periods.

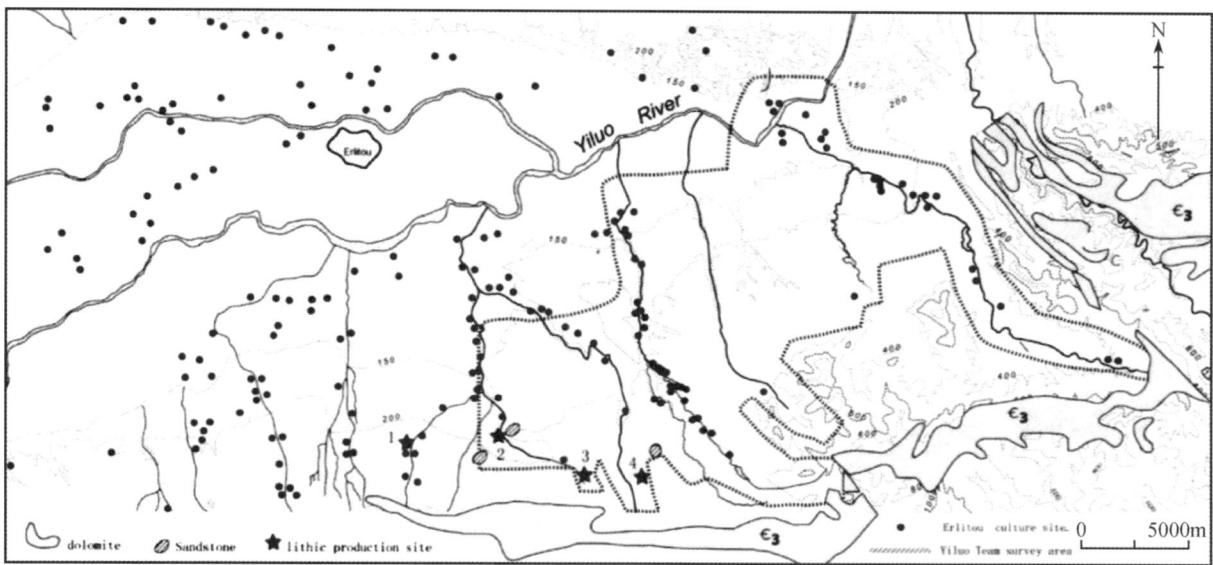

Figure 8.3 Distribution of Erlitou culture sites in the Yiluo region, showing the locations of spade production sites in relation to dolomite resource. Oolitic dolomite outcrops are in embedded in the dolomite deposits. Sites are surveyed by the Yiluo Team and Erlitou team (Erlitou Team survey results based on Erlitou Working Team 2005)

Spade production sites: 1. Zhaiwan; 2. Huizui; 3. Xiahousi; 4. Xikouzi

Two other sites appear to have been occupied only during the Erlitou period. If our survey data are reliable, there seems to have been a dramatic increase in spade production in the region, as the number of manufacturing centres increased from probably two during the Longshan period to four at the time of Erlitou. However, this needs to be tested in the future.

Considering the large area of the Yiluo basin, within which most settlements were not near lithic resources, the oolitic dolomite outcrops along a 12 km range of the Songshan Mountains were by no means a widely available raw material. However, since we have not surveyed the entire northern range of the Songshan Mountains, it is difficult to estimate how many more stone tool production sites still await discovery. The oolitic dolomite rock bed occurs in Upper Cambrian deposits along the northern side of the Songshan Mountains; its western part ends a few kilometres to the southwest of Zhaiwan, while its eastern part stretches many kilometres into the mountain ranges. So, it is possible more oolitic dolomite outcrops are available in the eastern areas. Nevertheless, not all oolitic dolomite outcrops would attract settlers and become sources of stone tools, since several factors may have restricted the suitability of a locale as a stone tool production centre. Given that the stonemasons were most likely agriculturalists with part-time craft specialization, and all so that stone raw material is heavy and difficult to transport over long distances, a ground stone production community should (1) have sizable farmland near the toolmakers' settlement, to provide sufficient agricultural supplies; (2) be located within a single day's return journey of the lithic sources; and (3) be close to sandstone sources for grinding slabs. The full-coverage regional surveys in the Yiluo basin (Erlitou Working Team 2005; Liu et al. 2002-2004) have not encountered many such optimal locations elsewhere, although more investigations have been planned to search for sites particularly suitable for lithic production.

Our surveys have revealed some interesting characteristics of the process of raw material procurement. A stone ball and a hammer stone of non-local materials, along with many oolitic dolomite flakes, were found scattered over a small site, Jiulongshuiku W (about 1500 sq. m in area), on a foothill, less than 100 m from an ancient quarry to the south of the Xikouzi site. It may have been a locale where stonemasons flaked the preforms after quarrying. No site has been found between the four spademaking settlements mentioned above and the dolomite outcrops, indicating direct access to the raw material by the production communities. The distance of 3-5 km between the settlements and outcrops appears to have been the optimal distance for craftsmen to complete several tasks for the raw material procurement within a day. These tasks include: walking to the lithic outcrops, quarrying the stone, roughly flaking the stone into preforms, and carrying the preforms home. The fact that our excavations at Huizui have yielded few large flakes (Chen 2005) supports the scenario that the first stage of manufacture, flaking preforms, may have been completed near the quarries before the raw material reached the tool production sites. This hypothesis nevertheless needs to be tested in the future.

That the production communities obtained the raw material directly from the mountains suggests that these communities may have controlled the access to these outcrops, many of which are situated on the pathways to the mountains. The relatively equidistant distribution of the four spade production settlements also suggests a competitive relationship between them. Huizui may have been in competition with its counterparts for controlling the raw material resources and for trading their products. This proposition will be tested in future by excavating the three other settlements, to see whether or not a similar manufacture process took place there.

3.1 Distribution of the oolitic dolomite spades

At Huizui 64% of spades were made of oolitic dolomite, while 36% were made of fine dolomite, siltstone, micaceous fine sandstone and fine sandstone. This suggests that oolitic dolomite was the chief material, but not the only material, for manufacturing spades used by Huizui people. In contrast, the predominant stone tool debitage from the lithic concentration areas, for example at Pit 04T1H1, is oolitic dolomite, indicating that oolitic dolomite was the exclusive raw material for the spades made for exporting to elsewhere. This phenomenon helps us to identify the spatial distribution of Huizui spade products in the region.

Unfortunately, the lithic materials used for ordinary tools are normally not identified in archaeological reports, so it is difficult to trace the distribution of certain stone products, even if their location of manufacture is known. In order to investigate the distribution sphere of oolitic dolomite spades, we examined stone artefact assemblages from seven Erlitou culture sites, including Huizui, in the Yiluo and Zhengzhou regions, distributed about 200 km from east to west (Table 8.1).

Table 8.1 Inventory of dolomite artefacts from eight Erlitou culture sites in the Yiluo and Zhengzhou regions

Site	No. of spades of all types of raw materials	No. of oolitic dolo mite spades (% of oolitic dolomite in all spades)	Distance from Huizui (as bird flies)	References
Huizui in Yanshi	11	7 (64%)		Henan Institute of Cultural Relics 1990
Erlitou in Yanshi	41	10 (24%)	15 km to NW	Data collected by Xie, Liye
Shaochai in Gongyi *	23	5 (22%)	20 km to NE	Henan Institute of Cultural Relics 1993
Huadizui in Gongyi	14	2 (14%)	35 km to NE	Identified by John Webb, 2006
Zaojiaoshu in Luoyang	6 examined (reported 16)	6 (100%)	30 km to W	Identified by John Webb, 2006
Zhengyao in Mianchi	24	3 (12.5%)	100 km to W	Henan Institute of Cultural Relics 1987
Nanwa in Dengfeng	9 examined (total number unknown)	5 (56%)	20 km to S, on the southern side of the Song Mountains	Identified by John Webb, 2006
Luodamiao in Zhengzhou	34 examined (reported 47)	0 (0%)	70 km to E on the eastern side of the Song Mountains	Henan Institute of Cultural Relics 1989

* The Shaochai spades include both Erlitou and Erligang periods, and it is not possible to separate them based on the data available us.

It would be ideal to analyse the ratios of oolitic dolomite spades in the stone tool assemblages from all these sites, in order to observe the correlations between the proportion of the raw material in tool assemblages and the distance from the production centre. However, since we were unable to obtain the complete assemblages of stone artefacts from these sites, our samples are not systematically collected. This prevents us from conducting further statistical analysis.

Oolitic dolomite spades have been identified from Erlitou culture sites up to 100 km from Huizui, as exemplified by Zhengyao at the western end of the Yiluo basin (Fig. 4). It is notable that dolomite spades account for a very low percentage in the spade assemblage (24%) at the Erlitou site as compared to other sites (Table 8.1). These data suggest that, as an urban population with rather heterogeneous origins, the Erlitou people obtained tools from various sources. It is also possible that Erlitou, as a political and economic centre, received tributary goods and labour from all surrounding regions where various raw materials were used for making spades. In any event, a part of the tool assemblage at the Erlitou site, no matter how small it might be, may have derived from Huizui.

The distribution of oolitic dolomite spades and other types of goods in the regional exchange networks is a complex issue, and more trace-element analyses on raw materials and artefacts are needed in order to establish detailed trade patterns.

3.2 Production and distribution of white pottery

White-ware shards, which are remains of prestige items, have been unearthed from the residential area at Huizui West. These white wares appear to have been used as ritual drinking vessels and status symbols during the Erlitou period, as they have been often found in burials of high elite at Erlitou, as well as of lesser elite in regional centres. At least seven Erlitou sites in western Henan have yielded such vessels, including Erlitou, Huizui, Shaochai (in Gongyi), Nanzhai (in Yichuan), Nanwa (in Dengfeng), Dongmagou (in Luoyang), and Zhengyao (in Mianchi). These sites were either primary or secondary centres of the Erlitou state, distributed in an area no more than 100 km in radius from Erlitou (Figure 8.4). It was previously hypothesised that white pottery was possibly made at locales near white clay sources, but the elite at Erlitou urban centre may have played an important role in

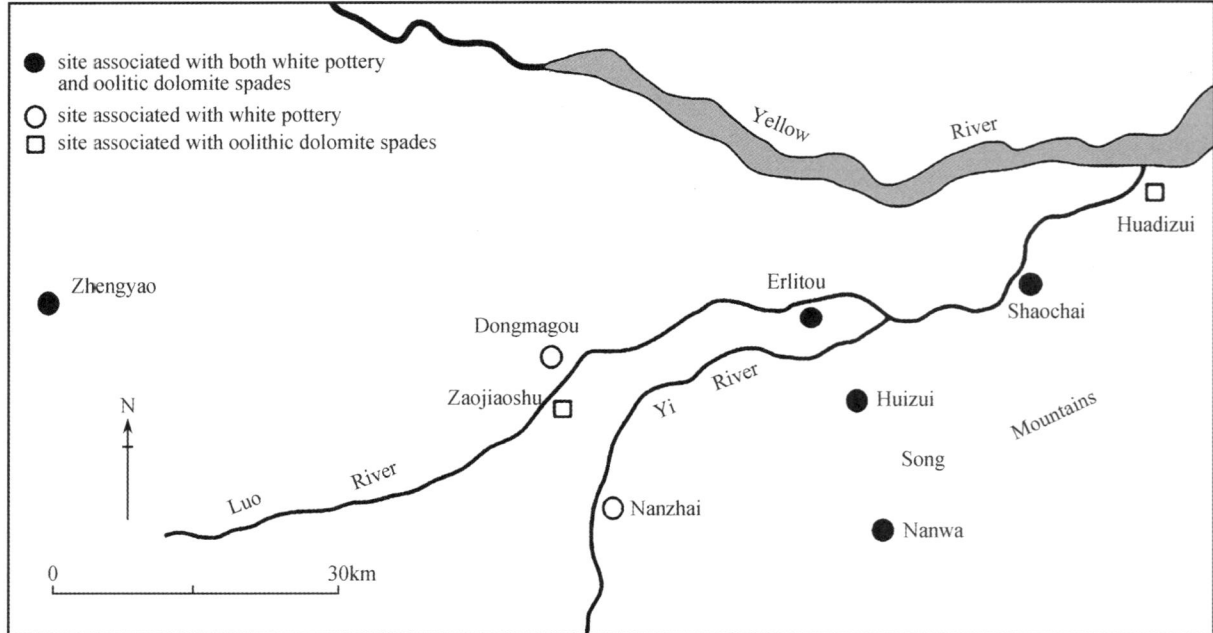

Figure 8.4 Location of Erlitou sites which yielded white pottery and oolitic dolomite spades around the Yiluo region

controlling the distribution of these prestige goods (Liu and Chen 2003).

White wares unearthed at different sites share similar stylistic characteristics, but no evidence of white ware production has been found at these sites, and their locations of manufacture are unknown. At the Nanwa site, archaeologists have found a wide range of artefacts made of white clay, including not only ritual vessels but also utilitarian items, such as fish-net sinkers and spindle whorls (Zhengzhou University and Zhengzhou Institute of Cultural Relics 2006). In addition, a layer of whitish soil, 30-40 cm in thickness, is widely distributed in the area near the Nanwa site, about 1 m below the ground, and the archaeologists suggest that this soil was used as clay for making white ware. It is possible, therefore, that Nanwa was a production centre of white pottery, which supplied white pottery vessels to Erlitou (Zhu Junxiao 2005 pers. comm.). This is a very interesting suggestion; but since no evidence of white ware production has been found at Nanwa, this proposition still needs to be tested.

Composition analysis has proven to be an effective tool in ceramic provenance studies. To investigate the provenance of white pottery, a total of 32 samples of white shards from Nanwa (14), Huizui (7, with 2 from the same pot, thus representing 6 objects), Erlitou (9), and Nanzhai (2) have been analysed for their elemental compositions. The analysis was performed using an ICP-MS (inductively coupled plasma mass spectrometry) method developed at the University of Queensland, which achieved reproducibility of 0.5%-3% (relative standard deviation) for most of the 40 trace elements routinely measured (Li et al. 2003; Li et al. 2006). Trace elements are present in clays (and ceramics) with concentrations typically below 1000 part per million (ppm). Compared with major elements (Si, Al, etc.) which are hosted in the constituent minerals of ceramic raw materials, the presence of trace elements in clay is effectively "accidental", and their concentrations largely depend on the compositions and geological histories of the original source rocks. As a result, trace elements are usually very powerful data for chemical grouping and differentiation of ceramics made of different sources of raw materials, as implied below.

Amongst the 14 shards from Nanwa, 6 small ones look to have the same colour and texture. They were possibly fragments from a single pot and thus not good for the purpose of representative sampling, but had to be included for analysis due to rarity of white ware shards. It turned out that these 6 shards have very similar concentrations for most of the 40 elements analysed, and thus form a sub-cluster independent of the other Nanwa shards (Figure 8.5). This observation further implies that they possibly belonged to the same artefact, or a few pots made from the same batch of clays. Although we cannot differentiate between the two possibilities, their identical elemental concentrations do give some idea of the high precision of the ICP-MS method, and the chemical homogeneity of the white wares.

Bearing in mind that they may possibly represent only 9 pots, the 14 shards from Nanwa show remarkably more restricted variation for contents in most of the 40 trace elements analysed when

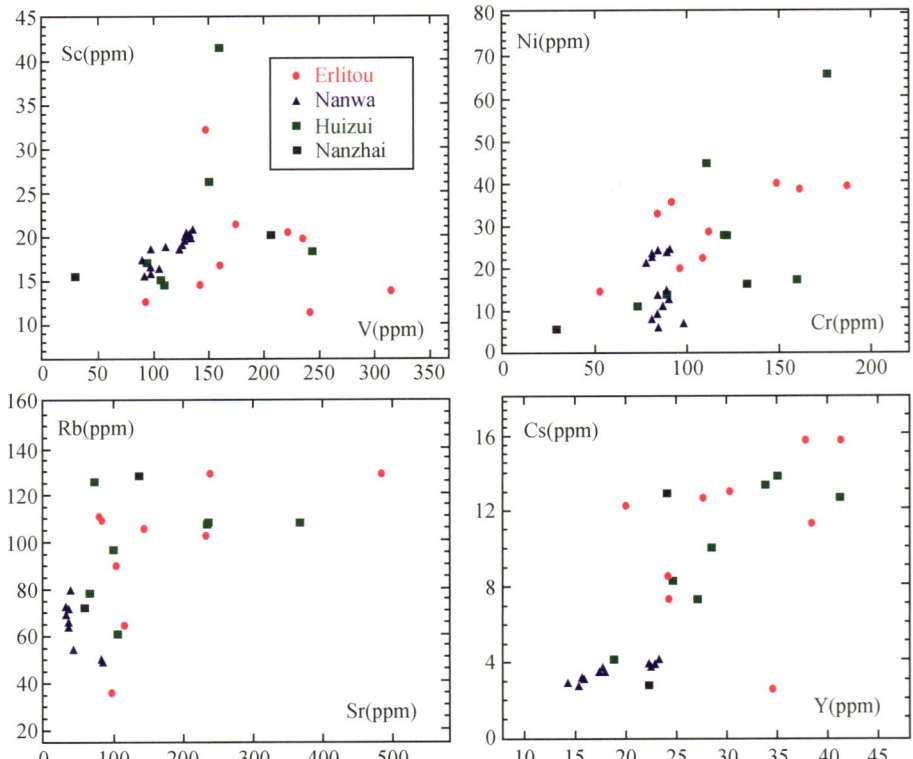

Figure 8.5 Chemical element grouping of white ware shards from the Nanwa site and comparison with other three sites of the Erlitou state

they are compared with samples from Huizui, Erlitou and Nanzhai. Consequently, Nanwa defines a considerably smaller field on binary plots of elemental compositions than the other three sites, (Figure 8.5). These observations have several implications.

Nanwa white wares were made of more restricted sources of raw materials, indicating more limited location of manufacture. The trace element features of Nanwa white wares thus support archaeologists' proposition that these ceramics were locally produced, and Nanwa was a production centre for white wares.

Many white wares from Huizui, Erlitou and Nanzhai fall out of the restricted field defined by Nanwa; they hardly look like Nanwa products. This indicates that Nanwa was not the only producer and supplier of white wares during the Erlitou period.

The above three sites are remarkably more scattered in the elemental compositions of their white wares than Nanwa. This demonstrates that they were made of more variable of raw materials. Therefore, the white wares at these sites possibly come from multiple locations of manufacture.

To date, no evidence has been discovered at Erlitou for manufacture of white wares, despite intensive archaeological surveys and excavations for over half a century. There are no signs of white ware manufacture at Huizui and Nanzhai either (although Nanzhai was a burial site and its residential area has not been found). In view of these situations and the trace element implications in sections

1-3, it is possible that the production of white wares was carried out at multiple locations outside the Erlitou urban centre, Nanwa being one of them. The white wares at Huizui, Erlitou and Nanzhai were probably not locally produced.

Some of the white wares from Huizui, Erlitou and Nanzhai fall in the small field defined by the Nanwa samples, suggesting that these three sites obtained some of their white wares from Nanwa. The samples from Huizui and Nanzhai do not seem to define the same field as the Erlitou white wares, although they partially overlap. These indicate variable sources of raw materials. Even if Erlitou was a redistribution centre, it is likely that Huizui and Nanzhai obtained their white wares not solely from Erlitou, but to some extent directly from production centre(s) apart from Nanwa that still await discovery.

It is noteworthy that the closely clustered distribution of the Nanwa white wares on the graph may be biased due to the small sample size. Larger numbers of white ware shards from a larger number of sites (when available) will be analysed to achieve a better chemical characterization and grouping based on more representative, systematic and comprehensive sampling.

Summarising the above implications, white pottery products may have been distributed among regional elite groups in a decentralized pattern. Although it was a part of the network for exchange of these prestige items, the Erlitou urban centre was unlikely to have totally monopolized the production and distribution of the white pottery.

Several sites yielded both white pottery and oolitic dolomite spades (Figure 8.4). This correlation points to the existence of regional exchange networks in the Erlitou hinterland, through which both utilitarian and prestige goods (including stone tools and elite ceramics) were traded. Among these sites, zaojiaoshu (100%) and Nanwa (56%) show high percentages of oolitic dolomite in their spade assemblages (Table 1). As Nanwa was likely making white pottery while Huizui produced dolomite spades, it is possible that people in these two settlements traded their products directly.

Local elite individuals, including some from Huizui, therefore, could have used these goods to express and negotiate for power, status, and wealth through exchange networks. As stone spades were the surplus products of Huizui, it is plausible that Huizui people exchanged spades for other goods, including both utilitarian and luxury items. White wares may have been sought by some individuals at Huizui to facilitate their participation in the elite circles of the region. This proposition, however, needs to be tested by trace-element analysis of white pottery and stone tools from a large number of sites in the Yiluo region.

4. CONCLUSION

Our research on the production and distribution of stone spades, and our analysis of white wares in the Erlitou hinterland, provide an opportunity to test Trigger's proposition on the modes of craft production in territorial states, described above. Based on our data we see a craft production system with multi-faceted operations, rather than a polarized two-tiered entity as Trigger suggested.

During the Erlitou period the state craft system may have indeed controlled the most valuable status symbols, such as ritual bronzes, whose distribution was strictly limited to the highest elite individuals, as such items have primarily been found at the Erlitou urban centre. These products, although providing wealth and legitimacy to the state rulers, were withheld from lesser elite groups in a broader region. The locale elite individuals, however, appear to have actively participated in power negotiations, by producing and exchanging other types of prestige items, such as white wares in the forms of drinking vessels for ritual purposes. These vessels were the protoforms of the major bronze vessels (Liu 2003), and continued to share the same forms with their bronze counterparts throughout the Erlitou period. To date, only Nanwa has been identified as a likely location of white pottery manufacture, and it is unclear if there were more settlements involved in such production. As an ongoing project, we are investigating the possibility that more than one site was in competition for making white wares in the Erlitou core area.

For spade production, although the products were utilitarian in function, the sources of raw material were not widely available to every village, and some communities/social groups may have taken advantage of their settlement locations to control access to the raw material. Production most likely operated on a household basis, and the products were not only meant to fulfil the subsistence needs of makers and their neighbours, but also helped some individuals to gain higher social status and wealth through trade.

The fact, that dolomite spades and white wares found their way to places some 100 km away from their locations of manufacture, indicates the existence of regionwide trade networks in the Erlitou hinterland (Figure 4). Through these networks both elite goods and utilitarian items were circulated, and lesser elite and commoners in the Erlitou hinterland created their own opportunities in the competition for power, prestige and wealth.

Archaeological evidence suggests that the Erlitou core area was a highly centralised political system, and the Erlitou site represents a well developed hierarchical society. It is very possible that some elite items, including white wares, were redistributed through the Erlitou high elite. However, our research also points to a heterarchical dimension in the Erlitou power structure. Independent craftsmen making both elite and non-elite artefacts in the hinterland did not just play a subordinate role in support of the urban elite, but actively pursued status and wealth through their craft skills.

There were many competing interests involving agencies at all levels of society during the period of state formation in the Erlitou core area. Our research on non-state craft specialisation opens a window for further research along this line of investigation.

Acknowledgements: This project is supported by a Discovery Project grant from the Australian Research Council (DP0450025). We are thankful to the members of our Yiluo Archaeology Team, John Webb, Arlene Rosen, Wei Ming, Gyoung-Ah Lee, Li Yongqiang, Xie Liye, Wang Facheng, Wang Hongzhang, Yang Junfeng, Zhang Pengfeng, Anne Ford, Sheahan Bestle, Geoffrey Hewitt, Liz Kilpatrick, and Charles Hartley, who have participated the Huizui excavation and regional survey since 2002. We are also grateful to several colleagues, Ma Xiaolin, Xu Hong, Han Guohe, Zhu Junxiao, Zhang Songlin, Shi Jiazhen, Yuan Guangkuo, and Thomas Bartlett, who generously provided information and expertise. However, we are responsible for any imperfections in this article.

REFERENCES

Adams, R.M. 1966. The Evolution of Urban Society: Early Mesopotamia and Prehispanic Mexico. Chicago: Aldine.

Bagley, R. 1990. Shang ritual bronzes: casting technique and vessel design. Archives of Asian Art 43: 6-20.

—. 1999. Shang archaeology. In M. Loewe and E. Shaughnessy eds, The Cambridge History of Ancient China, pp. 124-231. Cambridge: Cambridge University Press.

Brumfiel, E. and T. Earle. 1987. Specialization, exchange, and complex societies: an introduction. In E. Brumfiel and T.Earle eds, Specialization, Exchange, and Complex Societies, pp. 1-9. Cambridge: Cambridge University Press.

Chang, K.-c. 1980. Shang Civilization. New Haven: Yale University Press.

Chen, X. 2005. Lithic production of early states in China: An examination of the development of craft specialization. Workshop on Early Chinese Civilization, University British Columbia, Vancouver, Canada.

Childe, V.G. 1936. Man Makes Himself. London: Watts and Co. —. 1950. The urban revolution. Town Planning Review 21(1): 3-17.

Costin, C.L. 2001. Craft production systems. In G. M. Feinman and T. D. Price eds, Archaeology at the Millennium: A Sourcebook, pp. 273-328. New York: Kluwer Academic/Plenum Publishers.

Erlitou Working Team, Institute of Archaeology, CASS. 2004. Henan Yanshishi Erlitou yizhi gongcheng ji gongdianqu waiwei daolu de kancha yu fajue (Survey and excavation of the palatial city and its outer roads at the Erlitou site in Yanshi, Henan). Kaogu 11: 3-13.

—. 2005. Henan Luoyang pendi 2001-2003 nian kaogu diaocha jianbao (Report of the 2001-2003 archaeological survey in the Luoyang basin, Henan). Kaogu 5: 18-37.

—. 2005. Henan Yanshi Erlitou yizhi zhongxinqu de kaogu xinfaxian (New finds from the central area of the Erlitou site in Yanshi, Henan). Kaogu 7: 15-20.

Ford, A. 2001. States and Stones: Ground Stone Tool Production at Huizui, China. Honours Thesis. Department of Archaeology, La Trobe University. Melbourne.

Henan 1st Team, I.o.A., CASS. 2004. Henan Yanshi Huizui yizhi dongzhoumu fajue jianbao (Excavation of an Eastern Zhou

Tomb on the Huizui Site in Yanshi, Henan). Kaogu 12: 27-32.

Institute of Archaeology, C. 1999. Yanshi Erlitou. Beijing: Zhongguo Dabaikequanshu Press.

Li, B., J. Zhao, K.D. Collerson and A. Greig. 2003. Application of ICP-MS trace element analysis in study of ancient Chinese ceramics. Chinese Science Bulletin 48(12): 1219-1224.

Li, B., J. Zhao, A. Greig, K.D. Collerson, Y. Feng, X. Sun, M. Guo and Z. Zhuo. 2006. Characterisation of Chinese Tang sancai from Gongxian and Yaozhou kilns using ICP-MS trace element and TIMS Sr-Nd isotopic analysis. Journal of Archaeological Science 33(1): 56-62.

Li, Y.-t. 2003. The Anyang Bronze Foundries: Archaeological Remains, Casting Technology, and Production Organization. Ph.D dissertation. Department of Anthropology, Harvard University. Cambridge, Mass.

Liu, L. 2003. "The products of minds as well as of hands": Production of prestige goods in the Neolithic and early state periods of China. Asian Perspectives 42(1): 1-40.

Liu, L. and X. Chen. 2003. State Formation in Early China. London: Duckworth.

Liu, L., X. Chen, Y.K. Lee, H. Wright and A. Rosen. 2002-2004. Settlement patterns and development of social complexity in the Yiluo region, north China. Journal of Field Archaeology 29(1-2): 75-100.

Schortman, E.M. and P.A. Urban. 2004. Modeling the roles of craft production in ancient political economies. Journal of Archaeological Research 12(2): 185-226.

Trigger, B. 1999. Shang political organization: A comparative approach. Journal of East Asian Archaeology 1(1-4): 43-62.

—. 2003. Understanding Early Civilizations — A Comparative Study. Cambridge: Cambridge University Press.

Xu, H., G. Chen and H. Zhao. 2004. Erlitou yizhi juluo xingtai de chubu kaocha (Preliminary investigation of settlement patterns of the Erlitou site). Kaogu 11: 23-31.

Zhengzhou University and Zhengzhou Institute of Cultural Relics. 2006. Henan Dengfeng Nanwa yizhi 2004 nian chun fajue jianbao (Brief report of excavation at the Nanwa site in Dengfeng, Henan, in Spring 2004). Zhongyuan Wenwu 3: 4-12, 22.

CHAPTER 9 SOIL MICROMORPHOLOGY, CHEMISTRY AND MAGNETIC SUSCEPTIBILITY STUDIES AT HUIZUI (YILUO REGION, HENAN PROVINCE, NORTHERN CHINA), WITH SPECIAL FOCUS ON A TYPICAL YANGSHAO FLOOR SEQUENCE[1]

1. INTRODUCTION

During 2005, two archaeological fieldwork seasons in and around Huizui, Yiluo Region, Henan Province, China, led to the microstratigraphic analysis of geoarchaeological samples from the Peiligang, Yangshao, Longshan and Erlitou Periods (see Samples and methods; Table 1 after main text; Map 1 for site locations). This microstratigraphic study is a recent component of the interdisciplinary Yiluo Project (2003-2006), investigating geoarchaeology, plant remains, settlement patterns, craft specialization, and the rise of Chinese civilization on this part of the Loess Plateau (Liu et al. 2002-2004). Analysis of microstratigraphy at Huizui, employing the techniques of soil micromorphology, chemistry and magnetic susceptibility, had the aims of characterizing the natural soils and sediments of the locality in order to identify occupation deposits, such as ash pit fills, 'white' floor sequences, and selected contexts of an enigmatic near-river soil-sediment accumulation. This paper mainly focuses upon a typical Yangshao floor sequence and several ash pits (Map 2 for sampling locations). Preliminary interpretations of other deposits are also given, in order to understand more accurately the Yangshao floor sequence, within its archaeological and landscape context.

---

[1] This chapter is written by Richard I. Macphail and John Crowther, post on *Indo-Pacific Prehistory Association Bulletin*, 2007(27):103-113.

1462 洛阳盆地中东部先秦时期遗址

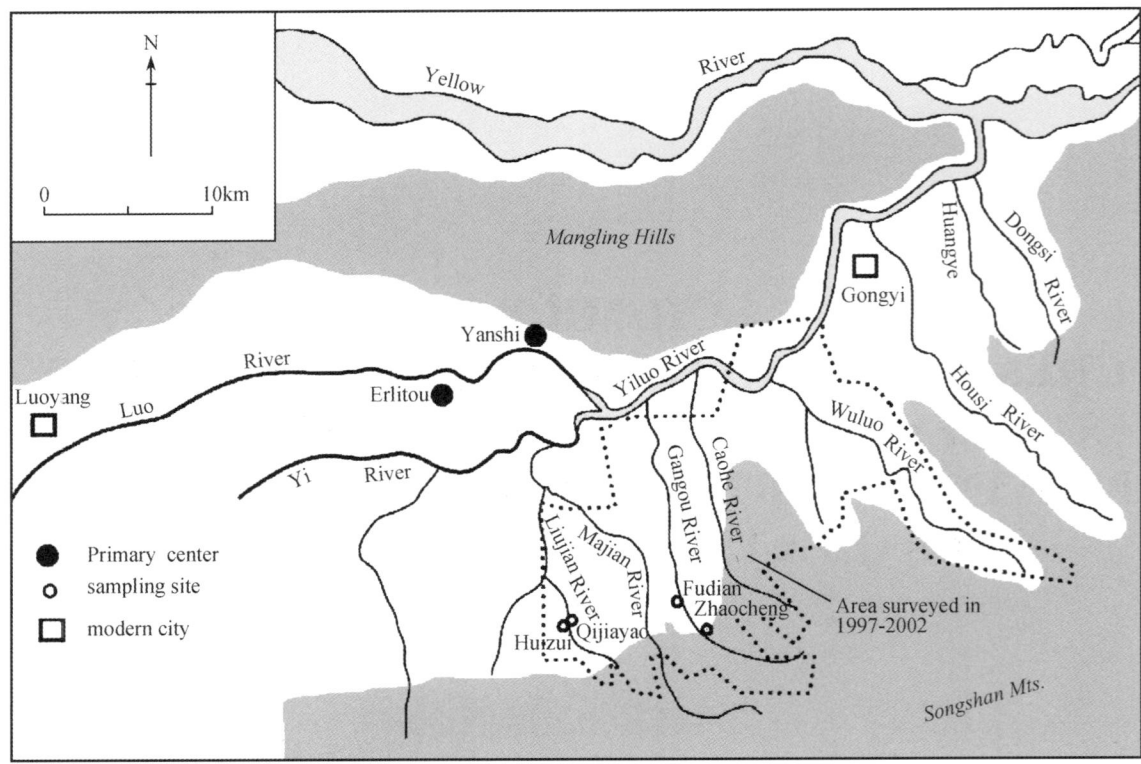

Map 9.1　The Yiluo Project: site locations

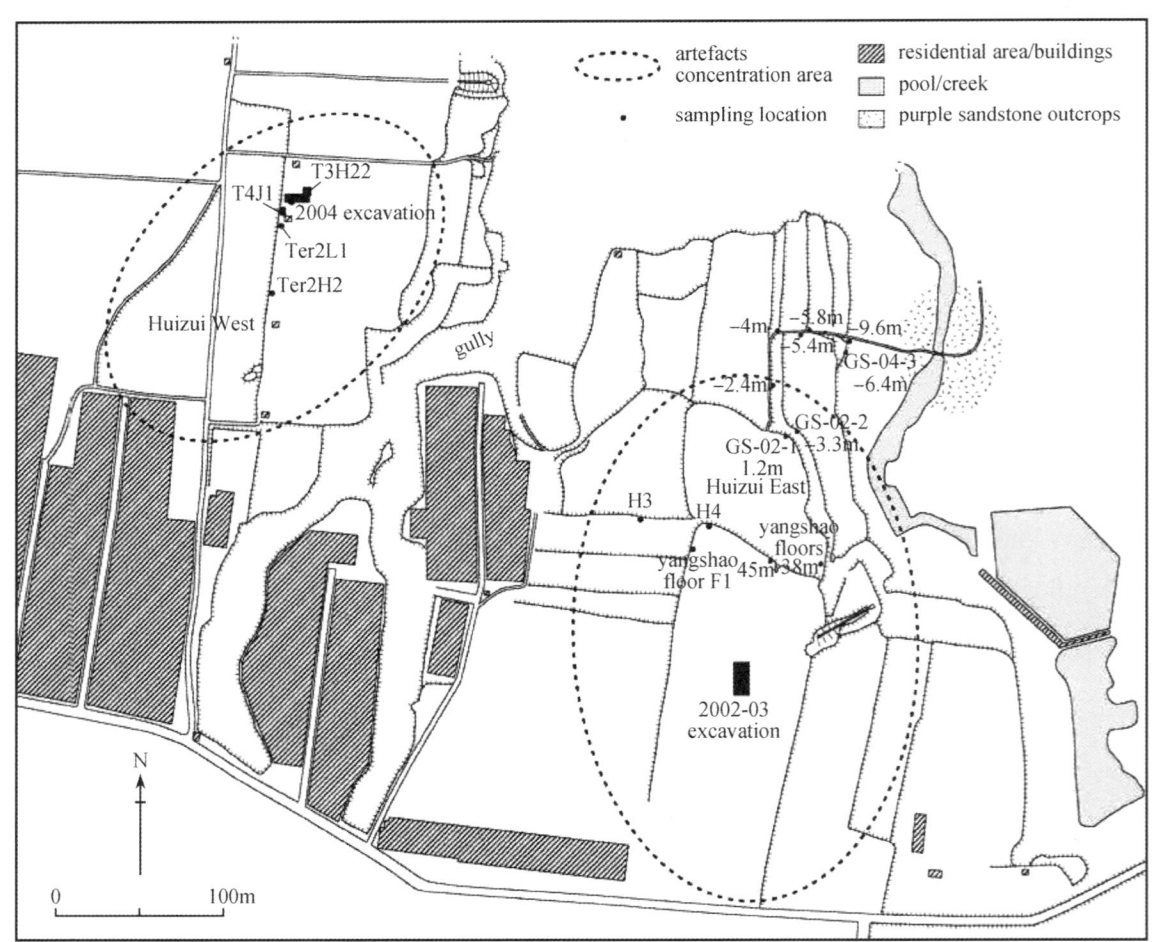

Map 9.2　Sampling locations at Huizui

CHAPTER 9 SOIL MICROMORPHOLOGY, CHEMISTRY AND MAGNETIC SUSCEPTIBILITY STUDIES AT HUIZUI (YILUO REGION, HENAN PROVINCE, NORTHERN CHINA), WITH SPECIAL FOCUS ON A TYPICAL YANGSHAO FLOOR SEQUENCE

2. SAMPLES AND METHODS

A selection of samples collected early in 2005 by Chen (Institute of Archaeology, Chinese Academy of Social Sciences, China) were received at UCL and assessed through soil micromorphology (the study of undisturbed soils and sediments in 20-30 μm thick thin sections; Courty et al. 1989) and bulk analyses (see below). This aided the sampling strategy of the Yiluo Project team that included Macphail during fieldwork carried out in November 2005.

In all, 44 undisturbed monolith (Figure 9.1) and 37 bulk samples were available for study. Discussion with coworkers led to the selective investigation of 31 thin sections and 25 bulk samples (Table 9.1), in order to answer selected archaeological questions.

Figure 9.1 Huizui Yangshao F1 floor sequences 05HYEHF1; ground-raising and preparation surfaces (Layers 1, 3, 5, and 7), floors (Layers 2, 4, 6 and 8) and burned daub (adobe) debris (Layer 9); samples M16-M19. Note biologically worked and homogenised upper deposits (Layer 11) and possible vertical wall or partition (white arrow)

Table 9.1 Huizui soil micromorphology (thin section) and bulk samples; preliminary interpretations

Site Code	Bulk analysis (Table 2)	Period and Context	Thin section (relative depth); preliminary interpretation
Qijiayao		***Peiligang soil and pits***	
05HYQGS2	43	Subsoil A2&Bt? Horizon	M43 0-75 mm: Deep loessic A2 soil horizon with rare bioworked fine charcoal throughout.
05HYQH1	44	Pit 1 - lower part near large shell	M44 0-75 mm: Loessic soil- (A2, Bt and calcareous Btk horizon) dominated fill with burned soil, pottery, charcoal, bone, and phosphate features indicative of disposal of human waste.

(continued)

Site Code	Bulk analysis (Table 2)	Period and Context	Thin section (relative depth); preliminary interpretation
(Fudian)		Peiligang fused ash	M34 reference sample: Wood ash, recemented (partially weathered) ash, burned bone, soil and burned soil.
Huizui		***Yangshao F1 floor sequences***	
05HYΞHF1		Layer 9: burned clay	M19A 0-75 mm: Burrowed fragments of burned daub presumed to be relict of burned adobe (daub) construction (red coloured because of both soil slaking and moderate burning).
05HYΞHF1	19/8	Layer 8: floor	M19A 0-75 mm (M19B): 2 tufa slabs, with plant pseudomorphs and plant remains, loess soil inclusions and staining. (high carbonate content; absence of magnetic susceptibility enhancement) (Parallel mineralogical studies* of floor slabs found quartz, chlorite, illite and iron oxide/hydroxides, consistent with the presence of loess).
05HYEHF1		Upper layer 7: floor preparation material?	M19B 75-150 mm: Mud plastered layer constructed from plant-tempered loess over loess-based plant-tempered adobe.
05HYEHF1		Layers 6a and 6b: uppermost and middle floor layer of floor series	M18A 10-85 mm: 2-3 tufa slabs, with very thin (charcoal) fine dusty clay surface layer between middle (6b) and uppermost (6a) layers.
05HYEHF1		Layer 6c: lowermost floor of floor series	M18B 85-140 mm: two tufa slabs.
05HYEHF1		Layer 6d: floor preparation material	M18B 140-170 mm: Mud plastered layer constructed from plant-tempered loess
05HYEHF1		Layer 5: yellowish clay leveling/ ground-raising deposit	Probable pale A2 horizon soil, as in M17A below.
05HYEHF1	17/4a	Layer 4a: dark fill	M17A 0-55 mm: ground-raising mixture of pale A2 horizon soil and burned daub (hence enhanced magnetic susceptibility).
05HYEHF1		Layer 4b: floor	M17B 95-105 mm: tufa slab (basal slab of three).
05HYEHF1	17/3a	Layer 3a: dark brown - floor preparation deposit	M17B 105-115 mm: Mud plastered layer constructed from loess; dark colour formed by the slaking of the loess and formation of clay textural pedofeatures features (no bulk evidence of added humic
05HYEHF1		Layer 3b:	mMa1t7teBr)115-165 mm: Adobe ground-raising deposit constructed from 'clean' loess.
05HYEHF1	16/3a	Layer 3a: brown - floor preparation deposit (lateral continuation of 17/3a)	No bulk signal of anthropogenic deposition or humic soil formation.
05HYEHF1	16/3b	Layer 3b: floor fill	No bulk signal of anthropogenic deposition or humic soil formation.
05HYEHF1		Layer 2: floor	M16A 0-5 mm: Floor constructed of a single slab of quarried tufa. M16B 5-75 mm: Thin plant-tempered 'mud-plastered' floor preparation surface made from loess (adobe), over occupation soil with enriched phosphate-P and enhanced magnetic susceptibility.
05HYEHF1	16/1	Layer 1: disturbed soil/deposit	M16B 80-155 mm: occupation soil, as above.
05HYHF1		Fragmented sample of floor	M1: Three coarse fragments of tufa ('floor')
05HYHF1		Floor	M2 0-30 mm: Floor constructed of quarried slab of tufa, over; 30-35 mm: plant-tempered 'mud-plastered' floor preparation surface composed of 'clean' loess.

CHAPTER 9 SOIL MICROMORPHOLOGY, CHEMISTRY AND MAGNETIC SUSCEPTIBILITY STUDIES AT HUIZUI (YILUO REGION, HENAN PROVINCE, NORTHERN CHINA), WITH SPECIAL FOCUS ON A TYPICAL YANGSHAO FLOOR SEQUENCE

(continued)

Site Code	Bulk analysis (Table 2)	Period and Context	Thin section (relative depth); preliminary interpretation
05HYEH3		Longshan ash pit	
05HYEH3S1	10	Ashpit	M31A 0-75 mm: Pit (quarry?) fill of likely ponded deposits composed of layered occupation soil, wood ash, and phytolith remains of plants; the last probably reflects inputs of cereal and plant processing waste and mats. Inputs of human cess and inwash of iron, calcium and phosphate under episodic wet conditions.
05HYEH3S2	11	Ashpit	M31B 75-150 mm: as above
05HYEH3		Mixed occupation soil below ash layers	M32 0-75 mm: Basal pit (quarry?) fill of disturbed topsoil and subsoil, and burrowed occupation deposits from overlying fill; inwash of iron, calcium and phosphate under episodic wet conditions.
05HYEH4		**Longshan ash pit**	
05HYH4S1	12	Series of thin ash and charcoal layers	M22A 0-75 mm: Very similar to ash pit fill H3 (see above), but includes more strongly burned materials, and 'mat' residues appear to include more fine anthropogenic inclusions ('dirtier'?).
05HYH4S2	13	Series of thin ash and charcoal layers	M22B 75-150 mm: as above
		Holocene, Yangshao and Longshan soil-sediment sequence at GS2	(see overleaf)
		Longshan fine laminated alluvium -	M38A 0-55 mm: Lenticular structured possible human trampled wet, gleyed anthropogenic sediment, containing many fine anthropogenic inclusions.
05HYEGS2	38b	Longshan soil-sediment with vertically oriented sherd	M38A 55-75 mm: as below M38B 75-150 mm: Massive, coarsely churned, wet, gleyed anthropogenic sediment, containing many coarse anthropogenic
05HYEGS2	39a	Yangshao soil-sediment towards base of soil-sediment sequence	iMnc3l9uAsio0n-s7.5 mm: massive silts with iron and manganese staining; occasional fine included anthropogenic material (probable post- depositional phosphate-enriched, along with Fe-Mn). M39plan: ditto, and as demonstrated by microprobe.
05HYEGS2	39b	Yangshao gravel deposits at base of soil-sediment sequence	M39B 75-150 mm: poorly laminated, silty muds with detrital organic matter fragments (75-100 mm), over unsorted gravel-rich fill containing rounded burned daub, and calcium carbonate-rich subsoil and tufa, with loess, charcoal and sand to silt size bone and phosphate nodules of anthropogenic origin (100-150 mm). M39base 0-75 mm: same sequence
05HYEGS2	40	Late Pleistocene/early Holocene (?) alluvial soil	M40A 0-75 mm: Gravel (0-15 mm) over (truncating?) uppermost part of soil (see below). M40B 75-150 mm: Late Pleistocene/early Holocene (?) alluvial gley soil formed from redeposited loess, with iron stained root channels and containing no anthropogenic inclusions.

(continued)

Site Code	Bulk analysis (Table 2)	Period and Context	Thin section (relative depth); preliminary interpretation
05HYEGS2		Laminated Holocene (Yangshao?) alluvium abutting truncated Late Pleistocene/Early Holocene soil	M30 0-75 mm: finely laminated silty alluvium abutting Late Pleistocene/early Holocene alluvial gley soil formed from redeposited loess, with iron stained root channels and containing no anthropogenic inclusions.
		Erlitou soil, ash pits and 'road'	
04HYHT4J1	4	Surface by well	M4 (fragments only): A truncated subsoil with indications of trampling and water spillage.
05HYHWTer2 H2	8 and 9 (6 and 7)	Ashpit 2 deposits	M8 0-75 mm: Strongly phosphate-enriched ash pit deposit containing very strongly burned materials (vitrified silica slags), ash, plant processing and human coprolites/cess.
T3H22	15	Erlitou Phase III Ashpit deposit	M15 (fragments only): ash- (wood ash) dominated, with strongly burned soil, daub, and cess, all resulting in the highest phosphate concentrations and the highest magnetic susceptibility (%χ conv) at Huizui.
05HYHWTer2 L1	37	Erlitou 'road'	M37 0-75 mm: compact, partially layered trampled soil containing many mainly fine anthropogenic inclusions, and formed under both wet and 'dry' conditions.

* Mineralogical studies by Dr John Webb, La Trobe University

Table 9.2 Huizui chemical (excluding phosphate fractionation) and magnetic susceptibility data

(continued on next page)

Sample	Brief description	LOI (%)	pH 1:2.5 water	Carbonate (est, %)§	Phosphate-P† (mg g^{-1})	Pb$ (mg g^{-1})	Zn$ (mg g^{-1})	Cu$ (mg g^{-1})	χ (10^{-8} SI)	χ max (10^{-8} SI)	χ conv¶ (%)
Peiligang soil and pits (Qijiayao; 05HYQ and 05HYQGS2)											
43	Subsoil A2&Bt?	1.08	8.6	5	0.871				23.8	298	7.99*
44	Pit 1	1.30	8.2	2	1.26				34.8	355	9.80*
Yangshao floor and construction sequence											
17/4a	Floor: Layer 4a	1.26	8.5	5	2.46				53.0	877	6.04*
17/3a	Floor: Layer 3a	0.782	8.8	>10	1.30	18.4	40.6	14.8	20.3	880	2.31
16/3a	Floor: Layer 3a	0.984	8.8	5	1.25				18.0	1000	1.80
16/3b	Floor: Layer 3b	1.09	8.7	5	1.29				22.3	911	2.45
16/1	Pre-floor: Layer 1	1.44	8.7	>10	3.13*	17.0	68.2	25.6	37.8	522	7.24*
Longshan ash pits											
10	Ash pit	2.25	8.6	5	7.24**				27.4	144	19.0**
11	Ash pit	2.13	8.7	>10	4.98*				16.4	179	9.16*
12	Ash pit	2.37	9.6	>10	5.21**				59.6	256	23.3***
13	Ash pit	1.99	9.6	>10	5.94**				68.7	294	23.4***

(continued)

Sample	Brief description	LOI (%)	pH 1:2.5 water	Carbonate (est, %)§	Phosphate-P† (mg g^{-1})	Pb$ (mg g^{-1})	Zn$ (mg g^{-1})	Cu$ (mg g^{-1})	χ (10^{-8} SI)	χ max (10^{-8} SI)	χ conv¶ (%)
Yangshao (Y) and Longshan (L) soil-sediment sequence at GS2 (05HYEGS2)											
38a	Alluvium (L)	1.76	9.4	>10	1.25	24.4	75.1	22.5	12.1	433	2.79
38b	Soil (L)	1.08	9.6	>10	1.90	20.0	60.0	20.0	9.7	269	3.61
39a	Basal soil (Y)	1.14	9.6	>10	3.59*	16.7	42.6	14.8	19.7	447	4.41
39b	Underlying gravel (Y)	1.25	9.4	>10	0.801	16.6	47.6	16.6	9.8	390	2.51
40	Underlying alluvial soil	1.04	9.1	5	1.07	18.8	50.1	18.8	10.3	542	1.90
Erlitou soil, ash pits, 'road' and floors											
4	Surface by well	1.08	8.3	>10	1.32				28.1	576	4.88
6	Ash pit	3.44	8.2	2	6.89**				103	309	33.3***
7	Ash pit	2.43	8.4	5	5.40**				192	462	41.6***
8	Ash pit	2.76	8.3	2	7.12**				56.6	255	22.2***
9	Ash pit	2.84	8.2	5	5.55**				99.4	331	30.0***
37	'Road'	1.61	8.6	5	3.54*				140	744	18.8**
14	Upper ash pit layer	1.98	8.6	>10	11.6***				164	406	40.4***
15	Lower ash pit layer	1.51	8.7	>10*	13.3***				142	279	50.9***

§ **Estimated carbonate:** * figure highlighted in bold appears to have a higher carbonate content than the other samples recorded as >10%, ** basedon acid insoluble residue determination for this sample (AIR = 32.4%).

† **Phosphate-P:** Figures highlighted in bold show signs of phosphate-P enrichment: * = enriched (2.50-4.99 mg g-1), ** = strongly enriched (5.00-9.99 mg g-1), *** = very strongly enriched (≥10.0 mg g-1) – phosphate fractionation data are presented in Table 3.

$ **Heavy metals (Pb, Zn & Cu):** None of the samples analysed shows clear signs of enrichment. ¶ χ: Figures highlighted in bold show signs of magnetic susceptibility enhancement: * = enhanced (χconv = 5.00-9.99%), ** = strongly enhanced (χconv= 10.0-19.9%), *** = very strongly enhanced (χconv ≥20.0%).

The microstratigraphic approach

Full details of the methods applied are given elsewhere (Goldberg and Macphail 2006; Macphail and Crowther 2004). Essentially, soil micromorphology (which included microprobe X-ray analysis), was combined with the bulk measurements of loss-on-ignition (LOI at 375ºC), fractionated phosphate (inorganic and organic P), magnetic susceptibility (including %χ conv) and the heavy metals copper (Cu), lead (Pb) and zinc (Zn) (Bethell and Máté 1989; Courty et al. 1989; Crowther 2003; Crowther and Barker 1995; Stoops 2003).

3. RESULTS AND DISCUSSION

Selected results are presented in Tables 1-2 and Figures 1-9, including a preliminary interpretation of each context studied (Table 9.1).

Figure 9.2 Scan of 15 cm long impregnated block (M18) that sampled Layer 5 – a plant-tempered adobe preparation surface (APS), and Layer 6 – a series of fossiliferous tufa floor layers (TFL) composed of quarried slabs of tufa; the basal slab and overlying thicker slabs showing natural horizontal splitting. Tufa is a type of limestone formed in calcareous springs

Figure 9.3 Scan of 14 cm long block (M19) that sampled Layer 7 – adobe ground-raising deposits (AGR) and plant-tempered adobe preparation surface (APS), Layer 8 – a series of fossiliferous tufa floor layer(s) (TFL), tufa slabs or slab showing natural horizontal splitting, and Layer 9 – burned daub (adobe) debris (BDD)

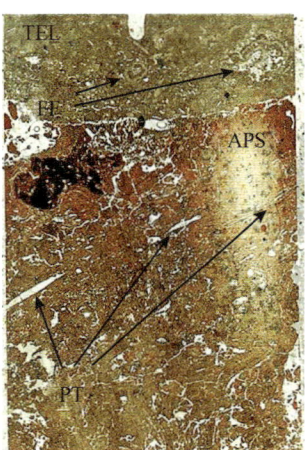
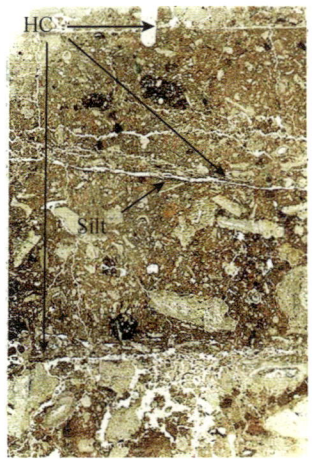

Figure 9.4 Scan of thin section M19B showing (Layer 7) voids pseudomorphic of plant-tempering (PT) and dark-coloured adobe preparation surface (APS) – a mud-plastered layer, and (Layer 8) tufa floor layers (TFL) containing fossil features (FF). Width is ~ 5cm

Figure 9.5 Scan of thin section M18A, tufa floor layers (Layer 6) containing loessic soil clasts and plant fossils, and showing horizontal cracks (HC) – natural horizontal splitting of the tabular tufa, and the location of fine-charcoal-rich loessic silt coating the base of one crack (Silt) – see text. Width is ~ 5cm

CHAPTER 9 SOIL MICROMORPHOLOGY, CHEMISTRY AND MAGNETIC SUSCEPTIBILITY STUDIES AT HUIZUI (YILUO REGION, HENAN PROVINCE, NORTHERN CHINA), WITH SPECIAL FOCUS ON A TYPICAL YANGSHAO FLOOR SEQUENCE

Figure 9.6 Photomicrograph of M1, fragmented sample of floor; detail of biochemical growth patterns in tufa. Crossed polarized light (XPL), frame width is ~ 2.3 mm

Figure 9.7 Photomicrograph of M18A, Floor Layer 6b, showing plant pseudomorphs and fossil remains formed by sparite (calcite) set in an impure micritic and microsparitic matrix (tufa) containing silt-size quartz (loess). XPL, frame width is ~ 4.6 mm

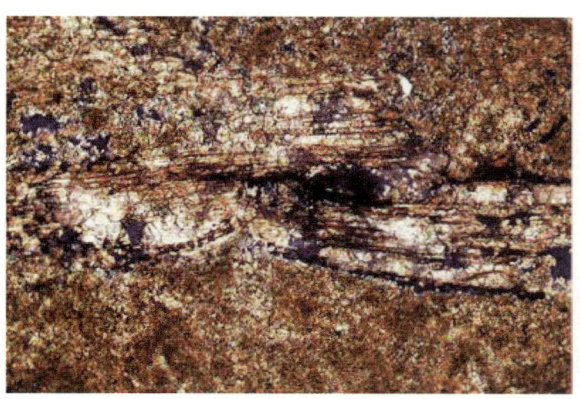

Figure 9.8 Photomicrograph of M18B, blackened plant tissues embedded in calcitic tufa as evidence of naturally included plant fragments. XPL, frame width is ~ 1.06 mm

Figure 9.9 Photomicrograph of M18B, plant-tempered mudplastered loess forming a floor preparation surface (arrows point out void pseudomorphs of plant tempering); the dense character of the matrix is due to soil slaking caused by the mudplastering process. XPL, frame width is ~ 4.6 mm

3.1 Post-deposition effects

The soil and landscape at and around Huizui has been highly manipulated by human populations for millennia. A Late Pleistocene/early Holocene alluvial soil (sample 40) at GS2 is considered a good example of a sterile 'control' sample. As would be expected, this 'natural' soil has a relatively low LOI (organic content), a low phosphate concentration and a very low magnetic susceptibility; its chief characteristics are a massive structure and iron stained porosity (relict root channels) typical of alluvial gley soils (Bouma et al. 1990). This soil has also been affected by later secondary calcium carbonate formation. The latter is believed to be the result of a general contamination of archaeological soils by calcium carbonate and other alkaline salts, which have produced anomalously high pH values (max. pH 9.6) across the site (see Table 9.2); all possibly linked to alkaline occupational deposits that were markedly present at Huizui at least since the Yangshao Period (see below). The effects of burrowing by fauna such as insects and small mammals has also to be considered (see Layer 11, Figure 9.1).

3.2 Local soils

Field and soil micromorphological observations of soils at Qijiayao (Peiligang pits; sample 43) and in soils below a Yangshao pit at Huizui (sample M32) indicate the typical presence of iron- and clay-epleted upper subsoil A2 horizons and the relatively more clay- and iron-rich lower subsoil Bw/B(t) horizons formed in silty clay loam loess under a broad-leaved woodland. These lower subsoils also often contain secondary calcium carbonate (B(t)k /Ck horizons), and at Zhaocheng, Pleistocene palaeosols are characterised by marked carbonate nodulular formation. This is typical of Holocene (and earlier) pedogenesis on loess, predominantly a wind blown silt (Duchaufour, 1982: 233-4, 282), with leaching and clay migration, and secondary carbonate formation at depth, forming a *Hapludalf* (Soil Survey Staff 1999) or *Orthic* (Calcic) Luvisol (FAO-Unesco 1988).

3.3 Peiligang occupation

At Fudian (Liu *et al.* 2002-2004: Figure 3) pit fill and reference ash pit deposits contain local topsoil and subsoil materials, in addition to bone, burned bone, ash, charcoal, pottery, burned soil and phosphate materials indicating the disposal of human waste (Table 9.1, M34, 43 and 44). There is evidence in the ash pit of fine soil mobilization induced by the weathering of ash and the release of potassium (K), as also reported from Neolithic pits in Europe (Courty and Fedoroff 1982; Slager and Van der Wetering 1977).

4. OCCUPATION AT HUIZUI

Off-site soil-sediments at GS2 (M39-40) and a floor sequence at 05HYEHF1 (Figure 9.1; M16A-M19B) were focused upon.

4.1 YANGSHAO FLOOR SEQUENCE（05HYEHF1）

At this constructional sequence a number of layers (1-11) was examined (Figure 9.1). The floor sequence is broadly composed of four or more white floors laid on prepared surfaces (Tables 1 and 2).

Layer 1 is composed of occupation soil (or ground-raising dump?) with a 2 mm thick compact, weakly layered soil spread immediately below the overlying white floor (Layer 2). This soil appears to be a 'plastered' soil layer and preparation surface, made from 'clean' loess. The white floor (Layer 2) is constructed from a 3 cm thick slab of fossiliferous tufa; in fact Layers 2, 4, 6 and 8 are all constructed from single or multiple 2-3 cm thick slabs of tufa that show natural horizontal splitting or jointing (see Figures 2-3). Bulk analysis of one example (Layer 8, Table 2) shows it to be highly calcareous (67.6% carbonate), but very impure (acid insoluble residue, 32.4%; mostly silts and clay), and has no signs whatsoever of phosphate enrichment or magnetic susceptibility enhancement. Soil micromorphology indicates that the silt and clay is present as included loess. Its sulphide content is also indicative of a natural waterlogged (gleyed) origin. Parallel elemental and mineralogical studies from this F1 floor sequence and the F4 floor at Huizui, found abundant calcite, with quartz, chlorite, illite and iron oxides/hydroxides, consistent with tufa forming alongside the inwash of loess (John Webb, La Trobe University, pers. comm., 2007).

Tufa as a constructional material

Tufa (cf. travertine) develops where spring water contains high amounts of dissolved calcium carbonate which precipitates as a mainly micritic limestone-like deposit. It also often forms around algae, lichens and mosses growing on site and produces pseudomorphs of plants in the form of microsparite- and sparite-size calcite, with some morphologies also reflecting the presence of bacteria and algae (Courty et al. 1989, 99, Figure 6.9b; Scholle and Scholle 2003: 349) (Figures 9.6-7). Tufa also often traps plant material and soil, at times, as found in the tufa floor slabs at Huizui (Figure 9.8). The presence of Quaternary tufa in the locality of Huizui is consistent with the weathering of loess and formation of calcium carbonate-rich Bk deep subsoil horizons and carbonate nodules in the area, and the likely formation of tufa associated with springs (cf. Avery 1990: 187-188). The ubiquitous presence of fossil traces of plants, organic remains and soil clasts, including both loess (see bulk analyses, above) and carbonate nodules, in the white floors, confirms their identification as quarried tufa slabs (Paul Goldberg, Boston University, pers. comm., 2006) (cf. Quaternary tufa-like beds in loess covered area of Kostenki, Russia; Holliday et al. 2007, Figure 6c). Although occasional burrowing by mesofauna is recorded in these floor layers, the fossil evidence cannot be mistaken for post-depositional rooting and secondary calcium carbonate formation, because such features do not cross boundaries between individual floor slabs of tufa (see Figures 2-3).

The natural splitting qualities of the tufa ('tabular formed tufa') presumably encouraged and aided quarrying. It is also evident that tufa slabs may also have been employed to create walls or partitions, as shown in Figure 9.1. (The complete absence of any chemical, mineralogical or micromorphological evidence of burning and the overwhelming indications of natural tufa formation demonstrate that none of the white floors investigated were manufactured from burned lime.)

Constructional sequence at 05HYEHF1 – layers 2-9

There is no evidence of occupation soils between floors, as for example formed when deposits are tracked-in by trampling, either by people or their animals (Macphail et al.2004). This implies that either floors were swept and/or covered (Goldberg and Macphail 2006; Macphail et al. 1997; Matthews et al. 1996, 2000). Within floor Layer 6 (Figure 9.5) there is a rare example of very fine charcoalrich silt deposition is recorded, but this may not be significant.

Instead of occupation deposits, soil Layer 3b between floor Layers 2 and 4b, is composed of unburned planttempered adobe (daub) manufactured from 'clean' loess (sample 16/3b) (see Figures 4 and 9). The plant-tempering material has now been mainly lost through oxidation from this ground-raising construction level, as is typical of plant tempered adobe and mudbrick (Courty et al. 1989; Goldberg and Macphail 2006), and reference Yangshao burned daub (M33). The dark soil Layer (3a) below floor Layer 4a, was expected to be humic, but in fact is chemically very poorly humic and carries no anthropogenic signal (Table 2, samples 16/3a, 17/3a); again, it is simply composed of 'clean' loess. The dark colour has been produced by the manufacture of another mud 'plastered' surface; the soil when wetted, became slaked, causing the clay constituents to separate and infill voids, hence giving it a dark reddish colour (Figures 4 and 9) (Macphail and Goldberg 2006). Mud plastered surfaces have been recorded from numerous sites, including Çatalhöyük, Turkey and from ethnographic examples from Turkey and India (Boivin 1999; Matthews et al. 1996, 2000). Mud 'plastered' preparation levels (Layers 6 and 8; M18B and M19B) below floors are similarly plant-tempered adobe deposits (Figure 9.9). Layer 5 in the construction sequence was termed a yellowish clay in the field. In thin section, it is quite clear that this is a leveling dump that is mainly composed of pale soil from a presumably local A2 soil horizon of the local loess soil (see above).

Layer 9 which overlies floor Layer 8, is made up of coarse fragments of rubefied (moderately burned; see Table 1) daub and biologically worked fine pieces of unburned daub (M18A). The burned daub is probably associated with the burned daub wall of the structure that underlies floor layer 10 (Figures 1 and 3). This debris again rests on a clean floor surface. Such deposits could imply the razing of the structure by fire, as carried out experimentally at Butser Ancient Farm, Hampshire, UK or as found in London as the result of the revolt by Boudicca in AD59-60 (Goldberg and Macphail 2006: Figures 11.9 and 12.8; Macphail *et al.* 2004). In Neolithic China, however, daub walls are believed to have been burned (hardened) for constructional purposes (Chen, pers. comm. 2005).

4.2 Longshan ash pit 05HYEH3

Ash pit deposits (samples 10 and 11) are moderately humic in comparison to other contexts at Huizui, and are enriched or strongly enriched in phosphate. They also show an enhanced or strongly enhanced magnetic susceptibility. In thin section (M31A and M31B), they are characterized mainly by layered deposits of wood ashy material that include fine moderately strongly burned soil, and occasional charcoal, and laminated phytoliths, including articulated phytoliths (e.g., from plant processing and the dumping of 'mats'). (As yet there is no consensus on the use of the floors in the 05HYEHF1 sequence, but if they were domestic and as they are 'clean' this could be the result of having been covered with mats.) The wood ash is identifiable from large lozenge shape calcite crystals and wood charcoal present (Courty et al. 1989). The presence of human(?) coprolitic fragments, bone, pottery and probable amorphous Fe-Ca-P staining, indicate general dumping of food and latrine waste. Little biological activity is recorded at these levels, possibly because of the high levels of alkali earths of ash origin that for example can be toxic to earthworms, and also because the layered character of the deposits is consistent with 05HYEH3 being an episodic ponded environment. Ephemerally waterlain occupation sediments in ditches, quarries, etc are not unusual in the archaeological record.

4.3 Longshan ash pit 05HYEH4

Chemically, this ash pit fill is similar to ash pit 05HYEH3, but records a more strongly enhanced magnetic susceptibility (samples 12 and 13). In the 150 mm sample examined in thin section (M22A and M22B) there are layers wood ash, mixed soil and long articulated phytoliths, and brown amorphous organic matter-stained layered articulated phytoliths. The last material is again believed to be from mats, but appear to be 'dirtier' than the 'mats' in 05HYEH3. There are recognizable phytoliths of grass stems, sedges and reeds (Rosen, pers. comm., 2006). The deposit was also affected by secondary iron staining and burrowing, and again may have developed under ponded conditions at times.

4.4 Yangshao and Longshan soil-sediment sequence at GS2 (05HYEGS2)

The section at GS2, comprises modern disturbed ground, below which there is a 2.30 m thick series of deposits (Table 1); this geological profile and others at lower and higher altitudes have been investigated by Rosen (this volume: Gigures 2-4). In brief, at 0.20-0.45 m a massive and iron-stained layer containing a Longshan sherd, is capped by laminated beds, and these deposits were examined in samples 38a and 38b, and M38A and 38B. At around 2.00 metres fine weakly iron-stained deposits overlay a pale leached fine layer over gravel; the last contains Yangshao pottery (samples 39a and 39b, respectively; M39A, M39B, M39base and M39plan). This gravel apparently truncates an assumed natural Late Pleistocene/early Holocene alluvial soil, and the vertical junction between the two layers and the soil below were sampled (samples 40, M40A and 40B). A control sample of the lateral junction between laminated alluvium and the alluvial soil was also collected (M30) some 0.4 m distant.

The characteristics of these soils and sediments are summarized in Table 2. Rooting is recorded in the lowermost grey alluvium which is devoid of anthropogenic material, unlike the Yangshao gravels and silty muds which overlie it. The latter contain sherds, sand to gravel size burned daub, carbonate nodules, tufa, bone, charcoal and phosphate nodules of anthropogenic origin (e.g., phosphate nodules that include of phytoliths and can be broadly termed as probable 'nightsoil' when of anthropogenic origin; Goldberg and Macphail 2006: 206). Due to post-depositional phosphate loss and groundwater movement (Thirly et al. 2006) phosphate is poorly recorded chemically, except for in sample 39a (Table 2) where secondary phosphate has apparently accumulated alongside iron and manganese (microprobe analysis). No enhancement in heavy metal concentrations was recorded, however, in this sequence.

The Longshan samples (M38A and 38B) examined two gleyed layers where an apparently laminated deposit (38a) is present over a massive heterogenous sediment (38b). The latter, includes large clasts of daub and burned daub (some with embedded charcoal), and smaller fragments of charcoal, fine bone and coprolite. Secondary iron-phosphate staining is present, and very dark, dusty clay void infills and coatings testify to the coarse turbation of this sediment under waterlogged conditions. The overlying and apparently laminated layer 39b, is equally rich in anthropogenic materials (daub, burned daub, bone, coprolite, charcoal, phosphate-stained charcoal-rich soil), but these are smaller and present as sand and coarse sand size material. In addition, occasional fine plant fragments, including 'soft' tissues, are present, and probably responsible for the highest LOI found in this sequence. On drying, however, the apparently laminated 'beds' have formed a lenticular structure. This, with the textural pedofeatures present that are again probably due to wet soil slaking and disturbance, suggest that a possible human trampled 'surface' layer formed in a waterlogged, fine anthropogenic sediment.

4.5 Erlitou contexts

A soil next to a well (sample 4), five ash pit deposits (samples 6-9, 14-15) and a 'road' (sample 37) were analysed. All deposits, with the exception of the soil, are enriched to very strongly enriched in phosphate-P (max. 13.3 mg g-1 in sample 15, highest measured at Huizui) and show strong to very strong magnetic susceptibility enhancement, producing a marked anthropogenic signal.

The soil by the well appears to be a mainly truncated subsoil material (M4, fragments only) with little evidence of activity apart from some very dusty clay infills. The last could be the result of soil slaking induced by trampling and spillage of water.

An example of an ash pit (M8) shows a very heterogeneous and biologically mixed fill composed of soil, daub, burned daub, bone, coprolites, with very abundant charred and ashed plant material including millet (in situ phytolith evidence; Rosen, pers comm.). Several silica slag fragments of vitrified (vesicular voids) material are evidence of moderately high temperature burned phytoliths, consistent with the very strongly enhanced magnetic susceptibility (samples 6-9). These inclusions indicate that plant (cereal?) processing, kitchen and latrine (nightsoil) waste have been dumped. The fill is not untypical of ash-rich deposits that have been studied in later prehistoric contexts in the UK (Macphail 2000; Macphail and Crowther 2002), but is less ash-rich compared with Longshan ash pits (see estimated carbonate in Table 2). M15 is wood ash dominated (excavated 'white layer') and charred bark is present; the included strongly burned soil, daub, and cess also contribute to the strong phosphate and magnetic susceptibility signal.

The 'road' sediment is very compact and although it includes coarse burned daub, much of the anthropogenic material is fine sand to medium sand-size; shell, charcoal, bone, rubefied burned bone, probably phosphatecemented bone rich aggregates (nightsoil) are present and contribute to the anthropogenic phosphate and magnetic susceptibility signal (sample 37). The fine-sorting is typical of trampled surfaces, and pseudolayering is expressed by charred organic matter and planar voids relict of oxidized plant remains that were horizontally oriented. From experiments and analysis of occupation surfaces, such deposits can develop by human trampling producing a beaten surface under relatively dry conditions; in the UK this was within roofed structures (Goldberg and Macphail 2006; Macphail et al. 2004). Here it is a 'beaten track'. Other layers within this road, however, show the development of dusty clay panning and clay void infills that more likely relate to passage when the road was muddy (Rentzel and Narten 2000).

5. CONCLUSIONS

Although 31 thin sections and 25 bulk samples were investigated from in and around Huizui after fieldwork in 2005, site interpretations are still at an early stage and need to be treated with caution. Soil micromorphology (with microprobe) was combined with analyses of LOI, fractionated phosphate, magnetic susceptibility including χ max, and the heavy metals Cu, Pb and Zn to produce a preliminary understanding of the microstratigraphy of soils and sediments from the Peiligang to Erlitou Periods. This produced a broad, albeit limited, dataset, which has allowed this article to focus upon our understanding of the constructional origins of a Yangshao floor sequence. Here, ground-raising was carried out using planttempered adobe manufactured from local 'clean' loess soils, with mud-plastered surfaces creating dark 'red' layers immediately below each white floor. The white floors themselves are not manufactured burned lime floors, but constructed from single to multiple slabs of tufa that may well have been quarried locally from tabular tufa formed along spring lines. Such slabs appear to be in excess of 3-4 m in size, the quarrying and transport of which imply a high degree of social organization. No quarries have yet been identified, however. No Yangshao occupation floor deposits were found (only ground-raising deposits), suggesting that either floors were of ritual use (Liu, pers. comm.) or were swept or mat-covered. The overall dataset also provides punctuated insights into the occupational and landscape history of the site, including likely manipulation of the fluvial system and the 'off-site' marked accumulation of anthropogenic soils and sediments under water-logged conditions.

Acknowledgements: The authors thank their chief co-workers at Huizui (Li Liu and John Webb, La Trobe University, Australia; Xingcan Chen, Institute of Archaeology, Chinese Academy of Social Sciences, China; and Arlene Rosen, University College London) for their collaboration and discussion, and gratefully acknowledge the Australian Research Council grant that supported this study. John Webb (La Trobe University) kindly allowed us to cite his mineralogical data. The authors also thank Gyoung-Ah Lee and Ming Wei (La Trobe University) for their assistance during fieldwork. Paul Goldberg's (Department of Archaeology, Boston University) comments on some of the thin sections are also gratefully acknowledged, as are the observations of Chris Hayward (Department of Geology, University of Cambridge).

REFERENCES

Avery, B.W. 1990. Soils of the British Isles: Wallingford, CAB International.

Bethell, P.H. and I. Máté. 1989. The use of soil phosphate analysis in archaeology: A critique. In J. Henderson (ed.), Scientific Analysis in Archaeology, 19, pp. 1-29. Oxford: Oxford University Committee.

Boivin, N.L., 1999. Life rythms and floor sequences: excavating time in rural Rajasthan and Neolithic Çatalhöyük. World Archaeology 31: 367-388.

Bouma, J., C.A. Fox, and R. Miedema. 1990. Micromorphology of hydromorphic soils: applications for soil genesis and land evaluation In Douglas, L.A. (ed.) Soil Micromorphology: A Basic and Applied Science, 19 Developments in Soil Science, pp 257-278. Amsterdam: Elsevier.

Courty, M.A., and N. Fedoroff. 1982. Micromorphology of a Holocene dwelling, Proceedings Nordic Archaeometry, PACT 7: 257-277.

Courty, M.A., P. Goldberg and R.I. Macphail. 1989. Soils and Micromorphology in Archaeology. Cambridge: Cambridge University Press.

Crowther. J. 2003. Potential magnetic susceptibility and fractional conversion studies of archaeological soils and sediments. Archaeometry 45: 685-701.

Crowther, J., and P. Barker. 1995. Magnetic susceptibility: distinguishing anthropogenic effects from the natural. Archaeological Prospection 2: 207-215.

Duchaufour, P. 1982. Pedology. London: Allen and Unwin.

FAO-Unesco. 1988. Soil Map of the World. Rome: FAO.

Goldberg, P. and R.I. Macphail. 2006. Practical and Theoretical Geoarchaeology. Oxford: Blackwell Publishing.

Holliday, V.T., Hoffecker, J., Goldberg, P., Macphail, R.I., Forman, S., Anikovich, M.V. and Sinitsyn, A.A. 2007. Geoarchaeology of the Kostenki-Borshchevo sites, Don River Valley, Russia. Geoarchaeology 22: 181-228.

Liu, L., X. Chen, Y.K. Lee, H. Wright and A. Rosen. 2002-2004. Settlement patterns and developing of social complexity in the Yiluo Region, north China. Journal of Field Archaeology 29: 75-100.

Lawson (ed.), Potterne 1982-5: Animal Husbandry in Later Prehistoric Wiltshire, 17 Archaeology Report, pp 47-70. Salisbury: Wessex Archaeology.

Macphail, R.I. 2000. Soils and microstratigraphy: a soil micromorphological and micro-chemical approach. In A.J.

Macphail, R.I., Courty, M.A., Hather, J., and Wattez, J., 1997. The soil micromorphological evidence of domestic occupation and stabling activities. In R. Maggi (ed.), Arene Candide: a Functional and Environmental Assessment of the Holocene Sequence (Excavations Bernabò Brea-Cardini 1940-50), pp 53-88. Roma: Memorie dell'Istituto Italiano di Paleontologia Umana.

Macphail, R.I., and J. Crowther. 2002. Battlesbury, Hampshire: soil micromorphology and chemistry (W4896). Unpublished report, Salisbury: Wessex Archaeology.

Macphail, R.I., and J. Crowther. 2004. Tower of London Moat: sediment micromorphology, particle size, chemistry and magnetic properties. In G. Keevil (ed.), Tower of London Moat Excavation, 1 Historic Royal Palaces Monograph, pp 41-43, 48-50, 78-79, 82-83, 155, 183-186, 202-204 and 271-284. Oxford: Oxford Archaeology.

Macphail, R.I., G.M. Cruise, M.J. Allen, J. Linderholm and P. Reynolds. 2004. Archaeological soil and pollen analysis of experimental floor deposits; with special reference to Butser Ancient Farm, Hampshire, UK. Journal of Archaeological Science 31: 175-191.

Matthews, W., C.A.I. French, T. Lawrence and D. Cutler. 1996. Multiple Surfaces: the Micromorphology. In I. Hodder (ed.), On the Surface: Çatalhöyük 1993-95, pp 301-342. Cambridge: McDonald Institute for Archaeological Research and British Institute of Archaeology at Ankara.

Matthews, W., C.A. Hastorf and B. Ergenekon. 2000. Ethnoarchaeology: studies in local villages aimed at understanding aspects of the Neolithic site. In I. Hodder (ed.), Towards Reflexive Method in Archaeology: the Example at Çatalhöyük, pp 177-188. Cambridge: McDonald Institute for Archaeological Research and British Institute of Archaeology at Ankara.

Rentzel, P., and G.-B. Narten. 2000. Zur Entstehung von Gehniveaus in sandig-lehmigen Ablagerungen - Experimente und archäologische Befunde (Activity surfaces in sandy-loamy deposits - experiments and archaeological examples), Jahresbericht 1999, pp 107-27. Basel: Archäologische Bodenforschung des Kantons Basel-Stadt.

Slager, S., and H.T.J. Van der Wetering. 1977. Soil formation in archaeological pits and adjacent loess soils in Southern Germany. Journal of Archaeological Science 4: 259-67. Soil Survey Staff. 1999. Soil Taxonomy. Washington D. C.: U.S. Department of Agriculture, U. S. Government Printing Office.

Stoops, G. 2003. Guidelines for Analysis and Description of Soil and Regolith Thin Sections. Madison, Wisconsin: Soil Science Society of America, Inc.

Thirly, M., J. Galbois, and J.-M. Schmitt. 2006. Unusual phosphate concretions related to groundwater flow in a continental environment. Journal of Sedimentary Research, 76: 866-877.

附　表

附表1　遗址登记表

序号	遗址信息 编号	名称	遗迹 灰坑	房址	墓葬	其他	旧石器	裴李岗文化 早期	裴李岗文化 晚期	仰韶文化 早期	仰韶文化 中期	仰韶文化 晚期	龙山文化 早期	龙山文化 晚期	二里头文化 一期	二里头文化 二期	二里头文化 三期	二里头文化 四期	二里岗文化 早期	二里岗文化 晚期	殷墟文化	西周 早期	西周 中期	西周 晚期	东周 春秋	东周 战国
1	014	西昌庙																								
2	036	刘坡									●										●				●	●
3	037	耀店东														●										●	●
4	038	平乐中州渠墓地															●								●	●
5	034	平乐A	H1											●		●	●	●	●							●
6	035	平乐B										●			●												
7	029	霍泉北																●								●	●
8	030	霍泉东北										●	●	●													
9	031	霍泉西南											●		●		○	●	●					●	●	●	●
10	032	金村东北													●			●	○						●	●	●
11	033	金村墓地																●	●							●	●
12	046	保庄西北	H1—H3										●		●										●	●	●
13	047	保庄北											●														
14	051	石桥北庄东北																						○			
15	028	丁沟南											●												●		○
16	027	丁沟新村南																				●				●	●
17	049	石桥东北															○	○								●	
18	050	石桥东南												○											○		○
19	012	帽郭A														●	●	●	●	●		●		○			

续表

遗址信息			遗迹				文化属性																	
							旧石器	裴李岗文化		仰韶文化			龙山文化		二里头文化				二里岗文化		殷墟文化	西周			东周	
序号	编号	名称	灰坑	房址	墓葬	其他		早期	晚期	早期	中期	晚期	早期	晚期	一期	二期	三期	四期	早期	晚期		早期	中期	晚期	春秋	战国
20	013	帽郭B																			●		●			
21	004	凹杨									○	●	○			●	●									○
22	003	扁担趄南									●	●	○			●	●	○								○
23	005	油王南										●					○						○			○
24	007	黑王															●	●	●		●						○
25	006	白王北									○							○									
26	008	分金沟																								○	
27	011	白马寺											○	○													
28	045	韩旗城址									●	●				●	●	●	●					●	●	●
29	039	永宁寺西南										●			○	●	●	●		●				●	●	●
30	040	龙虎滩北															●	●									●
31	048	寺里碑东									○	●			○	●	○		●	●	●			●	●	●
32	041	景阳岗	H1—H3											○												
33	043	白村东北									●					●				○				●	●	
34	054	新庄东南																								
35	052	南蔡庄西北									○						●										
36	053	南蔡庄西																								
37	055	羊二庄东南									○																
38	061	山神庙													○												
39	058	坟庄东																									
40	059	杜楼																									
41	060	赫田寨西北									○						●	○		●						○	○
42	001	史家湾北	H1									○					●	●							●	●	
43	002	杨湾西															●	●							○	●	○	●
44	009	陈屯老村												●	●	○	●	●	●	●	●	●	○	○	●	○	●
45	010	枣园北																						○			○	●
46	042	宋湾东南																									○

续表

序号	遗址信息			遗迹				文化属性																	
	编号	名称		灰坑	房址	墓葬	其他	旧石器	裴李岗文化		仰韶文化			龙山文化		二里头文化				二里岗文化		殷墟文化	西周			东周	
									早期	晚期	早期	中期	晚期	早期	晚期	一期	二期	三期	四期	早期	晚期		早期	中期	晚期	春秋	战国
47	044	渔骨西南																									
48	057	古城西																									
49	056	古城东北																								●
50	062	偃师商城																	○	●	●	●	○	○			
51	063	塔庄																								○
52	064	槐庙南									○															
53	065	北窑东北	H1								●	○						●	●			●	○			
54	066	汤泉沟									●	●	○				●	●	●							
55	067	凤凰沟																●								
56	069	石头沟北												●												
57	071	山圪垯北										○		○												
58	068	化村北																									
59	072	山圪垯																									
60	073	王窑												●												
61	070	忠义村黄家										●	○	●				●								
62、63	074	寺沟										●	●	●	●	●	○	●	●	●	○		●	○		●	●	
62	Y151	寺沟南	H1—H5								●	●										●	●	●	●		
63	Y152	寺沟东南	H1—H7								●	●										●	●	●	●		
64a	075	石家庄										●															
64b	Y153	石家庄西南																					○				
65	Y154	高岭																									●
66	Y156	南瓦窑												○	●												●
67	Y157	康北古城	H1			W1																		●		●	●
68	Y158	康沟												●										●	●	●	
69	Y159	董沟												○													○
70	Y160	洪沟						●																			
71	Y161	神北														○			○	○							

续表

遗址信息			遗迹			文化属性															
						旧石器	裴李岗文化		仰韶文化			龙山文化		二里头文化				二里岗文化		殷墟文化	西周			东周	
序号	编号	名称	灰坑	房址	墓葬	其他		早期	晚期	早期	中期	晚期	早期	晚期	一期	二期	三期	四期	早期	晚期		早期	中期	晚期	春秋	战国
72	076	西石桥东	H1						○	●				●		●		●								●
73	077	孙家岗	H1							●							●	●						●	●	●
74	080	佃庄东																								○
75	087	大郝寨东									○			○				○								○	
76	088	关庄东南																					●				
77	089	关公冢									●	●		●									●				
78	090	二里头										○				●	●	●	●	●					●		
79	091	四角楼											●														
80	092	北许南											●													○	
81	093	圪当头东北											●	●			●	●	●								●
82	094	合堆头寨										●	●			●	●	●	●		●					●	○
83	020	桂连凹南	H1										●					●	●	●		●				●	●
84	021	桂连凹东北											○					●	●					○		○	○
85	019	纲常	H1								●		●					●			●						○
86	024	齐村西南											●	○													
87	023	齐村东南											●														
88	025	夏庄西北										○	●											○			○
89	026	二郎庙北											○							○							
90	018	太平庄北											●											○			●
91	022	穆庄										○	●				●	●	●		●			●		●	●
92	015	潘寨老寨东	H1									●	●			●	●	●	●		●				●	●	●
93	086	西马庄西北													●												
94	016	西石罢										○	●		○		●		●	○		●		○		●	●
95	017	火龙庙	H1								○													○		●	●
96	083	大郎庙南											●													●	●
97	084	东马庄西																	●					○		○	○
98	078	牛王庙东北																								○	
99	079	西三家																	●								●

续表

遗址信息			遗迹				文化属性																	
序号	编号	名称	灰坑	房址	墓葬	其他	旧石器	裴李岗文化		仰韶文化			龙山文化		二里头文化				二里岗文化		殷墟文化	西周			东周	
								早期	晚期	早期	中期	晚期	早期	晚期	一期	二期	三期	四期	早期	晚期		早期	中期	晚期	春秋	战国
100	081	金钟寺								●		●		●		●		●						●	●	
101	085	碑楼南										●													●	●
102	082	罗圪垱								○	○															
103	179	刁窑东												●		●		●							●	
104	180	刘窑东							●		○	●														
105	178	诸葛水库北			M1																					
106	176	梁村南																						●	○	
107	177	道湛东南								●		●				●		●						●	●	●
108	160	杨闸东南	H1、H2								○														○	
109	161	杨闸东	H1									●					○								○	
110	162	王沟东	H1									●													○	
111	163	杨河西									○		●				○						○			
112	159	酒流沟水库西	H1、H2									●		●	●	●	●		●					●	●	●
113	158	酒流沟水库北														●	●	●		○					●	○
114	175	刘沟东北	H1、H2																					●	●	○
115	157	刘家窑	H1																					●	●	
116	170	袁沟西																							○	
117	172	袁沟东		Y1																						
118	173	袁沟东南													●	●	●	●							●	●
119	166	袁沟B	H1—H4							●	●				●	●	●			●	●			●	●	
120	165	袁沟A	H1、H2																						○	○
121	171	偏桥西南																								
122	164	毛村东	H1、H2		M1					●			●		●	●	●	●			●				●	●
123	174	常村西南									○									○				○	○	
124	169	常村东								○																

续表

遗址信息			遗迹				旧石器	裴李岗文化		仰韶文化			龙山文化		二里头				二里岗文化		殷墟文化	西周			东周	
序号	编号	名称	灰坑	房址	墓葬	其他		早期	晚期	早期	中期	晚期	早期	晚期	一期	二期	三期	四期	早期	晚期		早期	中期	晚期	春秋	战国
125	168	偏桥北																							●	
126	167	俎家庄东北																								○
127	156	俎家庄北										●						●		●					●		○
128	155	大王村西北															○										
129	154	南寨上村东	H1、H2									●	●				●	○				●		○			
130	151	南寨西村南															○					●	●	○			○
131	192	马寨													●												
132	193	孙家窑西	H1—H4		M1						○	●								●							
133	194	贾庄坡西南																●	○		●							
134	197	东朱村东南											●					●	○	●							
135	196	东朱村东北													●					●							
136	195	王湾西北	H1—H3										●	●	○												
137	191	韩寨北									○	○															
138	190	杨裴屯西南										●	●		●	○							●		○	●	
139	188	沙沟西										●	●	●	●	○	●		●				○			●	●
140	189	西湾北	H1													○											
141	185	寇店西										●			●				●								
142	184	刘李寨A										○			●	●	○	●		○		●				●	●
143	186	陈家窑	H1									●	●						●						○	●	●
144	187	刘李寨B																								●	●
145	183	宫家窑										●	●	●	●	●	○	●	○								○
146	181	刘李寨东北	H1																							●	●
147	182	刘李寨西北	H1										●													●	
148	139	九贤												○													
149	138	苏家窑南																									
150	137	苏家窑西北	H1—H5									●	●		●											●	●
151	152	武屯东南								○				○	●	●											●

续表

遗址信息			遗迹				文化属性															
							旧石器	裴李岗文化		仰韶文化			龙山文化		二里头文化				二里冈文化		殷墟文化	西周			东周	
序号	编号	名称	灰坑	房址	墓葬	其他		早期	晚期	早期	中期	晚期	早期	晚期	一期	二期	三期	四期	早期	晚期		早期	中期	晚期	春秋	战国
152	153	武屯南	H1—H4											●												
153	135	西庞村西北									●														●	
154	150	东陇村北										●														○
155	141	白草坡西南								○													○			○
156	142	辛庄东北									○																○
157	136	东陇村南									○			●													
158	144	杨村东南											●					●	●	●	○	○				○	○
159	145	杨村北	H1、H2								●	●			●		●	●	●			○			●	●
160	146	魏家窑北										●					●	●	●	●	●				●	●
161	147	掘山													●				●	●						●
162	148	西窑沟																					○				
163	149	窑沟												●												○	
164	209	肖村南寨														○		●	●							○	
165	207	肖周东											●					●	●	●		●				○	●
166	208	肖村西寨西北	H1、H2															●	●			●				●
167	206	经周东北																								○	
168	211	宁村西北										○												○			●
169	210	吕桥东南																●	●	●						●	●
170	205	吕桥	H1																●								
171	204	吕桥北										○													○		○
172	203	郭家岭北																									
173	125	邓寨北																									
174	140	辛屯东南	H1、H2								●		●			●	●	●	●	●						●	
175	124	石牛沟										●		●			●	○	●	●							●	
176	143	新彭店东																								●	
177	134	高崖西	H1—H3								●				●	●		●	●	●		●			●		●

续表

序号	编号	名称	灰坑	房址	墓葬	其他	旧石器	裴李岗文化早期	裴李岗文化晚期	仰韶文化早期	仰韶文化中期	仰韶文化晚期	龙山文化早期	龙山文化晚期	二里头一期	二里头二期	二里头三期	二里头四期	二里岗早期	二里岗晚期	殷墟文化	西周早期	西周中期	西周晚期	东周春秋	东周战国
178	132	高崖东北	H1																							
179	133	丁湖店西南																								○
180	131	半个寨西南																								○
181	130	五岔沟西北																								
182	129	五岔沟北																								
183	218	铁铬东南			M1																		○			
184	215	杨寨西南	H1								●			●												
185	219	铁铬东												●												
186	214	杨寨西									●			●		●	●	●						●	○	
187	220	铁村南										●			●											
188	213	马寨西	H1—H7									●	●	●		●	●	●	●	●	●					●
189	216	寨湾东南	H1—H8									●		●		●	●	●	●	●	●				●	
190	217	寨湾东北	H1—H7	F1—F4								●		●			●	●		●				●	●	
191	212	曹寨北	H1—H6									●	●	●												
192	222	西张庄东南											○													
193	221	西张庄东北	H1—H5								●															
194	202	韩村南B											○													
195	201	韩村南A										●		●		●	●	●						●		●
196	200	符家寨西									●			○			●	●								
197	199	符家寨北												●		●	●	●								○
198	198	符家寨东北	H1									●		●			●	●								●
199	123	张村东南	H1									●		●												○
200	122	裴村E										●														
201	118	裴村A	H1									●				●	●									
202	119	裴村B	H1									●					●	●	●							
203	120	裴村C	H1								○					●	●	●		●						○
204	121	裴村D	H1														●	●		●						○

续表

遗址信息			遗迹				文化属性															
							旧石器	裴李岗文化		仰韶文化			龙山文化		二里头文化				二里岗文化		殷墟文化	西周			东周	
序号	编号	名称	灰坑	房址	墓葬	其他		早期	晚期	早期	中期	晚期	早期	晚期	一期	二期	三期	四期	早期	晚期		早期	中期	晚期	春秋	战国
205	116	程子沟南										●		●					●								
206	117	程子沟													●		●	●					○				
207	115	崔河北									○															○	
208	114	郝寨东北	H1														●										
209	127	陶化店东南	H1								○						●	●	●							○	
210	126	陶化店水库	H1、H2									●					●	●						○		○	
211	Y226	邢寨东北									○				●									○		○	
212	Y225	邢村东																●	●							○	
213	Y182	夏后寺													●		●	●	●	○							
214	Y183	九龙水库东南												○				○									
215	Y184	邢村北	H1—H3												●			●		●		●				○	
216	Y185	扒头水库东南											●		●			●		●		●				●	●
217	Y181	扒头东南	H1												●		○			●						●	●
218	Y180	扒头西南											●		●			●		●		●					
219	Y179	任才村东南										○			●									●		○	
220	Y178	任才村西南										○			●		●	○		●				●		○	
221	Y186	卢村南													○												
222	Y227	卢村西南													●					●				○		○	
223	Y177	卢村西										○			○			○									
224	Y176	卢村西北													●									○	●	●	
225	Y224	双泉东南	H1												○									○		○	
226	Y169	卢村东北												●												○	
227	Y168	卢村北	H1、H2											●													
228	Y167	高祖庙	H1								○			●											○		
229	Y174	双泉东南																									
230	Y172	双泉南	H1											●													

续表

序号	遗址信息		遗迹				文化属性																	
	编号	名称	灰坑	房址	墓葬	其他	旧石器	裴李岗文化		仰韶文化			龙山文化		二里头文化				二里岗文化		殷墟文化	西周			东周	
								早期	晚期	早期	中期	晚期	早期	晚期	一期	二期	三期	四期	早期	晚期		早期	中期	晚期	春秋	战国
231	Y173	泉寨东																								○
232	Y170	泉寨西																								●
233	Y171	双泉西南							○	●	●															
234	Y175	双泉西北									○															
235	Y164	西齐家窑东南									○												○		○	
236	Y187	浏涧河水库东							●	●	●															
237	Y165	西齐家窑									●	●													●	●
238	Y127	灰嘴										●	●	●	●	●	●	●					●		●	
238	Y127	灰嘴										●	●	●	●	●	●	●					●		●	
239	Y166	西齐家窑东北	H1—H3											●												
240	Y188	西齐家窑西北										○		●												
241	Y192	灰嘴北													●											
242	Y189	郑窑南	H1、H2								●						●	●					○			●
243	Y191	陶家村东													●									○			●
244	Y190	刘国故城	H1、H2								●														●	●
245	Y140	郑窑	H1																						●春秋	
246	Y193	搞嫠台水库东																								○
247	Y194	郑村西	H1												●											○
248	Y195	涧东村																								○
249	Y196A	涧东村北	H1—H3													●	●	●			●			○		
250	Y196B	涧东村西北	H1											●			●	●			●			○		

续表

遗址信息			遗迹				文化属性																			
							旧石器	裴李岗文化		仰韶文化			龙山文化		二里头文化				二里岗文化		殷墟文化	西周			东周	
序号	编号	名称	灰坑	房址	墓葬	其他		早期	晚期	早期	中期	晚期	早期	晚期	一期	二期	三期	四期	早期	晚期		早期	中期	晚期	春秋	战国
251	Y228	姬家村南																							○	●
252	Y223	九龙角																							○	
253	Y203	水牢西					○																			
254	Y202	东管茅东南																					●				●
255	Y201	东管茅东	H1																			●				○	
256	Y200	西口孜	H1—H6								●	●										●		●		○	
257	Y199	老周寨	H1								●	●										●		●		○	
258	Y198	老屯寨	H1—H3									○	●			●	●	●		●	●				●	●
259	Y204	屯寨西北	H1, H2									○		●												●
260	Y206	布村东南	H1, H2									○														
261	Y197	布村东									●	●	●	●		●	●	●								○	
262	Y207	新寨北嘴										●	○														
263	Y208	马河北									●	●		●		●	●	●	○								●
264	Y205	马河	H1—H3											●		●	●	●		●	●					●
265	Y210	花张东北									●	●		●		●	●	○	●		○		○			●
266	Y209	王湾西北										●		●		●	●	●	○	●						○	
267	Y222	柏谷坞东												○					○	●							
268	Y215	金屯东												●		○	●	●								○	
269	Y214	北吴家湾												●												○	
270	Y213	南吴家湾东南										○							●	○	○		○			○	
271	Y211	林小寨												○												○	
272	Y212	林小寨西南												●												○	
273	Y221	邱河西										○		●												○	
274	Y220	凤凰台南																						●		○	
275	Y217	老吊桥寨																						●	●		

续表

遗址信息			遗迹				文化属性															
							旧石器	裴李岗文化		仰韶文化			龙山文化		二里头文化				二里岗文化		殷墟文化	西周			东周	
序号	编号	名称	灰坑	房址	墓葬	其他		早期	晚期	早期	中期	晚期	早期	晚期	一期	二期	三期	四期	早期	晚期		早期	中期	晚期	春秋	战国
276	Y216	吊桥寨东南																			●					●
277	Y218	北寨东南	H1																				○			○
278	Y219	北寨北																					●			○
279	113	陈河东北																								
280	112	陈河北	H1—H5									●					●	●							●	●
281	111	化寨东				Z1																			●	
282	109	盆窑寨东南	H1、H2								●	●				●	●	●								●
283	110	盆窑寨西南																								
284	101	东王河东南									●	●		●	●	●	●		●							●
285	100	东王河北											●													○
286	099	东王河									○				○					○							
287	108	陶化店水库东									○				○												
288	104	李家湾东南											●	●	●					●		●					●
289	128	铺刘北										●	●		●			●	●							●	●
290	107	吴家湾东南										●	●		●			●	●		●					○	
291	105	段西村西北												○		●											○
292	106	段东村东北										●	●	●	●												
293	098	苗湾东南										●	●		●							●					
294	097	苗湾C										●	●	●	●					●					●		●
295	096	苗湾B												●						●					●		
296	095	苗湾A											○	○												○	
297	Y122	李家窑西南											●	●												○	
298	Y121	邢村东	H1—H4																							●
299	Y123	半个寨	H1																								
300	Y120	邢村																									
301	Y119	赵城水库东																									●

序号	编号	名称	灰坑	房址	墓葬	其他	旧石器	裴李岗文化 早期	裴李岗文化 晚期	仰韶文化 早期	仰韶文化 中期	仰韶文化 晚期	龙山文化 早期	龙山文化 晚期	二里头文化 一期	二里头文化 二期	二里头文化 三期	二里头文化 四期	二里岗文化 早期	二里岗文化 晚期	殷墟文化	西周 早期	西周 中期	西周 晚期	东周 春秋	东周 战国
302	Y077	赵城	H1、H2		M1																		●		●	
303	Y079	赵城西南	H1																						○	
304	Y078	赵城西							○																	
305	Y117	刘村西南																					○			
306	Y116	赵城西北																							○	
307	Y115	高村东北															○									
308	Y118	府店东南	H1						●	○																
309	Y080	小相寨东南										●		●											○	●
310	Y114	颜良寨水库西南	H1											●					●						○	
311	Y084	小相西												●											●	●
312	Y087	颜良寨水库西	H1—H6										●												●	●
313	Y124	府店东	H1											●												
314	Y085	小相西北	H1									●		●			○		●	●	●					●
315	Y086	颜良寨西南	H1										●		●						●					
316	Y113	府北村北								○																
317	Y088	颜良村西											○					○			○					○	
318	Y089	冯寨西南	H1—H10	F1											●										●	●
319	Y107	滑国故城	H1																						○	○	
320	Y112	滑城河东	H1											●												
321	Y091	冯寨西	H1															○		●							●
322	Y090	冯寨西北	H1										●		●					●	○						
323	Y059	杨寨西	H1—H5																							●	
324	Y058	杨寨西北	H1、H2										●							●	●						
325	Y061	南村寨东南																○	●	●				○		○	

续表

序号	遗址信息		遗迹				文化属性																
	编号	名称	灰坑	房址	墓葬	其他	旧石器	裴李岗文化		仰韶文化			龙山文化		二里头文化				二里岗文化		殷墟文化	西周			东周	
								早期	晚期	早期	中期	晚期	早期	晚期	一期	二期	三期	四期	早期	晚期		早期	中期	晚期	春秋	战国
326	Y057	南村寨																							○	
327	Y060	南村寨南											●													
328	Y109	渭城河西									●	●						●								●
329	Y108	渭城河北	H1、H2								●	●	●		●			●					●			●
330	Y111	府西东北	H1										○	●		○	●	●							○	○
331	Y110	府西村北	H1											●	●	○										●
332	Y062	南村寨西											●			●									●	●
333	Y063	南村寨西南											●		○	○										
334	Y064	桑沟水库北											●		●			●							●	
335	Y065	桑沟老村									●		●						●	○						
336	Y126	桑沟五队北	H1、H2										●	●												
337	Y105	三官庙窑厂东南												○		○										●
338	Y066	桑沟南											●													
339	Y068	桑沟西											●					●								
340	Y106	三官庙窑厂											●		●	●	●		●				●			●
341	Y067	桑沟西北											●				●									
342	Y104	三官庙北											○		●		●									
343	Y103	马屯西村南													●	●	●						●		●	
344	Y069	马屯新村	H1—H7										●		●	●	●									●
345	Y102	马屯老村											●					●							●	●
346	Y070	马屯北	H1										○													○
347	Y071	王屯											●											○		
348	Y101	贾屯	H1										●		●	●									●	●
349	Y100	孙家峒南													●	●	●			●	●				●	○
350	Y099	李彦沟东	H1—H5										●		●	●										●
351	Y072	罗彦庄西南/肖家沟				G1									○						○					○

续表

序号	编号	名称	遗迹				文化属性																
			灰坑	房址	墓葬	其他	旧石器	裴李岗文化		仰韶文化			龙山文化		二里头文化				二里岗文化		殷墟文化	西周			东周	
								早期	晚期	早期	中期	晚期	早期	晚期	一期	二期	三期	四期	早期	晚期		早期	中期	晚期	春秋	战国
352	Y098	顾家屯南	H1																							●
353	Y097	顾家屯东南																							●	●
354	Y096	顾家屯东																							●	●
355	Y095	石家沟东南			M1																		●		●	
356	Y094	石家沟东																				○				
357	Y073	念子庄西北	H1																				●		●	
358	Y093	石家沟东北	H1、H2													●	●				●			●		
359	Y092	石家沟												●		○	○			○					
360	Y074	老村北																●	●	●					●	●
361	Y083	干沟猪场	H1、H2												●	●	●	●	●	●				○	
362	Y076	干沟南												●			●	●	●	●					
363	Y075	刘乐寨西南	H1—H9																				●			●
364	Y082	回龙湾西南																							●	●
365	Y081	回龙湾				K1																				●
366	102	肖村北									○					○										
367	103	木阁沟东南										○				○	○									
368	Y135	曹闸													●										○	
369	Y136	王屿													●										○	
370	Y134	南沟	H1								○	○														
371	Y229	虎山坡南					○																			
372	Y133	曹河水库西											●												○	
373	Y230	曹林东南																○						●		
374	Y137	北后沟东													●										○	
375	Y138	北后沟北											●													○
376	Y139	北后沟西北	H1—H3										●													○

续表

遗址信息			遗迹			文化属性																
						旧石器	裴李岗文化		仰韶文化			龙山文化		二里头文化				二里岗文化		殷墟文化	西周			东周	
序号	编号	名称	灰坑	房址	墓葬	其他		早期	晚期	早期	中期	晚期	早期	晚期	一期	二期	三期	四期	早期	晚期		早期	中期	晚期	春秋	战国
377	Y132	新后沟窑厂东	H1、H2													●	●	●								○
378	Y131	新后沟东																								○
379	Y130	新后沟	H1—H3							○									●							●
380	Y129	后沟	H1																							●
381	Y128	鲁庄东北																								
382	Y125	南罗									○											○				
383	Y155	八陵西								●	●	●	●												●	●
384	Y051	鏊坡									●	●													○	●
385	Y052	堤东	H1、H2										●	●												
386	Y053	龙骨堆	H1、H2	M1							●	●												●	●
387	Y054	金钟寺										○	○													
388	Y043	天坡水库东北	H1—H6									●			●	●	●									●
389	Y049	天坡	H1—H5									●													●	
390	Y050	羽林庄南	H1—H6						●			●	●													
391	Y045	新移							○																	
392	Y038	大南沟				●																				
393	Y039	上庄东南	H1—H4						●							●										
394	Y037	上庄南	H1—H7									●				●	●	●							●	●
395	Y055	北地沟																								
396	Y040	涉村上古朵																							○	
397	Y036	涉村南沟															●								○	
398	Y035	涉村东										●														●
399	Y041	东山原								●																
400	Y028	铁生沟西南								●																
401	Y029	铁生沟	H1、H2	M1						○														●	
402	Y030	夹津口									●	●														

续表

遗址信息			遗迹				文化属性																	
							旧石器	裴李岗文化		仰韶文化			龙山文化		二里头文化				二里岗文化		殷墟文化	西周			东周	
序号	编号	名称	灰坑	房址	墓葬	其他		早期	晚期	早期	中期	晚期	早期	晚期	一期	二期	三期	四期	早期	晚期		早期	中期	晚期	春秋	战国
403	Y044	北营																								
404	Y047	双河																					○			○
405	Y031	双河东南																					○			●
406	Y034	寺院沟																								●
407	Y042	坞罗西坡2	H1—H4		M1					●					●	●										
408	Y033	坞罗西坡1	H1—H4							●				●		●	●	●		●						
409	Y032	坞罗南店		F1—F2							○	●	●	●						●	●				●	
410	Y025	坞罗水库西1	H1、H2											●												●
411	Y026	坞罗水库西2																								
412	Y027	罗口南																								●
413	Y022	罗口	H1—H9												●	●	●	●	●	●						
414	Y056	火葬场南/山川西南					○																			
415	Y021	喂庄东南高地															○									
416	Y020	喂庄东南									●	●							●		○				●
417	Y023	喂庄东南角										●	○													
418	Y024	喂庄南										○														
419	Y017	罗口砖厂东北		H1							●	●					●			●	●	○				●
420	Y019	喂庄西	H1、H2																				○			○
421	Y018	喂庄西南	H1—H3																				●		●	●
422	Y013	费窑南2																						●		●
423	Y014	费窑南3																								
424	Y012	费窑南1															○				○					
425	Y011	费窑西南	H1—H7																	●	●					

续表

序号	遗址信息		遗迹				文化属性																		
	编号	名称	灰坑	房址	墓葬	其他	旧石器	裴李岗文化		仰韶文化			龙山文化		二里头文化				二里岗文化		殷墟文化	西周			东周	
								早期	晚期	早期	中期	晚期	早期	晚期	一期	二期	三期	四期	早期	晚期		早期	中期	晚期	春秋	战国
426	Y016	官庄西																								
427	Y010	永熙陵北																								
428	Y015	芝田东南																								
429	Y007	电厂东南1																								○
430	Y003	清易镇东2	H1																							○
431	Y004	清易镇东3																								
432	Y009	电厂南																								○
433	Y008	电厂东南2															●	●	●								○
434	Y002	清易镇东1																								○
435	Y048	电厂西																●									
436	Y001	范堂东南																								
437	Y163	稍柴西南																								
438	Y046	南石路南													○												
439	Y1001	稍柴	H1—H10												○	●	●	●	●	●	●	●			●	○	
440	Y1003	南石	H1	F1								●	○	●		●				●			●		●	
441	Y1005	小訾殿南												●	○	○				○						○
442	Y1004	小訾殿北												●		○	○									
443	Y005	稍柴电厂北路东														○										
444	Y1002	稍柴南																								
445	Y162	稍柴东南																								○
446	Y006	稍柴东A																								
447	Y142	稍柴东B																								
448	Y141	东沟																								
449	Y143	东沟西																								○
450	Y144	亚茂沟													●											
451	Y145	小南沟西南	H1												●											

附表 1495

续表

遗址信息			遗迹				文化属性																	
							旧石器	裴李岗文化		仰韶文化			龙山文化		二里头文化				二里岗文化		殷墟文化	西周			东周	
序号	编号	名称	灰坑	房址	墓葬	其他		早期	晚期	早期	中期	晚期	早期	晚期	一期	二期	三期	四期	早期	晚期		早期	中期	晚期	春秋	战国
452	Y146	东沟北												●												○
453	Y147	东沟西北	H1											●												○
454	Y148	东沟东												●												○
455	Y150	益家窑					○																			
456	Y149	牌坊沟																		○					●	●

附表2 遗迹登记表

序号	遗址信息 编号	名称	遗迹 编号	类型	具体位置	形状	尺寸（单位：米）	填土	包含物及特征	标本	年代	发现时间	备注
2	036	刘坡		灰坑					以龙山陶片为主。可辨认器形有中口罐、粗砂罐、盆、小口高领瓮、圈足盘、盖等	无		2003.6.15	
5	034	平乐A	H1	灰坑					以龙山晚期腹底片为主，有少量磨光黑陶。可辨认器形有中口罐、双腹盘、盖等	1. 罐	龙山晚期	2003.6.13	
12	046	保庄西北	H1	灰坑	保庄西北冲沟东侧				仅少量陶片标本。可辨认器形有罐、盆、器盖等	1. 蚌刀	龙山晚期	2001.12.18	
			H2	灰坑	保庄西北冲沟东侧					1. 罐形鼎 2. 器盖	仰韶晚期	2001.12.18	
			H3	灰坑						1. 折腹盆	龙山晚期	2001.12.18	
32	041	景阳岗	H1	灰坑	景阳岗台地东南断崖以南，宋湾村北				以东周陶片为主，也含仰韶、龙山文化的陶片。可辨认器形有刀、罐	1. 陶刀 2. 罐	春秋	2001.10.8	
			H2	灰坑	景阳岗南断崖，G207路东				可辨认器形有深腹罐、圆腹罐、鬲、甗、缸、捏口罐、盆、刻槽盆、大口尊等	无	二里头	2001.10.8	
			H3	灰坑	景阳岗南断崖，G207路东					无	二里头	2001.10.8	
42	001	史家湾北	H1	灰坑	张古洞至史家湾村路西侧废窑厂		坑口距地表2.5米	灰褐土	以二里头文化四期陶片为主。另发现猪上颌骨残块。陶片可辨认器形有深腹罐、圆腹罐、大口尊、高领尊等	无	二里头四期	2001.3.8	
53	065	北崟东北	H1	灰坑	北崟东北				陶片数量较多。可辨认器形有篮、甗、假腹豆、小口高领罐	1. 罐 2. 篮 3. 甗	二里岗早、晚之间	2002.3.3	

续表

序号	遗址信息		遗迹		具体位置	形状尺寸			包含物及特征		标本	年代	发现时间	备注
	编号	名称	编号	类型		形状	尺寸（单位：米）	填土	包含物					
62	Y151	寺沟南	H1	灰坑	寺沟村南台地西断崖剖面南端						1.大口罐 2.小罐 3.器盖 4.圈足	龙山晚期	2001.6.10	浮选土样
			H2	灰坑	寺沟村南台地东断崖剖面北端				可辨认器形有中口罐、瓿		无	龙山晚期	2001.6.10	浮选土样
			H3	灰坑	寺沟村南台地西断崖剖面中部				可辨认器形有中口罐、小口高领瓮、小盖		无	龙山晚期	2001.6.10	浮选土样
			H4	灰坑	寺沟村南台地西断崖剖面南部						1、2.鬲	龙山晚期	2011	
			H5	灰坑	寺沟村南台地西断崖剖面北部						无	西周	2011	
			H1	灰坑	铁路北台地东剖面南端				含有鱼骨、蚌壳、兽骨		无	仰韶晚期	2001.6.11	现已被省道S314破坏，浮选土样
			H2	灰坑	铁路北台地东剖面中南部				可辨认器形有鬶、泥质折沿罐、堆纹罐、缸、罐、盆、钵、小口高领瓮、碗		1—6.缸 7.罐 8.盆 9.钵	龙山早期	2001.6.11	现已被省道S314破坏，浮选土样
63	Y152	寺沟东南	H3	灰坑	铁路南二级台地东西向剖面东部				二里头时期，和龙山早期的堆纹罐及横篮纹陶片		1.圆腹罐	二里头	2001.6.11	浮选土样
			H4	灰坑	铁路南一级台地东西向剖面中部						1.鬲	周	2001.6.11	
			H5	灰坑	铁路南二级台地东西向剖面东中部						无	周	2007.11.12	浮选土样
			H6	灰坑	铁路南二级台地东西向剖面中部						无	周	2007.11.12	浮选土样

续表

序号	遗址信息 编号	名称	遗迹 编号	类型	具体位置	形状尺寸 形状	尺寸（单位：米）	填土	包含物及特征 包含物	标本	年代	发现时间	备注
63	Y152	寺沟东南	H7	灰坑	铁路南二级台地南部北向剖面南部，小路北					1.石刀坯	周	2011	浮选土样
66	Y156	南瓦窑	H1	灰坑	路南一南北向断崖剖面					1、2.罐 3、4.钵	仰韶早期	2001.6.15	浮选土样
			W1	瓮棺葬	路北东西向断崖剖面中部					1.盆 2.罐	仰韶早期	2017.6.18	
68	Y158	康沟		灰坑	石榴沟北断崖剖面					无	东周	2001.6.15	
71	Y161	神北		灰坑	东西向台地剖面					无	龙山晚期	2001.6.15	
72		西石桥东	H1	灰坑	东石桥公坟北断崖			黄褐土泛灰	含有兽骨、烧土块和龙山文化陶片。可辨认器形有甑、罐、盆、甗、斝等	1.甑 2.盆 3.罐 4.斝 5.甗 6.盘	龙山晚期	2001.3.11	
73		孙家岗	H1	灰坑	孙家岗西北公坟附近		坑口距地表约1米	浅灰褐土	包含兽骨和陶片。陶片可辨认器形有夹砂罐、夹砂折肩罐	1.夹砂罐	仰韶晚期	2001.3.11	地理坐标：北纬34°42′331″；东经112°35′655″
83	076	桂连凹南	H1	灰坑	遗址西南部的景石路240米的东高村北				以二里头文化陶片为主，纹饰包括篮纹、绳纹和附加堆纹等。可辨认器形有深腹罐、缸、小口尊等	1.深腹罐	二里头二期	2001.3.17	开口于表土层下
85	019	纲常	H1	灰坑	取土场北壁		坑口距地表0.4—0.5米，坑口宽约3米，深0.5—0.6米	黑灰土	均为龙山文化陶片。可辨认器形有大口罐、中口罐、甑、高领罐、圈足盘、小口高领瓮等	1.中口罐 2.罐 3.甑	龙山晚期	2001.3.17	

续表

序号	遗址信息			遗迹			形状尺寸		填土	包含物及特征		年代	发现时间	备注
	编号	名称	编号	类型	具体位置	形状	尺寸（单位：米）			包含物	标本			
92	015	潘寨老寨东	H1	灰坑	土坑刮面		长2米，深0.5米		深褐色土	见有极为丰富的泥质陶片和夹砂陶片，另发现石器1件。可辨认器形有罐、盆等	1.石杵 2.盆 3.罐	龙山晚期	2001.3.15	
95	017	火龙庙	H1	灰坑	西石坝村南，耕地台地断面				深褐色土	含烧土粒和一定数量的陶片。可辨认器形有鬲、罐、瓮等	1、2.鬲 3、4.罐	春秋	2001.3.14	
100	081	金钟寺		灰坑							无		2001.3.12	
105	178	诸葛水库北	M1	墓葬	诸葛水库北，原偃师水泥厂南墙外沟西壁				夹有红烧土块的红褐土，底层下为黄褐生土，头骨周围为深褐土	见有死者头骨、肩胛骨、锁骨等	无	仰韶早期	2001.4.1	地理坐标：北纬34°34′37″；东经112°31′37″
108	160	杨闸东南	H1	灰坑	杨闸东南路东断崖		坑底距地表约2.5米，宽约3米		灰褐土	包含少量黑灰陶陶片。生土层有红砂岩。可辨认器形有小口高领瓮、夹砂小罐、折腹盆、盖等	无	龙山晚期	2001.3.29	
			H2	灰坑	杨闸南东一干渠南侧高地		口部直径约1.5米			包含黑灰陶陶片，另发现蚌片。可辨认器形有夹砂小口高领罐、中口罐、罐、双腹盆、豆、盖等	1.罐 2.大口罐	龙山晚期	2001.3.29	
109	161	杨闸东	H1	灰坑	杨闸东台地		坑口距地表1米，宽约1.5米，深约1米		黄褐土泛灰	均为仰韶文化陶片。可辨认器形有夹砂小罐、泥质灰口缸、盆、彩陶盆、圈足盘、豆等	1.钵 2.缸	仰韶晚期	2001.3.29	

续表

序号	遗址信息		遗迹		具体位置	形状尺寸		填土	包含物及特征		年代	发现时间	备注
	编号	名称	编号	类型		形状	尺寸（单位：米）		包含物	标本			
110	162	王沟东	H1	灰坑	杨河村西台地		坑口距地表0.5米，宽1.5—2.0米	灰褐土	见有陶片和小件石器，石器有石斧1件，陶片均为碎片，无口沿。可辨认的陶器器形有深腹罐、豆等	1.石斧 2.深腹罐 3.豆	二里头二期晚段至三期早段	2001.3.29	
112	159	酒流沟水库西	H1	灰坑	酒流沟水库西		坑口距地表约2.5米	灰褐杂土	包含较大红烧土块，仰韶陶片，可辨认器形有小口罐、小口高领瓮、盖等	1.小口罐	仰韶晚期	2001.3.28	
			H2	灰坑	酒流沟水库西		宽0.7—0.8米，深约2.5米	红褐土	以仰韶晚期陶片为主，另外发现有猪牙和猪下颌骨，陶片较碎，可辨认器形有罐、敛口钵、盆、钵、盖等	无	仰韶晚期	2001.3.28	
114	175	刘沟东北	H1	灰坑	刘沟东北果园东北角外，房屋以东2米余			红褐土	以东周陶片为主，含烧土粒。可辨认器形有鬲、盆、罐等	1.鬲 2、3.盆	春秋	2001.3.31	地理坐标：北纬34°34′168″；东经112°22′702″
			H2	灰坑	刘沟东北果园东北角外，水道东断面，与H26距离约3米			红褐土	含烧土粒	无	东周	2001.3.31	地理坐标：北纬34°34′168″；东经112°22′702″
115	157	刘家峪	H1	灰坑	刘家峪东断崖		长4.5米，厚1米以上		可辨认器形有罐、鬲、盆、瓮等	1、2、8.盆 3—6.鬲 7.罐	战国	2001.3.27	

续表

遗址信息			遗迹		具体位置	形状尺寸		填土	包含物及特征		年代	发现时间	备注
序号	编号	名称	编号	类型		形状	尺寸（单位：米）		包含物	标本			
119	166	袁沟B	H1	灰坑	袁沟村北，河以西台地，北距毛村遗址约50米		坑口距地表0.3—0.7米	黄褐色土	以仰韶文化陶片为主，见一完整深腹罐（尊）。可辨认器形有平唇夹砂罐（夹砂敷肓弦纹附加堆纹罐）	1、2. 罐	仰韶中期（大河村三期）	2003.3.12	
			H2	灰坑	袁沟村北，河以西台地，北距毛村遗址约51米		坑口距地表约0.3米	黄褐色土	可辨认器形有簋、深腹罐等	1. 簋	二里岗早期	2003.3.12	
			H3	灰坑	袁沟村北，河以西台地				均为龙山晚期陶片。可辨认器形有罐、小口高领瓮	1. 瓮	龙山晚期	2003.3.12	
			H4	灰坑	袁沟村北，河以西台地				以仰韶中晚期陶片为主。可辨认器形有夹砂弦纹罐、夹砂敛口瓮等	1. 盆	仰韶中期偏晚（大河村二、三期）	2003.3.12	
120	165	袁沟A	H1	灰坑					陶片较少，见有二期遗物。可辨认器物有圆腹罐、深腹罐、高领尊	无	二里头三、四期	2003.3.11	
			H2	灰坑					陶片数量较多，可辨认器形有盆	无	东周	2003.3.11	
122	164	毛村东	H1	灰坑					见有兽骨和二里头陶片。发现的小件遗物有牛脊椎横突1件，可辨认器形有捏口罐、缸、深腹罐、缸等	1. 捏口罐 2. 缸	二里头四期	2003.3.11	
			H2	灰坑					见有石器、兽骨和二里头陶片。发现的小件遗物有石片1片，石杵1件，肩胛骨1块（不明）。可辨认器形有深腹罐等	1. 石杵	二里头二期	2003.3.11	

续表

序号	遗址信息			遗迹		具体位置	形状尺寸		填土	包含物及特征		年代	发现时间	备注
	编号	名称		编号	类型		形状	尺寸（单位：米）		包含物	标本			
122	164			Y1	窑址	台地南面，M1东约8米		坑壁距地表约0.35米，直径超过1米，现存深约0.4米	窑壁青灰色，陶窑上部土似经扰动	见有汉代陶片和二里头文化陶片。可辨认器形有二里头文化方格纹深腹罐	1. 深腹罐	二里头早期	2003.3.11	
		毛村东		M1	墓葬	毛村东、东南靠河台地南边		坑口距地表深0.5～1米，宽约0.5米	黄褐土，有黄绿水锈	见有兽骨和1件二里头鏊陶盆，发现的完整鸡冠耳鏊，兽骨3块，有狗胚骨、猪下颌骨、中型哺乳动物骨骼碎块（盆骨、髓骨）	1. 盆	二里头早期	2003.3.11	
129	154	南寨上村东		H1	灰坑	上村东砖厂西壁			深灰褐土	含有较多黑灰（草木灰）。可辨认器形有鼎、中口罐、盖等	1. 石器 2、3. 罐	龙山晚期	2001.3.25	
				H2	灰坑			坑口距地表2米		采集到少量陶片，其中含二里头文化的鬲、爵足根等遗物	无	商周	2001.3.25	
				H1	灰坑	村西冲沟东		深约1.1～3.2米，宽3米	青灰土，含水锈	包含大量二里头文化陶片。可辨认器形有鬲、罐、缸、大口尊、盆、壶等	1、2. 鬲 3. 尊 4. 缸 5. 壶 6. 盏	二里头四期	2003.3.17	
132	193	孙家窑西		H2	灰坑	H1南约70米，靠近冲沟口		坑口距地表0.3米	黄褐土	以仰韶早期或中期为主，其中含仰韶中期红陶片，橘黄陶。可辨认器形有鬲、盆、盏、钵	1. 鼎 2. 钵	仰韶早中期	2003.3.17	
				H3	灰坑	孙家窑村三岔路口南约20米，东部断崖上	坑口约为圆形，剖面约为袋形	坑口距地表约0.9米，底距地表约1.55米，宽1.5米	黄褐土	发现了两片白衣彩陶，含鱼纹，几何纹彩陶盆。可辨认器形有彩陶盆、小口尖底瓶	1. 尖底瓶 2. 盆	仰韶早期	2003.3.17	
				H4	灰坑	位于H2西约8米			黄灰土，含绿水锈	可辨认器形有小口尖底瓶	无	仰韶	2003.3.17	

续表

遗址信息			遗迹		具体位置	形状尺寸		填土	包含物及特征		年代	发现时间	备注
序号	编号	名称	编号	类型		形状	尺寸（单位：米）		包含物	标本			
132	193	孙家窑西	M1	墓葬	H3东约1米		墓口距地表约1米，墓底距地表约1.5米，墓长约1米，墓底距地表约1.5米	黄褐土	见有2件红陶线纹薄胎尖底瓶，瓶内有少量细小骨屑，瓶内和瓶外均是黄褐土	1、2.尖底瓶	仰韶中期偏早	2003.3.17	
136	195	王湾西北	H1	灰坑	村北崖地西台地	袋状	坑口距地表约2.2米，宽约1.11米，坑深约0.6米	浅灰土	含有石器、兽骨和仰韶文化陶片。发现的小件遗物有石片1片，另有猪骨8块	1.石片 2.盆	仰韶晚期	2003.3.19	
			H2	灰坑	H1东约15米		坑口距地表约1.8米，宽约0.5米，坑深约0.8米	黄褐土	均为仰韶文化陶片。可辨认器形有夹砂罐、彩陶盆、钵、碗、小口高颈瓮、尖底瓶	1.钵	仰韶中期偏晚	2003.3.19	
			H3	灰坑	H1北约1.5米	坑壁较直	宽约3.8米，厚约1米，深1.2—2.2米	以黄褐土为主，夹数层薄灰层土	含有大量烧土块、无标本。可辨认器形有夹砂罐、盆等	无	仰韶晚期	2003.3.19	
140	189	西湾北	H1	灰坑	西湾东北通往沙沟村道路临河处以北断崖上		宽1.4—1.6米，深约1—2.2米，堆积厚约1.2米			无	二里头	2003.3.17	
145	183	宫家窑	H1	灰坑	宫家窑村北断崖		坑口距地表0.3米，宽1.5米，深0.6—0.7米	浅灰土夹烧土粒炭粒，下为生土		无	不详	2003.2.27	

续表

遗址信息		遗迹		具体位置	形状尺寸		填土	包含物及特征	标本	年代	发现时间	备注
序号	编号	名称	编号	类型		形状	尺寸（单位：米）					
146	181	刘李东北	H1	灰坑	刘李东北近河西岸				均为二里岗文化陶片。可辨认器形有鬲、卷沿方唇鬲、卷沿薄胎鬲、小尊、盆等	1.鬲 2.尊	二里岗早期	2001.3.26	地理坐标：北纬34°35′998″；东经112°37′773″
			H1	灰坑	苏家窑西北台地西断崖		开口于耕土下，距地表0.5—0.6米	黑灰土	见有陶片和小件石器，石器有双缺口石刀和石片，可辨认器形有豆等	1、2.石片 3、4.豆	龙山晚期	2001.3.27	
			H2	灰坑	苏家窑西北台地西断崖		坑口距地表0.5—0.6米，深约2米	灰黄杂土	小件遗物发现有石片。可辨认的器形为大口罐	1、2.石片 3.罐	龙山晚期	2001.3.27	
150	137	苏家窑西北	H3	灰坑	苏家窑西北台地北断崖		坑口距地表1米，口宽1.5米，深0.6—0.7米		见有陶片和小件石器，石器有石刀2件，可辨认器形有夹砂罐、盆、器盖等	1、2.石刀 3.器盖 4.罐 5.盆	仰韶晚期晚段	2001.3.27	
			H4	灰坑	苏家窑西北台地西断崖，H14南约40米		深0.7米	黑灰土	见有石器、兽骨和陶器。石器为石片，兽骨为猪左侧肩胛骨。可辨认器形有盆、小口高颈瓮等	1.石片 2.盆	龙山晚期早段	2001.3.27	
			H5	灰坑	苏家窑西台地东断崖		坑口距地表1.4米	灰褐土夹红烧土	包含龙山文化泥质陶片和夹砂陶片	无	龙山早期	2001.3.27	
152	153	武屯南	H1	灰坑	沙河沟西岸，紧靠武屯村南，砖厂东壁剖面	斜直壁，微袋	坑口距地表2米，宽2米，残深1米	灰褐土、黑灰土、烧土成层状分布	陶片包括泥质和夹砂两种。辨认器形有小口高颈瓮、豆、盖等。另发现了猪骨4块、蚌镰和蚌壳等遗物	1.穿孔蚌刀 2.蚌料	龙山晚期	2001.3.25	

续表

序号	遗址信息 编号	名称	遗迹 编号	类型	具体位置	形状	尺寸（单位：米）	填土	包含物	标本	年代	发现时间	备注
152	153	武屯南	H2	灰坑	砖厂取土坑北壁，距H1约10米处断崖剖面		开口于耕土下，距地表0.3—0.4米	灰褐土	均为龙山文化陶片，可辨认器形有鼎（鼎可早至仰韶）、罐、大镂领瓮、高领瓮等	1、2.高领瓮 3.罐 4.鼎	龙山晚期	2001.3.25	
			H3	灰坑	H1、H2以北约20—25米处砖厂取土沟北壁		开口于地表	灰褐土	均为龙山文化陶片，可辨器形有大口罐等。另发现石器1件	1.石斧 2、3.罐	龙山晚期	2001.3.25	
			H4	灰坑	砖厂北取土沟壁上，与H3距离约8米		开口于地表	灰褐土	以龙山文化陶片为主，器形主要有中口罐、盆、折腹盆、小口高领瓮等	1、2.盆	龙山晚期	2001.3.25	
159	145	杨村北	H1	灰坑	杨村东北，南北路南头之断崖上		宽0.8—1.1米，深0.9米	灰褐土		无	龙山晚期	2003.3.8	
			H2	灰坑	H1之北约10米		宽0.8—1.2米，深1.5—1.7米			无	龙山晚期	2003.3.8	
161	147	掘山		文化层						无	龙山晚期	2003.3.9	
166	208	肖村西寨西北	H1	灰坑	遗址东部，取土场东约80米的阶地		坑口距地表0.3米，宽2.2米，深度不详	黑灰土	以二里头文化陶片为主，所含陶片均为碎片，未见典型标本	无	二里头四期晚段	2003.3.20	
			H2	灰坑	遗址中部，取土场东剖面南部		坑口距地表1.3米，宽约3米，深约1米	黄褐土夹灰黑土	以东周陶片为主，发现的小件遗物有猪骨2块。可辨认器形有盆	1.盆	东周	2003.3.20	
170	205	吕桥	H1	灰坑	村西南冲沟东侧断崖上		开口于地表下，深1.7—1.8米	灰褐土夹黑灰土	以二里头文化第四期陶片为主。可辨认器形有圆腹罐、深腹罐、盆、大口尊等	1、2.圆腹罐 3、4.深腹罐 5.盆	二里头四期晚段	2003.2.25	

续表

序号	遗址信息 编号	名称	遗迹 编号	类型	具体位置	形状	尺寸（单位：米）	填土	包含物及特征 包含物	标本	年代	发现时间	备注
174	140	军屯东南	H1	灰坑	公坟南，浅沟南侧剖面	直壁	坑口距地表约0.5米，宽1.7—1.8米	黄褐泛灰土，含白色丝纤维	见有二里头四期至二里岗陶片。可辨认器形有罐、盆、瓮、缸、大口尊、甑等	1.缸 2、4.大口尊 3.甑	二里岗早期	2003.2.25	
175			H2	灰坑	H1东3米	斜壁圜底	深约0.9米	灰褐泛黄土	含大量黑灰、红烧土粒，小件遗物发现了废石料	1.废石料	二里头四期偏晚	2003.2.25	
	124	石牛沟		灰坑						无		2003.2.20	
177	134	高崖西	H1	灰坑	高崖村西断崖上		坑口距地表约0.6米，宽0.7—0.9米，深0.6—0.8米	灰土	均为龙山晚期陶片。可辨认器形有中口罐	1.罐	龙山晚期	2003.3.8	
			H2	灰坑	H1向西1米				以龙山文化陶片为主。可辨认器形有尖底瓶	1.矮领瓮	龙山晚期	2003.3.8	
			H3	灰坑	高崖村西断崖上				以仰韶文化陶片为主，无标本。可辨认器形有尖底瓶	无	仰韶	2003.3.8	
178	132	高崖东北	H1	灰坑	高崖东北断崖东部	袋状	宽1.4米，深1米	灰黄土	见有蚌器和二里头陶片。小件遗物发现的有穿孔残蚌刀，个别为二里头文化	1.蚌刀	二里头	2003.3.3	
183	218	铁岩东南	M1	墓葬	台地中央地带	死者头西脚东，从剖面看，应是仰身直肢，骨骼保存尚好	墓口距地表约0.35米，宽约2.3米，墓底深约0.7米	红褐色土	墓中填土内另有少量较小红陶片，可辨认器形为夹砂唇罐。另发现有人类顶骨碎块	1.石料 2.石片 3.罐	仰韶中期	2003.3.22	

续表

序号	遗址信息 编号	名称	遗迹 编号	类型	具体位置	形状	尺寸（单位：米）	填土	包含物及特征	标本	年代	发现时间	备注
184	215	杨寨西南	H1	灰坑					小件遗物有石铲1件。可辨认器形有中口高领瓮、器盖等	1.残石铲 2.罐	龙山晚期	2003.3.21	
			H1	灰坑	曹寨村西南		坑口距地表1.3米，口宽约0.8米，底宽约1.5米，深约3米	浅灰土	包含较大红烧土块，小件遗物发现的有石器2件。可辨认器形有泥质彩陶罐、夹砂弦纹罐、彩陶钵、盆、尖底瓶、盖，含仰韶文化中期典型庙底沟类型三角纹白衣黑彩彩陶盆	1.残石器 2.石料 3.盆 4—6.罐	仰韶晚期	2003.3.21	
			H2	灰坑	马寨老寨东寨墙处		深约0.6米		均为龙山早期陶片。可辨认器形有横篮纹罐、双腹盆、器盖	1.器盖	龙山早期	2003.3.21	
			H3	灰坑	马寨老寨东寨墙处，H2南约12米		坑口距地表约1.1米，宽约1.1米，底宽约1.6米		小件发现的有猪骨和牛牙各1件。陶片以黑褐陶为主。可辨认器形有罐、中口高领瓮、圈足盘、小口高领瓮	1.罐 2.圈足盘	龙山晚期	2003.3.21	
188	213	马寨西	H4	灰坑	马寨村西老寨处北寨墙中间处		坑口距地表2.2米，口宽1米，底宽1.4米，深约0.6米		小件遗物发现的有泥质陶罐。可辨认器形有泥质彩陶罐、钵、小口高领盆、缸、尖底器、器盖等。其中三件陶器层层相套，外部为缸，中间钵，内层罐，用黄褐土中间隔开，似乎具有特殊意义	1.刮削器 2.缸 3.器盖 4.罐 5.罐 6.瓮 7.钵	仰韶晚期	2003.3.21	
			H5	灰坑	马寨村西南老寨沟以南的遗址最南部河东断崖上	圆底	坑口距地表0.45米，宽约1.4米，底深约1.05米	黄土	包含石器、兽骨和龙山晚期陶片。发现的小件遗物有石片1片，猪骨1块。可辨认器形有鬲（足根）、泥质罐、盆、双腹盆等	1.残石器 2.盆 3.鬲	龙山晚期	2003.3.21	

续表

序号	遗址信息		遗迹		具体位置	形状尺寸			包含物及特征			年代	发现时间	备注
	编号	名称	编号	类型		形状	尺寸（单位：米）	填土	包含物	标本			
188	213	马寨西	H6	灰坑	马寨村西南老寨沟南岸		坑口距地表约0.2米，口宽约1.7米，底宽约3.3米，底深约2.7米	坑内黑灰、浅灰和黄褐土相间杂	包含石器、兽骨和龙山晚期陶片。发现的小件遗物有焙烧石灰石2块、羊骨1块。陶片中有仰韶文化陶片混入，可辨认的陶器形有大口罐、中口罐、小口高领瓮等	1、2.焙烧石灰石 3.中口罐 4.大口罐	龙山晚期	2003.3.21	
			H7	灰坑	H6西约3米		坑口距地表约0.3米，宽约2.2米，底深约0.7米		以殷墟二期陶片为主，可辨认器形有殷墟二里头文化高领罐	1.高领罐 2.鬲	殷墟二期	2003.3.21	
189	216	寨湾东南	H1	灰坑	寨湾东南	圜底	坑口距地表1—1.4米，宽1.5米，底深约2米	灰土夹生土块和红、黑烧土块	以二里头文化陶片为主。可辨认的陶器形有深腹罐、圆腹罐等	1.石戈 2.石片 3.石片 4.石料 5.圆腹罐 6.盆	二里头二期	2003.3.21	
			H2	灰坑	寨湾东南		坑口距地表约0.8米，宽约0.7米，底深约1.3米	灰褐土	无典型口沿标本。可辨认器形有尊、高领尊等	无	二里头二期	2003.3.21	
			H3	灰坑	寨湾东南		坑口距地表约1米，宽约1.2米，底宽约1.36米，底深1.4—1.5米	浅灰土	以二里头文化陶片为主。可辨认器形有深腹罐、捏口罐、高领尊、豆等	1.高领尊	二里头二期	2003.3.21	

续表

序号	遗址信息		遗迹		具体位置	形状尺寸		填土	包含物及特征		年代	发现时间	备注
	编号	名称	编号	类型		形状	尺寸（单位：米）		包含物	标本			
189	216	寨沟东南	H4	灰坑	寨沟东南		坑口距地表1米，宽3.6米，底深1.9—2米，底宽约3米	灰褐土	见有石器和龙山陶片。发现的小件遗物有石铲坯1件。可辨认器形有小口高领瓮、盆、杯等	1.石坯 2.高领瓮 3.杯 4.盆	龙山晚期	2003.3.21	
			H5	灰坑	H3北约3.8米	圜底	坑口距地表1.2米，宽1.1米，底深约1.9米	灰褐土	含有石器、蚌器和龙山文化陶片。发现的小件遗物有残石铲，蚌器。无陶器口沿标本，有夹砂褐陶篮纹陶片（含仰韶陶片）	1.残石铲 2.蚌器	龙山晚期	2003.3.21	
			H6	灰坑	寨沟东南		坑口距地表约1.4米，长达16米，厚约1米	灰黑土	均为二里头文化陶片。可辨认器形有深腹罐、矮领瓮、器盖等	1.深腹罐 2.矮领瓮 3.器盖	二里头四期	2003.3.21	
			H7	灰坑	寨沟东南		坑口距地表至少1.4米，范围不明	黄灰土	见有平放的肢骨，可能为墓葬。可辨认器形有横篮纹鼎、花边附加堆纹罐	无	龙山早期	2003.3.21	
			H8	灰坑	寨沟东南	袋状	坑口距地表1米，底宽约2米，底深1.3—1.7米	灰黑土夹黄褐土	以龙山文化早期陶片为主，含仰韶泥质彩形陶罐1件。可辨认的器形有罐、鼎、钵、盖等	1.石片 2、3.鼎 4.罐	龙山早期	2003.3.21	
190	217	寨沟东北	H1	灰坑	寨沟村东南，南北向生产路与农田田南缘交接处西边		坑口距地表1.1米，口宽约0.7米，底宽约1米，底深约0.7米	灰土，有水浸痕	发现的小件遗物有小玉凿1件，可辨认器形有圈足盘、瓮、豆等	1.玉凿铲 2.豆	龙山晚期	2003.3.22	

续表

遗址信息			遗迹		具体位置	形状尺寸		填土	包含物及特征		年代	发现时间	备注
序号	编号	名称	编号	类型		形状	尺寸（单位：米）		包含物	标本			
190	217	寨湾东北	H2	灰坑	距H1约1.3米		坑口距地表约0.3米，坑口宽约2.3米，底宽约1.6米，底深约0.6米	灰土		无	龙山晚期	2003.3.22	
			H3	灰坑	寨湾村东、小庙东北取土形成的凹坑西壁偏西处		坑口距地表约0.5米，口宽约0.7米，底宽约2米，深约1.7米	坚硬黄土和较软灰土相杂	发现的小件遗物有石料2件。可辨认器形有甗、大口罐、捏口罐	1、2.石料 3.甗	二里头二、三期	2003.3.22	
			H4	灰坑	取土凹坑南壁中央	袋形	剖面暴露的上口宽约2.3米，深1.8米，下口宽约2.4米，深约2.3米	灰黑夹黄褐土	以龙山晚期陶片为主。可辨认器形有鼎、盆、瓮、甗等	1.鼎 2.甗	龙山晚期	2003.3.22	
			H5	灰坑	H4东约5米	壁、底较直	口深约0.3米，底深1.9米，宽约2.3米	灰黑土和黄褐土同杂		无	西周	2003.3.22	右上部被破坏，地表即是
			H6	灰坑			宽约1米，底低于H5底部约1米，底宽约2米	灰土	可辨认器形有深腹罐，其余以龙山晚期陶片为主	1.深腹罐	二里头二期晚段	2003.3.22	
			H7	灰坑					以龙山晚期陶片为主。可辨认器形有小口高领瓮	1.瓮	龙山晚期	2003.3.22	

续表

序号	遗址信息		遗迹		具体位置	形状尺寸			包含物及特征		标本	年代	发现时间	备注
	编号	名称	编号	类型		形状	尺寸（单位：米）	填土	包含物					
190	217	寨窑东北	F1	房址	H2西约0.2米		坑口距地表约0.4米，口宽约2.6米，底宽约2.7米，底深约0.88米	灰土，左下角有下角有灶，底壁的红烧土均较坚硬，烧土厚约3厘米	以二里头遗存为主。无典型龙山陶片口沿标本		1.环 2.缸	二里头	2003.3.22	
			F2	房址	H3右侧		坑口距地表约0.2米，口宽约4米，底宽约4.1米，底深约1.2米	黄褐土，右下角有灶，红烧土厚约3厘米	含龙山早、晚期陶片，无典型口沿标本		无	东周	2003.3.22	
			F3	房址	F2东侧		口宽约4.1米，左边底略弧，底宽约3.8米，底深约1.2米，左边略弧	上层黄褐土，下层为厚约0.3米的灰土	含有殷墟时期瓷片		1.瓮	东周	2003.3.22	上部已被破坏，地表即是
			F4	房址	F3东约4米		口宽4.2米，底宽4.2米，底深0.7米	浅灰土	仅见1件陶片。可辨认器形为瓮		无	西周	2003.3.22	上部被F2破坏，地表即是
191	212	曹寨北	H1	灰坑	曹寨村北，沟东断崖上	圆底	坑口距地表约1米，宽约1.5米，深约0.5米	灰土，有水浸痕	以二里头三期陶片为主。可辨认器形有大口尊、缸、盆等		1.缸	二里头三期	2003.3.20	

续表

序号	遗址信息		遗迹		具体位置	形状尺寸		填土	包含物及特征		年代	发现时间	备注
	编号	名称	编号	类型		形状	尺寸（单位：米）		包含物	标本			
191	212	曹寨北	H2	灰坑	龙少路以北的沟东断崖处，北距H1约10米		坑口距地表约1.7米，宽约0.6米，深约0.6米	红褐土		无	龙山	2003.3.20	
			H3	灰坑	H1北约150米东西向断崖		坑口距地表约1.2米，宽约2米，深度在1.3米以上	灰黑土	以二里头三期陶片为主。可辨认器形有圆腹罐、豆等	1.圆腹罐	二里头三期	2003.3.20	
			H4	灰坑	崖地最西北角阶地偏西处取土坑南端西侧		坑口距地表约0.8米，坑口宽约2.2米，坑底宽约2.6米，深度在1米以上	灰黑土	含有较为丰富的泥质陶片和夹砂陶片，无典型标本。可辨认器形有中口罐	无	龙山晚期	2003.3.20	
			H5	灰坑	H4东约6米	圜底	坑口距地表0.2—0.8米，坑底0.5米，宽约2.2米	灰黑土（其下尚有黄褐土堆积，深度不详）	以龙山晚期陶片为主。可辨认器形有大口罐、罐等	1.罐	龙山晚期	2003.3.20	
			H6	灰坑	西北台地北部		坑口距地表1.1米	黄褐土	以龙山晚期文化为主。可辨认器形有矮领瓮、小口高领瓮、大口罐、盖等	1.罐 2.瓮	龙山晚期	2003.3.20	
193	221	西张庄东北	H1	灰坑	遗址南面断崖		坑口距地表1.1米，宽1.1—1.6米，深约2.2米	浅灰土	以龙山文化早期陶片为主。可辨认器形有2片仰韶陶片有宽折沿盆（双腹盆）、小口高领瓮等	1.盆	龙山早期	2003.3.22	

续表

序号	遗址信息 编号	名称	遗迹 编号	类型	具体位置	形状尺寸 形状	尺寸（单位：米）	填土	包含物及特征 包含物	标本	年代	发现时间	备注
193	221	西张庄东北	H2	灰坑	遗址西南部，H1东北约15米				均为仰韶文化陶片。可辨认器形有泥质形彩陶罐、夹砂陶罐	1.彩陶罐	仰韶晚期	2003.3.22	
			H3	灰坑	砖场挖土形成的注地西南部东面断崖		坑口距地表约0.8米，口宽约0.7米，底宽约1.4米，深约2.1米		见有少量的泥质陶片和夹砂陶片，另有白灰墙皮1件。陶片均为碎片，无口沿标本，可辨认器形有盆、夹砂陶罐等	无	仰韶晚期	2003.3.22	
			H4	灰坑					以仰韶晚期陶片为主，多黑皮褐陶。可辨认器形有泥质陶罐（黑皮陶）、夹砂陶罐等	1、2.罐	仰韶晚期至龙山早期	2003.3.22	
			H5	灰坑					均为仰韶文化陶片。可辨认器形有泥质斜唇弦纹罐	1、2.罐	仰韶晚期	2003.3.22	
198	198	符家寨东北	H1	灰坑	村东北部，北道边	袋状	宽约2米，残深0.5米	浅灰褐土	以仰韶文化中期偏晚段陶片为主。可辨认器形有鼎、夹砂罐、碗，夹砂钵、钵等，含大量烧土块	1.钵 2.罐	仰韶中期偏晚（大河村二期）	2003.2.28	
199	123	张村东南	H1	灰坑	四角楼张村东南，废弃水渠南坡北台地西侧南北向小路西的断崖上				以龙山文化早期陶片为主，可辨认器形有横篮纹缸、大口罐	1.缸 2.罐	龙山早期	2003.2.19	
201	118	裴村A	H1	灰坑	裴村东南，四角楼张村正东小型冲沟北岸的台地上				含有兽骨和仰韶陶片。兽骨有1件鹿肩胛骨（疑似卜骨）则较多；陶片则较多，可辨认器形有夹砂弦纹鼓肩罐	1.罐	仰韶中期（大河村二、三期之间）	2003.2.19	
202	119	裴村B	H1	灰坑	裴村东北墙鼓合水库西岸				以龙山陶片为主，仅见个别仰韶陶片	无	龙山	2003.2.19	

续表

序号	遗址信息 编号	遗址信息 名称	遗迹 编号	遗迹 类型	具体位置	形状尺寸 形状	形状尺寸 尺寸（单位：米）	填土	包含物及特征 包含物	包含物及特征 标本	年代	发现时间	备注
204	121	裴村D	H1	灰坑	裴村北小型冲沟附近				以龙山文化晚期陶片为主，可辨认的器形有中口罐	1.罐	龙山晚期	2003.2.19	
208	114	郝寨东北	H1	灰坑	浏河主河道处的北岸沟西台地上				以二里头二期陶片为主。可辨认器形有盆	1.、2.盆	二里头二期	2003.2.16	
209	127	陶化店东南	H1	灰坑	郝寨北东北的尖嘴状台地上				以仰韶陶片为主。可辨认器形有钵、彩陶盆等	1.钵	仰韶	2003.3.3	
210	126	陶化店水库	H1	灰坑	浏河西侧姬家村通往火焦路道路北侧的断崖上		宽1.2米，深0.5—0.6米	浅灰褐土	均为仰韶文化陶片。可辨认器形有夹砂弦纹罐、小口高领瓮、盆等	1.瓮 2.罐	仰韶中期偏晚（大河村三期）	2003.3.2	
			H2	灰坑	半岛北侧二层台地上		宽2.3—2.4米，深0.7米		以仰韶中期偏晚陶片为主。可辨认器形有夹砂罐、盆、钵、器盖等	1.盆 2.罐	仰韶中期偏晚（大河村三期）	2003.3.2	
212	Y225	邢村东		灰坑	H1东约50米					无	龙山晚期	2005.6.25	
213	Y182	夏后寺		灰坑	地坎下部暴露有灰坑					无	二里头	2002.6.8	
			H1	灰坑	泄洪渠两侧剖面					无	二里岗	2007.11.6	浮选土样
215	Y184	邢村北	H2	灰坑	浏河南岸一取土坑南剖面东部					无	二里岗	2007.11.6	浮选土样
			H3	灰坑	浏河南岸一取土坑南剖面中部					无	二里岗	2007.11.6	浮选土样
217	Y181	扒头东南	H1	灰坑	浏河南岸一取土坑南剖面偏西					无	二里岗	2007.11.6	浮选土样

续表

序号	遗址信息		遗迹		具体位置	形状尺寸			包含物及特征		年代	发现时间	备注
	编号	名称	编号	类型		形状	尺寸（单位：米）	填土	包含物	标本			
219	Y179	任才村东南		灰坑	路南断崖剖面					无	龙山晚期	2002.6.7	
225	Y224	双泉东北		灰坑	卢村至双泉的小路西，临沟断崖剖面上					无	龙山晚期	2002.6.5	
227		卢村北	H1	灰坑	庙岭东公路西侧断崖剖面				采集陶片35片，可辨认器形有鼎、喇叭口罐、小口瓮、刻槽盆、罐	1. 白烧石	龙山早期	2002.6.2	浮选土样
			H1	灰坑	庙岭东公路东侧断崖剖面				采集3片陶片，可辨认器形有罩	1. 鼎 2、3. 罐 4. 刻槽盆	龙山早期	2002.6.2	
228	Y168	高祖庙	H2	灰坑	庙岭南东西向断崖剖面				内含白灰面及陶片、灰烬等，采集到陶片标本	无	龙山早期	2002.6.2	浮选土样
230	Y167	双泉南	H1	灰坑	村南一东西向断崖剖面				可辨认器形有中口罐、小口高领罐	无	龙山晚期	2002.6.5	浮选土样
237	Y172	西齐家窑	H1	瓮棺葬	路边断崖剖面				葬具为弦纹陶瓮，发现有人骨，未采集	1、2. 中口罐	仰韶中、晚期	2002.6.2	
238	Y165	灰嘴		灰坑	路南东西向断崖剖面					无	不详	2000.12.28	
239	Y127	西齐家窑东北	H1	灰坑	路北南北向断崖剖面					无	龙山晚期	2002.6.2	浮选土样
	Y166		H2	灰坑	路北南北向断崖剖面					无	龙山晚期	2002.6.2	
			H3	灰坑	路北南北向断崖剖面					无	龙山晚期	2002.6.2	
240	Y188	西齐家窑西北		灰坑	2006年冬季，所挖的高压线铁塔基坑剖面上		坑口距现地表2米			无	东周	2002.6.10	

续表

序号	遗址信息		遗迹		具体位置	形状尺寸			包含物及特征		年代	发现时间	备注
	遗址编号	名称	编号	类型		形状	尺寸（单位：米）	填土	包含物	标本			
242	Y189	郑窑南	H1	灰坑	遗址西部断崖剖面					1.罐	仰韶	2017.7.12	
			H2	灰坑	遗址西部断崖剖面					1.鬲 2.盆	东周	2017.7.12	
				地层、房基						无	不详	2017.7.12	
244	Y190	刘国故城	H1	灰坑	遗址中北部东西向剖面					无	东周	2006.11.21	浮选土样
			H2	灰坑	遗址中北部东西向剖面					无	东周	2006.11.21	浮选土样
245	Y140	郑窑	H1	灰坑	郑窑砖厂西北角断崖剖面					1.深腹罐 2~4.鬲 5.瓿 6.高领罐	二里岗	2001.1.14	浮选土样
248	Y195	涧东村	H1	灰坑	村南路西东西向断崖剖面					无	东周	2007.11.10	浮选土样
		涧东村北	H1	灰坑	涧东村北路沟西壁剖面北端					无	二里头	2007.6.16	浮选土样
249	Y196A		H2	灰坑	涧东村北路沟西壁剖面中部					无	二里头	2007.6.16	浮选土样
			H3	灰坑	涧东村北路沟西壁剖面偏丙					无	二里头	2007.6.16	浮选土样
250	Y196B	涧东村西北	H1	灰坑	河边断崖剖面，现代窖打破			可辨认器形有大口罐、器盖		1.大口罐 2.器盖	龙山晚期	2002.6.12	浮选土样
254	Y202	东管茅东	H1	灰坑	砖厂西南部断崖剖面上					无	仰韶晚期	2007.11.6	浮选土样

续表

序号	遗址信息		遗迹		具体位置	形状尺寸			包含物及特征		年代	发现时间	备注
	编号	名称	编号	类型		形状	尺寸（单位：米）	填土	包含物	标本			
255	Y201	西口矻	H1	灰坑	砖厂取土坑剖面				可辨认器形有深腹罐、圆腹罐、豆	1. 圆腹罐	二里头三、四期	2002.6.14	浮选土样
			H2	灰坑	砖厂取土坑剖面				可辨认器形有甑、缸	1、2. 甑 3. 石镰	二里头三期晚段	2002.6.14	浮选土样
			H3	灰坑	砖厂取土坑剖面				可辨认器形有甑、鬲、深腹罐、圆腹罐、捏口罐、缸、盆、豆	1、2. 深腹罐 3. 圆腹罐 4. 甑 5. 捏口罐 6. 缸 7. 三足盘 8. 石镰	二里头三期早段	2002.6.14	
			H4	灰坑	砖厂取土坑剖面				可辨认器形有捏口罐、三足皿、瓮、缸	1. 瓮 2. 三足盘 3、4. 石铲坯	二里头三期	2002.6.14	浮选土样
			H5	灰坑	砖厂路边东北角					无	二里头	2007.11.6	浮选土样
			H6	灰坑	砖厂路边东北角					无	二里头	2007.11.6	浮选土样
256	Y200	老周寨	H1	灰坑	老寨南断崖剖面					无	仰韶晚期	2007.11.6	浮选土样
257	Y199	老屯寨	H1	灰坑	老屯寨弃后取土坑剖面					1. 大口罐	龙山晚期	2002.6.13	浮选土样
			H2	灰坑	老屯寨西南角					无	仰韶晚期	2007.11.6	浮选土样
			H3	灰坑	老屯寨东北部取土坑剖面					无	仰韶晚期	2007.11.6	浮选土样
258	Y198	屯寨西北	H1	灰坑	屯寨西北小冲沟北壁窑洞顶部					无	二里岗	2007.11.6	浮选土样
			H2	灰坑	屯寨西北小冲沟北壁东部剖面					无	二里岗	2007.11.6	浮选土样

续表

序号	遗址信息		遗迹		具体位置	形状尺寸			包含物及特征		年代	发现时间	备注
	编号	名称	编号	类型		形状	尺寸（单位：米）	填土	包含物	标本			
259	Y204	布村东南	H1	灰坑	遗址西南部一个断崖剖面					无	仰韶晚期	2007.11.6	浮选土样
			H2	灰坑	遗址西南部一个断崖剖面					无	东周	2007.11.6	浮选土样
261	Y197	新寨北嘴		灰坑	沟嘴北部断崖剖面					无	不详	2002.6.12	
			H1	灰坑	遗址所在台地东南部的断崖剖面上				可辨认器形有大口罐、小口高领瓮、双腹盆、扁壶、盘、豆	1. 盆 2、3. 扁壶 4—7. 瓮 8、9. 折腹盆 10、11. 豆	龙山晚期	2002.6.16	浮选土样
265	Y210	张湾西北	H2	灰坑	遗址所在台地东南部的断崖剖面上				可辨认器形有泥质罐、大口罐、小口高领瓮、豆、钵	1、2. 大口罐 3、4、7. 瓮 5、6. 豆 8. 钵	龙山晚期	2002.6.16	浮选土样
			H3	灰坑	遗址所在台地东南部的断崖剖面上					1. 石片	龙山晚期	2011.7.14	浮选土样
270	Y213	南吴家湾东南		灰坑	陈河村至吊桥寨村的小路东侧的断崖剖面上					无	不详	2002.6.17	
274	Y220	凤凰台南		灰坑	电线杆独立台地剖面					无	龙山晚期	2002.6.18	
275	Y217	老吊桥寨		灰坑	路东断崖剖面北部					无	西周	2002.6.17	
277	Y218	北寨东南	H1	灰坑	北断面断崖剖面					无	仰韶晚期	2007.11.6	浮选土样
278	Y219	北寨北		灰坑						无	龙山晚期	2002.6.18	

续表

序号	遗址信息			遗迹		具体位置	形状尺寸			包含物及特征			年代	发现时间	备注
	编号	名称		编号	类型		形状	尺寸（单位：米）	填土	包含物	标本			
280	112	陈河北		H1	灰坑	村北断崖		文化堆积厚1—3米		以二里头文化二期陶片为主。可辨认器形有花边圆腹罐、深腹罐腹片等	1.圆腹罐	二里头二期	2002.12.5	
				H2	灰坑	村北断崖		文化堆积厚1—3米		以二里头文化第四期陶片为主，多腹片。可辨认器形有圆腹罐、深腹罐、矮领瓮、大口尊	1.深腹罐	二里头四期	2002.12.5	
				H3	灰坑	村北断崖		文化堆积厚1—3米		以二里头文化四期陶片为主。可辨认器形有深腹罐、平底盆等	无	二里头四期	2002.12.5	
				H4	灰坑	村北断崖		文化堆积厚1—3米		以二里头文化三期陶片为主。可辨认器形有圆腹罐、深腹罐等	无	二里头三期	2002.12.5	
				H5	灰坑	村北断崖		文化堆积厚1—3米		坑内堆积较丰富	无	二里头	2002.12.5	
281	111	化寨东		Z1	灶址	村东台地		现存高度约0.5米，直径约0.38米，厚约0.01米	灶底坚硬、光亮、黑色，厚约1厘米，灶四周均为红烧土		无	二里头	2002.12.5	
282	109	盆窑寨东南		H1	灰坑	马涧河南岸遗址中部略偏西处的断崖上		文化层堆积厚约1米		均为仰韶文化陶片。可辨认器形有罐形鼎、罐形缸、敛口钵，花边附加堆纹	1、2.罐形鼎3、4.缸5.敛口钵	仰韶晚期晚段	2003.3.4	

续表

序号	遗址信息 编号	遗址信息 名称	遗迹 编号	遗迹 类型	具体位置	形状尺寸 形状	形状尺寸 尺寸（单位：米）	包含物及特征 填土	包含物及特征 包含物	包含物及特征 标本	年代	发现时间	备注
282	109	盆窑寨东南	H2	灰坑	马涧河南岸，村东约50米处的断崖上				以东周陶片为主	1、2.豆 3.盆 4、5.罐 6.平底盆	战国	2003.3.4	
295	096	苗湾B		灰坑						无		2002.3.11	
296	095	苗湾A		灰坑						无		2002.3.11	
297	Y122	李家岔西南		灰坑	村西南台地断崖剖面					无	东周	2002.6.12	
298	Y121	邢村东	H1	灰坑	邢村东，路北高台地					无	仰韶晚期	2000.6.11	浮选土样
			H2	灰坑	邢村东，路北高台地					无	仰韶晚期	2000.6.11	
			H3	灰坑	邢村东，路北高台地					无	仰韶晚期	2000.6.11	
			H4	灰坑	邢村东，北中部一个东西向断崖上					无	仰韶晚期	2007.11.7	浮选土样
299	Y123	半个寨	H1	灰坑	村北断崖剖面					无	龙山早期	2007.11.7	浮选土样
300	Y120	邢村	H1	灰坑	遗址东北角					无	商周	2000.6.11	
302	Y077	赵城	H1	灰坑	大坝北部护坝房下面的断崖剖面上，H2右侧					1、2.砺石坯料	仰韶晚期	2005.11.6	浮选土样、植硅石土样
			H2	灰坑	大坝北部护坝房下面的断崖剖面上，H1左侧					无	仰韶晚期	2005.11.6	浮选土样、植硅石土样
				壕沟	遗址东北部					无	周	2005.11.6	
			M1	墓葬	大坝北部护坝房下面的断崖剖面，H1右侧				左侧下肢骨	无	仰韶晚期	2005.11.6	

续表

序号	遗址信息		遗迹			形状尺寸			包含物及特征		年代	发现时间	备注
	编号	名称	编号	类型	具体位置	形状	尺寸（单位：米）	填土	包含物	标本			
303	Y079	赵城西南	H1	灰坑	赵城村南、南北向下沟大路东侧断崖剖面上		坑口距地表约2米，底距下面路面约3米			无	仰韶早期	2007.7.19	浮选土样、残留物土样
304	Y078	赵城西	H1	灰坑	赵城老村东大路路沟南壁剖面					无	仰韶中期偏早	2000.1.19	
306	Y116	赵城西北		灰坑	东一干渠渡槽北河边断崖剖面					无	东周	2000.6.9	
308	Y118	府店东南	H1	灰坑	干沟河西岸一南部东西向断坎					1.碗	裴李岗晚期	2000.6.10	浮选土样
309	Y080	小相西南		灰坑	台地剖面				含龙山文化陶片	无	龙山	2000.1.19	
310	Y114	颜良寨水库西南	H1	灰坑	干沟河西岸一南北向断崖剖面					1.碗	龙山晚期	2000.6.9	浮选土样
312	Y087	颜良寨水库西	H1	灰坑	营君路（X002）东侧断崖剖面偏南				可辨认器形有大口罐、瓮	1.大口罐	龙山晚期	2000.1.23	浮选土样
			H2	灰坑	营君路（X002）东侧断崖剖面偏南				可辨认器形有圈足盘、壶	1.壶 2.器盖	龙山晚期	2000.1.23	浮选土样
			H3	灰坑	营君路（X002）东侧断崖剖面偏南				可辨认器形有大口罐、器盖	无	龙山晚期	2000.1.23	浮选土样
			H4	灰坑	营君路（X002）东侧断崖剖面偏北				可辨认器形有大口罐、小口高领瓮、觚、器盖	1.壶	龙山晚期	2011	浮选土样
			H5	灰坑	营君路（X002）东侧断崖剖面偏北				可辨认器形有泥质罐、大口罐、豆	1、2.大口罐	龙山晚期	2011	浮选土样
			H6	灰坑	台地西部断崖剖面				可辨认器形有泥质折沿罐、大口罐、小口高领瓮、圈足盘	1.罐 2.器盖 3.豆	龙山晚期	2011	浮选土样

续表

序号	遗址信息		遗迹		具体位置	形状尺寸		填土	包含物及特征		年代	发现时间	备注
	编号	名称	编号	类型		形状	尺寸（单位：米）		包含物	标本			
313	Y124	府店东	H1	灰坑	台地西部南北向断崖剖面中部			红色土	含有陶片、石器等。陶片多为红陶片，石器多为石锤、石料及石片	1—3.罐 4—6.钵 7.三足钵 8.碗 9、11.镰 10.石珠 12、13.磨盘	裴李岗晚期	2001.5.30	浮选土样
315	Y086	颜良寨西南	H1	灰坑	村西南二级台地东西向剖面					无	二里岗	2007.11.8	浮选土样
316	Y113	府北村北	H1	灰坑	府北村北，干沟河西岸下沟小路坡道断崖剖面					无	龙山	2000.6.8	
				房基	南北向剖面					无	不详	2000.6.8	
317	Y088	颜良村西		文化层	颜良村西北原砖厂西壁剖面			黑红土		无	裴李岗晚期至仰韶早期	2017.7.16	
			H1	灰坑	冯寨西南，干沟河东岸二级台地断崖剖面最南端					无	龙山晚期	2000.1.24	
318	Y089	冯寨西南	H2	灰坑	冯寨西南，干沟河东岸二级台地断崖剖面南端					无	龙山晚期	2000.1.24	
			H3	灰坑	冯寨西南，干沟河东岸一二级台地断崖剖面南端				可辨认器形有大口罐、小口高领瓮、豆	1.豆	龙山期	2000.1.24	浮选土样

续表

序号	遗址信息			遗迹		具体位置	形状尺寸			包含物及特征		年代	发现时间	备注
	编号	名称		编号	类型		形状	尺寸（单位：米）	填土	包含物	标本			
318	Y089	冯寨西南		H4	灰坑	冯寨西南、干沟河东岸一二级台地断崖剖面中部				可辨认器形有双腹盆	无	龙山晚期	2000.1.24	浮选土样
				H5	灰坑	冯寨西南、干沟河东岸一二级台地断崖剖面中部				可辨认器形有大口罐、豆	无	龙山晚期	2000.1.24	浮选土样
				H6	灰坑	冯寨西南、干沟河东岸一二级台地断崖剖面中部					无	龙山晚期	2000.1.24	
				H7	灰坑	冯寨西南、干沟河东岸一二级台地断崖剖面中部					无	龙山晚期	2000.1.24	
				H8	灰坑	冯寨西南、干沟河东岸一二级台地北部				可辨认器形有蛋壳杯	1. 杯	龙山晚期	2000.1.24	浮选土样
				H9	灰坑	冯寨西南、干沟河东岸一二级台地北部				无口沿标本，可辨认器形有小口高领瓮	无	龙山晚期	2000.1.24	浮选土样
				H10	灰坑	冯寨西南、干沟河东岸一二级台地北部				无口沿标本，可辨认器形有小口高领瓮	1、2. 石斧	龙山晚期	2000.1.24	
				F1	房址	冯寨西南、干沟河东岸一二级台地断崖剖面中部					无	龙山晚期	2000.1.24	
319	Y107	滑国故城		H1	灰坑	村子西北角沟之东壁					无	东周	2007	浮选土样
320	Y112	滑城河东		H1	灰坑	滑城河村东、干沟河西岸断崖剖面		坑口距地表约1.5米		可辨认器形有鼎、小口高领罐、圈足盘、浅盘豆、碗	1—3. 鼎 4. 豆 5. 碗 6. 卜骨	龙山早期	2000.6.8	浮选土样

续表

序号	遗址信息		遗迹		具体位置	形状尺寸		填土	包含物及特征		年代	发现时间	备注
	编号	名称	编号	类型		形状	尺寸（单位：米）		包含物	标本			
322	Y090	冯寨西北	H1	灰坑	冯寨西北，干沟河与冯杨寨沟交汇处台地断崖剖面				可辨认器形有小口高领瓮	无	龙山晚期	2000.1.24	
323	Y059	杨寨西	H1	灰坑	废弃的蓄水池西壁剖面				可辨认器形有鬲、罐	1.鬲	殷墟	2000.1.8	浮选土样
			H2	灰坑	台地中部的一个南北向梯田断面上					无	东周	2007.11.9	浮选土样
			H3	灰坑	台地中部的一个南北向梯田断面上					1.瓮	东周	2007.11.9	浮选土样
			H4	灰坑	台地中部的一个南北向梯田断面上					无	东周	2007.11.9	浮选土样
			H5	灰坑	台地中部的一个南北向梯田断面上					无	东周	2007.11.9	
324	Y058	杨寨西北	H1	灰坑	杨寨西北，废弃的蓄水池西壁剖面				出土陶片、骨片（刻有"工"）及象牙类的精美簪子	无	二里岗	2000.1.8	浮选土样
			H2	灰坑	杨寨西北，废弃的蓄水池北壁剖面（东北角）					无	二里岗	2007.11.9	浮选土样
325	Y061	南村寨南东南		灰坑	南村寨南大冲沟的断崖剖面					无	二里头	2000.1.8	
327	Y060	南村寨南		灰坑	南村寨南大冲沟与冯杨寨沟交汇处的断崖剖面					无	龙山	2000.1.8	
328	Y109	渭城河西		灰坑	台地南部断崖剖面					无	仰韶晚期	2000.6.7	

续表

序号	遗址信息		遗迹			形状尺寸		填土	包含物及特征		年代	发现时间	备注
	编号	名称	编号	类型	具体位置	形状	尺寸（单位：米）		包含物	标本			
329	Y108	潍城河北	H1	灰坑	遗址西北面断崖剖面					无	周	2007.11.9	浮选土样
			H2	灰坑	遗址东南部断崖剖面					无	仰韶晚期	2007.11.9	浮选土样
330	Y111	府西村东北	H1	灰坑	府店西西河岸断崖剖面				出土蚌贝，二里岗晚期文化风格的遗物。可辨认器形有鬲、深腹罐、缸、盆、大口尊、器盖	1—3.深腹罐 4.鬲 5.器盖	二里岗	2000.6.8	浮选土样
331	Y110	府西村北	H1	灰坑	府店西河拐弯处的取土大坑中部，现已被工厂所压				可辨认器形有大口罐、小口高领瓮、碗	1.碗 2.瓮	龙山晚期	2000.6.8	浮选土样
332	Y062	南村寨西		灰坑	临沟的二三级台地剖面都有					无	二里头	2000.1.8	
334	Y064	秦沟水库北		灰坑	临河的一二级台地剖面有					无	东周	2000.1.8	
335	Y065	秦沟老村		灰坑	断崖剖面					无	东周	2000.1.8	
				灰坑	东南一西北向小路的东壁上					无	龙山	2017.7.16	
336	Y126	秦沟五队北	H1	灰坑						无	不详	2007.11.9	
			H2	灰坑						无	不详	2007.11.9	
337	Y105	三官庙窑厂东南		灰坑	窑厂正南隔路的高台地上					无	仰韶	2000.6.6	
338	Y066	秦沟南		灰坑	秦沟一、六队南小冲沟剖面					无	仰韶晚期	2000.1.9	

续表

序号	遗址信息		遗迹		具体位置	形状尺寸			包含物及特征		标本	年代	发现时间	备注
	编号	名称	编号	类型		形状	尺寸（单位：米）	填土	包含物					
344	Y069	马屯新村	H1	灰坑	村东南北向大路东断崖剖面南部	袋状					无	龙山	2000.1.9	
			H2	灰坑	村东南北向大路东断崖剖面南部	袋状					无	龙山	2000.1.9	浮选土样
			H3	灰坑	村东南北向大路东断崖剖面南部	袋状					无	龙山	2000.1.9	浮选土样
			H4	灰坑	村东南北向大路东断崖剖面路向东拐弯处路北部	袋状					无	龙山	2007.11.9	浮选土样
			H5	灰坑	村东南北向大路东断崖剖面南部	袋状					无	龙山	2000.1.9	
			H6	灰坑	村东大坡路北剖面	袋状					无	龙山	2007.11.9	浮选土样
			H7	灰坑	村中南北向大路西	袋状			见二里冈下层薄胎鬲		无	二里冈	2011	浮选土样
346	Y070	马屯北	H1	灰坑	马屯村西北，一输水管道所开的沟槽南壁上	袋状	坑口距地表约0.9米，深1.6米，底长2.7米		坑内堆积大量炭化粟，厚约20厘米，保存状态良好		无	二里头	2000.1.9	
347	Y071	王门	H1	灰坑	村西北靠近红岩沟处的断崖						无	二里头	2000.1.10	
348	Y101	贾屯	H1	灰坑	临河的一二级台地南北向断崖剖面						无	东周	2007.11.8	浮选土样
			H1	灰坑	李家沟村东三四级台地						无	二里冈	1997.12.27	浮选土样
350	Y099	李家沟东	H2	灰坑	村东西大路中部转弯处南侧偏西南北向断崖剖面南端				可辨认器形有鬲、尊		1.尊	二里冈	2011.7.17	浮选土样

续表

序号	遗址信息		遗迹		具体位置	形状尺寸			包含物及特征		年代	发现时间	备注
	编号	名称	编号	类型		形状	尺寸（单位：米）	填土	包含物	标本			
350	Y099	李家沟东	H3	灰坑	村东东西大路中部转弯处南侧偏西南北向断崖剖面南端				可辨认器形有深腹罐、圆腹罐、刻槽盆、大口尊	1. 大口尊	二里头四期	2011.7.17	浮选土样
			H4	灰坑	大路中部转弯处南侧偏西南北向断崖南端转向东西剖面				可辨认器形有鬲、大口尊	1、2. 鬲 3. 大口尊	二里岗晚期	2011.7.17	浮选土样
			H5	灰坑	大路中部转弯处南侧偏西南北向断崖南端转向东西剖面					无	二里岗	2011.7.17	浮选土样
			G1	灰沟	李家沟村东西大路坡道南壁剖面上					无	二里岗	2007.11.8	浮选土样
351	Y072	罗彦庄西南肖家沟	H1	灰坑	肖家沟村西南、红岩沟北岸断崖剖面					无	不详	2000.1.13	
352	Y098	顾家屯东南	H1	灰坑	断崖剖面					无	不详	2007.11.8	浮选土样、残留物分析
354	Y096	顾家屯东	M1	窑葬	小庙下面的沟壁剖面上					无	仰韶	2000.6.4	
355	Y095	石家沟东南	H1	灰坑	台地周边断崖剖面					无	不详	2000.6.4	
357	Y073	念子庄西北	H1	灰坑	念子庄西北第三条冲沟北、已近成土柱的河中台地					1. 圈足 2. 碗	龙山	2000.1.13	浮选土样
358	Y093	石家沟东北	H1	灰坑	石家沟村东北台地南部剖面				可辨器形鬲、盆	1. 鬲 2. 盆	殷墟	2017.7.18	
			H2	灰坑	石家沟村东北台地南部剖面				可辨器形有鬲	1. 鬲	东周	2017.7.18	

续表

序号	遗址信息			遗迹		具体位置	形状尺寸			包含物及特征		年代	发现时间	备注
	编号	名称		编号	类型		形状	尺寸（单位：米）	填土	包含物	标本			
360	Y074	干沟猪场			灰坑、墓葬、文化层	干沟猪场西约200米的南北向断崖剖面					无	不详	2000.1.13	
361	Y083	回龙湾新村东		H1	灰坑	村东一条东西向小冲沟剖面					1.深腹罐 2.盆 3.石锤	二里头	2000.1.20	
				H2	灰坑	西侧的断崖上					无	不详	2000.1.20	
363	Y075	刘乐寨西南		H1	灰坑	刘乐寨南干沟河东岸一级台地剖面最南端东西向剖面				可辨认器形有鼎、罐、盆、钵、碗、器盖	无	仰韶	2000.1.18	
				H2	灰坑	刘乐寨南干沟河东岸一级台地剖面最南端剖面东拐处				可辨认器形有鼎、夹砂罐、碗	1.鼎 2.碗	仰韶晚期	2000.1.18	
				H3	灰坑	刘乐寨南干沟河东岸一级台地剖面最南端H2西、H4南					1.鼎 2.花边缸	仰韶晚期	2000.1.18	
				H4	灰坑	刘乐寨南干沟河东岸一级台地剖面中部，H3北、H5南				含有二里岗时期和战国时期陶片	1.簋 2.刮削器	战国	2000.1.18	
				H5	灰坑	刘乐寨南干沟河东岸一级台地剖面中部，H4北、H7南					无	西周	2000.1.18	
				H6	灰坑	干沟河东岸一级台地剖面最南端剖面东拐处H1西，H2东				可辨认器形有夹砂罐、花边缸	1.花边缸 2.环	仰韶晚期	2000.1.18	

续表

序号	遗址信息		遗迹			形状尺寸			包含物及特征			年代	发现时间	备注
	编号	名称	编号	类型	具体位置	形状	尺寸（单位：米）	填土	包含物		标本			
363	Y075	刘乐寨西南	H7	灰坑	刘乐寨南干沟河东岸一级台地剖面中部H5北、H8南						无	仰韶晚期	2000.1.18	
			H8	灰坑	刘乐寨南干沟河东岸一级台地剖面北端H7北、H9南				可辨认器形有夹砂罐、钵、盆		无	仰韶晚期	2000.1.18	
			H9	灰坑	刘乐寨南干沟河东岸一级台地剖面北端H8北				含有仰韶陶片，另见有1件二里岗文化早期鬲		1.鬲 2.石球	二里岗	2000.1.18	
365	Y081	回龙湾	K1	窑址	村子中部						无	不详	2007.11.9	浮选土样
368	Y135	曹河		灰坑	里河入水库处东北角，北距公路约15米处						无	龙山	2001.1.1	
370	Y134	南沟		灰坑	姚家门对岸高台地，断崖剖面						无	龙山晚期	2000.12.31	
371	Y229	虎山坡南		灰坑	遗址西侧靠近洪渠处的剖面						无	仰韶早期	2005.6.3	浮选土样
		北后沟西北	H1	灰坑	北后沟西北，现代窑洞内顶部						无	仰韶晚期	2001.1.2	浮选土样
	Y139		H2	灰坑	北后沟西北，现代窑洞内顶部						无	仰韶晚期	2001.1.2	浮选土样
376			H3	灰坑	北后沟西北，现代窑洞顶部口顶端						无	仰韶晚期	2007.11.10	浮选土样

续表

序号	遗址信息		遗迹			形状尺寸		包含物及特征			年代	发现时间	备注
	编号	名称	编号	类型	具体位置	形状	尺寸（单位：米）	填土	包含物	标本			
377	Y132	新后沟瓷厂东	H1	灰坑	新后沟瓷厂东南角，现代窑洞顶端临河台地西南部					1. 深腹罐 2~5. 圆腹罐 6、7. 大口尊	二里头	2000.12.31	浮选土样
			H2	灰坑	新后沟瓷厂东临河台地北剖面中部					无	二里头	2007.11.10	浮选土样
378	Y131	新后沟东		灰坑	新后沟村东靠近曹河南岸					无	龙山	2000.12.31	
379	Y130	新后沟	H1	灰坑	废弃的砖厂内				陶片口沿较碎小，可辨认器形有中口罐、豆	无	龙山晚期	2000.12.31	浮选土样
			H2	灰坑	废弃的砖厂内					无	龙山晚期	2000.12.31	浮选土样
			H3	灰坑	废弃的砖厂内				未采集陶片，见有人骨，有木炭	无	龙山晚期	2000.12.31	
381	Y128	鲁庄东北	H1	灰坑	南部沟口附近断崖剖面					无	周汉	2000.12.28	
385	Y052	堤东	H1	灰坑	苹果园东侧的东西向小断崖剖面					1. 罐	仰韶晚期	2007.11.12	浮选土样
			H2	灰坑	南北向小断崖剖面					无	仰韶晚期	2007.11.12	浮选土样
386	Y053	龙骨堆	H1	灰坑	堤东村东北孤岛形台地，东西向小断崖剖面中部					无	仰韶	2007.11.12	浮选土样
			H2	灰坑	堤东村东北孤岛形台地，西南部		长约5米，深约4米			1. 盆 2、3. 尖底瓶 4. 钵	仰韶中期	2017.6.16	
387	Y054	金钟寺		灰坑						无	不详	1999.1.13	

续表

序号	遗址信息		遗迹		具体位置	形状尺寸		填土	包含物及特征		年代	发现时间	备注
	编号	名称	编号	类型		形状	尺寸（单位：米）		包含物	标本			
388	Y043	天坡水库东北	H1	灰坑	天坡水库东北，原西村砖厂内				可辨认器形有鬲、簋等	1、3.鬲 2、4.深腹罐 5.腹片	二里岗	1999.1.9	浮选土样
			H2	灰坑	天坡水库东北，原西村砖厂内				可辨认器形有鬲、小罐、缸、瓮	1.鬲 2、4.深腹罐 3.小盆	二里岗	1999.1.9	植硅石土样
			H3	灰坑	天坡水库东北，原西村砖厂内					无	二里岗	1999.1.9	浮选土样
			H5	灰坑	天坡水库东北，原西村砖厂内，中部靠东南侧				可辨认器形有簋、鬲、甑、尊	1.缸 2、4.罐 3.深腹罐 5.鬲	二里岗	2001.5.30	浮选土样
			H6	灰坑	天坡水库东北，原西村砖厂内，中部砖窑门上方					无	二里岗	2001.5.30	浮选土样、植硅石土样
389	Y049	天坡	H1	灰坑	天坡村东原天坡砖厂内，西壁断崖剖面				可辨认器形有圈足盘、钵	1.罐 2.钵 3.彩陶片	仰韶晚期	1999.1.11	浮选土样
			H2	灰坑	天坡村东原天坡砖厂内，西壁断崖剖面				可辨认器形有鼎、彩陶碗	1.鼎 2.彩陶片	仰韶晚期	1999.1.11	浮选土样、植硅石土样
			H3	灰坑	天坡村东原天坡砖厂内，西壁断崖剖面					无	仰韶晚期	1999.1.11	浮选土样
			H4	灰坑	天坡村东原天坡砖厂内，西壁断崖剖面				可辨认器形有碗	1.杯	仰韶晚期	2007.11.12	浮选土样
			H5	灰坑	天坡村东原天坡砖厂内，取土坑内西南部					无	仰韶晚期	2007.11.12	浮选土样

续表

序号	遗址信息		遗迹		具体位置	形状尺寸		包含物及特征			年代	发现时间	备注
	编号	名称	编号	类型		形状	尺寸（单位：米）	填土	包含物	标本			
390	Y050	羽林庄南	H1	灰坑	羽林庄南，取土坑南壁西端				可辨认器形有泥质彩陶罐	无	仰韶晚期	1999.1.12	
			H2	灰坑	羽林庄南，取土坑南壁中部					无	仰韶晚期	1999.1.12	
			H3	灰坑	羽林庄南，取土坑南壁中部					无	仰韶晚期	1999.1.12	
			H4	灰坑	羽林庄南，取土坑南壁东部					无	仰韶晚期	1999.1.12	浮选土样、硅石土样
			H5	灰坑	羽林庄南，取土坑东壁南端					无	仰韶晚期	1999.1.12	浮选土样、硅石土样
			H6	灰坑	羽林庄南，取土坑东壁中部				可辨认器形有鼎、钵、尖底瓶、附加堆纹缸、小口高领罐等	1.罐 2.盆 3.彩陶片 4.腹片	仰韶晚期	2007.11.12	浮选土样、残留物土样
			M1	墓葬	羽林庄南，取土坑南壁西端					1.环	仰韶晚期	1999.1.12	
391	Y045	新移	H1	灰坑	遗址西北部断崖					无	跛墀早期	1999.1.10	
393	Y039	上庄东南	H1	灰坑	上庄东南三级台地断崖剖面路东					无	仰韶晚期	1999.1.7	
			H2	灰坑	上庄东南三级台地断崖剖面路西					无	仰韶晚期	1999.1.7	
			H3	灰坑	上庄东南三级台地断崖剖面路西中部					无	仰韶晚期	2007.11.13	浮选土样
			H4	灰坑	上庄东南三级台地断崖剖面路西中部偏西					无	仰韶晚期	2007.11.13	浮选土样

续表

遗址信息			遗迹		具体位置	形状尺寸		包含物及特征			年代	发现时间	备注
序号	编号	名称	编号	类型		形状	尺寸（单位：米）	填土	包含物	标本			
394	Y037	上庄南	H1	灰坑	上庄西南二级台地断崖剖面东端，H5西				可辨认器形有深腹罐、花边圆腹罐、缸、瓮、盆、大口尊、尊等	1. 圆腹罐 2、3、5. 深腹罐 4. 盆 6—8. 大口尊	二里头四期	1999.1.7	浮选土样
			H2	灰坑	上庄西南断崖剖面中部，H1西、H3东					无	二里头四期	1999.1.7	浮选土样
			H3	灰坑	上庄西南二级台地断崖剖面中部，H2西、H4东					1、2. 盆	东周	1999.1.7	
			H4	灰坑	上庄西南二级台地断崖剖面西端，H3西					无	二里头	1999.1.7	
			H5	灰坑	上庄西南二级台地断崖剖面东端，H1东					1. 深腹罐 2. 圆腹罐	二里岗	1999.1.7	植硅石土样
			H6	灰坑	东部断崖剖面					无	二里头	2007.11.13	浮选土样
			H7	灰坑	东部断崖剖面					无	二里头	2007.11.13	浮选土样
395	Y055	北地沟	H1	灰坑	上古朵村东临河台地中部小断崖剖面			红褐土	含烧土颗粒及灰烬	无	仰韶早期	2017.6.22	浮选、残留物分析土样
			H2	灰坑	村西新建砖窑剖面					无	裴李岗	2007.11.13	
401	Y029	铁生沟	H1	灰坑	东部废窑厂剖面					1—3. 鼎 4、5. 钵 6. 石刀	裴李岗	2017.6.14	
			M1	墓葬	新砖厂东侧偏北剖面，社区东南，成人墓				仅存下半段肢骨，未发现随葬品	无	裴李岗晚期	2015.3	

续表

序号	遗址信息			遗迹		具体位置	形状尺寸		填土	包含物及特征		标本	年代	发现时间	备注
	编号	名称		编号	类型		形状	尺寸（单位：米）		包含物					
402	Y030	夹津口			灰坑	二级台地南北断崖剖面						无	不详	1999.1.3	
406	Y034	寺院沟			灰坑							无	龙山晚期	1999.1.4	2个
407	Y042	坞罗西坡2		H1	灰坑	寺院沟西三级台地						无	裴李岗晚期	1999.1.13	浮选土样
				H2	灰坑	寺院沟西三级台地						无	裴李岗晚期	2007.11.13	浮选土样
				H3	灰坑	寺院沟西三级台地	袋状			见有三足钵足及大量兽骨等，堆积较为丰富		无	仰韶早期	2014.4.12	
				H4	灰坑	寺院沟西三级台地						无	裴李岗晚期	2017.6.15	
				M1	墓葬	寺院沟西三级台地						无	裴李岗晚期	不详	
408	Y033	坞罗西坡1		H1	灰坑	村北剖面						无	二里岗晚期	1999.1.4	
409	Y032	坞罗南店		H1	灰坑	南店村南断崖剖面最西端	袋状	底径约1.8米	灰土	可辨认器形有罐、器盖		1. 器盖 2. 罐 3. 蚌刀	龙山晚期	1999.1.4	浮选土样，植硅石土样
				H2	灰坑	南店村南断崖剖面中部，F1东、H3西	袋状	底径约3米	灰土及红烧土	可辨认器形有泥质罐、大口罐、折腹盆		1. 折腹盆	龙山晚期	1999.1.4	
				H3	灰坑	南店村南断崖剖面中部，H2东、F2西	袋状			可辨认器形有罐、小口高领瓮、器盖		无	龙山晚期	1999.1.4	
				H4	灰坑	南店村南断崖剖面东部，F2东	袋状			可辨认器形有大口罐、小罐、小口高领瓮、器盖		1、2. 大口罐	龙山晚期	1999.1.4	

续表

遗址信息		遗迹		具体位置	形状尺寸		包含物及特征			年代	发现时间	备注
序号	编号	名称	编号	类型		形状	尺寸（单位：米）	填土	包含物	标本			
409	Y032	坞罗南店	F1	房址	南店村南断崖剖面西部，H1东、H2西	袋状地穴式	底径约2.9米	填土上层灰色，下层红黄色，墙壁未经烧烤，地面为硬面		无	龙山晚期	1999.1.4	浮选土样、植硅石土样
			F2	房址	南店村南断崖剖面东部，H3东、H4西	袋状地穴式	底径约3.8米	填灰土及烧土块，墙壁经烧烤成红烧土层		无	龙山晚期	1999.1.4	
410	Y025	坞罗水库西1	H1	灰坑	坞罗水库西岸断崖剖面					1. 罐	仰韶晚期	1999.1.2	
			H2	灰坑	坞罗水库西岸断崖剖面					1、2. 瓮 3. 石斧	仰韶晚期	1999.1.2	
			H1	灰坑	村东口路北				可辨认器形有大口罐、小口高领罐	1.中口罐	龙山晚期	1999.1.1	浮选土样、植硅石土样
			H2	灰坑	魏家坑院东壁剖面北部					无	龙山晚期	1999.1.1	浮选土样、植硅石土样
413	Y022	罗口	H3	灰坑	魏家坑院东壁剖面中部				可辨认器形有泥质折沿罐、大口罐、石磨盘、蚌刀	1.中口罐 2.石磨盘 3、4.蚌刀	龙山晚期	1999.1.1	植硅石土样
			H4	灰坑	魏家坑院南壁剖面东部				口沿2件	1.深腹罐	二里头四期	1999.1.1	植硅石土样
			H5	灰坑	魏家坑院东壁剖面南部					无	龙山晚期	1999.1.1	

续表

遗址信息		遗迹		具体位置	形状尺寸		包含物及特征		年代	发现时间	备注
序号	编号	名称	编号	类型		形状	尺寸（单位：米）	填土	包含物	标本			

序号	编号	名称	编号	类型	具体位置	形状	尺寸	填土	包含物	标本	年代	发现时间	备注
413	Y022	罗口	H6	灰坑	魏家坑古院南壁剖面中部				见有陶片，陶片表面有石灰状残留物	无	龙山	1999.1.1	
			H7	灰坑	村东北断崖剖面，八队沟西100米				可辨认器形有深腹罐、盆、束颈盆、大口尊	1. 2.深腹罐 3.束颈盆 4.盆	二里岗晚期	2008.6.16	
			H8	灰坑	村子东南部，八队沟周围断崖剖面上					无	不详	2008.6.16	
			H9	灰坑	村子东南部，八队沟周围断崖剖面上					无	不详	2008.6.16	
				墓葬						无	周	1999.1.1	
416	Y020	喂庄东南		灰坑	坞罗河北岸断崖剖面					无	龙山	2008.6.19	
417	Y023	喂庄东南角		灰坑	村南坞罗河拐弯处西岸断崖剖面					无	仰韶晚期	1999.1.1	
418	Y024	喂庄南		灰坑、文化层	路东的断崖剖面上					无	仰韶	1999.1.1	
419	Y017	罗口砖厂东北	H1	灰坑	台地北壁剖面		直径约10米			无	汉代	1998.12.31	
			H1	灰坑	台地拐角处					1.夹砂罐 2.泥质彩陶罐	仰韶晚期	2001.6.4	浮选土样
420	Y019	喂庄西	H2	灰坑	H1南面					无	仰韶晚期	2001.6.4	浮选土样，植硅石土样

续表

序号	遗址信息 编号	遗址信息 名称	遗迹 编号	遗迹 类型	具体位置	形状尺寸 形状	形状尺寸 尺寸（单位：米）	包含物及特征 填土	包含物及特征 包含物	包含物及特征 标本	年代	发现时间	备注
421	Y018	喂庄西南	H1	灰坑	砖厂取土仅留一块台地西剖面南端					1.鼎 2.罐 3.陶片	仰韶晚期	1998.12.31	浮选土样，植硅石土样
			H2	灰坑	砖厂取土仅留一块台地西剖面中间					无	仰韶晚期	1998.12.31	浮选土样，植硅石土样
			H3	灰坑	砖厂取土仅留一块台地西剖面北端					无	仰韶晚期	1998.12.31	浮选土样
				墓葬	砖厂取土仅留一块台地北剖面东端	瓮棺葬				无	不详	1998.12.31	2座
425	Y011	费窑西南	H1	灰坑	取土大坑的北壁剖面					无	二里岗	1998.12.28	浮选土样，硅石土样
			H2	灰坑	取土大坑的北壁剖面					无	二里岗	1998.12.28	
			H3	灰坑	取土大坑的北壁剖面					无	二里岗	1998.12.28	
			H4	灰坑	取土大坑的西壁偏北剖面					无	二里岗	1998.12.28	
			H5	灰坑	取土大坑的北壁剖面					无	二里岗	1998.12.28	
			H6	灰坑	取土大坑的西壁剖面					无	二里岗	2007.11.14	浮选土样
			H7	灰坑	取土大坑的西壁剖面					无	二里岗	2007.11.14	浮选土样
430	Y003	清易镇东2	H1	灰坑	遗址南部断崖东西向断崖剖面上					无	东周	2007.11.14	浮选土样
439	Y1001	稍柴	H1	灰坑	老村东西大路东头大坡处路南断面最东端					1.深腹罐 2.圆腹罐 3.高领尊 4.器盖	二里头二期	1998.12.24	浮选土样
			H2	灰坑	老村东西大路东头大坡处路南断面中段，H1西					无	二里头二期	1998.12.24	

续表

序号	遗址信息		遗迹		具体位置	形状尺寸			包含物及特征			年代	发现时间	备注
	编号	名称	编号	类型		形状	尺寸（单位：米）	填土	包含物	标本				
439	Y1001	稍柴	H3	灰坑	老村东西大路东头大坡处路南断面西端，H2西					无	二里头	1998.12.28	浮选土样
			H4	灰坑	老村东西大路东头大坡处路南断面中段，H2西、H3东面					无	二里头四期	1998.12.28	
			H5	灰坑	老村东西大路东头大坡处路北张力家院内西南角				含有陶片、蚌片、石制品及猪骨头	1、2.深腹罐 3—6.圆腹罐 7.缸 8.三足盘 9.甑 10.盆	二里头二期	2001.6.7	
			H6	灰坑	老大队部西三孔窑洞、东窑洞南剖面				含有陶片、猪骨、兽骨及蚌片。陶片以二里头文化二期为主，少量四期	1.高领尊	二里头	2001.6.7	
			H7	灰坑	老大队部西三孔窑洞、中窑洞南剖面					1.鬲 2.盆	二里头二期	2001.6.7	
			H8	灰坑	老大队部西三孔窑洞、西窑洞南剖面					无	二里头二期	2001.6.7	
			H9	灰坑	老村东去河滩大路西侧断崖豁口北剖面					1.石镰 2.砺石 3.圆腹罐	二里头	2006.7.18	
			H10	灰坑	老村东去河滩大路西侧断崖豁口南剖面					1.大口尊	二里头	2013	

续表

序号	遗址信息		遗迹			形状尺寸			包含物及特征			年代	发现时间	备注
	编号	名称	编号	类型	具体位置	形状	尺寸（单位：米）	填土	包含物	标本				
440	Y1003	南石	H1	灰坑	小訾殿村北路南断崖剖面距村北口约30米	袋状				1.鼎	仰韶晚期	2017.6.18	
			F1	房址	小訾殿村北台地东剖面南端					1.甗	龙山晚期	1998.12.28	浮选土样
442	Y1004	小訾殿北		灰坑	小訾殿村北台地西断崖剖面北端					无	龙山晚期	1997.12.31	
446	Y006	稍柴东A		墓葬	路北断崖剖面				大量裸露的人骨	无	不详	1998.12.27	
451	Y145	小南沟西南	H1	灰坑	路边断崖剖面					无	龙山晚期	2001.6.8	
453	Y147	东沟西北	H1	灰坑	东沟村西北，路边断崖剖面					1.盆	龙山晚期	2001.6.8	

附表3 遗物登记表

续表

遗址信息			遗迹	登记号	器型	质地	图号		时代
序号	编号	名称					插图号	图版号	
2	036	刘坡		1	小盆	陶	图2.4b，1	图版三八七，1	二里头三期晚
				2	捏口罐	陶	图2.4b，10	图版四一一，1	二里岗早期
				3	捏口罐	陶	图2.4b，5		二里岗
				4	罐	陶	图2.4b，6		殷墟
				5	盆	陶	图2.4b，3	图版四四二，1	战国
				6	盆	陶	图2.4b，9		战国
				7	盆	陶	图2.4b，4	图版四四二，2	战国
				8	盆	陶	图2.4b，7	图版四四二，3	战国
				9	盆	陶	图2.4b，2	图版四四二，4	战国
				10	盆	陶	图2.4b，8	图版四四二，5	战国
				11	瓮	陶	图2.4b，11		战国
				12	瓮	陶	图2.4c，7	图版四四二，6	战国
				13	豆	陶	图2.4c，2	图版四四三，1	战国
				14	豆	陶	图2.4c，1		战国
				15	豆	陶	图2.4c，3	图版四四三，2	战国
				16	豆	陶	图2.4c，4		战国
				17	罐	陶	图2.4c，6		战国
				18	板瓦	陶	图2.4c，5	图版四四三，3	战国
5	034	平乐A		1	石锛	石	图2.6b，7	图版二三七，1	不详
				2	中口罐	陶	图2.6b，3		龙山晚期
				3	斝	陶	图2.6b，2		龙山晚期
				4	圆陶片	陶	图2.6b，4		龙山晚期
				5	捏口罐	陶	图2.6b，6	图版三九五，3	二里头四期晚
				6	盆形鼎	陶	图2.6b，5	图版三九五，4	二里头四期
				7	壶	陶		图版四四三，4	战国
			H1	1	罐	陶	图2.6b，1		龙山晚期
7	029	翟泉北		1	罐	陶	图2.8b，3		仰韶晚期
8	030	翟泉东北		1	鬲	陶	图2.8b，4		东周
9	031	翟泉西南		1	石戈	石	图2.8b，5	图版二三七，2	不详
				2	石环	石	图2.8b，6	图版二三七，3	不详
				3	小口尖底瓶	陶	图2.8b，1		仰韶中、晚期
				4	钵	陶	图2.8b，2		仰韶中、晚期
				5	盆	陶	图2.8b，7		东周
12	046	保庄西北		1	石刀	石		图版二三七，4	不详
				2	瓮	陶	图2.13b，2		龙山晚期
				3	罐	陶	图2.13b，3		龙山晚期

续表

遗址信息			遗迹	登记号	器型	质地	图号		时代
序号	编号	名称					插图号	图版号	
12	046	保庄西北		4	罐	陶	图2.13b，5	图版四二四，1	西周晚期
				5	罐	陶	图2.13b，6	图版四二四，2	西周晚期
				6	鬲	陶	图2.13b，4		战国
				7	鬲	陶	图2.13b，11		战国
				8	罐	陶	图2.13b，7	图版四四三，5	战国
				9	盆	陶	图2.13b，8		战国
				10	盆	陶	图2.13b，12	图版四四三，6	战国
			H1	1	刀	蚌	图2.13b，1	图版三五六，6	龙山晚期
			H2	1	罐形鼎	陶	图2.13b，9	图版三二四，2	仰韶晚期
				2	器盖	陶	图2.13b，10	图版三二四，3	仰韶晚期
			H3	1	折腹盆	陶	图2.13b，13	图版三五七，1	龙山晚期
13	047	保庄北		1	鼎	陶	图2.14b，1		仰韶晚期
				2	缸	陶	图2.14b，2	图版三二四，4	仰韶晚期
				3	圈足盘	陶	图2.14b，3	图版三五七，2	龙山晚期
				4	罐	陶	图2.14b，4		龙山晚期
				5	钵	陶	图2.14b，7	图版三二四，5	仰韶晚期
				6	鬲	陶	图2.14b，5	图版四二四，3	西周晚期
				7	盆	陶	图2.14b，9	图版四二四，4	西周晚期
				8	鬲	陶	图2.14b，8	图版四三〇，1	春秋
				9	罐	陶	图2.14b，12	图版四三〇，2	春秋
				10	鬲	陶	图2.14b，10	图版四三〇，3	春秋
				11	罐	陶	图2.14b，11	图版四三〇，4	春秋
				12	豆	陶	图2.14b，6		春秋
15	028	丁沟南		1	彩陶片	陶	图2.16b，7	图版三二四，6	仰韶晚期
				2	罐	陶	图2.16b，1		仰韶晚期
				3	豆	陶	图2.16b，4		仰韶晚期
				4	罐	陶	图2.16b，2		西周晚期
				5	罐	陶	图2.16b，3		西周晚期
17	049	石桥东北		1	鬲	陶	图2.16b，5	图版四三〇，5	春秋
				2	鬲	陶	图2.16b，6	图版四三〇，6	春秋
19	012	帽郭A		1	石锛	石	图2.21b，1	图版二三七，5	不详
				2	石铲	石	图2.21b，5	图版二三七，6	不详
				3	石凿	石	图2.21b，2	图版二三八，1	不详
				4	石铲	石	图2.21b，4	图版二三八，2	不详
				5	石料	石	图2.21b，8	图版二三八，3	不详
				6	石杵	石	图2.21b，3	图版二三八，4	不详
				7	石铲	石	图2.21b，6	图版二三八，5	不详

续表

遗址信息			遗迹	登记号	器型	质地	图号		时代
序号	编号	名称					插图号	图版号	
19	012	帽郭A		8	砺石	石	图2.21b, 7	图版二三八, 6	不详
				9	鬲	陶	图2.21c, 1	图版三九五, 5	二里头四期晚
				10	罐	陶	图2.21c, 3		二里头二至四期
				11	盆	陶	图2.21c, 4	图版三九五, 6	二里头四期早
				12	瓮	陶	图2.21c, 2	图版三九六, 1	二里头四期晚
				13	深腹罐	陶	图2.21c, 8	图版三八七, 2	二里头三期晚
				14	捏口罐	陶	图2.21c, 9	图版三八七, 3	二里头三期晚
				15	高领罐	陶	图2.21c, 10	图版三九六, 2	二里头四期晚
				16	盆	陶	图2.21c, 5	图版三七六, 5	二里头二期早
				17	盆	陶	图2.21c, 6	图版三八七, 4	二里头三期
				18	缸	陶	图2.21c, 7	图版三八七, 5	二里头三期
				19	盆	陶	图2.21c, 11	图版三九六, 3	二里头四期
				20	圆陶片	陶	图2.21d, 7		二里岗
				21	鬲	陶	图2.21d, 2	图版四一一, 2	二里岗早期
				22	鬲	陶	图2.21d, 3		二里岗早期
				23	鬲	陶	图2.21d, 4		二里岗早期
				24	鬲	陶	图2.21d, 9		二里岗早期
				25	鬲	陶	图2.21d, 5		二里岗早期
				26	鬲	陶	图2.21d, 1	图版四一九, 1	殷墟
				27	簋	陶	图2.21d, 6	图版四一九, 2	殷墟
				28	簋	陶	图2.21d, 10	图版四一九, 3	殷墟
				29	罐	陶	图2.21d, 8	图版四一九, 4	殷墟
				30	蚌器	蚌			不详
				31	蚌器	蚌			不详
				32	蚌料	蚌			不详
20	013	帽郭B		1	瓮	陶	图2.22b, 2	图版四一九, 5	殷墟
				2	罐	陶	图2.22b, 1	图版四一九, 6	殷墟
				3	簋	陶	图2.22b, 3	图版四二四, 5	西周
				4	盆	陶	图2.22b, 5		西周
				5	瓮	陶	图2.22b, 4	图版四二四, 6	西周
21	004	凹杨		1	圆陶片	陶	图2.23b, 1	图版三二二, 4	仰韶中、晚期
				2	石铲	石	图2.23b, 6		仰韶
				3	石凿	石	图2.23b, 7		仰韶
				4	陶器腹片	陶	图2.23b, 5		龙山晚期
				5	敛口钵	陶	图2.23b, 2		仰韶中、晚期
				6	折腹盆	陶	图2.23b, 18		仰韶中、晚期

续表

遗址信息			遗迹	登记号	器型	质地	图号		时代
序号	编号	名称					插图号	图版号	
21	004	凹杨		7	豆	陶	图2.23b, 17		仰韶中、晚期
				8	敛口钵	陶	图2.23b, 14		仰韶中、晚期
				9	折腹盆	陶	图2.23b, 3		仰韶中、晚期
				10	小口尖底瓶	陶	图2.23b, 4		仰韶中、晚期
				11	大口罐	陶	图2.23b, 15		仰韶中、晚期
				12	罐形鼎	陶	图2.23b, 16		仰韶中、晚期
				13	大口罐	陶	图2.23b, 10		仰韶中、晚期
				14	小口罐	陶	图2.23b, 13	图版三二五, 1	仰韶晚期
				15	瓮	陶	图2.23b, 8		仰韶中、晚期
				16	盆	陶	图2.23b, 11		仰韶中、晚期
				17	盆	陶	图2.23b, 12		仰韶中、晚期
				18	盆	陶	图2.23b, 9		仰韶中、晚期
22	003	扁担赵南		1	石斧	石	图2.24b, 5		不详
				2	罐	陶	图2.24b, 3		仰韶中、晚期
				3	盆	陶	图2.24b, 6		仰韶中、晚期
				4	罐	陶	图2.24b, 1		仰韶中、晚期
				5	罐	陶	图2.24b, 2		仰韶中、晚期
				6	器盖	陶	图2.24b, 4		二里头
				7	平底盆	陶	图2.24b, 8	图版三七六, 6	二里头二期早
				8	圆腹罐	陶	图2.24b, 7		二里头
				9	蚌器	蚌			不详
24	007	黑王		1	石斧	石	图2.26b, 1		不详
				2	瓮	陶	图2.26b, 3		仰韶晚期
				3	敛口钵	陶	图2.26b, 2		仰韶晚期
				4	圆腹罐	陶	图2.26b, 7		二里头
				5	深腹罐	陶	图2.26b, 5		二里头
				6	深腹罐	陶	图2.26b, 9		二里头
				7	鬲	陶	图2.26b, 8		二里岗晚期
				8	大口尊	陶	图2.26b, 6		二里岗晚期
				9	盆	陶	图2.26b, 4	图版四六二, 1	东周
				10	盆	陶	图2.26b, 10		东周
25	006	白王北		1	石斧	石	图2.27b, 4	图版二三九, 1	不详
				2	石镰	石	图2.27b, 2	图版二三九, 2	不详
				3	瓮	陶	图2.27b, 3		二里头三、四期
				4	罐	陶	图2.27b, 1		二里头三、四期
30	040	龙虎滩北		1	罐	陶	图2.32b, 3	图版四六二, 2	东周

续表

遗址信息			遗迹	登记号	器型	质地	图号		时代
序号	编号	名称					插图号	图版号	
30	040	龙虎滩北		2	器盖	陶	图2.32b，2		东周
				3	圆陶片	陶	图2.32b，1	图版四六二，3	东周
31	048	寺里碑东		1	鬲	陶	图2.32b，4	图版四四四，1	战国
32	041	景阳岗		1	石环坯	石	图2.34b，1	图版二三九，3	不详
				2	石凿	石	图2.34b，5	图版二三九，4	不详
				3	双缺口石刀	石	图2.34b，2	图版三五〇，1	仰韶
				4	圆陶片	陶	图2.34b，11	图版三二五，2	仰韶晚期
				5	圆陶片	陶	图2.34b，3	图版三二二，5	仰韶中、晚期
				6	罐	陶	图2.34b，7		仰韶晚期
				7	罐	陶	图2.34b，8		仰韶晚期
				8	盆	陶	图2.34b，4	图版三二五，3	仰韶晚期
				9	彩陶片	陶	图2.34b，6	图版三〇七，3	仰韶中期
				10	鬲	陶	图2.34b，13		西周
				11	罐	陶	图2.34b，10		龙山
				12	罐	陶	图2.34b，9		仰韶晚期至龙山早期
				13	盆	陶	图2.34b，14		龙山
				14	瓮	陶	图2.34b，12		龙山
				15	盆	陶	图2.34d，2	图版三九六，4	二里头四期晚
				16	缸	陶	图2.34d，3	图版三九六，5	二里头四期晚
				17	圆腹罐	陶		图版三八七，6	二里头三期晚
				18	圆腹罐	陶	图2.34d，6	图版三九六，6	二里头四期早
				19	深腹罐	陶	图2.34d，5	图版三九七，1	二里头四期早
				20	深腹罐	陶	图2.34d，4	图版三九七，2	二里头四期早
				21	深腹罐	陶	图2.34d，8		二里头
				22	鬲	陶	图2.34d，1		二里头
				23	鬲	陶	图2.34d，9	图版三九七，3	二里头四期晚
				24	圆腹罐	陶	图2.34d，7	图版三九七，4	二里头四期晚
				25	捏口罐	陶	图2.34e，1	图版三九七，5	二里头四期晚
				26	捏口罐	陶	图2.34e，2	图版三九七，6	二里头四期晚
				27	圆腹罐	陶	图2.34e，8		二里头
				28	圆腹罐	陶	图2.34e，9		二里头
				29	鼎	陶	图2.34e，5	图版三九八，1	二里头四期早
				30	捏口罐	陶	图2.34e，6		二里头
				31	骨料	骨	图2.34c，8		不详
				32	圆腹罐	陶	图2.34e，7	图版三九八，2	二里头四期早

续表

遗址信息			遗迹	登记号	器型	质地	图号		时代
序号	编号	名称					插图号	图版号	
32	041	景阳岗		33	刻槽盆	陶	图2.34e，12	图版三九八，3	二里头四期晚
				34	四系罐	陶	图2.34e，13	图版三九八，4	二里头四期晚
				35	盆	陶	图2.34e，4	图版三八八，1	二里头三期晚
				36	盆	陶	图2.34e，3		二里头
				37	盆	陶	图2.34c，7	图版四二五，1	西周晚期
				38	大口尊	陶	图2.34e，10	图版三八八，2	二里头三期早
				39	大口尊	陶	图2.34e，11	图版三九八，5	二里头四期晚
				40	鬲	陶	图2.34c，1		西周晚期
				41	罐	陶	图2.34c，4	图版四二五，2	西周晚期
				42	簋	陶	图2.34c，6		西周晚期
				43	罐	陶	图2.34c，3		东周
			H1	1	陶刀	陶	图2.34c，2	图版四三一，1	春秋
				2	罐	陶	图2.34c，5	图版四三一，2	春秋
33	043	白村东北		1	罐	陶	图2.35b，1	图版三二五，4	仰韶晚期
				2	盆	陶	图2.35b，2	图版三二五，5	仰韶晚期
41	060	赫田寨西北		1	鬲	陶	图2.43b，2		二里岗
				2	簋	陶	图2.43b，3		二里岗
				3	盆	陶	图2.43b，1	图版四一四，1	二里岗晚期
42	001	史家湾北		1	深腹罐	陶	图2.45b，7		二里头四期
				2	圆腹罐	陶	图2.45b，8	图版三九八，6	二里头四期晚
				3	盆	陶	图2.45b，9		二里头四期
				4	盆	陶	图2.45b，10		二里头四期
				5	簋	陶	图2.45b，1		西周
				6	簋	陶	图2.45b，2		西周
				7	簋	陶	图2.45b，4		西周
				8	簋	陶	图2.45b，3		西周
				9	簋	陶	图2.45b，5		西周
				10	簋	陶	图2.45b，6	图版四二五，3	西周
				11	簋	陶	图2.45b，11		西周
				12	罐	陶	图2.45b，12		西周
				13	罐	陶	图2.45b，13	图版四二五，4	西周
43	002	杨湾西		1	簋	陶	图2.46b，9		西周
				2	簋	陶	图2.46b，8		西周
				3	簋	陶	图2.46b，3	图版四二五，5	西周
				4	簋	陶	图2.46b，1	图版四二五，6	西周
				5	罐	陶	图2.46b，5		春秋早期

续表

遗址信息			遗迹	登记号	器型	质地	图号		时代
序号	编号	名称					插图号	图版号	
43	002	杨湾西		6	罐	陶	图2.46b, 4	图版四二六, 1	西周
				7	簋	陶	图2.46b, 2		西周
				8	盆	陶	图2.46b, 10	图版四四四, 2	战国
				9	盆	陶	图2.46b, 14		汉
				10	盆	陶	图2.46b, 11	图版四四四, 3	战国
				11	盆	陶	图2.46b, 12	图版四四四, 4	战国
				12	壶	陶	图2.46b, 6	图版四四四, 5	战国
				13	壶	陶	图2.46b, 7	图版四四四, 6	战国
				14	盆	陶	图2.46b, 13	图版四四五, 1	战国
44	009	陈屯老村		1	深腹罐	陶	图2.47b, 13	图版三七七, 1	二里头二期晚
				2	盆	陶	图2.47b, 3		战国
				3	盆	陶	图2.47b, 2	图版四四五, 2	战国
				4	盆	陶	图2.47b, 1	图版四四五, 3	战国
				5	圆陶片	陶	图2.47b, 5		战国
45	010	枣园北		1	鬲	陶	图2.47b, 10	图版四一一, 3	二里岗早期
				2	簋	陶	图2.47b, 12		二里岗早期
				3	盆	陶	图2.47b, 9		二里岗早期
				4	簋	陶	图2.47b, 11	图版四一一, 4	二里岗早期
				5	簋	陶	图2.47b, 7		二里岗早期
				6	盆	陶	图2.47b, 6		战国
				7	盆	陶	图2.47b, 8		战国
				8	盆	陶	图2.47b, 14	图版四四五, 4	战国
				9	盆	陶	图2.47b, 4	图版四四五, 5	战国
47	044	渔骨西南		1	骨料	骨	图2.50b, 1		不详
48	057	古城西		1	罐	陶	图2.50b, 2		二里头
53	065	北窑东北		1	鬲	陶	图2.57b, 3		二里岗晚期
				2	鬲	陶	图2.57b, 2	图版四一一, 5	二里岗早期
				3	鬲	陶	图2.57b, 1	图版四一四, 3	二里岗晚期
				4	盆	陶	图2.57b, 7	图版四一四, 4	二里岗晚期
				5	盆	陶	图2.57b, 6	图版四一四, 5	二里岗晚期
				6	盆	陶	图2.57b, 5		二里岗
				7	高领罐	陶	图2.57b, 10		二里岗
			H1	1	簋	陶	图2.57b, 9	图版四一四, 2	二里岗晚期
			H1	2	簋	陶	图2.57b, 8		二里岗
			H1	3	甗	陶	图2.57b, 4		二里岗

续表

遗址信息			遗迹	登记号	器型	质地	图号		时代
序号	编号	名称					插图号	图版号	
59	072	山圪垱		1	鼎	陶	图2.63b，1	图版三五一，1	龙山早期
				2	罐	陶	图2.63b，2	图版三五一，2	龙山早期
62/63	074	寺沟		1	石铲	石	图2.66b，1	图版二三九，5	不详
				2	石凿	石	图2.66b，2	图版二三九，6	不详
				3	石锛	石	图2.66b，3	图版二四〇，1	不详
				4	圆陶片	陶	图2.66b，4	图版三二五，6	仰韶晚期
				5	盆	陶	图2.66b，6		仰韶中、晚期
				6	罐	陶	图2.66b，10		仰韶中、晚期
				7	罐	陶	图2.66b，11		二里头晚期
				8	罐	陶	图2.66c，3		西周
				9	罐	陶	图2.66b，7	图版三二六，1	仰韶晚期
				10	盆	陶	图2.66b，5	图版三二六，2	仰韶晚期
				11	罐	陶	图2.66b，13		龙山早期
				12	罐	陶	图2.66b，8	图版三五一，3	龙山早期
				13	罐	陶	图2.66b，9		仰韶中、晚期
				14	罐	陶	图2.66b，12	图版三五一，4	龙山早期
				15	鬲	陶	图2.66c，7	图版四二〇，1	殷墟
				16	罐	陶	图2.66c，13	图版四二〇，2	殷墟
				17	罐	陶	图2.66c，4	图版四二〇，3	殷墟
				18	罐	陶	图2.66c，11		殷墟
				19	罐	陶	图2.66c，6	图版四二〇，4	殷墟
				20	鬲	陶	图2.66c，10		西周
				21	鬲	陶	图2.66c，9	图版四二六，2	西周
				22	鬲	陶	图2.66c，8	图版四二六，3	西周
				23	盆	陶	图2.66c，16	图版四二六，4	西周
				24	罐	陶	图2.66c，12		西周
				25	盆	陶	图2.66c，14		西周
				26	罐	陶	图2.66c，5		西周
				27	盆	陶	图2.66c，15		东周
				28	豆	陶	图2.66c，2		东周
				29	豆	陶	图2.66c，1		东周
62	Y151	寺沟南		1	彩陶罐	陶	图2.67b，1		仰韶晚期
				2	石片	石			不详
				3	甑	陶			龙山晚期
				4	瓮	陶	图2.67b，15		龙山晚期
				5	瓮	陶	图2.67b，14		龙山晚期

续表

遗址信息			遗迹	登记号	器型	质地	图号		时代
序号	编号	名称					插图号	图版号	
62	Y151	寺沟南		6	陶轮盘	陶	图2.67b，5		不详
				7	鬲	陶	图2.67b，13		西周早中期
				8	鬲	陶	图2.67b，12		西周早中期
				9	鬲	陶	图2.67b，6		西周早中期
				10	鬲	陶	图2.67b，7		西周早中期
				11	罐	陶	图2.67b，10		西周早中期
			H1	1	中口罐	陶	图2.67b，2		龙山晚期
				2	小罐	陶	图2.67b，3		龙山晚期
				3	器盖	陶	图2.67b，9		龙山晚期
				4	圈足	陶	图2.67b，4		龙山晚期
			H4	1	鬲	陶	图2.67b，8		西周早中期
				2	鬲	陶	图2.67b，11		西周早中期
63	Y152	寺沟东南		1	罐	陶	图2.68b，4		仰韶
				2	盆	陶	图2.68b，2		仰韶
				3	盆	陶	图2.68b，3		仰韶
				4	钵	陶	图2.68b，5		仰韶
				5	尖底瓶	陶			仰韶
				6	罐	陶	图2.68b，16		龙山早期
				7	瓮	陶	图2.68b，15		龙山
				9	深腹罐	陶	图2.68b，19		二里头
				10	深腹罐	陶	图2.68b，20		二里头
				11	鼎	陶	图2.68b，17		二里头
				12	鬲	陶	图2.68c，7		西周
				13	鬲	陶	图2.68c，5		西周晚期
				14	鬲	陶	图2.68c，6		西周晚期
				15	鬲	陶	图2.68c，3		西周晚期
				16	鬲	陶	图2.68c，2		西周晚期
				17	鬲	陶	图2.68c，1		西周晚期
				18	鬲	陶	图2.68c，4		西周
				19	罐	陶	图2.68c，11		西周
				20	罐	陶	图2.68c，10		西周
				21	罐	陶	图2.68c，14		西周晚期
				22	罐	陶	图2.68c，15		西周
				23	罐	陶	图2.68c，12		西周晚期
				24	罐	陶	图2.68c，13		西周晚期
				25	罐	陶	图2.68c，9		西周晚期

续表

遗址信息			遗迹	登记号	器型	质地	图号		时代
序号	编号	名称					插图号	图版号	
63	Y152	寺沟东南		26	豆	陶	图2.68c，16		西周晚期
				27	豆	陶	图2.68c，17		西周晚期
				28	器座	陶	图2.68c，19		不详
				29	网坠	陶	图2.68b，14		二里头
				30	石斧	石			不详
				31	石刀	石			不详
				32	石废料	石			不详
				33	石球	石	图2.68b，1		不详
				35	砺石	石			不详
				36	鬲	陶	图2.68c，18		不详
			H2	1	缸	陶	图2.68b，7		龙山早期
				2	缸	陶	图2.68b，9		龙山早期
				3	缸	陶	图2.68b，11		龙山早期
				4	缸	陶	图2.68b，10		龙山早期
				5	缸	陶	图2.68b，12		龙山早期
				6	缸	陶	图2.68b，13		龙山早期
				7	罐	陶			龙山早期
				8	盆	陶	图2.68b，8		龙山早期
				9	钵	陶	图2.68b，6		龙山早期
			H3	1	圆腹罐	陶	图2.68b，18		二里头二期
			H4	1	鬲	陶	图2.68c，8		西周
			H7	1	石刀坯	石			不详
64a	075	石家庄		1	钵	陶	图2.69b，1		仰韶中、晚期
				2	盆	陶	图2.69b，2		仰韶中、晚期
				3	鬲	陶	图2.69b，3		战国
65	Y154	高岭		1	鼎	陶	图2.71b，12		战国
				2	石斧	石			不详
66	Y156	南瓦窑		1	罐	陶	图2.71b，2		仰韶
				2	罐	陶	图2.71b，5		仰韶
				3	罐	陶	图2.71b，1		仰韶
				4	钵	陶	图2.71b，11		仰韶
				5	缸	陶	图2.71b，7		仰韶
				6	钵	陶	图2.71b，8		仰韶
				7	碗	陶	图2.71b，6		仰韶

续表

序号	遗址信息 编号	名称	遗迹	登记号	器型	质地	图号 插图号	图版号	时代
66	Y156	南瓦窑	H1	1	罐	陶	图2.71b, 3		仰韶
				2	罐	陶	图2.71b, 4		仰韶
				3	钵	陶	图2.71b, 10		仰韶
				4	钵	陶	图2.71b, 9		仰韶
			W1	1	盆	陶	图2.71b, 13		仰韶早期
				2	罐	陶	图2.71b, 14		仰韶早期
67	Y157	康北古城		1	碗	陶	图2.73b, 2		东周
				2	盆	陶	图2.73b, 1		东周
				3	豆	陶	图2.73b, 3		东周
				4	豆	陶	图2.73b, 5		东周
68	Y158	康沟		1	鬲	陶	图2.73b, 7		西周中晚期
				2	鬲	陶	图2.73b, 8		西周中晚期
				3	鬲	陶	图2.73b, 6		西周中晚期
				4	缸	陶	图2.73b, 4		西周中晚期
				5	罐	陶	图2.73b, 9		西周晚期
				6	豆	陶	图2.73b, 13		西周晚期
				7	豆	陶	图2.73b, 10		西周晚期
				8	鬲	陶	图2.73b, 11		东周
				9	盆	陶	图2.73b, 12		东周
				10	砺石	石			不详
71	Y161	神北		1	彩陶片	陶			仰韶晚期
				2	圈足盘	陶	图2.77b, 2		仰韶晚期
				3	石锤	石			不详
				4	石铲坯	石	图2.77b, 1		不详
72	076	西石桥东		1	砺石	石	图2.80b, 5	图版二四〇, 2	不详
				2	石料	石	图2.80b, 6		不详
				3	碗	陶	图2.80b, 13	图版三〇三, 6	裴李岗晚期至仰韶早期
				4	鼎	陶	图2.80b, 3	图版三〇七, 4	仰韶中期
				5	罐	陶	图2.80b, 12		仰韶早中期
				6	盆	陶	图2.80b, 7		仰韶早中期
				7	罐	陶	图2.80b, 8		仰韶早中期
				8	钵	陶	图2.80b, 9		仰韶早中期
				9	钵	陶	图2.80b, 2		仰韶早中期
				10	盆	陶	图2.80b, 4		仰韶早中期
				11	钵	陶	图2.80b, 10		仰韶早中期

续表

遗址信息			遗迹	登记号	器型	质地	图号		时代
序号	编号	名称					插图号	图版号	
72	076	西石桥东		12	钵	陶	图2.80b，1		仰韶早中期
				13	钵	陶	图2.80b，11	图版三二六，3	仰韶晚期
				14	圆腹罐	陶		图版三九九，1	二里头四期早
				15	圆腹罐	陶	图2.80c，9		二里头
				16	圆腹罐	陶	图2.80c，12	图版三九九，2	二里头四期晚
				17	圆腹罐	陶	图2.80c，10		二里头
				18	圆腹罐	陶	图2.80c，11		二里头
				19	缸	陶	图2.80c，8	图版三八八，3	二里头三期晚
				20	瓮	陶	图2.80c，13	图版三九九，3	二里头四期晚
				21	盆	陶	图2.80c，7	图版三九九，4	二里头四期晚
				22	鬲	陶	图2.80d，12	图版四二六，5	西周晚期
				23	鬲	陶	图2.80d，2		战国
				24	鬲	陶	图2.80d，1		战国
				25	盆	陶	图2.80d，10		战国
				26	盆	陶	图2.80d，5		战国
				27	盆	陶	图2.80d，9	图版四四五，6	战国
				28	盆	陶	图2.80d，4		战国
				29	盆	陶	图2.80d，11		战国
				30	盆	陶	图2.80d，13		战国
				31	盆	陶	图2.80d，7	图版四四六，1、2	战国
				32	豆	陶	图2.80d，6		战国
				33	壶	陶		图版四四六，3	战国
				34	盆	陶		图版四四六，4	战国
				35	盆	陶		图版四四六，5	战国
				36	骨料	骨	图2.80b，14		不详
				37	罐	陶		图版三五八，2	龙山晚期
				38	盆	陶	图2.80d，3		战国
				39	盆	陶	图2.80d，8		战国
				40	罐	陶	图2.80d，14		战国
			H1	1	甗	陶	图2.80c，1	图版三五七，3	龙山晚期
				2	盆	陶	图2.80c，5	图版三五七，4	龙山晚期
				3	罍	陶	图2.80c，3	图版三五七，5	龙山晚期
				4	罐	陶	图2.80c，6	图版三五七，6	龙山晚期
				5	觚	陶	图2.80c，2	图版三五八，1	龙山晚期
				6	盘	陶	图2.80c，4		龙山晚期

续表

遗址信息			遗迹	登记号	器型	质地	图号		时代
序号	编号	名称					插图号	图版号	
73	077	孙家岗		1	石杵	石	图2.81b, 4	图版二四〇, 3	不详
				2	石杵	石	图2.81b, 5	图版二四〇, 4	不详
				3	深腹罐	陶	图2.81b, 9	图版三九九, 5	二里头四期晚（岳石风格）
				4	束颈盆	陶	图2.81b, 2	图版三九九, 6	二里头四期晚
				5	圆腹罐	陶	图2.81b, 6	图版四〇〇, 1	二里头四期晚
				6	圆腹罐	陶	图2.81b, 11	图版四〇〇, 2	二里头四期晚
				7	盆	陶	图2.81b, 3	图版三八八, 4	二里头三期早
				8	大口尊	陶	图2.81b, 1	图版四〇〇, 3	二里头四期晚
				9	瓮	陶	图2.81b, 8		二里头四期
				10	壶	陶	图2.81b, 10	图版三九五, 2	二里头三期晚至四期早
				11	鬲	陶	图2.81b, 12	图版四一四, 6	二里岗晚期
				12	捏口罐	陶	图2.81b, 7		二里岗晚期
				13	罐	陶	图2.81b, 14		二里岗晚期
				14	鬲	陶	图2.81b, 15	图版四二〇, 5	殷墟
				15	盆	陶	图2.81c, 4	图版四四六, 6	战国
				16	盆	陶	图2.81c, 8	图版四三一, 3	春秋
				17	盆	陶	图2.81c, 10	图版四四七, 1	战国
				18	盆	陶	图2.81c, 5	图版四三一, 4	春秋
				19	豆	陶	图2.81c, 12		战国
				20	罐	陶	图2.81c, 9	图版四四七, 2	战国
				21	罐	陶	图2.81c, 11	图版四四七, 3	战国
				22	罐	陶	图2.81c, 7	图版四三一, 5	春秋
				23	鬲	陶	图2.81c, 1		春秋
				24	鬲	陶	图2.81c, 6	图版四三一, 6	春秋
				25	鬲	陶	图2.81c, 13	图版四四七, 4	战国
				26	鬲	陶	图2.81c, 15	图版四四七, 5	战国
				27	豆	陶	图2.81c, 14	图版四三二, 1	春秋
				28	豆	陶	图2.81c, 2	图版四四七, 6	战国
				29	盆	陶	图2.81c, 3	图版四四八, 1	战国
				30	鬲	陶	图2.81c, 16	图版四四八, 2	战国
				31	鬲	陶	图2.81c, 17	图版四四八, 3	战国
				32	板瓦	陶	图2.81c, 18	图版四六二, 4	东周
				33	穿孔陶片	陶	图2.81c, 19	图版四六二, 5	东周
			H1	1	夹砂罐	陶	图2.81b, 13	图版三二六, 4	仰韶晚期

续表

遗址信息			遗迹	登记号	器型	质地	图号		时代
序号	编号	名称					插图号	图版号	
74	080	佃庄东		1	纺轮	陶	图2.82b，4	图版四六二，6	东周
				2	宽沿盆	陶	图2.82b，3		战国
76	088	关庄东南		1	簋	陶	图2.82b，1		殷墟
				2	罐	陶	图2.82b，2	图版四二六，6	西周
77	089	关公冢		1	罐	陶	图2.82b，9	图版三二六，5	仰韶晚期
				2	簋	陶	图2.82b，7	图版四二七，1	西周
				3	簋	陶	图2.82b，8	图版四二七，2	西周
				4	簋	陶	图2.82b，6	图版四二七，3	西周
				5	罐	陶	图2.82b，10		西周
				6	簋	陶	图2.82b，5	图版四二七，4	西周
82	094	谷堆头寨		1	石球	石	图2.90b，1	图版二四〇，5	不详
				2	敛口钵	陶	图2.90b，10		仰韶晚期
				3	敛口钵	陶	图2.90b，6		仰韶晚期
				4	罐	陶	图2.90b，5	图版三五八，3	龙山晚期
				5	罐	陶	图2.90b，9		龙山晚期
				6	罐	陶	图2.90b，7		二里头三、四期
				7	罐	陶	图2.90b，8		西周晚期
				8	盆	陶	图2.90b，4		西周晚期
				9	罐	陶	图2.90b，3		西周晚期
				10	纺轮	陶	图2.90b，2		不详
83	020	桂连凹南		1	石锛	石	图2.92b，1	图版二四〇，6	不详
				2	石斧	石	图2.92b，2	图版二四一，1	不详
				3	残石器	石	图2.92b，4	图版二四一，2	不详
				4	残石器	石	图2.92b，3	图版二四一，3	不详
				5	石片	石	图2.92b，5	图版二四一，4	不详
				6	残石器	石	图2.92b，6	图版二四一，5	不详
				7	鼎	陶	图2.92c，1	图版三七七，3	二里头二期早
				8	圆腹罐	陶	图2.92c，3	图版三八八，5	二里头三期晚
				9	圆腹罐	陶	图2.92c，4		二里头
				10	深腹罐	陶	图2.92c，2	图版三八八，6	二里头三期晚
				11	捏口罐	陶	图2.92c，13	图版四〇〇，4	二里头四期早
				12	圆腹罐	陶	图2.92c，6	图版四〇〇，5	二里头四期早
				13	深腹盆	陶	图2.92c，5	图版三七七，4	二里头二期早
				14	瓮	陶	图2.92c，9	图版三八九，1	二里头三期晚
				15	圆腹罐	陶	图2.92c，10	图版四〇〇，6	二里头四期早
				16	缸	陶	图2.92c，11	图版三七七，5	二里头二期晚

续表

遗址信息			遗迹	登记号	器型	质地	图号		时代
序号	编号	名称					插图号	图版号	
83	020	桂连凹南		17	器盖	陶	图2.92c，7		二里头
				18	鼎	陶	图2.92d，1	图版四四八，4	战国
				19	鬲	陶	图2.92d，4		春秋
				20	鬲	陶	图2.92d，5		春秋
				21	鬲	陶		图版四三二，2	春秋
				22	盆	陶	图2.92d，2		战国
				23	盆	陶	图2.92d，7		春秋晚期
				24	盆	陶	图2.92d，6		春秋晚期
				25	瓮	陶	图2.92d，10		战国
				26	瓮	陶	图2.92d，3	图版四四八，5	战国
				27	盆	陶	图2.92d，8	图版四四八，6	战国
				28	三足盘	陶	图2.92c，8	图版三七七，6	二里头二期早
			H1	1	深腹罐	陶	图2.92c，12	图版三七七，2	二里头二期晚
84	021	桂连凹东北		1	盆	陶	图2.92d，9	图版三七八，1	二里头二期晚
85	019	纲常		1	石斧	石	图2.94b，1	图版二四一，6	不详
				2	石刀	石	图2.94b，2	图版二四二，1	不详
				3	石刀	石		图版二四二，2	不详
				4	尖底瓶	陶	图2.94b，3	图版三〇七，5	仰韶中期
				5	敛口钵	陶	图2.94b，5	图版三二六，6	仰韶晚期
				6	敛口钵	陶	图2.94b，6	图版三二七，1	仰韶晚期
				7	罐	陶	图2.94b，7		仰韶中、晚期
				8	盆	陶	图2.94b，8		仰韶中、晚期
				9	盆	陶	图2.94b，9		仰韶中、晚期
				10	瓮	陶	图2.94b，11		仰韶中、晚期
				11	盆	陶	图2.94b，10	图版三〇七，6	仰韶中期
				12	瓮	陶	图2.94b，4		仰韶中、晚期
				13	罐	陶	图2.94c，8	图版三五八，6	龙山晚期
				14	瓮	陶	图2.94c，5		龙山晚期
				15	盆	陶	图2.94c，4	图版三五九，1	龙山晚期
				16	圈足盆	陶	图2.94c，6		龙山晚期
				17	碗	陶	图2.94c，7		龙山晚期
				18	罐	陶	图2.94c，1	图版三七八，2	二里头二期早
				19	豆	陶	图2.94c，10		春秋
				20	罐	陶		图版四四九，1	战国
				21	罐	陶		图版四四九，2	战国

续表

遗址信息			遗迹	登记号	器型	质地	图号		时代
序号	编号	名称					插图号	图版号	
85	019	纲常	H1	1	中口罐	陶	图2.94c，9	图版三五八，4	龙山晚期
				2	罐	陶	图2.94c，2		龙山晚期
				3	甑	陶	图2.94c，3	图版三五八，5	龙山晚期
87	023	齐村东南		1	石片	石	图2.96b，1		不详
				2	小口尖底瓶	陶	图2.96b，3	图版三○八，1	仰韶中期
				3	缸	陶	图2.96b，4	图版三二七，2	仰韶晚期
				4	罐	陶	图2.96b，5		仰韶中、晚期
88	025	夏庄西北		1	石斧	石	图2.96b，2	图版二四二，3	不详
				2	鬲	陶	图2.96b，6	图版四一五，1	二里岗晚期
				3	圆陶片	陶	图2.96b，7	图版二四二，4	不详
90	018	太平庄北		1	瓮	陶	图2.96b，8	图版四四九，3	战国
				2	瓮	陶	图2.96b，9	图版四四九，4	战国
				3	盆	陶	图2.96b，10		战国
91	022	穆庄		1	石片	石	图2.100b，1	图版二四二，5	不详
				2	石器	石	图2.100b，2	图版二四二，6	不详
				3	鬲	陶	图2.100b，4	图版四二○，6	殷墟
				4	鬲	陶	图2.100b，11		西周晚期
				5	盆	陶	图2.100b，5		西周晚期
				6	罐	陶	图2.100b，6	图版四二七，5	西周晚期
				7	罐	陶	图2.100b，7		西周晚期
				8	盆	陶		图版四四九，5	战国
				9	盆	陶	图2.100b，13		战国
				10	豆	陶	图2.100b，9		战国
				11	盆	陶	图2.100b，14	图版四四九，6	战国
				12	圆陶片	陶	图2.100b，12		东周至汉
				13	盆	陶	图2.100b，10	图版四六五，1	汉
				14	盆	陶	图2.100b，3	图版四五○，1	战国
				15	盆	陶	图2.100b，15	图版四五○，2	战国
				16	盆	陶	图2.100b，8	图版四六五，2	汉
92	015	潘寨老寨东		1	纺轮	陶	图2.101b，4		不详
			H1	1	石杵	石	图2.101b，5		龙山
				2	盆	陶	图2.101b，1	图版三○八，2	仰韶中期
				3	罐	陶	图2.101b，2	图版三二七，3	仰韶晚期
93	086	西马庄西北		1	刀坯	石		图版二四三，1	不详
				2	罐	陶	图2.101b，3	图版三五一，5	龙山早期
				3	刻划陶片	陶		图版四○一，1	二里头四期

续表

遗址信息			遗迹	登记号	器型	质地	图号		时代
序号	编号	名称					插图号	图版号	
94	016	西石罢		1	石斧	石	图2.103b，1	图版二四三，2	不详
				2	残石器	石	图2.103b，3	图版二四三，3	不详
				3	石片	石	图2.103b，4	图版二四三，4	不详
				4	石斧	石	图2.103b，5	图版二四三，5	不详
				5	石镰	石	图2.103b，2	图版二四三，6	不详
				6	罐	陶	图2.103e，6		春秋
				7	碗	陶	图2.103c，9		仰韶晚期
				8	罐	陶	图2.103c，8	图版三二七，4	仰韶晚期
				9	盆	陶	图2.103c，10	图版三二七，5	仰韶晚期
				10	钵	陶	图2.103c，12		仰韶晚期
				11	豆	陶	图2.103c，1		仰韶晚期
				12	钵	陶	图2.103c，2		仰韶晚期
				13	盆	陶	图2.103e，4		战国
				14	夹砂罐	陶	图2.103c，4		仰韶晚期
				15	大口罐	陶	图2.103c，6	图版三二七，6	仰韶晚期
				16	夹砂罐	陶	图2.103c，3	图版三二八，1	仰韶晚期
				17	夹砂罐	陶	图2.103c，5		仰韶晚期
				18	缸	陶	图2.103c，13		仰韶晚期
				19	钵	陶	图2.103c，11		仰韶晚期
				20	彩陶罐	陶	图2.103c，7	图版三二八，2	仰韶晚期
				21	鼎	陶	图2.103d，8	图版三五一，6	龙山早期
				22	鼎	陶	图2.103d，11		龙山早期
				23	鼎	陶	图2.103d，10		龙山早期
				24	盆	陶	图2.103e，5		战国
				25	鼎	陶	图2.103d，9	图版三五二，1	龙山早期
				26	罐	陶	图2.103d，7		龙山早期
				27	盆	陶	图2.103d，1		龙山早期
				28	缸	陶	图2.103d，3	图版三五二，2	龙山早期
				29	缸	陶	图2.103d，2	图版三五二，3	龙山早期
				30	盆	陶	图2.103d，4		龙山早期
				31	罐	陶	图2.103d，5		龙山早期
				32	折腹盆	陶	图2.103d，6		龙山早期
				33	鬲	陶	图2.103e，1	图版四二一，1	殷墟晚期
				34	鬲	陶	图2.103e，2		殷墟晚期
				35	罐	陶	图2.103e，9	图版四二一，2	殷墟晚期
				36	罐	陶	图2.103e，8	图版四二一，3	殷墟晚期

续表

遗址信息			遗迹	登记号	器型	质地	图号		时代
序号	编号	名称					插图号	图版号	
94	016	西石罨		37	鬲	陶		图版四三二，3	春秋
				38	鬲	陶			春秋
				39	罐	陶			春秋
				40	鬲	陶	图2.103e，11		东周
				41	盆	陶	图2.103e，13		春秋
				42	盆	陶	图2.103e，7		战国
				43	盆	陶	图2.103e，10	图版四六三，1	东周
				44	罐	陶	图2.103e，3		春秋
				45	罐	陶	图2.103e，12		春秋
95	017	火龙庙	H1	1	鬲	陶	图2.104b，2	图版四三二，4	春秋
				2	鬲	陶	图2.104b，1	图版四三二，5	春秋
				3	罐	陶	图2.104b，3		春秋
				4	罐	陶	图2.104b，4	图版四三二，6	春秋
96	083	大郎庙南		1	圈足盘	陶	图2.105b，1	图版三五九，2	龙山晚期
				2	钵	陶	图2.105b，3		龙山晚期
				3	罐	陶	图2.105b，5		龙山晚期
				4	瓮	陶	图2.105b，7	图版三五九，3	龙山晚期
				5	豆	陶	图2.105b，6		龙山晚期
				6	蚌料	蚌		图版二四四，1	不详
				7	圆腹罐	陶	图2.105b，8	图版四○一，2	二里头四期晚
				8	大口尊	陶	图2.105b，2	图版四○一，3	二里头四期晚
				9	高领尊	陶	图2.105b，10	图版四○一，4	二里头四期晚
				10	深腹罐	陶	图2.105b，4		二里头
97	084	东马庄西		1	豆	陶	图2.105b，11		战国
				2	盆	陶	图2.105b，12		战国
				3	盆	陶	图2.105b，13		战国
				4	盆	陶	图2.105b，14		战国
				5	敛口盆	陶	图2.105b，9		战国
				6	罐	陶	图2.105b，15		战国
99	079	西三冢		1	盆	陶	图2.108b，1		战国
				2	鬲	陶	图2.108b，2		战国
				3	鬲	陶	图2.108b，3		战国
100	081	金钟寺		1	石刀	石		图版二四四，2	不详
				2	石斧	石		图版二四四，3	不详
				3	石斧	石		图版二四四，4	不详
				4	石斧	石	图2.109b，1	图版二四四，5	不详

续表

遗址信息			遗迹	登记号	器型	质地	图号		时代
序号	编号	名称					插图号	图版号	
100	081	金钟寺		5	石纺轮	石	图2.109b，2	图版二四四，6	不详
				6	小口尖底瓶	陶	图2.109b，4		仰韶
				7	小口尖底瓶	陶	图2.109b，3		仰韶
				8	小口尖底瓶	陶	图2.109b，5	图版三〇四，1	仰韶早期
				9	小口尖底瓶	陶	图2.109b，8	图版三〇四，2	仰韶早期
				10	小口尖底瓶	陶	图2.109b，6	图版三〇八，3	仰韶中期
				11	小口尖底瓶	陶	图2.109b，7		仰韶
				12	小口尖底瓶	陶	图2.109b，9	图版三〇八，4	仰韶中期
				13	小口尖底瓶	陶	图2.109b，10		仰韶
				14	钵	陶	图2.109c，8		仰韶
				15	釜形鼎	陶	图2.109c，4		仰韶
				16	鼎	陶	图2.109c，3		仰韶
				17	缸	陶	图2.109c，7		仰韶
				18	缸	陶	图2.109c，2		仰韶
				19	豆	陶	图2.109c，5		仰韶
				20	缸	陶	图2.109c，9		仰韶
				21	瓮	陶	图2.109c，10		仰韶
				22	瓮	陶	图2.109c，1	图版三〇八，5	仰韶中期
				23	盆	陶	图2.109c，14	图版三〇八，6	仰韶中期
				24	折腹盆	陶	图2.109c，6	图版三〇九，1	仰韶中期
				25	折腹盆	陶	图2.109c，11	图版三二八，3	仰韶晚期
				26	折腹盆	陶	图2.109c，12	图版三二八，4	仰韶晚期
				27	盆	陶	图2.109c，15	图版三〇九，2	仰韶中期
				28	罐	陶	图2.109d，1	图版三〇九，3	仰韶中期
				29	罐	陶	图2.109c，13	图版三〇九，4	仰韶中期
				30	刻槽盆	陶	图2.109d，10		龙山早期
				31	鼎	陶	图2.109d，4		仰韶
				32	鼎	陶	图2.109d，5	图版三〇九，5	仰韶中期
				33	鼎	陶	图2.109d，6	图版三二八，5	仰韶晚期
				34	碗	陶	图2.109d，11	图版三〇四，3	仰韶早期
				35	盆	陶	图2.109d，9		仰韶
				36	器盖	陶	图2.109d，3		仰韶
				37	器盖	陶	图2.109d，12		仰韶
				38	壶	陶	图2.109d，2		仰韶
				39	大口罐	陶	图2.109d，7		龙山
				40	大口罐	陶	图2.109d，8		龙山

续表

遗址信息			遗迹	登记号	器型	质地	图号		时代
序号	编号	名称					插图号	图版号	
100	081	金钟寺		41	罐	陶	图2.109d,14	图版三二八,6	仰韶晚期
				42	大口罐	陶	图2.109d,16		龙山
				43	大口罐	陶	图2.109d,15		龙山
				44	罐	陶	图2.109d,13	图版三二九,1	仰韶晚期
				45	高领瓮	陶	图2.109d,17		仰韶
				46	矮领瓮	陶	图2.109f,2	图版三二九,2	仰韶晚期
				47	矮领瓮	陶	图2.109f,4	图版三〇九,6	仰韶中期
				48	矮领瓮	陶	图2.109f,1		仰韶
				49	矮领瓮	陶	图2.109f,5		仰韶
				50	矮领瓮	陶	图2.109f,6		仰韶
				51	盆	陶	图2.109f,8	图版三二九,3	仰韶晚期
				52	罐	陶	图2.109f,7		仰韶
				53	器盖	陶	图2.109f,10		仰韶
				54	罐	陶	图2.109f,9		龙山晚期
				55	罐	陶	图2.109f,14		龙山晚期
				56	罐	陶	图2.109f,3		仰韶
				57	罐	陶	图2.109f,15		仰韶
				58	盆	陶	图2.109f,13		仰韶
				59	罐	陶	图2.109f,12		仰韶
				60	盆	陶	图2.109f,11		仰韶
				61	盆	陶	图2.109f,16	图版三二九,4	仰韶晚期
				62	盆	陶	图2.109e,1	图版三一〇,1	仰韶中期
				63	盆	陶	图2.109e,2		仰韶
				64	盆	陶	图2.109e,3		仰韶
				65	盆	陶	图2.109e,5		仰韶
				66	盆	陶	图2.109e,6	图版三一〇,2	仰韶中期
				67	盆	陶	图2.109e,7	图版三二九,5	仰韶晚期
				68	罐	陶	图2.109e,8		龙山早期
				69	缸	陶	图2.109e,4		仰韶
				70	碗	陶	图2.109e,12		仰韶
				71	罐	陶	图2.109e,9	图版三五九,4	龙山晚期
				72	钵	陶	图2.109c,16	图版三一〇,3	仰韶中期
				73	罐	陶	图2.109e,10	图版三五九,5	龙山晚期
				74	罐	陶	图2.109e,11	图版三五九,6	龙山晚期
				75	深腹罐	陶	图2.109g,1	图版三七八,3	二里头二期早
				76	鬲	陶	图2.109g,4		西周晚期

续表

遗址信息			遗迹	登记号	器型	质地	图号		时代
序号	编号	名称					插图号	图版号	
100	081	金钟寺		77	甗	陶	图2.109g，2	图版四二七，6	西周晚期
				78	罐	陶	图2.109g，5		春秋
				79	甗	陶	图2.109g，3	图版四二八，1	西周晚期
				80	罐	陶	图2.109g，6		春秋
				81	鬲	陶	图2.109g，7		春秋
				82	钵	陶	图2.109b，12	图版三〇四，4	仰韶早期
				83	罐	陶	图2.109b，11	图版三〇四，5	仰韶早期
101	085	碑楼南		1	石镰	石	图2.110b，1	图版二四五，1	不详
				2	大口罐	陶	图2.110b，3		龙山晚期
				3	鬲	陶	图2.110b，5	图版四三三，1	春秋
				4	鬲	陶	图2.110b，4	图版四五〇，3	战国
				5	鬲	陶	图2.110b，7	图版四五〇，4	战国
				6	鬲	陶	图2.110b，8		战国
				7	罐	陶	图2.110b，9		战国
				8	盆	陶	图2.110b，10		战国
				9	盆	陶	图2.110b，2	图版四五〇，5	战国
				10	盆	陶	图2.110b，6	图版四五〇，6	战国
102	082	罗圪塔		1	石斧	石	图2.111b，1	图版二四五，2	不详
				2	石饼	石	图2.111b，2	图版二四五，3	不详
				3	石器	石		图版二四五，4	不详
				4	深腹罐	陶	图2.111c，12	图版三七五，5	龙山晚期至二里头早期
				5	高领罐	陶	图2.111c，10	图版三六〇，1	龙山晚期
				6	深腹罐	陶	图2.111c，4	图版三七八，4	二里头二期早
				7	深腹罐	陶	图2.111c，1	图版三八九，2	二里头三期晚
				8	深腹罐	陶	图2.111c，2	图版三八九，3	二里头三期晚
				9	圆腹罐	陶	图2.111c，3	图版四〇一，5	二里头四期晚
				10	捏口罐	陶	图2.111c，11		二里头
				11	甗	陶	图2.111c，14	图版四〇一，6	二里头四期晚
				12	盆	陶	图2.111c，7	图版三八九，4	二里头三期早
				13	盆	陶	图2.111c，13	图版四〇二，1	二里头四期晚
				14	三足盘	陶	图2.111c，15	图版三八九，5	二里头三期早
				15	刻槽盆	陶	图2.111c，8	图版三七八，5	二里头二期早
				16	刻槽盆	陶	图2.111c，9	图版三七八，6	二里头二期晚
				17	敛口罐	陶	图2.111c，6	图版四〇二，2	二里头四期晚
				18	盆	陶	图2.111c，5	图版三八九，6	二里头三期晚
				19	矮领瓮	陶	图2.111c，16	图版四〇二，3	二里头四期晚

续表

遗址信息			遗迹	登记号	器型	质地	图号		时代
序号	编号	名称					插图号	图版号	
103	179	刁窑东		1	盆	陶	图2.114b, 1	图版四三三, 2	春秋
104	180	刘窑东		1	盆	陶	图2.114b, 3	图版三一〇, 4	仰韶中期
				2	盆	陶	图2.114b, 2	图版三二九, 6	仰韶晚期
105	178	诸葛水库北		1	釜形鼎	陶	图2.116b, 1	图版三〇六, 1	仰韶早中期
				2	罐	陶	图2.116b, 2	图版三〇六, 2	仰韶早中期
				3	钵	陶	图2.116b, 9	图版三〇六, 3	仰韶早中期
				4	钵	陶	图2.116b, 4	图版三〇六, 4	仰韶早中期
				5	钵	陶	图2.116b, 10		仰韶早中期
				6	钵	陶	图2.116b, 5	图版三〇六, 5	仰韶早中期
				7	盆	陶	图2.116b, 3	图版三〇六, 6	仰韶早中期
				8	盆	陶	图2.116b, 7	图版三〇四, 6	仰韶早期
				9	盆	陶	图2.116b, 6	图版三〇五, 1	仰韶早期
				10	盆	陶	图2.116b, 8	图版三〇七, 1	仰韶早中期
				11	尖底瓶	陶	图2.116b, 12	图版三〇七, 2	仰韶早中期
				12	罐	陶	图2.116b, 11	图版三〇五, 2	仰韶早期
107	177	道湛东南		1	鬲	陶	图2.118b, 1	图版四二八, 2	西周晚期
108	160	杨冈东南	H2	1	罐	陶	图2.119b, 2	图版三六〇, 2	龙山晚期
				2	大口罐	陶	图2.119b, 5	图版三六〇, 3	龙山晚期
109	161	杨冈东	H1	1	钵	陶	图2.119b, 4		仰韶晚期
				2	缸	陶	图2.119b, 8	图版三三〇, 1	仰韶晚期
110	162	王沟东		1	罐	陶	图2.119b, 9	图版四二八, 3	西周
				2	罐	陶	图2.119b, 1	图版四五一, 1	战国
			H1	1	石斧	石	图2.119b, 7	图版三七九, 1	二里头二期
				2	深腹罐	陶	图2.119b, 3	图版三七九, 2	二里头二期
				3	豆	陶	图2.119b, 6	图版三七九, 3	二里头二期
112	159	酒流沟水库西		1	石锄	石	图2.123b, 4	图版二四五, 5	不详
				2	石器	石		图版二四五, 6	不详
				3	石器	石		图版二四六, 1	不详
				4	石斧	石	图2.123b, 5	图版二四六, 2	不详
				5	石环	石	图2.123b, 1	图版二四六, 3	不详
				6	鼎	陶	图2.123b, 3	图版三三〇, 2	仰韶晚期
				7	鼎	陶	图2.123b, 6		仰韶中、晚期
				8	罐	陶			仰韶晚期
				9	钵	陶	图2.123b, 7	图版三三〇, 3	仰韶晚期
				10	罐	陶	图2.123b, 2		仰韶中、晚期
				11	罐	陶	图2.123b, 9	图版三三〇, 4	仰韶晚期

续表

遗址信息			遗迹	登记号	器型	质地	图号		时代
序号	编号	名称					插图号	图版号	
112	159	酒流沟水库西		12	盆形鼎	陶	图2.123b，10	图版三五二，4	龙山早期
				13	罐形鼎	陶	图2.123b，12	图版三五二，5	龙山早期
				14	罐	陶	图2.123b，14		龙山晚期
				15	罐	陶	图2.123b，13	图版三三〇，5	仰韶晚期
				16	盆	陶	图2.123b，11	图版三六〇，4	龙山晚期
			H1	1	小口罐	陶	图2.123b，8		仰韶晚期
113	158	酒流沟水库北		1	石凿	石	图2.124b，6	图版二四六，4	不详
				2	石斧	石	图2.124b，7	图版二四六，5	不详
				3	盆	陶	图2.124b，2		仰韶晚期
				4	彩陶片	陶	图2.124b，5		仰韶晚期
				5	鬲	陶	图2.124b，9	图版四二八，4	西周晚期
				6	瓮	陶	图2.124b，3		西周晚期
				7	豆	陶	图2.124b，11		战国
				8	罐	陶	图2.124b，1	图版四三三，3	春秋
				9	鬲	陶	图2.124b，10	图版四五一，2	战国
				10	罐	陶	图2.124b，4	图版四三三，4	春秋
				11	纺轮	陶	图2.124b，8	图版四六三，2	东周
114	175	刘沟东北	H1	1	鬲	陶	图2.125b，9	图版四三三，5	春秋
				2	盆	陶	图2.125b，11	图版四三三，6	春秋
				3	盆	陶	图2.125b，10	图版四三四，1	春秋
115	157	刘家窑	H1	1	盆	陶	图2.125b，1	图版四五一，3	战国
				2	盆	陶	图2.125b，2	图版四五一，4	战国
				3	鬲	陶	图2.125b，3	图版四五一，5	战国
				4	鬲	陶	图2.125b，4	图版四五一，6	战国
				5	鬲	陶	图2.125b，5	图版四五二，1	战国
				6	鬲	陶	图2.125b，6	图版四五二，2	战国
				7	罐	陶	图2.125b，7	图版四五二，3	战国
				8	盆	陶	图2.125b，8		战国
116	170	袁沟西		1	圆陶片	陶	图2.128b，10		疑似东周
118	173	袁沟东南		1	石铲	石	图2.128b，9	图版二四六，6	不详
				2	罐	陶	图2.128b，1	图版三六〇，5	龙山晚期
				3	罐	陶	图2.128b，3	图版三六〇，6	龙山晚期
				4	盆	陶	图2.128b，8	图版四五二，4	战国
				5	盆	陶	图2.128b，2	图版四五二，5	战国
				6	罐	陶	图2.128b，5	图版四五二，6	战国
				7	罐	陶	图2.128b，4		战国

续表

遗址信息			遗迹	登记号	器型	质地	图号		时代
序号	编号	名称					插图号	图版号	
118	173	袁沟东南		8	盆	陶	图2.128b, 7	图版四三四, 2	春秋
				9	鬲	陶	图2.128b, 6	图版四五三, 1	战国
119	166	袁沟B		1	钵	陶	图2.131b, 1		仰韶中、晚期
				2	罐	陶	图2.131b, 2		仰韶中、晚期
				3	罐	陶	图2.131b, 7	图版三六一, 2	龙山晚期
			H1	1	罐	陶	图2.131b, 5		仰韶晚期
				2	罐	陶	图2.131b, 4	图版三三〇, 6	仰韶晚期
			H2	1	簋	陶	图2.131b, 8	图版四一一, 6	二里岗早期
			H3	1	瓮	陶	图2.131b, 6	图版三六一, 1	龙山晚期
			H4	1	盆	陶	图2.131b, 3	图版三一〇, 5	仰韶中期
120	165	袁沟A		1	石铲（坯）	石	图2.132b, 1	图版二四七, 1	不详
				2	石斧	石		图版二四七, 2	不详
				3	器盖	陶	图2.132b, 8	图版四〇二, 4	二里头四期晚
				4	刻槽盆	陶	图2.132b, 6	图版三九〇, 1	二里头三期早
				5	簋	陶	图2.132b, 2		殷墟晚期
				6	盆	陶	图2.132b, 5		殷墟晚期
				7	盆	陶	图2.132b, 3	图版四二一, 4	殷墟晚期
				8	盆	陶	图2.132b, 4	图版四二一, 5	殷墟晚期
				9	盆	陶	图2.132b, 7	图版四五三, 2	战国
122	164	毛村东		1	石杵	石		图版二四七, 3	不详
				2	石锤	石		图版二四七, 4	不详
				3	残石器	石		图版二四七, 5	不详
				4	石凿	石	图2.134b, 1	图版二四七, 6	不详
				5	石片	石		图版二四八, 1	不详
				6	石铲	石	图2.134b, 2	图版二四八, 2	不详
				7	石片	石		图版二四八, 3	不详
				8	石凿	石	图2.134b, 3	图版二四八, 4	不详
				9	豆	陶	图2.134d, 2		战国
				10	罐	陶	图2.134c, 1	图版三六一, 3	龙山晚期
				11	罐	陶	图2.134c, 2	图版三六一, 4	龙山晚期
				12	高领瓮	陶	图2.134c, 16	图版三六一, 5	龙山晚期
				13	鼎	陶	图2.134c, 4	图版三九〇, 2	二里头三期晚
				14	深腹罐	陶	图2.134c, 6	图版三八〇, 2	二里头二期早
				15	深腹罐	陶	图2.134c, 5	图版三八〇, 3	二里头二期早
				16	圆腹罐	陶	图2.134c, 7	图版四〇二, 6	二里头四期晚
				17	高领尊	陶	图2.134c, 8	图版三八〇, 4	二里头二期早

续表

遗址信息			遗迹	登记号	器型	质地	图号		时代
序号	编号	名称					插图号	图版号	
122	164	毛村东		18	高领罐	陶	图2.134c，9	图版四〇三，1	二里头四期晚
				19	高领瓮	陶	图2.134c，11	图版四〇三，2	二里头四期晚
				20	高领瓮	陶	图2.134c，15	图版三八〇，5	二里头二期晚
				21	盆	陶	图2.134c，17		二里头
				22	敛口罐	陶	图2.134c，10		二里头
				23	器盖	陶	图2.134c，13	图版三八〇，6	二里头二期晚
				24	鬲	陶	图2.134c，18	图版四一五，2	二里岗晚期
				25	鬲	陶	图2.134d，1		春秋
				26	鬲	陶	图2.134d，4		春秋
				27	鬲	陶	图2.134d，5	图版四三四，3	春秋
				28	鬲	陶	图2.134d，7		春秋
				29	罐	陶	图2.134d，8	图版四三四，4	春秋
				30	罐	陶	图2.134d，6		春秋
				31	罐	陶	图2.134d，13	图版四三四，5	春秋
				32	罐	陶	图2.134d，10	图版四三四，6	春秋
				33	盆	陶	图2.134d，11	图版四三五，1	春秋
				34	缸	陶	图2.134d，3	图版四三五，2	春秋
				35	鬲	陶	图2.134d，12	图版四五三，3	战国
				36	鬲	陶	图2.134d，9	图版四五三，4	战国
			H1	1	捏口罐	陶	图2.134c，3	图版四〇二，5	二里头四期晚
				2	缸	陶		图版三七九，6	二里头二期晚
			H2	1	石杵	石		图版三八〇，1	二里头二期
			Y1	1	深腹罐	陶	图2.134c，12	图版三七九，4	二里头二期
			M1	1	盆	陶	图2.134c，14	图版三七九，5	二里头二期晚
123	174	常村西南		1	盆	陶	图2.135b，2	图版三二二，6	仰韶中、晚期
124	169	常村东		1	高领瓮	陶	图2.135b，1	图版三六一，6	龙山晚期
125	168	偏桥北		1	石片	石		图版二四八，5	不详
				2	甗	陶	图2.135b，5	图版四〇三，3	二里头四期
				3	鬲	陶	图2.135b，4		春秋晚期
				4	盆	陶	图2.135b，6		春秋晚期
126	167	咀家庄东南		1	石锛	石	图2.135b，7	图版二四八，6	不详
				2	鬲	陶	图2.135b，3		二里岗晚期
127	156	咀家庄北		1	盆	陶	图2.139b，15	图版三七六，1	二里头早期
				2	罐	陶	图2.139b，11	图版三二三，1	仰韶中、晚期
				3	瓮	陶	图2.139b，5		龙山晚期
				4	蚌刀	蚌	图2.139b，14	图版二四九，1	不详

续表

遗址信息			遗迹	登记号	器型	质地	图号		时代
序号	编号	名称					插图号	图版号	
129	154	南寨上村东		1	罐	陶	图2.139b，1		仰韶晚期
				2	盆	陶	图2.139b，2		仰韶晚期
				3	鬲	陶	图2.139b，9		殷墟晚期
				4	罐	陶	图2.139b，12		殷墟晚期
				5	鬲	陶	图2.139b，3		西周
				6	鬲	陶	图2.139b，4		西周
				7	圆陶片	陶	图2.139b，7		龙山晚期
			H1	1	石器	石			龙山晚期
				2	罐	陶	图2.139b，13		龙山晚期
				3	罐	陶	图2.139b，6	图版三六二，1	龙山晚期
130	151	南寨西村南		1	石铲	石	图2.139b，8	图版二四九，2	不详
				2	罐	陶	图2.139b，10		仰韶晚期
131	192	马寨		1	罐	陶	图2.144b，15		龙山晚期
132	193	孙家窑西		1	罐	陶	图2.144b，4	图版三一〇，6	仰韶中期
				2	罐	陶	图2.144b，3		仰韶中期
			H1	1	鬲	陶	图2.144b，5		二里头四期
				2	鬲	陶	图2.144b，1		二里头四期
				3	尊	陶	图2.144b，11	图版四〇三，4	二里头四期
				4	缸	陶	图2.144b，12	图版四〇三，5	二里头四期
				5	壶	陶	图2.144b，10		二里头四期
				6	盉	陶	图2.144b，2		二里头四期
			H2	1	鼎	陶	图2.144b，8		仰韶早中期
				2	钵	陶	图2.144b，14		仰韶早中期
			H3	1	尖底瓶	陶	图2.144b，6	图版三〇五，5	仰韶早期
				2	盆	陶	图2.144b，7	图版三〇五，6	仰韶早期
			M1	1	尖底瓶	陶	图2.144b，13	图版三〇五，3	仰韶早期
				2	尖底瓶	陶	图2.144b，9	图版三〇五，4	仰韶早期
135	196	东朱村东北		1	鬲	陶	图2.148b，6	图版四〇三，6	二里头四期晚
				2	盆	陶	图2.148b，2	图版四〇四，1	二里头四期晚
				3	罐	陶	图2.148b，5	图版四〇四，2	二里头四期晚
				4	高领罐	陶	图2.148b，3		二里头晚期
				5	高领罐	陶	图2.148b，1	图版四〇四，3	二里头四期晚
				6	瓮	陶	图2.148b，4	图版四〇四，4	二里头四期晚
				7	瓮	陶	图2.148b，7	图版四〇四，5	二里头四期晚
136	195	王湾西北		1	双缺口石刀	石		图版三五〇，2	仰韶
				2	砺石	石		图版二四九，3	不详

续表

遗址信息			遗迹	登记号	器型	质地	图号		时代
序号	编号	名称					插图号	图版号	
136	195	王湾西北		3	钵	陶	图2.148b, 8	图版三三一, 3	仰韶晚期
				4	罐	陶	图2.148b, 10	图版三一一, 1	仰韶中期
				5	器盖	陶	图2.148b, 9	图版三一一, 2	仰韶中期
			H1	1	石片	石		图版三三一, 1	仰韶晚期
				2	盆	陶	图2.148b, 11		仰韶晚期
			H2	1	钵	陶	图2.148b, 12	图版三三一, 2	仰韶晚期
137	191	韩寨北		1	盆	陶	图2.150b, 2	图版四五三, 5	战国
138	190	杨裴屯西南		1	盆	陶	图2.150b, 4	图版三六二, 2	龙山晚期
				2	鬲	陶	图2.150b, 8		殷墟
				3	罐	陶	图2.150b, 7	图版四二一, 6	殷墟
				4	鬲	陶	图2.150b, 1	图版四三五, 3	春秋
				5	豆	陶	图2.150b, 9	图版四三五, 4	春秋
				6	罐	陶	图2.150b, 3	图版四三五, 5	春秋
				7	罐	陶	图2.150b, 5	图版四三五, 6	春秋
				8	盆	陶	图2.150b, 6	图版四三六, 1	春秋
				9	豆	陶	图2.150b, 10		春秋
				10	三足皿	陶	图2.150b, 11	图版三六二, 3	龙山晚期
139	188	沙沟西		1	鬲	陶	图2.152b, 1	图版四一二, 1	二里岗早期
				2	鬲	陶	图2.152b, 3	图版四一五, 3	二里岗晚期
				3	捏口罐	陶	图2.152b, 4		二里岗
				4	罐	陶	图2.152b, 5	图版四一五, 4	二里岗晚期
				5	盆	陶	图2.152b, 8	图版四一二, 2	二里岗早期
				6	鬲	陶	图2.152b, 2		西周晚期
				7	鬲	陶	图2.152b, 7	图版四三六, 2	春秋
				8	鬲	陶	图2.152b, 6	图版四三六, 3	春秋
				9	盆	陶	图2.152b, 9	图版四三六, 4	春秋
				10	盆	陶	图2.152b, 10	图版四三六, 5	春秋
				11	盆	陶	图2.152c, 1		战国
				12	鬲	陶	图2.152c, 2	图版四五三, 6	战国
				13	盆	陶	图2.152c, 3	图版四五四, 1	战国
				14	鬲	陶	图2.152c, 4	图版四五四, 2	战国
				15	豆	陶	图2.152c, 7	图版四五四, 3	战国
				16	豆	陶	图2.152c, 9	图版四五四, 4	战国
				17	豆	陶	图2.152c, 8		战国
140	189	西湾北		1	罐	陶	图2.152c, 5	图版三八一, 1	二里头二期晚
				2	鬲	陶	图2.152c, 6		殷墟

续表

遗址信息			遗迹	登记号	器型	质地	图号		时代
序号	编号	名称					插图号	图版号	
141	185	寇店西刘李寨A		1	鼎	陶	图2.154b，1	图版三一一，3	仰韶中期
				2	钵	陶	图2.154b，4	图版三一一，4	仰韶中期
				3	钵	陶	图2.154b，3	图版三一一，5	仰韶中期
				4	盒	陶	图2.154b，2	图版三一一，6	战国
				5	盆	陶	图2.154b，5	图版三一二，1	仰韶中期
				6	盆	陶	图2.154b，6	图版三一二，2	仰韶中期
				7	盆	陶	图2.154b，7	图版三一二，3	仰韶中期
142	186			1	盆	陶		图版四五四，5	战国
143	184	陈家窑		1	石锛	石	图2.156b，3	图版二四九，4	不详
				2	穿孔石器	石	图2.156b，2	图版二四九，5	不详
				3	石锛	石		图版二四九，6	不详
				4	环	陶	图2.156b，1	图版三一二，4	仰韶中期
				5	盆	陶	图2.156b，4	图版三一二，5	仰韶中期
				6	钵	陶	图2.156b，5	图版三一二，6	仰韶中期
				7	盆	陶	图2.156b，6		仰韶中期
				8	鼎	陶	图2.156b，10	图版三一三，1	仰韶中期
				9	鼎	陶	图2.156b，7		仰韶中期
				10	罐	陶	图2.156b，8	图版三一三，2	仰韶中期
				11	罐	陶	图2.156b，9	图版三一三，3	仰韶中期
				12	罐	陶	图2.156b，11	图版三一三，4	仰韶中期
				13	鬲	陶	图2.156c，1	图版四〇四，6	二里头四期晚
				14	盆	陶	图2.156c，2	图版四〇五，1	二里头四期晚
				15	大口尊	陶	图2.156c，4	图版四〇五，2	二里头四期晚
				16	缸	陶	图2.156c，5	图版四〇五，3	二里头四期晚
				17	水管	陶	图2.156c，3	图版四〇五，4	二里头四期晚
				18	陶垫	陶	图2.156c，10		二里头
				19	盆	陶	图2.156c，6	图版四六五，3	汉
				20	壶	陶	图2.156c，9	图版四六五，4	汉
				21	鬲	陶	图2.156c，7	图版四三六，6	春秋
				22	鬲	陶	图2.156c，8	图版四三七，1	春秋
144	187	刘李寨B		1	簋	陶		图版四一五，5	二里岗晚期
145	183	宫家窑		1	残石器	石		图版二五〇，1	不详
				2	石镰	石		图版二五〇，2	不详
				3	石片	石			不详
				4	石料	石			不详
				5	石球	石	图2.158b，1	图版二五〇，3	不详

续表

遗址信息			遗迹	登记号	器型	质地	图号		时代
序号	编号	名称					插图号	图版号	
145	183	宫家窑		6	环	陶	图2.158b，4	图版三二三，2	仰韶中、晚期
				7	鼎	陶	图2.158b，5	图版三一三，5	仰韶中期
				8	鼎	陶	图2.158b，2		仰韶中、晚期
				9	鼎	陶	图2.158b，3		仰韶中、晚期
				10	罐	陶	图2.158b，6		仰韶中、晚期
				11	罐	陶	图2.158b，8	图版三一三，6	仰韶中期
				12	罐	陶	图2.158b，10	图版三一四，1	仰韶中期
				13	罐	陶	图2.158b，9		仰韶中、晚期
				14	穿孔陶片	陶	图2.158b，7	图版三二三，3	仰韶中、晚期
				15	深腹罐	陶	图2.158c，8	图版四〇五，5	二里头四期晚
				16	深腹罐	陶	图2.158c，3	图版三九〇，3	二里头三期晚
				17	深腹罐	陶	图2.158c，4	图版三九〇，4	二里头三期晚
				18	鬲	陶	图2.158c，1		春秋
				19	鼎	陶	图2.158c，2		春秋
				20	鬲	陶	图2.158c，10		春秋晚期
				21	盆	陶	图2.158c，6	图版四六五，5	汉
				22	盆	陶	图2.158c，5	图版四五四，6	战国
				23	盆	陶	图2.158c，12	图版四六五，6	汉
				24	罐	陶	图2.158c，9		汉
				25	罐	陶	图2.158c，7	图版四五五，1	战国
				26	尖底瓶	陶	图2.158c，11	图版三二三，4	仰韶中、晚期
146	181	刘李东北		1	石斧	石	图2.159b，1	图版二五〇，4	不详
				2	石斧	石		图版二五〇，5	不详
				3	石斧	石			不详
				4	盆	陶	图2.159d，6		二里岗早期
				5	罐	陶	图2.159b，2	图版三三一，4	仰韶晚期
				6	罐	陶	图2.159b，3		仰韶晚期
				7	罐	陶	图2.159b，4	图版三六二，4	龙山晚期
				8	罐	陶	图2.159b，5	图版三六二，5	龙山晚期
				9	罐	陶	图2.159b，6	图版三三一，5	仰韶晚期
				10	罐	陶	图2.159b，7	图版三三一，6	仰韶晚期
				11	罐	陶	图2.159b，8	图版三三二，1	仰韶晚期
				12	罐	陶	图2.159b，9	图版三三二，2	仰韶晚期
				13	罐	陶	图2.159b，10	图版三三二，3	仰韶晚期
				14	罐	陶	图2.159b，11	图版三三二，4	仰韶晚期
				15	罐	陶	图2.159c，1	图版三三二，5	仰韶晚期

续表

遗址信息			遗迹	登记号	器型	质地	图号		时代
序号	编号	名称					插图号	图版号	
146	181	刘李东北		16	罐	陶	图2.159c，2	图版三三二，6	仰韶晚期
				17	罐	陶	图2.159c，4	图版三三三，1	仰韶晚期
				18	罐	陶	图2.159c，3		仰韶晚期
				19	瓮	陶	图2.159c，5	图版三三三，2	仰韶晚期
				20	瓮	陶	图2.159c，6		仰韶晚期
				21	盆	陶	图2.159c，9	图版三三三，3	仰韶晚期
				22	缸	陶	图2.159c，8	图版三三三，4	仰韶晚期
				23	缸	陶	图2.159c，7	图版三三三，5	仰韶晚期
				24	钵	陶	图2.159c，10	图版三三三，6	仰韶晚期
				25	钵	陶	图2.159c，11	图版三三四，1	仰韶晚期
				26	壶	陶	图2.159c，13		仰韶晚期
				27	器盖	陶	图2.159c，12		仰韶中期
				28	深腹罐	陶	图2.159d，4		二里岗早期
				29	鬲	陶	图2.159d，1		二里岗晚期
				30	罐形鼎	陶	图2.159d，3	图版四一二，4	二里岗早期
			H1	1	鬲	陶	图2.159d，2	图版四一五，6	二里岗晚期
				2	尊	陶	图2.159d，5	图版四一二，3	二里岗早期
147	182	刘李西北		1	罐	陶	图2.160b，6	图版三三四，2	仰韶晚期
				2	罐	陶	图2.160b，5	图版三三四，3	仰韶晚期
				3	盆	陶	图2.160b，4	图版三三四，4	仰韶晚期
				4	碗	陶	图2.160b，3	图版三三四，5	仰韶晚期
				5	瓮	陶	图2.160b，1	图版四三七，2	春秋
				6	盆	陶	图2.160b，2	图版四三七，3	春秋
148	139	九贤		1	双缺口石刀	石		图版三五〇，3	仰韶
				2	双缺口石刀	石		图版三五〇，4	仰韶
				3	缸	陶	图2.161b，2		仰韶晚期
				4	罐	陶	图2.161b，4	图版三三四，6	仰韶晚期
				5	罐	陶	图2.161b，5	图版三三五，1	仰韶晚期
				6	罐	陶	图2.161b，1	图版三一四，2	仰韶中期
				7	罐	陶	图2.161b，8	图版三五二，6	龙山早期
				8	罐	陶	图2.161b，7	图版三三五，2	仰韶晚期
				9	罐	陶	图2.161b，10	图版三五三，1	龙山早期
				10	罐	陶	图2.161b，11		仰韶晚期
				11	三足器	陶	图2.161b，3		殷墟
				12	鬲	陶	图2.161b，9	图版四二二，1	殷墟
				13	杯	陶	图2.161b，6		仰韶晚期

续表

遗址信息			遗迹	登记号	器型	质地	图号		时代
序号	编号	名称					插图号	图版号	
150	137	苏家窑西北		1	罐	陶	图2.163b，12	图版三三五，5	仰韶晚期
				2	盆	陶	图2.163b，2		仰韶晚期
				3	纺轮	陶	图2.163b，1		仰韶晚期
				4	盆	陶	图2.163b，6	图版三五三，2	龙山早期
				5	罐	陶	图2.163b，5		龙山
				6	罐	陶	图2.163b，3	图版三五三，3	龙山早期
				7	罐	陶	图2.163b，11	图版三五三，4	龙山早期
				8	罐	陶	图2.163c，14	图版四五五，2	战国
				9	罐	陶	图2.163c，6	图版四三七，4	春秋
				10	罐	陶	图2.163c，8	图版四五五，3	战国
				11	豆	陶	图2.163c，5	图版四三七，5	春秋
				12	盆	陶	图2.163c，7	图版四六三，3	东周
				13	豆	陶	图2.163c，3	图版四五五，4	战国
				14	豆	陶	图2.163c，1	图版四五五，5	战国
				15	豆	陶	图2.163c，4	图版四五五，6	战国
				16	豆	陶	图2.163c，2	图版四五六，1	战国
				17	盆	陶	图2.163c，10	图版四五六，2	战国
				18	盆	陶	图2.163c，9		战国
				19	罐	陶	图2.163c，15		战国
				20	鬲	陶	图2.163c，12	图版四五六，3	战国
				21	鬲	陶	图2.163c，11	图版四五六，4	战国
				22	鬲	陶	图2.163c，13	图版四五六，5	战国
			H1	1	石片	石			龙山晚期
				2	石片	石		图版三六二，6	龙山晚期
				3	豆	陶	图2.163b，8	图版三六三，1	龙山晚期
				4	豆	陶	图2.163b，7		龙山晚期
			H2	1	石片	石		图版三六三，2	龙山晚期
				2	石片	石		图版三六三，3	龙山晚期
				3	罐	陶	图2.163b，13	图版三六三，4	龙山晚期
			H3	1	石刀	石		图版三三五，3	仰韶晚期
				2	石刀	石		图版三三五，4	仰韶晚期
				3	器盖	陶	图2.163b，4		仰韶晚期
				4	罐	陶	图2.163b，10		仰韶晚期
				5	盆	陶	图2.163b，14		仰韶晚期
			H4	1	石片	石		图版三六三，5	龙山晚期
				2	盆	陶	图2.163b，9		仰韶

续表

遗址信息			遗迹	登记号	器型	质地	图号		时代
序号	编号	名称					插图号	图版号	
151	152	武屯东南		1	石器	石		图版二五〇，6	不详
				2	石料	石			不详
				3	碗	陶	图2.164b，13	图版三三五，6	仰韶晚期
				4	钵	陶	图2.164b，2	图版三三六，1	仰韶晚期
				5	钵	陶	图2.164b，3	图版三一四，3	仰韶中期
				6	钵	陶	图2.164b，6	图版三一四，4	仰韶中期
				7	鼎	陶	图2.164b，4	图版三一四，5	仰韶中期
				8	鼎	陶	图2.164b，5	图版三一四，6	仰韶中期
				9	鼎	陶	图2.164b，7	图版三一五，1	仰韶中期
				10	尖底瓶	陶	图2.164b，1	图版三一五，2	仰韶中期
				11	罐	陶	图2.164b，8	图版三一五，3	仰韶中期
				12	罐	陶	图2.164b，9	图版三一五，4	仰韶中期
				13	罐	陶	图2.164b，10	图版三一五，5	仰韶中期
				14	罐	陶	图2.164b，11	图版三一五，6	仰韶中期
				15	罐	陶	图2.164b，12	图版三一六，1	仰韶中期
				16	罐	陶	图2.164c，12	图版三一六，2	仰韶中期
				17	罐	陶	图2.164c，1		仰韶晚期
				18	罐	陶	图2.164c，2		仰韶中期
				19	罐	陶	图2.164c，5	图版三一六，3	仰韶中期
				20	罐	陶	图2.164c，6		战国
				21	罐	陶	图2.164c，3		龙山晚期
				22	罐	陶	图2.164c，4	图版三三六，2	仰韶晚期
				23	盆	陶	图2.164c，9	图版三一六，4	仰韶中期
				24	盆	陶	图2.164c，8	图版三一六，5	仰韶中期
				25	盆	陶	图2.164c，10	图版三三六，3	仰韶晚期
				26	盆	陶	图2.164c，11	图版三三六，4	仰韶晚期
				27	刀	陶	图2.164c，7	图版三一六，6	仰韶中期
				28	盆	陶	图2.164d，8	图版三一七，1	仰韶中期
				29	盆	陶	图2.164d，9	图版三一七，2	仰韶中期
				30	罐	陶	图2.164d，1		仰韶中期
				31	盖	陶	图2.164d，5		仰韶中期
				32	缸	陶	图2.164d，7		仰韶晚期
				33	圈足盘	陶	图2.164d，2	图版三六三，6	龙山晚期
				34	斝	陶	图2.164d，3		龙山晚期
				35	深腹罐	陶	图2.164d，4	图版三八一，2	二里头二期早
				36	罐	陶	图2.164d，6	图版四五六，6	战国

续表

遗址信息			遗迹	登记号	器型	质地	图号		时代
序号	编号	名称					插图号	图版号	
152	153	武屯南		1	石斧	石	图2.165b，1	图版二五一，1	不详
				2	石片	石		图版二五一，2	不详
				3	罐	陶	图2.165b，4	图版三六五，3	龙山晚期
				4	罐	陶		图版四三七，6	春秋
				5	盆	陶	图2.165b，12	图版四三八，2	春秋
			H1	1	穿孔蚌刀	蚌	图2.165b，3	图版三六四，1	龙山晚期
				2	蚌料	蚌		图版三六四，2	龙山晚期
			H2	1	高领瓮	陶	图2.165b，8	图版三六四，3	龙山晚期
				2	高领瓮	陶	图2.165b，10	图版三六四，4	龙山晚期
				3	罐	陶	图2.165b，9	图版三六四，5	龙山晚期
				4	鼎	陶	图2.165b，13		龙山晚期
			H3	1	石斧	石	图2.165b，2		龙山
				2	罐	陶	图2.165b，11	图版三六四，6	龙山晚期
				3	罐	陶	图2.165b，5	图版三七五，6	龙山晚期至二里头早期
			H4	1	盆	陶	图2.165b，7	图版三六五，1	龙山晚期
				2	盆	陶	图2.165b，6	图版三六五，2	龙山晚期
153	135	西庞村西北		1	鼎	陶	图2.166b，1	图版三一七，3	仰韶中期
				2	盆	陶	图2.166b，5	图版三一七，4	仰韶中期
				3	鼎	陶	图2.166b，3	图版三一七，5	仰韶中期
				4	鼎	陶	图2.166b，2		仰韶中期
154	150	东庞村北		1	石刀	石		图版二五一，3	不详
				2	鼎	陶	图2.166b，4	图版三三六，5	仰韶晚期
157	136	东庞村南		1	盆	陶	图2.170b，1		仰韶早中期
				2	盆	陶	图2.170b，2	图版四二八，5	西周
158	144	杨村东南		1	簋	陶	图2.170b，6	图版四〇五，6	二里头四期晚
				2	深腹罐	陶	图2.170b，5		二里头
				3	鬲	陶	图2.170b，3	图版四一二，5	二里岗早期
				4	罐	陶	图2.170b，4	图版四五七，1	战国
				5	鬲	陶	图2.170b，7		殷末周初
				6	盆	陶	图2.170b，8	图版四三八，3	春秋
159	145	杨村北		1	石杵	石	图2.172b，1	图版二五一，4	不详
				2	石镰	石	图2.172b，3	图版二五一，5	不详
				3	石斧	石		图版二五一，6	不详
				4	鼎	陶	图2.172b，4		龙山晚期

续表

遗址信息			遗迹	登记号	器型	质地	图号		时代
序号	编号	名称					插图号	图版号	
159	145	杨村北		5	罐	陶	图2.172b, 7		龙山晚期
				6	罐	陶	图2.172b, 8		龙山晚期
				7	圈足	陶	图2.172b, 5	图版三六五, 4	龙山晚期
				8	网坠	陶	图2.172b, 2		二里头
				9	大口尊	陶	图2.172b, 6	图版四〇六, 1	二里头四期晚
				10	盆	陶	图2.172b, 10		二里头三、四期
				11	罐	陶	图2.172b, 9	图版四〇六, 2	二里头四期晚
				12	鬲	陶	图2.172c, 1		春秋
				13	鬲	陶	图2.172c, 2		春秋
				14	豆	陶	图2.172c, 5		春秋
				15	盆	陶	图2.172c, 7	图版四三八, 4	春秋
				16	盆	陶	图2.172c, 8	图版四三八, 5	春秋
				17	盆	陶	图2.172c, 10		春秋
				18	盆	陶	图2.172c, 11		春秋
				19	盆	陶	图2.172c, 12	图版四三八, 6	春秋
				20	盆	陶	图2.172c, 3	图版四三九, 1	春秋
				21	鬲	陶	图2.172c, 6	图版四五七, 2	战国
				22	鬲	陶	图2.172c, 9	图版四五七, 3	战国
				23	鬲	陶	图2.172c, 4	图版四五七, 4	战国
161	147	掘山		1	石杵	石	图2.174b, 10	图版二五二, 1	不详
				2	石坯	石		图版二五二, 2	不详
				3	石片	石			不详
				4	石片	石			不详
				5	石片	石		图版二五二, 3	不详
				6	石球	石	图2.174b, 1	图版二五二, 4	不详
				7	器盖	陶	图2.174b, 6	图版三六五, 5	龙山晚期
				8	器盖	陶	图2.174b, 7	图版三三六, 6	仰韶晚期
				9	鼎	陶	图2.174b, 3	图版三五三, 5	龙山早期
				10	罐	陶	图2.174b, 11	图版三五三, 6	龙山早期
				11	罐	陶	图2.174b, 5	图版三六五, 6	龙山晚期
				12	罐	陶	图2.174b, 9	图版三六六, 1	龙山晚期
				13	罐	陶	图2.174b, 8	图版三六六, 2	龙山晚期
				14	缸	陶	图2.174b, 4	图版四一二, 6	二里岗早期
				15	鬲	陶	图2.174c, 14	图版四三九, 2	春秋
				16	鬲	陶	图2.174c, 5	图版四三九, 3	春秋
				17	罐	陶	图2.174c, 10		春秋

续表

遗址信息			遗迹	登记号	器型	质地	图号		时代
序号	编号	名称					插图号	图版号	
161	147	掘山		18	鬲	陶	图2.174c，16		春秋
				19	鬲	陶	图2.174c，15	图版四三九，4	春秋
				20	鬲	陶	图2.174c，4	图版四三九，5	春秋
				21	鬲	陶	图2.174c，2	图版四三九，6	春秋
				22	鬲	陶	图2.174c，6	图版四四〇，1	春秋
				23	盆	陶	图2.174c，7	图版四五七，5	战国
				24	盆	陶	图2.174c，1	图版四五七，6	战国
				25	罐	陶	图2.174c，8	图版四四〇，2	春秋
				26	罐	陶	图2.174c，9	图版四四〇，3	春秋
				27	罐	陶	图2.174c，17	图版四四〇，4	春秋
				28	罐	陶	图2.174c，11	图版四四〇，5	春秋
				29	罐	陶	图2.174c，3	图版四四〇，6	春秋
				30	罐	陶	图2.174c，12		春秋
				31	豆	陶	图2.174d，1		战国
				32	豆	陶	图2.174b，13		龙山晚期
				33	豆	陶	图2.174d，2		战国
				34	豆	陶	图2.174d，3		战国
				35	豆	陶	图2.174d，10		战国
				36	豆	陶	图2.174d，4		战国
				37	豆	陶	图2.174b，14		龙山晚期
				38	罐	陶	图2.174d，9	图版四四一，1	春秋
				39	盆	陶	图2.174b，15	图版三一七，6	仰韶中期
				40	罐	陶	图2.174b，12		仰韶中、晚期
				41	盆	陶	图2.174c，13	图版四五八，1	战国
				42	盆	陶	图2.174d，13	图版四五八，2	战国
				43	盆	陶	图2.174d，14	图版四五八，3	战国
				44	盆	陶	图2.174d，8	图版四五八，4	战国
				45	罐	陶	图2.174d，5	图版四五八，5	战国
				46	罐	陶	图2.174d，6	图版四五八，6	战国
				47	瓮	陶	图2.174d，12	图版四五九，1	战国
				48	瓮	陶	图2.174d，7	图版四五九，2	战国
				49	瓮	陶	图2.174d，11	图版四五九，3	战国
				50	圆陶片	陶	图2.174b，2		龙山晚期
165	207	经周东		1	石锛	石	图2.179b，1	图版二五二，5	不详
				2	深腹罐	陶	图2.179b，5	图版四〇六，3	二里头四期晚
				3	豆	陶	图2.179b，2	图版四二八，6	西周

续表

遗址信息			遗迹	登记号	器型	质地	图号		时代
序号	编号	名称					插图号	图版号	
165	207	经周东		4	鬲	陶	图2.179b，6		春秋
				5	盆	陶	图2.179b，7	图版四五九，4	战国
				6	豆	陶	图2.179b，4	图版四四一，2	春秋
				7	豆	陶	图2.179b，3	图版四四一，3	春秋
166	208	肖村西寨西北		1	砍砸器	石	图2.180b，6	图版二五二，6	不详
				2	鬲	陶	图2.180b，1	图版四一六，1	二里岗晚期
				3	罐	陶	图2.180b，2		二里岗
				4	簋	陶	图2.180b，7		二里岗
				5	盆	陶	图2.180b，5		二里岗
				6	尊	陶	图2.180b，3	图版四一六，2	二里岗晚期
				7	罐	陶	图2.180b，8	图版四二二，2	殷墟
			H2	1	盆	陶	图2.180b，4	图版四五九，5	战国
169	210	吕桥东南		1	罐	陶	图2.183b，5	图版四四一，4	春秋
				2	豆	陶	图2.183b，1		战国
				3	豆	陶	图2.183b，2		春秋
				4	豆	陶	图2.183b，3	图版四五九，6	战国
				5	豆	陶	图2.183b，4	图版四六〇，1	战国
170	205	吕桥		1	捏口罐	陶	图2.183b，6		二里头四期
				2	瓮	陶	图2.183b，16		二里头四期
				3	罐	陶	图2.183b，7		二里头四期
			H1	1	圆腹罐	陶	图2.183b，9	图版四〇六，4	二里头四期晚
				2	圆腹罐	陶	图2.183b，10		二里头四期晚
				3	深腹罐	陶	图2.183b，8	图版四〇六，5	二里头四期晚
				4	深腹罐	陶	图2.183b，11	图版四〇六，6	二里头四期晚
				5	盆	陶	图2.183b，14	图版四〇七，1	二里头四期晚
171	204	吕桥北		1	鬲	陶	图2.183b，12		二里岗早期
				2	瓮	陶	图2.183b，13		战汉
				3	盆	陶	图2.183b，15		战汉
174	140	军屯东南		1	高领瓮	陶	图2.188b，2	图版四〇七，4	二里头四期晚
				2	盆	陶	图2.188b，4	图版四一三，1	二里岗早期
			H1	1	缸	陶	图2.188b，5	图版四〇七，2	二里头四期晚
				2	大口尊	陶	图2.188b，3	图版四〇七，3	二里头四期晚
				3	甑	陶	图2.188b，1		二里头四期
				4	大口尊	陶	图2.188b，6		二里头四期
			H2	1	废料	石			二里头四期
175	124	石牛沟		1	石铲	石	图2.189b，1	图版二五三，1	不详

续表

遗址信息			遗迹	登记号	器型	质地	图号		时代
序号	编号	名称					插图号	图版号	
175	124	石牛沟		2	鼎	陶	图2.189b, 4	图版三九〇, 5	二里头三期晚
				3	深腹罐	陶	图2.189b, 2	图版三八一, 3	二里头二期早
				4	深腹罐	陶	图2.189b, 3	图版三九〇, 6	二里头三期早
				5	刻槽盆	陶	图2.189b, 7	图版三九一, 1	二里头三期晚
				6	圆腹罐	陶	图2.189b, 8	图版三八一, 4	二里头二期晚
				7	盆	陶	图2.189b, 5	图版三九一, 2	二里头三期早
				8	尊	陶	图2.189b, 6		二里头
176	143	新彭店东		1	刀坯	石		图版二五三, 2	不详
				2	尖底瓶	陶	图2.189b, 9	图版三一八, 1	仰韶中期
				3	尖底瓶	陶	图2.189b, 10		仰韶中期
				4	豆	陶	图2.189b, 11		春秋
				5	盆	陶	图2.189b, 12	图版四四一, 5	春秋
177	134	高崖西		1	石片	石			不详
				2	石杵	石		图版二五三, 3	不详
				3	石铲	石	图2.191b, 8	图版二五三, 4	不详
				4	钵	陶	图2.191b, 1		仰韶中、晚期
				5	碗	陶	图2.191b, 2		仰韶中、晚期
				6	豆	陶	图2.191b, 3		仰韶中、晚期
				7	罐	陶	图2.191b, 4	图版三三七, 1	仰韶晚期
				8	缸	陶	图2.191b, 12	图版三三七, 2	仰韶晚期
				9	鼎	陶	图2.191b, 6		仰韶中、晚期
				10	盆	陶	图2.191b, 7		仰韶中、晚期
				11	器盖	陶	图2.191b, 5	图版三六六, 5	龙山晚期
				12	罐	陶	图2.191b, 13	图版三六六, 6	龙山晚期
				13	罐	陶	图2.191b, 9	图版三六七, 1	龙山晚期
				14	罐	陶	图2.191b, 11		龙山晚期
				15	矮领瓮	陶	图2.191c, 9		二里头
				16	高领瓮	陶	图2.191b, 15	图版三六七, 2	龙山晚期
				17	豆	陶	图2.191c, 18	图版四〇七, 5	二里头四期晚
				18	器盖	陶	图2.191c, 10	图版三八一, 5	二里头二期早
				19	圆腹罐	陶	图2.191c, 11	图版三八一, 6	二里头二期晚
				20	刻槽盆	陶	图2.191c, 15	图版三九一, 3	二里头三期早
				21	圆腹罐	陶	图2.191c, 14	图版三八二, 1	二里头二期晚
				22	捏口罐	陶	图2.191c, 16	图版四〇七, 6	二里头四期早
				23	深腹罐	陶	图2.191c, 19	图版三八二, 2	二里头二期早
				24	深腹罐	陶	图2.191c, 13	图版三八二, 3	二里头二期早

续表

遗址信息			遗迹	登记号	器型	质地	图号		时代
序号	编号	名称					插图号	图版号	
177	134	高崖西		25	鬲	陶	图2.191c,12	图版四〇八,1	二里头四期晚
				26	爵	陶	图2.191c,6	图版三八二,4	二里头二期早
				27	深腹罐	陶	图2.191c,17		二里头
				28	刻槽盆	陶	图2.191c,8	图版三八二,5	二里头二期晚
				29	鬲	陶	图2.191c,5	图版四二二,3	殷墟
				30	鬲	陶	图2.191c,1		殷墟
				31	鬲	陶	图2.191c,20		西周晚期
				32	豆	陶	图2.191c,2	图版四二九,1	西周晚期
				33	盆	陶	图2.191c,3		西周晚期
				34	盆	陶	图2.191c,21	图版四二九,2	西周晚期
				35	鬲	陶	图2.191c,4		战国
				36	鬲	陶	图2.191c,7	图版四六〇,2	战国
			H1	1	罐	陶	图2.191b,14	图版三六六,3	龙山晚期
			H2	1	矮领瓮	陶	图2.191b,10	图版三六六,4	龙山晚期
178	132	高崖东北		1	罐	陶	图2.192b,4	图版三三七,3	仰韶晚期
				2	缸	陶	图2.192b,2		仰韶晚期
				3	瓮	陶	图2.192b,1		仰韶晚期
				4	圆陶片	陶	图2.192b,3		二里头
				5	盆	陶	图2.192b,9	图版四一三,2	二里岗早期
				6	鬲	陶	图2.192b,12	图版四一六,3	二里岗晚期
				7	圆腹罐	陶	图2.192b,6	图版四〇八,2	二里岗
				8	圆腹罐	陶	图2.192b,7	图版四一六,4	二里岗晚期
				9	鬲	陶	图2.192b,8	图版四一六,5	二里岗晚期
				10	圆腹罐	陶	图2.192b,5	图版四一六,6	二里岗晚期
				11	圈足	陶	图2.192b,10		二里岗
				12	鬲	陶	图2.192b,11	图版四一三,3	二里岗早期
			H1	1	蚌刀	蚌	图2.192b,13		二里头
180	131	半个寨西南		1	罐	陶	图2.194b,1	图版三六七,3	龙山晚期
181	130	五岔沟西北		1	罐	陶	图2.194b,2	图版三六七,4	龙山晚期
183	218	铁窑东南		1	石料	石		图版二五三,5	不详
				2	石铲	石		图版二五三,6	不详
				3	石凿	石		图版二五四,1	不详
				4	尖底瓶	陶	图2.198b,1		仰韶中、晚期
				5	钵	陶	图2.198b,2		仰韶中、晚期
				6	鼎	陶	图2.198b,4	图版三七六,2	二里头早期
				7	罐	陶	图2.198b,3	图版三六七,5	龙山晚期

续表

遗址信息			遗迹	登记号	器型	质地	图号		时代
序号	编号	名称					插图号	图版号	
				8	圈足	陶	图2.198b, 8		龙山
183	218	铁窑东南	M1	1	石料	石		图版三一八, 2	仰韶中期
				2	石片	石		图版三一八, 3	仰韶中期
				3	罐	陶	图2.198b, 5	图版三一八, 4	仰韶中期
184	215	杨寨西南		1	石片	石		图版二五四, 2	不详
				2	石片	石		图版二五四, 3	不详
				3	钵	陶	图2.198b, 7		仰韶晚期
				4	缸	陶	图2.198b, 9	图版三三七, 4	仰韶晚期
			H1	1	残石铲	石	图2.198b, 12	图版三六七, 6	龙山晚期
				2	罐	陶	图2.198b, 6	图版三七六, 3	龙山晚期
185	219	铁窑东		1	罐	陶	图2.198b, 10	图版三三七, 5	仰韶晚期
				2	缸	陶	图2.198b, 11		仰韶晚期
186	214	杨寨西		1	罐	陶	图2.201b, 1	图版三三七, 6	仰韶晚期
				2	罐	陶	图2.201b, 5		龙山晚期
				3	罐	陶	图2.201b, 2	图版三六八, 1	龙山晚期
				4	罐	陶	图2.201b, 3	图版三六八, 2	龙山晚期
				5	罐	陶	图2.201b, 4	图版三六八, 3	龙山晚期
				6	罐	陶	图2.201b, 7	图版三六八, 4	龙山晚期
				7	罐	陶	图2.201b, 8	图版三六八, 5	龙山晚期
				8	夹砂罐	陶	图2.201b, 6	图版三六八, 6	龙山晚期
				9	斝	陶	图2.201b, 10		龙山晚期
				10	甑	陶	图2.201b, 11	图版三六九, 1	龙山晚期
				11	瓮	陶	图2.201b, 9		龙山晚期
				12	高领罐	陶	图2.201b, 12		龙山晚期
				13	壶	陶	图2.201c, 1		龙山晚期
				14	圈足盘	陶	图2.201c, 2	图版三六九, 2	龙山晚期
				15	盘	陶	图2.201c, 3	图版三六九, 3	龙山晚期
				16	盆	陶	图2.201c, 6		周
				17	瓮	陶	图2.201c, 5	图版三六九, 4	龙山晚期
				18	器盖	陶	图2.201c, 4	图版三六九, 5	龙山晚期
				19	圆腹罐	陶	图2.201c, 13		二里头
				20	深腹罐	陶	图2.201c, 7	图版三八二, 6	二里头二期晚
				21	深腹罐	陶	图2.201c, 8	图版三八三, 1	二里头二期晚
				22	深腹罐	陶	图2.201c, 9	图版三八三, 2	二里头二期晚
				23	圆腹罐	陶	图2.201c, 10	图版三九一, 4	二里头三期晚
				24	圆腹罐	陶	图2.201c, 11	图版四〇八, 3	二里头四期早

续表

遗址信息			遗迹	登记号	器型	质地	图号		时代
序号	编号	名称					插图号	图版号	
186	214	杨寨西		25	圆腹罐	陶	图2.201c,12	图版三九一,5	二里头三期晚
				26	高领罐	陶	图2.201d,1	图版三九一,6	二里头三期晚
				27	大口尊	陶	图2.201d,2		二里头
				28	甗	陶	图2.201d,5	图版四〇八,4	二里头四期早
				29	盆	陶	图2.201d,3	图版四〇八,5	二里头四期早
				30	刻槽盆	陶	图2.201d,4	图版三九二,1	二里头三期早
				31	鬲	陶	图2.201d,6	图版四二九,3	西周
				32	瓮	陶	图2.201d,7	图版四二九,4	西周
				33	蚌锥	蚌	图2.201d,8	图版二五四,4	不详
187	220	铁村南		1	罐	陶	图2.202b,1		仰韶晚期
				2	罐	陶	图2.202b,2		仰韶晚期
				3	罐	陶	图2.202b,4		仰韶晚期
				4	罐	陶	图2.202b,3		仰韶晚期
				5	罐	陶	图2.202b,5		仰韶晚期
				6	高领罐	陶	图2.202b,13	图版三三八,1	仰韶晚期
				7	盆	陶	图2.202b,12		二里头二至四期
				8	鬲	陶	图2.202b,7		殷墟
				9	鬲	陶	图2.202b,6		殷墟
				10	鬲	陶	图2.202b,9	图版四一七,1	二里岗晚期
				11	鬲	陶	图2.202b,8	图版四一七,2	二里岗晚期
				12	盆	陶	图2.202b,10	图版四一七,3	二里岗晚期
				13	鬲	陶	图2.202b,11	图版四一三,4	二里岗早期
188	213	马寨西		1	石刀	石		图版二五四,5	不详
				2	石刀	石		图版二五四,6	不详
				3	石刀	石			仰韶
				4	鼎	陶	图2.203b,13	图版三一八,5	仰韶中期
				5	罐	陶	图2.203b,14		仰韶晚期
				6	罐	陶	图2.203b,15		仰韶晚期
				7	罐	陶	图2.203b,11	图版三一八,6	仰韶中期
				8	盆	陶	图2.203b,16		仰韶中、晚期
				9	缸	陶	图2.203c,7	图版三五四,2	龙山早期
				10	鼎	陶	图2.203c,9	图版三五四,3	龙山早期
				11	盆	陶	图2.203c,4	图版三七一,2	龙山晚期
				12	深腹罐	陶	图2.203d,1	图版三八六,5	二里头二、三期
				13	盆	陶	图2.203d,4	图版四六〇,3	战国
				14	瓮	陶	图2.203c,5	图版三七一,3	龙山晚期

续表

遗址信息			遗迹	登记号	器型	质地	图号		时代
序号	编号	名称					插图号	图版号	
188	213	马寨西		15	罐	陶	图2.203b, 4		仰韶晚期
			H1	1	残石器	石		图版三三八, 2	仰韶晚期
				2	石料	石		图版三三八, 3	仰韶晚期
				3	盆	陶	图2.203b, 12	图版三三八, 4	仰韶晚期
				4	罐	陶	图2.203b, 9		仰韶晚期
				5	罐	陶	图2.203b, 10	图版三三八, 5	仰韶晚期
				6	罐	陶	图2.203b, 6	图版三三八, 6	仰韶晚期
			H2	1	器盖	陶	图2.203c, 2	图版三五四, 1	龙山早期
			H3	1	罐	陶	图2.203c, 8	图版三六九, 6	龙山晚期
				2	圈足盘	陶	图2.203c, 6	图版三七〇, 1	龙山晚期
			H4	1	刮削器	石	图2.203b, 1	图版三三九, 1	仰韶晚期
				2	缸	陶	图2.203b, 3	图版三三九, 2	仰韶晚期
				3	器盖	陶	图2.203b, 8	图版三三九, 3	仰韶晚期
				4	罐	陶	图2.203b, 5	图版三三九, 4	仰韶晚期
				5	罐	陶		图版三三九, 5	仰韶晚期
				6	瓮	陶	图2.203b, 2		仰韶晚期
				7	钵	陶	图2.203b, 7	图版三三九, 6	仰韶晚期
			H5	1	残石器	石		图版三七〇, 2	龙山晚期
				2	盆	陶	图2.203c, 3	图版三七〇, 3	龙山晚期
				3	鬶	陶	图2.203c, 1	图版三七〇, 4	龙山晚期
			H6	1	焙烧石灰石	石		图版三七〇, 5	龙山晚期
				2	焙烧石灰石	石		图版三七〇, 6	龙山晚期
				3	中口罐	陶	图2.203c, 10		龙山晚期
				4	大口罐	陶	图2.203c, 11	图版三七一, 1	龙山晚期
			H7	1	高领罐	陶	图2.203d, 2	图版三八六, 6	二里头二、三期
				2	鬲	陶	图2.203d, 3	图版四二二, 4	殷墟早期
189	216	寨湾东南		1	石锛坯	石	图2.204b, 1	图版二五五, 1	不详
				2	石斧	石	图2.204b, 5	图版二五五, 2	不详
				3	石料	石		图版二五五, 3	不详
				4	石铲	石	图2.204b, 2	图版二五五, 4	不详
				5	石铲	石		图版二五五, 5	不详
				6	石刀	石	图2.204b, 3	图版二五五, 6	不详
				7	石器	石		图版二五六, 1	不详
				8	石斧	石	图2.204b, 4	图版二五六, 2	不详
				9	石斧	石	图2.204b, 6	图版二五六, 3	不详
				10	石器	石		图版二五六, 4	不详

续表

遗址信息			遗迹	登记号	器型	质地	图号		时代
序号	编号	名称					插图号	图版号	
189	216	寨湾东南		11	石刀	石		图版二五六，5	不详
				12	石凿	石		图版二五六，6	不详
				13	石料	石		图版二五七，1	不详
				14	鼎	陶	图2.204c，1		仰韶晚期
				15	罐	陶	图2.204c，3		仰韶晚期
				16	盆	陶	图2.204c，2		仰韶晚期
				17	罐	陶	图2.204c，5	图版三四〇，2	龙山
				18	罐	陶	图2.204c，6		龙山
				19	罐	陶	图2.204c，4		龙山
				20	盆	陶	图2.204c，9		龙山
				21	盆	陶	图2.204c，7		龙山
				22	鬲	陶	图2.204e，1	图版四〇八，6	二里头四期晚
				23	深腹罐	陶	图2.204e，2	图版四〇九，1	二里头四期晚
				24	深腹罐	陶	图2.204e，3	图版四〇九，2	二里头四期晚
				25	深腹罐	陶	图2.204e，9	图版三九二，2	二里头三期早
				26	圆腹罐	陶	图2.204e，6	图版三八四，3	二里头二期晚
				27	鼎	陶	图2.204e，5	图版三八四，4	二里头二期早
				28	盆	陶	图2.204e，4	图版三八四，5	二里头二期晚
				29	敛口罐	陶	图2.204e，7	图版四〇九，3	二里头四期晚
				30	高领尊	陶	图2.204e，13		二里头
				31	敛口罐	陶	图2.204e，8		二里头
				32	鬲	陶	图2.204e，12	图版四一七，4	二里岗晚期
				33	鬲	陶	图2.204e，10	图版四一七，5	二里岗晚期
				34	鬲	陶	图2.204e，11		二里岗晚期
				35	簋	陶	图2.204e，14		二里岗晚期
			H1	1	石戈	石	图2.204d，1	图版三八三，3	二里头二期
				2	石片	石		图版三八三，4	二里头二期
				3	石片	石			二里头二期
				4	石料	石		图版三八三，5	二里头二期
				5	圆腹罐	陶	图2.204d，4	图版三八三，6	二里头二期
				6	盆	陶	图2.204d，8	图版三八四，1	二里头二期
			H3	1	高领尊	陶	图2.204d，5		二里头
			H4	1	石坯	石		图版三七一，4	龙山晚期
				2	高领瓮	陶	图2.204c，11		龙山晚期
				3	杯	陶	图2.204c，8		龙山晚期
				4	盆	陶	图2.204c，14	图版三七一，5	龙山晚期

续表

遗址信息			遗迹	登记号	器型	质地	图号		时代
序号	编号	名称					插图号	图版号	
189	216	寨湾东南	H5	1	残石锛	石	图2.204d，2		龙山晚期
				2	蚌器	蚌	图2.204d，3		龙山晚期
			H6	1	深腹罐	陶	图2.204d，9	图版三八四，2	二里头二期
				2	矮领瓮	陶	图2.204d，6		二里头二期
				3	器盖	陶	图2.204d，7	图版三七六，4	二里头一期晚
			H8	1	石片	石		图版三五四，4	龙山早期
				2	鼎	陶	图2.204c，10	图版三五四，5	龙山早期
				3	鼎	陶	图2.204c，12	图版三五四，6	龙山早期
				4	罐	陶	图2.204c，13	图版三四〇，1	仰韶晚期
190	217	寨湾东北		1	石铲	石		图版二五七，2	不详
				2	石器	石		图版二五七，3	不详
				3	石片	石		图版二五七，4	不详
				4	器盖	陶	图2.205b，9	图版三四〇，4	仰韶晚期
				5	罐	陶	图2.205b，8	图版三四〇，5	仰韶晚期
				6	罐	陶	图2.205b，7		仰韶晚期
				7	罐	陶	图2.205b，11		仰韶晚期
				8	盆	陶			龙山晚期
				9	罐	陶	图2.205b，10		龙山晚期
				10	深腹罐	陶	图2.205c，15	图版三九二，4	二里头三期早
				11	深腹罐	陶	图2.205c，14		二里头二三期
				12	鼎	陶	图2.205c，11	图版三九二，5	二里头三期晚
				13	大口尊	陶	图2.205c，4		二里头二三期
				14	敛口罐	陶	图2.205c，16		二里头二三期
				15	罐	陶	图2.205c，8		二里头二三期
				16	鼎	陶	图2.205c，13		二里头二三期
				17	罐	陶	图2.205c，7		二里头二三期
				18	尊	陶	图2.205c，9		二里头二三期
				19	尊	陶	图2.205c，10		二里头二三期
				20	盆	陶	图2.205c，5	图版三九二，6	二里头三期晚
				21	甗	陶	图2.205c，12		二里头二三期
				22	缸	陶	图2.205c，1	图版四〇九，4	二里头四期晚
				23	缸	陶	图2.205c，2	图版四〇九，5	二里头四期晚
				24	缸	陶	图2.205c，3	图版四〇九，6	二里头四期晚
				25	罐	陶	图2.205d，4		殷墟
				26	罐	陶	图2.205d，3	图版四二二，6	殷墟
				27	罐	陶	图2.205d，11		殷墟

续表

遗址信息			遗迹	登记号	器型	质地	图号		时代
序号	编号	名称					插图号	图版号	
190	217	寨湾东北		28	罐	陶	图2.205d，7	图版四二三，1	殷墟
				29	罐	陶	图2.205d，10	图版四二三，2	殷墟
				30	盆	陶	图2.205d，5	图版四二三，3	殷墟
				31	鬲	陶	图2.205d，1		殷墟
				32	罐	陶	图2.205d，2		殷墟
				33	罐	陶	图2.205d，9		春秋
				34	罐	陶	图2.205d，8	图版四四一，6	春秋
				35	罐	陶	图2.205b，6		龙山晚期
				36	盆	陶			殷墟
				37	簋	陶			殷墟
				38	圈足器	陶		图版四六三，4	东周
				39	壶	陶		图版四六三，5	东周
				40	鬲	陶			殷墟
				41	鬲	陶		图版四二三，4	殷墟
				42	鬲	陶		图版四二三，5	殷墟
				43	鬲	陶			殷墟
				44	鬲	陶			殷墟
				45	鬲	陶		图版四二三，6	殷墟
				46	鬲	陶			殷墟
				47	鬲	陶			殷墟
				48	鬲	陶			殷墟
				49	鬲	陶			殷墟
				50	鬲	陶			殷墟
				51	鼎	陶		图版三五五，1	龙山早期
				52	盆	陶		图版四六三，6	东周
				53	盆	陶		图版四六四，1	东周
				54	盆	陶		图版四六四，2	东周
				55	罐	陶			殷墟
				56	簋	陶		图版四六四，3	东周
				57	腹片	陶			二里头
			H1	1	玉凿/锛	玉	图2.205b，13	图版三七一，6	龙山晚期
				2	豆	陶	图2.205b，12	图版三七二，1	龙山晚期
			H3	1	石料	石		图版三七二，2	龙山晚期
				2	石料	石			龙山晚期
				3	觚	陶	图2.205b，5		龙山晚期

续表

遗址信息			遗迹	登记号	器型	质地	图号		时代
序号	编号	名称					插图号	图版号	
190	217	寨湾东北	H4	1	鼎	陶	图2.205b, 2		龙山晚期
				2	鬶	陶	图2.205b, 4		龙山晚期
			H6	1	深腹罐	陶	图2.205c, 6	图版三八四, 6	二里头二期
			H7	1	瓮	陶	图2.205b, 3	图版三七二, 3	龙山晚期
			F1	1	环	陶	图2.205b, 1	图版三四〇, 3	仰韶晚期
				2	缸	陶		图版三九二, 3	二里头三期早
			F3	1	瓮	陶	图2.205d, 6	图版四二二, 5	殷墟
191	212	曹寨北		1	石凿	石	图2.206b, 1	图版二五七, 5	不详
				2	鼎	陶	图2.206b, 2	图版四一〇, 1	二里头四期晚
				3	刻槽盆	陶	图2.206b, 5	图版三九三, 3、4	二里头三期晚
				4	盆	陶	图2.206b, 8		二里头晚期
				5	盆	陶	图2.206b, 3	图版四一〇, 2	二里头四期晚
				6	鬲	陶	图2.206b, 10	图版四一七, 6	二里岗晚期
			H1	1	缸	陶	图2.206b, 11	图版三九三, 1	二里头三期
			H3	1	圆腹罐	陶	图2.206b, 7	图版三九三, 2	二里头三期
			H5	1	罐	陶	图2.206b, 6	图版三七二, 4	龙山晚期
			H6	1	罐	陶	图2.206b, 9	图版三七二, 5	龙山晚期
				2	瓮	陶	图2.206b, 4	图版三七二, 6	龙山晚期
192	222	西张庄东南		1	钵	陶	图2.207b, 4	图版三四〇, 6	仰韶晚期
				2	钵	陶	图2.207b, 8	图版三四一, 1	仰韶晚期
193	221	西张庄东北		1	器盖	陶	图2.207b, 2		仰韶晚期
				2	蚌环	蚌	图2.207b, 10		不详
			H1	1	盆	陶	图2.207b, 9	图版三五五, 2	龙山早期
			H2	1	彩陶罐	陶	图2.207b, 3	图版三四一, 2	仰韶晚期
			H4	1	罐	陶	图2.207b, 5		仰韶晚期
				2	罐	陶	图2.207b, 1	图版三四一, 3	仰韶晚期
			H5	1	罐	陶	图2.207b, 6		仰韶晚期
				2	罐	陶	图2.207b, 7	图版三四一, 4	仰韶晚期
194	202	韩村南B		1	罐	陶	图2.210b, 1	图版三四一, 5	仰韶晚期
				2	碗	陶	图2.210b, 2		仰韶晚期
195	201	韩村南A		1	尊	陶	图2.210b, 3	图版三九三, 5	二里头三期早
				2	深腹罐	陶	图2.210b, 5	图版四一〇, 3	二里头四期晚
				3	罐	陶	图2.210b, 10	图版四一八, 1	二里岗晚期
				4	捏口罐	陶	图2.210b, 4		二里岗晚期
				5	大口尊	陶	图2.210b, 6	图版四一八, 2	二里岗晚期

续表

遗址信息			遗迹	登记号	器型	质地	图号		时代
序号	编号	名称					插图号	图版号	
196	200	符家寨西		1	鼎	陶	图2.210b,7	图版三四一,6	仰韶晚期
				2	罐	陶	图2.210b,8	图版三五五,3	龙山早期
				3	瓮	陶	图2.210b,9		仰韶晚期
198	198	符家寨东北		1	石铲	石	图2.213b,6	图版二五七,6	不详
				2	钵	陶	图2.213b,2	图版三一九,2	仰韶中期
				3	豆	陶	图2.213b,15	图版三四二,1	仰韶晚期
				4	盆	陶	图2.213b,9	图版三四二,2	仰韶晚期
				5	盆	陶	图2.213b,7	图版三四二,3	仰韶晚期
				6	罐	陶	图2.213b,8	图版三四二,4	仰韶晚期
				7	罐	陶	图2.213b,13	图版三四二,5	仰韶晚期
				8	罐	陶	图2.213b,4	图版三一九,3	仰韶中期
				9	缸	陶	图2.213b,1		仰韶中、晚期
				10	瓮	陶	图2.213b,3	图版三四二,6	仰韶晚期
				11	鼎	陶	图2.213b,14	图版三四三,1	仰韶晚期
				12	陶饼	陶	图2.213b,5		仰韶
				13	深腹罐	陶	图2.213b,11	图版四一三,5	二里岗早期
				14	鬲	陶	图2.213b,12	图版四六〇,4	战国
			H1	1	钵	陶	图2.213b,16		仰韶中期
				2	罐	陶	图2.213b,10	图版三一九,1	仰韶中期
199	123	张村东南		1	罐	陶	图2.214b,13	图版三四三,2	仰韶晚期
				2	罐	陶	图2.214b,19		二里头四期晚
				3	鬲	陶	图2.214b,7		二里岗晚期
				4	深腹罐	陶	图2.214b,11		二里头二、三期
			H1	1	缸	陶	图2.214b,15	图版三五五,4	龙山早期
				2	罐	陶	图2.214b,8	图版三五五,5	龙山早期
200	122	裴村E		1	石铲	石		图版二五八,1	不详
				2	鬲	陶	图2.214b,5	图版四一〇,4	二里头四期晚
				3	深腹罐	陶	图2.214b,16	图版四一〇,5	二里头四期晚
				4	罐	陶	图2.214b,18		战国
201	118	裴村A		1	盆	陶	图2.214b,3	图版三一九,4	仰韶中期
				2	折沿缸	陶	图2.214b,2		仰韶中、晚期
				3	骨料	骨	图2.214b,9	图版二五八,2	不详
			H1	1	罐	陶	图2.214b,4		仰韶中期
202	119	裴村B		1	钵	陶	图2.214b,6		仰韶晚期
				2	盆	陶	图2.214b,17	图版三七三,1	龙山晚期
				3	豆	陶	图2.214b,14	图版三七三,2	龙山晚期

续表

遗址信息			遗迹	登记号	器型	质地	图号		时代
序号	编号	名称					插图号	图版号	
202	119	裴村B		4	碗	陶	图2.214b，20	图版三四三，3	仰韶晚期
203	120	裴村C		1	折沿缸	陶	图2.214b，1	图版三四三，4	仰韶晚期
204	121	裴村D		1	骨匕	骨	图2.214b，10	图版二五八，3	不详
			H1	1	罐	陶	图2.214b，12	图版三七三，3	龙山晚期
205	116	程子沟南		1	罐	陶	图2.220b，5		仰韶晚期
				2	豆	陶	图2.220b，9		龙山晚期
				3	罐	陶	图2.220b，12	图版四二九，5	西周
206	117	程子沟		1	折沿罐	陶	图2.220b，4		龙山晚期
				2	陶拍	陶	图2.220b，1		二里头
				3	捏口罐	陶	图2.220b，2	图版三八五，1	二里头二期晚
				4	圆腹罐	陶	图2.220b，8		二里头一至三期
				5	深腹罐	陶	图2.220b，11	图版三八五，2	二里头二期早
				6	深腹罐	陶	图2.220b，7	图版三八五，3	二里头二期晚
				7	鼎	陶	图2.220b，6		二里头一至三期
				8	甑	陶	图2.220b，10	图版三八五，4	二里头二期晚
				9	缸	陶	图2.220b，3	图版三八五，5	二里头二期晚
207	115	崔河北		1	鬲	陶	图2.222b，1		殷墟
				2	碗	陶	图2.222b，2	图版四六〇，5	战国
208	114	郝寨东北	H1	1	盆	陶	图2.222b，3	图版三八五，6	二里头二期
				2	盆	陶	图2.222b，7	图版三八六，1	二里头二期
209	127	陶化店东南	H1	1	钵	陶	图2.222b，9	图版三四三，5	仰韶晚期
210	126	陶化店水库		1	罐	陶	图2.222b，4	图版三一九，6	仰韶中期
			H1	1	瓮	陶	图2.222b，10	图版三一九，5	仰韶中期
				2	罐	陶	图2.222b，5	图版三四三，6	仰韶晚期
			H2	1	盆	陶	图2.222b，6	图版三四四，1	仰韶晚期
				2	罐	陶	图2.222b，8	图版三四四，2	仰韶晚期
212	Y225	邢村东		1	盆	陶	图2.228b，3		龙山晚期
213	Y182	夏后寺		1	深腹罐	陶	图2.228b，5		二里头
				2	深腹罐	陶	图2.228b，4		二里头
				3	深腹罐	陶	图2.228b，6		二里头
				4	深腹罐	陶	图2.228b，7		二里头
				5	鼎	陶	图2.228b，11		二里头
				6	鼎	陶	图2.228b，12		二里头
				7	圆腹罐	陶	图2.228b，10		二里头
				8	圆腹罐	陶	图2.228b，8		二里头
				9	圆腹罐	陶	图2.228b，9		二里头

续表

遗址信息			遗迹	登记号	器型	质地	图号		时代
序号	编号	名称					插图号	图版号	
213	Y182	夏后寺		10	甗	陶	图2.228b，13		二里头
				11	缸	陶	图2.228c，9		二里头
				12	尊	陶	图2.228c，8		二里头
				13	盆	陶	图2.228c，3		二里头
				14	盆	陶	图2.228c，2		二里头
				15	敛口罐	陶	图2.228c，1		二里头
				16	敛口罐	陶	图2.228c，7		二里头
				17	敛口罐	陶	图2.228c，10		二里头
				18	鬲	陶	图2.228c，4		殷墟晚期
				19	盆	陶	图2.228c，6		殷墟晚期
				20	罐	陶	图2.228c，5		殷墟晚期
				21	石斧	石	图2.228b，1		不详
				22	石斧	石	图2.228b，2		不详
				23	石斧	石			不详
				24	石斧	石			不详
				25	石锛	石			不详
				26	石锤	石			不详
				27	石杵	石			不详
				28	石铲坯	石			不详
				29	石铲坯	石			不详
				30	石铲坯	石			不详
				31	石铲坯	石			不详
				32	石铲坯	石			不详
				33	石铲坯	石		图版二五八，4	不详
				34	石铲坯	石		图版二五八，5	不详
				35	石铲坯	石		图版二五八，6	不详
				36	石铲坯	石		图版二五九，1	不详
				37	去薄石片	石			不详
				38	石铲坯	石		图版二五九，2	不详
				39	石铲坯	石		图版二五九，3	不详
				40	去薄石片	石			不详
				41	去薄石片	石			不详
				42	石铲坯	石		图版二五九，4	不详
				43	石铲坯	石		图版二五九，5	不详
				44	石铲坯	石		图版二五九，6	不详
				45	石铲坯	石		图版二六〇，1	不详

续表

序号	遗址信息		遗迹	登记号	器型	质地	图号		时代
	编号	名称					插图号	图版号	
213	Y182	夏后寺		46	石铲坯	石		图版二六〇，2	不详
				47	石铲坯	石		图版二六〇，3	不详
				48	石铲坯	石		图版二六〇，4	不详
				49	石铲坯	石		图版二六〇，5	不详
				50	石铲坯	石		图版二六〇，6	不详
				51	石铲坯	石		图版二六一，1	不详
				52	石铲坯	石		图版二六一，2	不详
				53	石铲坯	石		图版二六一，3	不详
				54	石铲坯	石		图版二六一，4	不详
				55	石铲坯	石		图版二六一，5	不详
				56	石器残件	石			不详
				57	石铲坯	石		图版二六一，6	不详
				58	砺石	石		图版二六二，1	不详
				59	砺石	石		图版二六二，2	不详
				60	白烧石	石		图版二六二，3	不详
214	Y183	九龙水库东南		1	豆	陶	图2.229b，2		战国
				2	石斧	石	图2.229b，1		不详
215	Y184	邢村北		1	鬲	陶	图2.229b，3		二里岗晚期
				2	捏口罐	陶	图2.229b，4		二里岗晚期
216	Y185	扒头水库南		1	鬲	陶	图2.229b，6		二里岗晚期
				2	鬲	陶	图2.229b，5		殷墟晚期
				3	鬲	陶	图2.229b，7		殷墟晚期
				4	石锤	石			不详
				5	石刀	石			不详
217	Y181	扒头东南		1	罐	陶	图2.232b，7		二里岗
				2	瓮	陶	图2.232b，3		二里岗
				3	大口尊	陶	图2.232b，4		二里岗
				4	敛口尊	陶	图2.232b，6		二里岗
				5	鬲	陶	图2.232b，8		二里岗晚期
				6	鬲	陶	图2.232b，5		二里岗
				7	鬲	陶	图2.232b，9		二里岗晚期
				8	盆	陶	图2.232b，2		二里岗
				9	石斧	石		图版二六二，4	不详
218	Y180	扒头西南		1	深腹罐	陶	图2.232b，1		二里岗晚期
219	Y179	任才村东南		1	中口罐	陶	图2.234b，2		龙山晚期
				2	瓮	陶	图2.234b，3		龙山晚期

续表

遗址信息			遗迹	登记号	器型	质地	图号		时代
序号	编号	名称					插图号	图版号	
219	Y179	任才村东南		3	盆	陶	图2.234b，4		春秋
220	Y178	任才村西南		1	瓮	陶	图2.234b，1		战国
221	Y186	卢村南		1	器盖	陶	图2.234b，7		龙山晚期
				2	豆	陶	图2.234b，5		龙山晚期
				3	鬲	陶	图2.234b，6		二里岗晚期
223	Y177	卢村西		1	小罐	陶	图2.238b，1		龙山晚期
				2	瓮	陶	图2.238b，2		龙山晚期
				3	折腹盆	陶	图2.238b，6		龙山晚期
				4	白烧石	石		图版二六二，5	不详
224	Y176	卢村西北		1	盆	陶	图2.238b，11		殷墟晚期
				2	鬲	陶	图2.238b，5		西周
				3	罐	陶	图2.238b，3		西周
				4	鬲	陶	图2.238b，4		东周
				5	鬲	陶	图2.238b，9		东周
				6	盆	陶	图2.238b，10		战国
				7	刮削器	石			不详
225	Y224	双泉东北		1	瓮	陶	图2.238b，8		龙山晚期
				2	盆	陶	图2.238b，7		龙山晚期
				3	石斧	石		图版二六二，6	不详
				4	石斧	石		图版二六三，1	不详
				5	石毛坯	石			不详
				6	石毛坯	石			不详
				7	石杵	石			不详
				8	刮削器	石			不详
			H1	1	白烧石	石			不详
226	Y169	卢村东北		1	盆	陶	图2.241b，2		仰韶晚期
227	Y168	卢村北	H1	1	鼎	陶			龙山早期
				2	罐	陶	图2.241b，1		龙山早期
				3	罐	陶	图2.241b，4		龙山早期
				4	刻槽盆	陶			龙山早期
228	Y167	高祖庙		1	罐	陶	图2.241b，3		龙山早期
230	Y172	双泉南		1	鼎	陶	图2.245b，1		龙山晚期
				2	斝	陶	图2.245b，2		龙山晚期
			H1	1	中口罐	陶	图2.245b，4		龙山晚期
				2	中口罐	陶	图2.245b，3		龙山晚期
233	Y171	双泉西南		1	小罐	陶	图2.245b，5		仰韶早期

续表

遗址信息			遗迹	登记号	器型	质地	图号		时代
序号	编号	名称					插图号	图版号	
233	Y171	双泉西南		2	小罐	陶	图2.245b，6		仰韶早期
236	Y187	浏涧河水库东		1	夹砂罐	陶	图2.251b，1		仰韶早期
				2	夹砂罐	陶	图2.251b，2		仰韶早期
				3	盆	陶	图2.251b，7		仰韶早期
				4	泥质罐	陶	图2.251b，4		仰韶早期
				5	泥质罐	陶	图2.251b，6		仰韶早期
				6	泥质罐	陶	图2.251b，5		仰韶早期
				7	钵	陶	图2.251b，3		仰韶早期
				8	石铲	石			不详
				9	石锤	石			不详
239	Y166	西齐家窑东北		1	中口罐	陶	图2.254b，4		龙山晚期
				2	中口罐	陶	图2.254b，7		龙山晚期
				3	刻槽盆	陶	图2.254b，3		龙山晚期
				4	器盖	陶	图2.254b，6		龙山晚期
				5	器盖	陶	图2.254b，5		龙山晚期
				6	石斧	石	图2.254b，1		不详
				7	石斧	石			不详
				8	石锛坯	石	图2.254b，2		不详
240	Y188	西齐家窑西北		1	瓮	陶	图2.255b，9		龙山晚期
				2	平底盆	陶	图2.255b，8		战国
				3	盆	陶	图2.255b，4		战国
				4	盆	陶	图2.255b，5		战国
				5	盆	陶	图2.255b，2		战国
				6	盆	陶	图2.255b，7		战国
				7	盆	陶	图2.255b，6		战国
				8	盆	陶	图2.255b，3		战国
				9	盆	陶	图2.255b，1		战国
				10	豆	陶	图2.255b，10		战国
				11	石器	石			不详
241	Y192	灰嘴北		1	罐	陶	图2.256b，11		西周
242	Y189	郑窑南		1	罐	陶	图2.256b，8		仰韶中期
				2	罐	陶	图2.256b，10		战国
				3	鬲	陶	图2.256b，4		战国
				4	盆	陶	图2.256b，5		战国
				5	豆	陶	图2.256b，7		战国
				6	石铲坯	石			不详

续表

序号	遗址信息		遗迹	登记号	器型	质地	图号		时代
	编号	名称					插图号	图版号	
242	Y189	郑窑南		7	石铲坯	石			不详
				8	石铲坯	石			不详
				9	石铲坯	石			不详
			H1	1	罐	陶	图2.256b，9		仰韶中期
			H2	1	鬲	陶	图2.256b，3		战国
				2	盆	陶	图2.256b，6		战国
243	Y191	陶家村东		1	深腹罐	陶	图2.256b，1		二里岗
				2	假腹豆	陶	图2.256b，2		二里岗
244	Y190	刘国故城		1	罐	陶	图2.259b，1		龙山晚期
				2	罐	陶	图2.259b，2		龙山晚期
				3	鬲	陶	图2.259b，9		春秋
				4	器盖	陶	图2.259b，7		东周
				5	罐	陶	图2.259b，4		战国
				6	罐	陶	图2.259b，5		战国
				7	罐	陶	图2.259b，3		战国
				8	瓮	陶	图2.259b，10		东周
				9	盆	陶	图2.259b，8		战国
				10	盆	陶	图2.259b，6		战国
				11	石锤	石			不详
245	Y140	郑窑		1	深腹罐	陶	图2.260b，14		二里头三、四期
				2	鼎	陶	图2.260b，15		二里头三、四期
				3	鬲	陶	图2.260b，8		东周
				4	盆	陶	图2.260b，16		东周
				5	豆	陶	图2.260b，3		东周
				6	豆	陶	图2.260b，2		东周
				7	豆	陶	图2.260b，1		东周
				8	瓮	陶	图2.260b，4		东周
				9	腹片	陶	图2.260b，5		东周
				10	罐	陶	图2.260b，13		东周
				11	石斧	石			不详
				12	刮削器	石			不详
				13	石毛坯	石			不详
				14	白烧石	石		图版二六三，2	不详
				15	石毛坯	石			不详

续表

遗址信息			遗迹	登记号	器型	质地	图号		时代
序号	编号	名称					插图号	图版号	
245	Y140	郑窑	H1	1	深腹罐	陶	图2.260b，6		二里岗晚期
				2	鬲	陶	图2.260b，9		二里岗晚期
				3	鬲	陶	图2.260b，10		二里岗晚期
				4	鬲	陶	图2.260b，11		二里岗晚期
				5	甗	陶	图2.260b，7		二里岗晚期
				6	高领罐	陶	图2.260b，12		二里岗晚期
247	Y194	郑村西		1	夹砂罐	陶	图2.262b，4		仰韶中、晚期
				2	鼎	陶	图2.262b，5		仰韶中、晚期
				3	鼎	陶	图2.262b，6		仰韶中、晚期
				4	泥质彩陶罐	陶	图2.262b，9		仰韶中、晚期
				5	泥质彩陶罐	陶	图2.262b，8		仰韶中、晚期
				6	盆	陶	图2.262b，3		仰韶中、晚期
				7	钵	陶	图2.262b，7		仰韶中、晚期
				8	圈足盘	陶	图2.262b，1		仰韶中、晚期
				9	圈足盘	陶	图2.262b，10		仰韶中、晚期
				10	圈足盘	陶	图2.262b，2		仰韶中、晚期
248	Y195	涧东村		1	砺石	石			不详
				2	砺石	石		图版二六三，3	不详
249	Y196A	涧东村北		1	深腹罐	陶	图2.264b，10		二里头二、四期
				2	深腹罐	陶	图2.264b，9		二里头二、四期
				3	圆腹罐	陶	图2.264b，3		二里头二、四期
				4	圆腹罐	陶	图2.264b，2		二里头二、四期
				5	甑	陶	图2.264b，1		二里头二、四期
				6	盆	陶	图2.264b，8		二里头二、四期
				7	刻槽盆	陶	图2.264b，7		二里头二、四期
				8	鬲	陶	图2.264b，4		西周早期
				9	石锛	石	图2.264b，5		不详
				10	石杵	石	图2.264b，6		不详
				11	石铲	石		图版二六三，4	不详
				12	石毛坯	石		图版二六三，5	不详
250	Y196B	涧东村西北		1	罐	陶	图2.265b，3		龙山晚期
				2	深腹罐	陶	图2.265b，5		二里头二至四期
				3	鼎	陶	图2.265b，6		二里头二至四期
				4	圆腹罐	陶	图2.265b，8		二里头二至四期
				5	圆腹罐	陶	图2.265b，4		二里头二至四期
				6	甑	陶	图2.265b，9		二里头二至四期

续表

遗址信息			遗迹	登记号	器型	质地	图号		时代
序号	编号	名称					插图号	图版号	
250	Y196B	涧东村西北		7	盆	陶	图2.265b，7		西周
				8	石斧	石		图版二六三，6	不详
				9	石斧	石			不详
				10	石铲	石			不详
				11	砍砸器	石			不详
				12	石核	石			不详
			H1	1	大口罐	陶	图2.265b，1		龙山晚期
				2	器盖	陶	图2.265b，2		龙山晚期
251	Y228	姬家村南		1	鬲	陶	图2.265b，10		殷墟晚期
				2	豆	陶	图2.265b，11		殷墟晚期
				3	簋	陶	图2.265b，12		殷墟晚期
252	Y223	九龙角水库西		1	石锤	石		图版二六四，1	不详
				2	石锤	石		图版二六四，2	不详
				3	石锤	石		图版二六四，3	不详
				4	砍砸器	石		图版二六四，4	不详
				5	砍砸器	石		图版二六四，5	不详
				6	石砧	石		图版二六四，6	不详
				7	砺石	石		图版二六五，1	不详
				8	石料	石		图版二六五，2	不详
253	Y203	东管茅东南		1	鬲	陶	图2.269b，1		殷墟早期
				2	罐	陶	图2.269b，2		西周早期
				3	罐	陶	图2.269b，3		西周早期
254	Y202	东管茅东		1	夹砂罐	陶	图2.270b，2		仰韶晚期
				2	夹砂罐	陶	图2.270b，3		仰韶晚期
				3	夹砂罐	陶	图2.270b，4		仰韶晚期
				4	鼎	陶	图2.270b，11		仰韶晚期
				5	鼎	陶	图2.270b，1		仰韶晚期
				6	泥质罐	陶	图2.270b，7		仰韶晚期
				7	泥质罐	陶	图2.270b，8		仰韶晚期
				8	泥质罐	陶	图2.270b，9		仰韶晚期
				9	泥质罐	陶	图2.270b，6		仰韶晚期
				10	瓮	陶	图2.270b，5		仰韶晚期
				11	缸	陶	图2.270b，10		仰韶晚期
				12	钵	陶	图2.270c，8		仰韶晚期
				13	钵	陶	图2.270c，7		仰韶晚期
				14	钵	陶	图2.270c，6		仰韶晚期

续表

遗址信息			遗迹	登记号	器型	质地	图号		时代
序号	编号	名称					插图号	图版号	
254	Y202	东管茅东		15	钵	陶	图2.270c，9		仰韶晚期
				16	碗	陶	图2.270c，4		仰韶晚期
				17	碗	陶	图2.270c，2		仰韶晚期
				18	碗	陶	图2.270c，3		仰韶晚期
				19	杯	陶	图2.270c，5		仰韶晚期
				20	小罐	陶	图2.270b，12		仰韶晚期
				21	盆	陶	图2.270c，11		殷墟
				22	盒	陶	图2.270c，1		战国
				23	盆	陶	图2.270c，12		战国
				24	盆	陶	图2.270c，10		战国
				25	环	陶	图2.270c，13		仰韶晚期
				26	石斧	石			不详
				27	石铲	石			不详
				28	石镰	石			不详
				29	石锤	石			不详
				30	砍砸器	石		图版二六五，3	不详
255	Y201	西口孜		1	深腹罐	陶	图2.271b，3		二里头三、四期
				2	深腹罐	陶	图2.271b，2		二里头三、四期
				3	深腹罐	陶	图2.271b，4		二里头三、四期
				4	鼎	陶	图2.271b，16		二里头三、四期
				5	圆腹罐	陶	图2.271b，12		二里头三、四期
				6	圆腹罐	陶	图2.271b，11		二里头三、四期
				7	圆腹罐	陶	图2.271b，13		二里头三、四期
				8	圆腹罐	陶	图2.271b，6		二里头三、四期
				9	圆腹罐	陶	图2.271b，8		二里头三、四期
				10	圆腹罐	陶	图2.271b，9		二里头三、四期
				11	甑	陶	图2.271c，4		二里头三、四期
				12	甑	陶	图2.271c，5		二里头三、四期
				13	缸	陶	图2.271b，15		二里头三、四期
				14	大口尊	陶	图2.271c，10		二里头三、四期
				15	石铲坯	石			不详
				16	去薄石片	石		图版二六五，5	不详
			H1	1	圆腹罐	陶	图2.271b，7		二里头三、四期
			H2	1	甑	陶	图2.271c，7		二里头三期
				2	甑	陶	图2.271c，1		二里头三期
				3	石镞	石	图2.271c，3		不详

续表

遗址信息			遗迹	登记号	器型	质地	图号		时代
序号	编号	名称					插图号	图版号	
255	Y201	西口孜	H3	1	深腹罐	陶	图2.271b，1		二里头四期
				2	深腹罐	陶	图2.271b，5		二里头四期
				3	圆腹罐	陶	图2.271b，10		二里头四期
				4	甑	陶	图2.271c，6		二里头四期
				5	捏口罐	陶	图2.271c，8		二里头四期
				6	缸	陶	图2.271b，14		二里头四期
				7	三足盘	陶	图2.271c，11		二里头四期
				8	石镰	石	图2.271c，2		不详
			H4	1	瓮	陶	图2.271c，9		二里头三期
				2	三足盘	陶	图2.271c，12		二里头三期
				3	石铲坯	石		图版二六五，4	不详
				4	石铲坯	石			不详
256	Y200	老周寨		1	罐	陶	图2.272b，3		仰韶中、晚期
				2	罐	陶	图2.272b，2		仰韶中、晚期
				3	釜形鼎	陶	图2.272b，6		仰韶中、晚期
				4	釜形鼎	陶	图2.272b，8		仰韶中、晚期
				5	釜形鼎	陶	图2.272b，4		仰韶中、晚期
				6	釜形鼎	陶	图2.272b，5		仰韶中、晚期
				7	釜形鼎	陶	图2.272b，7		仰韶中、晚期
				8	缸	陶	图2.272b，9		仰韶中、晚期
				9	盆	陶	图2.272b，10		仰韶中、晚期
				10	盆	陶	图2.272b，13		仰韶中、晚期
				11	盆	陶	图2.272b，12		仰韶中、晚期
				12	盆	陶	图2.272b，11		仰韶中、晚期
				13	钵	陶	图2.272b，16		仰韶中、晚期
				14	钵	陶	图2.272b，15		仰韶中、晚期
				15	尖底瓶	陶	图2.272b，14		仰韶中、晚期
				16	罐	陶	图2.272b，1		仰韶中、晚期
				17	罐	陶	图2.272b，18		西周
				18	罐	陶	图2.272b，17		西周
				19	石斧	石			不详
				20	石锤	石			不详
				21	石锤	石			不详
				22	石锤	石			不详
				23	石锤	石			不详
				24	石锤	石			不详

遗址信息			遗迹	登记号	器型	质地	图号		时代
序号	编号	名称					插图号	图版号	
256	Y200	老周寨		25	石铲坯	石		图版二六五，6	不详
				26	石铲坯	石			不详
				27	石铲坯	石			不详
				28	石锤	石			不详
				29	砍砸器	石			不详
				30	砍砸器	石			不详
				31	砍砸器	石			不详
				32	砍砸器	石			不详
				33	砺石	石			不详
				34	刮削器	石			不详
257	Y199	老屯寨		1	夹砂罐	陶	图2.273b，11		仰韶中、晚期
				2	瓮	陶	图2.273b，9		仰韶中、晚期
				3	瓮	陶	图2.273b，10		仰韶中、晚期
				4	泥质彩陶罐	陶	图2.273b，5		仰韶中、晚期
				5	钵	陶	图2.273b，6		仰韶中、晚期
				6	钵	陶	图2.273b，7		仰韶中、晚期
				7	罐	陶	图2.273c，1		龙山
				8	中口罐	陶	图2.273c，2		龙山
				9	中口罐	陶	图2.273c，7		龙山
				10	中口罐	陶	图2.273c，6		龙山
				11	器盖	陶	图2.273c，9		龙山
				12	瓮	陶	图2.273c，3		龙山
				13	瓮	陶	图2.273c，4		龙山
				14	壶	陶	图2.273c，5		龙山
				15	石锤	石	图2.273b，1		不详
				16	鬲	陶	图2.273c，10		殷墟
				17	纺轮	陶	图2.273b，3		仰韶中、晚期
				18	砺石	石	图2.273b，2		不详
				19	石铲	石	图2.273b，8		不详
				20	石铲	石	图2.273b，4		不详
			H1	1	大口罐	陶	图2.273c，8		龙山
258	Y198	屯寨西北		1	鬲	陶	图2.274b，2		二里岗晚期
				2	捏口罐	陶	图2.274b，8		二里岗晚期
				3	捏口罐	陶	图2.274b，7		二里岗晚期
				4	鬲	陶	图2.274b，1		殷墟晚期
				5	鬲	陶	图2.274b，3		殷墟晚期

续表

遗址信息			遗迹	登记号	器型	质地	图号		时代
序号	编号	名称					插图号	图版号	
258	Y198	屯寨西北		6	鬲	陶	图2.274b，5		西周晚期
				7	鬲	陶	图2.274b，6		西周晚期
				8	鬲	陶	图2.274b，4		西周晚期
				9	罐	陶	图2.274b，14		东周
				10	罐	陶	图2.274b，9		战国
				11	罐	陶	图2.274b，13		战国
				12	盆	陶	图2.274b，12		战国
				13	盆	陶	图2.274b，11		战国
				14	筒瓦	石	图2.274b，10		东周
259	Y204	布村东南		1	夹砂罐	陶	图2.275b，8		仰韶晚期
				2	刻槽盆	陶			仰韶晚期
				3	泥质罐	陶	图2.275b，2		仰韶晚期
				4	泥质罐	陶	图2.275b，1		仰韶晚期
				5	豆	陶	图2.275b，6		仰韶晚期
				6	钵	陶	图2.275b，4		仰韶晚期
				7	钵	陶	图2.275b，5		仰韶晚期
				8	盆	陶	图2.275b，7		战国
				9	盆	陶	图2.275b，3		战国
				10	石锤	石		图版二六六，1	不详
261	Y197	新寨北嘴		1	泥质罐	陶	图2.277b，7		仰韶晚期
				2	泥质彩陶罐	陶	图2.277b，4		仰韶晚期
				3	钵	陶	图2.277b，1		仰韶晚期
				4	尖底瓶	陶	图2.277b，2		仰韶晚期
				5	尖底瓶	陶	图2.277b，3		仰韶晚期
				6	鼎	陶	图2.277b，5		二里头二至四期
				7	圆陶片	陶	图2.277b，6		二里头二至四期
				8	石斧	石			不详
				9	石斧	石			不详
				10	石刀	石			不详
				11	石刀	石			不详
				12	石毛坯	石			不详
262	Y207	马河北		1	罐	陶	图2.278b，3		仰韶晚期
				2	盆	陶	图2.278b，2		仰韶晚期
				3	圈足盘	陶	图2.278b，5		仰韶晚期
				4	圈足	陶	图2.278b，4		仰韶晚期
263	Y208	马河		1	石凿	石			不详

续表

序号	遗址信息 编号	遗址信息 名称	遗迹	登记号	器型	质地	图号 插图号	图号 图版号	时代
263	Y208	马河		2	鬲	陶	图2.278b，1		战国
264	Y205	花张东北		1	盆	陶	图2.278b，6		战国
				2	缸	陶	图2.278b，7		战国
265	Y210	张湾西北		1	鼎	陶	图2.281b，5		仰韶中、晚期
				2	夹砂罐	陶	图2.281b，3		仰韶中、晚期
				3	盆	陶	图2.281b，4		仰韶中、晚期
				4	泥质彩陶罐	陶	图2.281b，6		仰韶中、晚期
				5	泥质彩陶罐	陶	图2.281b，7		仰韶中、晚期
				6	盆	陶	图2.281b，8		仰韶中、晚期
				7	罐	陶	图2.281c，10		龙山晚期
				8	器盖	陶	图2.281c，9		龙山晚期
				9	豆	陶	图2.281c，4		龙山晚期
				10	壶	陶	图2.281d，2		龙山晚期
				11	深腹罐	陶	图2.281e，7		二里头
				12	圆腹罐	陶	图2.281e，2		二里头
				13	圆腹罐	陶	图2.281e，3		二里头
				14	圆腹罐	陶	图2.281e，4		二里头
				15	圆腹罐	陶	图2.281e，5		二里头
				16	圆腹罐	陶	图2.281e，6		二里头
				17	缸	陶	图2.281e，9		二里头
				18	鬲	陶	图2.281e，1		西周
				19	罐	陶	图2.281e，8		东周
				20	石斧	石	图2.281b，1		不详
				21	石斧	石		图版二六六，2	不详
				22	石刀	石	图2.281b，2		不详
				23	石铲	石		图版二六六，3	不详
				24	石铲	石		图版二六六，4	不详
			H1	1	盆	陶	图2.281d，1		龙山晚期
				2	扁壶	陶	图2.281c，7	图版三七三，4	龙山晚期
				3	扁壶	陶	图2.281c，8	图版三七三，5	龙山晚期
				4	瓮	陶	图2.281d，8	图版三七三，6	龙山晚期
				5	瓮	陶	图2.281d，7		龙山晚期
				6	瓮	陶	图2.281d，4		龙山晚期
				7	瓮	陶	图2.281d，6		龙山晚期
				8	折腹盆	陶	图2.281d，9	图版三七四，1	龙山晚期
				9	折腹盆	陶	图2.281d，10		龙山晚期

续表

遗址信息			遗迹	登记号	器型	质地	图号		时代
序号	编号	名称					插图号	图版号	
265	Y210	张湾西北	H1	10	豆	陶	图2.281c，1		龙山晚期
				11	豆	陶	图2.281c，5		龙山晚期
			H2	1	大口罐	陶	图2.281c，11		龙山晚期
				2	大口罐	陶	图2.281c，6		龙山晚期
				3	瓮	陶	图2.281d，5		龙山晚期
				4	瓮	陶	图2.281d，3		龙山晚期
				5	豆	陶	图2.281c，2		龙山晚期
				6	豆	陶	图2.281c，3		龙山晚期
				7	瓮	陶			龙山晚期
				8	钵	陶	图2.281d，11		龙山晚期
			H3	1	石片	石			不详
266	Y209	王湾西北		1	夹砂罐	陶	图2.282b，1		仰韶中、晚期
				2	釜形鼎	陶	图2.282b，7		仰韶中、晚期
				3	鼎	陶	图2.282b，3		仰韶中、晚期
				4	缸	陶	图2.282b，2		仰韶中、晚期
				5	泥质彩陶罐	陶	图2.282b，4		仰韶中、晚期
				6	泥质彩陶罐	陶	图2.282b，5		仰韶中、晚期
				7	泥质彩陶罐	陶	图2.282b，6		仰韶中、晚期
				8	钵	陶	图2.282b，9		仰韶中、晚期
				9	钵	陶	图2.282b，8		仰韶中、晚期
				10	豆	陶	图2.282b，10		仰韶中、晚期
				11	圆陶片	陶	图2.282b，11		仰韶中、晚期
				12	鬲	陶	图2.282b，12		殷墟
				13	石斧	石			不详
				14	石斧	石			不详
267	Y222	柏谷坞东		1	鬲足	陶	图2.283b，1		二里岗
268	Y215	金屯东		1	瓮	陶	图2.283b，3		仰韶晚期
				2	盆	陶	图2.283b，2		仰韶晚期
269	Y214	北吴家湾		1	泥质罐	陶	图2.283b，4		仰韶中、晚期
				2	钵	陶	图2.283b，6		仰韶中、晚期
				3	钵	陶	图2.283b，7		仰韶中、晚期
				4	钵	陶	图2.283b，5		仰韶中、晚期
				5	中口罐	陶	图2.283b，11		龙山晚期
				6	罐	陶	图2.283b，9		龙山晚期
				7	瓮	陶	图2.283b，8		龙山晚期
				8	甗	陶	图2.283b，10		二里头

续表

遗址信息			遗迹	登记号	器型	质地	图号		时代
序号	编号	名称					插图号	图版号	
269	Y214	北吴家湾		9	假腹豆	陶	图2.283b，12		二里岗
270	Y213	南吴家塆东南		1	鼎	陶	图2.286b，3		仰韶晚期
				2	泥质彩陶罐	陶	图2.286b，1		仰韶晚期
				3	泥质彩陶罐	陶	图2.286b，2		仰韶晚期
				4	缸	陶	图2.286b，4		仰韶晚期
				5	盆	陶	图2.286b，14		仰韶晚期
				6	盆	陶	图2.286b，5		仰韶晚期
				7	钵	陶	图2.286b，6		仰韶晚期
				8	豆	陶	图2.286b，7		仰韶晚期
				9	尖底瓶	陶	图2.286b，12		仰韶晚期
				10	罐	陶	图2.286b，9		龙山晚期
				11	瓮	陶	图2.286b，8		龙山晚期
				12	盆	陶	图2.286b，15		二里头
				13	鬲	陶	图2.286b，13		二里岗晚期
				14	鬲	陶	图2.286b，10		二里岗
				15	瓿	陶	图2.286b，11		二里岗
				16	罐	陶	图2.286b，16		东周
				17	白烧石	石		图版二六六，5	不详
271	Y211	林小寨		1	高领罐	陶	图2.286b，17		二里头
273	Y221	邱河西		1	器盖	陶	图2.289b，1	图版三二〇，1	仰韶中期
				2	杯	陶	图2.289b，7		龙山晚期
				3	豆	陶	图2.289b，5		龙山晚期
				4	豆	陶	图2.289b，3		龙山晚期
				5	圆腹罐	陶	图2.289b，2		二里头三、四期
				6	大口尊	陶	图2.289b，4		二里头三、四期
				7	鬲	陶	图2.289b，6		东周
				8	盆	陶	图2.289b，9		东周
				9	石凿	石			不详
274	Y220	凤凰台南		1	罐	陶	图2.289b，11		龙山晚期
				2	瓮	陶	图2.289b，10		龙山晚期
				3	盆	陶	图2.289b，8		龙山晚期
275	Y217	老吊桥寨		1	鬲	陶			西周中晚期
276	Y216	吊桥寨东南		1	鼎	陶	图2.292b，6		仰韶晚期
				2	缸	陶	图2.292b，3		仰韶晚期
				3	泥质彩陶罐	陶	图2.292b，7		仰韶晚期
				4	泥质彩陶罐	陶	图2.292b，8		仰韶晚期

续表

遗址信息			遗迹	登记号	器型	质地	图号		时代
序号	编号	名称					插图号	图版号	
276	Y216	吊桥寨东南		5	盆	陶	图2.292b, 10		仰韶晚期
				6	钵	陶	图2.292b, 2		仰韶晚期
				7	豆	陶	图2.292b, 4		仰韶晚期
				8	钵	陶	图2.292b, 9		仰韶晚期
				9	杯	陶	图2.292b, 1		仰韶晚期
				10	罐	陶	图2.292b, 11		龙山晚期
				11	豆	陶	图2.292b, 5		龙山晚期
				12	鬲	陶	图2.292c, 2		西周
				13	鬲	陶	图2.292c, 3		西周
				14	罐	陶	图2.292c, 14		二里岗晚期
				15	盆	陶	图2.292c, 7		西周
				16	盆	陶	图2.292c, 10		殷墟
				17	鬲	陶	图2.292c, 1		西周
				18	鬲	陶	图2.292c, 5		战国
				19	鬲	陶	图2.292c, 6		战国
				20	鬲	陶	图2.292c, 4		战国
				21	罐	陶	图2.292c, 13		战国
				22	盆	陶	图2.292c, 11		战国
				23	盆	陶	图2.292c, 8		战国
				24	盆	陶	图2.292c, 9		战国
				25	纺轮	陶	图2.292c, 12		不详
				26	石斧	石		图版二六六, 6	不详
				27	石斧	石			不详
				28	砍砸器	石			不详
				29	石杵	石		图版二六七, 1	不详
				30	砺石	石		图版二六七, 2	不详
				31	石锤	石		图版二六七, 3	不详
				32	石锤	石			不详
				33	石锤	石			不详
277	Y218	北寨东南		1	罐	陶	图2.293b, 5		龙山早期
				2	鼎	陶	图2.293b, 6		仰韶中、晚期
				3	罐	陶	图2.293b, 4		仰韶中、晚期
				4	钵	陶	图2.293b, 7		仰韶中、晚期
				5	钵	陶	图2.293b, 2		仰韶中、晚期
				6	钵	陶	图2.293b, 3		仰韶中、晚期
				7	钵	陶	图2.293b, 1		仰韶中、晚期

续表

遗址信息			遗迹	登记号	器型	质地	图号		时代
序号	编号	名称					插图号	图版号	
278	Y219	北寨北		1	鼎	陶	图2.294b,6		仰韶晚期
				2	鼎	陶	图2.294b,9		仰韶晚期
				3	鼎	陶	图2.294b,7		仰韶晚期
				4	鼎	陶	图2.294b,8		仰韶晚期
				5	罐	陶	图2.294b,4		仰韶晚期
				6	瓮	陶	图2.294b,3		仰韶晚期
				7	盆	陶	图2.294b,5		仰韶晚期
				8	钵	陶	图2.294b,1		仰韶晚期
				9	钵	陶	图2.294b,2		仰韶晚期
				10	石锤	石		图版二六七,4	不详
279	113	陈河东北		1	石坯	石		图版二六七,5	不详
				2	鬲	陶	图2.295b,17		西周
				3	簋	陶	图2.295b,1		西周
				4	簋	陶	图2.295b,2		西周
				5	罐	陶	图2.295b,3		西周
				6	罐	陶	图2.295b,4		西周
280	112	陈河北		1	石器	石		图版二六七,6	不详
				2	石斧	石		图版二六八,1	不详
				3	石片	石		图版二六八,2	不详
				4	石料	石		图版二六八,3	不详
				5	圆腹罐	陶	图2.295b,8	图版三八六,3	二里头二期晚
				6	圆腹罐	陶	图2.295b,7	图版三九三,6	二里头三期早
				7	深腹罐	陶	图2.295b,9	图版三九四,1	二里头三期晚
				8	鬲	陶	图2.295b,11		二里岗早期
				9	簋	陶	图2.295b,5		二里岗早期
			H1	1	圆腹罐	陶	图2.295b,6	图版三八六,2	二里头二期
			H2	1	深腹罐	陶	图2.295b,10		二里头四期
281	111	化寨东		1	圆腹罐	陶	图2.295b,13	图版三九四,2	二里头三期晚
				2	深腹罐	陶	图2.295b,14	图版三九四,3	二里头三期晚
				3	鬲	陶	图2.295b,12	图版四六四,4	东周
				4	盆	陶	图2.295b,16	图版四六〇,6	战国
				5	罐	陶	图2.295b,15	图版四六一,1	战国
282	109	盆窑寨东南		1	石铲	石		图版二六八,4	不详
				2	罐形鼎	陶	图2.298b,6	图版三四四,5	仰韶晚期
				3	罐形鼎	陶	图2.298b,1	图版三四四,6	仰韶晚期

续表

遗址信息			遗迹	登记号	器型	质地	图号		时代
序号	编号	名称					插图号	图版号	
282	109	盆窑寨东南		4	罐	陶	图2.298b，4	图版三四五，1	仰韶晚期
				5	鬲	陶	图2.298c，1		西周晚期
				6	罐	陶	图2.298c，3		战国
				7	罐	陶	图2.298c，2		战国
				8	盆	陶	图2.298c，6	图版四六一，5	战国
				9	盆	陶	图2.298c，8		战国
				10	鬲	陶	图2.298c，5		战国
				11	蚌料	蚌		图版二六八，5	不详
			H1	1	罐形鼎	陶	图2.298b，3	图版三四四，3	仰韶晚期
				2	罐形鼎	陶	图2.298b，2	图版三四四，4	仰韶晚期
				3	缸	陶	图2.298b，7		仰韶晚期
				4	缸	陶	图2.298b，5		仰韶晚期
				5	敛口钵	陶	图2.298b，8		仰韶晚期
			H2	1	豆	陶	图2.298c，12	图版四六一，2	战国
				2	豆	陶	图2.298c，4		战国
				3	盆	陶	图2.298c，7		战国
				4	罐	陶	图2.298c，10	图版四六一，3	战国
				5	罐	陶	图2.298c，9		战国
				6	平底盆	陶	图2.298c，11	图版四六一，4	战国
284	101	东王河东南		1	盂	陶	图2.300b，1	图版三四五，2	仰韶晚期
				2	鼎	陶	图2.300b，4		龙山早期
				3	缸	陶	图2.300b，3	图版三五五，6	龙山早期
				4	瓮	陶	图2.300b，2	图版三九四，4	二里头三期早
				5	深腹罐	陶	图2.300b，5	图版三八六，4	二里头二期晚
285	100	东王河北		1	石料	石		图版二六八，6	不详
				2	砍砸器	石		图版二六九，1	不详
				3	砍砸器	石		图版二六九，2	不详
				4	砍砸器	石		图版二六九，3	不详
				5	石锤	石		图版二六九，4	不详
				6	石料	石		图版二六九，5	不详
				7	小口罐	陶	图2.300b，6	图版三四五，3	仰韶晚期
				8	盆	陶	图2.300b，7		战国
				9	盆	陶	图2.300b，8	图版四六一，6	战国
				10	罐	陶	图2.300b，9		战国
286	099	东王河		1	烧石	石		图版二六九，6	不详
				2	高柄杯	陶	图2.300b，10	图版三七四，2	龙山晚期

续表

遗址信息			遗迹	登记号	器型	质地	图号		时代
序号	编号	名称					插图号	图版号	
287	108	陶化店水库东		1	器盖	陶	图2.300b, 11	图版三九四, 5	二里头三期
288	104	李家湾东南		1	鬲	陶	图2.305b, 14	图版四一八, 3	二里岗晚期
				2	豆	陶	图2.305b, 7	图版四一八, 4	二里岗晚期
				3	盆	陶	图2.305b, 5	图版四一三, 6	二里岗早期
				4	圆陶片	陶	图2.305b, 9		不详
289	128	铺刘北		1	鬲	陶	图2.305b, 15		战国
290	107	吴家湾东南		1	残石器	石		图版二七〇, 1	不详
				2	盆	陶	图2.305b, 13	图版四一八, 5	二里岗晚期
				3	盆	陶	图2.305b, 12		春秋晚战国早
291	105	段西村西北		1	钵	陶	图2.305b, 4	图版三四五, 4	仰韶晚期
292	106	段东村东北		1	罐形鼎	陶	图2.305b, 8	图版三四五, 5	仰韶晚期
				2	夹砂罐	陶	图2.305b, 1	图版三四五, 6	仰韶晚期
				3	敛口缸	陶	图2.305b, 10	图版三四六, 1	仰韶晚期
				4	盆	陶	图2.305b, 11	图版三四六, 2	仰韶晚期
				5	泥质罐	陶	图2.305b, 2	图版三四六, 3	仰韶晚期
				6	泥质罐	陶	图2.305b, 3	图版三四六, 4	仰韶晚期
				7	骨镞	骨	图2.305b, 6	图版二七〇, 2	不详
293	098	苗湾东南		1	罐	陶	图2.310b, 9		仰韶中、晚期
				2	刀	陶	图2.310b, 7	图版三二〇, 2	仰韶中期
				3	盆	陶	图2.310b, 3		仰韶中、晚期
				4	盆	陶	图2.310b, 4		仰韶中、晚期
				5	盆	陶	图2.310b, 5		仰韶中、晚期
				6	盆	陶	图2.310b, 6		仰韶中、晚期
294	097	苗湾C		1	鼎	陶	图2.310b, 10	图版三四六, 5	仰韶晚期
				2	泥质彩陶罐	陶	图2.310b, 8	图版三四六, 6	仰韶晚期
				3	盆	陶	图2.310b, 2		仰韶中、晚期
				4	盆	陶	图2.310b, 1		仰韶中、晚期
				5	钵	陶	图2.310b, 11		仰韶中、晚期
295	096	苗湾B		1	石杵	石	图2.312b, 10	图版二七〇, 3	不详
				2	鼎	陶	图2.312b, 2		仰韶中、晚期
				3	鼎	陶	图2.312b, 4	图版三四七, 1	仰韶晚期
				4	鼎	陶	图2.312b, 5		仰韶中、晚期
				5	小口尖底瓶	陶	图2.312b, 7		仰韶中、晚期
				6	小口尖底瓶	陶	图2.312b, 8		仰韶中、晚期
				7	小口尖底瓶	陶	图2.312b, 11		仰韶中、晚期
				8	盆	陶	图2.312b, 1		仰韶中、晚期

续表

遗址信息			遗迹	登记号	器型	质地	图号		时代
序号	编号	名称					插图号	图版号	
295	096	苗湾B		9	敛口瓮	陶	图2.312b，12		仰韶中、晚期
				10	罐	陶	图2.312b，14		仰韶中、晚期
				11	罐	陶	图2.312b，15		仰韶中、晚期
				12	罐	陶	图2.312b，13		仰韶中、晚期
				13	罐	陶	图2.312b，9		仰韶中、晚期
				14	罐	陶	图2.312b，3	图版三四七，2	仰韶晚期
				15	罐	陶	图2.312b，6	图版三二〇，3	仰韶中期
				16	盆	陶	图2.312c，3		仰韶中、晚期
				17	盆	陶	图2.312c，4		仰韶中、晚期
				18	碗	陶	图2.312c，8		仰韶中、晚期
				19	敛口盆	陶	图2.312c，1		仰韶中、晚期
				20	敛口盆	陶	图2.312c，5	图版三二〇，4	仰韶中期
				21	敛口盆	陶	图2.312c，9	图版三四七，3	仰韶晚期
				22	敛口盆	陶	图2.312c，6	图版三二〇，5	仰韶中期
				23	敛口盆	陶	图2.312c，12		仰韶中、晚期
				24	敛口盆	陶	图2.312c，7	图版三二〇，6	仰韶中期
				25	罐	陶	图2.312c，13		仰韶中、晚期
				26	盆	陶	图2.312c，10		仰韶中、晚期
				27	鼎	陶	图2.312c，14	图版三四七，4	仰韶晚期
				28	罐	陶	图2.312c，11	图版三四七，5	仰韶晚期
				29	鬲	陶	图2.312c，2	图版四二九，6	西周
296	095	苗湾A		1	罐	陶	图2.313b，5		仰韶中、晚期
				2	豆	陶	图2.313b，9		仰韶中、晚期
				3	彩陶罐	陶	图2.313b，1	图版三四七，6	仰韶晚期
				4	彩陶罐	陶	图2.313b，3	图版三二一，1	仰韶中期
				5	彩陶罐	陶	图2.313b，2	图版三二一，2	仰韶中期
				6	彩陶罐	陶	图2.313b，7	图版三四八，1	仰韶晚期
				7	彩陶罐	陶	图2.313b，4	图版三四八，2	仰韶晚期
				8	盆	陶	图2.313b，6	图版三四八，3	仰韶晚期
				9	盆	陶	图2.313b，8	图版三四八，4	仰韶晚期
				10	矮领瓮	陶	图2.313b，10	图版三四八，5	仰韶晚期
				11	高领瓮	陶	图2.313b，15		仰韶中、晚期
				12	矮领瓮	陶	图2.313b，11		仰韶中、晚期
				13	鼎	陶	图2.313b，14		仰韶中、晚期
				14	罐	陶	图2.313b，12		仰韶中、晚期
				15	罐	陶	图2.313b，13	图版三二一，3	仰韶中期

续表

遗址信息			遗迹	登记号	器型	质地	图号		时代
序号	编号	名称					插图号	图版号	
296	095	苗湾A		16	盆	陶	图2.313c，1		仰韶中、晚期
				17	钵	陶	图2.313c，2		仰韶中、晚期
				18	钵	陶	图2.313c，3	图版三二一，4	仰韶中期
				19	钵	陶	图2.313c，5	图版三四八，6	仰韶晚期
				20	折腹盆	陶	图2.313c，8	图版三二一，5	仰韶中期
				21	钵	陶	图2.313c，4		仰韶中、晚期
				22	瓮	陶	图2.313c，10		仰韶中、晚期
				23	鼎	陶	图2.313c，7	图版三五六，1	龙山早期
				24	鼎	陶	图2.313c，11	图版三五六，2	龙山早期
				25	鼎	陶	图2.313c，9	图版三五六，3	龙山早期
				26	鼎	陶	图2.313c，12	图版三五六，4	龙山早期
				27	盘	陶	图2.313c，13		龙山早期
				28	折腹钵	陶	图2.313c，15		龙山早期
				29	折腹钵	陶	图2.313c，14	图版三五六，5	龙山早期
				30	罐	陶	图2.313c，6		龙山早期
298	Y121	邢村东		1	夹砂罐	陶	图2.316b，8		仰韶晚期
				2	鼎	陶	图2.316b，4		仰韶晚期
				3	鼎	陶	图2.316b，5		仰韶晚期
				4	缸	陶	图2.316b，7		龙山晚期
				5	罐	陶	图2.316b，6		仰韶晚期
				6	罐	陶	图2.316b，3		仰韶晚期
				7	罐	陶	图2.316b，2		仰韶晚期
				8	杯形器	陶	图2.316b，1	图版三四九，1	仰韶晚期
				9	石斧	石		图版二七〇，4	不详
				10	砺石	石		图版二七〇，5	不详
299	Y123	半个寨		1	鼎	陶	图2.317b，5		龙山早期
				2	鼎	陶	图2.317b，10		仰韶中、晚期
				3	盆	陶	图2.317b，4		仰韶中、晚期
				4	盆	陶	图2.317b，3		仰韶中、晚期
				5	瓮	陶	图2.317b，11		仰韶中、晚期
				6	钵	陶	图2.317b，8		仰韶中、晚期
				7	钵	陶	图2.317b，6		仰韶中、晚期
				8	钵	陶	图2.317b，7		仰韶中、晚期
				9	钵	陶	图2.317b，9		仰韶中、晚期
				10	中口罐	陶	图2.317c，7		龙山
				11	中口罐	陶	图2.317c，3		龙山

续表

遗址信息			遗迹	登记号	器型	质地	图号		时代
序号	编号	名称					插图号	图版号	
299	Y123	半个寨		12	中口罐	陶	图2.317c, 6		龙山
				13	中口罐	陶	图2.317c, 2		龙山
				14	中口罐	陶	图2.317c, 5		龙山
				15	瓮	陶			龙山
				16	器盖	陶	图2.317c, 4		龙山
				17	纺轮	陶	图2.317c, 1		龙山
				18	石锛坯	石	图2.317b, 2	图版二七〇, 6	不详
				19	石凿	石	图2.317b, 1	图版二七一, 1	不详
300	Y120	邢村		1	鬲	陶	图2.318b, 1		二里岗晚期
301	Y119	赵城水库东		1	鼎	陶	图2.318b, 2		仰韶晚期
				2	罐	陶	图2.318b, 3		仰韶晚期
				3	罐	陶	图2.318b, 5		仰韶晚期
				4	环	陶	图2.318b, 4		仰韶晚期
302	Y077	赵城		1	瓮	陶	图2.320c, 10		仰韶中、晚期
				2	瓮	陶	图2.320c, 14		仰韶中、晚期
				3	瓮	陶	图2.320c, 11		仰韶中、晚期
				4	瓮	陶	图2.320c, 13		仰韶中、晚期
				5	瓮	陶	图2.320c, 8		仰韶中、晚期
				6	瓮	陶	图2.320c, 9		仰韶中、晚期
				7	瓮	陶	图2.320c, 12		仰韶中、晚期
				8	夹砂罐	陶	图2.320c, 7		仰韶中、晚期
				9	夹砂罐	陶	图2.320c, 5		仰韶中、晚期
				10	夹砂罐	陶	图2.320c, 2		仰韶中、晚期
				11	夹砂罐	陶	图2.320c, 4	图版三二三, 5	仰韶中、晚期
				12	夹砂罐	陶	图2.320c, 6	图版三二三, 6	仰韶中、晚期
				13	夹砂罐	陶	图2.320c, 3	图版三二四, 1	仰韶中、晚期
				14	鼎	陶	图2.320c, 1		仰韶中、晚期
				15	鼎	陶	图2.320c, 15		仰韶中、晚期
				16	彩陶罐	陶	图2.320d, 6		仰韶中、晚期
				17	彩陶罐	陶	图2.320d, 7		仰韶中、晚期
				18	泥质罐	陶	图2.320d, 16		仰韶中、晚期
				19	彩陶罐	陶	图2.320d, 10		仰韶中、晚期
				20	盆	陶	图2.320d, 14		仰韶中、晚期
				21	盆	陶	图2.320d, 9		仰韶中、晚期
				22	盆	陶	图2.320d, 15		仰韶中、晚期
				23	盆	陶	图2.320d, 11		仰韶中、晚期

续表

遗址信息			遗迹	登记号	器型	质地	图号		时代
序号	编号	名称					插图号	图版号	
				24	盆	陶	图2.320d，12		仰韶中、晚期
				25	盆	陶	图2.320d，13		仰韶中、晚期
				26	彩陶罐	陶	图2.320d，8		仰韶中、晚期
				27	尖底瓶	陶	图2.320d，3		仰韶中、晚期
				28	尖底瓶	陶	图2.320d，4		仰韶中、晚期
				29	尖底瓶	陶	图2.320d，5		仰韶中、晚期
				30	钵	陶	图2.320d，1		仰韶中、晚期
				31	钵	陶	图2.320d，2		仰韶早期
				32	豆	陶	图2.320e，6		仰韶中、晚期
				33	碗	陶	图2.320e，9		仰韶中、晚期
				34	碗	陶	图2.320e，8		仰韶中、晚期
				35	碗	陶	图2.320e，7		仰韶中、晚期
				36	碗	陶	图2.320e，10		仰韶中、晚期
				37	盆	陶	图2.320e，11		仰韶中、晚期
				38	彩陶片	陶			仰韶中、晚期
				39	彩陶片	陶			仰韶中、晚期
				40	彩陶片	陶			仰韶中、晚期
302	Y077	赵城		41	彩陶片	陶			仰韶中、晚期
				42	彩陶片	陶			仰韶中、晚期
				43	罐	陶	图2.320e，14		龙山
				44	罐	陶	图2.320e，13		龙山
				45	圈足	陶	图2.320e，12		龙山
				46	纺轮	陶	图2.320e，1		仰韶中、晚期
				47	环	陶	图2.320e，2		仰韶中、晚期
				48	环	陶	图2.320e，5		仰韶中、晚期
				49	环	陶	图2.320e，4		仰韶中、晚期
				50	环	陶	图2.320e，3		仰韶中、晚期
				51	白灰面	陶			仰韶
				52	石斧	石			不详
				53	石斧	石			不详
				54	石斧	石	图2.320b，3	图版二七一，4	不详
				55	石斧	石	图2.320b，1	图版二七一，5	不详
				56	石斧	石	图2.320b，2	图版二七一，6	不详
				57	石斧	石			不详
				58	石刀	石			不详
				59	石磨棒	石		图版二七二，1	不详

续表

遗址信息			遗迹	登记号	器型	质地	图号		时代
序号	编号	名称					插图号	图版号	
302	Y077	赵城		60	石料	石		图版二七二，2	不详
				61	石料	石		图版二七二，3	不详
				62	石料	石		图版二七二，4	不详
				63	石网坠	石	图2.320b，4	图版二七二，5	不详
				64	石球	石		图版二七二，6	不详
				65	石环	石	图2.320b，7	图版二七三，1	不详
				66	石环	石	图2.320b，6	图版二七三，2	不详
				67	石杵	石			不详
				68	颜料块	石	图2.320b，5	图版二七三，3	不详
				69	砺石	石			不详
				70	石铲坯	石			不详
				71	石铲坯	石		图版二七三，4	不详
			H1	1	砺石坯料	石		图版二七一，2	不详
				2	砺石坯料	石		图版二七一，3	不详
303	Y079	赵城西南		1	盆	陶	图2.321b，6		仰韶
				2	盆	陶	图2.321b，2		春秋
304	Y078	赵城西		1	鼎	陶	图2.321b，4		仰韶中期
				2	盆	陶	图2.321b，1		仰韶中期
				3	盆	陶	图2.321b，3		仰韶中期
				4	盆	陶	图2.321b，7		仰韶中期
				5	环	陶	图2.321b，5		仰韶中期
306	Y116	赵城西北		1	鬲	陶	图2.324b，2		西周
				2	罐	陶	图2.324b，1		东周
307	Y115	高村东北		1	鬲	陶	图2.324b，6		二里岗
				2	鬲	陶	图2.324b，4		二里岗
				3	鬲	陶	图2.324b，5		二里岗
308	Y118	府店东南		1	深腹罐	陶	图2.324b，10		裴李岗晚期或仰韶早期
				2	深腹罐	陶			裴李岗晚期或仰韶早期
				3	三足钵	陶	图2.324b，3		裴李岗晚期或仰韶早期
				4	钵	陶	图2.324b，9		裴李岗晚期或仰韶早期
				5	钵	陶	图2.324b，8		裴李岗晚期或仰韶早期

续表

遗址信息			遗迹	登记号	器型	质地	图号		时代
序号	编号	名称					插图号	图版号	
308	Y118	府店东南	H1	1	碗	陶	图2.324b，7		裴李岗晚期或仰韶早期
309	Y080	小相西南		1	鼎	陶	图2.327b，3		仰韶晚期
				2	泥质罐	陶	图2.327b，1		仰韶晚期
				3	大口罐	陶	图2.327b，5		龙山晚期
				4	斝	陶	图2.327b，2		龙山晚期
				5	器盖	陶	图2.327b，6	图版三七四，3	龙山晚期
				6	鬲	陶	图2.327b，4		东周
				7	豆柄	陶	图2.327b，7		东周
				8	石料	石			不详
310	Y114	颜良寨水库西南		1	石饼	石			不详
				2	石钺	石		图版二七三，5	不详
				3	石铲坯	石		图版二七三，6	不详
				4	石条形器	石	图2.328b，5	图版二七四，1	不详
				5	燧石块	石		图版二七四，2	不详
				6	中口罐	陶	图2.328b，10		龙山晚期
				7	中口罐	陶	图2.328b，6		龙山晚期
				8	中口罐	陶	图2.328b，4		龙山晚期
				9	小罐	陶	图2.328b，3		龙山晚期
				10	鼎	陶	图2.328b，11		龙山晚期
				11	斝	陶			龙山晚期
				12	斝	陶			龙山晚期
				13	斝	陶			龙山晚期
				14	瓮	陶	图2.328b，7		龙山晚期
				15	瓮	陶	图2.328b，8		龙山晚期
				16	瓮	陶	图2.328b，9		龙山晚期
				17	泥质罐	陶	图2.328c，6		龙山晚期
				18	折腹盆	陶	图2.328c，7		龙山晚期
				19	碗	陶	图2.328c，3		龙山晚期
				20	器盖	陶	图2.328c，4	图版三七四，4	龙山晚期
				21	钵	陶	图2.328c，2		龙山晚期
				22	豆	陶	图2.328c，1		龙山晚期
				23	深腹罐	陶	图2.328d，1		二里岗晚期
				24	圆腹罐	陶	图2.328d，4		二里岗晚期
				25	盆	陶	图2.328d，5		二里岗晚期
				26	盆	陶	图2.328d，7		二里岗晚期

续表

遗址信息			遗迹	登记号	器型	质地	图号		时代
序号	编号	名称					插图号	图版号	
310	Y114	颜良寨水库西南		27	鬲	陶	图2.328d，6		东周
				28	罐	陶	图2.328d，8		东周
				29	豆	陶	图2.328d，2		东周
				30	豆	陶	图2.328d，3		东周
				31	石斧	石	图2.328b，2	图版二七四，3	不详
				32	石斧	石		图版二七四，4	不详
				33	石斧	石		图版二七四，5	不详
				34	石斧	石		图版二七四，6	不详
				35	石刀坯	石	图2.328b，1	图版二七五，1	不详
				36	石刀坯	石		图版二七五，2	不详
				37	石刀坯	石		图版二七五，3	不详
				38	石镰坯	石		图版二七五，4	不详
				39	石凿	石			不详
				40	石凿	石		图版二七五，5	不详
				41	石锤	石		图版二七五，6	不详
				42	石锤	石		图版二七六，1	不详
				43	石杵	石		图版二七六，2	不详
				44	石杵	石		图版二七六，3	不详
				45	石杵	石			不详
			H1	1	碗	陶	图2.328c，5		龙山晚期
311	Y084	小相西		1	鬲	陶	图2.329b，1		东周
				2	盆	陶	图2.329b，3		东周
				3	罐	陶	图2.329b，2		东周
				4	器耳	陶	图2.329b，4		东周
				5	罐	陶			东周
				6	石饼	陶		图版二七六，4	不详
312	Y087	颜良寨水库西		1	大口罐	陶	图2.330b，2		龙山晚期
				2	大口罐	陶	图2.330b，1		龙山晚期
				3	大口罐	陶	图2.330b，3		龙山晚期
				4	中口罐	陶	图2.330b，11		龙山晚期
				5	瓮	陶	图2.330b，9		龙山晚期
				6	罐	陶	图2.330b，8		龙山晚期
				7	罐	陶	图2.330b，7		龙山晚期
				8	折腹盆	陶	图2.330b，13		龙山晚期
				9	碗	陶	图2.330b，10		龙山晚期
				10	盆	陶	图2.330c，1		二里头

续表

遗址信息			遗迹	登记号	器型	质地	图号		时代
序号	编号	名称					插图号	图版号	
				11	瓮	陶	图2.330c，16		春秋晚期
				12	鬲	陶	图2.330c，15		东周
				13	鬲	陶	图2.330c，17		东周
				14	罐	陶	图2.330c，10		东周
				15	罐	陶	图2.330c，9		春秋
				16	鬲	陶	图2.330c，5		春秋
				17	瓮	陶	图2.330c，6		春秋晚战国早
				18	豆	陶	图2.330c，11		东周
				19	盆	陶	图2.330c，7		战国
				20	豆	陶	图2.330c，12		战国
				21	豆	陶	图2.330c，13		战国
				22	豆	陶	图2.330c，14		战国
				23	石斧	石		图版二七六，5	不详
				24	石斧	石		图版二七六，6	不详
				25	石斧	石		图版二七七，1	不详
				26	石斧	石		图版二七七，2	不详
312	Y087	颜良寨水库西		27	石刀坯	石		图版二七七，3	不详
				28	石刀坯	石		图版二七七，4	不详
				29	石料	石		图版二七七，5	不详
				30	石刀坯	石			不详
				31	石刀坯	石			不详
				32	石镰	石		图版二七七，6	不详
				33	石铲	石		图版二七八，1	不详
				34	石残毛坯	石		图版二七八，2	不详
				35	石饼	石			不详
				36	石刮削器	石			不详
			H1	1	大口罐	陶	图2.330b，6		龙山晚期
			H2	1	壶	陶	图2.330c，3		龙山晚期
				2	器盖	陶	图2.330c，2		龙山晚期
			H4	1	壶	陶	图2.330c，4		龙山晚期
			H5	1	大口罐	陶	图2.330b，4		龙山晚期
				2	大口罐	陶	图2.330b，12		龙山晚期
			H6	1	器盖	陶			龙山晚期
				2	罐	陶	图2.330b，5		龙山晚期
				3	豆	陶	图2.330c，8		龙山晚期

续表

遗址信息			遗迹	登记号	器型	质地	图号		时代
序号	编号	名称					插图号	图版号	
313	Y124	府店东	H1	1	鼎	陶	图2.331b, 9		裴李岗
				2	钵	陶	图2.331b, 10		裴李岗
				3	三足钵	陶	图2.331b, 4		裴李岗
				4	碗	陶	图2.331b, 14		裴李岗
				1	罐	陶	图2.331b, 8		裴李岗
				2	罐	陶	图2.331b, 7		裴李岗
				3	罐	陶	图2.331b, 6		裴李岗
				4	钵	陶	图2.331b, 12		裴李岗
				5	钵	陶	图2.331b, 13		裴李岗
				6	钵	陶	图2.331b, 11		裴李岗
				7	三足钵	陶	图2.331b, 5		裴李岗
				8	碗	陶	图2.331b, 15		裴李岗
				9	石镰	石	图2.331b, 1	图版二七八, 3	不详
				10	石珠	石	图2.331b, 3	图版二七八, 4	不详
				11	石镰	石	图2.331b, 2	图版二七八, 5	不详
				12	磨盘	石		图版二七八, 6	不详
				13	磨盘	石			不详
314	Y085	小相西北		1	瓮	陶	图2.332b, 1		二里头
				2	盆	陶	图2.332b, 4		二里头
				3	深腹罐	陶	图2.332b, 3		二里岗晚期
				4	盆	陶	图2.332b, 9		殷墟晚期
				5	盆	陶	图2.332b, 7		殷墟晚期
				6	瓮	陶	图2.332b, 8		春秋晚期
				7	盆	陶	图2.332b, 6		春秋晚期
				8	盆	陶	图2.332b, 5		春秋晚期
				9	豆	陶	图2.332b, 2		春秋晚期
315	Y086	颜良寨西南		1	鬲	陶	图2.333b, 5		二里岗早期
				2	罐	陶	图2.333b, 4		二里岗晚期
				3	簋	陶	图2.333b, 2		二里岗晚期
				4	大口尊	陶	图2.333b, 1		二里岗晚期
				5	罐	陶			二里岗早期
				6	鼎	陶	图2.333b, 3		春秋
317	Y088	颜良村西		1	罐	陶	图2.335b, 2		东周
				2	罐	陶	图2.335b, 1		东周
318	Y089	冯寨西南		1	大口罐	陶	图2.335b, 8		龙山晚期
				2	瓮	陶	图2.335b, 6		龙山晚期

续表

遗址信息			遗迹	登记号	器型	质地	图号		时代
序号	编号	名称					插图号	图版号	
318	Y089	冯寨西南		3	杯	陶	图2.335b，3		龙山晚期
				4	器盖	陶	图2.335b，7		龙山晚期
			F1	1	石斧	石	图2.335b，5	图版二七九，1	不详
				2	石斧	石		图版二七九，2	不详
			H3	1	豆	陶	图2.335b，4		龙山晚期
			H9	1	杯	陶			龙山晚期
319	Y107	滑国故城		1	罐	陶	图2.337b，7		东周
				2	罐	陶	图2.337b，9		东周
				3	罐	陶	图2.337b，6		东周
				4	罐	陶	图2.337b，4		东周
				5	罐	陶	图2.337b，3		东周
				6	罐	陶	图2.337b，5		东周
				7	盆	陶	图2.337b，8		东周
				8	盆	陶	图2.337c，1		东周
				9	盆	陶	图2.337c，4		东周
				10	盆	陶	图2.337c，2		东周
				11	盆	陶	图2.337c，3		东周
				12	瓮	陶	图2.337c，6		东周
				13	瓮	陶	图2.337c，5		东周
				14	盘	陶	图2.337c，9		东周
				15	瓦	陶	图2.337c，8		东周
				16	瓦	陶	图2.337c，7		东周
				17	瓦	陶	图2.337c，10		东周
				18	石斧	石		图版二七九，3	不详
				19	石尖状器	石	图2.337b，1	图版二七九，4	不详
				20	石杵	石		图版二七九，5	不详
				21	石杵	石		图版二七九，6	不详
				22	石研磨器	石	图2.337b，2	图版二八〇，1	不详
320	Y112	滑城河东		1	深腹罐	陶	图2.338b，6		二里岗晚期
				2	方形石器	石	图2.338b，1	图版二八〇，2	不详
				3	盘状器	石		图版二八〇，3	不详
			H1	1	鼎	陶	图2.338b，7		龙山早期
				2	鼎	陶	图2.338b，2		龙山早期
				3	鼎	陶	图2.338b，3		龙山早期
				4	豆	陶	图2.338b，5		龙山早期
				5	碗	陶	图2.338b，4		龙山早期
				6	卜骨	骨			不详

续表

序号	遗址信息		遗迹	登记号	器型	质地	图号		时代
	编号	名称					插图号	图版号	
322	Y090	冯寨西北		1	钵	陶	图2.340b，7		仰韶中、晚期
				2	豆	陶	图2.340b，5		仰韶中、晚期
				3	大口罐	陶	图2.340b，4		龙山晚期
				4	大口罐	陶	图2.340b，3		龙山晚期
				5	折腹盆	陶	图2.340b，2		龙山晚期
				6	折腹盆	陶	图2.340b，1		龙山晚期
				7	杯	陶	图2.340b，8		龙山晚期
				8	瓮	陶	图2.340b，6		西周
				9	簋	陶	图2.340b，12		西周
323	Y059	杨寨西		1	罐	陶	图2.340b，9		殷墟
			H1	1	鬲	陶	图2.340b，10		殷墟早期
			H3	1	瓮	陶	图2.340b，11		春秋
324	Y058	杨寨西北		1	深腹罐	陶	图2.342b，7		二里岗
				2	鬲	陶	图2.342b，3		二里岗
				3	鬲	陶	图2.342b，1		二里岗
				4	鬲	陶	图2.342b，2		二里岗
				5	鬲	陶	图2.342b，4		二里岗
				6	大口尊	陶	图2.342b，5		二里岗
				7	盆	陶	图2.342b，6		二里岗
325	Y061	南村寨东南		1	鼎	陶	图2.343b，10		仰韶中、晚期
				2	缸	陶	图2.343b，4		仰韶中、晚期
				3	罐	陶	图2.343b，12		仰韶中、晚期
				4	钵	陶	图2.343b，6		仰韶中、晚期
				5	深腹罐	陶	图2.343b，11		二里头三、四期
				6	鼎	陶	图2.343b，3		二里头三、四期
				7	瓮	陶	图2.343b，5		二里头三、四期
				8	刻槽盆	陶	图2.343b，9		二里头三、四期
				9	鬲	陶	图2.343b，7		二里岗早期
				10	鬲	陶	图2.343b，2		二里岗早期
				11	盆形鼎	陶	图2.343b，8		二里岗早期
				12	器盖	陶	图2.343b，13		二里头三、四期
				13	石斧	石	图2.343b，1	图版二八〇，4	不详
327	Y060	南村寨南		1	斝	陶	图2.345b，9		龙山晚期
				2	罐	陶	图2.345b，11		龙山晚期
				3	鬲	陶	图2.345b，8		二里岗晚期
				4	缸	陶	图2.345b，10		二里岗晚期

续表

遗址信息			遗迹	登记号	器型	质地	图号		时代
序号	编号	名称					插图号	图版号	
328	Y109	滑城河西		1	罐	陶	图2.345b，7		仰韶中、晚期
				2	罐	陶	图2.345b，1		仰韶中、晚期
				3	盆	陶	图2.345b，2		仰韶中、晚期
				4	钵	陶	图2.345b，5		仰韶中、晚期
				5	大口罐	陶	图2.345b，6		龙山
				6	大口罐	陶	图2.345b，4		龙山
				7	盆	陶	图2.345b，3		龙山
				8	石楔	石			不详
				9	石斧	石		图版二八〇，5	不详
				10	石楔	石		图版二八〇，6	不详
329	Y108	滑城河北		1	罐	陶	图2.347b，4		仰韶中、晚期
				2	鼎	陶	图2.347b，3		仰韶中、晚期
				3	鼎	陶	图2.347b，2		仰韶中、晚期
				4	鼎	陶	图2.347b，1		仰韶中、晚期
				5	缸	陶	图2.347b，5		龙山
				6	斝	陶	图2.347b，6		龙山
				7	盆	陶	图2.347b，12		仰韶中、晚期
				8	钵	陶	图2.347b，7		仰韶中、晚期
				9	钵	陶	图2.347b，8		仰韶中、晚期
				10	尖底瓶	陶	图2.347b，11		仰韶中、晚期
				11	大口罐	陶	图2.347c，1		龙山
				12	瓮	陶	图2.347c，4		龙山
				13	器盖	陶	图2.347c，5		龙山
				14	圆腹罐	陶	图2.347c，7		二里头
				15	鼎	陶	图2.347c，3		二里头
				16	大口尊	陶	图2.347c，2		二里头
				17	鬲	陶	图2.347c，6		二里岗早期
				18	环	陶	图2.347b，10		仰韶中、晚期
				19	环	陶	图2.347b，9		仰韶中、晚期
				20	石饼	石			不详
				21	石斧	石			不详
330	Y111	府西村东北		1	瓮	陶	图2.348b，3		仰韶晚期
				2	圆腹罐	陶	图2.348b，14		二里头四期
				3	盆	陶	图2.348b，4		二里头四期
				4	深腹罐	陶	图2.348b，5		二里岗晚期
				5	捏口罐	陶	图2.348b，13		二里岗晚期

续表

遗址信息			遗迹	登记号	器型	质地	图号		时代
序号	编号	名称					插图号	图版号	
33C	Y111	府西村东北		6	罐	陶	图2.348b，12		西周
				7	鬲	陶	图2.348b，7		战国
				8	盆	陶	图2.348b，8		战国
				9	豆	陶	图2.348b，2		战国
				10	残石器	石		图版二八一，1	不详
				11	石杵	石			不详
			H1	1	深腹罐	陶	图2.348b，9		二里岗晚期
				2	深腹罐	陶	图2.348b，6		二里岗晚期
				3	深腹罐	陶	图2.348b，10		二里岗晚期
				4	鬲	陶	图2.348b，1		二里岗晚期
				5	器盖	陶	图2.348b，11		二里岗晚期
331	Y110	府西村北		1	大口罐	陶	图2.349b，10		龙山晚期
				2	大口罐	陶	图2.349b，11		龙山晚期
				3	大口罐	陶	图2.349b，7		龙山晚期
				4	大口罐	陶	图2.349b，9		龙山晚期
				5	大口罐	陶	图2.349b，6		龙山晚期
				6	鼎	陶	图2.349c，3		龙山晚期
				7	单把杯	陶	图2.349b，8	图版三七四，6	龙山晚期
				8	鼎	陶	图2.349c，4		龙山晚期
				9	甗	陶	图2.349c，7		龙山晚期
				10	瓮	陶	图2.349c，2		龙山晚期
				11	大口罐	陶			龙山晚期
				12	瓮	陶	图2.349c，10		龙山晚期
				13	折腹盆	陶	图2.349c，5		龙山晚期
				14	折腹盆	陶	图2.349c，6		龙山晚期
				15	折腹盆	陶			龙山晚期
				16	豆	陶	图2.349c，12		龙山晚期
				17	豆	陶	图2.349c，13		龙山晚期
				18	豆	陶	图2.349c，9		龙山晚期
				19	盘	陶	图2.349c，15		龙山晚期
				20	豆	陶	图2.349c，11		龙山晚期
				21	拍	陶	图2.349c，8		龙山晚期
				22	斝	陶	图2.349d，1		二里头
				23	盆	陶	图2.349d，9		二里头
				24	鬲	陶	图2.349d，2		二里头
				25	鬲	陶	图2.349d，8		东周

续表

遗址信息			遗迹	登记号	器型	质地	图号		时代
序号	编号	名称					插图号	图版号	
331	Y110	府西村北		26	罐	陶	图2.349d，6		东周
				27	瓮	陶	图2.349d，3		东周
				28	罐	陶	图2.349d，7		东周
				29	豆	陶	图2.349d，5	图版四六四，5	东周
				30	豆	陶	图2.349d，4		东周
				31	石斧	石	图2.349b，1	图版二八一，2	不详
				32	石斧	石	图2.349b，5	图版二八一，3	不详
				33	石矛（刀）	石	图2.349b，2	图版二八一，4	不详
				34	石斧	石		图版二八一，5	不详
				35	石斧	石		图版二八一，6	不详
				36	石斧	石			不详
				37	石斧	石		图版二八二，1	不详
				38	石斧坯	石	图2.349b，4		不详
				39	石镰	石		图版二八二，2	不详
				40	石凿	石		图版二八二，3	不详
				41	石杵	石		图版二八二，4	不详
				42	石杵	石		图版二八二，5	不详
				43	石锤	石		图版二八二，6	不详
				44	石锤	石		图版二八三，1	不详
				45	石铲	石		图版二八三，2	不详
				46	砺石	石		图版二八三，3	不详
				47	石刮削器	石			不详
				48	石刮削器	石			不详
				49	石毛坯	石	图2.349b，3	图版二八三，5、6	不详
				50	石毛坯	石		图版二八三，4	不详
			H1	1	碗	陶	图2.349c，14	图版三七四，5	龙山晚期
				2	瓮	陶	图2.349c，1		龙山晚期
332	Y062	南村寨西		1	盆	陶	图2.350b，6		二里头
				2	高领瓮	陶	图2.350b，8		二里岗
				3	罐	陶	图2.350b，5		战国
				4	罐	陶	图2.350b，7		战国
				5	盆	陶	图2.350b，4		战国
				6	石刀	石	图2.350b，2	图版二八四，1	不详
				7	石锤	石	图2.350b，1	图版二八四，2	不详
333	Y063	南村寨西南		1	钵	陶	图2.350b，10		龙山
334	Y064	桑沟水库北		1	鬲	陶	图2.350b，9		战国

续表

遗址信息			遗迹	登记号	器型	质地	图号		时代
序号	编号	名称					插图号	图版号	
335	Y065	桑沟老村		1	鬲	陶	图2.350b，3		春秋
336	Y126	桑沟五队北		1	鼎	陶	图2.354b，7		龙山早期
				2	缸	陶	图2.354b，3		仰韶晚期
				3	罐	陶		图版三七五，1	龙山晚期
337	Y105	三官庙窑厂东南		1	瓮	陶	图2.354b，8		仰韶中、晚期
				2	盆	陶	图2.354b，4		仰韶中、晚期
				3	瓮	陶	图2.354b，5		仰韶中、晚期
				4	尖底瓶	陶	图2.354b，6		仰韶中、晚期
				5	瓮	陶	图2.354b，11		西周
				6	瓮	陶	图2.354b，9		西周
				7	盆	陶	图2.354b，10		东周
				8	盆	陶	图2.354b，2		东周
				9	环	陶	图2.354b，1		仰韶中、晚期
				10	角器	骨	图2.354b，12		不详
338	Y066	桑沟南		1	鼎	陶	图2.356b，1		仰韶晚期
				2	鼎	陶	图2.356b，2		仰韶晚期
				3	罐	陶	图2.356b，4		仰韶晚期
				4	尖底瓶	陶	图2.356b，7		仰韶晚期
				5	盆	陶	图2.356b，3		仰韶晚期
				6	盆	陶	图2.356b，8		仰韶晚期
				7	彩陶片	陶	图2.356b，5		仰韶晚期
				8	豆	陶	图2.356b，6		战国
				9	石斧	石		图版二八四，3	不详
340	Y106	三官庙窑厂		1	中口罐	陶	图2.358b，1		龙山晚期
				2	中口罐	陶	图2.358b，4		龙山晚期
				3	中口罐	陶	图2.358b，2		龙山晚期
				4	瓮	陶	图2.358b，5		龙山晚期
				5	瓮	陶	图2.358b，6		龙山晚期
				6	瓮	陶	图2.358b，3		龙山晚期
				7	豆	陶	图2.358b，7		龙山晚期
				8	中口罐	陶			龙山晚期
				9	鬲	陶	图2.358c，5		战国
				10	鬲	陶	图2.358c，3		战国
				11	鬲	陶	图2.358c，2		战国
				12	鬲	陶	图2.358c，4		战国
				13	鬲	陶	图2.358c，6		战国

续表

遗址信息			遗迹	登记号	器型	质地	图号		时代
序号	编号	名称					插图号	图版号	
340	Y106	三官庙窑厂		14	鬲	陶	图2.358c, 1		战国
				15	鼎	陶	图2.358c, 12		战国
				16	罐	陶			战国
				17	罐	陶	图2.358c, 10		战国
				18	罐	陶	图2.358c, 9		战国
				19	罐	陶	图2.358c, 7		战国
				20	罐	陶	图2.358c, 8		战国
				21	罐	陶	图2.358c, 11		战国
				22	盆	陶	图2.358d, 11		战国
				23	盆	陶	图2.358d, 2		战国
				24	壶	陶	图2.358d, 8		战国
				25	豆	陶	图2.358d, 12		战国
				26	豆	陶	图2.358d, 3		战国
				27	豆	陶	图2.358d, 6		战国
				28	豆	陶	图2.358d, 4		战国
				29	豆	陶	图2.358d, 9		战国
				30	豆	陶	图2.358d, 5		战国
				31	器盖	陶	图2.358d, 1		战国
				32	盒	陶	图2.358d, 7		战国
				33	筒瓦	陶	图2.358d, 10		战国
				34	石杵	石		图版二八四, 4	不详
342	Y104	三官庙北		1	豆	陶	图2.360b, 1		仰韶晚期
				2	甗	陶	图2.360b, 5		东周
				3	骨匕	骨			不详
343	Y103	马屯西村南		1	圆腹罐	陶	图2.360b, 2		二里头
				2	圆腹罐	陶	图2.360b, 3		二里头
				3	缸	陶	图2.360b, 4		二里头
344	Y069	马屯新村		1	泥质彩陶罐	陶	图2.362b, 1		仰韶晚期
				2	碗	陶	图2.362b, 3	图版三七五, 2	龙山晚期
				3	碗	陶	图2.362b, 5		龙山晚期
				4	甗	陶	图2.362b, 6		龙山晚期
				5	罐	陶	图2.362b, 4		龙山晚期
				6	陶片	陶	图2.362b, 7		龙山晚期
				7	鬲	陶	图2.362b, 8		二里岗早期
				8	石铲	石	图2.362b, 2	图版二八四, 5	不详
				9	角锥	角		图版二八四, 6	不详

续表

遗址信息			遗迹	登记号	器型	质地	图号		时代
序号	编号	名称					插图号	图版号	
345	Y102	马屯老村		1	钵	陶	图2.363b，2		仰韶晚期
				2	彩陶片	陶	图2.363b，3		仰韶晚期
				3	瓮	陶	图2.363b，6		龙山晚期
				4	小盆	陶	图2.363b，7		龙山晚期
				5	残陶片	陶	图2.363b，4		龙山晚期
346	Y070	马屯北		1	深腹罐	陶	图2.363b，8		二里头
				2	深腹罐	陶	图2.363b，9		二里头
				3	罐	陶	图2.363b，5		战国
				4	石铲	石	图2.363b，1	图版二八五，1	不详
348	Y101	贾屯		1	鬲	陶	图2.366b，1		殷墟晚期
				2	罐	陶	图2.366b，5		春秋
				3	罐	陶	图2.366b，4		春秋
				4	罐	陶	图2.366b，2		春秋
				5	盆	陶	图2.366b，3		春秋
350	Y099	李家沟东		1	中口罐	陶	图2.368b，8		龙山晚期
				2	中口罐	陶	图2.368b，9		龙山晚期
				3	瓮	陶	图2.368b，11		龙山晚期
				4	折腹盆	陶	图2.368b，10		龙山晚期
				5	平底盆	陶	图2.368b，5		龙山晚期
				6	深腹罐	陶	图2.368c，8		二里头二至四期
				7	深腹罐	陶	图2.368c，7		二里头二至四期
				8	圆腹罐	陶	图2.368c，2		二里头二至四期
				9	圆腹罐	陶	图2.368c，3		二里头三期
				10	圆腹罐	陶	图2.368c，4		二里头二至四期
				11	甑	陶	图2.368c，9		二里头三期
				12	甑	陶	图2.368c，6		二里头二至四期
				13	甑	陶	图2.368c，5		二里头二至四期
				14	缸	陶	图2.368c，1		二里头二至四期
				15	盆	陶	图2.368d，6	图版三九四，6	二里头三期早
				16	盆	陶	图2.368d，7		二里头三期
				17	盆	陶	图2.368d，1		二里头二至四期
				18	大口尊	陶	图2.368d，2		二里头二至四期
				19	大口尊	陶	图2.368d，4		二里头二至四期
				20	矮领尊	陶	图2.368d，5		二里头二至四期
				21	瓮	陶	图2.368e，10		二里头二至四期
				22	盉	陶			二里头二至四期

续表

遗址信息			遗迹	登记号	器型	质地	图号		时代
序号	编号	名称					插图号	图版号	
350	Y099	李家沟东		23	深腹罐	陶	图2.368e，2		二里岗晚期
				24	鬲	陶	图2.368e，4		二里岗晚期
				25	鬲	陶	图2.368e，3		二里岗晚期
				26	甗	陶	图2.368e，1		二里岗晚期
				27	深腹罐	陶	图2.368e，9		二里岗晚期
				28	深腹罐	陶	图2.368e，8		二里岗晚期
				29	深腹罐	陶	图2.368e，7		二里岗晚期
				30	盆	陶	图2.368f，3		二里岗晚期
				31	盆	陶	图2.368f，6		二里岗晚期
				32	折腹盆	陶	图2.368f，5		二里岗晚期
				33	盆	陶	图2.368f，1		二里岗晚期
				34	器盖	陶	图2.368f，4		二里岗晚期
				35	环	陶	图2.368b，7		龙山晚期
				36	权	陶			不详
				37	斝	陶			二里头二至四期
				38	石镰	石	图2.368b，1	图版二八五，2	不详
				39	石镰	石	图2.368b，4	图版二八五，3	不详
				40	石铲	石	图2.368b，3	图版二八五，4	不详
				41	砺石	石	图2.368b，6	图版二八五，5	不详
				42	石坠	石	图2.368b，2	图版二八五，6	不详
				43	砺石	石		图版二八六，1	不详
				44	砺石	石		图版二八六，2	不详
				45	石铲坯	石		图版二八六，3	不详
				46	石铲坯	石		图版二八六，4	不详
				47	石铲坯	石		图版二八六，5	不详
				48	石铲坯	石		图版二八六，6	不详
				49	石刮削器	石		图版二八七，1	不详
				50	石杵	石			不详
			H2	1	尊	陶	图2.368f，2		二里岗晚期
			H3	1	大口尊	陶	图2.368d，3		二里头四期
			H4	1	鬲	陶	图2.368e，5		二里岗晚期
				2	鬲	陶	图2.368e，6		二里岗晚期
				3	大口尊	陶	图2.368f，7		二里岗晚期
351	Y072	罗彦庄西南/肖家沟		1	罐	陶	图2.369b，8		商

续表

遗址信息			遗迹	登记号	器型	质地	图号		时代
序号	编号	名称					插图号	图版号	
352	Y098	顾家屯南		1	彩陶片	陶	图2.369b，4		仰韶晚期
				2	豆	陶	图2.369b，6		龙山晚期
				3	石英片	石	图2.369b，1	图版二八七，2	不详
				4	石镰坯	石			不详
				5	石刀坯	石	图2.369b，3	图版二八七，3	不详
353	Y097	顾家屯东南		1	鬲	陶	图2.369b，7		东周
				2	瓮	陶	图2.369b，5		东周
				3	盆	陶	图2.369b，9		东周
				4	豆	陶	图2.369b，2		东周
354	Y096	顾家屯东		1	器盖	陶	图2.372b，3	图版三二一，6	仰韶中期
				2	甑	陶	图2.372b，2		东周
				3	石镰	石	图2.372b，1	图版二八七，4	不详
355	Y095	石家沟东南		1	鬲	陶	图2.372b，4		西周
357	Y073	念子庄西北		1	中口罐	陶	图2.375b，4		龙山晚期
				2	中口罐	陶	图2.375b，3		龙山晚期
				3	碗	陶	图2.375b，6	图版三七五，3	龙山晚期
				4	中口罐	陶	图2.375b，2		龙山晚期
				5	中口罐	陶	图2.375b，1		龙山晚期
				6	瓮	陶	图2.375b，8		西周
			H1	1	圈足	陶	图2.375b，5		龙山晚期
				2	碗	陶	图2.375b，7		龙山晚期
358	Y093	石家沟东北		1	圆腹罐	陶	图2.376b，2		二里头三、四期
				2	刻槽盆	陶	图2.376b，5		二里头三、四期
				3	瓮	陶	图2.376b，10		二里头三、四期
				4	豆	陶	图2.376b，1		二里头三、四期
				5	深腹罐	陶	图2.376b，7		二里岗
				6	石斧	石	图2.376b，4	图版二八七，5	不详
				7	石斧	石	图2.376b，3	图版二八七，6	不详
			H1	1	鬲	陶	图2.376b，9		殷墟
				2	盆	陶	图2.376b，8		殷墟
			H2	1	鬲	陶	图2.376b，6		战国
359	Y092	石家沟老村北		1	圆腹罐	陶	图2.377b，2		二里头
				2	鬲	陶	图2.377b，3		二里岗晚期
				3	鬲	陶	图2.377b，1		二里岗晚期
				4	假腹豆	陶	图2.377b，6		二里岗晚期

续表

遗址信息			遗迹	登记号	器型	质地	图号		时代
序号	编号	名称					插图号	图版号	
360	Y074	干沟猪场		1	深腹罐	陶	图2.377b，10		二里头三、四期
				2	鬲	陶	图2.377b，7		二里头三、四期
				3	鬲	陶	图2.377b，8		二里岗早期
				4	鬲	陶	图2.377b，4		东周
				5	鬲	陶	图2.377b，5		东周
				6	瓮	陶	图2.377b，9		东周
				7	石刮削器	石			不详
361	Y083	回龙湾新村东		1	深腹罐	陶	图2.379b，12		二里头三、四期
				2	深腹罐	陶	图2.379b，6		二里头三、四期
				3	深腹罐	陶	图2.379b，5		二里头三、四期
				4	圆腹罐	陶	图2.379b，3		二里头三、四期
				5	鼎	陶	图2.379b，8		二里头三、四期
				6	鼎	陶	图2.379b，7		二里头三、四期
				7	刻槽盆	陶	图2.379b，2		二里头三、四期
				8	鬲	陶	图2.379b，1		二里岗晚期
				9	盆	陶	图2.379b，10		二里岗晚期
				10	大口尊	陶	图2.379b，11		二里岗晚期
				11	豆	陶	图2.379b，4		春秋
			H1	1	深腹罐	陶	图2.379b，9		二里头三、四期
				2	盆	陶	图2.379b，13		二里头三、四期
				3	石锤	石			不详
362	Y076	干沟南		1	深腹罐	陶	图2.380b，3		二里头
				2	碗	陶	图2.380b，1		东周
				3	盆	陶	图2.380b，2		东周
363	Y075	刘乐寨西南		1	鼎	陶	图2.381b，4		仰韶晚期
				2	夹砂罐	陶	图2.381b，11		仰韶晚期
				3	泥质彩陶罐	陶	图2.381b，9		仰韶晚期
				4	豆	陶	图2.381b，8		战国
				7	石锤	石		图版二八八，3	不详
			H2	1	鼎	陶	图2.381b，3		仰韶晚期
				2	碗	陶	图2.381b，2	图版三四九，2	仰韶晚期
			H3	1	鼎	陶	图2.381b，7		仰韶晚期
				2	花边缸	陶	图2.381b，5		仰韶晚期
			H4	1	簋	陶	图2.381b，12		二里岗
				2	刮削器	石		图版二八八，1	不详

续表

遗址信息			遗迹	登记号	器型	质地	图号		时代
序号	编号	名称					插图号	图版号	
363	Y075	刘乐寨西南	H6	1	花边缸	陶	图2.381b, 6		仰韶晚期
				2	环	陶	图2.381b, 1		仰韶晚期
			H9	1	鬲	陶	图2.381b, 10		二里岗
				2	石球	石		图版二八八, 2	不详
364	Y082	回龙湾南		1	石刀	石		图版二八八, 4	不详
365	Y081	回龙湾		1	罐	陶	图2.383b, 1		战国
				2	盆	陶	图2.383b, 2		战国
				3	豆	陶	图2.383b, 3		战国
368	Y135	曹冏		1	兽面石刻	石	图2.387b, 1		不详
				2	石毛坯	石			不详
370	Y134	南沟		1	中口罐	陶	图2.387b, 5		龙山晚期
				2	中口罐	陶	图2.387b, 6		龙山晚期
				3	中口罐	陶			龙山晚期
				4	中口罐	陶	图2.387b, 3		龙山晚期
				5	瓮	陶	图2.387b, 4		龙山晚期
				6	器盖	陶	图2.387b, 7		龙山晚期
				7	碗	陶	图2.387b, 2		龙山晚期
372	Y133	曹河水库西		1	瓮	陶			仰韶晚期
374	Y137	北后沟东		1	鬲	陶	图2.393b, 1		二里岗
				2	鬲	陶			二里岗
				3	石球	石	图2.393b, 2		不详
				4	砺石	石			不详
376	Y139	北后沟西北		1	夹砂弦纹罐	陶	图2.394b, 4		仰韶晚期
				2	缸	陶	图2.394b, 13		仰韶晚期
				3	夹砂弦纹罐	陶	图2.394b, 7		仰韶晚期
				4	泥质彩陶罐	陶	图2.394b, 6		仰韶晚期
				5	缸	陶	图2.394b, 12		仰韶晚期
				6	缸	陶	图2.394b, 3		仰韶晚期
				7	缸	陶	图2.394b, 11		仰韶晚期
				8	缸	陶	图2.394b, 10		仰韶晚期
				9	钵	陶	图2.394b, 8		仰韶晚期
				10	豆	陶	图2.394b, 5		仰韶晚期
				11	盆	陶	图2.394b, 9		仰韶晚期
				12	彩陶片	陶			仰韶晚期
				13	罐	陶	图2.394b, 14		龙山早期
				14	石斧	石			不详

续表

遗址信息			遗迹	登记号	器型	质地	图号		时代
序号	编号	名称					插图号	图版号	
376	Y139	北后沟西北		15	砺石	石	图2.394b, 2		不详
				16	石凿	石	图2.394b, 1		不详
				17	石砍砸器	石		图版二八八, 5	不详
				18	磨石	石			不详
377	Y132	新后沟窑厂东		1	深腹罐	陶	图2.395b, 8		二里头
				2	深腹罐	陶	图2.395b, 7		二里头
				3	圆腹罐	陶	图2.395b, 5		二里头
				4	大口尊	陶	图2.395c, 2		二里头
				5	大口尊	陶	图2.395c, 1		二里头
				6	矮领瓮	陶	图2.395c, 6		二里头
				7	豆	陶	图2.395c, 3		二里头
				8	砺石	石			不详
				9	燧石核	石			不详
				10	砺石	石		图版二八八, 6	不详
				11	砺石	石		图版二八九, 1	不详
			H1	1	深腹罐	陶	图2.395b, 6		二里头三期
				2	圆腹罐	陶	图2.395b, 3		二里头三期
				3	圆腹罐	陶	图2.395b, 4		二里头四期
				4	圆腹罐	陶	图2.395b, 2		二里头三期
				5	圆腹罐	陶	图2.395b, 1		二里头
				6	大口尊	陶	图2.395c, 4		二里头
				7	大口尊	陶	图2.395c, 5		二里头三期
378	Y131	新后沟东		1	深腹罐	陶	图2.396b, 8		二里岗
				2	鬲	陶	图2.396b, 10		二里岗
				3	盆	陶	图2.396b, 9		二里岗
379	Y130	新后沟		1	罐	陶	图2.396b, 5		龙山晚期
				2	器盖	陶	图2.396b, 3		龙山晚期
				3	瓮	陶	图2.396b, 7		龙山晚期
				4	盆	陶	图2.396b, 6		龙山晚期
				5	碗	陶	图2.396b, 4		龙山晚期
				6	石刀	石	图2.396b, 2		龙山晚期
				7	石铲半成品	石	图2.396b, 1		龙山晚期
				8	打制石片	石		图版二八九, 2	不详
				9	打制石片	石		图版二八九, 3	不详
				10	打制石片	石		图版二八九, 4	不详
				11	白烧石	石		图版二八九, 5	不详

续表

遗址信息			遗迹	登记号	器型	质地	图号		时代
序号	编号	名称					插图号	图版号	
380	Y129	后沟		1	筒瓦	陶			汉
				2	盆	陶	图2.398b，6		汉
				3	瓦	陶	图2.398b，4		汉
				4	筒瓦	陶	图2.398b，5		汉
				5	板瓦	陶	图2.398b，1		汉
				6	板瓦	陶	图2.398b，2		汉
381	Y128	鲁庄东北		1	板瓦	陶	图2.398b，3		汉
382	Y125	南罗		1	瓮	陶	图2.401b，1		西周
				2	圈足	陶	图2.401b，2		东周
				3	平底盆	陶	图2.401b，3		东周
384	Y051	鳌坡		1	甑	陶	图2.403b，5	图版四六四，6	东周
				2	盆	陶	图2.403b，7		东周
				3	盆	陶	图2.403b，6		东周
				4	豆	陶	图2.403b，4		东周
				5	豆	陶	图2.403b，1		东周
				6	瓦当	陶	图2.403b，2		东周
				7	垫	陶	图2.403b，3		东周
385	Y052	提东		1	鼎	陶	图2.404b，3		仰韶晚期
				2	鼎	陶	图2.404b，4		仰韶晚期
				3	瓮	陶	图2.404b，8		仰韶晚期
				4	彩陶罐	陶			仰韶晚期
				5	瓮	陶	图2.404b，11		仰韶晚期
				6	盆	陶	图2.404b，6		仰韶晚期
				7	彩陶片	陶	图2.404b，5		仰韶晚期
				8	杯形器	陶	图2.404b，9		龙山早期
				9	鼎	陶	图2.404b，2		龙山早期
				10	鼎	陶	图2.404b，1		龙山早期
				11	罐	陶	图2.404b，10		仰韶晚期
				12	砺石	石	图2.404b，12		不详
			H1	1	罐	陶	图2.404b，7		仰韶中、晚期
386	Y053	龙骨堆		1	鼎	陶	图2.405b，1		仰韶中、晚期
				2	盆	陶	图2.405b，2		仰韶中、晚期
				3	钵	陶	图2.405b，3		仰韶中、晚期
				4	钵	陶	图2.405b，6		仰韶中、晚期
				5	钵	陶	图2.405b，10		仰韶中、晚期
				6	碗	陶	图2.405b，4		仰韶中、晚期

续表

遗址信息			遗迹	登记号	器型	质地	图号		时代
序号	编号	名称					插图号	图版号	
				7	环	陶	图2.405b，5		仰韶中、晚期
386	Y053	龙骨堆	H2	1	盆	陶	图2.405b，11		仰韶中、晚期
				2	尖底瓶	陶	图2.405b，8		仰韶中、晚期
				3	尖底瓶	陶	图2.405b，7		仰韶中、晚期
				4	钵	陶	图2.405b，9		仰韶中、晚期
388	Y043	天坡水库东北		1	鬲	陶	图2.407b，9		二里岗
				2	鬲	陶	图2.407b，11		二里岗
				3	鬲	陶	图2.407b，3		二里岗
				4	深腹罐	陶	图2.407b，7		二里岗
				5	深腹罐	陶	图2.407b，4		二里岗
				6	鬲	陶	图2.407b，8		二里岗
				7	鬲	陶	图2.407b，5		二里岗
				8	鬲	陶	图2.407b，6		二里岗
				9	鬲	陶	图2.407b，10		二里岗
				10	鬲	陶	图2.407b，12		二里岗
				11	鬲	陶	图2.407b，15		二里岗
				12	鬲	陶	图2.407b，16		二里岗
				13	鬲	陶	图2.407b，13		二里岗
				14	鬲	陶	图2.407b，14		二里岗
				15	鬲	陶	图2.407b，18		二里岗
				16	鬲	陶	图2.407b，17		二里岗
				17	鼎足	陶	图2.407b，20		二里岗
				18	深腹罐	陶	图2.407c，10		二里岗
				19	甗	陶	图2.407c，4	图版四一八，6	二里岗晚期
				20	捏口罐	陶	图2.407c，7		二里岗
				21	捏口罐	陶	图2.407c，6		二里岗
				22	爵	陶	图2.407d，4		二里岗
				23	盆	陶	图2.407d，3		二里岗
				24	盆	陶	图2.407d，5		二里岗
				25	束颈盆	陶	图2.407d，6		二里岗
				26	盆	陶	图2.407d，2		二里岗
				27	束颈盆	陶	图2.407d，9		二里岗
				28	束颈盆	陶	图2.407d，10		二里岗
				29	簋	陶	图2.407d，7		二里岗
				30	大口尊	陶	图2.407d，8		二里岗
				31	瓮	陶	图2.407d，11		二里岗

续表

遗址信息			遗迹	登记号	器型	质地	图号		时代
序号	编号	名称					插图号	图版号	
388	Y043	天坡水库东北		32	罐	陶	图2.407d，13		二里岗
				33	石锛坯	石		图版二八九，6	不详
				34	石刀	石	图2.407b，1	图版二九○，1	不详
				35	石铲	石		图版二九○，2	不详
				36	石铲	石			不详
				37	石镰	石	图2.407b，2	图版二九○，3	不详
				38	大型砺石	石		图版二九○，4	不详
				39	大型砺石	石		图版二九○，5	不详
				40	大型砺石	石			不详
				41	大型砺石	石		图版二九○，6	不详
				42	大型砺石	石		图版二九一，1	不详
				43	大型砺石	石		图版二九一，2	不详
				44	大型砺石	石		图版二九一，3	不详
				45	大型砺石	石		图版二九一，4	不详
				46	石锤	石		图版二九一，5	不详
				47	石锤	石		图版二九一，6	不详
				48	石锤	石		图版二九二，1	不详
				49	石锤	石		图版二九二，2	不详
				50	石锤	石		图版二九二，3	不详
				51	中型砺石	石		图版二九三，2	不详
				52	中型砺石	石		图版二九三，3	不详
				53	中型砺石	石		图版二九三，4	不详
				54	石料	石		图版二九五，6	不详
				55	手持磨石	石		图版二九四，1	不详
				56	手持磨石	石		图版二九四，2	不详
				57	手持磨石	石		图版二九四，3	不详
				58	中型砺石	石		图版二九三，5	不详
				59	砺石	石		图版二九四，6	不详
				60	砺石	石		图版二九五，1	不详
				61	手持磨石	石		图版二九四，4	不详
				62	石料	石		图版二九六，1	不详
				63	中型砺石	石		图版二九三，6	不详
				64	砺石	石		图版二九五，2	不详
				65	手持磨石	石		图版二九四，5	不详
				66	石料	石		图版二九六，2	不详
				67	石砧	石		图版二九五，3	不详

续表

遗址信息			遗迹	登记号	器型	质地	图号		时代
序号	编号	名称					插图号	图版号	
388	Y043	天坡水库东北		68	石砧	石		图版二九五,4	不详
				69	石锤	石		图版二九二,4	不详
				70	石料	石		图版二九六,3	不详
				71	石料	石		图版二九六,4	不详
				72	石锤	石		图版二九二,5	不详
				73	石锤	石		图版二九二,6	不详
				74	石锤	石		图版二九三,1	不详
				75	石灰岩片	石		图版二九五,5	不详
				76	石灰皮	石			不详
			H1	1	鬲	陶	图2.407c,8		二里岗
				2	深腹罐	陶	图2.407c,1		二里岗
				3	鬲	陶	图2.407c,2		二里岗
				4	深腹罐	陶			二里岗
				5	腹片	陶			二里岗
			H2	1	鬲	陶	图2.407c,5		二里岗
				2	深腹罐	陶	图2.407c,11		二里岗
				3	小盆	陶	图2.407c,3		二里岗
			H5	1	缸	陶	图2.407d,1		二里岗
				2	罐	陶	图2.407d,14		二里岗
				3	深腹罐	陶	图2.407c,9		二里岗
				4	罐	陶	图2.407d,12		二里岗
				5	鬲	陶	图2.407b,19		二里岗
389	Y049	天坡		1	罐	陶	图2.408b,5		仰韶晚期
				2	罐	陶	图2.408b,9		仰韶晚期
				3	罐	陶	图2.408b,7		仰韶晚期
				4	尖底瓶	陶	图2.408b,11		仰韶晚期
				5	钵	陶	图2.408b,1		仰韶晚期
				6	钵	陶	图2.408b,2		仰韶晚期
				7	钵	陶	图2.408b,3		仰韶晚期
				8	豆	陶	图2.408b,10		仰韶晚期
				9	刀	陶	图2.408b,14		仰韶晚期
			H1	1	罐	陶	图2.408b,6		仰韶晚期
				2	钵	陶	图2.408b,4		仰韶晚期
				3	彩陶片	陶	图2.408b,13		仰韶晚期
			H2	1	鼎	陶	图2.408b,8		仰韶晚期
				2	彩陶片	陶	图2.408b,12		仰韶晚期

续表

遗址信息			遗迹	登记号	器型	质地	图号		时代
序号	编号	名称					插图号	图版号	
389	Y049	天坡	H4	1	杯	陶	图2.408b，15		仰韶晚期
390	Y050	羽林庄南		1	圈足盘	陶	图2.409b，20		仰韶中、晚期
				2	鼎	陶	图2.409b，19		仰韶中、晚期
				3	罐	陶	图2.409b，17		仰韶中、晚期
				4	罐	陶	图2.409b，18		仰韶中、晚期
				5	豆	陶	图2.409b，5		仰韶中、晚期
				6	罐	陶	图2.409b，13		仰韶中、晚期
				7	罐	陶	图2.409b，12		仰韶中、晚期
				8	罐	陶	图2.409b，14		仰韶中、晚期
				9	尖底瓶	陶	图2.409b，10		仰韶中、晚期
				10	罐	陶	图2.409b，16		仰韶中、晚期
				11	器盖	陶	图2.409b，11		仰韶中、晚期
				12	彩陶片	陶	图2.409b，6		仰韶中、晚期
				13	彩陶片	陶	图2.409b，9		仰韶中、晚期
				14	彩陶片	陶	图2.409b，7		仰韶中、晚期
				15	环	陶	图2.409b，2		仰韶中、晚期
				16	石刀	石		图版二九六，5	不详
				17	石饼	石			不详
				18	石环	石	图2.409b，1	图版二九六，6	不详
			H6	1	罐	陶	图2.409b，15		仰韶中、晚期
				2	盆	陶	图2.409b，4		仰韶中、晚期
				3	彩陶片	陶	图2.409b，8		仰韶中、晚期
				4	腹片	陶			仰韶中、晚期
			M1	1	环	陶	图2.409b，3		仰韶中、晚期
391	Y045	新移		1	盆	陶	图2.409b，21		殷墟早期
392	Y038	大南沟		1	尖底瓶	陶	图2.412b，1		仰韶
393	Y039	上庄东南		1	鼎	陶	图2.412b，2		仰韶晚期
				2	盆	陶	图2.412b，3		仰韶晚期
				3	石片	石			不详
394	Y037	上庄南		1	罐	陶	图2.414b，6		仰韶晚期
				2	彩陶罐	陶	图2.414b，10		仰韶晚期
				3	盆	陶	图2.414b，3		仰韶晚期
				4	深腹罐	陶	图2.414b，8		二里头三、四期
				5	深腹罐	陶	图2.414b，4		二里头三、四期
				6	圆腹罐	陶	图2.414c，12		二里头三、四期
				7	圆腹罐	陶	图2.414c，10		二里头三、四期

续表

遗址信息			遗迹	登记号	器型	质地	图号		时代
序号	编号	名称					插图号	图版号	
394	Y037	上庄南		8	圆腹罐	陶	图2.414c，9		二里头三、四期
				9	高领罐	陶	图2.414c，8		二里头三、四期
				10	高领罐	陶	图2.414c，6		二里头三、四期
				11	大口尊	陶	图2.414c，1		二里头三、四期
				12	大口尊	陶	图2.414c，2		二里头三、四期
				13	豆	陶	图2.414c，13		二里岗晚期
				14	鬲	陶	图2.414d，1		东周
				15	盆	陶	图2.414d，4		东周
				16	石斧	石	图2.414b，1	图版二九七，1	不详
				17	石环形器坯	石	图2.414b，2	图版二九七，2	不详
			H1	1	圆腹罐	陶	图2.414c，4		二里头三、四期
				2	深腹罐	陶	图2.414b，7		二里头三、四期
				3	深腹罐	陶	图2.414b，5		二里头三、四期
				4	盆	陶	图2.414c，5		二里头三、四期
				5	深腹罐	陶	图2.414b，9		二里头三、四期
				6	大口尊	陶	图2.414c，11		二里头三、四期
				7	大口尊	陶	图2.414c，7		二里头三、四期
				8	大口尊	陶	图2.414c，3		二里头三、四期
			H3	1	盆	陶	图2.414d，2		东周
				2	盆	陶	图2.414d，6		东周
			H5	1	深腹罐	陶	图2.414d，3		二里岗晚期
				2	圆腹罐	陶	图2.414d，5		二里岗晚期
395	Y055	北地沟		1	鼎	陶	图2.415b，1		仰韶
397	Y036	涉村南南沟		1	石核	石	图2.415b，6		旧石器
				2	石片	石	图2.415b，7	图版三〇三，1	旧石器
398	Y035	涉村东		1	罐	陶	图2.415b，4		仰韶早期
				2	深腹罐/鬲	陶	图2.415b，5		二里岗晚期
				3	石刮削器	石	图2.415b，3		不详
399	Y041	东山原		1	钵	陶	图2.415b，2		仰韶晚期
				2	钵	陶	图2.415b，8		仰韶晚期
400	Y028	铁生沟西南		1	盆	陶			汉
401	Y029	铁生沟		1	鼎	陶	图2.421b，10		裴李岗
				2	鼎	陶	图2.421b，8		裴李岗
				3	垫	陶	图2.421b，13		裴李岗
				4	燧石核	石	图2.421b，5	图版二九七，4	不详
				5	小石锛	石	图2.421b，3	图版二九七，5	不详

续表

遗址信息			遗迹	登记号	器型	质地	图号		时代
序号	编号	名称					插图号	图版号	
401	Y029	铁生沟	H2	6	石刀	石	图2.421b, 2	图版二九七, 6	不详
				7	石饼	石	图2.421b, 4	图版二九八, 1	不详
				8	石磨盘	石	图2.421b, 1	图版二九八, 2	裴李岗
				9	打制石片	石			不详
				1	鼎	陶	图2.421b, 7		裴李岗
				2	鼎	陶	图2.421b, 9		裴李岗
				3	鼎	陶	图2.421b, 6		裴李岗
				4	钵	陶	图2.421b, 11		裴李岗
				5	钵	陶	图2.421b, 12		裴李岗
				6	石刀	石		图版二九七, 3	不详
402	Y030	夹津口		1	碗	陶	图2.422b, 5		仰韶
				2	钵	陶	图2.422b, 2		仰韶
				3	钵	陶	图2.422b, 1		仰韶
403	Y044	北营		1	鼎足	陶	图2.422b, 4		裴李岗晚期
				2	罐	陶	图2.422b, 7		裴李岗晚期
				3	壶	陶	图2.422b, 3		裴李岗晚期
				4	石铲	石	图2.422b, 6	图版二九八, 3	不详
				5	石刀	石			不详
406	Y034	寺院沟		1	瓮	陶	图2.426b, 1		龙山晚期
				2	瓮	陶	图2.426b, 2		龙山晚期
				3	盆	陶	图2.426b, 4		龙山晚期
				4	折腹盆	陶	图2.426b, 3		龙山晚期
				5	豆	陶	图2.426b, 5		龙山晚期
				6	石楔	石	图2.426b, 6	图版二九八, 4	不详
407	Y042	坞罗西坡2		1	罐	陶	图2.427b, 1		裴李岗晚期
				2	罐	陶	图2.427b, 2		裴李岗晚期
				3	刀	陶	图2.427b, 6		裴李岗晚期
				4	球	陶	图2.427b, 3	图版三○三, 2	裴李岗晚期
				5	磨石	石	图2.427b, 5	图版三○三, 3	裴李岗晚期
				6	石磨棒	石		图版三○三, 4	裴李岗晚期
				7	磨石	石		图版三○三, 5	裴李岗晚期
				8	石球	石	图2.427b, 4		裴李岗晚期
				9	砺石	石			裴李岗晚期
408	Y033	坞罗西坡1		1	深腹罐	陶	图2.428b, 5		二里头三、四期
				2	鼎	陶	图2.428b, 2		二里头三、四期
				3	圆腹罐	陶	图2.428b, 6		二里头三、四期

续表

遗址信息			遗迹	登记号	器型	质地	图号		时代
序号	编号	名称					插图号	图版号	
408	Y033	坞罗西坡1		4	鼎	陶	图2.428b，3		二里头三、四期
				5	缸	陶	图2.428b，7		二里头三、四期
				6	豆	陶	图2.428b，1	图版四一〇，6	二里头四期晚
				7	大口尊	陶	图2.428b，4		二里头三、四期
409	Y032	坞罗南店		1	鼎	陶	图2.429b，1		战国
				2	豆	陶	图2.429b，5		战国
				3	盆	陶	图2.429b，4		战国
				4	盆	陶	图2.429b，2		战国
				5	残石器	石			不详
			H1	1	器盖	陶	图2.429b，6		龙山晚期
				2	瓮	陶	图2.429b，3		龙山晚期
				3	蚌刀	蚌			不详
			H2	1	折腹盆	陶	图2.429b，8	图版三七五，4	龙山晚期
			H4	1	大口罐	陶	图2.429b，9		龙山晚期
				2	大口罐	陶	图2.429b，7		龙山晚期
410	Y025	坞罗水库西1		1	鼎足	陶	图2.430b，1		仰韶中、晚期
				2	鼎足	陶	图2.430b，2		仰韶中、晚期
				3	罐	陶	图2.430b，9		仰韶中、晚期
				4	钵	陶	图2.430b，6		仰韶中、晚期
				5	钵	陶	图2.430b，5		仰韶中、晚期
				6	圈足	陶	图2.430b，3		龙山晚期
				7	簋	陶	图2.430b，10		殷墟晚期
				8	石研磨器	石	图2.430b，11	图版二九八，5	不详
				9	石锤	石			不详
				10	砺石	石			不详
			H1	1	罐		图2.430b，4		仰韶晚期
			H2	1	瓮	陶	图2.430b，8		仰韶晚期
				2	瓮	陶	图2.430b，7		仰韶晚期
				3	石斧	石			不详
413	Y022	罗口		1	罐	陶	图2.433c，9		仰韶晚期
				2	中口罐	陶	图2.433c，8		龙山晚期
				3	中口罐	陶	图2.433c，12		龙山晚期
				4	中口罐	陶	图2.433c，2		龙山晚期
				5	小口高领罐	陶	图2.433c，11		龙山晚期
				6	瓮	陶			龙山晚期
				7	印纹陶片	陶	图2.433e，8		西周

续表

遗址信息			遗迹	登记号	器型	质地	图号		时代
序号	编号	名称					插图号	图版号	
413	Y022	罗口		8	深腹罐	陶	图2.433c，6		二里头
				9	鬲	陶	图2.433d，1		二里岗晚期
				10	簋	陶	图2.433d，2		二里岗晚期
				11	残陶片	陶	图2.433c，4		二里头
				12	盆形鼎	陶	图2.433d，5		二里岗晚期
				13	盆	陶	图2.433d，6		二里岗晚期
				14	盆	陶	图2.433d，7		二里岗晚期
				15	盆	陶	图2.433d，8		二里岗晚期
				16	捏口罐	陶	图2.433d，3		二里岗晚期
				17	鬲	陶	图2.433e，2		春秋
				18	鬲	陶	图2.433e，1		春秋
				19	瓮	陶	图2.433e，5		春秋
				20	瓮	陶	图2.433e，6		春秋
				21	瓮	陶	图2.433e，7		春秋
				22	罐	陶	图2.433e，4		春秋
				23	豆	陶	图2.433e，3		春秋
				24	纺轮	陶	图2.433c，7		龙山晚期
				25	纺轮	陶	图2.433c，10		龙山晚期
				26	石斧坯	石	图2.433b，7		不详
				27	石斧	石	图2.433b，1	图版二九九，1	不详
				28	石斧	石		图版二九九，2	不详
				29	石斧	石			不详
				30	石凿	石			不详
				31	石刀	石	图2.433b，5	图版二九九，3	不详
				32	石镰	石		图版二九九，4	不详
				33	石铲	石	图2.433b，4	图版二九九，5	不详
				34	石饼	石	图2.433b，2	图版二九九，6	不详
				35	石饼	石	图2.433b，3	图版三〇〇，1	不详
			H1	1	中口罐	陶	图2.433c，3		龙山晚期
			H3	1	中口罐	陶	图2.433c，1		龙山晚期
				2	石磨盘	石	图2.433b，6	图版二九八，6	不详
				3	蚌刀	蚌			不详
				4	蚌刀	蚌			不详
			H4	1	深腹罐	陶	图2.433c，5		二里头四期

续表

序号	遗址信息 编号	名称	遗迹	登记号	器型	质地	图号 插图号	图版号	时代
413	Y022	罗口	H7	1	深腹罐	陶	图2.433d,10		二里岗晚期
				2	深腹罐	陶	图2.433d,11		二里岗晚期
				3	束颈盆	陶	图2.433d,4		二里岗晚期
				4	盆	陶	图2.433d,9		二里岗晚期
414	Y056	火葬场南/山川西南		1	石核	石			不详
416	Y020	喂庄东南		1	罐	陶	图2.436b,7		仰韶晚期
				2	陶片	陶	图2.436b,3		仰韶晚期
				3	圆腹罐	陶	图2.436b,6		二里头
				4	陶片	陶	图2.436b,4		二里头
				5	鬲	陶	图2.436b,2		二里岗晚期
				6	捏口罐	陶	图2.436b,5		二里岗晚期
				7	豆	陶	图2.436b,1		西周
				8	盆	陶	图2.436b,11		战国
				9	圆陶片	陶	图2.436b,10		不详
				10	石铲	石	图2.436b,8	图版三〇〇,2	不详
				11	石铲	石	图2.436b,9	图版三〇〇,3	不详
417	Y023	喂庄东南角		1	鼎	陶	图2.437b,1		仰韶晚期
				2	罐	陶	图2.437b,7		仰韶晚期
				3	罐	陶	图2.437b,2		仰韶晚期
				4	钵	陶	图2.437b,6		仰韶晚期
				5	豆	陶	图2.437b,4		仰韶晚期
				6	豆	陶	图2.437b,5		仰韶晚期
				7	彩陶片	陶	图2.437b,3		仰韶晚期
				8	石砍砸器	石			不详
				9	石环坯	石	图2.437b,8		不详
420	Y019	喂庄西		1	夹砂罐	陶	图2.440b,5		仰韶中、晚期
				2	夹砂罐	陶	图2.440b,7		仰韶中、晚期
				3	夹砂罐	陶	图2.440b,1		仰韶中、晚期
				4	器盖	陶	图2.440b,2	图版三二二,1	仰韶中期
				5	碗	陶	图2.440b,3		仰韶中、晚期
				6	石斧	石		图版三〇〇,4	不详
				7	石砍砸器	石		图版三〇〇,5	不详
			H1	1	夹砂罐	陶	图2.440b,6		仰韶中、晚期
				2	泥质彩陶罐	陶	图2.440b,4		仰韶中、晚期

续表

遗址信息			遗迹	登记号	器型	质地	图号		时代
序号	编号	名称					插图号	图版号	
421	Y018	喂庄西南		1	鼎	陶		图版三四九，3	仰韶晚期
				2	鼎	陶			仰韶晚期
				3	鼎	陶	图2.441c，3		仰韶中、晚期
				4	夹砂罐	陶	图2.441c，8		仰韶中、晚期
				5	夹砂罐	陶	图2.441c，10		仰韶中、晚期
				6	夹砂罐	陶	图2.441c，9		仰韶中、晚期
				7	瓮	陶	图2.441c，2		仰韶中、晚期
				8	瓮	陶		图版三四九，4	仰韶晚期
				9	瓮	陶	图2.441c，4		仰韶中、晚期
				10	器盖	陶	图2.441c，7	图版三二二，2	仰韶中期
				11	罐	陶	图2.441d，11		仰韶中、晚期
				12	罐	陶	图2.441d，1		仰韶中、晚期
				13	罐	陶	图2.441d，2		仰韶中、晚期
				14	罐	陶	图2.441d，3		仰韶中、晚期
				15	罐	陶	图2.441d，4		仰韶中、晚期
				16	罐	陶	图2.441d，6		仰韶中、晚期
				17	罐	陶	图2.441d，7		仰韶中、晚期
				18	罐	陶	图2.441d，8		仰韶中、晚期
				19	罐	陶	图2.441d，9		仰韶中、晚期
				20	罐	陶	图2.441d，14		仰韶中、晚期
				21	罐	陶	图2.441d，10		仰韶中、晚期
				22	罐	陶	图2.441d，5		仰韶中、晚期
				23	罐	陶	图2.441d，13		仰韶中、晚期
				24	杯	陶	图2.441c，1		仰韶中、晚期
				25	缸	陶	图2.441e，2		仰韶中、晚期
				26	缸	陶	图2.441e，3		仰韶中、晚期
				27	缸	陶	图2.441e，1		仰韶中、晚期
				28	盆	陶	图2.441e，4		仰韶中、晚期
				29	盆	陶	图2.441e，5		仰韶中、晚期
				30	盆	陶		图版三四九，5	仰韶晚期
				31	钵	陶	图2.441e，8		仰韶中、晚期
				32	钵	陶	图2.441e，6		仰韶中、晚期
				33	钵	陶	图2.441e，7		仰韶中、晚期
				34	杯	陶	图2.441c，5		仰韶中、晚期
				35	彩陶片	陶	图2.441e，10		仰韶中、晚期
				36	彩陶片	陶	图2.441e，12		仰韶中、晚期

续表

遗址信息			遗迹	登记号	器型	质地	图号		时代
序号	编号	名称					插图号	图版号	
421	Y018	喂庄西南		37	彩陶片	陶	图2.441e，13		仰韶中、晚期
				38	彩陶片	陶	图2.441e，11		仰韶中、晚期
				39	瓮	陶			龙山晚期
				40	圈足	陶		图版三四九，6	仰韶晚期
				41	蚌刀	蚌			不详
				42	石斧	石	图2.441b，4	图版三〇〇，6	不详
				43	石砍砸器	石			不详
				44	砺石	石	图2.441b，8		不详
				45	石刀	石	图2.441b，5	图版三五〇，5	仰韶
				46	石刀	石	图2.441b，6	图版三五〇，6	仰韶
				47	石刀坯	石	图2.441b，1		不详
				48	石铲	石			不详
				49	小石锛	石	图2.441b，3	图版三〇一，1	不详
				50	石刮削器	石		图版三〇一，2	不详
				51	石砍砸器	石			不详
				52	石饼	石	图2.441b，2	图版三〇一，3	不详
				53	石刮削器	石			不详
				54	石刮削器	石			不详
				55	石刮削器	石			不详
				56	石毛坯	石			不详
				57	砺石	石	图2.441b，7	图版三〇一，4	不详
				58	石锤	石			不详
				59	石磨盘	石			不详
				60	石磨盘	石			不详
				61	石锤	石		图版三〇一，5	不详
				62	石锤	石			不详
			H1	1	鼎	陶	图2.441c，6		仰韶中、晚期
				2	罐	陶	图2.441d，12		仰韶中、晚期
				3	陶片	陶	图2.441e，9		仰韶中、晚期
425	Y011	费窑西南		1	鬲	陶	图2.445b，2		二里岗晚期
				2	鬲	陶	图2.445b，1		二里岗晚期
				3	鬲	陶	图2.445b，3		二里岗晚期
				4	深腹罐	陶	图2.445b，9		二里岗晚期
				5	深腹罐	陶	图2.445b，10		二里岗晚期
				6	大口尊	陶	图2.445b，12		二里岗晚期
				7	大口尊	陶	图2.445b，5		二里岗晚期

续表

遗址信息			遗迹	登记号	器型	质地	图号		时代
序号	编号	名称					插图号	图版号	
425	Y011	费窑西南		8	矮领尊	陶	图2.445b, 4		二里岗晚期
				9	盆	陶	图2.445b, 14		二里岗晚期
				10	盆	陶	图2.445b, 13		二里岗晚期
				11	盆	陶	图2.445b, 11		二里岗晚期
				12	簋	陶	图2.445b, 7		二里岗晚期
				13	簋	石	图2.445b, 8		二里岗晚期
				14	砍砸器	石	图2.445b, 6	图版三〇一, 6	不详
430	Y003	清易镇东2		1	瓮	陶	图2.450b, 4		春秋
				2	瓮	陶	图2.450b, 3		春秋
				3	瓮	陶	图2.450b, 1		东周
				4	盆	陶	图2.450b, 2		东周
433	Y008	电厂东南2		1	盆	陶	图2.453b, 1		二里头二至四期
				2	陶片	陶	图2.453b, 2		二里头二至四期
435	Y048	电厂西		1	圆腹罐	陶	图2.453b, 3		二里头
439	Y1001	稍柴		1	钵	陶	图2.458c, 1	图版三二二, 3	仰韶中期
				2	深腹罐	陶	图2.458c, 2		二里头
				3	深腹罐	陶	图2.458c, 3		二里头
				4	鼎	陶	图2.458d, 9		二里头
				5	圆腹罐	陶	图2.458c, 7		二里头
				6	圆腹罐	陶	图2.458c, 6		二里头
				7	鼎	陶	图2.458d, 8		二里头
				8	鼎	陶	图2.458d, 7		二里头
				9	鼎	陶	图2.458d, 4		二里头
				10	鼎	陶	图2.458d, 3		二里头
				11	刻槽盆	陶	图2.458e, 9		二里头
				12	豆	陶	图2.458e, 4		二里头
				13	豆	陶	图2.458e, 7		二里头
				14	深腹罐	陶	图2.458f, 6		二里岗晚期
				15	深腹罐	陶	图2.458f, 5		二里岗晚期
				16	鬲	陶	图2.458f, 4		二里岗晚期
				17	鬲	蚌	图2.458f, 1		二里岗晚期
				18	高领罐	陶	图2.458f, 2		二里岗晚期
				19	簋	陶	图2.458f, 7		二里岗晚期
				20	蚌刀	蚌			不详
				21	假腹豆	陶	图2.458f, 15		二里岗晚期
				22	缸	陶	图2.458f, 12		二里岗晚期

续表

遗址信息			遗迹	登记号	器型	质地	图号		时代
序号	编号	名称					插图号	图版号	
439	Y1001	稍柴		23	高领罐	陶	图2.458f, 9		二里岗晚期
				24	鬲	陶	图2.458f, 14		殷墟
				25	鬲	陶	图2.458f, 3		周
				26	鬲	陶	图2.458f, 11		周
				27	盆	陶	图2.458e, 3		二里头
				28	盆	陶	图2.458f, 13		周
				29	花纹陶片	陶	图2.458e, 6		二里头
				30	石刀	石	图2.458b, 1		不详
				31	石刀坯	石	图2.458b, 3	图版三○二, 3	不详
				32	蚌刀	蚌			不详
				33	片状残断石器	石			不详
				34	蚌刀	蚌			不详
			H1	1	深腹罐	陶	图2.458c, 4		二里头二期
				2	圆腹罐	陶	图2.458c, 5		二里头二期
				3	高领尊	陶	图2.458d, 2		二里头二期
				4	器盖	陶	图2.458e, 8		二里头二期
			H5	1	深腹罐	陶	图2.458c, 13		二里头二期
				2	深腹罐	陶	图2.458c, 14		二里头二期
				3	圆腹罐	陶	图2.458c, 12		二里头二期
				4	圆腹罐	陶	图2.458c, 9		二里头二期
				5	圆腹罐	陶	图2.458c, 11		二里头二期
				6	圆腹罐	陶	图2.458c, 8		二里头二期
				7	缸	陶	图2.458e, 1		二里头二期
				8	三足盘	陶	图2.458e, 2		二里头二期
				9	甑	陶	图2.458d, 6	图版三九五, 1	二里头三期早
				10	盆	陶	图2.458e, 5		二里头二期
			H6	1	高领尊	陶	图2.458d, 1		二里头二至四期
			H7	1	深腹罐	陶	图2.458f, 8		二里岗晚期
				2	盆	陶	图2.458f, 10		二里岗晚期
			H9	1	石镰	石	图2.458b, 2	图版三○二, 1	不详
				2	砺石	石	图2.458b, 4	图版三○二, 2	不详
				3	圆腹罐	陶	图2.458c, 10		二里头
			H10	1	大口尊	陶	图2.458d, 5		二里头
440	Y1003	南石		1	盆	陶	图2.459b, 1		龙山晚期
				2	石铲	石	图2.459b, 5	图版三○二, 4	不详

续表

遗址信息			遗迹	登记号	器型	质地	图号		时代
序号	编号	名称					插图号	图版号	
440	Y1003	南石		3	砺石	石	图2.459b，2		不详
			H1	1	鼎	陶	图2.459b，4		仰韶晚期
			F1	1	瓮	陶	图2.459b，3		龙山晚期
441	Y1005	小訾殿南		1	罐	陶	图2.460b，3		龙山晚期
				2	罐	陶	图2.460b，8		西周
				3	盆	陶	图2.460b，4		西周
				4	罐	陶	图2.460b，5		春秋
				5	石砍砸器	石			不详
442	Y1004	小訾殿北		1	中口罐	陶	图2.460b，7		龙山晚期
				2	石片	石	图2.460b，1	图版三〇二，5	不详
				3	石片	石	图2.460b，2	图版三〇二，6	不详
444	Y1002	稍柴南		1	鬲	陶			东周
				2	石刀	石			不详
				3	蚌刀	蚌			不详
				4	蚌刀	蚌			不详
451	Y145	小南沟西南		1	中口罐	陶	图2.469b，3		龙山晚期
				2	中口罐	陶	图2.469b，5		龙山晚期
				3	中口罐	陶	图2.469b，4		龙山晚期
				4	瓮	陶	图2.469b，6		龙山晚期
				5	盆	陶	图2.469b，7		龙山晚期
				6	折腹盆	陶	图2.469b，9		龙山晚期
				7	折腹盆	陶	图2.469b，10		龙山晚期
				8	折腹盆	陶	图2.469b，8		龙山晚期
				9	环	陶	图2.469b，1		龙山晚期
453	Y147	东沟西北	H1	1	盆	陶	图2.469b，2		龙山晚期
456	Y149	牌坊沟		1	罐	陶	图2.472b，3		二里岗
				2	盆	陶	图2.472b，5		二里岗
				3	盆	陶	图2.472b，4		二里岗
				4	鬲	陶	图2.472b，1		西周
				5	罐	陶	图2.472b，6		战国
				6	豆	陶	图2.472b，2		战国
				7	蚌刀	蚌			不详
				8	蚌刀	蚌			不详
				9	蚌刀	蚌			不详
				10	蚌刀	蚌			不详

编 后 记

经过中澳美伊洛河流域联合考古队11年（1997—2007年）、二里头工作队3年（2001—2003年）的野外调查，10年（2007—2016年）的酝酿，4年（2016—2019年）繁杂的基础资料整理和报告编纂与修订审校，在田野项目结束12年之后，《洛阳盆地中东部先秦时期遗址——1997—2007年区域系统调查报告》的编纂工作终于结束。

进入中国社会科学院考古研究所工作后不久的1999年10月，我跟随时任夏商周考古研究室副主任、二里头工作队队长许宏博士同赴二里头遗址，开始了新一轮的考古勘探与发掘工作。此后16年间，除了在中国社会科学院研究生院求学和短时间借调发掘外，一直在二里头遗址参与田野发掘、资料整理和报告编写工作。而那一年，中澳美伊洛河流域联合考古队对伊洛河下游洛阳盆地东部开展的区域系统调查工作已经进行了3年。

2001年春季，出于探索二里头遗址和区域聚落形态的目的，在许宏队长的带领下，二里头工作队开始对遗址所在的洛阳盆地中部区域进行系统调查，至2003年夏季，野外工作基本结束。2005年，经过初步整理，该区域的调查简报正式发表，相关工作遂告一段落。2006年春季，二里头遗址的田野发掘工作暂时结束，发掘报告的编纂工作开展起来，而调查报告的整理和出版，一时难以列入工作日程。2014年秋季，《二里头（1999~2006）》正式出版后，我从二里头工作队调入了河南二队（偃师商城队），调查报告的整理和编纂工作在陈星灿所长、许宏研究员和刘莉教授的协调下，重新提上了两队的工作日程。

20余年来，随着中国考古学研究的逐步转型，区域系统调查的资料成为研究者探索中国古代文明和早期国家形成之路的必备资料，且国内相关机构在同一时期开展的调查工作资料多已刊发这一现状，时时刻刻鞭策着我们尽快系统发表相关资料。同样，调查工作开展以来的20余年，也正是中国经济飞速发展和城市化进程快速推进的阶段，当年调查时保存相对完好的遗址，在城市化的背景下面临着新一轮的蚕食、占压及破坏。2016年4月，在"中国社会科学院哲学社会科学创新工程"的资助下，为筹备二里头遗址发掘60周年和二里头遗址博物馆开馆等纪念活动，在时任中国社会科学院考古研究所副所长陈星灿研究员、美国斯坦福大学东亚文化系刘莉教授和夏商周考古研究室主任许宏研究员等3位调查工作主持人的统筹协调下，本报告编纂工作团队成立，并获得经费支持，资料整理工作得以顺利进行。

相关章节的分工如下：第一章、第二章二里头工作队调查遗址条目和第三章由陈国梁执笔；第二章中澳美伊洛河流域联合考古队调查条目由李永强执笔；第四章由刘莉等领衔执笔

（含英文，下同）；第五章由乔玉执笔；第六章由李炅娥（Gyoung-Ah Lee）等领衔执笔；第七章由约翰·韦伯（John Webb）等执笔；第八章由刘莉、陈星灿、李宝平执笔；第九章由Richard I. Macphail、John Crowther执笔；其中第六至九章中文部分由邓玲玲翻译。整整3年时间，1000多个日日夜夜，在团队成员的共同努力下，终于完成了报告的全部编纂工作，并得以付梓出版。由于整理时间紧迫，涉及的遗迹、遗物和相关信息繁杂，报告编撰过程中，编者对于具体资料的理解和判定不尽一致，错误之处在所难免，尚望业界同仁多多谅解，并给予指正。

在此，对调查工作的多个资助方、项目主持人、众多参与者们所付出的辛劳，中国社会科学院考古研究所各部门及驻洛各工作队（尤其是河南一队、河南二队和二里头队）和相关人员一如既往的支持，表示深深的谢意，并对科学出版社及责任编辑张亚娜女士团队紧张和辛勤的工作表达深深的敬意。

陈国梁

代为记

2019年4月于河南偃师塔庄村